Geography and Man's Environment

Geography and Man's Environment

Arthur N. Strahler
Alan H. Strahler

JOHN WILEY & SONS
New York ☐ Santa Barbara ☐ London ☐ Sydney ☐ Toronto

Cover and text design: Eileen Thaxton

Cover photograph: aerial of Breckenridge, Colorado at dusk (Shorty Wilcox/The Image Bank)

Library of Congress Cataloging in Publication Data:

Strahler, Arthur Newell, 1918-
  Geography and man's environment.

  Includes index.
  1. Physical geography — Text-books — 1945-
2. Conservation of natural resources. 3. Environmental protection. I. Strahler, Alan H., joint author. II. Title.

GB55.S834   910'.02   76-30759
ISBN 0-471-01870-8

Printed in the United States of America

10 9 8 7 6 5 4 3 2 1

Preface

In *Geography and Man's Environment,* we have evolved a new concept in geography textbooks, both in content and in structure. The content closely interweaves environmental problems and issues with principles of science necessary to their understanding. By presenting science topics simultaneously with environmental implications, we hope to have achieved a book that is readily teachable and holds student interest. At the same time, the text emphasizes the key role of geography in the understanding of environmental problems and their solutions. The broad scope of many environmental problems, however, necessitates incorporating many topics that are not usually part of the standard physical geography course—among these are pollution of air and water, ecosystem dynamics, natural resource use, and the exploitation of energy resources by Man. Inclusion of these and related environmental topics has required us to shorten the treatment of some conventional physical geography topics. We hope our book will be strengthened by this new, more relevant material.

For the structure of *Geography and Man's Environment* we have also adopted a new format. Our text consists of a large number of short *study units,* each dealing with a specific topic and equivalent to about one-third or one-fourth of a conventional textbook chapter. Each study unit opens with a nontechnical essay on a subject selected for its human interest. Some essays deal with contemporary environmental issues and problems, some with natural environmental hazards, and others with historical or biographical themes. The opening essays are intended to be read for pleasure, as well as for a message of value. The main text portions of each unit contain not only science principles and other factual information, but also discussions of environmental problems and case histories. In addition, many of the study units contain a brief *science supplement,* adding depth to various science topics. These supplements can be included or omitted by the instructor, depending upon the amount of lecture time available.

Organizing our book into short study units achieves two objectives. First, it provides maximum flexibility for the instructor. Because each study unit is focused on a specific topic, instructors can choose quickly and easily the study units best suited to their courses. (Sample lists of study units for courses with different emphases are in the table of contents. Second, this organization should be easier for students to master because lengthy chapters are avoided. Instead, students view their reading objectives as easily attainable, because short passages provide closely interwoven science principles, practical applications, and human concerns.

Geography and Man's Environment is divided into eight parts, each containing from 5 to 12 study units. *Part I, Man and Atmosphere,* covers systematically the essentials of atmospheric processes. The 12 study units emphasize two distinct facets of environmental science: (1) natural environmental hazards and Man's attempt to reduce them; (2) the environmental impact of Man on the atmosphere through industrial activity and urbanization. Forms of urban air pollution, as well as possible inadvertent global climate modifications, are examined in depth.

Part II, Man's Water Resources, treats the hydrosphere in 8 study units with particular emphasis upon water as a vital natural resource susceptible to various forms of pollution and depletion. *Part III, Man and the Lithosphere* devotes 5 units to the earth's crust as a source of material substances in the soil that are vital to life on earth, as well as the source of severe environmental hazards in the form of volcanic activity and earthquakes. Plate tectonics provides a unifying theory for the many and varied geologic activities within the lithosphere. Mineral resources are the subject of the closing study unit.

Part IV, Man and Geomorphic Processes, with 12 study units, places special emphasis on the way in which Man's activities upset normal geomorphic processes and lead to such unwanted effects as soil erosion and valley sedimentation. Units dealing with river floods and coastal storm erosion present changing viewpoints as to the most desirable human response to these environmental hazards.

An important feature of our book, setting it apart from conventional physical geography texts, is a major section on ecosystems and the ways in which they are modified and impacted by human activity. This material comprises *Part V, Man and Ecosystems,* with 10 study units. Agricultural ecosystems and the use of cultural energy in their modern operation are topics of vital importance as the world enters upon a prolonged crisis in food production. Equally important is an understanding of Man's impact upon ecosystems through pollutant substances and various physical forms of ecosystem modification and degradation.

In *Part VI, Man, Soils, and Climate,* we present a new approach to the global scope of climates, soils, and vegetation classes. Instead of including complete standard classification schemes, we have selected six different environmental regions to represent environments exploited by Man on earth. Selected regions range in latitude from arctic tundra to equatorial rainforest, and in water availability from very moist to very dry climates. The first study unit, dealing with soil fertility, introduces the modern United States soil taxonomy (former Seventh Approximation) and emphasizes both base status and availability of soil moisture as they affect agricultural productivity. The remaining 6 study units are designed to show the opportunities and restraints that each environmental region offers to Man, explaining characteristic soils and biomes and stressing ecosystem productivity and agricultural resources.

Part VII, Man and Scenery–The Wilderness Resource, is a new departure in landscape interpretation, based upon the wilderness ethic as a rising force in conflict with prevailing doctrines of natural resource exploitation and land reclamation. Several American landscape types are viewed in terms of their intrinsic value as wild areas. The 5 study units deal with river gorges, alpine zones, rugged coastlines, mountainous deserts, and ancient mountain roots. Geomorphic expressions of folding, faulting, and the erosive action of streams, waves, glaciers, and winds are given new meaning through the need to understand and appreciate the unique qualities of each wilderness landscape we seek to preserve and enjoy. Human impact upon these varied landscapes is viewed as a major management problem.

Part VIII, Man's Energy Resources, treats the nature and extent of the various useful forms of energy, including fossil fuels, nuclear fuels, geothermal energy, and solar energy. Six study units apply basic science principles to each important form of energy. We also evaluate present and future contributions of each energy resource, along with the environmental impacts of fuel extraction, processing, and consumption. We include energy resources because the topic is one of major concern to scientists in many fields. Geography students are in a unique position to understand the full impacts of energy resource development and utilization through applications of physical geography and ecology.

We have concluded our book with a brief *Epilogue,* touching upon certain broad facets of the relationship between the human race and the global system of environment and resource.

The *Bibliography* consists of a limited number of carefully selected references emphasizing environmental topics related to each study unit. Entries are largely limited to readily accessible journals and books.

We are grateful to Professor F. Kenneth Hare, Department of Geography, University of Toronto, for critical reading of the manuscript of Parts I to III, and to Professor Henry D. Foth, Department of Crop and Soil Sciences, Michigan State University, for reading those units containing material relating to soils. The many suggestions and corrections offered by these reviewers resulted in a more accurate text.

A note on sexism in textbooks: According to a recently issued publisher's report, *sexism* in its broader sense means any arbitrary stereotyping of males and females by reason of their gender. Both women and men have been leading contributors to geography. Except in those cases where the work of a an individual geographer is cited, we have been careful to avoid using either feminine or masculine pronouns.

We are, however, confronted with a much more serious problem—that of selecting a word to denote collectively the individuals of the human race, including persons of both sexes. We are told that leaders in the fight for women's rights take the position that the word *Man* is now so closely associated with a male human being that it is no longer broad enough to be applied to persons of either sex or to the human race. We have also been advised that *Mankind* and *Man-made* are unacceptable on the same grounds. Our dilemma as authors is particularly acute because the entire emphasis of environmental studies is on the interaction and conflict between the human race and the natural environment. Whatever word we select to denote humanity at large will be repeated hundreds of times over in the pages of this book.

Our decision is to use the proper name *Man,* always capitalized, to denote collectively all individuals or any group of individuals of the human race. *Man* is the English translation of the Latin name *Homo* for the genus to which all individuals of the human race belong. Although there have been other *sapiens.* We feel that *Man* is no more a sexist word than, for example, *American, Canadian,* or *Navajo,* all of which are proper names for groups of persons including both sexes. We also capitalize two terms used repeatedly in environmental studies: *Man-made* and *Man-induced.*

Arthur N. Strahler
Alan H. Strahler

Biographical Note

ARTHUR N. STRAHLER (b. 1918) received his B.A. degree in 1938 from the College of Wooster, Ohio, and his Ph.D. degree in geology from Columbia University in 1944. He is a fellow of the Geological Society of America and the Association of American Geographers. He was appointed to the Columbia University faculty in 1941, serving as Professor of Geomorphology from 1958 to 1967 and as Chairman of the Department of Geology from 1959 to 1962. He is the author of several widely used textbooks of physical geography, environmental science, and the earth sciences.

ALAN H. STRAHLER (b. 1943) received his B.A. degree in 1964 and his Ph.D. degree in 1969 from The Johns Hopkins University, Department of Geography and Environmental Engineering. His published research lies in the fields of quantitative plant geography and forest ecology. He is Assistant Professor in the Department of Geography of the University of California at Santa Barbara. From 1973 to 1974 he held an appointment as Bullard Forest Research Fellow at Harvard University. He is the coauthor of textbooks on physical geography and environmental science.

Selected Course Plans

Geography and Man's Environment has been designed to allow maximum flexibility in meeting the instructor's needs. By selecting only those study units that are appropriate, the instructor can closely tailor our text to suit course requirements. With this end in mind, we have drafted three sample course plans to serve as examples of courses with different orientations. Each course includes 54 study units, slightly more than one unit per lecture for a one-semester course meeting three times per week. Selected study units for each course are indicated by columns of dots in the table of contents. Remaining units can be omitted or assigned as outside reading. Science supplements may also be included or omitted at the instructor's discretion.

The total text length of all 65 units, exclusive of the opening essays and science supplements, is about equal to the total text length of Strahler, *Introduction to Physical Geography,* 3rd edition, used in many one-semester courses. Thus some instructors may choose to cover all study units of *Geography and Man's Environment* in one intensive semester.

Environmental physical geography: A course offering wide coverage of physical geography topics with environmental emphasis. Units omitted deal largely with natural resources and with biological aspects of ecosystems. This plan offers an alternative to the conventional, highly structured physical geography course.

Man and the environment: A course directed toward the functioning of human and natural ecosystems in interaction within their environments. Pollution and environmental impact topics are emphasized, including energy resources and their development. Units omitted deal largely with physical environmental hazards, scenic landscapes, and mineral resources.

Man and earth resources: A course emphasizing the nature, origin, and extent of renewable and nonrenewable resources of both materials and energy, along with the environmental impacts of resource use. Units omitted deal largely with natural environment hazards and certain forms of human impact on physical systems.

Contents

	Environmental Physical Geography	Man and the Environment	Man and Earth Resources

	Environmental Physical Geography	Man and the Environment	Man and Earth Resources

Geography and Man's Environment

Introduction

Environment Makes the News

On May 12, 1976, newspaper headlines and TV carried the first sketchy reports of a great marine disaster. A huge tanker carrying crude oil from the Persian Gulf to a European refinery had run aground on the Spanish coast near the port of La Coruna. The great ship exploded and began to burn, quickly releasing thousands of tons of toxic oil into the coastal waters. To the 5000 fishermen of La Coruna who make a living reaping a rich harvest of mussels, oysters, and clams, the event was a stunning blow. Much of this sea life, highly prized throughout Western Europe as a gourmet food supply, was doomed. Said one restaurant owner: "With our beaches badly polluted and our best seafood poisoned, what can we offer the tourists? All we can do is close our doors and go." Oceanographers ventured the opinion that some of the 100,000 tons of crude oil leaking from the shattered hulk would eventually be carried by ocean currents to places as far off as the Caribbean

Sea. To understand the full environmental impact of this huge oil spill you need to know some basic facts about the composition of petroleum and the way in which it has accumulated. You also need to know something about life systems of the shallow coastal waters, and the paths of ocean water circulation in the North Atlantic. Can anything be done to reduce the possibility of more oil spills?

For Londoners, December 8, 1952, was the fifth day in a row of heavy smog, better described as poison fog. Hospitals were crowded with seriously ill persons unable to breathe effectively. Many who had chronic respiratory diseases succumbed to an environmental stress from which they could not escape. This incident is not news; many of you have heard it before. The recurrent crisis of air pollution over urbanized areas is never very far from the minds of city dwellers. It is obvious that Man has played a leading role in degrading atmospheric quality over large cities. Understanding the smog problem requires a knowledge of basic principles of atmospheric science. These principles are explained in

The tanker vessel *Urquiola* burns after running aground in La Coruna Bay on the Atlantic coast of Spain. (Alain Nogues/ Sygma.)

1

The grounded tanker finally broke in two, releasing 90,000 tons of crude oil into the waters of La Coruna Bay. (Alain Nogues/Sygma.)

early study units of this book and will help you to be more effective in formulating action programs to improve the quality of air over cities.

In May 1971, the Food and Drug Administration announced that swordfish should not be eaten because an extensive sampling of canned swordfish in markets revealed the presence of mercury in amounts too great to be considered safe for human consumption. To what extent, if any, are Man's industrial processes responsible for the concentration of mercury in the tissues of swordfish? Is it possible that the mercury level in these fishes is no higher now than it has been for centuries in the past? To get the answers to these and other problems of mercury

contamination requires that we tap a number of sciences. First, of course, is biological science. The food chain must be traced back to its source. But we must also look to geology for the prime sources of mercury compounds and to hydrology (water science) for an understanding of the transport processes by which it enters the sea water.

As far back as 1947 the pumping of drinking water from wells in Kings County, on Long Island, New York (the Borough of Brooklyn) was finally discontinued because the fresh water beneath the surface had become contaminated by salt water drawn in from beneath the adjacent ocean. Since then, this large urban community has had to be supplied with fresh water brought from reservoirs in the Catskill Mountains, far upstate. Will the same fate overtake Long Island communities farther to the east? Planning for Long Island's future urban development depends very heavily upon the question of availability of adequate supplies of fresh water. Already serious problems of contamination by salt water and detergents have arisen. To understand what is happening on Long Island requires a knowledge of the basic principles of water beneath the ground surface. We shall explain these principles, so that you can recommend effective action to head off the disaster of a failing water supply.

In November 1970, a great surge of sea water, generated by a powerful tropical cyclone in the Bay of Bengal, swept over a densely populated low-lying coastal area in Bangladesh (then East Pakistan). The sudden, 20-foot rise of water level drowned many tens of thousands of persons and destroyed over 200,000 houses along with all rice crops in the area. Disasters of the same origin are known to have occurred in this region in the past. Here is an area where the physical environment has dealt harshly with humans, and through little fault on their part. So we must recognize that humans, along with all other life forms, have always been subjected to environmental stresses over which they have no control.

Geography and the Environment

Geography is a discipline that links the social sciences with the natural sciences. The phrase "Man and the land" is often used to convey the essence of geography. While the relationship of humans to their earthly environment is a core concept in geography, an equally important idea is that the relationship has a certain distribution in space. Geographers recognize that the quality of the life layer varies from place to place in terms of richness or poverty of life forms capable of being supported. Geographers recognize environmental regions, each with a particular set of qualities for life support. A given environmen-

tal region usually has certain definite locations on the globe in terms of latitude and continental position. It has a characteristic combination of soil type and native plant cover and offers a certain set of opportunities to Man to derive vital supplies of fresh water and food. Some environmental regions are richly endowed with water and food; others are very poorly endowed. The poorly endowed environments are too cold, too dry, or too rocky to support much life. A major goal of geography is to evaluate each environmental region in terms of its life-support capacity. We shall sample several of these environments in study units of Part VI, dealing with soil fertility in relation to climate.

Environment and Society

Environmental influences include in the broadest sense forces and restraints that arise from Man's accumulated cultural resources contained in elaborately developed social structures. These structures of society are industrial, political, religious, or esthetic in nature. No problem of the environment can be approached and solved without taking into account value judgments that are weighed against the consequences to our total culture. Cleaning up the air over cities and the water of lakes and streams requires an enormous output of human energy and tangible resources. Resources so expended must be drawn against other alternative resource uses. To what extent are we willing to change our life styles to restore quality of environment? Are we willing to relinquish the automobile in favor of mass rapid-transit systems? Are we willing to put a larger share of our incomes into pollution abatement programs from which we will derive no immediate pleasure or entertainment? Are we willing as a society to submit to rigid population control? To do justice to such social questions would require a book much longer than this one. Although we cannot examine these questions in detail here, we can at least provide a background so that you, as a member of our society, can constructively participate in the decision-making processes needed to resolve these important social issues.

Understanding the Environment

To understand the environment you will need to study each of the global realms: atmosphere, hydrosphere, lithosphere, and biosphere. When you are making decisions about environmental action, there is no substitute for a real understanding of the working of the earth's natural physical and biological systems. Perhaps it is accurate to say that most of the environmental problems facing the human race today have developed in the absence of the sustained application of principles of science and technology that have been at our disposal. Had society chosen to put this knowledge to use we might have headed off most of the troubles in which we now find ourselves. But now society is awakening and responding. National priorities are changing in response to the demands of a troubled society.

Resources and the Environment

Are Man's resources of materials and energy adequate for the future? The raw materials of industry, in the form of mineral concentrations, have accumulated through exceedingly slow geologic processes acting over millions of years of time. Yet we are using these resources at an alarming rate. Inevitably the world supplies of certain key minerals will run low or give out entirely. Use of industrial mineral resources, particularly the metals, has an important impact upon the environment. After use, these materials are largely disposed of as wastes, which create problems of pollution of air, water, and soil. Extraction of the minerals in many cases leaves gaping pits and scars upon the land.

The fossil fuels (petroleum, natural gas, and coal) now supply most of our energy for industrial processes, transportation, and heating. Here, again, we are rapidly consuming energy resources that required vast spans of geologic time to create. World supplies of fossil fuels will eventually run out, and we must turn to other sources, such as solar energy and geothermal energy. The combustion of fossil fuels has had an important impact upon the environment. One area of impact is upon the atmosphere; another is upon the face of the solid earth, as huge strip mines scarify the lands and pipelines cut across wilderness areas. Because of their environmental impacts, we shall want to make a study of energy resources and their use.

Industrialization has added a new dimension to the environment, namely, the introduction of new substances into the air, water, and ground—substances that were never present in the preindustrial era. One striking example is the radioactive substances spewed into the atmosphere by nuclear explosions and eventually returning as fallout into soil and surface waters of the lands and into the oceans. Another example is the production and use of synthetic compounds, such as insecticides and herbicides, which enter the natural cycles of water transport and the food chains of life forms.

Throughout this book you will find numerous examples of Man's impact upon the environment. These examples cover many facets of the environment and bring into play many areas of knowledge of processes of the atmosphere, hydrosphere, lithosphere, and biosphere. Interactions usually occur in such a way that more than one field of science must be drawn upon for an understanding of the problem and its solution.

Man and Nature

As natural areas of the earth are invaded by the human race and converted into farms, cities, highways, and vacation places, the remaining wilderness areas shrink. A new movement is building throughout the land to save the few wild areas that remain. The idea behind this movement can be called the **wilderness ethic.** Its supporters have run headlong into conflict with those who have followed the frontier tradition, based on a deep-seated conviction that natural resources should be used and that natural landscapes should be modified to provide farmland, timber, and water supplies. We will probe this conflict of interests and examine a number of the remaining wilderness regions of America.

These are some, but by no means all, of the principles, problems, and issues you will become familiar with as you read this book. Our environment is highly complex and involves many separate areas of study, but the common themes are unexpected technological impact, the interrelated nature of the ecosystem, the exploitation of earth resources, and the changing environmental attitudes. These themes occur and recur throughout the study units to follow. Preparing this book to cover such a multitude of topics in a simple, understandable fashion has been a challenge for us as authors. But the more important challenge is yours—to take an active role in assessing environmental problems and participating, as geographers, North Americans, and world citizens, in their solution.

Environmental Science

It seems clear enough from the examples we have given that there is a field of study we can label **environmental science.** Perhaps this label is just another term for applied science generally. In any case it is a field of such enormous scope that even a general overview would require many textbooks and many semesters of courses. The word "environment" is so common in the everyday vocabulary that we shall have to qualify its meaning very carefully to fit the needs of geography.

Environment, defined most broadly as "that which surrounds," requires a receiving object. What is surrounded? Surrounded by what? Primarily, the concern of all geographers is with the environment of Man. But Man cannot exist or be understood in isolation from the other forms of animal life and from plant life. Therefore, we must deal with the environment of all life forms within the life-bearing layer, or **biosphere** of planet earth. This shallow **life layer** lies at or close to vital interfaces between the basic earth realms: the **atmosphere** (gaseous realm), the **hydrosphere** (liquid water realm), and **lithosphere** (solid mineral realm).

While study of the environment of life forms is concentrated on the life layer itself, understanding of the flow of matter and energy that operates in that layer requires that we probe rather deeply into the overlying and underlying layers. To understand the exchanges of heat and water at the earth's surface requires understanding of processes operating in the entire lower atmospheric layer, and also of the action of upper atmospheric layers upon the sun's radiant energy as it travels earthward. To understand the properties of mineral matter exposed at the earth's surface requires study of the geologic processes of change that operate in a deep crustal layer of the solid earth.

Environmental Hazards and Stresses

The list of severe environmental hazards and natural disasters is well known to all of us: volcanic eruptions, earthquakes, landslides, tornadoes, hurricanes and typhoons, river floods, blizzards, forest fires. But protective and evasive action is possible if we have advance knowledge. We shall be foolish if we don't take the opportunity to arm ourselves with information about these forms of environmental hazards. Where do such things occur? When can they be expected? Can warning systems be made effective? What should we do when disaster threatens? Broadly speaking, such information comes under the heading of **environmental protection.** We will explain how and where these dangerous natural phenomena operate.

Other environmental stresses are less lethal in terms of human life toll, but nevertheless of severe economic importance. For example, take these weather phenomena: drought, dust storms, and hail in the Great Plains region of the interior United States. Can we act to alleviate these stresses? Rainmaking shows potentiality for success in favorable situations; hail formation may yet be reduced in intensity by artificial means; and treatment methods applied to the ground surface can to some extent reduce the blowing of dust and sand. Evidently, Man has various means of exerting at least some limited controls over the environmental processes. We group these activities under the heading of **planned environmental modification.** Success in programs of this type requires knowledge of the fundamental processes of the atmosphere and of water on and beneath the lands.

Environment and Ecology

Organisms, whether of one species or many, whether belonging to the plant kingdom or to the animal kingdom, interact not only with the physical environments which they occupy, but with each other as well. Study of these interactions—in the form of exchanges of matter, energy, and stimuli of various sorts—between life forms and the environment is the science of **ecology,** very broadly defined. The total assemblage of components interacting with a group of organisms is known as an **ecological system,** or more simply, an **ecosystem.** The root eco comes from a Greek word connoting a house in the sense of household, which implies that a family lives together and interacts within a functional physical structure. Ecosystems have inputs of matter and energy, used to build biological structures (the biomass), to reproduce, and to maintain necessary internal energy levels. Matter and energy are also exported from an ecosystem. An ecosystem tends to achieve a balance of the various processes and activities within it. For the most part these balances are quite sensitive and can easily be upset or destroyed. We will investigate the many ways in which human activity impacts natural ecosystems.

Facing page: Steel works in Wales. (Gerry Cranham/Rapho-Researchers.)

PART 1 Man and the Atmosphere

Unit 1
Solar Radiation and the Ozone Layer

Concorde and the Ozone Layer

On the morning of January 22, 1976, millions of American TV viewers glanced up from their cups of coffee and morning papers to watch a historic moment for commercial aviation. Two supersonic aircraft—British- and French-built Concordes—were taking off simultaneously to begin the first scheduled supersonic passenger service with flights from London and Paris to South America and the Middle East. Coordinated by an open telephone line between Paris and London, Captain Norman Todd of British Airways and Pilot Pierre Chamoine of Air France advanced their throttles at the same moment to provide a magnificent, split-screen television view of the

Air France's Concorde takes off on its Paris–Washington run. (Air France Photo.)

two huge $60-million jets accelerating down their runways and roaring off into the sky above.

Yet even as the two planes began their acceleration to speeds of more than twice that of sound and their ascent to heights of greater than 50,000 ft, the future of scheduled supersonic air transport in America was being pondered by the United States Secretary of Transportation, William T. Coleman, Jr. After weighing the arguments voiced in a series of special hearings held earlier in the month, it was up to Coleman to decide whether or not to allow British Airways and Air France to begin scheduled supersonic service to New York's Kennedy and Washington's Dulles airports.

The hearings had brought into focus two main areas of concern about the environmental impact of the Concorde and supersonic transport flights. One major issue was that of the ozone layer. Earlier studies by the Department of Transportation and the National Academy of Sciences had confirmed that significant amounts of nitrogen oxides would be released from the exhausts of a large fleet of SSTs operating at high altitudes in the stratosphere in the northern hemisphere. The studies showed that the nitrogen oxides would act to reduce the amount of ozone in the stratosphere, thereby lessening the effectiveness of the ozone layer in shielding the earth's surface from harmful ultraviolet radiation. A second important issue was that of noise—not the noise of the sonic booms that are created when any aircraft exceeds the speed of sound, but rather the incredible roar of the four huge jet engines during takeoff.

On board the aircraft, however, all was serene. Traveling at more than twice the speed of sound, the supersonic flights were smooth and uneventful. The passengers, paying a fare some fifty percent higher than that of normal first-class air travel, were greatly impressed by their flight. The Duke of Kent, cousin of the Queen of England, termed the flight "absolutely magnificent," adding, "It is a great moment for British and French aviation." On board the Air

France flight to Rio, Lee Elman, a New York investment banker, found the flight far superior to his previous air trips and termed it a "lyrical journey."

On the ground below, however, response to the flight was quite different. Outside Heathrow Airport, officials of the British Aircraft Noise Council commented on the Concorde's takeoff noise. "The sound was excruciating—it was above the level of pain," stated Geoffrey Holmes, an environmental health officer. Instruments had measured the Concorde's takeoff roar at 134 perceived noise decibels—an amount exceeding the permitted level in the Heathrow runway area by some 24 decibels.

It was, of course, the noise issue that had originally been a major factor in the congressional decision to withhold support for the development of a Boeing supersonic transport in 1970. Environmentalists argued that the SST, flying over continents, would create sonic booms that would startle and inconvenience millions of Americans, only to benefit a few select business executives and wealthy private individuals with the convenience of saving a few hours of air-travel time. In addition, there was widespread concern over the amount of tax dollars which would have to be committed to the development of the Boeing prototype. Having already bailed out Lockheed, Congress was in no mood to make an open-ended commitment for financial support to a project with such obvious environmental drawbacks.

In retrospect, it seems fortunate that Congress made the decision to stop American development of commercial SST technology, for in the next few years atmospheric scientists were to demonstrate that large numbers of supersonic transports, flying high in the stratosphere, could act to reduce the amount of ozone by as much as 30%, depending on assumptions concerning the number of flights and aircraft, the exhaust emissions of their engines, and their cruising altitudes.

Studies of the effects of such an ozone reduction on human health have shown that a a 5% reduction in the amount of ozone in the atmosphere could cause between 20,000 and 60,000 additional cases of skin cancer in the United States alone. Fortunately, skin cancer is one of the most readily curable

forms of cancer known. Approximately 90 to 95% of the persons treated for skin cancer remain cancer-free more than five years following treatment.

In addition to human health problems, biologists have been concerned about reduction in growth of major food crops by exposure to ultraviolet radiation, as well as dangers of increased biological mutations in plant and animal species. Concern has also been raised about the effects of ultraviolet radiation on the growth of plankton in the open ocean, because these tiny floating organisms form the base of the oceanic food-chain pyramid.

Yet in spite of such obvious environmental problems of the SST's high takeoff and landing noise levels and the threat of destruction of the ozone layer, Transportation Secretary Coleman decided to permit six scheduled Concorde flights daily to the United States during a 16-month test period. Under Coleman's decision, both Air France and British Airways were permitted to operate two flights daily into New York's Kennedy Airport and one flight daily to Dulles Airport near Washington, D.C. Although the operations of the Concorde are considerably noisier than those of more conventional jet aircraft, Coleman felt that the impact on local areas would be minor. In addition, Coleman also ruled that the ozone layer would not be adversely affected by the Concorde flights.

Economic and diplomatic considerations were also important in Coleman's analysis. As he wrote in the 62-page decision, released on February 4, 1976, "To ban the Concorde and thereby threaten the enormous European investment in capital and prestige, would, perhaps justifiably, be perceived by our allies in Europe as discriminatory. Such discrepant treatment would be justifiable only to ward off a substantial and immediate danger of harm, and the danger posed by these flights does not, in my opinion, fall into this category."

Was Coleman correct? Will those Concorde flights have little impact on the ozone layer? A fuller discussion of the issues surrounding the SST controversy must wait until we have made an examination of the atmosphere and the balance of energy within it, which is the subject of this study unit.

Concept of a Radiation Balance

All life processes on Planet Earth are supported by radiant energy coming from the sun. The planetary circulation systems of atmosphere and oceans are driven by solar energy. Exchanges of water vapor and liquid water from place to place over the globe depend on this single energy source. We shall develop the concept of a **radiation balance,** in

which energy absorbed by our planet is matched by the planetary output of energy into outer space.

Solar energy is intercepted by our spherical planet, and the level of heat energy tends to be raised. At the same time, our planet radiates energy into outer space, a process that tends to diminish the level of heat energy. Incoming and outgoing radiation processes are simultaneously in action (Figure 1.1). In one place and time more energy is

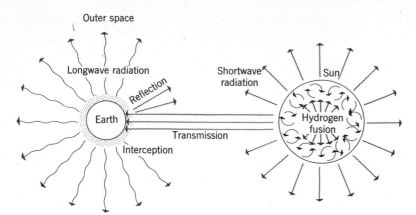

Figure 1.1 A schematic diagram of the global energy balance.

being gained than lost; in another place and time more energy is being lost than gained.

The equatorial region receives much more energy through solar radiation than is lost directly to space. In contrast, polar regions lose much more energy by radiation into space than is received. So mechanisms of energy transfer must be included in the global energy system. These mechanisms must be adequate to export energy from the region of surplus and to carry that energy into the regions of deficiency. On our planet, motions of the atmosphere and oceans act as heat-transfer mechanisms.

Solar Radiation

Our sun is a star of about average size and temperature as compared with the overall range of stars. The highly heated, incandescent gas that comprises the sun's surface emits a form of energy known as **electromagnetic radiation.** This form of energy transfer can be thought of as a collection, or spectrum, of waves of a wide range of lengths traveling at the uniform velocity of 186,000 mi (300,000 km) per second. The energy travels in straight lines radially outward from sun through space without energy loss. However, the rays are diverging as they move away from the sun. Consequently, the intensity of radiation within a beam of given cross section (such as 1 sq in.) decreases rapidly with increasing distance from the sun. The earth intercepts only about one two-billionth of the sun's total energy output.

The sun's electromagnetic spectrum can be divided into three major portions, based on wavelength, a concept explained in Figure 1.2. The group of wavelengths known as **ultraviolet rays** consists of the shortest waves; this wave band carries about 9% of the total energy of the solar spectrum. **Visible light rays,** of somewhat longer wavelength than the ultraviolet group, carry 41% of the total energy. The third energy band consists of **infrared rays,** with wavelengths longer than visible light. Energy carried by infrared rays amounts to 50% of the total. Figure 1.3 shows the solar energy spectrum with its three bands.

Ultraviolet rays are well known to all of us through their ability to cause sunburn, a form of skin cell damage. Many kinds of bacteria are killed by exposure to ultraviolet radia-

tion. Specialized types of electric light bulbs emit ultraviolet rays and are used to disinfect surfaces that may bear disease-producing bacteria. Prolonged exposure to the sun's rays can bring on skin cancer in humans. The ultraviolet radiation band of the solar spectrum is thus of vital environmental significance to Man.

The solar radiation spectrum also includes **X rays** and **gamma rays,** which are of shorter wavelengths than ultraviolet rays. The energy carried by the X-ray and gamma-ray bands is only a small fraction of the total solar energy spectrum, and we have included it with the figure of 9% given above for the ultraviolet band. X rays and gamma rays are forms of **ionizing radiation;** they are intense energy beams capable of tearing off electrons from the atoms they strike. Ionizing radiation not only can destroy living cells, but can induce damage to genetic materials within cells and can cause cancer. Fortunately, almost all of the solar X rays and gamma rays are absorbed high in the earth's atmosphere.

Figure 1.2 Wavelength, L, is the crest-to-crest distance between successive wave crests.

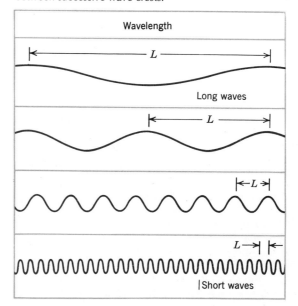

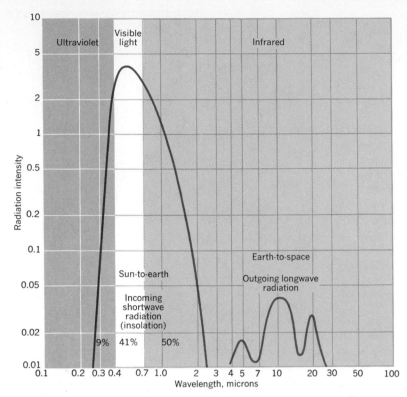

Figure 1.3 Intensity of incoming shortwave radiation at the top of the atmosphere (left); longwave radiation from earth to outer space (right). Wavelength is measured in microns; one micron equals one ten-thousandth of a centimeter, 0.0001 cm. Scales on this graph increase by powers of ten.

As solar radiation penetrates the earth's atmosphere, the solar spectrum is gradually changed in terms of both the total energy and its distribution within the three wavelength bands. To understand this process, we must investigate the composition and structure of the atmosphere.

The Atmosphere

The earth's **atmosphere** consists of a mixture of various gases surrounding the earth to a height of many miles. Held to the earth by gravitational attraction, this envelope of air is densest at sea level and thins upward rapidly. Although almost all of the atmosphere, some 99%, lies within 18 mi (29 km) of the earth's surface, the upper limit of the atmosphere can be drawn approximately at a height of 6000 mi (10,000 km), a distance approaching the diameter of the earth itself. From the earth's surface upward to an altitude of about 50 mi (80 km) the chemical composition of the atmosphere is highly uniform throughout in terms of the proportions of its gases.

Pure, dry air consists largely of nitrogen, about 78% by volume, and oxygen, about 21% (Figure 1.4). The remaining 1% of the air is mostly argon, an inactive gas of little importance in natural processes. In addition, there is a very small amount of carbon dioxide, amounting to about 0.033%. In analyzing a number of major environmental problems we will find that carbon dioxide is extremely important to life on earth despite its very small degree of concentration in the air.

Nitrogen and oxygen of the lower atmosphere are perfectly diffused together so as to give pure, dry air a definite set of physical properties, as if it were a single gas.

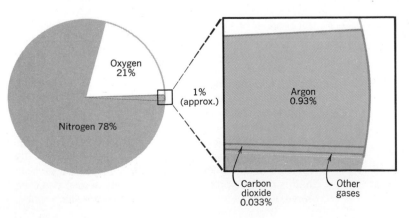

Figure 1.4 Components of the lower atmosphere. Figures tell percentage by volume.

The atmosphere is subdivided into layers according to temperatures and zones of temperature change. Of greatest importance to Man and other life forms is the lowermost layer, called the **troposphere.** If we sent up a sounding balloon carrying a recording thermometer, and repeated this operation many times, we would obtain an average or representative profile of temperature. We would find that air temperature falls rather steadily with increasing altitude. The average rate of temperature decrease is about 3½ F°/1000 ft (6.4 C°/km) of ascent. This rate is known as the **environmental temperature lapse rate.** When used repeatedly, we shorten this ponderous term to **lapse rate.**

Figure 1.5 shows a typical air sounding into the troposphere at midlatitudes (45° N) on a summer day. Altitude is plotted on the vertical axis, temperature on the horizontal axis. The resulting curve is a sloping line. Temperature drops uniformly with altitude to a height of about 8 mi (13 km). The lapse rate then changes abruptly. Instead of continuing to fall, temperature here remains constant with increasing altitude. This level of change is the **tropopause;** it marks a transition into the next higher temperature zone, known as the **stratosphere.** Upward into the stratosphere the temperature shows a gradual increase.

The lowermost atmospheric layer, the troposphere, is of most direct importance to humans in their environment at the bottom of the atmosphere. Almost all phenomena of weather and climate that physically affect Man take place within the troposphere (Figure 1.6).

In addition to pure, dry air, the troposphere contains **water vapor,** a colorless, odorless gaseous form of water that mixes perfectly with the other gases of the air. The quantity of water vapor present in the atmosphere is of primary importance in weather phenomena. Water vapor can condense into clouds and fog. When condensation is rapid, rain, snow, hail, or sleet are produced and fall to earth. Where water vapor is present only in small proportions, extremely dry deserts may result.

Water vapor performs another important environmental

Figure 1.6   The troposphere, seen in its proper perspective from an orbiting space vehicle, is a very shallow layer holding the earth's cloud cover and most of the free water vapor. (NASA Gemini V photo.)

function. Both water vapor and carbon dioxide are gases capable of absorbing heat in the radiant form coming from the sun and from the earth's surface. Water vapor thus gives to the troposphere the qualities of an insulating blanket, which inhibits the escape of heat from the earth's surface.

The troposphere contains myriads of tiny dust particles, so small and light that the slightest movements of the air keep them aloft. They have been swept into the air from dry desert plains, lake beds and beaches, or ejected from explosive volcanoes. Strong winds blowing over the ocean lift droplets of spray into the air. These may dry out, leaving as residues extremely minute crystals of salt which are carried high into the air. Forest and brush fires are another important source of atmospheric dust particles. Countless meteors, vaporizing from the heat of friction as they enter the upper layers of air, have contributed dust particles. Industrial processes involving combustion of fuels are also a major source of atmospheric dust.

Dust in the troposphere contributes to the occurrence of twilight and the red colors of sunrise and sunset, but the most important function of dust particles cannot be seen and is rarely appreciated. Certain types of dust particles serve as nuclei, or centers, around which water vapor

Figure 1.5   A typical summer altitude-temperature curve in midlatitudes.

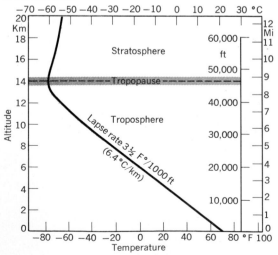

condenses to produce cloud particles. In contrast, the stratosphere is almost entirely free of water vapor and has little dust. Clouds are rare in the stratosphere, but there are high-speed winds in broad zones.

The Ozone Layer

As the sun's radiation penetrates the earth's atmosphere, its energy is absorbed or diverted in various ways. At an altitude of 95 mi (150 km), the radiation spectrum possesses almost 100% of its original energy but, by the time rays have penetrated to an altitude of 55 mi (88 km), absorption of gamma rays and X rays is almost complete, and some of the ultraviolet radiation has been absorbed as well.

As solar rays penetrate more deeply into the atmosphere, they reach the stratosphere. Here, we find the **ozone layer,** produced by absorption of solar radiation. This layer sets in an altitude of about 35 mi (55 km) and extends down to about 9 mi (15 km). The ozone layer is a region of concentration of the form of oxygen molecule known as **ozone** (O_3) in which three oxygen atoms are combined instead of the usual two atoms (O_2). Ozone is produced by the action of ultraviolet rays on ordinary oxygen atoms.

The ozone layer serves as a shield, protecting the troposphere and earth's surface from most of the ultraviolet radiation found in the sun's rays. If these ultraviolet rays were to reach the earth's surface in full intensity, all exposed bacteria would be destroyed; plant and animal tissues would be severely damaged. In this protective role the presence of the ozone layer is an essential factor in Man's environment.

Incoming Solar Radiation

As solar radiation penetrates into deeper and denser atmospheric layers, gas molecules cause the visible light rays to be turned aside in all possible directions, a process known as **scattering.** Dust and cloud particles in the troposphere cause further scattering, described as **diffuse reflection.** Scattering and diffuse reflection send some energy into outer space and some down to the earth's surface. As a result of all forms of wave scattering, about 5% of the total energy of incoming solar radiation is returned to space and forever lost, as shown in Figure 1.7.

Another form of energy loss, **absorption,** takes place as the sun's rays penetrate the atmosphere. Both carbon dioxide and water vapor are capable of absorbing infrared radiation directly. Because absorption results in a rise of temperature of the air, some direct heating of the lower atmosphere takes place during incoming solar radiation. Although carbon dioxide remains a constant quantity in the air, the water vapor content varies greatly from place to place. The amount of absorption thus varies markedly from one global environment to another.

All forms of direct energy absorption—by air molecules, including molecules of water vapor and carbon dioxide, and by dust—are estimated to total 15% for typical conditions of clear, dry air. When skies are clear, reflection and absorption combined may total about 20%, leaving as much as 80% to reach the ground. Clouds also absorb radiation, so that total absorption may run much higher when a cloud cover is present (Figure 1.7).

Yet another form of energy loss must be brought into the picture. The upper surfaces of clouds are extremely good reflectors of solar radiation. Air travelers are well

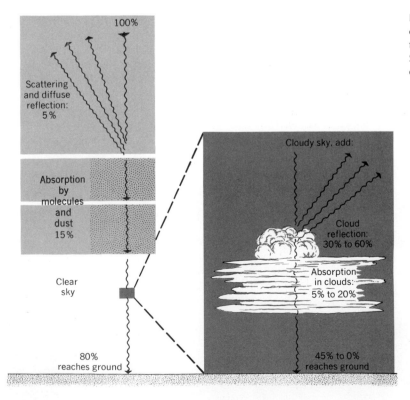

Figure 1.7 Losses of incoming solar energy are much less with clear skies (left) than with cloud cover (right). (From A. N. Strahler [1971] *The Earth Sciences,* 2nd ed., Harper & Row, New York.)

aware of how painfully brilliant the sunlit upper surface of a cloud deck can be when seen from above. **Cloud reflection** can account for a direct turning back into space of from 30 to 60% of the total incoming radiation (Figure 1.7). So we see that, under conditions of a heavy cloud layer, the combined reflection and absorption from clouds alone can account for a loss of 35 to 80% of the incoming radiation and allow from 45% to nearly zero to reach the ground. A world average value for reflection of the total incoming energy from clouds to space is about 21%. World average absorption by clouds is much less— about 3%.

The surfaces of the land and ocean reflect some solar radiation directly back into space. This small quantity, about 6% as a world average, may be combined with cloud reflection in evaluating total reflection losses. Figure 1.8 lists the percentages given so far for the energy losses by reflection and absorption. Altogether, the losses to space by reflection add up to 32% of the total incoming solar radiation.

The percentage of solar radiation reflected back by a surface is its **albedo.** This is an important property of the earth's surface, because it determines how fast a surface heats up when exposed to solar radiation. The albedo of a water surface is very low (2%) for nearly vertical rays but high for low-angle rays. It is also extremely high for snow or ice (45 to 85%). For fields, forests, and bare ground the albedos are of intermediate value, ranging from as low as 3% to as high as 25%.

A major concern of environmentalists investigating climate changes and droughts is the possible role of Man in changing the ground surface albedo by destruction of the vegetation cover and other forms of surface modification.

SST Emissions and the Ozone Layer

It was at the time of the congressional hearings on further funding of the Boeing SST that the first questions were raised concerning the impact of supersonic aircraft on the ozone layer. Harold H. Johnston, an atmospheric scientist at the University of California at Berkeley, was first to publish a series of calculations which suggested a fleet of 500 Boeing SSTs would reduce global ozone by a value between 3 and 23% over all the earth's surface, and by as much as 50% near areas of intensive air travel. Soon afterwards, J. E. McDonald presented findings that suggested a reduction as small as 1% would increase skin cancer cases in the U.S. by about 8,000 per year. Many questions were raised immediately about the validity of the mathematical models that Johnston used to predict such a severe impact.

As a result, Congress requested the Department of Transportation (DOT) to carry out a definitive study to determine whether or not SST-type aircraft would produce significant ozone reductions. In response to this request, the DOT initiated its Climatic Impact Assessment Program which was focused on the problem of ozone depletion by nitrogen oxides. After four years of study, including the development of several very sophisticated models of atmospheric chemical reactions, the DOT study essentially confirmed Johnston's earlier work. Although the new models predicted somewhat lower percentages of ozone reductions, the study nonetheless confirmed that great numbers of large high-flying SSTs would severely deplete the amount of ozone in the stratosphere and could produce a significant health impact.

In addition to the DOT study, the National Academy of

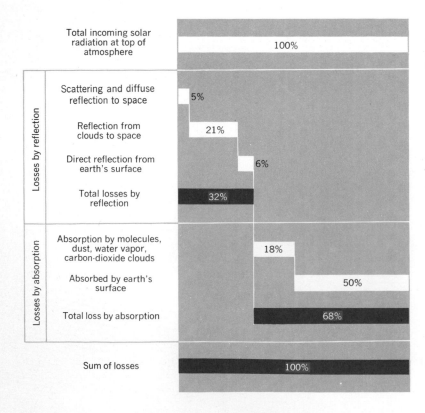

Figure 1.8 A summary of the energy losses by reflection and absorption as solar energy penetrates the atmosphere to reach the earth's surface.

Sciences and the National Academy of Engineering also undertook a study of the environmental impact of supersonic flight on the stratosphere. Using methods similar to to those in the DOT study, the NAS-NAE committee also reached the conclusion that large numbers of large, high-flying SSTs would significantly reduce the amount of ozone in the stratosphere. In fact, the NAS-NAE study predicted about twice as much ozone reduction as did the DOT research program.

Since the completion of these studies, additional research has been underway to confirm the validity of the mathematical models that were used. By probing with sensitive instruments, borne aloft by balloon or rocket, scientists have recently measured the amounts of ozone and other chemical substances involved in the complicated reactions that form and destroy ozone. Thus far, the measurements have supported the computer models to an unexpectedly high degree. Thus, the best scientific evidence to date tends to confirm the potential impact of stratospheric flight on the ozone layer.

The amount of impact predicted is quite sensitive, however, to the number of airplanes in service and to the amount of nitrogen oxides emitted from the engines during each mile of flight. For example, a fleet of 500 Boeing SSTs, operating essentially as described in the environmental impact statement produced for the project in 1971, would decrease ozone by 12% and thereby increase skin cancer cases by 120,000 per year. in contrast, a fleet of 125 Concorde-type SSTs would reduce the ozone in the northern hemisphere by only 0.5%, thus increasing skin cancer cases in the U.S. by about 1% per year. This difference arises because the Concorde is a smaller airplane; it burns less fuel and flies at lower altitudes than were planned for the Boeing SST. In addition, only eight Concorde aircraft have thus far been purchased by the airlines, and only 16 are planned to be built at the present time. If we add to this total the 14 Soviet SSTs which are now scheduled to be built, the impact of this small fleet on the ozone layer should be quite small.

A further reduction in impact can be achieved by redesigning jet engines to produce considerably lowered levels of nitrogen oxide emissions. Already, experimental fuel injection systems have been developed for jet engines which reduce nitrogen oxide emissions by a factor of 10 or more. Thus it seems possible that a modest fleet of smaller SSTs with modified engines could still usher aviation into the supersonic age with little or no impact on the ozone layer.

Chlorofluorocarbons and the Ozone Layer

Recently a new threat to the ozone layer has emerged. Propellants used in spray-can dispensers and fluids used in air conditioners and refrigerators belong to a class of synthetic chemicals called **chlorofluorocarbons.** They are relatively simple compounds of the elements chlorine, fluorine, and carbon. These compounds are very stable and have practically no toxic effect on life processes. Until 1974 scientists had not discovered what processes, if any, acted to remove them from the atmosphere. It now appears that chlorofluorocarbons can be broken down by the ultraviolet rays of solar radiation, and that this process must occur in the stratosphere, where ozone is also formed. Chlorine released in the breakdown process can destroy ozone in much the same way that nitrogen oxides from SST exhausts can destroy ozone. Recent scientific studies indicate that if chlorofluorocarbon production continues to grow at the present rate, the compound will enter the stratosphere in quantities capable of seriously depleting the ozone layer.

Much of the chlorofluorocarbon production of the world is for uses that many persons would consider nonessential. For example, the U.S. consumes about one-half of the annual world production of 1.7 billion pounds of chlorofluorocarbons. About one-half of that one-half (about one-quarter of the world production) is used to propel "personal care products"—deodorants, hair sprays, shaving creams, and countless other consumer cosmetic products. For many of these uses, alternative propellants are available; for others, a return to older and simpler means of application may be warranted. Already, many cosmetic firms are marketing deodorants and hair sprays in conventional nonaerosol applicators.

Our Science Supplement gives further details of the way in which chlorofluorocarbons impact the ozone layer. Some of the results of computer model studies are reviewed as well. The subject continues to arouse controversy among scientists.

Our first study unit has traced the progress of incoming solar radiation. This is only one side of the global energy balance. In the next unit we will investigate energy outgoing from the earth's surface and lost eventually to space. In this way we will have gained an understanding of the total global radiation balance.

SCIENCE
SUPPLEMENT

Destruction of the Ozone Layer by Chlorofluorocarbons

It was in 1974, as atmospheric scientists were proceeding in their research on the possible impacts of nitrogen-oxide jet-engine exhausts on the ozone layer, that a new and startling series of chemical reactions for ozone destruction in the upper stratosphere was proposed. Two University of Michigan scientists, Ralph J. Cicerone and Richard S. Stolarski, reported that chlorine atoms could work in the same way as nitrogen oxides to deplete the concentration of ozone in the stratosphere. Shortly afterward, chemists Mario J. Molina and Frank S. Rowland of the University of California at Irvine published another important idea. They proposed that chlorine atoms could be conveyed to the stratosphere in the form of chlorofluorocarbons, a number of chemical compounds known commercially as freons.

Chlorofluorocarbons can be degraded only by the split-

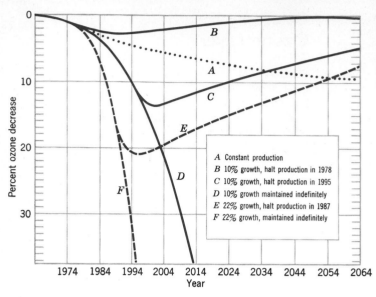

Figure 1.9 Predictions of ozone decrease derived by computer analysis at Harvard University. (After S. C. Wofsky, M. B. McElroy, and N. D. Sze [1975] Freon consumption: Implications for atmospheric ozone, *Science,* vol. 187, p. 535.)

A Constant production
B 10% growth, halt production in 1978
C 10% growth, halt production in 1995
D 10% growth maintained indefinitely
E 22% growth, halt production in 1987
F 22% growth, maintained indefinitely

ting apart of the chlorofluorocarbon molecule through absorption of ultraviolet energy from solar radiation. Because this form of energy is normally absorbed by ozone, the chlorofluorocarbon molecule cannot be broken apart at lower altitudes in the atmosphere. Instead, splitting must occur in the stratosphere—at the same altitudes where ozone is rapidly formed and reformed through normal atmospheric processes.

In predicting the impact of chlorofluorocarbons on the ozone layer, atmospheric scientists were greatly aided by existing models for analyzing the impact of nitrogen oxides. As it turns out, the action of the chlorine atom, released by splitting of the chlorofluorocarbon molecules, chemically parallels that of the nitrous oxide (NO) molecule. Thus, existing computer models developed to assess SST impact could be readily modified to include the effects of chlorine.

The possible impact of chlorofluorocarbons on the ozone layer is shown in Figure 1.9. It presents the results of computer calculations carried out by three Harvard scientists using a model similar to that used to evaluate the effects of SST exhaust on the ozone layer.

The figure shows two important points. First, there is a considerable lag between the time at which there is a change in chlorofluorocarbon production, and the time at which that change will be reflected in the behavior of the ozone layer. For example, curve C assumes that chlorofluorocarbon production increases at 10% per year till 1987, at which time production halts. Although production stops in 1987, the ozone quantity continues to fall, eventually reaching a minimum at about the year 2000. Thus, 13 years elapse between the time at which production halts and the ozone layer begins its recovery. This lag reflects the time necessary for chlorofluorocarbon molecules released at the earth's surface to diffuse upward into the stratosphere. The lag also reflects the fact that chlorofluorocarbons sealed in cooling systems may not be re-

leased to the atmosphere until some years after their initial manufacture.

A second important point is that the impact is quite sensitive to the annual growth rate of chlorofluorocarbon production. In the period 1960 to 1972, chlorofluorocarbon production grew about 22% per year. Should this trend continue indefinitely (curve F) ozone will be drastically reduced within a 10 to 15-year period. Under assumptions of a 10% growth rate, however, the impact is somewhat less severe, as shown by curves B, C, and D. Curve A shows that even if chlorofluorocarbon production is maintained at the present level without increase, there will still be a significant impact, but the decline will be much slower. Of course, these predictions for such a severe impact are just that—predictions by competent atmospheric chemists based on complicated computer models. These predictions, however, do seem likely to be accurate at the present time. Research programs are now underway to test the validity of these models by measuring actual concentrations of chlorofluorocarbons and related molecules at various altitudes in the stratosphere. The theoretical and observed results are thus far very close.

In September, 1976, the National Academy of Sciences reported to the President and the Congress of the United States that a 13-member study panel had substantiated the earlier conclusions of atmospheric chemists. The NAS panel recommended that, while the continued use of chlorofluorocarbons for two more years would not bring serious consequences, steps should be taken to reduce future chlorofluorocarbon releases. At the same time, Russell Train, the head of the Environmental Protection Agency, urged that consumers give up the use of freon propellants in sprays used in the home. Although further research may shed new light on this topic, continued use of chlorofluorocarbons seems likely, on the basis of evidence at present, to have the potential to significantly reduce ozone concentrations in the earth's atmosphere.

Unit 2
Longwave Radiation and the Global Energy Balance

Seeing in the Dark — Remote Sensing of Infrared Radiation

Environmental research has adopted many new tools and techniques for learning more about the earth's surface. Remote sensing is the gathering of information by indirect methods. Using an aircraft or an orbiting space vehicle as an instrument platform, the remote sensing system is usually situated high above the earth's surface. The sensing instruments pick up various forms of radiation emitted by the earth, or they pick up reflected signals sent down to earth by emitters mounted on the platforms.

One important class of remote sensing information is *infrared sensing,* in which special cameras and lenses record the longwave radiation emitted by ground surfaces and water surfaces. Photography is often done at night, when no reflected light rays from sunlight are present. In this way, images can be obtained in total darkness.

A major step forward in remote sensing of the environment was taken by NASA in July 1972, with the launching of the first *Earth Resources Technology Satellite,* designated ERTS-1. This one-ton satellite orbits the earth at a height of about 570 miles and its observations cover the entire earth every 18 days. The complex cameras of ERTS-1 transmit images to receiving radio stations on earth. In the first 10 months of operation, ERTS-1 generated remote sensing imagery for more than 1½ million photographs and mapped more than 75% of the earth's land areas. A new dimension was added to remote sensing by launching in May 1973 of *Skylab,* a manned orbiting space laboratory. Cameras on *Skylab* allow photos of high resolution to be taken at will and the films returned to earth.

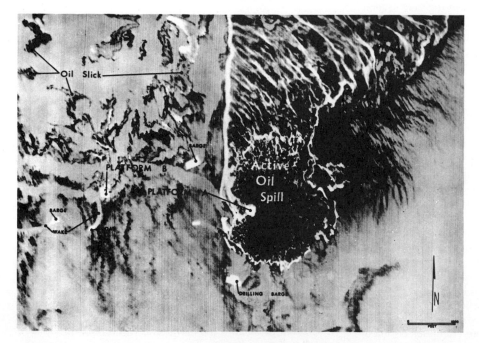

Shown here is the Santa Barbara Oil Spill of February 1969. Its spread was studied by geographers by means of this infrared image. Warmer areas of ocean surface appear lighter; cooler areas are darker. Patterns show clearly the central area from which the oil is welling up and the drift of the oil layer northward with the slowly moving current. (Courtesy of North American Rockwell Corporation; labels by Geography Remote Sensing Unit, University of California at Santa Barbara.)

15

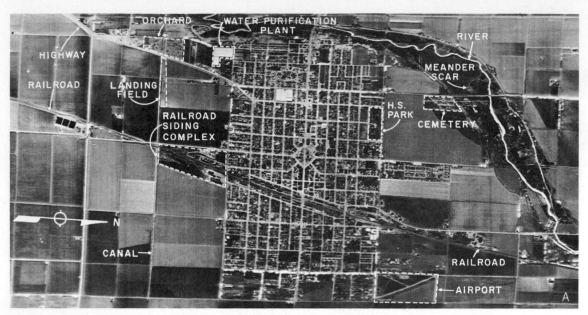

This infrared image of the city of Brawley, California, was obtained between 2 and 4 A.M. under conditions of total darkness. Pavements and streams appear bright on the print because they are warm and radiate infrared rays more intensely. In contrast, moist soil surfaces of fields are cooler and appear dark. (Courtesy of Environmental Analysis Department HRB—Singer, Inc.)

Shortwave and Longwave Radiation

The three wavelength bands of the solar radiation spectrum, shown in Figure 1.3, are described collectively as **shortwave radiation.** Very little energy of the solar spectrum is of wavelengths longer than about 3 microns. This spectrum represents the radiant output of an extremely hot object—the sun's surface temperature registers several thousand degrees on the Celsius scale. Any substance having heat, however, sends out electromagnetic radiation, and our comparatively cold planet is no exception. Radiation emitted by the earth into outer space is entirely in the longer infrared wavelengths—longer than about 4 microns—as shown by the curve on the right-hand side of the graph, Figure 1.3. In contrast to the shortwave radiation of the sun, this terrestrial energy output is described as **longwave radiation.**

Outgoing Longwave Radiation

The solid ground and the ocean surface possess heat derived originally from absorption of the sun's rays. These surfaces continually radiate longwave energy back into the atmosphere. The process is known as **ground radiation.** The atmosphere also radiates longwave energy both downward to the ground and outward into space, where it is lost. Be sure to understand that longwave radiation is quite different from reflection. Reflected rays are turned back directly without being absorbed. Longwave radiation from both ground and atmosphere continues during the night, when no solar radiation is being received.

Longwave radiation from the earth's land and ocean surfaces spans a wavelength range of 4 to 30 microns, as shown in Figure 1.3. The emission of longwave radiation into outer space takes place largely in a wavelength band between 8 and 13 microns, often referred to as a **window.** There are also lesser windows in the range of 4 to 6 microns and 17 to 21 microns. These windows show as peaks on the longwave radiation curve in Figure 1.3. Between the windows most of the longwave radiation leaving the ground is absorbed by water vapor and carbon dioxide, and this absorbed energy is converted into heat, warming the atmosphere that absorbs it.

As Figure 1.3 shows, the intensity of longwave energy leaving our planet is only a small fraction of the shortwave solar energy. Keep in mind that longwave radiation is constantly emitted from the entire spherical surface of the earth, whereas solar radiation falls only on one hemisphere. A single hemisphere presents the equivalent of only a cross section of the sphere to full sunlight. Also, do not forget that about 32% of the incoming solar radiation is reflected directly back into space. Only the remaining 68% that is absorbed must be disposed of by longwave radiation. On the average, year in and year out, for the planet as a whole, the quantity of absorbed solar energy is balanced by an equal longwave emission to space.

Part of the ground radiation absorbed by the atmosphere is radiated back toward the earth surface, a process called **counterradiation.** For this reason, the lower atmosphere, with its water vapor and carbon dioxide, acts as a blanket that returns heat to the earth. This mechanism helps to keep surface temperatures from dropping excessively dur-

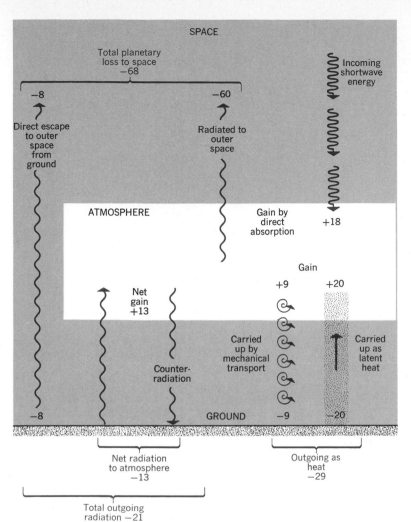

Figure 2.1 Energy passes from ground to atmosphere by longwave radiation, by mechanical transport, and as latent heat. From the atmosphere energy passes out into space by longwave emission.

ing the night or in winter at middle and high latitudes.

Somewhat the same principle is used in greenhouses and in homes using solar heating. Here, the glass windows permit entry of shortwave energy. Accumulated heat cannot escape by mixing with cooler air outside. Meteorologists use the expression **greenhouse effect** to describe this atmospheric heating principle. Cloud layers are even more important in producing a blanketing effect to retain heat in the lower atmosphere, since they are excellent absorbers and emitters of longwave radiation.

Figure 2.1 shows the components of outgoing longwave radiation for the planet as a whole, using the same percentage units as for the incoming radiation. A small percentage (8%) passes directly out into space, while the remainder is absorbed by the atmosphere. In turn, the atmosphere emits longwave radiation, both to outer space and back to the earth's surface as counterradiation.

Upward Transport of Heat

Now a new concept enters the radiation balance picture. Much of the heat energy passing from the ground to the atmosphere is carried upward by two mechanisms other than longwave radiation. First, sensible heat is conducted

upward by turbulent motions of the air. (**Sensible heat** is the heat of a substance as measured by its temperature, i.e., ''heat you can feel.'') As Figure 2.1 shows, sensible heat transport amounts to about 9 percentage units. Second, heat is conducted upward in water vapor that has evaporated from land and ocean surfaces. This kind of heat is in a hidden form, not indicated by the thermometer; it is known as latent heat. A full explanation is given in Unit 6. Latent-heat transport accounts for about 20 percentage units.

Summarizing the information of the previous paragraphs, energy leaving the ground (both land and water surfaces) is divided up as follows.

	Percent
Longwave radiation (net value)	21
Mechanical transport as sensible heat	9
Transport as latent heat	20
Total	50

Recall from Figure 1.8 that 50% is the amount of energy absorbed by the ground. We have now balanced the annual energy budget insofar as the ground surface is concerned. This is the environment of vital importance to Man and all life forms.

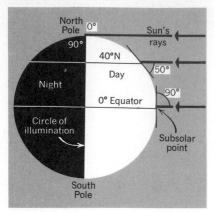

Figure 2.2   How the sun's rays strike the earth at time of equinox.

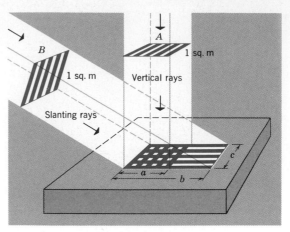

Figure 2.3   The angle of the sun's rays determines the intensity of solar radiation absorbed by the ground. The energy of vertical rays A is concentrated in square a, but the same energy in the slanting rays B is spread over a rectangle, b.

The atmosphere in turn disposes of its heat by longwave radiation into outer space. Together with direct longwave emission from the ground, the total emission to space is 68%. Add this figure to 32% losses by reflection (the earth's albedo), and the total is 100%. The global radiation budget stands balanced.

Latitude and Solar Radiation

The concept of latitude is very important in understanding the earth's radiation balance. (Our Science Supplement explains latitude.) The earth spins on an axis that is more or less perpendicular to the sun's rays. As a result, rays strike the earth most directly in the low latitudes, and particularly in the equatorial zone. Over the polar zones the sun's rays strike at a very low angle. These relationships are shown in Figure 2.2, which shows conditions that prevail twice each year at the times of the equinoxes.

Notice, first, that one half of the globe is receiving solar rays (daytime); the other half is in shadow (nighttime). Separating the lighted and shadowed hemispheres is the **circle of illumination.** Under the equinox conditions shown, the circle of illumination passes through the two poles. The point at which the sun's noon rays are perpen-

dicular to the earth, or **subsolar point,** is located exactly at the equator. Here the angle between sun's rays and the earth surface is 90°. At both poles, the sun's rays graze the surface. As the earth turns, the equator receives the maximum intensity of solar energy; the poles receive none. At an intermediate latitude, such as 40° N, the rays of the sun at noon make an angle with the surface equal to 90° minus the latitude.

Figure 2.3 shows that where the sun's rays are perpendicular to the ground surface, the intensity of solar radiation is the greatest possible. Where the sun's rays strike the ground surface at a slanting angle, the same amount of energy must be spread over a larger area, so that the intensity is diminished.

Net Radiation and Latitude

We are now going to examine the **net radiation,** which is the difference between all incoming energy and all outgoing energy carried by both shortwave and longwave radiation. Our analysis of the radiation balance has already

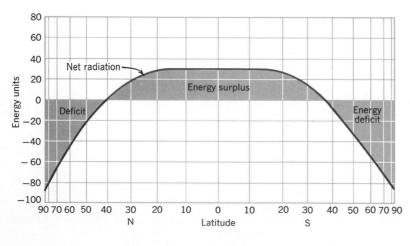

Figure 2.4   Net radiation from pole to pole shows two polar regions of energy deficit, matching a large low-latitude region of energy surplus.

shown that for the entire globe as a unit, the net radiation is zero on an annual basis. However, in some places, energy is coming in faster than it is going out, and the energy balance is a positive quantity, or **energy surplus.** In other places energy is going out faster than it is coming in, and the energy balance is a negative quantity, or **energy deficit.**

Figure 2.4 is a global profile of the net radiation from pole to pole. Between about lat. 40° N and lat. 40° S there is an energy surplus, as you would expect, because at low latitudes solar radiation is intense throughout the year. Poleward of lat. 40° N and S a deficit sets in and becomes more and more severe as the poles are reached. The two areas labeled ''deficit'' have a combined area on the graph equal to the area labeled ''surplus.'' In other words, the net

radiation for the entire globe is zero.

It is obvious from Figure 2.4 that the earth's radiation balance can be maintained only if heat is transported from the low-latitude belt of surplus to the two high-latitude regions of deficit. This poleward movement of heat is described as **meridional transport.** ''Meridional'' means moving north or south along the meridians of longitude (explained in Science Supplement). The rate of meridional heat transport is greatest in midlatitudes between the 30th and 50th parallels.

The meridional flow of heat is carried out by circulation of the atmosphere and oceans. In the atmosphere, heat is transported both as sensible heat and as latent heat. Meridional energy transport will be a topic for further investigation in our next study unit.

SCIENCE SUPPLEMENT

Latitude and Longitude

Points are located on the globe by use of intersecting sets of circles—meridians and parallels (Figure 2.5). **Meridians** are half circles drawn from pole to pole; they run north-south. Parallels are full circles lying in parallel planes at right angles to the earth's axis; they run east-west. The **equator** is the longest of the parallels.

Latitude is a measure of the position of a given point in terms of the angular distance between the equator and the poles. Latitude is an indicator of how far north or south of the equator a given point is situated. Latitude is measured in degrees of arc from the equator (0°) toward either pole, where the value reaches 90°. All points north of the equator—in the northern hemisphere, that is—are designated as north latitude; all points south of the equator—in the southern hemisphere—are designated as south latitude. Figure 2.6 shows how latitude is measured. The point *P* lies at latitude 50 degrees north, which we can abbreviate to lat. 50° N. Notice that latitude is actually measured along a meridian; it is an arc of that meridian.

Longitude is a measure of the position of a point east-

ward or westward with respect to a chosen reference meridian, called the **prime meridian.** As Figure 2.6 shows, longitude is the arc of a parallel of latitude between a given point and the prime meridian. The point *P* lies at longitude 60 degrees west (long. 60° W). The prime meridian is also referred to as the Greenwich meridian. This meridian has the value long. 0°. The longitude of any given point on the globe is measured eastward or westward from this meridian, whichever is the shorter arc. Longitude may thus range from 0° to 180°, either east or west. When both the latitude and longitude of a place are given, it is accurately and precisely located on the earth's surface.

Global environments change greatly when traced from equator to poles. Latitude zones shown in Figure 2.7 are assigned names for convenience in describing environmental conditions. The zone limits are arbitrary, of course, and should not be considered as precisely fixed. The band at the right shows the true proportions of earth's surface area lying in each latitude zone.

You should be aware that many environmentalists use the expression **tropical zone** (or **tropics**) to refer to all of the area lying between the tropics of cancer and capricorn. Because this low-latitude region is enormous in global

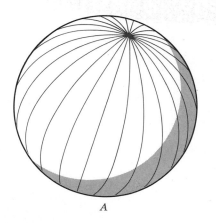
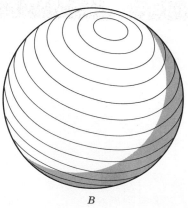

A *B*

Figure 2.5 Meridians (A) and parallels (B).

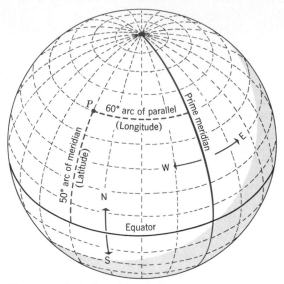

Figure 2.6   Latitude and longitude.

area and includes several extremely unlike classes of climate, vegetation, and soils, we find it practical to recognize an equatorial zone flanked by two tropical zones. The midlatitude zone is often called the "temperate zone," but this expression is extremely misleading with regard to climates prevailing in those latitudes.

The Seasons

The earth's axis is inclined by an angle of 23½° from a perpendicular position with respect to the plane of the earth's orbit. As Figure 2.8 shows, there is one point in the orbit at which the axis leans toward the sun; at an opposite

point the axis leans away from the sun. At two intermediate points the axis leans neither toward nor away from the sun, although the axis remains always inclined at the constant angle of 23½° from the perpendicular.

On June 21 or 22 the earth is so located in its orbit that the north polar end of its axis leans at the maximum angle 23½° toward the sun. The northern hemisphere is tipped toward the sun. This event is named the **summer solstice.** Six months later, on December 21 or 22, the earth is in an equivalent position on the opposite point in its orbit. At this time, known as the **winter solstice,** the axis again is at a maximum inclination with respect to a line drawn to the sun, but now it is the southern hemisphere that is tipped toward the sun.

Midway between the dates of the solstices occur the **equinoxes,** at which time the earth's axis makes a 90° angle with a line drawn to the sun, and neither the north nor south pole has any inclination toward the sun. The **vernal equinox** occurs on March 20 or 21; the **autumnal equinox** occurs on September 22 or 23. Conditions are identical on the two equinoxes insofar as earth-sun relationships are concerned.

Winter solstice conditions are shown in Figure 2.9. Because the maximum inclination of the axis is away from the sun, the entire area lying inside the **arctic circle,** lat. 66½° N, is in shadow. Even though the earth rotates through a full circle during one day, this area poleward of the arctic circle remains in darkness. In the southern hemisphere during winter solstice all of the area lying south of the **antarctic circle,** lat. 66½° S, is under the sun's rays and enjoys 24 hours of day. The subsolar point lies on the **tropic of capricorn,** lat. 23½° S.

At summer solstice, conditions are exactly reversed from those of winter solstice. As Figure 2.9 shows, the subsolar

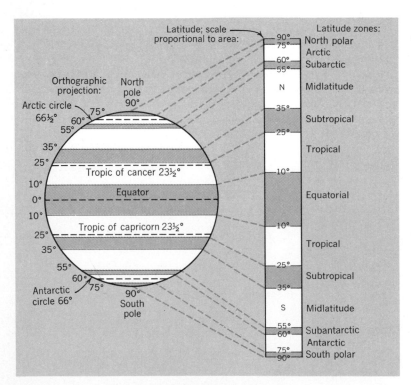

Figure 2.7   A global system of latitude zones.

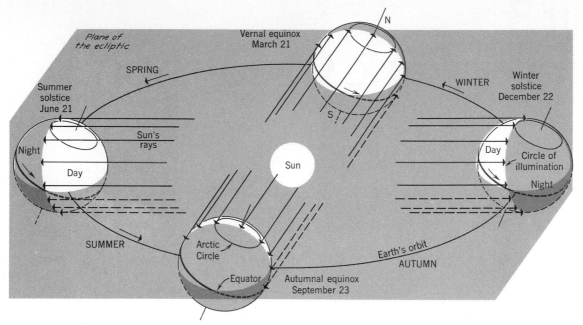

Figure 2.8 The seasons.

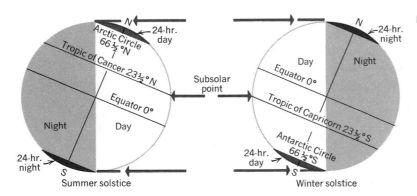

Figure 2.9 Solstice conditions.

point now lies on the **tropic of cancer,** lat. 23½° N. Now the region poleward of the arctic circle experiences a 24-hour day; that poleward of the antarctic circle experiences a 24-hour night. From one solstice to the next, the subsolar point has shifted over a latitude range of 47°.

The progression of changes from equinox to solstice to equinox and back to solstice initiates the **astronomical seasons:** spring, summer, autumn, and winter. The inflow of energy from the sun is thus varied in an annual cycle, and climatic seasons are generated.

Unit 3
Atmospheric Circulation

Krakatoa and Sun Glows

In 1883 the world was still a big place. The island of Java a few degrees south of the equator lies some 8000 miles distant by the most direct great-circle path from Chelsea, England, a neighborhood of many artists in metropolitan London. In addition, London lies 3500 miles north of the equator. Landscape painters who lived in Chelsea could not have dreamed that an event occurring on August 27, 1883, on a small island between Java and Sumatra would soon make its impression on their canvases. That event was the explosive demolition of the volcano Krakatoa, throwing out about 13 cubic miles of rock in a single act of self-destruction. Fine volcanic dust, representing about the equivalent of one cubic mile of solid rock, was blown upward into the atmosphere to a height of 20 miles, which is well into the stratosphere. Most of these particles were extremely minute—on the order of one ten-thousandth of an inch in diameter—so that they were able to drift for years in the upper atmosphere before gradually settling to earth.

The global travel of these particles was swift and astounding. Traveling from east to west in the equatorial zone, the volcanic dust completed one full circuit of the earth in only two weeks, which is an average speed of over 1600 miles per day, or about 70 miles per hour. The presence of the dust in the stratosphere was enough to detect with the unaided eye. Its presence made the sun and moon take on a blue, purple, or green hue.

This pall of volcanic dust continued to circle the globe in the equatorial zone, but then it started to spread north and south into higher latitudes. Within weeks the effects began to show up in midlatitudes of North America and Europe—and they were spectacular effects. Gorgeous red sunsets immediately caught the public attention. One news report (which we frankly find hard to believe) says that on October 30 the red glow in the western sky at sunset was so brilliant that fire engines were called out in both Poughkeepsie, New York, and New Haven, Connecticut, to seek and battle what appeared to be a huge conflagration. But the brilliant red sunset glow continued almost unabated for months thereafter. It was then that British artists furiously painted what were to be known later as the "Chelsea sunsets."

Scientists of that time were divided as to the cause of the red sunsets, which they referred to as *sun glows*. Many opposed the idea that the dust came

Taal Volcano, Luzon, Philippines, eruption of 1917. (Josephus Daniels, Rapho/Photo Researchers.)

from the volcano Krakatoa. First, the dissidents argued, the volume of dust required to produce the phenomenon must be vastly greater than a volcano could eject in such a short time. Second, the speed of travel of the supposed dust veil was incredibly fast. There was just no way it could move that fast in the high atmosphere. One know-it-all scientist dismissed the air transport idea with the statement "We know little of velocities of air currents at great height, but they are probably slight." These opponents of the volcanic-dust theory suggested instead that the earth may have passed through a cosmic cloud of some sort, or through the tail of a comet.

Eventually, the volcanic theory was accepted and for the first time the rapidity with which the upper atmosphere circulated on a global basis was fully appreciated. In this unit we will investigate the global circulation of the atmosphere. We will seek answers to two questions: First, why did the volcanic dust travel from east to west (westward) in the equatorial region? Second, by what mechanism could the dust be spread poleward into the mid-latitude regions of North America and Europe?

The volcanic dust veil of Krakatoa had an important environmental effect, besides merely producing beautiful sunsets. That is a topic we will take up in our next study unit.

Data Source: Fred M. Bullard (1962) *Volcanoes: In History, in Theory, in Eruption*, University of Texas Press, Austin, pp. 48–50.

Global Circulation and Heat Transport

Air and ocean water play a basic role in the planetary environment. Large-scale circulation of air transports heat, both as sensible heat and as latent heat present in water vapor. At the close of the last Study Unit we made this point: Because of the global radiation imbalance—a surplus in low latitudes and a deficit in high latitudes—atmospheric circulation must transport heat across the parallels of latitude from the region of surplus to the regions of deficit. Figure 3.1 shows this meridional transport in schematic form. Notice that circulation of ocean waters is also involved in transport of sensible heat. But this oceanic circulation is a secondary mechanism, driven largely by surface winds.

Pressure and Winds

Wind is air motion with respect to the earth's surface, and it is dominantly horizontal motion. (Dominantly vertical air motions are referred to by other terms, such as updrafts or downdrafts.) To explain winds, we must first consider atmospheric pressure and its variations from place to place.

Although we are not constantly aware of it, air is a tangible, material substance, exerting **atmospheric pressure** on every solid or liquid surface exposed to it. At sea level, this pressure is about 15 pounds per square inch (about 1 kg/sq cm). Because this pressure is exactly counterbalanced by the pressure of air within liquids, hollow objects, or porous substances, its ever-present weight goes unnoticed. The pressure on 1 sq in. of surface can be thought of as the actual weight of a column of air 1 in. in cross section extending upward to the outer limits of the atmosphere. Air is readily compressible. That which lies lowest is most greatly compressed and is, therefore, densest. In an upward direction, both density and pressure of the air fall off rapidly.

Pressure of the atmosphere is nicely demonstrated by a classic experiment of physics first performed by Torricelli in the year 1643. A glass tube about 3 ft (1 m) long, sealed at one end, is completely filled with mercury. The open end is temporarily held closed. Then the tube is inverted and the end is immersed into a dish of mercury. When the opening is uncovered, the mercury in the tube falls a few inches, but then remains fixed at a level about 30 in. (76 cm) above the surface of the mercury in the dish (Figure 3.2). Atmospheric pressure now balances the weight of the mercury column. When the air pressure increases or decreases, the mercury level rises or falls correspondingly. Here, then, is a device—a **barometer**—for measuring air pressure and its variations.

Figure 3.3 shows how pressure falls with increasing altitude. For every 900 ft (275 m) of rise in altitude, the mercury column falls 1/30 of its height. As the graph shows, by a steepening of the curve, the rate of drop of the mercury becomes less and less with increasing altitude.

Figure 3.1 The global energy balance is maintained by transport of heat from low to high latitudes.

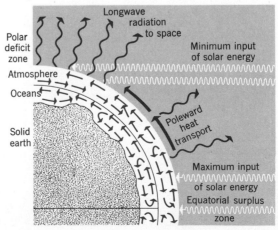

23

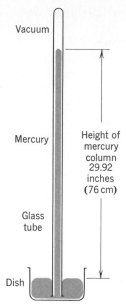

Figure 3.2   The mercurial barometer of Torricelli.

Beyond a height of 30 mi (50 km), the decrease is extremely slight.

If the earth were a perfectly smooth sphere and did not turn on its axis, the atmosphere would come to a perfect state of rest with the pressure being the same everywhere at sea level and at any given level above that base. This condition is illustrated in the upper diagram of Figure

Figure 3.3   Atmospheric pressure decreases with increasing altitude, but the rate of decrease falls off rapidly.

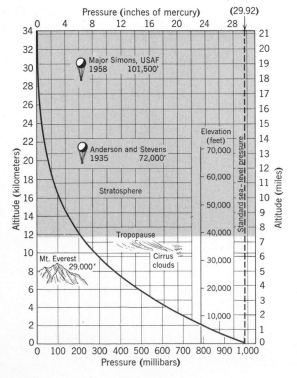

3.4, which is a cross section of a portion of the lower atmosphere. (For convenience, we remove earth curvature and show the earth's surface as a flat, horizontal plane.)

Suppose, now, that the sea-level air pressure should be increased in the region of A. Compared with the original average pressure, this condition is described as **high pressure.** Suppose that at the same time the pressure in the region of C should be decreased. Here the condition is one of **low pressure.** There now exists a **pressure gradient,** shown schematically by the sloping line connecting the tops of the three mercury columns. Pressure gradient is always from high pressure to low pressure.

The important principle is that air will tend to move in the direction from high pressure to low pressure, following the direction of the pressure gradient. In this way wind is generated.

Winds on a Nonrotating Planet

Now let us apply this principle to an imaginary nonrotating planet which is heated uniformly around the equatorial belt (where a radiation surplus exists) but cooled severely at both polar regions (where a radiation deficit exists). Figure 3.5 shows this ideal case. Heated air at the equator will expand and become less dense (all gases expand in volume when heated). Because the air is now less dense than average, the atmospheric pressure at the earth's surface will be lower than average (L). The heated air will rise and upon reaching high levels in the atmosphere will spread out, moving poleward. Chilled air over the poles will increase in density, creating high pressure at the earth's surface (H). The chilled air will sink and then spread horizontally, traveling toward the equatorial belt of low pressure. Once the air flow is established, a system of **meridional winds** results, as shown in Figure 3.5. The global winds will now be formed into two **cells** of motion, one in each hemisphere. As long as heat continues to be supplied to the equatorial belt, the wind system will remain in operation. We have here a **heat engine;** that is, a mechanical system driven by an input of heat energy.

Figure 3.4   Air tends to move in the direction of the pressure gradient—from high pressure toward low pressure.

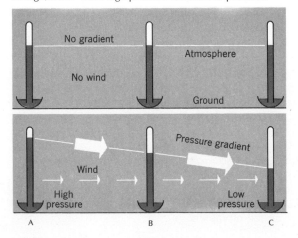

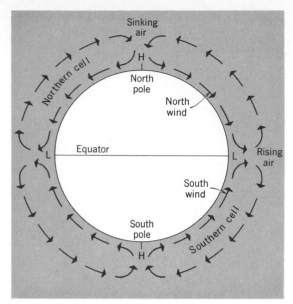

Figure 3.5   On an imagined nonrotating earth a simple system of meridional winds would operate in two cells.

Our model of a nonrotating earth serves to explain one very real feature of the earth's atmospheric circulation. There does exist an equatorial belt of low pressure, or **equatorial low,** within which heated air rises to high levels. What actually happens to this rising air as it begins to move poleward in the upper atmosphere can only be understood by bringing into account another force influencing air motions on a real earth.

Figure 3.6   The Coriolis force acts to turn winds or ocean currents to the right in the northern hemisphere and to the left in the southern hemisphere.

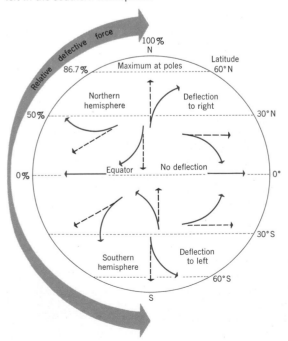

The Coriolis Force and its Effect on Winds

If the earth did not rotate on its axis, winds would follow the direction of the pressure gradient. However, earth rotation produces a force, the **Coriolis force,** which tends to turn the flow of air. The direction of action of this turning force can be stated thus: any object or fluid moving horizontally in the northern hemisphere tends to be deflected to the right of its path of motion, regardless of the compass direction of the path. In the southern hemisphere a similar deflection is toward the left of the path of motion. The Coriolis force is absent at the equator but increases in strength toward the poles.

On Figure 3.6 the small arrows show how an initial straight line of motion is modified by the Coriolis force. Note especially that the compass direction is not of any consequence: if we face down the direction of motion, turning will always be toward the right hand in the northern hemisphere. Because the turning force is very weak, its action is conspicuous only in freely moving fluids such as air or water. Consequently, both winds and ocean current patterns are greatly affected by the Coriolis force.

The Hadley Cell Circulation

Introducing the Coriolis force into our simple model of meridional circulation, consider what happens to air that begins to move poleward at high levels from the equatorial belt. As Figure 3.7 shows, a parcel of air starting at point A and beginning to move north begins to be affected by the Coriolis force a short distance north of the equator. Its path is then turned eastward in traveling from A to B. Upon reaching point C, the flow runs due east along the parallels of latitude. (In the southern hemisphere deflection toward the left also results in eastward flow.)

With no further poleward progress possible, the air tends to accumulate in a subtropical zone at about latitude 20° to 30°. The piling up of air causes a sinking motion, or **subsidence,** to develop in this zone, which in turn creates a belt of increased pressure. This belt is called the **subtropical high-pressure belt.** Air reaching low levels is now required to move away from the downsinking zone. Part of this air moves poleward, but much of it moves equatorward, as shown in the right-hand diagram of Figure 3.7. Equatorward motion results in deflection to the west, setting up an easterly wind system. These winds are known as the **tropical easterlies.** The eastward-moving air converges over the equator in the **intertropical convergence zone (ITC)** and is accompanied by a general rise to complete the entire circuit.

Taking into account only the north to south, south to north, and vertical components of air movement—in other words only the meridional flow—we find a cell of atmospheric circulation dominating the tropical and equatorial zones. This system has been named the **Hadley cell** in honor of George Hadley, who postulated its existence in 1735. Ideally there are two matching Hadley cells, one for each hemisphere.

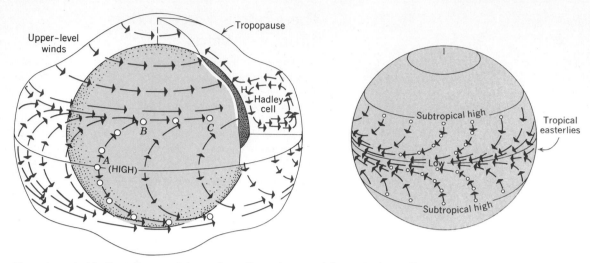

Figure 3.7   An idealized diagram of the Hadley cell circulation and the tropical easterlies.

The Global Westerly Winds

Air spreading poleward from the subtropical high-pressure belt is deflected to the right by the Coriolis force in the nothern hemisphere. Within a short distance the motion is turned to follow the parallels of latitude, moving from west to east and forming the **westerly winds,** or **westerlies.** In the southern hemisphere deflection to the left as air moves south also leads to westerly winds in that hemisphere.

Figure 3.8 shows in a simplified way the westerly winds in relation to the subtropical high-pressure belt and the tropical easterlies. Notice that a number of high-pressure centers, or cells, comprise the high-pressure belt. The westerly winds persist into the polar region, where they form a

Figure 3.8   Idealized patterns of global atmospheric circulation.

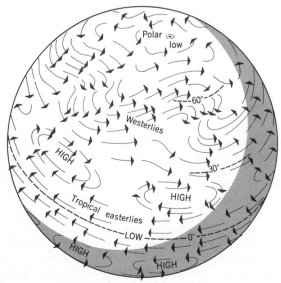

great vortex. Atmospheric pressure falls rapidly toward the polar region, where the **polar low** is situated.

Westerly winds around the polar lows involve the entire depth of the troposphere. The troposphere is much thinner, however, at high latitudes than at low latitudes. Over the polar regions the troposphere is only about 5½ mi (9 km) in thickness, whereas over the equator its thickness is about 10 mi (16 km). (This difference in thickness is shown in Figure 3.7.) Because the tropopause is comparatively low in high latitudes, aircraft fly in that region within the stratosphere at normal cruising altitudes, which are in the range of 6 to 7 mi (9 to 12 km) for commercial jets such as the Boeing 707 and 727 aircraft. The ozone layer, which we have explained in Unit 1, is also much lower in altitude over polar regions than over low latitudes. This means that jet engine emissions from SST aircraft will take place in a comparatively concentrated region of the stratospheric ozone layer when making transpolar flights.

Upper-air Waves and the Jet Stream

The uniform flow of the westerly winds is frequently disturbed by the formation of large undulations, called **upper-air waves.** As shown in detail in Figure 3.9, these waves grow in amplitude and finally are cut off. The waves develop in a zone of contact between cold air of the polar region and warm air of tropical origin.

It is by means of the upper-air waves that warm air of low latitudes is carried far north at the same time that cold air of polar regions is brought equatorward. In this way, horizontal mixing develops on a vast scale and provides heat exchange between the equatorial region of energy surplus and the polar regions of energy deficit.

Associated with the development of such upper-air waves at altitudes of 30,000 to 40,000 ft (10 to 12 km) are

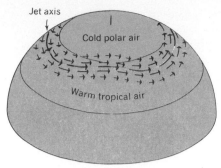

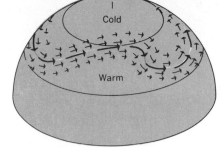

A. Jet stream begins to undulate.

B. Upper-air waves begin to form.

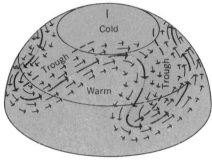

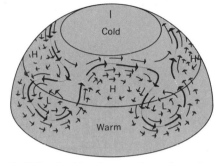

C. Waves strongly developed.

D. Cells of cold and warm air are formed.

Figure 3.9 Development of upper-air waves in the westerlies. (Data of J. Namias, National Weather Service. From A. N. Strahler [1971] *The Earth Sciences,* 2nd ed., Harper & Row, New York.)

narrow zones in which wind streams attain velocities up to 250 mi (450 km) per hour. This phenomenon is named the **jet stream.** It consists of pulselike movements of air following broadly curving tracks. In cross section, the jet resembles a stream of water moving through a hose.

The jet stream is an important factor in the operation of jet aircraft in the range of their normal cruising altitudes. In addition to strongly increasing or decreasing the ground speed of the aircraft, the jet stream carries a form of air turbulence that at times reaches hazardous levels. This is clear air turbulence (CAT); it is avoided when known to be severe.

Ocean Currents

An **ocean current** is any persistent, dominantly horizontal flow of ocean water. Ocean currents are important regulators of thermal environments at the earth's surface. On a global scale, the vast current systems aid in exchange of heat between low and high latitudes and are essential in sustaining the global energy balance. On a local scale, warm water currents bring a moderating influence to coasts in arctic latitudes; cool currents greatly alleviate the heat of tropical deserts along narrow coastal belts.

Practically all of the important surface currents of the oceans are set in motion by prevailing surface winds. Energy is transferred from wind to water by the frictional

drag of the air blowing over the water surface. Because of the Coriolis force, the water drift is impelled toward the right of its path of motion (northern hemisphere): therefore the current at the water surface is in a direction about 45° to the right of the wind direction.

To illustrate global surface water circulation, we can refer to an idealized ocean extending across the equator to latitudes of 60° or 70° on either side (Figure 3.10). Perhaps the most outstanding features are the circular movements, called **gyres,** around the subtropical highs. The gyres are centered about lat. 25° to 30° N and S. An **equatorial current** with westward flow marks the belt of the tropical easterlies. The equatorial currents are separated by an equatorial countercurrent. A slow, eastward movement of water over the zone of the westerlies is named the **west-wind drift.** It covers a broad belt between lat. 35° and 45° in the northern hemisphere and between lat. 30° and 60° in the southern hemisphere.

Along the west sides of the oceans in low latitudes the equatorial current turns poleward, forming a warm current paralleling the coast. Examples are the Gulf Stream (Florida stream or Caribbean stream) and the Japan current (Kuroshio). These currents bring higher than average temperatures along these coasts.

The west-wind drift, upon approaching the east side of the ocean, is deflected both south and north along the coast. The equatorward flow is a cool current, accompanied by upwelling of colder water from greater depths. It

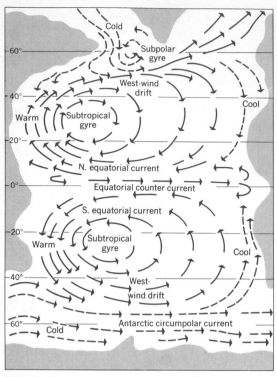

Figure 3.10   Two great gyres, one in each hemisphere, dominate the circulation of shallow ocean waters.

is well illustrated by the Humboldt current (Peru current) off the coast of Chile and Peru; by the Benguela current off the southwest African coast; by the California current off the west coast of the United States; and by the Canaries current, off the Spanish and North African coast.

The antarctic region has a relatively simple current scheme consisting of a single antarctic circumpolar current moving clockwise around the antarctic continent in lat. 50° to 65° S, in a continuous expanse of open ocean.

Oceanic circulation also involves the complex motions of water masses with different characteristics of temperature and salinity. Sinking and upwelling are both important motions in certain areas of the oceans.

The Global Circulation and Man's Environment

We have outlined the major mechanical circuits within which sensible heat is transported from low latitudes to high latitudes. In low latitudes the Hadley cell transports heat from the equatorial zone to the subtropical zone. Upper-air waves take up the transport and move warm air poleward in exchange for cold air. Ocean currents perform a similar function through the turning of the great gyres.

The global atmospheric circulation also transports heat in the latent form held by water vapor. This heat is released by condensation, a process we shall examine in Unit 5. The movement of water vapor also represents a mass transport of water and is a part of the world's water balance. This topic is also the subject of a later unit.

Winds of the lower troposphere have great environmental significance. Arriving at a mountainous coastal zone after a long travel path over a great ocean, these winds carry a large amount of water vapor, and this is deposited as precipitation on the coast. In this way, the distribution of our water resources is partly determined by the atmospheric circulation patterns. Winds also transport atmospheric pollutants, carrying them tens and hundreds of miles from the source of pollution.

Unit 4
Man and the Global
Heat Balance

Greenland Defeats the Norsemen

It had been another bad year—1395 A.D.—for the Eastern Settlement of Norsemen on Greenland's southern tip. Burying grandfather just could not be done in an approved manner. He had been kept in cold storage throughout the winter and spring, but now it was midsummer and the soil in the little cemetery had thawed only two feet down; below that the earth remained solidly frozen. Besides, there were no wooden planks with which to make his coffin. Floating ice from the north had for years prevented Norse vessels from making their usual trips across Davis Strait to secure lumber from the forests of Newfoundland. So there was nothing to do but wrap the corpse in a shroud and place it in a shallow grave.

The above anecdote has some threads of truth, based on modern scholarly research into the settlement of Greenland by the Norsemen. About 1000 A.D. a period of exceptionally mild climate had set in over northern latitudes. This period has been called the Secondary Climatic Optimum. Sea ice retreated from northern waters of the Atlantic and the Norsemen were able to settle first in Iceland, then colonize the Greenland coast in two settlements. Herds of sheep and cattle thrived in the Greenland colonies. Even grain cultivation was possible to a limited extent.

The Norse colonies thrived during the eleventh and twelfth centuries, but then a cooling trend set in. Sea ice, drifting in large slabs, began to move past the south Greenland coast in increasing amounts, making hazardous the passage of Viking ships bringing supplies from Norway. Finally, the ice cut off all

An artist's reconstruction of Vikings boarding their ships to begin a perilous colonizing expedition to Iceland or Greenland. (From *The Viking*, by Bertil Almgren, copyright © 1966 by Tre Tryckare, AB, Gothenburg, Sweden. Reproduced by permission.)

communication with the motherland. The period of summer thaw became shorter; permanently frozen ground, called permafrost, set in at shallow depths in the soil.

Excavation of Greenland graves by a Danish archaeological expedition in the 1920s showed that graves were deep in the early period of mild climate and that the coffins and shrouds of the dead were penetrated by plant roots. Later burials were shallow and lacked coffins. Under present conditions even the shallow remains are preserved by permafrost. The archaeologists found evidence that the last of the surviving colonists were in poor physical condition; their stature was small and their teeth were severely worn down from grinding upon coarse plant foods of little nutritional value. By 1400 or thereabouts, the Norse colonies ceased to exist.

About 1450 A.D. a colder-than-average climate period had set in over the northern hemisphere. This period has been called the Little Ice Age. Sea ice advanced far southward over the North Atlantic Ocean. Forests disappeared from Iceland, to be replaced by tundra. Much agricultural land had to be abandoned in northern Europe. As winters became more severe, alpine glaciers grew in bulk and advanced to lower levels, filling valleys that were previously empty.

The Little Ice Age ended about 1850 with a return to a warmer climate. Throughout the early 1900s average air temperatures continued to rise. The arctic ice pack underwent rapid shrinkage. Alpine glaciers receded to higher levels, leaving empty the lower parts of troughs they had occupied in the Little Ice Age. Temperature records show that this warm period may have peaked about in 1940, for since then average air temperatures have been going down in northern latitudes.

There seems to be no doubt that global air temperatures undergo cycles of change. Until recently, these changes have been through natural causes, not fully understood. But Man has now entered the climate-modification program, and we have reason to think that Man-induced changes in the atmosphere, largely through the large-scale combustion of fossil fuels, may be partly responsible for climate changes currently in progress. In this study unit, we will investigate basic principles of heating of the atmosphere, then follow with an investigation of Man's impact upon the atmosphere and its possible global consequences.

DATA SOURCE: C. E. P. Brooks (1949) *Climate Through the Ages,* McGraw-Hill Book Co., New York, pp. 356–358; H. H. Lamb (1966) *The Changing Climate,* Methuen & Co., London, pp. 4–12, 64–66.

The Thermal Environment

Temperature is a measure of sensible heat; temperature measures the heat energy level of air, water, or soil. Organisms respond directly to heating and cooling of the environmental substance that surrounds them. We can refer to this influence as the **thermal environment.**

Our study of the radiation balance has shown that temperature changes result from the gain or loss of energy by the absorption or emission of radiant energy. When a substance absorbs radiant energy, the surface temperature of that substance is raised. This process of absorption represents a transformation of radiant energy into the energy of sensible heat, which is the physical property measured by the thermometer. Heat can also enter or leave a substance by conduction or can be lost as latent heat during evaporation. (Latent heat is explained in Unit 5.)

We are all familiar with natural cycles of temperature change. There is a daily rhythm of rise and fall of air temperature as well as a seasonal rhythm. There are also systematic average changes in air temperatures from equatorial to polar latitudes and from oceanic to continental surfaces. These temperature changes require that the lower atmosphere and the surfaces of the lands and oceans receive and give up heat in daily and seasonal cycles. There must also be great differences in the quantities of heat received and given up annually in low latitudes as compared with high latitudes. Seasonal temperature cycles and the influence of latitude on air temperature will be dominant themes of this study unit.

Solar Radiation and Latitude

To understand how the annual cycle of air temperature is influenced by latitude, we must begin with a look at the annual cycle of intensity of incoming solar radiation. If equinox conditions (described in Unit 2, see Figure 2.2) prevailed throughout the year, there would be no seasons. Moreover, the poles would receive no direct solar radiation whatsoever. Because of the tilt of the earth's axis, this simple equinox situation is greatly changed.

Because of the changing conditions from one winter solstice to the opposite summer solstice and back, the intensity of incoming solar radiation shows an annual cycle that is very weakly developed near the equator, but very strongly developed in high latitudes. Figure 4.1 is a graph of the intensity of solar radiation at selected latitudes in the northern hemisphere. The radiation unit used here is the **langley,** defined as the energy in calories falling upon one square centimeter of surface area. The scale numbers give langleys per day. The data apply to solar energy as

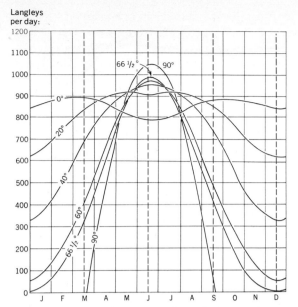

Langleys per day:

Figure 4.1 Curves of incoming solar radiation at various latitudes in the northern hemisphere. (From A. N. Strahler [1971] *The Earth Sciences,* 2nd ed., Harper & Row, New York.)

it would be measured beyond the limits of the earth's atmosphere.

You will notice that the energy curve for the north pole, 90° N, shows zero radiation at winter solstice, but a very high value at summer solstice. In fact, the summer peak value at the north pole is substantially greater than on the equator at any time of year. The important concept is this: because the earth's axis is inclined, solar radiation is dis-

Figure 4.2 Total annual insolation from equator to pole (solid line) compared with insolation on a globe with axis perpendicular to the ecliptic plane (dashed line).

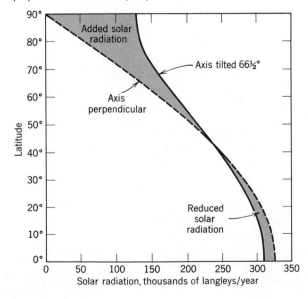

tributed toward high latitudes so that the polar regions receive a substantial annual quantity. At the same time, the annual total at the equator is somewhat reduced. These facts are shown in graph form in Figure 4.2.

Actually, the amount of tilt of the axis changes somewhat throughout a cycle of about 40,000 years' duration. In this cycle, the tilt angle changes over a range of about 2°. We should add that the distance separating earth from sun also varies in a cyclic way. Combining the two cycles, scientists can show that the solar energy received at a given parallel in the northern hemisphere undergoes a substantial cyclic fluctuation. This fluctuation has been made the basis of a theory of climate cycles of sufficient magnitude to control glaciations (ice ages). Major peaks of higher solar radiation intensity occur at intervals of about 80,000 to 90,000 years. It has been suggested that during each of these peak periods, the added heat was sufficient to cause the ice sheets to melt away, terminating a glacial episode. During periods of reduced solar radiation, air temperatures were lowered and ice sheets were able to grow.

The Annual Cycle of Air Temperature

The annual cycle of incoming solar radiation generates an annual cycle of the net radiation which, in turn, causes an annual cycle in average monthly air temperatures. In this way, the climatic seasons are generated. (Recall from Unit 2 that net radiation is the difference between all incoming radiation and all outgoing radiation; both shortwave and longwave energy forms are included.)

Figure 4.3 shows the yearly cycle of net radiation for four stations, ranging in latitude from the equator almost to the arctic circle. Figure 4.4 shows mean monthly air temperatures for these same stations. Starting with Manaus, a city on the Amazon River in Brazil, let us compare the net radiation graph with the air temperature graph.

At Manaus, almost on the equator, the net radiation shows a large surplus in every month. The average surplus is about 200 langleys per day (200 ly/day), but there are two minor maxima, approximately coinciding with the equinox, when the sun is nearly straight overhead. A look at the temperature graph of Manaus shows monotonously uniform air temperatures, averaging about 82° F (28° C) for the year. The **annual temperature range,** or difference between the highest mean monthly temperature and lowest mean monthly temperature, is only 3 F° (1.7 C°). In other words, near the equator one month is about like the next, thermally speaking. There are no temperature seasons.

We go next to Aswan, United Arab Republic (Egypt), on the Nile River at lat. 24° N. Here we are in a very dry desert. The net radiation curve has a strong annual cycle, and the surplus is large in every month. The surplus rises to more than 250 ly/day in June and July, but falls to less than 100 ly/day in December and January. The temperature graph shows a corresponding annual cycle, with an annual range of about 30 F° (17 C°). June, July, and August are terribly hot, averaging over 90° F (32° C).

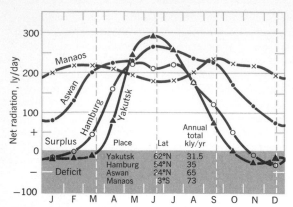

Figure 4.3 Net radiation for four stations ranging from the equatorial zone to the arctic zone. (Data by courtesy of David H. Miller.)

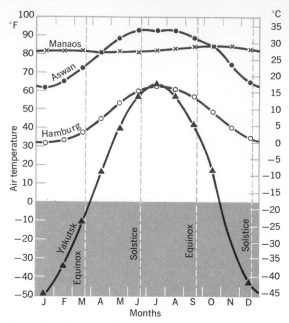

Figure 4.4 The annual cycles of monthly mean temperatures for the same stations shown in Figure 4.3.

Moving further north, we come to Hamburg, Germany, lat. 54° N. The net radiation cycle is strongly developed. The surplus lasts for 9 months, and there is a deficit for 3 winter months. The temperature cycle reflects the reduced total intensity of solar radiation at this latitude. Summer months reach a maximum of just over 60° F (16° C); winter months reach a minimum of just about freezing (32° F; 0° C). The annual range is 30 F° (17 C°).

Finally, we travel to Yakutsk, Siberia, lat. 62° N. During the long, dark winters, there is an energy deficit; it lasts about 6 months. During this time, air temperatures drop to extremely low levels. For three of the winter months monthly mean temperatures are between −30 and −50° F (−35 and −45° C). Yakutsk is one of the coldest places on earth. In summer, when daylight lasts most of the 24 hours, the energy surplus rises to a strong peak, reaching 300 ly/day. This is a value higher than any of the other three stations. As a result, air temperatures show a phenomenal spring rise to summer-month values of over 55° F (13° C). In July the temperature is about the same as for Hamburg. The annual range at Yakutsk is enormous— over 110 F° (61 C°). No other region on earth, even the south pole, has so great an annual range.

Carbon Dioxide and Global Climate Change

Atmospheric changes induced by Man fall into four categories with respect to basic causes: (1) changes in concentrations of the natural component gases of the lower atmosphere; (2) changes in the water vapor content of the troposphere and stratosphere; (3) alteration of surface characteristics of the lands and oceans in such a way as to change the interaction between the atmosphere and those surfaces; (4) introduction of finely divided solid substances into the lower atmosphere, along with gases not normally found in substantial amounts in the unpolluted atmosphere.

Under preindustrial conditions of recent centuries, the atmospheric content of carbon dioxide (CO_2) was fixed at

a level of roughly 0.029 percent by volume (290 parts per million). The problem is, of course, that Man has recently begun to extract and burn hydrocarbon fuels at a rapid rate, releasing into the atmosphere the combustion products (principally water and CO_2) and also a great deal of heat. How does this activity affect our environment?

During the past 110 years, atmospheric CO_2 has increased about 10%. (Figure 4.5 shows this increase.) In addition, the rate of increase in this period, while slow at first, has become much more rapid toward the end of the period. Projection of the present curve of increase into the future shows a CO_2 value exceeding 370 parts per million in the year 2000. At that time, if the predictions are correct, the content of CO_2 will have increased by about 25% over the 1860 value.

Consider now the environmental effects to be anticipated from an increase of atmospheric CO_2. Because CO_2 is an absorber and emitter of longwave radiation, its presence in larger proportions would raise the level of absorption of both incoming and outgoing radiation, changing the energy balance. The result would be to raise the average level of sensible heat in the atmosphere. In other words, a general air temperature rise is the anticipated result. We shall look next at available temperature data to see if such an increase has occurred.

Figure 4.6 shows the northern hemisphere change in mean air temperature for the past century. From 1880 to 1940, when fuel consumption was rising rapidly, the average temperature increased by about 0.6 F° (0.4 C°). This relationship follows the predicted pattern for the effect of increased CO_2. Since 1940, however, the graph shows a drop in temperature, despite the rising rate of fuel combustion. Assuming that atmospheric warming because of increased CO_2 is a valid effect in principle, some other factor, working in the opposite direction, has entered the picture, and its cooling effect has outweighed that of warming by CO_2.

Since the data in Figure 4.6 were made public, atmospheric scientists have shown that average air temperatures in the southern hemisphere have changed in an opposite manner in recent decades. Since about 1960, southern hemisphere temperatures have risen on the order of 1 F° (0.6 C°) in the latitude range from 60° south to the south pole. This new information suggests that the cause of cooling documented in northern latitudes is confined to that hemisphere and is not global in scope. Thus, we must turn to consider a cause of temperature change that can be largely confined to one hemisphere or the other.

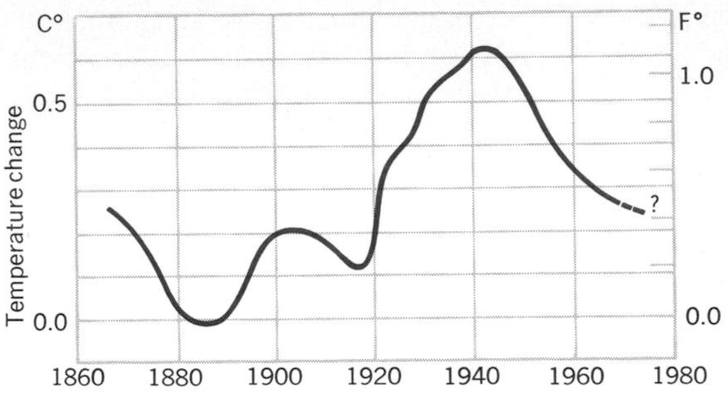

Figure 4.6 Changes in the mean annual air temperature in the zone between the equator and lat. 80° N. (Generalized from data of J. M. Mitchell, Jr. and NOAA.)

Volcanic Dust and Climate Change

In Unit 1 we investigated the effect of the atmosphere upon incoming solar radiation, noting that the sun's rays can be scattered by gas molecules and by dust and cloud particles. The average diameter of the volcanic dust particles released into the stratosphere by the eruption of Krakatoa and other volcanoes is about 2 microns (0.002 mm). Particles of this size both scatter and absorb the solar rays. The effect of absorption is to raise the temperature of the stratosphere. However, the Krakatoa dust veil reduced by about 20% the intensity of solar energy reaching the lower atmosphere in the first year following the explosion. For each of the next three years, the reduction was about 10%. Eventually most of the dust settled into the lower atmosphere, and the blocking effect disappeared. A number of other large volcanic eruptions followed Krakatoa in the 1880s and 1890s, but their effect as

stratospheric dust producers seems to have been relatively less important.

Some atmospheric scientists agree that the climatic effect of a stratospheric dust veil is to cause a cooling effect—that is, a lowering of the average atmospheric temperatures near the earth's surface. This effect might be global, as in the case of Krakatoa. If the erupting volcano were situated at high latitude, however, the dust veil might be limited largely to that hemisphere and confined to circulating in the upper-air westerly winds around the polar low. In that case, temperatures would be lowered in the affected hemisphere. Less solar energy reaching the lower atmosphere would account for a drop in average air temperatures. Note that the stratospheric dust layer does not block outgoing longwave radiation, so it would not intensify the greenhouse effect.

It might seem like a simple task to compile some global average air temperatures before and after Krakatoa's explosion and see what temperature changes actually occurred. Records are very poor, however, for the middle and late 1800s. Volcanic activity was exceptionally low the world over in the 35-year period from 1912 to 1947. Temperature records of good quality, shown in Figure 4.6, document a warming trend in this period, with the average northern hemisphere temperature rising about one-half of a Celsius degree. Some scientists attribute this rise to the recovery of temperatures previously depressed by the Krakatoa dust veil. Others relate this warming trend to the increase in carbon dioxide we have already evaluated.

The sharp decline in northern hemisphere temperatures since 1940 may represent cooling caused by a large increase in stratospheric dust produced by the eruptions of Hekla in Iceland (1947), Mt. Spurr in Alaska (1953), Agung in Bali (1963), and a number of other lesser eruptions. Opinions differ on this point.

Dr. Reid Bryson, an atmospheric scientist, has suggested that the cooling trend since 1940 is in large part the result of a sharp increase in quantities of dust of industrial origin which are carried high into the atmosphere; he speaks of this effect as the "human volcano." Bryson points to the catastrophic rise in quantity of dusts settling upon the snowfields of the high Caucasus Mountains. This dust is thought to be of industrial origin, carried eastward by the prevailing westerly winds. The amount of dust deposited

Figure 4.5 Increase in atmospheric CO_2 since 1860, with predicted increase to the year 2000.

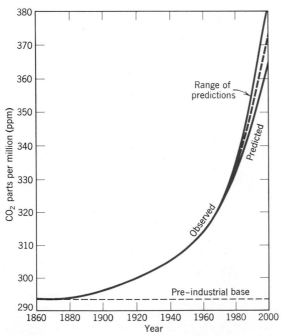

annually here has increased about 19-fold since 1930. If Bryson's explanation is valid, we can expect falling global temperatures in future decades as the "human volcano" spews more and more dust into the atmosphere. Perhaps a new ice age is in the offing, and if so, perhaps it is being brought on by humans and not by volcanoes. (Caution: Other mechanisms have been proposed as the cause of ice ages, and these will be mentioned in Unit 6.)

SCIENCE SUPPLEMENT

Testimony of the Glacial Ice Layers

Ice layers of the Greenland and Antarctic ice sheets provide a means of monitoring atmospheric air temperatures and of comparing the modern record with temperatures going back many thousands of years. Each year a layer of new snow is added to the surface of the ice sheet. Year after year these layers accumulate. Under pressure of overlying layers the snow is transformed into glacial ice. Scientists drill a hole into the ice, extracting a cylindrical ice core. It is possible to estimate the age of the ice in years at any point in the core by the depth of the sample point and a knowledge of the flow pattern of the ice. Determining the atmospheric temperature that prevailed at the time of the formation of the snow crystals is more difficult.

As you know, the water molecules of which ice is composed consist of two hydrogen atoms and one oxygen atom, with the formula H_2O. Air temperature at the time of ice formation is determined by examining relative quantities of two forms of oxygen atoms that are present in the sample. The common oxygen atom has 16 neutrons in its nucleus, whereas an uncommon form of the oxygen atom has 18 neutrons. These two different forms of oxygen are referred to as **isotopes.** The common oxygen isotope is designated by the symbol O^{16}; the uncommon isotope by the symbol O^{18}.

When ice crystals are formed in clouds, the water molecules within those crystals contain a certain ratio of O^{18} to O^{16} which depends upon the temperature of the surrounding air as the crystals form. A lowering of temperature results in a decreasing proportion of O^{18} in the ice molecules. Once the ice crystals are formed, however, the ratio of the two oxygen isotopes is permanently locked in. Consequently, a given snow or ice layer carries with it a permanent record of average atmospheric temperature prevailing during the year in which it was formed. It is not possible to assign a specific temperature value to a particular isotope ratio, but temperature fluctuations from warmer to colder periods and vice versa can be readily recognized from a succession of samples taken at intervals along an ice core.

Figure 4.7 shows ice-core data derived from the Greenland Ice Sheet in 1966. The bar graph at the right shows the relative amount of O^{18} present in each segment of the ice core. The farther the graph projects to the left, the colder the atmospheric temperature; the farther it projects to the right, the warmer the temperature. The center line represents an arbitrary median value. Shown at the left is a smooth curve fitted to the isotope data by a mathematical procedure known as "Fourier analysis." This particular analysis was designed to reveal cycles of a medium range of time periods. The total record shown here represents a time span of about 800 years, going back from the present to the year 1200 A.D.

We notice at once that the smooth curve shows the warming trend of the first half of the present century, which can be attributed to an increase in carbon dioxide from fuel combustion. The cooling trend that has set in since about 1940 also shows clearly.

When we look back into earlier centuries, we find a series of cycles of temperature variation of approximately the same amplitude as the latest variations. Cycles with periods of 78 and 181 years have been recognized by Fourier analysis of these isotope data. The important point is that air-temperature fluctuations of the past 800 years are of the same order of magnitude that we observe in our

Figure 4.7   Variations in oxygen-isotope ratio within an ice core from the Greenland Ice Sheet. (From S. J. Johnsen, et al. [1970] *Nature*, vol. 227, No. 5257, Figure 1.)

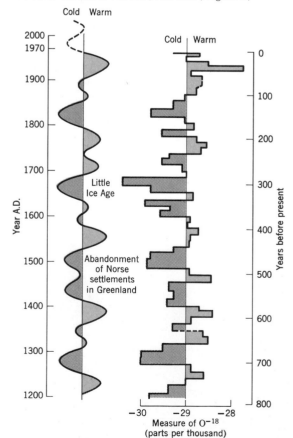

century. In other words, the recent trends of warming and cooling are within the normal range found throughout the record. What we have interpreted as Man-made changes in global atmospheric temperature may, in fact, be caused by natural variations in the radiation balance.

A leading geochemist, Professor Wallace Broecker, warned in 1975 that the cooling trend from 1940 to the present may be only temporary and may soon bottom out. If so, the rapid increase in atmospheric CO_2 may again assert its effect, causing the pre-1940 warming trend to take over again. Broecker finds evidence that the recent cooling trend is attributable to a natural cyclic change in climate rather than to increased atmospheric dust. As we have just shown, cyclic changes of this same order of magnitude have been going on for centuries. According to Broecker, the present cooling cycle is about due to undergo a reversal and will reinforce the Manmade warming trend attributed to an increase of CO_2. When this reinforcement does occur, global air temperatures will rise rapidly, Broecker suggests. An average yearly temperature increase of nearly 1 C° (2 F°) may occur by the year 2010.

And so we see, the best-informed scientists can come up with different models of future global climate change, which lead to different climatic predictions. Most scientists, however, do agree completely with one conclusion. As Professor Broecker puts it: "Our efforts to understand and eventually to predict these changes must be redoubled."

Unit 5
Man-induced Precipitation

Rainmaking as a Weapon of War

Rainmaking has been an honored calling for centuries. Many respected rainmakers practiced their art in primitive agricultural societies struggling to raise crops in marginal regions where rainfall is often delayed and crops imperiled by drought. Rainmaking has also had its share of con artists, taking the farmer's money and making a fast exit when the skies failed to produce. But rainmaking as a military weapon is something new—something the United States can proudly hail as its own secret invention.

In the years from 1967 to 1972, during which the United States was heavily involved in the Vietnam War, North Vietnamese troops and supplies, streaming down the Ho Chi Minh Trail, headed south under cover of tropical rainforest in mountainous terrain. Bombing with massive doses of high explosives seemed to have limited deterrent effect on this supply system, so the Department of Defense decided to try a new tack—rainmaking. The object was to create torrential downpours that would hinder the enemy's transport operations by flooding and washing out his truck trails.

Starting in 1966, the Office of Defense Research and Engineering proposed a rainmaking plan based upon techniques developed at the Naval Ordinance Test Station at China Lake, California. Upon receiving approval, the Department of Defense undertook a field-test program in the Laos Panhandle. The technique consisted of "seeding" suitable cloud formations from aircraft. Seeding consists of releasing myriads of tiny particles that induce the formation of ice crystals to serve as condensation nuclei. Droplets formed on these nuclei grow rapidly to produce raindrops in substantial quantities. The technique was already well known through civilian experiments, using such seeding agents as silver iodide and dry ice (solid carbon dioxide). By November 1966, the experiments in Laos were concluded and the results evaluated.

The decision to go ahead with large-scale cloud seeding as a military weapon in Vietnam seemed to demand the utmost secrecy, especially for this

reason: the United States was a leader in developing the international exchange of meteorological information with many other countries. The World Meteorological Organization had become a model for the free exchange of weather information of great value to the participating nations in improving weather forecasting. If the military rainmaking effort became known to other nations, the United States would probably be criticized severely, and international cooperation would suffer a serious setback. Eventually, the decision was made to proceed with rainmaking in Vietnam, and under the utmost secrecy.

Beginning early in 1967, and in subsequent years thereafter, rainmaking operations were conducted in the Vietnam theater during the favorable rainy mon-

This French rainmaker is exploding a charge of dynamite lifted into the storm cloud by a balloon. (New York Public Library Picture Collection.)

36

soon season, when warm, moist masses of air, moving into Southeast Asia, are heavily charged with water vapor. Described as reconnaissance in nature, aircraft sorties released seeding agents over the Ho Chi Minh Trail. A total of more than 2000 such sorties were flown and nearly 50,000 canisters of seeding agents were released. The efficacy of the program remains in doubt, largely because the precipitation at ground level could not be monitored. It was reported that the rainfall was increased by some 10 to 15% over the normal average monsoon fall. There was no evidence to suggest that the rainmaking had an important effect on traffic on supply trails. The 7-year program cost about $21 million.

By early 1974, the military rainmaking program had been made public through reports made by the Department of Defense to members of the Senate Foreign Relations Committee. Senator Claiborne Pell, who had asked for the briefing, made public the information and introduced legislation seeking agreements with other countries to prohibit the use of rainmaking as a weapon of war. In July 1973, the Senate passed a modified version of Senator Pell's original resolution. The Executive Branch, however, was not then receptive to action of this sort and supported the Defense Department in efforts to limit further discussions on the subject.

Then, in August 1974, the Soviet Union made a sweeping proposal to the United Nations General Assembly to ban a wide range of activities that might influence unfavorably the earth's environment. The proposal would have banned interference with natural processes of the atmosphere and oceans, as well as hydrologic systems (such as rivers) on the lands. The United States was embarrassed by this proposal, which came as a surprise. The UN, however, quickly passed a resolution to proceed with a draft of a convention along the lines proposed by the Soviets.

Shortly thereafter, the United States and the Soviet Union submitted to the Geneva disarmament talks a joint proposal for a pact outlawing weather modification or other forms of environmental modification as weapons. Debate on the draft in 1976 paved the way for submission of a joint proposal to the UN General Assembly in the same year.

Whatever the outcome of the newest efforts to protect the global environment by international cooperation, there is no question that a new awareness is widely felt of potential dangers of weather modification programs. In this study unit we investigate the science principles underlying the occurrence of rainfall under natural conditions in the atmosphere. We will also look into some attempts to increase rainfall over agricultural regions and over watersheds from which public water supplies are drawn.

DATA SOURCE: Deborah Shapley (1974) Weather warfare: Pentagon conceded 7-year Vietnam effort, *Science,* vol. 184, pp. 1059–1061; Gordon J. MacDonald (1975) Weather modification as a weapon, *Technology Review,* vol. 78, no. 1, pp. 57–63.

Water in the Atmosphere

Both heat and water are vital ingredients of the environment of the biosphere, or life layer. Plant and animal life of the lands, on which humans depend for much of their food, require fresh water. People use fresh water in many ways. The only basic source of fresh water is from the atmosphere through condensation of water vapor. In this study unit, we are concerned with water in the vapor state in the atmosphere and the processes by which it passes into the liquid or solid state and ultimately arrives at the surface of the ocean and the lands through the process of precipitation.

Water also leaves the land and ocean surfaces by evaporation and so returns to the atmosphere. Evidently, the global pathways of movement of water form a complex network. There is a global water balance, just as there is an energy balance; the water balance deals with the flow of matter and so complements the energy balance.

The amount of water vapor that may be present in the air at a given time varies widely from place to place. It ranges from almost nothing in the cold, dry air of arctic regions in winter to as much as 4 or 5% of a given volume of air in the humid equatorial zone.

Humidity

The general term **humidity** refers to the amount of water vapor present in the air. At any specified temperature, the quantity of moisture that can be held by the air has a definite limit. This limit is the saturation quantity. The proportion of the amount of water vapor present at a given temperature relative to the maximum quantity that could be present is the **relative humidity,** which is expressed as a percentage. For **saturated air,** the relative humidity is 100%; when half of the total possible quantity of vapor is present, relative humidity is 50%, and so on.

A change in relative humidity of the atmosphere can be caused in one of two ways. If an exposed water surface is present, the humidity can be increased by evaporation. This process is slow since it requires that the water vapor diffuse upward through the air. The second way is through a change of temperature. Even through no water vapor is added, a lowering of temperature results in a rise of relative humidity. This change is automatic because the capacity of the air to hold water vapor is lowered by cooling. After cooling, the existing amount of vapor represents a higher percentage of the total capacity of the air. Similarly, a rise of air temperature results in decreased relative hu-

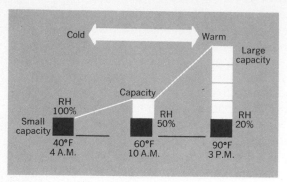

Figure 5.1 Relative humidity changes with temperature because capacity of warm air is greater than for cold air.

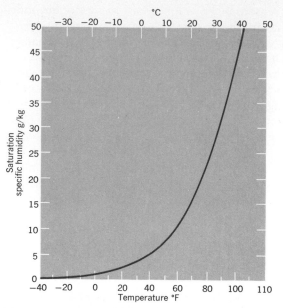

Figure 5.2 Maximum specific humidity of a mass of air increases sharply with rising temperature.

midity, even though no water vapor has been taken away.

The simple example shown in Figure 5.1 may help to illustrate these principles. At 10 A.M., the air temperature is 60° F (16° C), and the relative humidity is 50%. By 3 P.M., the air has become warmed by the sun to 90° F (32° C). The relative humidity has automatically dropped to 20%, which is very dry air. Next, the air becomes chilled during the night, and by 4 A.M., its temperature has fallen to 40° F (5° C). Now the relative humidity has automatically risen to 100%, and the air is saturated. Any further cooling will cause **condensation** of the excess vapor into liquid or solid form. As the air temperature continues to fall, the humidity remains at 100%, but condensation continues and may take the form of minute droplets of dew or fog. If the temperature falls below freezing, condensation occurs as frost on exposed surfaces.

Dew point is the critical temperature at which air becomes saturated during cooling. Below the dew point, condensation occurs normally. An excellent illustration of condensation caused by cooling is seen in the summer, when beads of moisture form on the outside surface of a pitcher or glass filled with ice water. Air immediately adjacent to the cold glass or metal surface is chilled enough to fall below the dew-point temperature and thus cause moisture to condense on the surface of the glass.

Specific Humidity

Although relative humidity is an important indicator of the state of water vapor in the air, it is a statement only of the relative quantity present compared to a saturation quantity. The actual quantity of moisture present is denoted by **specific humidity,** defined as the mass of water vapor contained in a given mass of air. Mass of water is given in grams; the unit mass of air is the kilogram. Specific humidity is stated in terms of grams per kilogram (gm/kg). For any specified air temperature, there is a maximum mass of water vapor which a kilogram of air can hold (the saturation quantity). Figure 5.2 is a graph showing this maximum moisture content of air for a wide range of temperature.

Specific humidity is often used to describe the moisture characteristics of a large mass of air. For example, ex-

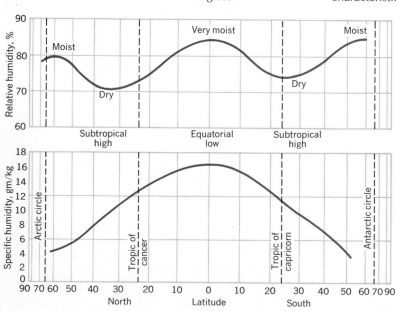

Figure 5.3 Pole-to-pole profiles of average relative humidity (above) and of specific humidity (below). (Data of Haurwitz and Austin, 1944.)

tremely cold, dry air over arctic regions in winter may have a specific humidity of as low as 0.2 gm/kg, whereas extremely warm moist air of equatorial regions often holds as much as 18 gm/kg. The total natural range on a world-wide basis is such that the largest values of specific humidity are from 100 to 200 times as great as the least.

Figure 5.3 is a graph showing how relative humidity and specific humidity vary with latitude. Notice that the relative humidity curve has two saddles, one over each of two subtropical high-pressure belts where the world's tropical deserts are found. Humidity is high in equatorial and arctic zones. In contrast, the specific humidity curve has a single peak, near the equator, and declines toward high latitudes.

In a real sense, specific humidity is the environmentalist's yardstick of a basic natural resource—water—to be applied from equatorial to polar regions. It is a measure of the quantity of water that can be extracted from the atmosphere as precipitation. Cold air can supply only a small quantity of rain or snow; warm air is capable of supplying very large quantities.

Condensation and the Adiabatic Process

Falling rain, snow, sleet, or hail are referred to collectively as **precipitation.** Only where large masses of air are experiencing a steady drop in temperature below the dew point can precipitation occur in appreciable amounts. Precipitation cannot be brought about by the simple process of chilling of the air through loss of heat by longwave radiation during the night. Precipitation requires that a large mass of air be rising to higher altitudes.

One of the most important laws of weather science is that rising air experiences a drop in temperature, even though no heat energy is lost to the outside. The drop of temperature is a result of the decrease in air pressure at higher altitudes, permitting the rising air to expand. Because individual molecules of the gas are more widely diffused and do not move so fast, the sensible temperature of the expanding gas is lowered. This process is described by the adjective **adiabatic,** which simply means "occurring without any gain or loss of heat." In the adiabatic process, heat energy as well as matter remain within the system. Expansion always results in a lower temperature; compression always results in a higher temperature.

Within a rising body of air, temperature drops at the rate of 5½ F° per 1000 ft of vertical rise. This rate is termed the **dry adiabatic lapse rate.** (In metric units, the rate is 1 C° per 100 m.) The dry rate applies only when no condensation is taking place. The dew-point temperature also declines gradually with rise of air: the rate is 1 F° per 1000 ft (0.2 C° per 100 m).

Adiabatic cooling rate should not be confused with the environmental lapse rate, explained in Unit 1. The environmental lapse rate applies only to nonrising air within which the air temperature is measured at successively higher levels.

Lapse rates can be shown on a simple graph in which altitude is plotted on the vertical scale and temperature on the horizontal scale (Figure 5.4). The chain of dots connected by arrows represents air rising as if it were a bubble. Suppose that a body of air near the ground has a temperature of 70° F (21° C) and that its dew-point temperature is 52° F (11° C); these are the conditions shown in Figure 5.4. If, now, a bubble of air undergoes a steady ascent, its air temperature will decrease much faster than its dew-point temperature. Consequently, the two lines on the graph are rapidly converging. At an altitude of 4000 ft (1200 m), the air temperature will have met the dew-point temperature. The air bubble has now reached the saturation temperature. Further rise results in condensation of water vapor into minute liquid particles, and so a cloud is produced. The flat base of the cloud is a common visual indicator of the level of condensation.

As the bubble of saturated air continues to rise, further condensation takes place, but now a new principle comes into effect. When water vapor condenses, heat in the latent form is transformed into sensible heat, which is added to the existing heat content of the air. **Latent heat** represents energy of rapid motions of the gas molecules of water vapor. This heat amounts to about 600 calories for each gram of water. Originally, this stored energy was obtained during the process of **evaporation** at the time the water vapor entered the atmosphere.

You know that evaporation of water cools the liquid surface from which evaporation is taking place. Evaporation of perspiration cools the skin. The desert water bag also works on this principle. Evaporation of water seeping through the coarse flax cloth of the bag cools the remaining water. The heat drawn off by evaporation enters the atmosphere along with the water vapor in the form of the rapid motion of the gaseous water molecules. When these same molecules come to rest on a liquid surface as water, the energy of their motion turns into sensible heat.

As condensation continues within a rising mass of air, the latent heat liberated by that condensation partly offsets the temperature drop by adiabatic cooling. As a result, the adiabatic rate is substantially reduced. The reduced rate,

Figure 5.4 Adiabatic decrease of temperature in a rising mass of air leads to condensation of water vapor and the formation of a cloud.

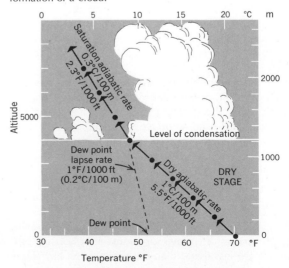

which commonly ranges between 2 and 4 F° per 1000 ft (0.3 and 0.7 C° per 100 m), is termed the **wet adiabatic lapse rate.** On the graph, this reduced rate is expressed by the more steeply inclined section of line above the level of condensation.

Clouds

A **cloud** is a dense mass of suspended water or ice particles in the diameter range of 20 to 50 microns. Each cloud particle has formed on a **nucleus** of solid matter, which is originally on the order of 1/10 to 1 micron in diameter. Nuclei of condensation must be present in large numbers, and they must be of such a composition as to attract water vapor molecules. In Unit 1 we referred to these minute, suspended particles collectively as atmospheric dust and noted that one source is the surface of the sea. Droplets of spray from the crests of waves are carried rapidly upward in turbulent air. Evaporation of the water leaves a solid residue of crystalline salt, which strongly attracts water molecules. You are probably familiar with the way in which ordinary table salt becomes moist when exposed to warm humid air. Another example is calcium chloride, a commercial salt, widely used to control dust on dirt roads; it attracts atmospheric water vapor and keeps the soil damp, even in dry weather.

Although we may campaign vigorously for "clean air," the term is only relative, since all air of the troposphere is charged with dust. As a result, there is no lack of suitable condensation nuclei. As we shall find in the discussion of air pollution, the heavy load of dust carried by polluted air over cities substantially aids in condensation and the formation of clouds and fog.

We are accustomed to finding that liquid water turns to ice when the surrounding temperature falls to the freezing point (32° F, 0° C) or below. However, water in such minute particles as those comprising clouds remains in the liquid state at temperatures far below freezing. Such water is described as **supercooled.** Clouds consist largely of water droplets at temperatures down to about 10° F (−12° C). Between 10 and −20° F (−12 to −30° C), the cloud is a mixture of water droplets and ice crystals. Below −20° F (−30° C), the cloud consists predominantly of ice crystals; below −40° F (−40° C), all of the cloud particles are ice crystals. Very high, thin clouds, formed at altitudes of 20,000 to 40,000 ft (6 to 12 km), are composed of ice particles.

On the basis of form, there are two major classes of clouds: **stratiform,** or layered clouds, and **cumuliform,** or globular clouds. The stratiform clouds are blanketlike and cover large areas. A common type is called **stratus.** The important point about a stratiform cloud layer is that it represents an air layer being forced to rise gradually over a stable underlying air layer of greater density. As forced rise continues, the rising layer of air is adiabatically cooled, and condensation is sustained over a large area. Stratiform clouds can yield substantial amounts of rain or snow.

The cumuliform clouds are globular masses representing bubblelike bodies of warmer air spontaneously rising because they are less dense than the surrounding air. These

Figure 5.5   Cumulus of fair weather. (National Weather Service.)

clouds go by the name **cumulus** (Figure 5.5). Some cumuliform clouds are small masses no higher than wide; others develop tall, stalklike shapes and penetrate high into the troposphere. The tall, dense form is called **cumulonimbus** (Figure 5.6). It comprises the thunderstorm, a weather disturbance with heavy rain and sometimes hail, to the accompaniment of lightning and thunder.

In later study units we shall explain the conditions under which both stratiform and cumuliform clouds are produced and the weather systems in which they yield their precipitation.

Precipitation Forms

During the rapid ascent of a mass of air in the saturated state, cloud particles grow rapidly and attain a diameter of 50 to 100 microns. They then coalesce through collisions and grow quickly into droplets of about 500 microns diameter (about 1/50 in.). Droplets of this size reaching the

Figure 5.6   Cumulonimbus, an isolated thunderstorm showing rain falling from base. (U.S. Navy.)

ground constitute a drizzle, one of the recognized forms of precipitation. Further coalescence increases drop size and yields **rain.** Average raindrops have diameters of about 1000 to 2000 microns (1/25 to 1/10 in.), but they can reach a maximum diameter of about 7000 microns (¼ in.). Above this value, they become unstable and break into smaller drops while falling.

One kind of rain forms directly by liquid condensation and droplet coalescence in warm clouds of the equatorial and tropical zones. Rain of middle and high latitudes, however, is largely the product of the melting of snow as it makes its way to lower, warmer levels.

Snow is produced in clouds that are a mixture of ice crystals and supercooled water droplets. The falling crystals serve as nuclei to intercept water droplets. As these adhere, the water film freezes and is added to the crystalline structure. The crystals readily clot together to form larger snowflakes, and these fall more rapidly from the cloud. When the underlying air layer is below the freezing temperature, snow reaches the ground as a solid form of precipitation; otherwise, it will melt and arrive as rain. A reverse process, the fall of raindrops through a cold air layer, results in freezing of rain and produces pellets or grains of ice. These are commonly referred to in North America as **sleet** but, among the British, sleet refers to a mixture of snow and rain.

Hail, another form of precipitation, consists of large pellets or spheres of ice. The formation of hail will be explained in our discussion of the thunderstorm (Unit 11.)

When rain falls on a frozen ground surface that is covered by an air layer of below-freezing temperature, the water freezes into clear ice after striking the ground or other surfaces such as trees, houses, or wires (Figure 5.7). The coating of ice that results is called a **glaze,** and an **ice storm** is said to have occurred. Actually, no ice falls, so that ice glaze is not a form of precipitation. Ice storms cause great damage, especially to telephone and power wires and to tree limbs. Roads and sidewalks are made extremely hazardous.

How Precipitation is Produced

Precipitation in substantial quantities is induced by two basic types of mechanisms. One is spontaneous rise of moist air; the other is forced rise of moist air.

Spontaneous rise of moist air is associated with **convection,** a form of atmospheric motion consisting of strong updrafts taking place within a **convection cell.** Air rises in the cell because it is less dense than the surrounding air. Perhaps a fair analogy is the updraft of heated air in a chimney but, unlike the steady air flow in a chimney, air motion in a convection cell takes place in pulses as bubblelike masses of air rise in succession.

To illustrate the convection process, let us suppose that on a clear, warm summer morning the sun is shining on a landscape consisting of patches of open fields and woodlands. Certain of these types of surfaces, such as bare ground, heat more rapidly and transmit radiant heat to the overlying air. Air over a warmer patch becomes warmed more than adjacent air and begins to rise as a bubble,

Figure 5.7 Heavily coated wires and branches caused heavy damage in eastern New York State in January 1943 as a result of this ice storm. (National Weather Service.)

much as a hot-air balloon rises after being released. Vertical movements of this type are often called "thermals" by sailplane pilots who use them to obtain lift.

As the air rises, it is cooled adiabatically so that eventually it is cooled below the dew point. Condensation begins at once, and the rising air column appears as a cumulus cloud. The flat base shows the critical level above which condensation is occurring (Figure 5.8). The bulging "cauliflower" top of the cloud represents the top of the rising warm air column, pushing into higher levels of the atmosphere. Usually, the small cumulus cloud dissolves after drifting some distance downwind. However, should this convection continue to develop, the cloud may grow to a dense cumulonimbus mass, or thunderstorm, from which heavy rain will fall.

Why, you ask, does such spontaneous cloud growth take place and continue beyond the initial cumulus stage, long after the original input of heat energy absorbed from the ground surface is gone? Actually, the unequal heating of the ground served only as a trigger effect to release a

Figure 5.8 The rise of a bubble of heated air forms a small cumulus cloud. (From A. N. Strahler [1971] *The Earth Sciences,* 2nd ed., Harper & Row, New York.)

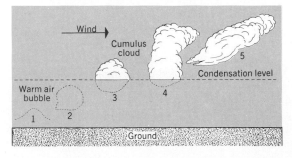

spontaneous updraft, fed by latent heat energy liberated from the condensing water vapor. Recall that for every gram of water formed by condensation, 600 calories of heat are released. This heat acts like fuel in a bonfire.

A mass of air capable of rising spontaneously during condensation is said to be **unstable.** In such air, the updraft tends to increase in intensity as time goes on, much as a bonfire blazes with increasing ferocity as the updraft draws in greater supplies of oxygen. Of course, at very high altitudes, the bulk of the water vapor has condensed and fallen as precipitation, so that the energy source is gone. When this happens the convection cell weakens and air rise finally ceases.

Unstable air, given to spontaneous convection in the form of heavy showers and thunderstorms, is most likely to be found in warm, humid areas such as the equatorial and tropical zones throughout the year, and the midlatitude regions during the summer season.

Orographic and Frontal Precipitation

Forced ascent of large masses of air occurs under two quite different sets of controlling conditions. Where prevailing winds encounter a mountain range, the air layer as a whole is forced to rise in order to surmount the barrier. Precipitation produced in this way is described as **orographic,** meaning "related to mountains." An explanation of orographic precipitation is given in the accompanying science supplement.

A layer of cold air may act in much the same way as a mountain barrier. Warm air in motion often encounters a cold air layer. The surface of contact of the two unlike masses of air is called a **weather front.** The cold air is denser than the warm and will remain close to the ground, acting as a barrier to progress of the warm air. The warm air is then forced to rise over the barrier. In a related type of mechanism, the cold air layer is in motion and forces the warm air to rise over it. Precipitation resulting from weather activity along fronts is explained in Unit 10.

Cloud Seeding

Early scientific experiments with rainmaking, using principles of atmospheric science, were conducted in the 1940s by Irving Langmuir and Vincent Schaefer. These researchers used the principle of **cloud seeding,** a natural process in cumulonimbus clouds wherein ice crystals falling from the cloud top serve to coagulate supercooled droplets to form raindrops.

Langmuir and Schaefer released dry-ice (solid CO_2) pellets into a stratus cloud and found that there resulted a rapid growth of ice particles at the expense of liquid particles in a layer of supercooled cloud particles. Their work was followed by that of Bernard Vonnegut in which silver iodide smoke was released to provide nuclei. When basic conditions were favorable, this method proved capable of intensifying condensation in dense cumulus clouds. The

latent heat thus released caused cumulonimbus clouds to form and to yield heavy precipitation. But for many years the efficacy of the method to increase precipitation remained in doubt.

Severe drought in south and central Florida in 1970 and 1971 led to intensification of cloud-seeding experiments begun in 1968 by Joanne Simpson and William L. Woodley of the Experimental Meteorological Laboratory of NOAA (National Oceanic and Atmospheric Administration). By dropping pyrotechnic flares into the tops of individual massive cumulus clouds, these investigators were able to increase rainfall sevenfold. A later project attempted to produce mergers between separate clouds, since larger clouds produce disproportionately more rain than smaller ones. Only occasional days are favorable for seeding experiments, and the optimum in results is to increase rainfall, not to break a severe drought.

Attempts to increase winter snowfall over high mountain ranges appear to have been effective. Here the orographic effect is important. In a carefully controlled experimental program, using sophisticated statistical methods involving randomized sampling, the effect of seeding was studied near Climax, Colorado, along the Continental Divide. Experiments were conducted in two stages—1960 to 1965 and 1965 to 1970—using ground-based silver iodide generators. Snowfall was carefully recorded at 70 observing stations. Under conditions when cloud tops were in the temperature range of 10° to −4° F (−11° to −20° C), the increase of snowfall following seeding amounted to 75 to 85%. Under colder cloud conditions, the results were variable and inconclusive.

Using the data and experience of the Climax experiments, *Project Skywater* was launched in 1969 in south-

Figure 5.9   This schematic diagram summarizes the exchanges of water vapor from pole to pole.

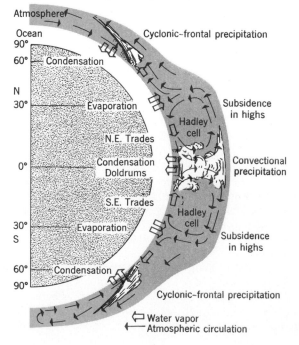

Atmosphere

Ocean
90°

60° Condensation

N
30° Evaporation

Cyclonic–frontal precipitation

Subsidence in highs

Hadley cell

N.E. Trades

0° Condensation
Doldrums

Convectional precipitation

S.E. Trades

30°
S   Evaporation

Hadley cell

Subsidence in highs

60° Condensation
90°

Cyclonic–frontal precipitation

⇦ Water vapor
← Atmospheric circulation

western Colorado, over the San Juan Mountains, in an effort to increase the winter snowpack. This cloud-seeding project is designed to create more snowmelt runoff for the Colorado River drainage system. At the same time, an ecological study is evaluating the effects of both the increased precipitation and the silver iodide fallout upon plants and animals of the mountain region.

Water Vapor and the Global Balances of Energy and Water

To conclude this study unit, let us take another look at the global energy balance so as to include the mechanism of heat transport in latent form. Figure 5.9 is a schematic diagram showing how evaporation and condensation are involved in energy exchange in each of the major latitude zones. We can now also visualize the pattern of transport of water vapor across the parallels of latitude; this is a transport of matter and is part of the global water balance.

The equatorial zone is characterized by a rise of moist, warm air in innumerable convection cells reaching to the upper limits of the troposphere. As condensation and precipitation occur here, enormous amounts of latent heat energy are liberated. This zone has been called the "fire box" of the globe in recognition of this intense production of sensible heat by condensation. Moving equatorward to replace the rising air are the tropical easterlies, or **trades,** part of the Hadley cell circulation. Water evaporates from the ocean surface over the subtropical highs and is carried equatorward in vapor form.

Next, we move into the midlatitudes, where upper-air waves constantly form and dissolve in the westerlies. Here, horizontal vortices exchange cold, polar air for warm, tropical air across the parallels of latitude. Water vapor is also transported poleward, carrying with it much latent heat. Condensation in storms along weather fronts removes water vapor from the troposphere toward high latitudes, so that the poleward movement of water vapor declines and reaches zero at the poles.

SCIENCE SUPPLEMENT
Cloud Forms and Cloud Classification

Cloud types are classified on the basis of two characteristics: form and altitude. The accompanying diagram, Figure 5.10, shows the four major cloud families and the individual cloud types within each family. Families A, B,

and C are defined in terms of height; Family D consists of clouds having extended vertical development and produced by convection. The prefix **nimbo** designates a cloud that is producing precipitation.

The high clouds, cirrus and related types, are composed of ice. Cirrus is a delicate wispy cloud; it does not interfere appreciably with the passage of sunlight. Middle clouds may be cumuliform or stratiform. Low clouds include dense nimbostratus, yielding rain or snow. Clouds with vertical development range from small cumulus of fair weather to great cumulonimbus towers.

Figure 5.10 Cloud families and cloud types.

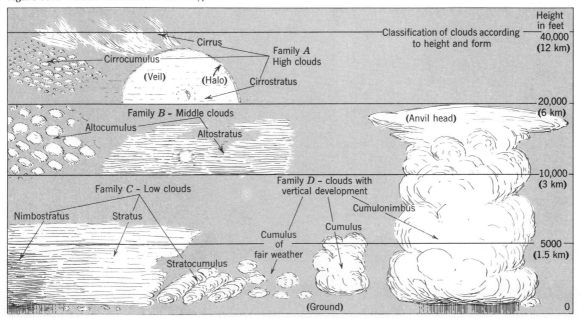

Orographic Precipitation and Rainshadows

The accompanying diagram, Figure 5.11, shows steps associated with production of orographic precipitation. Moist air arrives at the coast after passing over a large ocean surface. As the air rises on the windward side of the range, it is cooled at the adiabatic rate. When cooling is sufficient, precipitation sets in. After passing over the mountain summit, the air begins to descend the lee side of the range. Now it undergoes a warming through the same adiabatic process and, having no source from which to draw up moisture, becomes very dry. Upon reaching sea level, it is much warmer than at the start. A belt of dry climate, often called a **rainshadow,** exists on the lee side of the range. Several great deserts of the earth are of this type.

Dry, warm **foehn winds** (Austrian Alps) and **chinook winds** (northwestern North America), which occur on the lee side of a mountain range, cause extremely rapid evaporation of snow or soil moisture. These winds result from turbulent mixing of lower and upper air in the lee of the range. The upper air, which has little moisture to begin with, is greatly dried and heated when swept down to low levels.

An excellent illustration of orographic precipitation and rainshadow occurs in the far west of the United States. The accompanying map, Figure 5.12, shows California's mean annual precipitation by lines called **isohyets.** Prevailing westerly winds bring moist air from the Pacific Ocean over the coast ranges of central and northern California and the great Sierra Nevada range, whose summits rise to 14,000 ft

(4000 m) above sea level. Heavy rainfall occurs on the windward slopes of these ranges, nourishing rich forests. Passing down the steep eastern face of the Sierras, air must descend nearly to sea level, even below sea level in Death Valley. The adiabatic heating so caused, and a consequent reduction in humidity, produces part of America's great desert zone, covering a strip of eastern California and all of Nevada.

Much orographic rainfall is actually of the convectional type, in that it takes the form of heavy convectional showers and thunderstorms. The convection is induced by the forced ascent of unstable air as it passes over the mountain barrier.

Figure 5.12 Mean annual precipitation for the State of California. Isohyets are in inches.

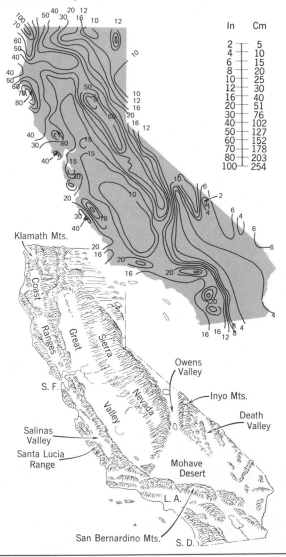

Figure 5.11 Orographic precipitation. (From A. N. Strahler [1971] *The Earth Sciences,* 2nd ed., Harper & Row, New York.)

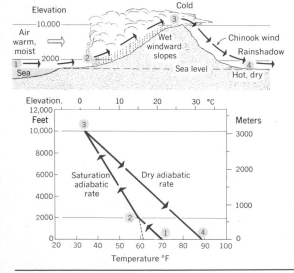

Unit 6
Man and the Ice Age

Human Evolution and the Ice Age

Modern Man is the child of a great Ice Age, evolving as a species under the influence of wide swings of climate from mild to severely cold. During this critical evolutionary period, probably fewer than one-half million individuals comprised the total human population at any one time. Although skilled in the use of fire during the Ice Age, Man as an animal species had little significant impact upon the atmospheric environment. Now the tables are turned; we are worried that the increasing combustion of enormous quantities of hydrocarbon fuels will set off either a new advance of glacial ice or will stimulate a warming of climate with equally serious consequences. With a little imagination, we can visualize our cities as either slowly engulfed by creeping ice or drowned by rising ocean water.

Homo sapiens, the species that includes all living races of humans, appeared on the scene early in middle Pleistocene time, about −500,000 years

(500,000 years before the present). A number of different varieties of this species, formerly considered as separate species, appeared in Europe. Neanderthal Man, who inhabited Europe from about −100,000 to −40,000 years was heavy-boned, short, and stocky. These people were able to make good stone tools, such as axes, scrapers, and points; they were capable hunters and food gatherers. Neanderthal Man is associated with the Middle Paleolithic culture, or "Old Stone Age."

At about −35,000 years, Neanderthal Man was replaced in Europe by a more advanced race of *Homo sapiens,* called Cro-Magnon Man. Cro-Magnon Man had a high forehead and small lower jaw, but a prominent chin, in contrast with the low forehead and massive jutting jaws of Neanderthal Man. Cro-Magnon Man stood erect, the skull resting directly over the top of the spine. Although these people belonged to the final stages of the Paleolithic culture, the quality of their finely chipped stone implements was very high and, moreover, they were able to shape ivory into tools, weapons, and ornaments.

A Neanderthal encampment. (Reproduced by permission from J. Augusta and Z. Burian, *Prehistoric Man,* Prague, Artia.)

Restoration of a winter scene in Europe in Pleistocene time showing the woolly mammoth and the woolly rhinoceros. (Field Museum of Natural History.)

Following the Ice Age, milder climate spread northward, and with it came forests. Now the Paleolithic culture was succeeded by the Neolithic culture, starting in the Near East. Hunting dominated the early Neolithic culture for a long period, but then newer races of this culture learned to make pottery and to domesticate animals, and gradually turned to agriculture.

In this unit we will investigate the Ice Age as a physical phenomenon by viewing the growth and disappearance of great ice sheets as responses to global climate change.

Ice Sheets and Glaciations

The Ice Age falls into a unit of geologic time called the **Pleistocene Epoch.** Lasting perhaps two million years, this time unit is hardly more than an instant in the total scale of geologic time—rocks containing abundant remains of advanced life forms range back in time over half a billion years.

The Ice Age consists of an alternating succession of two events: glaciation and interglaciation. A **glaciation** is a period of growth of a continental ice sheet, during which time the ice sheet spreads southward into midlatitudes over North America and Europe, with lesser advances in Siberia and South America. An **interglaciation** is a mild climatic period following ice sheet recession, perhaps to the point of disappearance. An **ice sheet** is an ice layer ranging in thickness from several hundred to several thousand feet and covering a landmass of subcontinental area.

Two great ice sheets of the present time are the Greenland Ice Sheet and the Antarctic Ice Sheet (Figure 6.1). Both of these ice bodies are closely limited to the landmasses of Greenland and Antarctica. We are currently experiencing an interglaciation (or interglacial stage), but this does not necessarily imply that no ice sheets exist. Antarctica has probably been covered by an ice sheet continuously for all of the Pleistocene Epoch and very much longer—perhaps for the last 20 million years.

Glaciers, whether ice sheets of continental dimensions or long narrow alpine glaciers, occupying previous valleys, are characterized by continuous, slow motion. Motion is partly by internal flow; the ice under heavy load behaves as a plastic substance and yields under the force of gravity. Our Science Supplement explains some principles of glacier dynamics.

Glaciation of North America and Europe

The full record of the Pleistocene Epoch includes at least four well-documented glaciations separated by interglaciations. There is some evidence that six glaciations may have occurred, and even perhaps more than six. We are primarily concerned, however, with the most recent of these, the **Wisconsin glaciation,** because of its strong environmental influence on climate, soils, and vegetation during the time when *Homo sapiens* first appeared on the scene in Europe.

The Wisconsin glaciation (or, as it is known in Europe, the Würm glaciation) began at about −75,000 years and ended about −10,000 years. The recession of the Wisconsin ice sheets by melting and evaporation, described as **deglaciation,** appears to have been a very rapid phenomenon in response to a rapidly warming climate.

Figures 6.2 and 6.3 show the extent to which North America and Europe were covered at the maximum known spread of the Wisconsin ice advance. Over North America, the dominant ice body was the Laurentide Ice Sheet, centered about over Hudson Bay. It began as an icecap, situated over the Labrador Highlands, which en-

Figure 6.1 The great ice sheet of Antarctica. In this oblique air view toward the head of the Shackleton Glacier we see in the distance the polar ice plateau. (U.S. Geological Survey photograph,)

larged and spread south, west, and northwest to reach the base of the Cordilleran ranges on the west and the arctic islands on the north. Over the Cordilleran ranges coalescent icecaps and alpine glaciers formed a single ice body

reaching down to the Pacific coast on the west and to the mountain foothills on the east. In the United States, all the land lying north of the Missouri and Ohio rivers was covered, as well as northern Pennsylvania and all of New York and New England.

In Europe, the Scandinavian Ice Sheet centered upon the Baltic Sea, covering the Scandinavian countries and

Figure 6.2 Pleistocene ice sheets of North America at their maximum spread reached as far south as the present Ohio and Missouri rivers. (After R. F. Flint.)

Figure 6.3 The Scandinavian ice sheet dominated northern Europe during the Pleistocene glaciations. Solid line shows limits of ice in the Wisconsin (Würm) glaciation; dotted line on land shows maximum extent in earlier glaciations. (After R. F. Flint.)

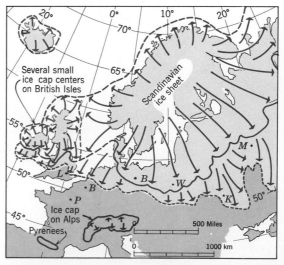

spreading as far south as central Germany. The British Isles were almost covered by an icecap that had several centers on highland areas and spread outward to coalesce with the Scandinavian ice sheet. The Alps at the same time were heavily inundated by enlarged alpine glaciers, fused into a single icecap. All high mountain areas of the world underwent greatly intensified alpine glaciation at the time of maximum ice-sheet advance. Today, only small remnant alpine glaciers exist as vestiges of these great valley glaciers. In less favorable mountain regions no glaciers remain.

Causes of Glaciations

We will not go into detail on merits and shortcomings of several contending hypotheses purporting to explain repeated glaciations and interglaciations. A few general statements are of environmental interest because they bring up certain of the same mechanisms of global climatic change we examined in Unit 5. The difference between this and our earlier discussion is one of time scale, since each episode of glaciation persisted many thousands of years.

Consider first that glaciation requires a substantial decrease in average global air and sea surface temperatures, enough to reduce rates of ice melting and evaporation and so allow ice to accumulate. Second, there must be an adequate supply of snowfall over highland areas serving as

the sites of development of the initial icecaps. A basic counteracting mechanism exists here, because lowered air and sea surface temperatures result in reduced evaporation and reduced moisture-holding capacity of the air.

Evidence of lowered global air temperatures during glaciations comes from both terrestrial and marine sources. One line of evidence is the lowered elevation of the **snowline,** or lower limit of snow accumulations lasting through the entire year (Figure 6.4). Figure 6.5 is a meridional profile along the Cordilleran ranges and Andes from 65° N to 60° S latitude, which shows the altitude of the snowline of today as compared with that during a glaciation. These snowlines are smoothed lines, evening out local differences in altitude due to varying local influences. In North America, the amount of lowering was about 5000 ft (1500 m). In the Andes at low latitudes the snowline was lowered about 2000 ft (600 m). Similar figures apply on other continents. The lowering of snowline is interpreted as representing a drop of mean annual global air temperature of between 9 and 13 F° (5 and 7 C°).

Lowering of the snowline must have been accompanied by a lowering of all life zones stratified according to altitude. This change would have required plants and animals to migrate to lower elevations or to lower latitudes to remain in the same thermal environments. A reverse effect would be caused by the rising of snowline during deglaciation.

An important basic factor contributing to onset of glaciation, whatever the primary mechanism of control, is the

Figure 6.4   Zone of perpetual snow within a few degrees of latitude of the equator. White Range, near Ancash, Peru. (Aero Service Division, Western Geophysical Co. of America.)

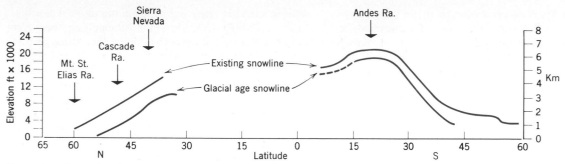

Figure 6.5 Generalized profile of the present snow line and lowered Pleistocene snow line of maximum glaciations. (Data of R. F. Flint [1957] *Glacial and Pleistocene Geology,* John Wiley, New York, p. 47. Figure 4.1.)

widespread presence of high mountain systems and high plateaus over the continents in Pleistocene time. These upland features could act as orographic traps for snowfall and also permit the snow accumulations to be retained at high elevations where air temperatures are prevailingly low. Once a large icecap had developed, it became its own orographic trap for continued precipitation. The Labrador highlands are an example, serving as the center for initial accumulation of the Laurentide ice sheet (see Figure 6.2).

One group of hypotheses of glaciation invokes a reduction in solar energy received by the earth. It has been proposed that glaciations occur when radiant output of the sun is reduced; a reduced planetary temperature would follow. Actually, no evidence has been found for past reductions in solar output on a scale sufficient to cause glaciation.

The quantity of solar radiation intercepted by the earth varies with cyclic changes in distance between earth and sun. The eccentricity of the earth's orbit causes the distance to vary yearly from a minimum at the closest approach (perihelion, January 3) to a maximum at the most distant point (aphelion, July 4). This changing distance has the effect of giving the south polar region a slightly larger input of solar energy during the summer of that hemisphere than the north polar region receives during the summer of its hemisphere. Without going into details, it can be added that there is a cycle of variation in eccentricity of the earth's orbit, and this results in a cycle of changing distance with a period of about 90,000 years in which the distance can deviate as much as about 5% from the mean value. Another astronomical cycle varies the inclination of the earth's axis with respect to the plane of the earth's orbit with a period of 40,000 years. When these astronomical cycles are combined, a curve of varying solar radiation can be computed for a selected latitude, such as 45° N or 55° N, and shows appreciable departures from the average value. There are a number of scientists who consider these changes in intensity of solar radiation at midlatitudes as sufficient to bring on a glaciation, or a deglaciation. The astronomical hypotheses are strongly debated.

Solar energy variation may play a role as a causative agent in glaciation in yet another way. Increased quantities of volcanic dust in the atmosphere may bring on a glaciation because more solar energy is absorbed in the stratosphere and radiated back into space and hence less is permitted to enter the lower atmosphere. The role of volcanic dusts in varying radiation received at low levels has been discussed in Unit 4. Evidence of intensified volcanic activity in phase with glaciations is rather uncertain and controversial.

An important and widely held theory attributes glaciation to a reduction of the carbon dioxide content of the atmosphere. The role of carbon dioxide in absorbing longwave radiation and thus warming the atmosphere has been explained in Unit 4. It is estimated that, if the carbon dioxide content of the atmosphere, which is now about 0.03% by volume, were reduced by half that amount, the earth's average surface temperature would drop about 7 F° (4 C°).

Another group of theories proposes shifts in the positions of the continents with respect to the poles, bringing various landmasses into polar positions favorable for the growth of ice sheets. Still another theory requires changes in oceanic currents, specifically the diversion or blocking of such warm currents as the Gulf Stream, which would have brought colder climates to the subarctic regions.

Pleistocene Changes of Sea Level

Journalists and other writers seeking a public audience have enjoyed speculating upon the consequences of a future interglacial climate warm enough to melt the world's glacial ice and return its water to the oceans. The Antarctic Ice Sheet alone holds enough ice (90% of the world's glacial ice) so that, if entirely melted, the world sea level would rise about 200 ft (60 m). Actually, because the load of this added water layer would depress somewhat the crust of the continental margins, the result might be an inundation to what is presently a level about 135 ft (40 m) higher than existing sea level. At the very outside, with all glacial ice melted, the maximum rise might be on the order of 200 ft (60 m). If you were to draw the 200-ft (60-m) contour on the map of the United States, using that as the new shoreline, you would find that a broad band of the Atlantic and Gulf coasts would be under water. Isolated clusters of high-rise buildings would project from beneath the ocean surf in many major cities such as Boston, New York, Philadelphia, Miami, and New Orleans. The entire Florida peninsula would be awash. West coast urban areas similarly affected would include Portland, Seattle, Tacoma, the San Francisco Bay area, and much of metropolitan Los Angeles.

The best available evidence indicates that stands of sea level higher than the present have not been of spectacular proportions in previous interglacial periods. During the last interglacial period before the Wisconsin glaciation, a sea-level stand about 18 ft (6 m) higher than today has been fairly well documented. This evidence means that much of the glacial ice of Greenland and Antarctica remained intact through that entire interglacial period. Even if we do experience a major warming period to the normal maximum extent reached previously, coastal drowning will not be so devastating an event as the journalists conjure up.

Perhaps more interesting, and certainly more real, is the great lowering of sea level that accompanied growth of the Wisconsin ice sheets. Various lines of evidence converge on a figure of −400 ft (−120 m) for the drawdown of sea level 15,000 years ago, not long before the last deglaciation set in. At that time a broad zone of the continental shelf off our Atlantic coast was exposed, and the shoreline lay some 60 to 125 mi (100 to 200 km) east of its present position. Remains of freshwater plants show that this exposed shelf was a richly vegetated landscape; animal remains show that it supported land animals, such as elephants (mastodons and mammoths). Although glacial ice stood not far away at the time, the climate was not as severe as one might suppose, being essentially like that of the subarctic lands of Canada, and at times not much different from that of northern New England today.

Holocene Environments

The elapsed time span of about 10,000 years since the Wisconsin deglaciation is called the **Holocene Epoch;** it began with rapid warming of ocean surface temperatures. Continental climate zones shifted rapidly poleward. Soil-forming processes began to act upon new parent matter of glacial deposits in midlatitudes. Plants became reestablished in glaciated areas in a succession of climate stages. First of these was known as the **Boreal stage.** Boreal refers to the present subarctic region where needleleaf forests dominate the vegetation. The history of climate and vegetation throughout the Holocene time has been interpreted through a study of spores and pollens found in layered order from bottom to top in postglacial bogs. (This study is called palynology.) Plant species can be identified and ages of samples can be determined. Interpretation of pollens indicates that the Boreal stage in midlatitudes had a vegetation similar to that now found in the subarctic zone; a dominant tree was spruce.

There followed a general warming of climate until the

Atlantic climatic stage was reached about −8000 years. Lasting for about 3000 years, the Atlantic stage had average air temperatures somewhat higher than those of today—perhaps on the order of 4.5 F° (2.5 C°) higher. We call such a period a **climatic optimum** with reference to the midlatitude zone of North America and Europe. There followed a period of temperatures below average, the **Subboreal climatic stage,** in which alpine glaciers showed a period of readvance. In this stage, which spanned the age range −5000 to −2000 years, sea level had reached a position close to that of the present, and coastal submergence of the continents was largely completed.

The past 2000 years, from the time of Christ to the present, shows climatic cycles on a finer scale than those we have described as Holocene climatic stages. This refinement in detail of climatic fluctuations is a consequence of the availability of historical records and of more detailed evidence generally. Recall from Unit 4 that a secondary climatic optimum occurred in the period 1000 to 1200 A.D. (−1000 to −800 years), and that this warm episode was followed by the Little Ice Age 1450–1850 A.D. (−550 to −150 years). During this time valley glaciers made new advances to lower levels. In the process, the ice overrode forests and so left a mark of its maximum extent.

Man and Glaciations

In our last study unit we examined conflicting predictions as to Man's role in causing global climate change. Cycles of glaciation and interglaciation demonstrate the power of natural forces to make drastic swings from cold to warm climates. Lesser climatic cycles of the Holocene Epoch also occurred through natural causes. Only following the Industrial Revolution do we recognize possible linkages between global air temperature change and Man's combustion of hydrocarbon fuels on a massive scale. There is general agreement that increased carbon dioxide tends to cause a rise in average temperatures; that an increase in input of industrial dusts reaching the upper atmosphere tends to lower average temperatures near the earth's surface. There seems also to be general agreement that average atmospheric temperatures in the northern hemisphere, rose steadily from about 1900 to 1940, then began to fall and are probably continuing to fall today. But we do not know to what extent these observed changes are parts of a natural cycle and to what extent they are influenced by the impacts of an industrial society.

We can only follow the advice unanimously agreed upon by scientists doing climatic research: intensify our efforts to monitor atmospheric changes; increase as rapidly as possible our understanding of how the global atmospheric processes work.

If the long-term global climate changes we have so far investigated seem to defy positive statements, the opposite is true of local climate changes, particularly over urban areas. Man's impact on the climate of cities is well documented and the causes are well understood. It is to those impacts we turn in the next two study units.

SCIENCE SUPPLEMENT

Glacier Dynamics

Most of us know ice only as a brittle, crystalline solid because we are accustomed to seeing it only in small quantities. Where a great thickness of ice exists, let us say 200 to 300 ft (60 to 90 m) or more, the ice at the bottom behaves as a plastic material and will slowly flow in such a way as to spread out the mass over a larger area, or to cause it to move downhill, as the case may be. This behavior characterizes **glaciers,** which may be defined as any large natural accumulations of land ice affected by present or past motion.

Conditions requisite to the accumulation of glacial ice are simply that snowfall of the winter shall, on the average, exceed the amount of melting and evaporation of snow that occurs in summer. (The term **ablation** is used by glaciologists to include both evaporation and melting of snow and ice.) Thus, each year a layer of snow is added to what has already accumulated. As the snow compacts, by surface melting and refreezing, it turns into a granular ice, then is compressed by overlying layers into hard crystalline ice. When the ice becomes so thick that the lower layers become plastic, outward or downhill flow commences, and an active glacier has come into being. Glaciers that form in high mountains are characteristically long and narrow because they occupy previously formed valleys. They bring the plastic ice from small collecting grounds high upon the range down to lower elevations, and consequently warmer temperatures, where the ice disappears by ablation. Such **alpine glaciers** are distinctive types.

In arctic and polar regions upland areas of many thousands of square miles may become buried under gigantic plates of ice whose thickness may reach several thousand feet. The term **icecap** is usually applied to an ice plate limited to high mountain and plateau areas. During glacial periods, an icecap spreads over surrounding lowlands, enveloping all landforms it encounters and ceasing its spread only when the rate of ablation at its outer edge balances the rate at which it is spreading. This extensive type of ice mass is an ice sheet.

Figure 6.6 is a schematic drawing comparing an alpine glacier with an icecap. Whereas the alpine glacier has a sloping floor, as does a water stream, the icecap may have a horizontal floor, or even an upwardly concave (saucer-shaped) floor. Flow of an icecap is induced by surface gradient of the ice. A simple analog is a spoonful of pancake batter poured on a flat skillet. As more batter is added at the center the pancake increases in size.

Further details of an alpine glacier as a flow system are shown in Figure 6.7. Input of matter takes place within the **zone of accumulation.** Layers of snow in stages of transformation to ice comprise the **firn.** Through flow, indicated by arrows, the ice moves both downvalley and into lower depths within the glacier. Upon entering the **zone of ablation,** flow lines turn surfaceward. Here ice is lost through

the upper boundary by evaporation and from the lower end, or **terminus,** by melting. Because of ablation, the lower glacier surface is deeply pitted and furrowed, in contrast to the smooth, white surface of the firn.

Glacier equilibrium is achieved when the rate of mass input in the firn zone is balanced by the rate of mass output in the ablation zone. Velocity of flow within the ice is adjusted to transport the mass through the system and the geometry of the glacier remains constant with time. By geometry we mean both volume and cross-sectional form of the glacier. In an equilibrium state the glacier terminus neither advances nor recedes.

A change in glacier equilibrium is caused by a change in the net input of snow in the accumulation zone, as averaged over several years' time. If there is an increase in input, the glacier thickens and flow velocity is increased. The glacier terminus then advances and the area of ablation is increased. Also, as the terminus reaches lower elevations, warmer air temperatures are encountered and ablation is accelerated. When ablation rate again matches accumulation rate within the system, the terminus is again stabilized. Should the net snow accumulation be reduced, the glacier will be reduced in thickness and will flow more

Figure 6.6 Schematic maps and a cross section of an alpine glacier and an icecap. (From A. N. Strahler [1972] *Planet Earth,* Harper & Row, New York.)

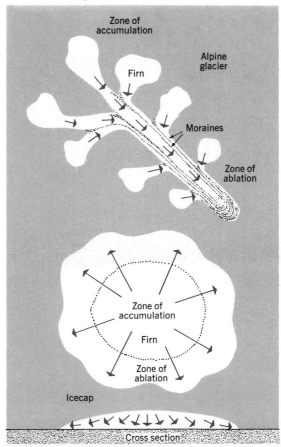

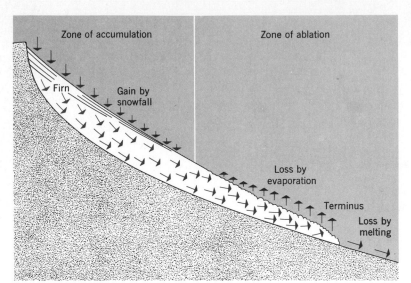

Figure 6.7   An idealized longitudinal cross section through an alpine glacier. (From A. N. Strahler [1972] *Planet Earth,* Harper & Row, New York.)

slowly. As a result, ablation exceeds the rate at which ice is supplied by flow and the terminus recedes to a higher position. In time, the terminus is again stabilized.

Alpine glaciers are rather sensitive indicators of changes in climatic factors that control both accumulation and ablation. Consequently, many modern glaciers are kept under surveillance by repeated topographical surveys, to determine their rates of advance or retreat and thus to draw inferences as to climatic changes occurring over decades of time.

Unit 7
Atmospheric Pollutants

Get the Lead Out?

Zoo animals in their cages might seem to be well protected against the onslaughts of environmental pollution, but recent events and research indicate that, on the contrary, they may be among its first victims. A 1971 news report in the journal *Science* tells of the plight of animals in the Staten Island Zoo. The first signs of trouble were experienced in November 1970, when an 11-month-old leopard developed some alarming symptoms—muscular weakness, refusal of food, and loss of hair. Taken to New York Medical College for diagnosis the sick leopard came under the observation of pathologist Ralph Strebel. No recognizable symptoms of any known disease were found, but the animal died only a day later.

Then, three weeks later, the victim's fraternal twin, a black leopard named Mr. Leo Pard, was found by zoo keepers lying paralyzed in his cage. Studied at New York Medical College, Leo showed no symptoms of any known animal disease, but he managed to survive under intensive care and was able to regain his muscular coordination. After six weeks he was well enough to return to his home at the Staten Island Zoo.

While under treatment, Leo had been tested for metal poisoning by Dennis Cranston, a toxicologist from the New York City Medical Examiner's Office. Extremely high levels of both lead and zinc were found in Leo's hair, blood, and feces. Then a check was made of the preserved internal organs of Leo's dead brother. The results were similar—high levels of lead and zinc there, too.

Now further tests were made for lead in other animals of the zoo. High concentrations of lead were found in other animals, ranging from primates down to reptiles. Looking back over the records, investigators found that a number of snakes in the zoo had died after showing such poor muscular coordination that they could not slither from place to place. Their preserved carcasses also showed high lead concentrations.

A search was begun for sources of lead poisoning in the zoo. Tests were made of water, food, and bedding materials used by the animals, but these proved to be free of lead. Analysis of paint used in cages showed presence of some lead, and that might seem at first to have been the answer. But then, high levels of lead were found outside the cages—in grass, leaves, and soil of the zoo grounds. These lead levels were as high as those observed close to major highways, where lead from automobile exhausts is the obvious source.

The pathologist who directed the investigation, Ralph Strebel, stated: "We can only conclude that most of the lead taken in by the animals resulted from atmospheric fallout." He went on to say: "The findings have ominous implications for the people of the city."

The Oakland–San Francisco Bay Bridge approach during morning rush hour. (Joe Munroe/Photo Researchers.)

Doubtless you are familiar with lead poisoning of small children living in old, dilapidated slum buildings. This form of poisoning comes from the ingestion of scaling layers of lead-based paint and lead-saturated plaster. But the evidence of the zoo animals suggested that lead from atmospheric fallout may be a factor in lead poisoning of city dwellers.

Later in 1971, *Science* carried a report that seemed to place increased suspicion upon atmospheric lead as a source of high lead concentration in children. Although this connection was strongly debated, there was clear evidence that atmospheric lead content was on the rise in urban areas and that its source was in emissions from combustion engines.

A group of New York City parents banded together at this time under the name of "Get the Lead Out Committee." They were concerned because lead levels were found to be high even in the blood of middle-class children not likely to have ingested lead from old paint and plaster. A group spokesman, Paul Du Brul, is quoted in *Science* as saying, "It's clear to me that there are too damn many kids with too damn much lead in their bodies." The committee intended to press for the removal of lead additives from gasoline. Said Du Brul, "We have to say 'No' to the automobile industry. We've already done inestimable damage to our children."

In 1972, a 330-page report on airborne lead in the environment was published by the prestigious National Academy of Sciences. In the general summary and conclusions, we read that while the exposure of urban dwellers to atmospheric lead pollution was fully recognized, ". . . the concentration of lead in the air of cities poses no identifiable threat to the general population." The report pointed, however, to two categories of persons for whom the exposure to airborne lead seems undesirable. One category includes persons exposed to heavy lead concentrations, for example, garage workers and traffic policemen. The second category is children. The report recognizes the high lead concentrations found in the blood samples of children, but notes, "The high blood lead concentrations cannot be ascribed specifically to the inhalation of lead, although it is a possibility."

As you know, federal efforts to control automobile emissions have resulted in a new gas pump in service stations: it serves nonleaded gasoline, and you must use it in your automobile if the exhaust is equipped with a catalytic converter.

In this study unit we will begin a study of air pollution. A knowledge of the various kinds of air pollutants will help you to understand the emission control regulations that are imposed upon your automobile.

Data Source: Robert J. Bazell (1971) Lead poisoning: Zoo animals may be the first victims, *Science*, vol. 173, pp. 130-131; Robert J. Bazell (1971) Lead poisoning: Combating the threat from the air, *Science*, vol. 174, pp. 574-576; Committee on Biologic Effects of Atmospheric Pollutants (1972) *Lead: Airborne lead in perspective*, National Research Council, National Academy of Sciences, Washington, D.C., pp. 209-211.

What is Environmental Pollution?

We may define Man-made **environmental pollution** as the introduction directly or indirectly through Man's activities into the atmosphere, hydrosphere, lithosphere, and biosphere of infusions of matter and energy at levels of quantity or intensity appreciably higher than natural levels and usually with undesirable or deleterious effects upon environments of the biosphere.

A **pollutant** is any form of energy or matter causing pollution. In **air pollution** the pollutants include gases and solid and liquid particles of both organic and inorganic chemical classification. **Water pollution** includes presence of disease-producing (pathogenic) bacteria and viruses (**biological pollution**) and of undesirable ions and compounds in solution (**chemical pollution**). Presence of suspended solids causing turbidity may be included as forms of water pollution. **Thermal pollution** of air and water, a form of energy infusion, raises the quantity of sensible heat in those fluids to abnormally high levels. **Noise pollution** illustrates energy infusion into the environment by sound-wave transmission.

In this study unit and the next, we investigate urban air pollution and some of its important impacts upon Man. Later study units will deal with water pollution. In each unit, we cover basic science principles that explain how pollutants are formed, how they are injected into air, water, and soil, and how they interact with life processes.

Particulate Matter in the Atmosphere

When discussing air pollution, the contents of the atmosphere can be placed into two basic categories or classes: particulate matter and gases. **Particulate matter** consists of particles of matter in either the liquid state or the solid state. In the language of air pollution science, these particles are usually called **particulates.**

Particulate matter injected into the atmosphere is of both natural and Man-made origins. From earlier study units, you are already familiar with a number of the natural forms of particulate matter: sea-salt crystals, mineral dust, and volcanic dust. These particulates play a vital role in the atmospheric processes by serving as nuclei of moisture condensation to form clouds. Another class of natural solid particulate matter is smoke from forest fires and grass fires. Living plants release pollens and spores into the air; these are organic compounds. From forest trees certain hydrocarbon compounds called **terpenes** are also released into the atmosphere in the form of minute droplets. These compounds are important in producing atmospheric haze that builds up naturally within stagnant air masses far from industrial air pollution sources.

Man-made particulate matter comes from many sources, but the major source is in combustion of hydrocarbon fuels—petroleum products, coal, peat, and wood. Combustion of solid wastes is another source. Other kinds of particulate matter are introduced into the atmosphere in manufacturing industrial chemicals, refining fossil fuels, mining and smelting ores, quarrying, cement manufacturing, and farming activities.

Sizes of Particulates

Particulates range in size from ultramicroscopic particles, consisting of a few molecules clustered together, to grains of ash or dust large enough to see individually under a magnifying glass. Figure 7.1 expresses the great range in sizes of particulates and the effects of size upon particle behavior. The scale of diameters runs from smallest at the left to largest at the right, using powers of ten. We can take the 1-micron line, near the middle of the graph, as an important dividing line. Particulates smaller than 1 micron in diameter, because of their very small size, behave very much like gas molecules. They are easily deflected by the impacts of gas molecules, a phenomenon called Brownian movement. These small particulates can remain suspended almost indefinitely in the atmosphere; they travel freely at the speed of the wind that moves them; they can rise to great heights and may enter the stratosphere. Particles that fall into this freely floating class are found in smoke; they also include the nuclei of condensation required for the formation of clouds. Fumes emitted in various chemical manufacturing processes and in ore smelting are also within this ultramicroscopic size class.

To the right of the 1-micron line on the graph of Figure 7.1 is a second distinct group of particulates—those large enough to fall steadily through the atmosphere under the force of gravity. They settle at constant velocities, depending upon size, the larger ones falling faster, of course. Notice that particles of fog, mist, drizzle, and rain are in this class, arranged in order of size. Industrial dusts belong mostly in this size class and include fly ash from smokestacks, coal dust, cement dust, milled flour, insecticide powders, paint pigments, and pollens. The natural mineral dust found in wind-produced dust storms over arid land surfaces is largely in this group of larger particulates. The process of particulate settling to reach the ground is termed **fallout.** Particulates of all sizes can also be swept down to the earth's surface by falling precipitation; this process is **washout** (or "scavenging"); it provides a means of clearing the atmosphere of particles too fine to settle out under gravity.

Upward Diffusion of Pollutants

If particulates larger than about 1 micron settle continually downward through the air, how do they arrive at high levels in the first place? The answer lies in atmospheric turbulence and convection. Wind consists of innumerable small eddies, resembling tight, corkscrew motions. The phenomenon is called **atmospheric turbulence.** Part of the motion in the eddies is in an upward direction. When the upward air speed is greater than the natural rate of fall of a particle, the particle is lifted. In this way, particulates gradually diffuse upward into the atmosphere through the same wind flow that also carries them long distances horizontally.

Convection, another mechanism of rise of particulates, consists of updrafts somewhat like the rise of hot air in a chimney. We will explain natural convection processes in Unit 11. Many industrial sources, particularly large smokestacks, emit hot air that rises rapidly in a column because the air is less dense than its surroundings. In this way pollutants can be carried up many hundreds of feet before the heat of the rising air column is lost to the surrounding air, halting further rise.

Figure 7.1 Sizes and physical properties of atmospheric particles. (Data from W. G. Frank, American Air Filter Company, Inc., Louisville, Ky. Reference: *Air Conservation* [1965] American Association for the Advancement of Science, Publ. 80, p. 110, Figure 5.)

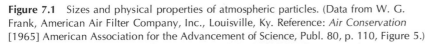

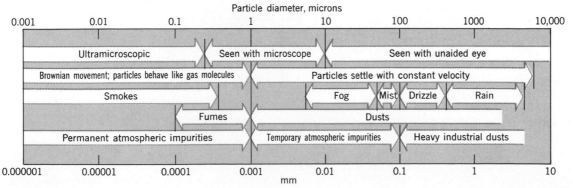

Primary and Secondary Particulates

We are now ready to investigate further the Man-made particulates in terms of their origin. Scientists dealing with air pollution recognize two classes of Man-made particulates: primary and secondary. **Primary particulates** are injected into the atmosphere from ground sources. The chemical and physical properties of primary particulates are acquired at ground-level sources. Most of the primary particulates are in the size range larger than 1 micron; they belong to a size grade that settles through the air under the force of gravity. The sources for primary particulates were listed in our earlier description of industrial dusts.

Secondary particulates are produced by chemical reactions that take place within the atmosphere. Gases are involved in the production of many secondary particulates; energy for certain of the chemical reactions is supplied by sunlight. The particulates themselves result from the attachment of the newly formed chemical compounds to the water films that surround solid condensation nuclei, already present in the atmosphere. Because these host particulates are of the free-floating ultramicroscopic size, smaller than 1 micron, the secondary particulates are for the most part also very small—between 0.1 and 1 micron. This very small size assures that secondary particulates will remain suspended in the air over cities for long periods of time, often increasing steadily in numbers to produce a distinctive and unpleasant Man-made haze known as **smog.** Removal of the primary particulates can only be accomplished by washout during precipitation, or by dilution as the particulates are carried downwind and mixed with large masses of cleaner air.

Gaseous Pollutants and Their Reactions

To understand how the secondary pollutants are formed, it is necessary first to list the important pollutant gases injected into the atmosphere from Man-made sources. For the most part, these are oxides of sulfur and nitrogen, along with ammonia and carbon monoxide. Because of their importance in urban air pollution monitoring and control, we list these gases with their chemical compositions as follows:

Name of Gas	Chemical Formula
Sulfur oxides	SO_2, SO_3
Nitrogen oxides	NO, NO_2, NO_3
	(often grouped as NO_x)
Ammonia	NH_3
Carbon monoxide	CO

Carbon dioxide gas (CO_2) is given off in large quantities during the combustion of fuels, but because it is not harmful to health and is one of the natural components of pure air, it is not regarded as a pollutant gas.

Besides the above gases, ground emissions that are important in the formation of secondary particulates include hydrocarbon compounds and various compounds of lead, chlorine, and bromine. These take the form of small solid particulates.

The two principal gases making up the pure atmosphere—oxygen (O_2) and nitrogen (N_2)—are of major importance in chemical reactions that produce secondary particulates.

Chemical reactions in the atmosphere which involve the above gases and are energized by sunlight are called

Figure 7.2   Air pollution emissions in the United States, 1968. Percentage by weight. (Reference: 1971 Annual Report of the Council on Environmental Quality, U.S. Govt. Printing Office, p. 64.)

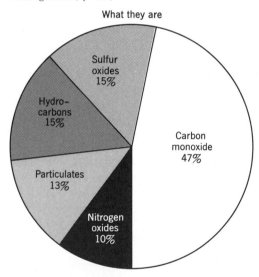

What they are

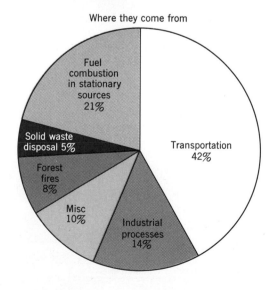

Where they come from

Table 7.1 Components of Air Pollution and Their Sources in the United States, 1968

Contaminants (millions of tons per year)[a]

Sources	Carbon Monoxide	Particulate Matter	Sulfur Oxides	Hydro-carbons	Nitrogen Oxides	Totals	
Transportation	64	1	1	17	8	91	(83)
Fuel combustion: stationary sources	2	9	24	1	10	46	(42)
Industrial processes	10	7	7	5	0.2	29	(26)
Solid waste disposal	8	1	0.1	2	1	11	(10)
Miscellaneous[b]	17	10	0.6	8	2	37	(34)
Total	100 (91)	28 (26)	33 (30)	32 (29)	21 (19)	214	(195)

SOURCE: NAPCA Inventory of Air Pollutant Emissions (1970). Reference: 1971 Annual Report of the Council on Environmental Quality, U.S. Government Printing Office, Table 1.
Note: Figures rounded off.
[a]Metric tons in parentheses.
[b]Largely from forest fires, agricultural burning, and coal waste fires.

photochemical reactions; they are the major source of irritating and dangerous pollutants in the smog of urban areas. Without actually stating these reactions by chemical equations, we can describe the important reactions in words.

Sulfur dioxide (SO_2) is a leading culprit in forming harmful products through photochemical reactions. The sulfur dioxide gas combines readily with atmospheric oxygen (O_2) and with the water films on suspended particulates to produce sulfuric acid (H_2SO_4). Sulfuric acid is extremely corrosive since it impairs the respiratory system of humans and damages a wide variety of materials with which it comes in contact.

Oxides of nitrogen (NO_x) are another group of major culprits in generating harmful products in urban smog. Nitrogen oxide can form nitric acid (HNO_3); like sulfuric acid, it is highly corrosive. Nitric acid can, in turn, react with ordinary salt (sodium chloride, $NaCl$), found in water films on particulates, to produce hydrochloric acid (HCl).

One of the most insidious gases produced in polluted air is ozone (O_3), a form of oxygen which we explained in Unit 1. Ozone is a poisonous gas, and it can also react with hydrocarbon compounds to produce other toxic compounds, for example, **ethylene,** a common pollutant in urban smog. One way in which ozone is produced is through a photochemical reaction. A molecule of nitrogen dioxide (NO_2) is split up by sunlight into two parts: nitric oxide (NO) and an oxygen atom (O). The oxygen atom quickly combines with a nearby molecule of oxygen gas (O_2), forming a molecule of ozone (O_3).

The principal components of air pollution, both primary particulates and gases, injected into the atmosphere in one year in the United States are listed in Table 7.1, together with their major sources. The data are shown in graphical form in Figure 7.2.

Air Pollution Standards

Late in 1970, the Federal Clean Air Act was signed into law, giving the Environmental Protection Agency authority to set national standards for tolerable limits of pollutants in the air. These standards are given in Table 7.2. Included in the act is provision for an emergency alert system that will signal the need to reduce fuel combustion and curtail the use of automobiles when the danger point is reached in a given city.

Table 7.2 Air Pollution Standards—Limits of Concentrations Permitted

Pollutant	Weight of Pollutants per Cubic Meter of Air
Carbon monoxide	10 milligrams maximum 8-hour concentration
Sulfur oxides	80 micrograms annual mean, 365 micrograms maximum 24-hour concentration
Hydrocarbon compounds	125 micrograms maximum 3-hour concentration
Nitrogen oxides	100 micrograms annual mean, 250 micrograms maximum 24-hour concentration
Photochemical oxidants	125 micrograms maximum 1-hour concentration
Particulates	75 micrograms annual mean, 260 micrograms maximum 24-hour concentration

Fog and Fog Dispersal

Fog is an environmental hazard, as those who drive the nation's city streets and highways know all too well. In marine navigation, fog brings grave danger of collision of one vessel with another or with an iceberg, or of running aground. To these classic perils of the sea are now added the perils of aircraft operation in and out of fogbound landing fields. A large city airport, closed down by fog, incurs enormous losses of revenues due to flight cancellations, to say nothing of loss of productive time to thousands of persons forced to wait in airports or to seek alternative means of transportation.

Fog is simply a stratiform cloud lying very close to the ground. One type, known as a **radiation fog,** is formed at night. This type of fog requires still air and clear skies above, so that the nocturnal net radiation loss is large and mixing cannot occur. When the air temperature near the ground falls below the dew point, fog is formed.

Another type, **advection fog,** results from the movement of warm, moist air over a cold or snow-covered ground surface. Losing heat to the ground, the air layer undergoes a drop of temperature below the dew point, and condensation sets in. A similar type of advection fog is formed over oceans where air from over a warm current blows across the cold surface of an adjacent cold current. Fogs of the Grand Banks off Newfoundland are largely of this origin because here the cold Labrador current comes in contact with warm waters of Gulf Stream origin.

Frequency of occurrence of dense fog varies greatly with region. The accompanying map, Figure 7.3, shows that for the United States and southern Canada, fog incidence is highest in coastal areas, especially adjacent to cold currents (Pacific Coast, New England), over large inland water bodies (Great Lakes), and over mountainous areas in humid climates (Appalachian region). In contrast, dense

Figure 7.4 Airborne cloud seeding cleared the fog from this runway at Elmendorf Air Base, Alaska. Note the dense fog remaining over the far end of the runway. (U.S. Air Force photograph.)

fogs are rare in interior continental regions, especially in the deserts and semiarid grasslands of the West.

Fog dispersal is a form of weather modification that has invited research and experimentation because of its great potential use at airports. Seeding experiments have shown that fog consisting of supercooled droplets can be cleared by seeding, using liquid propane or dry ice (Figure 7.4). Seeding causes rapid transformation of water droplets into ice particles. The very cold fogs to which this method applies are only a small percentage of all fogs that occur in middle and high latitudes. Warm fogs require other methods for dispersal, and these have met with some success, but at high cost.

Figure 7.3 Greatly generalized map of the 48 contiguous United States and southern Canada showing number of days annually with dense fog. (Data of J. N. Myers, NOAA, National Weather Service, and Dept. of Mines & Technical Survey, Atlas of Canada.)

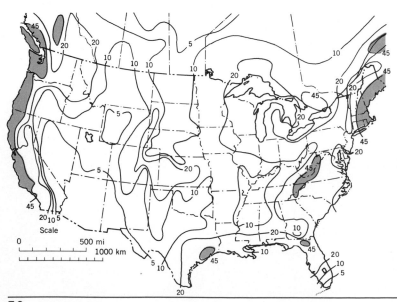

Unit 8
Air Pollution Meteorology

The Ordeal of Donora, Pennsylvania

October 26, 1948: Tuesday morning at Donora dawned cold and damp. A fog had settled in and the air was dead calm. Nothing in this situation was unusual for the small western Pennsylvania community crowded into the flat floor of the winding valley of the Monongahela River, not far south of Pittsburgh. Nor was Donora an unusual town in this region, where steel mills, railroads, and highways compete for space beside the river, crowding the workers' soot-stained frame homes against the steeply rising valley walls.

What the people of Donora did not know on that raw Tuesday morning was that a five-day health crisis lay ahead, ordained by inexorable weather controls. A high-pressure system had stagnated over the region. Slowly sinking air from aloft literally put

a lid over Donora, trapping a cold 1000-foot thick air layer in the narrow confines of the valley. As Tuesday progressed into Wednesday, the fog thickened. Smoke from the mills poured sulfide fumes and soot into the stagnant air, turning it into a sickening pea-soup mess reeking of sulfur. Illness spread rapidly among the coughing and wheezing inhabitants of Donora. Altogether, 43% of the population became ill, and of these about 60% were age 65 and older. Hospitals were soon overcrowded, but the ill kept arriving. A large proportion of the elderly patients were seriously ill. In all, 20 persons died; of these deaths, 17 occurred on the third day of the poison fog. After the fifth day, relief came in the form of a rapidly moving cold front, sweeping away the dangerous air layer.

The type of air pollution experienced by Donora had a very similar forerunner in the Meuse Valley of Belgium. Here in December 1930, a temperature in-

Johnstown, an industrial city on the Conemaugh River in western Pennsylvania. Mills share the narrow valley bottom with workers' homes and railroad lines. (Grant Heilman.)

version trapped pollutants in a 15-mile length of a steep-sided valley. As at Donora, industrial plants spewed forth their poison into a stagnant, cold air layer. Besides having coke ovens, steel mills, and blast furnaces, this valley was the site of zinc smelters and sulfuric acid plants — intense sources of sulfur dioxide gas. Uniting with fog droplets, this gas formed sulfuric acid, capable of a crippling impact upon the human respiratory system. More than 600 persons became ill in the Meuse Valley in the few days that the poison fog lasted; there were 63 deaths directly attributable to breathing the polluted air. But

the worst urban disaster from poison fog was yet to come. The City of London received a massive attack in 1952. For several days in December of that year a thick, heavily polluted fog hung over the city. Adverse effects of that poison fog caused a total of 4000 deaths, mostly through respiratory diseases brought on or aggravated by the pollutants.

To understand how poison fogs accumulate, some basic principles of air pollution and weather science need to be investigated. In this unit and the next, we will study atmospheric pollutants and the atmospheric situations in which they can accumulate.

Spontaneous Rise of Polluted Air

With a knowledge of the ingredients of polluted air, we can now turn to the ways in which polluted air is dispersed or trapped above an urban area.

When the normal environmental lapse rate of 3½° F per 1000 ft (0.6° C per 100 m) is present, there is resistance to mixing by vertical movements. This situation is shown at the left side of Figure 8.1. Air that is forced to rise will cool adiabatically at a rate faster than the normal lapse rate. The air will then be denser than surrounding air and will tend to sink back to its original level if allowed to do so. Under these stable conditions, work must be done to lift air to a higher level, and in the absence of a mechanism for performing that work, the air mass remains at rest.

Consider next, a case in which the environmental lapse rate is steepened by heating of an air layer near the ground. This condition could come about because of excess heat conducted from hot pavements or roof tops (Figure 8.1, right). When the temperature gradient (lapse rate) of the heated air becomes greater than the dry adiabatic rate of 5.4 F° per 1000 ft (1.0 C° per 100 m), an unstable condition exists. A bubble of warm air can begin to rise, like a helium-filled balloon. Assume that lapse rate lessens with increased altitude, as shown by the curved line in Figure 8.1. Cooled at the dry adiabatic rate, the temperature of the rising bubble then falls faster than does the temperature of the surrounding air. When the bubble has

reached an altitude at which its temperature (and therefore also its density) matches that of the surrounding air, it can rise no further.

Now suppose that instead of the bubble of warm air we substitute the hot air from a smokestack (Figure 8.1). The spontaneous rise follows essentially the same pattern, although initially faster and in the form of a vertical jet. Carrying up with it the pollutants of combustion, the rising hot air gradually cools and reaches a level of stability, where it spreads laterally. Cooling by longwave radiation and mixing with the surrounding air will reinforce the adiabatic cooling, since a truly adiabatic system would not be realistic in nature.

Spontaneous rise of columns of warmer air goes by the general term of convection. As warm air rises, cooler air sinks nearby to replace it. In this way, a mixing action affects the lower atmosphere by carrying the pollutants upward and diluting them.

Inversion and Smog

Unfortunately, many urban areas experience from time to time an atmospheric condition that conspires to trap pollutants in a shallow layer. This condition is a temperature inversion. We can explain this phenomenon with a simple example.

During the night, when the sky is clear and the air calm,

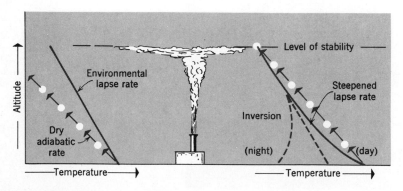

Figure 8.1   Relation of dry adiabatic lapse rate *(circles)* to different environmental lapse rates.

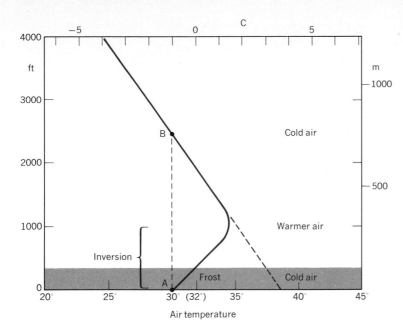

Figure 8.2 A low-level temperature inversion. In this case a layer of air close to the ground has dropped below the freezing temperature, while the air above remains warmer.

the ground surface rapidly radiates longwave energy into the atmosphere above it. Surface temperatures drop rapidly, and the overlying air layer becomes colder. When we plot temperature against altitude, as in Figure 8.2, the straight, slanting line of the normal environmental lapse rate becomes bent to the left in a "J" hook. In the case shown, the air temperature at the surface, point A, has dropped to 30° F (−1° C). This value is the same as at point B, some 2500 ft (750 m) aloft. As we move up from ground level, temperatures become warmer up to about 1000 ft (300 m). Here the curve reverses itself and the normal lapse rate takes over.

The lower, reversed portion of the lapse rate curve is called a **low-level temperature inversion.** In the case we have shown you temperature of the lowermost air has fallen below the freezing point (32° F, 0° C). For sensitive plants, this condition is a **killing frost** when it occurs during the growing season. Killing frost can be prevented in citrus groves by setting up an air circulation that mixes the cold basal air with warmer air above.

A low-level temperature inversion represents an unusually stable air structure. When this type of inversion develops over an urban area, conditions favor accumulation of pollutants. A heavy smog or highly toxic fog can develop, as shown in Figure 8.3. The upper limit of the inversion layer coincides with the **cap,** or **lid,** below which pollutants are held. The lid may be situated at a height of perhaps 500 to 1000 ft (150 to 300 m) above the ground.

Figure 8.4 shows for the United States the frequency with which low-level inversions may be expected during the fall. Strong temperature inversions conducive to air pollution are also caused in late spring and early summer over coastal cities such as New York, Toronto, and Chicago by cool sea or lake breezes that bring a stable, cool air layer over a narrow coastal zone.

Related to the low-level inversion, but caused in a somewhat different manner, is the **upper-level inversion,** illustrated in Figure 8.5. Air subsides within a center of high atmospheric pressure. The subsiding air diverges at low levels. Winds are calm or very gentle. As the air subsides, it is adiabatically warmed so that the normal temperature lapse rate is displaced to the right in the temperature-altitude graph, as shown in Figure 8.5 by the diagonal arrows. Below the level at which subsidence is occurring, the air layer remains stagnant. The temperature curve consequently develops a kink in which a part of the curve shows an inversion. For reasons already explained, the layer of inverted temperature structure strongly resists mixing and acts as a lid to prevent the continued upward movement and dispersal of pollutants.

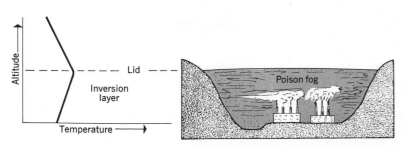

Figure 8.3 A low-level inversion *(left)* was the predisposing condition for poison fog accumulation at Donora, Pennsylvania, in October 1948. (From A. N. Strahler [1972] *Planet Earth,* Harper & Row, New York.)

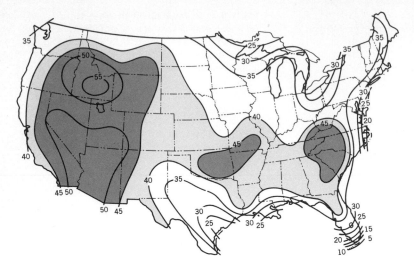

Figure 8.4 Frequency of low-level inversions (under 500 ft; 150 m) in the autumn season. Figures show average percentage of hours of inversion daily. (After D. H. Pack [1964] *Science,* vol. 146, p. 1125. © 1964 by the American Association for the Advancement of Science.)

Urban Pollution Domes and Pollution Plumes

Pollutants trapped beneath an inversion lid form a broad **pollution dome** centered over a city when winds are very light or near calm (Figure 8.6). When there is general air movement in response to a pressure gradient, however, pollutants are carried far downwind to form a **pollution plume.** Figure 8.7 has two maps showing plumes from the

major cities of the Atlantic seaboard. The V-lines show zones of fallout beneath the plumes, while the small dot at the open end of the V shows the distance traveled by the air in one day from the source. The left-hand map shows the effects of weak southerly winds on a day in June. In this situation pollution from one city affects another and generally the pollutants remain over the land, contaminating suburban and rural areas over a wide zone. The right-hand map, for a day in February, shows the effect of strong westerly winds, causing the pollution to be carried directly to sea.

Harmful Effects of Air Pollution

A list of the harmful effects of atmospheric pollutants upon plant and animal life and upon inorganic substances would be a very long one if fully developed. We can only suggest some of these effects. For humans in cities both sulfur dioxide and hydrocarbon compounds, altered by photochemical reaction to produce sulfuric acid and ethylene, respectively, are irritants to the eyes and to the respiratory system. Nitrogen dioxide is also an eye

Figure 8.5 An upper-air inversion caused by subsidence. (From A. N. Strahler [1972] *Planet Earth,* Harper & Row, New York.)

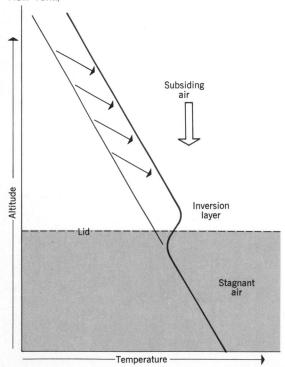

Figure 8.6 Schematic diagram of (A) pollution over a city under conditions of calm, stable air, and (B) a downwind pollution plume formed when a regional wind is blowing.

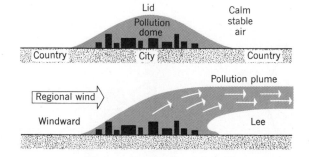

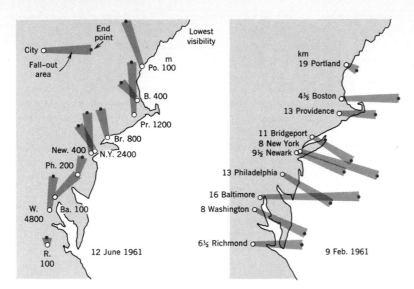

Figure 8.7 Pollution plumes from cities on the eastern seaboard under conditions of weak, southerly winds *(left)* and strong westerly winds *(right)*. The dot at end of each plume represents approximate distance traveled by pollutants at the end of a 24-hour period. (After H. E. Landsberg [1962] in *Symposium — Air Over Cities,* Sanitary Engineering Center Tech. Report A62-5, Cincinnati, Ohio.)

and lung irritant when present in sufficient quantities. Ozone acts as an irritant in smog and would be lethal if it occurred in large concentrations.

For persons suffering from respiratory ailments, such as bronchitis and emphysema, the breathing of heavily polluted air can bring on disability and even death, as statistics clearly show. During the London fog of December 1952, the death rate approximately doubled, while an increased death rate over the average rate persisted for weeks after the event. In a more recent London fog, that of December 1962, more than 300 deaths were attributed to the breathing of polluted air. Particularly hard hit were tthe very young and the old. There is also a suspected linkage between breathing of atmospheric pollutants and lung cancer, since the incidence of that disease is higher in cities than in other areas. In addition, the accumulation of atmospheric hydrocarbon compounds on lung tissues may predispose to the onset of lung cancer.

Carbon monoxide is a cause of death when inhaled in sufficient quantities. Everyone knows that the carbon monoxide from automobile exhaust will kill in a short time when breathed in a closed garage. Carbon monoxide levels are a general indicator of the degree of air pollution from vehicular exhausts, but concentrations rarely reach sufficient levels in the open air to be a threat to life. Nevertheless, the long-continued inhalation of small amounts of carbon monoxide is suspected of harmful effects, as yet unevaluated.

Ozone in urban smog has a most deleterious effect upon plant tissues, and in some cases has caused the death or severe damage of ornamental trees and shrubs. Sulfur dioxide is injurious to certain plants and is a cause of loss of productivity in truck gardens and orchards in polluted air. Atmospheric sulfuric acid in cities has in places largely wiped out lichen growth.

Although secondary in the sense that the loss is in dollars, rather than in lives and health of animals and plants, the deterioration of various materials subjected to polluted air forms an important category of harmful effects. Building stones and masonry are susceptible to corrosive action of sulfuric acid derived from the atmosphere. Metals, fabrics, leather, rubber, and paint deteriorate and discolor under the impact of exposure to urban air pollutants. In particular, natural rubber is vulnerable to ozone, which causes rubber to harden and crack. The sulfuric acid produced from sulfur dioxide corrodes exposed metals, particularly steel and copper. Not the least of the economic losses from pollution are simply those from soilage of clothing, automobiles, furniture, and interior floors, walls, and ceilings. The cleaning bill totaled for a large city is truly staggering, especially when calculated to include the labor and cleaning agents expended by householders.

Lead and other toxic metals in the polluted atmosphere are a particular source of concern for human health in the future. The lead-bearing particles from auto exhausts tend to concentrate in the grass, leaves, and soil near major highways. There is good reason to suppose that humans ingest lead particles directly from the air and that they may prove to be a health hazard. Although lead poisoning from atmospheric sources has not yet been documented in humans, there is now evidence that it has caused the deaths of animals in city zoos. Tests have shown high levels of lead in the tissues of the dead animals and no source other than atmospheric particles has been found for the ingested lead. Animals in outdoor cages showed higher lead levels than animals kept indoors. These findings are ominous in tone and tend to reinforce the conclusion of the Air Pollution Control Office of the Environmental Protection Agency that atmospheric lead pollution is a possible health hazard. Reduction of lead additives to gasoline has been a corrective step.

Radioactive substances in the atmosphere are a special form of environmental hazard because of the genetic damage that is done to plant and animal tissues exposed to dangerous radiation. This form of environmental hazard is discussed in Unit 63.

Smoke Plumes and Air Stability

Observation of smoke plumes from tall stacks of large industrial combustion plants can tell you a lot about the degree of stability or instability of the atmosphere on a given day. Figure 8.8 shows the smooth, level, downwind flow of smoke indicating a high degree of stability with low wind speed; it is described as a **fanning plume.** When air stability is close to neutral and winds are greater than about 20 mi (32 km) per hour, the **coning plume** develops, showing some moderate diffusion and mixing in the downwind direction. Under conditions of instability the **looping plume** develops. The vertical fluctuations are an indication of the large size of turbulent eddies.

Typically, since wind speeds and turbulence are higher during the afternoon than at night, a smoke plume will assume the fanning form during the night and early morning hours, but change to the coning or looping forms during the late morning hours. When turbulence is severe, smoke can be carried down to ground levels in the looping plume. As stack height is increased the concentration of smoke reaching the ground is lessened and the horizontal distance from the stack at which the smoke touches ground is lengthened. Under conditions of dead calm with stable air, the smoke from the stack goes straight up and will be seen to spread laterally at a sharply defined level, which coincides with the inversion lid.

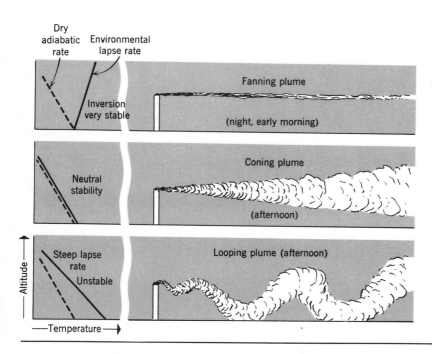

Figure 8.8 Three types of smoke plumes reflecting the degree of stability of the lower air layer. (After E. V. Somers [1971] in *Air Pollution Control,* Part I, W. Strauss, ed., Wiley-Interscience, New York, p. 25, Figure 13.)

Unit 9
The Changing Climate
of Cities

Metutopia — the Meteorologically Utopian City

Megalopolis we already know about, and then there is *BosWash* on the eastern seaboard and *SanSan* on the coast of California. But where and what is *Metutopia? Metutopia*—the meteorologically utopian city—is in the mind of Professor Helmut Landsberg, a leading atmospheric scientist with a special interest in the meteorology of cities. He told us about *Metutopia* in an address in 1972 before the American Meteorological Society Conference on Urban Environment. He asked:

Why towns, and if towns, what kind of towns? Let me admit at once that towns have a *raison*

d'être as convenient centers of communications, as hubs and transit points of traffic, as agglomerations of sufficient population to support cultural, educational, and sports enterprises as well as large stores. Thus the only major question remaining is, how should a town be built and function?

Professor Landsberg first talked about a hydrologic topic, that of avoiding construction on low-lying areas where flooding by rivers can be expected. This is a subject we will take up in a later study unit. He concluded, "So meteorological rule number one is not to use the flood plains, and a little more land above them, for houses and buildings. . . . In my utopian town such land would be devoted to parks and recreational activities—for example, golf courses and perhaps even home gardens."

Landsberg then explained how a "heat island" forms over cities, raising the air temperature several

Columbia is a new small city. (Columbia, Maryland, Chamber of Commerce.)

degrees higher than that over the surrounding rural countryside. He has a remedy:

Just as in the case of the floods, the summer heat-island problem suggests that in our utopian town we would leave as much of the surface as possible covered by vegetation. This is in stark contrast to the ever denser land utilization now prevalent in urban areas. While it is true that there is usually some park land set aside, present planners assume that it is sufficient to have it as grass land that may double in use as playgrounds.

Yet our observations have shown that grass, while better than pavement, often dries out in summer and does not mitigate the heat island effect nearly as much as trees and shrubs. Trees have well nigh disappeared from the inner cities. Even in the suburbs or the so-called planned towns the bulldozer is the first piece of equipment to appear and in order to ease construction old trees are eradicated. Ironically, in those same areas the new houseowners plant measly little saplings in the hope that they might grow back into shade trees perhaps by the time the mortgage is paid off.

In the utopian town—let me call it *Metutopia*—we would postulate preservation of as many natural trees as possible. Those that succumb would be replaced and wherever feasible new trees would be added. But we would also reduce the needs for surface space, much of which is now occupied by parking lots. In the first place these needs will be lowered by reduced use of cars as a mode of transportation, and whatever cars remain necessary will be parked underground or under buildings. Even parking garages are preferable as a compromise over parking lots. Business and apartment buildings in Metutopia would be required to provide for necessary parking below their establishment. Similarly, tall buildings using less land surface than low structures will be the rule rather than the exception. Pedestrian traffic will move through tunnels or under colonnades. Buildings will have open vegetated spaces between them. Instead of having four times the ground area of a building covered by parking space and access roads, as is often the case at present, that part of the grounds will be developed as a park.

Aside from reducing the heat-island effects, the spacing of buildings will have beneficial results for ventilation. In higher latitudes during the cold season, when spare heat might do some good, much better use will be made than at present of rejected heat from furnaces, factory smokestacks, and cooling towers. Instead of dissipating this heat into the atmosphere—and perhaps producing unwanted weather modifications elsewhere downwind from the urban scene—this heat is to be channeled through smoke sewers under uncovered sidewalks, streets, highways, and bridges to melt snows that cause accidents and traffic jams. This will eliminate the need for expensive snow clearing equipment, standby crews, and ecology-damaging salts.

Professor Landsberg continued his talk with a discussion of urban air pollution, a subject we have covered in previous study units. He then turned to optimum standards in building construction:

Housing and buildings, according to the climatic zone in which the town is located, will be constructed to minimize consumption of energy and heat rejection. Superior insulation will be required to reduce demands for heating and cooling. In sunny areas and during summer, reflecting outside paints will increase albedos, and all glass surfaces, including windows with exposure to the sun, will have outside reflecting shutters or shading devices to avoid the trapping of heat. In cold climates and in winter, maximal heat absorption from radiation through low albedos and glass sides will be attempted. A "chameleon" type of house for the mid-latitude dwellings with seasonally changeable absorption still has to be invented. In the development of a new style of housing adapted to climatological conditions, opportunities for wholly or partially using solar energy for space and water heating will have to be exploited. Cooling problems are more difficult to handle, but the soil heat pump may yet be improved to become practicable. Indeed, we should not entirely spurn the habits of the desert lizards that, in intense heat, find comfort a few decimeters below the surface. In some climatic regions more underground construction is definitely to be encouraged.

But for our *Metutopia* it is also indispensable to look at the available climatic information on the "air resource." In many otherwise pleasant climatic settings this resource has been overexploited if not depleted. A horrible example is the Los Angeles Basin. Other areas are in acute danger of becoming similarly afflicted, such as portions of Arizona. Even if one takes an optimistic outlook—and I do not entirely—that all the laws, ordinances, and regulations on pollution will be complied with or can be enforced, the still increasing population may keep improvements in many older communities marginal. Our observations in Columbia, Md., a planned new town, have taught us how fast urbanization creates also an urban atmospheric environment with all its characteristics, including pollution.

And how large should *Metutopia* be? Professor Landsberg offered this opinion: "Others will have to address themselves to the question of optimal size for a city. But to the meteorologist it is obvious from the available analyses of present towns that the atmospheric effects emerge measurably with 10,000 inhabitants and become very pronounced, perhaps uncontrollable, with a million inhabitants."

Urban planning is a subject that deeply interests many geographers. Designing a new city with a minimum of air pollution and other unwanted climatic changes is an important aspect of urban planning. In this study unit we will learn how climate has already been changed for the worse over our large cities.

DATA SOURCE: Helmut Landsberg (1973) The meteorologically utopian city, *Bulletin, American Meteorological Society*, vol. 54, pp. 86-89. (Permission to quote from this publication has been obtained from the author and from the American Meteorological Society.)

Urbanization and the Balances of Radiation and Heat

We can use principles of energy radiation and air temperature, covered in earlier units, to understand how urbanization affects local climate. We can anticipate the impact of Man as his spreading cities replace a richly vegetated countryside with blacktop and concrete. Thermal properties of the land surface change. The vertical walls of buildings not only add to surfaces of reflection and radiation, but they also change the aerodynamic character of the surface, altering the flow patterns of air and the speed of winds.

In the urban environment the absorption of solar radiation causes higher ground temperatures for two reasons: First, since foliage of plants is largely absent, the full quantity of solar energy falls upon the bare ground. Absence of foliage also means absence of transpiration, which is a form of evaporation taking place from leaf pores. In a forest or grassland, transpiration produces a cooling of the lower air layer through the upward transport of latent heat. Second, because roofs and pavements of concrete and asphalt hold no moisture, evaporative cooling does not occur as it would from a moist soil.

The thermal effect is that of converting the city into a hot desert. The midday summer temperatures close to the pavement of a city may be almost as extreme as that of a desert floor. This surface heat is conducted into the ground and stored there. An additional thermal factor is that vertical masonry surfaces absorb solar radiation or reflect it to the ground and to other vertical surfaces. The absorbed heat is then radiated back into the air between buildings.

As a result of these changes in the radiation balance, the central region of a city typically shows summer air temperatures several degrees higher than for the surrounding suburbs and countryside. Figure 9.1 is a map of the Washington, D.C. area showing air temperatures for the afternoon of a typical day in August. The lines of equal temperature, called **isotherms,** delineate a **heat island.**

You might suppose that at night the city air temperatures would fall below those of the surrounding countryside, because longwave radiation from bare, dry surfaces would

cause rapid heat loss, as it does in the desert. Instead, we find that the heat island persists through the night because of the availability of a large quantity of heat stored in the pavements, masonry, and ground during the daytime hours. In winter additional heat is radiated by walls and roofs of buildings, which conduct heat from the inside. Even in summer, Man adds to the city heat output through use of air conditioners and refrigerators, which expend enormous amounts of energy at a time when the outside air is at its warmest.

A mechanical side effect of the heat island is to increase convectional circulation at night. A general rise of the warm air extends to the upper limit of the polluted air layer. As shown in Figure 9.2, the air then spreads radially outward from the city to reach the surrounding countryside. Cooler air moving into the city at lower levels constitutes a weak **country breeze.**

Figure 9.1 A heat island over Washington, D.C. Air temperatures were taken at 10 p.m. on a day in early August. (Data of H. E. Landsberg.)

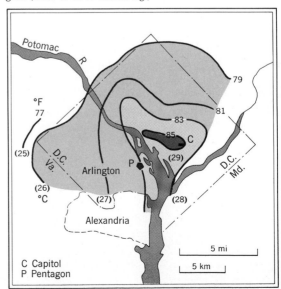

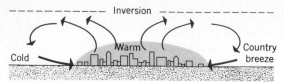

Figure 9.2   Air flow at night within an urban heat island. Dense, cold air from the surrounding countryside flows inward to replace rising, outspreading warm air. (After H. E. Landsberg [1970] *Science,* vol. 170, p. 1271, Figure 5.)

The heat-island effect of cities is augmented by the presence of large buildings, which act to reduce wind speeds by as much as 10 to 30% as compared with flat ground surfaces. For example, wind speeds observed in Central Park in New York City averaged about 3 mi (5 km) per hour less than at La Guardia Airport. These differences existed throughout each quarter of the year and the average reduction was 23%. The Central Park weather station is actually quite far from buildings that surround the park, so that the effect would be even more pronounced among blocks of high buildings.

Urbanization and Air Quality

One important physical effect of urban air pollution is that it reduces visibility and illumination. A smog layer can cut illumination by 10% in summer and 20% in winter. Ultraviolet radiation is absorbed by smog, which at times completely prevents these wavelengths from reaching the ground. Reduced ultraviolet radiation may prove to be of importance in permitting increased bacterial activity at ground level.

City smog cuts horizontal visibility from one-fifth to one-tenth of the distance normal for clean air. Where atmospheric moisture is sufficient, the hygroscopic particles acquire water films and can lead to formation of true fog with near-zero visibility. Over cities, winter fogs are much more frequent than over the surrounding countryside. Coastal airports, such as La Guardia (New York), Newark (New Jersey), and Boston suffer severely from a high incidence of fogs augmented by urban air pollution.

A related effect of the urban heat island is the general increase in cloudiness and precipitation over a city, as compared with the surrounding countryside. This increase

Table 9.1 Climate of a City as Compared with that of the Surrounding Countryside

Radiation	
Total insolation	15 to 20% less
Ultraviolet (winter)	30% less
Ultraviolet (summer)	5% less
Sunshine duration	5 to 15% less
Temperature	
Annual mean	0.9 to 1.8 F° (0.5 to 1.0 C°) higher
Winter minimum	1.8 to 3.6 F° (1.0 to 2.0 C°) higher
Relative humidity	2 to 3% less
Cloudiness	
Cloud cover	5 to 10% more
Fog in winter	100% more
Fog in summer	30% more
Precipitation	
Total quantity	5 to 10% more
Snowfall	5% less
Particulate matter	10 times more
Gaseous pollutants	5 to 25 times more
Wind speed	
Annual mean	20 to 30% lower
Extreme gusts	10 to 20% lower
Calms	5 to 20% more frequent

SOURCE: Data of H. E. Landsberg (1970) *Meteorological Monographs,* vol. 11, p. 91, Table 1.

results from intensified convection generated by heating of the lower air. For example, it has been found that thunderstorms over the city of London produce 30% more rainfall than thunderstorms over the surrounding country. Increased precipitation over an urban area is estimated to average from 5 to 10% over the normal for the region in which it lies.

Table 9.1 summarizes the main climatic differences between a city and the surrounding countryside. Keep in mind that this summary is a generalization applied to highly industrialized nations in midlatitudes, and there are differences among cities with respect to magnitude of a given effect.

Unit 10 Wave Cyclones of Midlatitudes

The Great Blizzard of '66 on the Northern Great Plains*

The hardy plainsmen of the northern Great Plains expect unusual and severe weather and are seldom disappointed in their expectation. Summertime brings dreaded, destructive tornadoes and violent thunderstorms accompanied by heavy hail sometimes larger than a baseball, or the kind of hail that, in minutes, wipes out a farmer's nearly realized dream of a wonderful bumper crop.

And winter, which comes early and stays late in the Big Country, brings the fearsome, angry, howling 'white death'—the hazardous prairie blizzard with 60-mile-per-hour, bonechilling winds, ladened with snow so fine, so strongly driven, that no crack or crevice is too small to admit what in time becomes an amazing mass.

Sometimes spring comes early, if only for a few days, with warm balmy chinook winds, rapidly melting snow, with a peek at solid earth again for the first time in months. Such was the promise at the close of February and the first day of March 1966, nature's hint that winter wouldn't last forever.

But the reprieve was short-lived. By midmorning of March 1st clouds began to gather and shut out the welcome sun. A preliminary warning issued by the Weather Bureau . . . was confirmed when on March 2nd a severe weather bulletin was broadcast by radio and television stations warning of an approaching storm . . . Cattle and other farm animals were brought in close to farmhouses, into large barns or corrals. Plans for trips of more than a few hours' duration were either cancelled or rescheduled to avoid the all-too-well-known dangers of exposure in a blizzard.

What prompted the early warning was a small and

Deep drifts stalled this rescue train during the great blizzard of '66. (Herman G. Stommel.)

Judge for yourself how deep the snowdrift is along
this line of telephone poles! (Herman G. Stommel.)

relatively insignificant low pressure system centered
in southwestern Montana. During the next 24 hours,
however, the low steadily deepened and moved
rapidly south-southeastward. At the same time an
arctic air mass with temperatures in the teens was
slowly advancing into northern Montana and North
Dakota.

Twelve hours later the low . . . had advanced into
central South Dakota. There it stalled. As the center
became more intense, increasing winds, now occasionally gusting to 70-80 miles per hour and driving
icy snow crystals, reduced visibilities to zero over
much of the northern Plains.

Bitter cold arctic air, pouring into the Dakotas following the prolonged blizzard, dropped temperatures well below zero by Sunday morning, March
6th, a morning which dawned clear and crisp to
present a fantastically beautiful fairy world of tremendous grey and white streaked, marble cake snow
drifts that occasionally nearly covered some two-
story buildings. Streets and farmyards were completely blocked by solid packed drifts offering stub-
born resistance to all but the heaviest types of snow
plows to penetrate them.

During the storm violent churning winds swept
bare some areas, while only a few yards away tower-
ing drifts built up downstream from what were sometimes only minor obstructions. Loose wind-borne
dirt, mixed with snow, resulted in a greyish mass of
snow-dirt, aptly dubbed "snirt."

The 1966 storm, with up to 80 mph winds occasionally gusting to 100 mph, continued unabated for
as long as four days in some areas. For the first time
in the history of many towns, schools were closed,
all business was suspended, newspapers failed to
publish, and all forms of traffic came to a complete
halt. Some roads were not cleared for two weeks.

Before it blew itself out, the Great Blizzard of '66
had claimed the lives of 18 persons. Two women . . .
froze to death while walking from stalled automobiles. A six-year-old . . . girl, fully clothed for
the outdoors, became separated from her two
brothers when the children went from their home to
a barn 60 feet away. She was found two days later
only a quarter of a mile from home, frozen to death.

The loss of livestock in Nebraska and the Dakotas
was appalling, with estimates including 74,500 head
of cattle, 54,000 sheep, and 2,400 hogs. On one
farm alone in eastern North Dakota, 7,000 turkeys
perished. Many cattle suffocated when barns became completely covered and sealed-in by huge
snow drifts. Large barns, into which stock were
herded before the storm struck, collapsed, resulting
in many dead and injured animals. The total loss of
livestock in these three states was estimated at over
$12 million. Many thousands of upland game
birds—grouse, pheasants, and partridge—were killed
by the storm.

The continual high winds piled snow in corrals
and feed lots. Cattle, as a result of milling around in
corrals, tramped down and compacted the snow as it
fell until the level of the snow became higher than
the fence. Then they wandered off and perished in
open fields or against fencelines.

All transportation had come to a standstill by the
second day of the storm. Three transcontinental
trains, trapped in railway cuts, became nearly covered in a short time with rock-hard packed snow,
defeating all efforts to free the trains until well after
the storm had ended. Five hundred passengers were
trapped for a time without heat or food. Automobile
travel, even early in the storm, was stopped by huge
drifts and near-zero visibility.

Power and telephone service were interrupted up
to several days in many areas by the high winds and
driven snow. Several aircraft hangers collapsed,
damaging and destroying a number of airplanes.
Many store windows were blown in. Snow, driven
into the attics during the storm, melted later with
distressing consequences. Chimney vents froze up,
causing a number of cases of gas poisoning in
homes.

The Great Blizzard of '66 was a type of storm
known to weather scientists as a wave cyclone. In
this study unit we will investigate the workings of
wave cyclones.

*This essay was written by Herman G. Stommel, State Cli-
matologist, ESSA, Bismarck, North Dakota. His complete article
was published in *Weatherwise*, vol. 19, no. 5, 1966. Passages
used here were reproduced by permission of the author and
Weatherwise, Inc.

Man and Weather

The atmosphere exerts stress, often severe, on Man and other life forms through weather disturbances involving hazards from high winds, cold, and precipitation. Severe storms can also generate environmental hazards through such events as storm waves, storm surges of the oceans, river floods, mudflows, and landslides.

Weather disturbances of lesser magnitude, however, are likely to be more beneficial—since they bring precipitation to the land surfaces and so recharge the vital supplies of fresh water on which Man and all other terrestrial life forms depend.

An understanding of weather disturbances of all intensities enables Man to predict their times and places of occurrence and so to give warnings and allow protective measures to be taken. This function of the atmospheric scientist can be placed under the heading of environmental protection. It is also possible to a limited degree for Man to modify some atmospheric processes deliberately to lessen the wind speeds of storms or to increase precipitation over drought areas. These activities come under the heading of planned weather modification. Here, again, we find that the relationship of Man with the atmosphere is one of interaction.

Surface Winds and the Coriolis Force

In Unit 3 we explained that a pressure gradient is the cause of winds and that the Coriolis force turns the flow path of the air toward the right in the northern hemisphere, but toward the left in the southern hemisphere. Close to the earth's surface the moving air encounters friction with the land or water surface beneath. This friction partly counteracts the Coriolis effect.

Figure 10.1 is a schematic map of a simple set of pressure conditions to illustrate how surface winds are related to pressure gradients. The map shows east-west zones of high and low pressure alternating from top to bottom. A trough of low pressure lies on the equator; ridges of high pressure lie to the north and south, one in each hemisphere. Farther poleward are belts of low pressure. (The profile at the right expresses the trough and two ridges.) Lines of equal atmospheric pressure, called **isobars,** run east-west across the map. The pressure gradient is shown by broad arrows.

The pressure gradient is always at right angles to the isobars. In the case shown in Figure 10.1, the gradient arrows point either due north or due south, but they always point in the direction of lower pressure.

Air moving from a ridge of high pressure toward lower pressure is turned by the Coriolis force to cross the isobars at an angle. The diagram shows the wind making an angle of 45° with the isobars. In nature the angle is subject to some variation, depending on the character of the ground surface.

Looking first at the northern hemisphere case, the deflection is to the right. The northward pressure gradient gives a

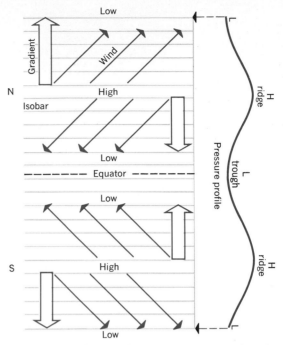

Figure 10.1 Surface winds cross isobars at an angle as the air moves from higher to lower pressure. Turn the figure sideways to view the pressure profile.

southwest wind. The southward gradient gives a northeast wind. In the southern hemisphere winds are deflected to the left and the pattern is the mirror image of that in the northern hemisphere. We turn next to the case of concentric isobars, using the same rules.

Cyclones and Anticyclones

In the language of meteorology, a center of low pressure is called a **cyclone**; a center of high pressure is an **anticyclone.** Cyclones and anticyclones may be stationary, or they may be rapidly moving pressure centers such as those that create severe weather disturbances.

Surface wind systems for cyclones and anticyclones in both hemispheres are shown in Figure 10.2. Winds in a cyclone in the northern hemisphere show an anticlockwise inspiral. In an anticyclone there is a clockwise outspiral. Note the reversal between the labels "anticlockwise" and "clockwise" in the southern hemisphere.

In both hemispheres the surface winds spiral inward on the center of the cyclone, so that the air near the center is forced to converge and to rise to high levels. For the anticyclone, by contrast, surface winds spiral out from the center. This motion represents a diverging of air flow and must be accompanied by a sinking (subsidence) of air in the center of the anticyclone to replace the outmoving air.

Much unsettled, cloudy weather we experience in midlatitudes is associated with traveling cyclones. Convergence of masses of air toward these centers is accompanied by lift of air and adiabatic cooling which, in turn, produces cloudiness and precipitation. By contrast, much of our fair sunny weather is associated with traveling anti-

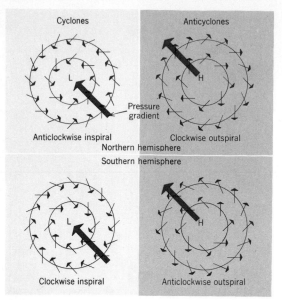

Figure 10.2 Surface winds spiral inward toward the center of a cyclone, but outward from the center of an anticyclone.

cyclones in which the air subsides and spreads outward, causing adiabatic warming. This process is unfavorable to the development of clouds and precipitation.

Many cyclones are very mild in intensity, passing with little more than a period of cloud cover and light rain or snow. On the other hand, when pressure gradients are strong, winds ranging in strength from moderate to gale force accompany the cyclone. In such a case, the disturbance can be called a **cyclonic storm.**

Large moving cyclones fall into two general classes. One is the wave cyclone of midlatitude and high latitude zones occuring in the region of global westerly winds. The wave cyclone ranges in severity from a weak disturbance to a powerful storm. A second major class includes cyclones of tropical and subtropical zones over ocean areas, forming in the belt of tropical easterly winds. These tropical cyclones range in intensity from mild disturbances to terribly destructive hurricanes or typhoons.

Air Masses

Cyclones of middle and high latitudes depend for their development on the coming together of large bodies of air of contrasting physical properties. A body of air in which the upward gradients of temperature and moisture are fairly uniform over a large area is known as an **air mass.** In horizontal extent a single air mass may be as large as a part of a continent; in vertical dimension it may extend through the troposphere. A given air mass is characterized by a distinctive combination of temperature, environmental lapse rate, and specific humidity. Air masses differ widely in temperature—from very warm to very cold—and in moisture content—from very dry to very moist.

A given air mass usually has a sharply defined boundary between itself and a neighboring air mass. This discontinuity is termed a **front.** We found an example of a front in the contact between polar and tropical air masses below the axis of the jet stream in upper-air waves, as shown in Figure 3.9. This feature is called the **polar front;** it is highly generalized in the figure. Fronts may be nearly vertical, as in the case of air masses having little motion relative to one another. Fronts may be inclined at an angle not far from the horizontal in cases where one air mass is sliding over another. A front may be almost stationary with respect to the earth's surface but, nevertheless, the adjacent air masses may be moving rapidly with respect to each other along the front.

The properties of an air mass are derived partly from the regions over which it passes. Because the entire troposphere is in more or less continuous motion, the particular air-mass properties at a given place may reflect the composite influence of a travel path covering thousands of miles and passing alternately over oceans and continents. This complexity of influences is particularly important in middle and high latitudes in the northern hemisphere, within the flow of the global westerlies.

Over vast tropical and equatorial areas, however, an air mass reflects quite simply the properties of an ocean or a land surface above which it moves slowly or tends to stagnate. Over a warm equatorial ocean surface, the lower levels of the overlying air mass develop a high water-vapor content. Over a large tropical desert, slowly subsiding air forms a warm air mass with low relative humidities. Over cold, snow-covered land surfaces in the arctic zone in winter, the lower layer of the air mass remains very cold with a very low water-vapor content. Meteorologists have designated as **source regions** those land or ocean surfaces that strongly impress their temperature and moisture characteristics on overlying air masses.

Air masses move from one region to another following the patterns of barometric pressure. During these migrations, lower levels of the air mass undergo gradual modification, taking up or losing heat to the surface beneath, and perhaps also taking up or losing water vapor.

Air masses are classified according to two categories of source regions: (1) the latitudinal position on the globe, which primarily determines thermal properties; and (2) the underlying surface, whether continent or ocean, determining the moisture content. With respect to latitudinal position, five types of air masses are as follows:

Air Mass	Symbol	Source Region
Arctic	A	Arctic ocean and fringing lands
Antarctic	AA	Antarctica
Polar	P	Continents and oceans, lat. 50–60° N and S
Tropical	T	Continents and oceans, lat. 20–35° N and S
Equatorial	E	Oceans close to equator

With respect to the type of underlying surface, two further subdivisions are imposed on the preceding.

Air Mass	Symbol	Source Region
Maritime	m	Oceans
Continental	c	Continents

By combining types based on latitudinal position with those based on underlying surface, a list of six important air masses results (Table 10.1). Figure 10.3 shows the global distribution of source regions of these air masses.

Maritime equatorial (mE) and maritime tropical (mT) air masses hold from 100 to 200 times as much water vapor as the extremely cold arctic and antarctic air masses, cA and cAA. The continental tropical air mass (cT) has its source region over subtropical deserts of the continents. Although it may have a substantial water-vapor content, it has low relative humidity when highly heated during the daytime. The polar maritime air mass (mP) originates over midlatitude oceans. Although the quantity of water vapor it holds is not large compared with the tropical air masses, the mP air mass can yield heavy precipitation. Much of this precipitation is of the orographic type, over mountain ranges on the western coasts of continents. The continental polar air mass (cP) originates over North America and Eurasia in the subarctic zone.

Table 10.1 Air Masses of the Globe

Air Mass	Symbol	Properties
Continental-arctic (and continental-antarctic)	cA (cAA)	Very cold, very dry (winter)
Continental polar	cP	Cold, dry (winter)
Maritime polar	mP	Cool, moist (winter)
Continental tropical	cT	Warm, dry
Maritime tropical	mT	Warm, moist
Maritime equatorial	mE	Warm, very moist

Cold and Warm Fronts

Figure 10.4 shows the structure of a front in which cold air is invading the warm-air zone. A front of this type is called a **cold front.** The colder air mass, being the denser, remains in contact with the ground and forces the warmer air mass to rise over it. The slope of the cold front surface is greatly exaggerated in steepness in the figure. Cold fronts are associated with strong atmospheric disturbance. As the unstable warm air is lifted by the advancing cold air layer, the warm air often develops strong convectional activity, forming cumulonimbus clouds. Thus severe thunderstorms are often associated with cold fronts.

Figure 10.5 illustrates a **warm front** in which warm air is moving into a region of colder air. Here, again, the cold air mass remains in contact with the ground and the warm

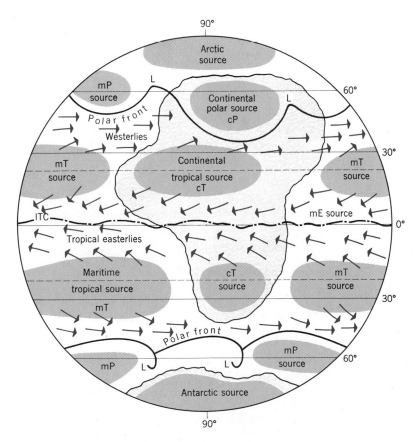

Figure 10.3 This schematic global diagram shows the source regions of the major air mass types.

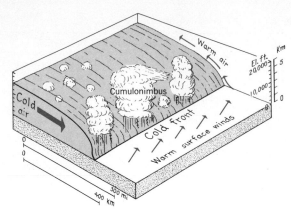

Figure 10.4   A cold front.

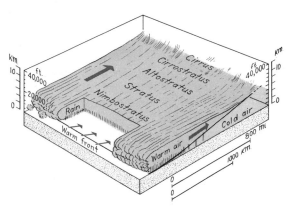

Figure 10.5   A warm front.

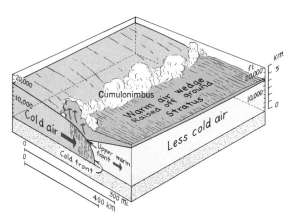

Figure 10.6   An occluded warm front.

air mass is forced to rise, as if it were ascending a long ramp. Warm fronts have much lower slopes than cold fronts. Moreover, warm fronts commonly represent stable atmospheric conditions and lack the turbulent air motions of the cold front. Typically, clouds are of the stratiform types, labeled on the diagram.

Cold fronts normally move along the ground at a faster rate than warm fronts. So, when both types are in the same neighborhood, the cold front overtakes the warm front. An **occluded front** then results (Figure 10.6). The colder air of the fast-moving cold front remains next to the ground, forcing both the warm air and the less cold air to rise over it. The warm air mass is lifted completely free of the ground.

Life Cycle of a Wave Cyclone

The dominant type of weather disturbance of middle and high latitudes is the **wave cyclone,** a vortex that repeatedly forms, intensifies, and dissolves along the frontal zone between cold and warm air masses. At the time of World War I, the Norwegian meteorologist, J. Bjerknes, recognized the existence of atmospheric fronts and developed his **wave theory** of cyclones.

As used by Bjerknes, the term "front" was particularly apt because of the resemblance of this feature to the fighting fronts in western Europe, then active. Just as vast armies met along a sharply defined front that moved back and forth, so masses of cold polar air meet in conflict with warm, moist tropical air. Instead of mixing freely, these unlike air masses remain clearly defined, but they interact along the polar front in great spiraling whorls.

A series of individual blocks (Figure 10.7) shows the sequence of stages in the life history of a wave cyclone. At the start of the cycle, the polar front is a smooth boundary along which air is moving in opposite directions. Block A shows a wave beginning to form along the polar front. Cold air is turned in a southerly direction and warm air in a northerly direction so that each invades the domain of the other.

In Block B the wave disturbance along the polar front has deepened and intensified. Cold air is now actively pushing southward along a cold front; warm air is actively moving northeastward along a warm front. Each front is convex in the direction of motion. The zone of precipitation is now considerable, but wider along the warm front than along the cold front. In a still later stage the more rapidly moving cold front has reduced the zone of warm air to a narrow sector.

In Block C, the cold front has overtaken the warm front, producing an occluded front. The warm air mass has been forced off the ground and is now isolated from the parent region of warm air to the south. Because the source of moisture and energy has been cut off, the cyclonic storm gradually dies out. In Block D the polar front is now reestablished as originally.

Wave Cyclones and the Global Energy Balance

Wave cyclones play a vital role in maintaining the global energy balance. The horizontal vortex of a wave cyclone draws cold polar air equatorward, while at the same time warm tropical air is carried poleward. In this way heat makes its way toward either polar region. This mixing process is referred to as **advection.** Anticyclones also aid

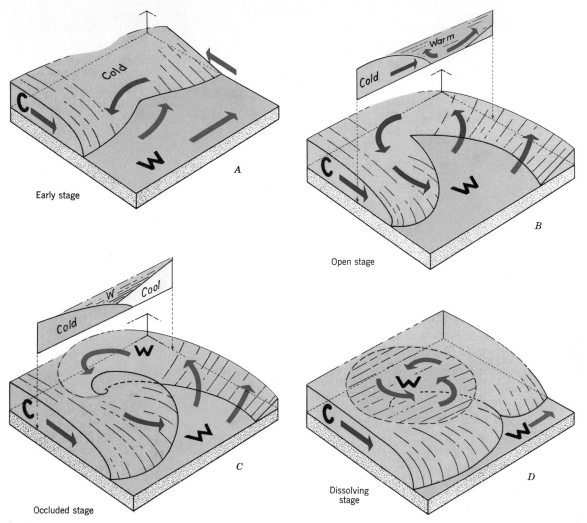

Figure 10.7 Four stages in the development of a wave cyclone.

in the advection process, turning like gear wheels in the opposite direction to adjacent cyclones. Even though their direction is opposite, anticyclones also act to move cold air toward the equator and warm air toward the poles.

Precipitation within a wave cyclone also acts to transport energy through the release of latent heat—heat that originally entered the tropical air masses through evaporation at low latitudes. Altogether, sufficient heat energy is

carried poleward to make up for the radiation deficit in high latitudes.

In our next study unit we will investigate two forms of violent weather typically connected with wave cyclones. One is the thunderstorm, with hail and lightning; the other is the deadly tornado. Both of these intense disturbances strongly impact Man and cultural features; both are highly destructive in narrow paths of travel.

SCIENCE SUPPLEMENT

The Anatomy of a Wave Cyclone

We can predict the changing weather conditions accompanying the passage of a wave cyclone in midlatitudes by examining some details of the internal structure of the storm. The accompanying simplified surface weather maps

depict conditions on successive days (Figure 10.8). The structure of the storm is defined by the isobars, labeled in millibars, the standard pressure units used on weather maps. Three kinds of fronts are shown by specialized line symbols. Areas in which precipitation is occurring are shown in color.

Map A shows the cyclone in an open stage, similar to that in Figure 10.7B. Note the following points. (1) Isobars

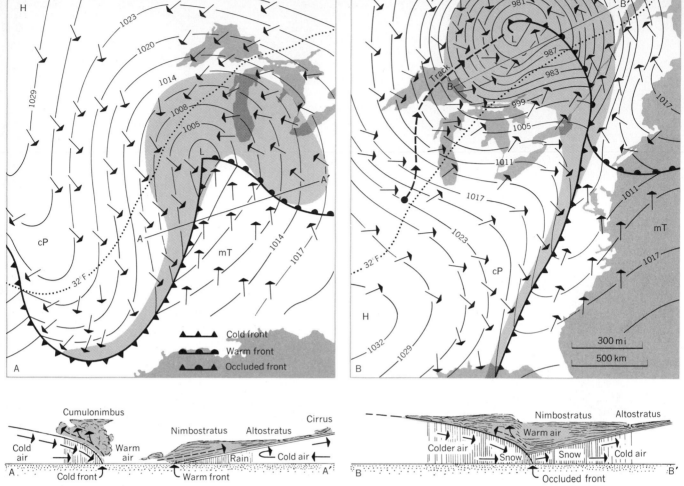

Figure 10.8 Simplified surface weather maps and cross sections through a wave cyclone. (A) Open stage. (B) Occluded stage.

of the low are closed to form an oval-shaped pattern. (2) Isobars make a sharp V where crossing cold and warm fronts. (3) Wind directions, indicated by arrows, are at an angle to the trend of the isobars and form a pattern of counterclockwise inspiraling. (4) In the warm-air sector there is northward flow of warm, moist tropical air toward the direction of the warm front. (5) There is a sudden shift of wind direction accompanying the passage of the cold front. This fact is indicated by the widely different wind directions at stations close to the cold front, but on opposite sides. There is also a sharp drop in temperature accompanying the passage of the cold front. (6) Precipitation is occurring over a broad zone near the warm front and in the central area of the cyclone, but extends as a thin band down the length of the cold front. Cloudiness prevails generally over the entire cyclone. (7) The low is followed on the west by a high (anticyclone) in which low temperatures and clear skies prevail. (8) The 32°F (0°C) isotherm crosses the cyclone diagonally from northeast to southwest, showing that the southeastern part is warmer than the northwestern part. (An **isotherm** is a line connecting

points on the map having the same temperature.)

A cross section through Map A along line *AA* shows how the fronts and clouds are related. Along the warm front is a broad layer of stratiform clouds. These take the form of a wedge with a thin leading edge of cirrus. Westward this thickens to altostratus, then to stratus, and finally to nimbostratus with steady rain. Within the warm air mass sector, the sky may partially clear with scattered cumulus. Along the cold front are cumulonimbus clouds associated with thunderstorms. These yield heavy rains, but only along a narrow belt.

The second weather map, Map B, shows conditions 24 hours later. The cyclone has moved rapidly northeastward, its track shown by a dashed line. The center has moved about 1000 mi (1600 km) in 24 hours, a speed of just over 40 mi (65 km) per hour. The cyclone has occluded. An occluded front replaces the separate warm and cold fronts in the central part of the disturbance. The high-pressure area, or tongue of cold polar air, has moved in to the west and south of the cyclone, and the cold front has pushed far south and east. Within the anticyclone the skies are clear

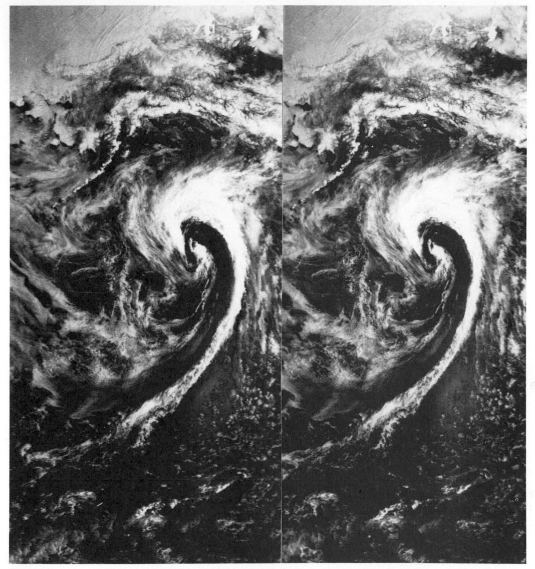

Figure 10.9   Stereoscopic satellite photographs of an occluded cyclone over the eastern Pacific Ocean. (NOAA-2 satellite image, courtesy of National Environmental Satellite Service.)

and winds are weak. A cross section below the map shows conditions along line *BB,* cutting through the occluded part of the storm. Notice that the warm air mass is being lifted higher off the ground and is giving heavy precipitation.

Wave cyclones in all stages of development are seen in weather satellite photographs. A good example is pictured in Figure 10.9. Two photographs have been placed side by side in such a way that a strong three-dimensional effect results when you view them together with a stereoscope. Try it—the effect is quite stunning.

An occluded cyclone over the eastern Pacific Ocean shows on this satellite image as a tight cloud spiral. The cold front makes a dense, narrow cloud band sweeping to the south and southwest of the cyclone center.

Since 1960, specialized orbiting satellites have been in operation, circling the globe continuously and sending back data. In addition to transmitting sharp TV pictures, these satellites record infrared radiation. They also record the vertical profile of temperatures in the atmosphere and the global distributions of ozone, water vapor, and precipitation.

Unit 11
Thunderstorms, Hail, and Tornadoes – Threats to Man

Two Great Tornado Outbreaks — 1884 and 1974

Tornadoes never fail to make the news. Most of that news is grim, but there are some remarkable incidents that draw special attention. For example, a wheat straw is found deeply implanted in a telephone pole, or a handbag is recovered miles from the point where a tornado snatched it from the owner's shoulder. Tornadoes that occur in large numbers on a given day attract much interest from meteorologists; such an occurrence is called a tornado outbreak. We shall look at two massive outbreaks separated by a span of 90 years.

> On February 19th, 1884, the States of Virginia, North Carolina, South Carolina, Georgia, Alabama, Mississippi, Tennessee, and Kentucky were visited with the most terrible devastation by wind ever experienced in this country. From 10 o'clock in the morning until 12 midnight sixty tornadoes occurred in different parts of the above-named states. Rough estimates placed the loss of property at from $3 million to $4 million; the loss of life at 800, and the number of wounded at 2,500. The number of people rendered homeless and destitute numbered from 10,000 to 15,000, many of whom were left in a starving condition. The number of buildings destroyed was about 10,000. Cattle, horses, hogs, and other domestic animals were destroyed in large numbers. (John Park Finley, 1887, *Tornadoes, What They Are*.)

Taking into account the great decline in purchasing value of the American dollar and the great increase in human population and building structures since 1884, we might multiply the above losses by a factor of 20 or more for a comparable tornado outbreak occurring in the same region today. By purest chance no tornado of the 1884 outbreak crossed a sizeable settlement—it was almost entirely a rural strike, and for that reason is overshadowed by some single terrible tornado disasters affecting cities. The number of tornadoes in the 1884 outbreak was estimated at 60, a very uncertain figure at best. Here are two eyewitness accounts:

> The funnel-shaped cloud was coming, with the lower edges curling, and as white as snow. I braced myself against the door, catching my sister with one hand. Instantly the wind caught us. The house was shattered in a flash, and we were thrown to the ground. I was deafened and stunned. When I came to my senses, the right leg of my breeches was torn off and gone, and, incredible as it sounds, the sole of my right shoe had been wrenched off and the upper stock of the shoe hung around my ankle. Had the house disappeared? There was not a trace of it left. The place where it stood was clean as a floor. There was not a morsel of food left, not a piece of crockery— literally nothing. The corn crib had gone and the corn with it. The destitution is complete. Not a stitch of clothing, food, or furniture is to be found where two days ago stood happy and prosperous homes. (*Atlanta Constitution*, 23 February, 1884.)

> The center of the storm struck the outskirts of Rockingham with such fury that people were unable to escape from their houses. Buildings were blown into fragments. Some bodies were found under the timbers, others were carried by the wind 150 to 300 yards. A woman was found clasping to her breast an infant scarcely a month old; both were dead. The bodies of victims were terribly

bruised and cut, presenting a ghastly appearance. The force of the wind was such that two millstones were moved 100 feet. Chickens and birds were picked clean, except the feathers on their heads. (*Wilmington* (N.C.) *Star* in *The Washington Post,* 22 February, 1884.)

Speaking of plucked chickens—it had occurred earlier to one Elias Loomis that he might estimate the wind speed in the funnel cloud of a tornado by experimentally blowing the feathers off a chicken. Loomis' experiment, carried out in 1842, was described as follows: A fresh-killed chicken was used as the projectile in a cannon (a six-pounder). Propelled by a charge of five ounces of gunpowder, the chicken was fired vertically upward, the muzzle velocity being about 340 miles per hour. The feathers were widely scattered; upon close examination they were found to have been pulled out clean. However, the chicken's body was torn into small fragments. The experiment really proved nothing. Biologists say that birds will release their feathers much more readily under emotional stress than normally, and it is quite probable that plucked chickens found after tornadoes have passed were denuded at much lower wind speeds than that used in the cannon experiment.

What is now called the Jumbo Outbreak of April 3–4, 1974, involved 148 tornadoes in 12 central states. Xenia, Ohio, was brutally struck, with the broad path of destruction running through the center of the city. Five schools within the city were destroyed. Fortunately, all other tornadoes of this period avoided large cities, but the toll ran to over 300 persons killed and over 5000 injured. The tornado season of 1974 was the worst ever recorded, with 944 tornadoes reported in the United States, bringing death to 360 persons and injury to over 6500.

The environmental impact of two kinds of severe storms—thunderstorms and tornadoes—is a major topic of this study unit.

DATA SOURCE: T. T. Fujita (1974) Jumbo tornado outbreak of 3 April 1974, *Weatherwise,* vol. 27, pp. 116–119; David M. Ludlum (1975) The great tornado outbreak on 19 February 1884, *Weatherwise,* vol. 28, pp. 84–88; B. Vonnegut (1975) Chicken plucking as a measure of tornado wind speed, *Weatherwise,* vol. 28, p. 217; A. Pearson and F. P. Ostby (1975) The tornado season of 1974, *Weatherwise,* vol. 28, pp. 5–11.

This wide swath of destruction through Xenia, Ohio, was cut by a tornado on the afternoon of April 4, 1974. The storm was one of 148 tornadoes that struck in 12 central states on two successive days, altogether killing over 300 persons and injuring over 5000 — the largest single tornado outbreak in the world's history. (Wide World Photos.)

Thunderstorms

Strong convectional activity manifests itself in the **thunderstorm,** an intense local storm associated with a tall, dense cumulonimbus cloud in which there are very strong updrafts of air. Thunder and lightning normally accompany the storm, and rainfall is heavy, often of cloudburst intensity, for a short period. Violent surface winds may occur at the onset of the storm. Hail is often produced within large thunderstorms.

A single thunderstorm consists of individual cells. Air rises within each cell as a succession of bubblelike air bodies, instead of as a continuous updraft from bottom to top (Figure 11.1). As each bubble rises, air in its wake is brought in from the surrounding region. Precipitation in the thunderstorm cell can be in the form of rain in the lower levels, mixed water and snow at intermediate levels, and snow at high levels.

Upon reaching high levels, which may be about 20,000 to 40,000 ft (6 to 12 km) or even higher, the rising rate diminishes, and the cloud top is dragged downwind to form an anvil top. Ice particles falling from the cloud top act as nuclei for condensation at lower levels in the process of cloud seeding. The rapid fall of raindrops adjacent to the rising air bubbles exerts a frictional drag on the air and sets in motion a downdraft. Striking the ground where precipitation is heaviest, this downdraft forms a local squall wind, which is sometimes strong enough to fell trees and do severe structural damage to buildings (Figure 11.2).

A single large thunderstorm consists of several adjacent cells, each experiencing activity in succession. As a result, the storm can have a long duration and can yield many heavy bursts of rain. Thunderstorm precipitation is characterized by its intensity combined with spotty distribution, so that an area a few miles across may receive a torrential

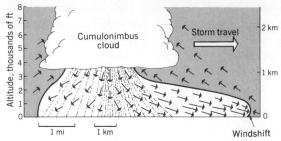

Figure 11.2   Downdraft beneath a thunderstorm. (After H. R. Byers and R. T. Braham [1949] *The Thunderstorm,* U.S. Govt. Printing Office, Washington, D.C.)

downpour whereas adjoining areas may receive little or none during the same period.

Because spontaneous convection is favored by a warm air mass with a high moisture content, thunderstorms are a dominant form of precipitation in the equatorial zone throughout the year, and in the rainy (monsoon) season of lands in the tropical zone. In midlatitudes thunderstorms are largely a summer phenomenon, while in arctic and polar regions their occurrence is rare.

Lightning

Another effect of convection cell activity is to generate **lightning,** one of the environmental hazards that results annually in the death of many persons and livestock as well as in the setting of forest fires and building fires. (See data in Table 11.1.) Lightning is a great electric arc—a gigantic spark—passing between cloud and ground, or between parts of a cloud mass. Although the mechanism of lightning generation is not fully understood, it is known that electrical charges become separated in different cloud levels. The lower portion of the cloud develops a negative charge; the ground beneath it a positive charge. When sufficient electrical potential has accumulated, an arc passes from cloud to ground, and returns to cloud, with many subsequent alternations of flow until the potential is dissipated. During lightning discharge, a current of as much as 60,000 to 100,000 amperes may develop.

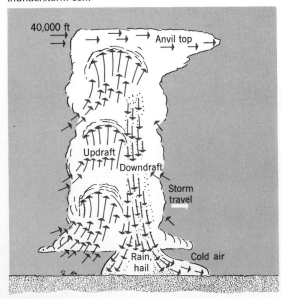

Figure 11.1   A schematic diagram of the interior of a thunderstorm cell.

Figure 11.3   Hailstones, larger than hens' eggs *(arrow).* (NOAA, National Weather Service.)

Figure 11.4 A severe hail storm devastated this corn crop. (NCAR photograph.)

Table 11.1 Losses of Life and Property in the United States Caused by Severe Weather Phenomena

Phenomenon	Average Annual Deaths	Average Annual Property Damage (millions of dollars)
Tornado[a]	125	75
Lightning	150[b]	100[b]
Hail	—	284[c]
Hurricane[a]	75	500

SOURCE: E. Kessler (1970) *Bulletin of American Meteorological Society.,* vol. 51, no. 10, p. 962.
[a]Data of Environmental Data Service, NOAA, for period 1955 to 1969.
[b]Period 1959–1965. Property damage includes building fires set by lightning.
[c]Period 1958–1967. Most is crop damage.

Hail

One of the most destructive products of the thunderstorm is the hail storm. **Hail** consists of rounded lumps of ice, having an internal structure of concentric layers, much like an onion. Ordinarily the ice is not clear but has a frosted appearance. Hailstones range from 0.2 to 2 in. (0.5 to 5 cm) in diameter (Figure 11.3). Large hailstones constitute an environmental hazard as they can be extremely destructive to crops and flimsy buildings (Figure 11.4).

Hail occurs only from the cumulonimbus cloud, inside of which are extremely strong updrafts of air. Raindrops are carried up to high altitudes, are frozen into ice pellets, then fall again through the cloud. Suspended in powerful updrafts, the hailstone grows by the attachment and freezing of droplets, much as ice accumulates on the leading edge of an airplane wing. Eventually the hailstone escapes from the updrafts and falls to earth.

Annual losses from crop destruction by hail storms are given in Table 11.1 as approaching $300 million. In 1970, insurance companies paid out about $70 million in damages, but uninsured losses ran much higher. Figure 11.4 shows a corn crop destroyed by a single hail storm.

Damage to wheat crops is particularly severe in a north-south belt of the High Plains, which runs through Nebraska, Kansas, and Oklahoma (Figure 11.5). There occur from four to five hail storms per year at any given place. A much larger region, extending eastward generally from the Rockies to the Ohio Valley, experiences two to four days per year of hail storms at any given place. Much of this larger region is under corn cultivation.

A small area of particularly high frequency of hail storms, over eight per year, is situated over the common corners of Wyoming and Nebraska, and a part of northeastern Colorado. This spot is known to atmospheric scientists as *Hail Alley.*

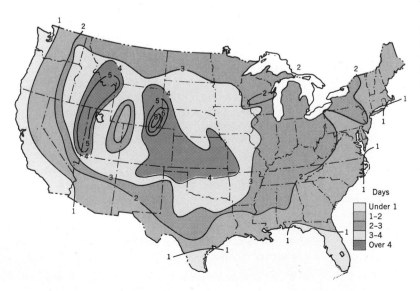

Figure 11.5 Average annual number of days with hail. This map is based on observations at 200 National Weather Service stations in the period 1899-1938. (After U.S. Dept. of Agriculture.)

Days
Under 1
1–2
2–3
3–4
Over 4

Hail-suppression Experiments

Some major hail-suppression programs have been in progress since the 1960s in the Soviet Union, where severe crop damage from hail storms has long been experienced over wide areas of farmlands. A major feature of the Soviet programs is the use of both artillery shells and rockets to inject cloud-seeding agents directly into the heart of cumulonimbus clouds where hail is beginning to form. Artilley shells explode in the cloud, each one releasing 100 to 200 g of silver iodide or lead iodide particles. Rockets carry larger loads—over 3 kg each—and release the seeding agent by burning a pyrotechnic mixture. The burning rocket casing descends through the cloud by parachute, releasing its contents on the way down.

By 1969, areal coverage of farmlands by hail-suppression activities had been extended to over 2.4 million hectares of farmland in the Soviet Union. It is reported that in the protected areas hail damage was only from one-third to one-fifth as great as in unprotected areas, whereas the cost of the protection amounted to only 2 to 3% of the value of the crops. In the year 1966, an expenditure of about 1 million rubles is said to have saved from destruction crops valued at 24 million rubles.

Generally speaking, American scientists are not fully satisfied with many of the claims of success arising from programs such as that described above. Experimental designs used are considered inadequate to allow the statistical significance of the results to be calculated.

High expectations were held for the National Hail Research Experiment (NHRE) begun in 1971 by the National Center for Atmospheric Research (NCAR) centered in Boulder, Colorado. This program includes an elaborate observational program to determine the physical activities taking place within cumulonimbus clouds that typically produce hail over the High Plains. These observations were expected to lead to the formulation of numerical models to predict hail formation. Field tests were to be conducted in reasonable expectation that the significance of the tests might be evaluated.

The NHRE program ran into unexpected delay because of the passage in 1972 of the Colorado Weather Modification Act. The new law was the outcome of a lengthy dispute between the Coors Company, a leading Colorado brewery, and citizens of the San Luis Valley of southern Colorado. Virtually the entire Moravian barley crop of that valley is purchased by the Coors Company. In a program to suppress hail over the valley, and so reduce barley crop damage, the Coors Company undertook commercial cloud seeding during the late summer period of crop ripening and harvesting. However, other users of land in the San Luis Valley, principally cattle ranchers, suspected that the cloud seeding, carried out for several years, had reduced summer precipitation to their detriment.

The resulting dispute over commercial cloud seeding led to drafting of the new state law, which requires that cloud seeding be rigidly controlled. Citizen support was strongly in favor of the legislation. In a referendum held in the San Luis counties, the vote was heavily opposed to uncontrol-led modification activities. Under the new Colorado law, the applicant wishing to undertake a weather modification program must show that the project is technically feasible, involves no risk of harm to people, property, or the environment, and is of economic benefit to the state. The NHRE research and experimental program met with these requirements, and a permit was granted by the State of Colorado to continue the five-year hail study project.

In 1976, as the five-year project drew to a close, its results were examined by a group of atmospheric scientists, convened by the National Academy of Sciences. It was agreed that no statistically significant reduction of hail had been achieved by the seeding experiments. Moreover, the basic hypothesis of hail formation on which the experiments were based was judged to be in error. Thus, future efforts will be devoted to basic research on hail-forming processes.

Tornadoes

Associated with frontal air-mass interactions in mid-latitudes is the smallest but most violent of all known storms, the tornado. It seems to be a typically American storm, being most frequent and violent in the United States, although occurring in Australia in substantial numbers and reported occasionally in other places in mid-latitudes. Storms reported as tornadoes also occur throughout tropical and subtropical zones.

The **tornado** is a small, intense cyclone in which the air is spiraling at tremendous speed. It appears as a dark **funnel cloud** (Figure 11.6), hanging from a dense cumulonimbus cloud. At its lower end the funnel may be from 300 to 1500 ft (90 to 460 m) in diameter. The funnel appears dark because of the density of condensing moisture, and the presence of dust and debris swept up by the wind.

Wind speeds in a tornado exceed anything known in other storms. Estimates of wind speed run to as high as 250 mi (400 km) per hour. As the tornado moves across the country the funnel writhes and twists. The end of the funnel cloud may alternately sweep the ground, causing complete destruction of anything in its path, then rise in the air to leave the ground below unharmed.

Tornado destruction occurs both from the great wind stress and from the sudden reduction of air pressure in the vortex of the cyclonic spiral. Closed houses literally explode. It is even reported that the corks will pop out of empty bottles, so great is the difference in air pressure.

Tornadoes occur as parts of cumulonimbus clouds. Usually those clouds form a line of thunderstorms (squall line) that travels in advance of a cold front. They seem to originate where turbulence is greatest. Tornadoes are commonest in the spring and summer but occur in any month, Figure 11.7. Where maritime polar (mP) air lifts warm, moist tropical (mT) air on a cold front, conditions may become favorable for tornadoes. They occur in greatest numbers in the central and southeastern states and are rare over mountainous and forested regions. They are

Figure 11.6 This funnel cloud was photographed by William L. Males at Cheyenne, Oklahoma, on May 4, 1961. The tornado was less than one mile from the observer when the picture was taken.

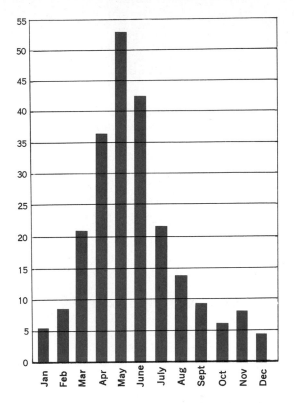

Figure 11.7 Average number of tornadoes reported in each month in the United States for the period 1916-1960. (From NOAA, National Weather Service.)

almost unknown from the Rocky Mountains westward and are relatively few on the eastern seaboard (Figure 11.8).

Devastation from a tornado is complete within the narrow limits of its path. Only the strongest buildings constructed of concrete and steel can resist major structural damage. Table 11.1 gives data on tornado deaths and property damage. Storm cellars built completely below ground provide satisfactory protection if they can be reached in time. Although a tornado can often be seen or heard approaching, a cold front passing during the hours of darkness, as it often does, may present no warning. The National Weather Service maintains a tornado forecasting and warning system. Whenever weather conditions conspire to favor tornado development, the danger area is alerted and systems for observing and reporting a tornado are set in readiness. Communities in the paths of tornadoes may thus be warned in time for inhabitants to take shelter.

In the next study unit, we continue with the subject of severe weather phenomena and their impact upon Man. We will be turning to the tropical zone to study hurricanes and typhoons.

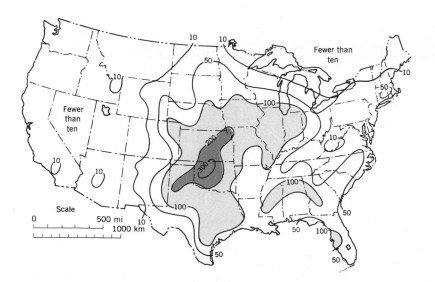

Figure 11.8 Distribution of tornadoes in the United States, 1955 to 1967. Figures tell number of tornadoes observed within 2-degree squares of latitude and longitude. (Data of M. E. Pautz, ESSA.)

SCIENCE SUPPLEMENT

Convection and Unstable Air Masses

To understand how cumulonimbus clouds develop and produce heavy rainfall, we must look further into the process of condensation and liberation of latent heat. Figure 11.9 will help to explain why spontaneous rise of air to produce intense convection can take place only when air mass properties are favorable.

Diagram A (left) is a plot of altitude against air temperature. The small circles represent a small parcel of air being forced to rise steadily higher, following the dry adiabatic rate of cooling shown. To the right of this line is a solid line showing the temperature of the undisturbed surrounding air; it decreases upward at the normal environmental lapse rate.

Suppose that the air parcel is lifted from a point near the ground, where its temperature is 90° F (32° C). After the air parcel has been carried up 2000 ft (600 m), its temperature has fallen about 11 F° (6 C°) and is now 79° F (26° C); whereas the surrounding air (environment) is warmer by 7 F° (4 C°), and has a temperature of 83° F (28° C). The air parcel would thus be cooler than the environment at 2000 ft (600 m) and denser than the surrounding air. If no longer forcibly carried upward, it would tend to sink back to the ground. These conditions represent a **stable air mass,** not likely to produce convection cells, because the air would resist lifting.

When the air layer near the ground is excessively heated, the environmental lapse rate is increased. Diagram B (right) shows a steep lapse rate of 7 F° per 1000 ft (1.3 C° per 100 m). (As the graph is constructed the steeper lapse rate is represented by a line of lower inclination.) The air parcel near the ground begins to rise spontaneously because it is less dense than air over adjacent, less intensely heated ground areas. Although cooled adiabatically while rising, the air parcel at 1000 ft (300 m) has a temperature of 85° F (29° C), but this is well above the temperature of the surrounding still air.

The air parcel, therefore, is lighter than the surrounding air and continues its rise. At 2000 ft (600 m), the dew point is reached and condensation sets in. Now the rising air parcel is cooled at a wet adiabatic rate, shown here as 3.2 F° per 1000 ft (0.6 C° per 100 m), because the latent heat liberated in condensation offsets the rate of drop due to expansion. At 3000 ft (900 m), the rising air parcel is still several degrees warmer than the environment, and therefore continues its spontaneous rise.

The air described here as spontaneously rising during condensation is said to be an **unstable air mass.** Generally, steep lapse rates in air holding a large quantity of water vapor are associated with instability. In such air, the updraft tends to increase in intensity as time goes on, much as a bonfire blazes with increasing ferocity as the updraft draws in greater supplies of oxygen. Of course, at very high altitudes, the bulk of the water vapor will have condensed and fallen as precipitation. With the energy source gone, the convection cell weakens and air rise finally ceases.

Figure 11.9 Stable and unstable air masses.

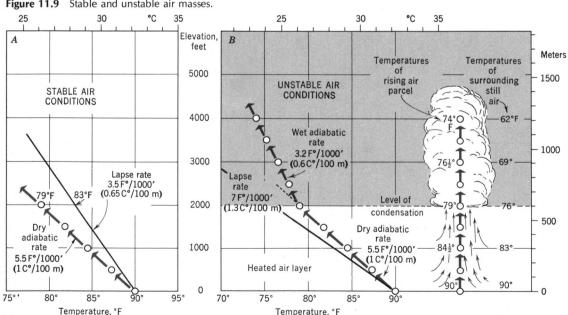

84

Unit 12
The Tropical Cyclone– An Environmental Hazard

The Deadliest Storm in History?

What may have been the greatest killer storm in three centuries of human record roared north out of the Bay of Bengal on November 12, 1970. It was aimed at the most vulnerable coastline in the world. Millions of persons inhabit the low-lying deltaic coast of what was then East Pakistan and the adjoining Bengal Province of India. Here the distributaries of the Ganges and Brahmaputra rivers branch repeatedly, dividing the coastal fringe into numerous low islands. Fishing and rice cultivation support a population as dense as in any agricultural region on earth, as well as supplying food to millions dwelling on higher ground farther inland.

The record of deaths in this portion of East Pakistan (now Bangladesh) from tropical cyclones is almost unbelievable: 1822, 40,000; 1876, 100,000; 1897, 175,000; 1970, 300,000. Most deaths were by drowning, as the ocean water moved landward in a great wave, called a *storm surge*. This kind of wave can cause the water to rise 20 feet or more within minutes. Few places on the coastal islands are as high as 20 feet, and there is little refuge save in the upper branches of some larger trees.

A district official living on one of the islands described his experience on the night of November 12, 1970:

At midnight we heard a great roar growing louder from the southeast. I looked out. It was pitch black, but in the distance I could see a glow. The glow got nearer and bigger and then I realized it was the crest of a huge wave. I was lucky because I live in a solidly built house and we went upstairs. But thousands were just swept away. The wave came as high as the first floor of my house. We

Survivors of the cyclone which struck the coast of Bangladesh in 1970 file past the body of a drowning victim. The great storm surge which accompanied the storm inundated these flat paddy fields under nearly 20 feet of water in a few minutes, leaving no escape for people or animals. (United Press International.)

were not poor people on this island but prosperous fishermen and paddy (rice) farmers. Now we are all street beggars. Everything has gone. All the cattle are dead, all the sheep and goats and most of the buffaloes. All the fishing vessels have been lost and all the nets. We are shy to beg from you, but please, I do beg you to get help for us. We have no drinking water—that we need above all. But we must have vaccines and other medicines too, and we need food.*

On the basis of later fact-finding investigations, the toll was assessed as follows: There were 200,000 confirmed burials; the missing were estimated as between 50,000 and 100,000 persons. Crop losses were valued at $63 million. Nearly 300,000 cattle perished and 400,000 homes were destroyed or damaged. Of the offshore fishing fleet, 9000 boats were destroyed; of the inland-water fleet, 90,000 boats. Because most of the protein in the diet of the 73 million persons of East Pakistan came from fish, the loss of 65% of the total fishing capacity pointed to a disastrous famine.

Storm surges accompanying hurricanes (our American word for tropical cyclones) are also well known along the Gulf Coast of Louisiana and Texas. The Galveston, Texas, disaster of September 8, 1900, was undoubtedly the worst of its kind on record.

*Quoted from a dispatch of the *Daily Telegraph,* London, as reprinted in *The New York Times,* November 17, 1970.

Here the rapid rise of water conspired with the wind. About 3000 houses were destroyed by the force of the wind, hurling the people inside them into water 10 to 15 feet deep. Of the 6000 who died in the pitch-black of night, most succumbed by drowning, but many were killed by flying planks and timbers as they clung to floating masses of wreckage.

The delta plain of Louisiana has had a history of hurricane disasters paralleling that of the Bay of Bengal in storm intensity, but with far fewer casualties. Audrey, a hurricane of June 1957, was a notable storm in this area. She came ashore about halfway between New Orleans and Galveston. Here, over a broad coastal zone only a few narrow beach ridges rise above the high-tide level, and these are only a few feet high. During the storm the water level rose steadily at a rate of about 1½ feet per hour, and most residents had ample time to heed the barrage of warnings urging them to evacuate their homes and move inland to higher ground. The water level finally reached a height of 8 to 12 feet above high tide, and upon that sea the storm waves and swell rode inland to smash houses and float them away. Even sealed concrete tombs were floated inland as far as 20 miles from their resting places. The number of dead in Louisiana was estimated at about 550 persons; the damage in that state alone was valued at $120 million.

In this study unit we investigate the workings of tropical cyclones. Man's attempts to reduce the severity of these killer storms will be a subject of special interest.

Weather Systems in Low Latitudes

Weather systems of the tropical and equatorial zones show some basic differences from those of midlatitudes. The Coriolis force is weak close to the equator, and there is a lack of strong contrast between air masses. Consequently, clearly defined fronts and large, intense wave cyclones are missing.

On the other hand, in low latitudes there is intense atmospheric activity in the form of convection cells because of the high moisture content of the maritime air masses in these low latitudes. In other words, there is an enormous reservoir of energy in the latent form. This same energy source powers the most formidable of all storms—the tropical cyclone.

Tropical Cyclones

One of the most powerful and destructive types of cyclonic storms is the **tropical cyclone,** otherwise known as the **hurricane** or **typhoon** (Figure 12.1). The storm develops over oceans in lat. 8° to 15° N and S, but not close to the equator, where the Coriolis force is extremely weak. A low-pressure center in the belt of tropical easterlies deepens and intensifies, growing into a deep but small, circular low.

High sea-surface temperatures that are over 80° F (27° C) in these latitudes are important in the environment of storm origin because warming of air at low level creates instability. Once formed, the storm moves westward through the trade-wind belt. It may then curve northwest and north, finally penetrating well into the belt of westerlies.

The tropical cyclone is an almost circular storm center of extremely low pressure into which winds are spiraling at high speed, accompanied by very heavy rainfall (Figure 12.2). Storm diameter may be 100 to 300 mi (150 to 500 km). Wind speeds range from 75 to 125 mi (120 to 200 km) per hour, and sometimes much higher. Atmospheric pressure in the storm center commonly falls to 950 mb or lower.

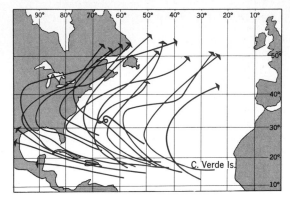

Figure 12.4 Tracks of some typical Atlantic hurricanes occurring during August.

Figure 12.1 Hurricane Gladys, photographed on October 8, 1968, from *Apollo 7* spacecraft at an altitude of about 110 mi (180 km). The storm center was near Tampa, Florida. (NASA photograph.)

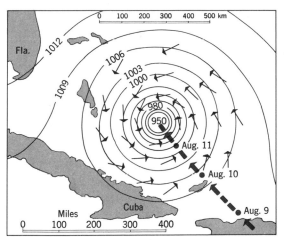

Figure 12.2 A hurricane of the West Indies.

A characteristic feature of the tropical cyclone is its **central eye,** in which calm prevails (Figure 12.3). The eye is a cloud-free vortex produced by the intense spiraling of the storm. In the eye, air descends from high altitude and is adiabatically warmed. Passage of the central eye may take about half an hour, after which the storm strikes with

renewed ferocity, but with winds in the opposite direction.

World distribution of tropical cyclones is limited to six regions, all of them over tropical and subtropical oceans: (1) West Indies, Gulf of Mexico, and Caribbean Sea; (2) western North Pacific, including the Philippine Islands, China Sea, and Japanese Islands; (3) Arabian Sea and Bay of Bengal; (4) eastern Pacific coastal region off Mexico and Central America; (5) south Indian Ocean, off Madagascar; and (6) western South Pacific, in the region of Samoa and Fiji Islands and the east and north coast of Australia. Curiously, these storms are unknown in the South Atlantic. Tropical cyclones never originate over land, although they often penetrate well into the margins of continents.

Tracks of tropical cyclones of the North Atlantic are shown in Figure 12.4. Most of the storms originate at 10° to 20° latitude, travel westward and northwestward through the trades, then turn northeast at about 30° to 35° latitude into the zone of the westerlies. Here the intensity lessens and the storms change into typical midlatitude wave cyclones. In the trade-wind belt the cyclones travel 6 to 12 mi (10 to 20 km) per hour.

The occurrence of tropical cyclones is restricted to certain seasons of year, and these vary according to the global location of the storm region. For hurricanes of the North Atlantic, the season runs from May through November, with maximum frequency in late summer or early autumn. The general rule is that tropical cyclones of the northern hemisphere occur in the season during which the intertropical convergence zone has moved north; those of the southern hemisphere occur when it has moved south.

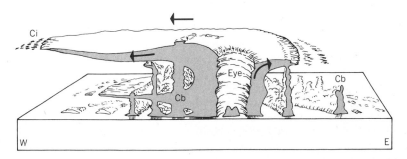

Figure 12.3 Schematic diagram of a hurricane. Cumulonimbus clouds in concentric rings rise through dense stratiform clouds. Width of the diagram represents about 600 mi (1000 km). (Redrawn from NOAA, National Weather Service, R. C. Gentry, 1964.)

Destruction by Tropical Cyclones

The environmental importance of tropical cyclones lies in their tremendously destructive effect on inhabited islands and coasts (Figure 12.5). Wholesale destruction of cities and their inhabitants has been reported on several occasions. A terrible hurricane that struck Barbados in the West Indies in 1780 is reported to have torn stone buildings from their foundations, destroyed forts, and carried cannons more than 100 ft from their locations. Trees were torn up and stripped of their bark. More than 6000 persons perished there.

The Storm Surge

Coastal destruction by storm waves and greatly raised sea level is perhaps the most serious effect of tropical cyclones. Where water level is raised by strong wind pressure, great storm surf attacks ground ordinarily far inland of the limits of wave action. A sudden rise of water level, known as **storm surge,** may take place as the hurricane moves over a coastline. Ships are lifted bodily and carried inland to become stranded. If high tide accompanies the storm, the limits reached by inundation are even higher. The terrible hurricane disaster at Galveston, Texas, in 1900 was wrought largely by a sudden storm surge, inundating the low coastal city and drowning about 6000 persons. At the mouth of the Hooghly River on the Bay of Bengal, 300,000 persons died as a result of inundation by a 40-ft (12 m) storm surge that accompanied a severe tropical cyclone in 1737. Low-lying coral atolls of the western Pacific may be entirely swept over by wind-driven seawater, washing away palm trees and houses and drowning the inhabitants.

Important, too, is the large quantity of rainfall produced by tropical cyclones. A considerable part of the summer rainfall of some coastal regions can be traced to a few such storms. While this rainfall is a valuable water resource, it may prove a menace as a producer of unwanted river floods and, in areas of steep mountain slopes, may give rise to disastrous mudslides and landslides.

Hurricane Modification

Take the punch out of a mighty hurricane; spare the coastal zone from the impact of 200-mph winds, from inundation beneath a 40-foot storm surge; save hundreds of lives, save millions in property damage. This dream of beneficial weather modification has long been with those atmospheric scientists who study hurricanes. The most obvious question is: Can it be done? A less obvious, but far more sophisticated question is: Should it be done?

Project Stormfury is a cooperative effort of the U.S. Navy and the National Oceanic and Atmospheric Administration (NOAA); it began in 1962. Under the direction of the National Hurricane Research Laboratory (NHRL) in Miami, plans were laid to carry out cloud seeding of hurricanes over the Atlantic Ocean. It was hoped that a technique could be found to lessen the hurricane intensity—particularly wind speeds—and that these techniques might later be applied to ameliorating storms as they come ashore on the American mainland. Keep in mind that the mission of Project Stormfury is strictly scientific: to add to Man's knowledge of the workings of hurricanes. Seeding of hurricanes that may soon impinge upon the mainland is forbidden.

In the first nine years of Project Stormfury only two hurricanes suitable for experimental seeding appeared on the scene. The hurricane used must be on a track such that it will probably remain at sea, far from the mainland. Hurricane Beulah, 1963, was one of these; but the scientific results were not clear cut. Changes in cloud structure and wind speed followed cloud seeding, but cause-and-effect relationships were debatable. Then, in August 1969, Debbie arrived on a suitable track. Five aircraft seeding passes were made through Debbie, seeding with silver iodide particles. Within five hours of completion of the seeding, winds had decreased by about 30%. During the following day, wind speeds increased, but five hours after a second seeding they decreased by 15%. It was supposed that the seeding caused rapid condensation of supercooled liquid particles in the storm clouds, rapidly draining off the reserves of latent heat. Scientists of NHRL analyzing the data were convinced that the reduction in wind speed was significant and was a response to the seeding. Other scientists were not convinced, but regarded the data as promising.

Since the seeding of Debbie, theoretical studies of hurricane dynamics have gone forward, using elaborate numerical models handled by computers. Seeding programs have been simulated by the computer. One recommenda-

Figure 12.5 This devastation along the south coast of Haiti was caused by Hurricane Flora on October 3, 1963. (Miami News photo.)

tion coming out of this activity has been to suggest that seeding in future field trials should be made farther out from the tall dense clouds immediately surrounding the central eye. Growth of the peripheral clouds might tend to draw off moisture supplies from the eye-wall clouds.

Abruptly, in 1972, military support of Project Stormfury was terminated. When the project resumes, experiments may be conducted in the Pacific Ocean, in an area where suitable tropical cyclones are more frequent than in the Atlantic.

Should seeding be used in an attempt to diminish the severity of hurricanes as they approach the coast of the mainland United States? In a 10-year period from 1961 to 1971 property damage from United States hurricanes averaged some $440 million annually. Single hurricanes in this period caused damage valued at $1.5 billion. In 1970 the Stanford Research Institute began a study of the decision-making process involved in seeding of hurricanes to reduce damage on land. Responsibility for damages is a major issue. Since there would be no way to be certain what amount of damage would have resulted if no seeding were done, any severe damage might be blamed upon the seeding. The decision to seed a hurricane would need to be made about 12 hours before the storm was due to arrive at the coast. There is a good possibility that the hurricane would be increasing in intensity through natural causes as it moved landward. If the increase were to overshadow a small reduction in intensity achieved by seeding, the residual increase might well be blamed on the seeding.

Legislation has been urged to clarify the responsibilities of those who make decisions to seed hurricanes, and to safeguard members of such decision-making boards from liability to public suits. Furthermore, within a particular state threatened by the hurricane, a local committee should assist the decision board in outlining the seeding program. Even so, the complications arising from any attempt to alleviate the intensity of a storm are unknown and forbidding to contemplate. Even the best attempts to predict the path and timetable of a hurricane can end in errors that bring severe criticism and blame for losses from the public sector. Small wonder, then, that hurricane modification as an applied science faces a troublesome future.

Man and the Atmosphere— Retrospect

At the close of this group of study units we can look back to analyze the broad pattern of concepts covered. As any coin with two sides, environmental science has two opposite but complementary phases. One is the impact or influence of the environment upon Man; the other is Man's influence or impact upon the environment.

The influences of the atmospheric environment upon Man are to a large extent favorable, even downright essential to survival. The atmosphere furnishes a favorable environment in which all life forms derive energy and materials needed to sustain growth. But, at various times and places, extremes of atmospheric activity are harmful, impacting Man and other life forms unfavorably. Severe weather phenomena are in this category. Perhaps we have placed more emphasis upon the harmful impacts of atmospheric phenomena than upon the day-to-day beneficial phenomena that sustain life; if so, we need to reorganize our perspective.

Turning over the environmental coin, we have given major emphasis to Man's impact upon the atmospheric environment. That impact largely concerns climate change. Two forms of climate change have been analyzed: inadvertent changes in global climate and deliberate Man-induced changes. Certain inadvertent (unintentional, or unplanned) changes have global scope; these changes are the most difficult to recognize and predict. Are we inducing a cooling trend or a warming trend? Are observed changes natural, or are they caused by Man's industrial activity? Those questions remain unanswered. Inadvertent changes in urban climates, on the other hand, are clearly evident and their causes well understood. The deliberate forms of change Man tries to impose upon the atmosphere deal entirely with temporal weather phenomena; for example, they are attempts to produce more rain, to produce less hail, to disperse fog, or to lessen storm wind intensities.

Our next group of study units deals with the hydrosphere, or global water realm, with special emphasis upon fresh water as a vital resource.

Facing page: The Grand Coulee Dam and Franklin D. Roosevelt
Lake. (U.S. Department of the Interior, Bureau of Reclamation.)

PART II

Man's Water Resources

Unit 13
The Hydrologic Cycle

Drought in the Sahel — the Sahara Desert Creeps Southward

Several West African nations lie in a perilous climatic belt called the Sahel. Because this belt lies along the southern border of the great Sahara Desert of North Africa, it is also referred to as the sub-Sahara region. Seven countries occupy much of the Sahel in western Africa: Senegal, Mauretania, Mali, Upper Volta, Niger, Nigeria, and Chad. All of these countries were struck a severe blow by drought, which began in 1968, became particularly severe in 1971 and 1972, was a major human catastrophe by 1974, and then in 1975 was ended.

The drought zone of the Sahel is, for the most part, a tropical grassland. It has a feast-or-famine climate. There is a short rainy season when the sun rides high in the sky (June, July, August), but a long dry season when the sun is low in the sky (November through April). To the north lies year-around drought of the Sahara Desert; to the south is a savanna region hav-

ing a much longer wet season with much heavier rainfall. Drought in the Sahel means a dearth in the annual rains on which the growth of grasses depends. Two groups of humans live on the natural resources of the Sahel: nomadic herders and grain farmers. Both groups depend upon the annual rains to turn the landscape green, rejuvenating the grasses upon which their cattle graze and supplying the soil moisture needed for the annual crop of grain. When the rains fail to appear, there are no grain crops to harvest and the cattle starve for lack of forage.

Water in another form is vital to people of the Sahel—fresh water to drink. Neither humans nor cattle survive long without drinking water. Streams of the Sahel flow copiously during the brief rainy season, but rapidly shrink as the dry season sets in. Water remains trapped in sand and gravel below the surface. This water fills holes scraped in low points in the stream beds. Water holes of this sort are essential to survival of humans and their cattle. Shallow dug wells can also supply water needs throughout the long dry season. But when the rains have failed

Famine in the Sahel. (Alain Nogues/Sygma.)

for three, four, or five successive years the subsurface water reserve is depleted. Water holes and shallow wells run dry.

In the worst stages of the Sahel drought nomads were forced to sell the remaining cattle that were their sole means of subsistence. Reduced to the status of refugees, these miserable humans crowded into camps close to the major cities. Here they might be fortunate enough to receive handouts of grain flown in from other nations on desperate relief missions. Despite relief supplies, many thousands of people died of starvation and disease in the Sahel. It is estimated that some 5 million cattle perished in the Sahel drought. The population of Ethiopia, far to

the east in the same climatic belt, also suffered heavily from this drought, with a death toll estimated at more than 50,000.

We will investigate the cause of the Sahelian drought in greater depth in this study unit. Clearly, something happened to the normal chain of atmospheric processes in which water is cycled from ocean to atmosphere as water vapor, then back to the earth's surface as rain.

Data Source: Thomas A. Johnson (1974) Sub-Sahara drought is termed worse, *New York Times,* vol. 123, no. 42,371 (January 26); John H. Douglas (1974) The omens of famine, *Science News,* vol. 105, pp. 306-308; Nicholas Wade (1974) Sahelian drought: No victory for Western aid, *Science,* vol. 185, pp. 234-237.

The Hydrologic Cycle

With this study unit we begin an investigation of the fresh water resources of the lands. Water of the lands is classified according to whether it is **surface water,** flowing exposed or ponded on the land, or **subsurface water,** occupying openings in the soil or rock. Water held in the soil within a few feet of the surface is the **soil water;** it is the particular concern of the plant ecologist, soil scientist, and agricultural engineer. Water held in the openings of the bedrock is referred to as ground water and is studied by the geologist.

Water of oceans, atmosphere, and lands moves in a great series of continuous interchanges of both geographic position and physical state which comprise the **hydrologic cycle** (Figure 13.1). A particular molecule of water might,

if we could trace it continuously, travel through any one of a number of possible circuits involving alternately the water vapor state and the liquid or solid state. The science of **hydrology** treats the global circuits of water as a complex but unified system on the earth.

The Global Water Balance

The pictorial diagram of the hydrologic cycle given in Figure 13.1 can be quantified for the earth as a whole. Figure 13.2 is a mass-flow diagram relating the principal pathways of the water circuit. We can start with the world ocean, which is the basic reservoir of free water. Evaporation from the ocean surfaces totals about 109,000 cu mi per year. (Metric equivalents are shown in a table in Figure 13.2). At the same time, evaporation from soil, plants, and water surfaces of the continents totals about 15,000 cu mi. Thus the total evaporation term is 124,000 cu mi; it represents the quantity of water which must be returned annually to the liquid or solid state.

Precipitation is unevenly divided between continents and oceans; 26,000 cu mi is received by the land surfaces and 98,000 cu mi by the ocean surfaces. Notice that the

Figure 13.1 The hydrologic cycle traces the various paths of water from oceans, through atmosphere, to lands, and return to oceans.

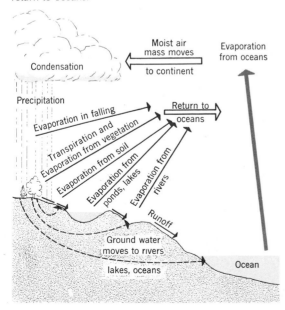

Figure 13.2 The global water balance. Figures give average annual water flux in and out of world land areas and world oceans. (Data of M. I. Budyko, 1971.)

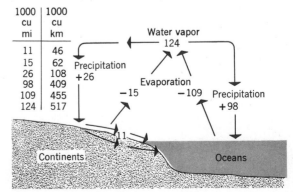

continents receive about 11,000 cu mi more water as precipitation than they lose by evaporation. This excess quantity flows over or under the ground surface to reach the
sea; it is collectively termed **runoff.**

We can state the **global water balance** as follows.

$$P = E + R$$

where P = precipitation
E = evaporation
R = runoff (positive when out of the continents,
negative when into the oceans)

Using the figures given for the continents

$$26,000 = 15,000 + 11,000$$

and for the oceans

$$98,000 = 109,000 - 11,000$$

For the globe as a whole, combining continents and ocean
basins, the runoff terms cancel out.

$$26,000 + 98,000 = 15,000 + 109,000$$

$$124,000 = 124,000$$

Global Water in Storage

The total global water resource is stored in the gaseous,
liquid, and solid states. Figure 13.3 gives a breakdown of
storage quantities. Water of the oceans constitutes over
97% of the total, as we would expect. Next comes water
in storage in glaciers, a little over 2%. Of the remaining
quantity, almost all is ground water, so that surface
water in lakes and streams is, indeed, a very small quantity. Yet it is this surface water, together with the very small
quantity of soil water, that sustains all life of the lands.
Some environmentalists consider that fresh surface water
will prove to be the limiting factor in the capacity of our
planet to support the rapidly expanding human population. The quantity of water vapor held in the atmosphere is
also very small—only about ten times greater than that
held in streams—yet this atmospheric moisture is the
source of all fresh water of the lands.

The Sahelian Drought—Natural or Man-made?

The Sahelian drought, commencing in 1968 and steadily
worsening through 1974, has been attributed by some to a
natural shifting of climate zones. In the news media, the
change is described as a southward creeping of the Sahara
Desert—advancing at a rate of 30 mi (50 km) per year.
Food and agricultural experts describe the climate change
as an equatorward shift of the tropical rainy monsoon.
Taking a quite different position, a few scientists have
proposed the hypothesis that the drought is in part, at least,
Man-made. Let us analyze both concepts.

Referring back to Unit 3, review the atmospheric circulation within the Hadley cell. There is a general rise of
warm, moist air over the equatorial trough of low pressure,
or intertropical convergence zone. This moist air mass
breaks out into numerous convection cells, so that heavy
thunderstorm rainfall is the rule, with from 80 to 100 in.
(200 to 250 cm) of rain received at the ground during the
year. Air subsiding from high levels in the subtropical belt
of high pressure is adiabatically warmed and is very dry.
This subsidence produces the Sahara Desert and other
great tropical deserts (Figure 13.4). Next, the wet equatorial and dry tropical belts must migrate northward at one
time of the year (June solstice) and southward at the opposite time of year (December solstice). In the latitude belt of
the Sahel (10° to 20° N) the annual migration of the tropical circulation system brings rain to the Sahel in the season
of high sun and dryness in the season of low sun.

If the amount of rain received by the Sahelian zone has
been decreasing year after year through a natural global
climatic change, the causing mechanism may be an expansion, or equatorward spread, of the dry subtropical
high pressure system along with a narrowing of the wet
equatorial belt. This change can be linked, in theory at
least, with the atmospheric cooling trend observed since
about 1940. Meteorologists suggest the possibility that the
cooling effect has been to strengthen and expand into
lower latitudes the circulation of the westerlies, pushing
the subtropical high pressure belt to lower latitudes. Cooling would also diminish the intensity of convectional activity in the equatorial zone, shrinking the width of that zone.

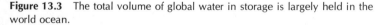

Figure 13.3   The total volume of global water in storage is largely held in the
world ocean.

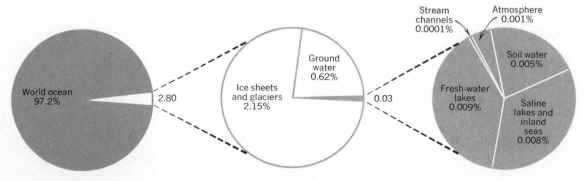

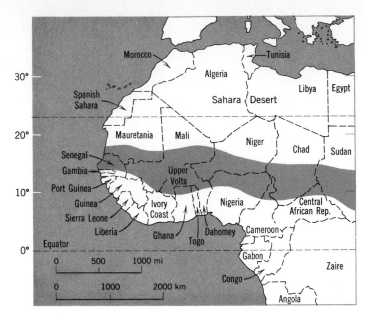

Figure 13.4 The Sahel, or Sahelian Zone, shown in color, lies south of the great Sahara Desert of North Africa.

With this shifting of climate belts, the Sahel would come under dominance of the desert climate.

Man-made drought is often termed **desertification.** The term refers particularly to the change in appearance of the land surface to resemble a desert, largely through the destruction of grasses and shrubs that previously existed. It is argued that, while the reduction in rainfall may well be a natural climate change, desertification is brought about by Man's abusive treatment of the land surface.

An American agronomist, Norman H. MacLeod, was studying NASA satellite color photographs of the Sahelian zone when he came across a most remarkable feature. In the drought-stricken area was a green area with a pentagonal outline (Figure 13.5). Upon visiting this area in the field, MacLeod discovered that it was enclosed by a barbed-wire fence (Figure 13.6). The green pentagon turned out to be a 250,000-acre cattle ranch, subdivided into five sectors. Cattle were allowed to graze one sector a year, rotating the pastures and allowing four intervening years for grasses to recover. The system had been in use for only five years, which corresponded to those of the drought period. Clearly, land use had made the difference, despite reduced rainfall.

This study unit has served as a transition between our study of the atmosphere, completed in Part I, and our study of the hydrosphere, which we have just begun. Rather than regard these two global realms as separate, we emphasize that they are interwoven in a most complex way through the hydrologic cycle.

Figure 13.5 An alert agronomist, Norman H. MacLeod, spotted this strange demarcation line between a green region (dark area at left) and barren parched land near the border between Niger and Mali, during the height of the Sahelian drought. (N. H. MacLeod.)

Figure 13.6 The straight line proved to be the boundary fence of the Ekrafane ranch, inside which carefully controlled grazing allowed the plant cover to survive through the drought. (N. H. MacLeod.)

The Global Water Balance by Latitude Zones

To get a better picture of the global fresh-water resource, we need to examine the water balance by latitude zones from equator to poles. Whereas the total global water must always be in true balance, this requirement does not apply to various individual regions. One region can have a water surplus; another can have a water deficit.

From a global water balance in terms of water volume per unit of time (cu mi/yr; cu km/yr), we now turn to water balance data in terms of water depth per unit of time (in./yr; cm/yr). Just as the first set of data tells us the total quantity of water transported into or out of a specified area in one year, so the second set tells us the intensity of water flow, independent of total surface area and total water quantity.

The water balance can be estimated for latitude belts of 10-degree width to reveal the response to the latitudinal changes in radiation and heat balances from equatorial zone to polar zones. Figure 13.7 shows the average annual values of precipitation, evaporation, and runoff. Units are water depth in millimeters per year.

The runoff term, R, in this case includes import or export of water in or out of the belt by ocean currents as well as by stream flow. Notice the equatorial zone of water surplus with positive values of R, in contrast to the dry subtropical belts, with an excess of evaporation. The runoff term, R, which is here negative in sign, represents the importation of water by ocean currents to furnish the quantity needed for evaporation.

Water surpluses occur poleward of the 40th parallel but the values of all three terms decline rapidly at high latitudes, going nearly to zero at the poles. The precipitation surpluses are sustained by importation of water vapor; evaporation surpluses by export of water vapor.

Figure 13.7 The water balance for 10-degree latitude zones. Data from several sources compiled by W. D. Sellers (1965) *Physical Climatology*, Univ. of Chicago Press, Chicago, p. 5, Table 1. (From A. N. Strahler [1971] *The Earth Sciences*, 2nd ed., Harper & Row, New York.)

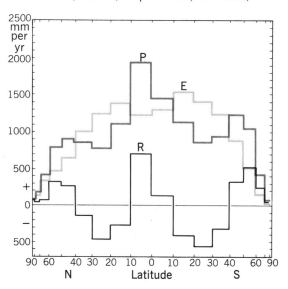

Unit 14
Surface Water as a Natural Resource

The Royal Flush

The affluence of American society has assumed astounding proportions. A long list of developing nations is striving to catch up. Affluence means big spending in all categories of energy and materials. With that big spending comes big wasting, too. Except for waste of energy resources, in no category is the squandering of precious resources more evident that in the use of fresh water. When it comes to the use of that costly fluid, every urban household in American contains a royal family, dedicated to the proposition that an endless flow of pure water is an inalienable birthright.

Water use in an average household runs as high as 80 gallons per day per family member in urban and suburban areas. Here, electricity is available and people have been educated to keep clean and smell nice by using lots of water for bathing. Most households have automatic clothes laundering and dishwashing appliances. In suburbia, the added preoccupation with two great national pursuits—lawn watering and car washing—drives up the daily per capita use. Those rural dwellings without electricity, and therefore no electric pump to drive a household water supply, may use as little as 10 gallons of water per day per person. When you have to work a pump handle to lift all the water you use, you get along with a lot less.

The accompanying diagram shows the approximate average apportionment of household water use among eight functions in homes in Akron, Ohio. The symbol of American affluence must indeed be the toilet, with 41% of the total. A single toilet flush uses from 3 to 6 gallons of water. The bathtub, shower and wash basin account for the second greatest use, 37%. A single tub bath may use 30 gallons, a single shower bath from 30 to 60 gallons.

Pure water fit to drink is a very expensive commodity, when we consider the capital investment and upkeep included in a municipal water supply system with its reservoirs and deep wells, conduits, filtration and purification plants, and pumping stations. As a city grows, its demands for water require extensions of the water supply system to more distant sources, usually in well-watered uplands. Serious trouble is beginning to brew as environmentalists object to the construction of new water diversion dams and reservoirs in scenic mountain gorges. In addition, water diversion from a river to a city can so seriously deplete the downstream river flow that the river ecosystem is often endangered as concen-

How water is used in an average home in Akron, Ohio. (U.S. Geological Survey.)

trations of pollutants increase to intolerable levels in the shrunken river volume.

In this group of study units devoted to Man's fresh water resource, we will touch upon many aspects of water supply and water pollution. To understand the pollution of water supplies and other environmental impacts of water use, we will need to build up a basic knowledge of principles of water movement over the land surfaces and within the ground.

DATA SOURCE: L. B. Leopold and W. B. Langbein (1960) *A primer on water*, U.S. Government Printing Office, Washington, D.C., 50 pp; J. H. Feth (1973) Water facts and figures for planners and managers, U.S. Geological Survey, Circular 601-1, 30 pp.

Overland Flow and Channel Flow

Rainfall and melting snow enter the soil through natural openings between soil grains and soil clumps. Moving downward under the force of gravity, this water becomes part of the subsurface water flow system. We shall trace the subsurface flow paths of the hydrologic cycle in Unit 15. At times when the soil is already saturated, or soil water is frozen, precipitation and snowmelt are blocked from downward passage. Then the excess water flows over the land surface to lower levels as **overland flow** (Figure 14.1).

Overland flow eventually contributes to a stream, which is a much deeper, more concentrated form of runoff (Figure 14.2). We define a **stream** as a long, narrow body of flowing water occupying a trenchlike depression, or channel, and moving to lower levels under the force of gravity.

The **channel** of a stream is a narrow trough, shaped by the forces of flowing water to be most effective in moving the quantities of water and sediment supplied to the stream. Channels may be so narrow that a person can jump across them, or as wide as 1 mi (1.5 km) for great rivers such as the Mississippi.

Both overland flow and stream flow are forms of runoff, which we defined in Unit 13 as the movement of surplus precipitation from the lands to the oceans in the hydrologic cycle.

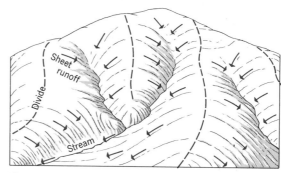

Figure 14.2   Overland flow from slopes in the headwater area of a stream system supplies water and rock debris to the smallest elements of the channel network.

Seeking to escape to progressively lower levels and eventually to the sea, runoff becomes organized into a **drainage system.** The system consists of a branched network of stream channels, as well as the sloping ground surfaces that contribute overland flow to those channels. The entire system is bounded by a drainage divide, outlining a more-or-less pear-shaped **drainage basin.** The drainage system is adjusted to dispose as efficiently as possible of the runoff and its contained load of mineral particles.

Figure 14.1   Overland flow on this sloping corn field is being generated during a summer thunderstorm. The flow is being received by a narrow stream channel in the foreground and conducted rapidly away toward the left. (Soil Conservation Service.)

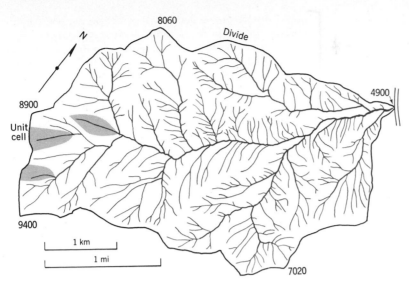

8060
Divide
N
8900
Unit cell
9400
4900
7020
1 km
1 mi

Figure 14.3 Channel network of a small drainage basin. Figures around the perimeter give elevation above sea level (feet). (Data of U.S. Geological Survey and Mark A. Melton.)

A typical stream network contributing to a single outlet is shown in Figure 14.3. Note that each fingertip tributary receives overland flow from a small area of land surface surrounding the channel. This area may be regarded as the unit cell of the drainage system. The entire land surface within the outer divide (perimeter) of the drainage basin constitutes the **watershed** for overland flow. A drainage system is a converging mechanism, funneling and integrating the weaker and more diffuse forms of runoff into progressively deeper and more intense paths of activity.

Channel Geometry and Stream Flow

The size of a stream channel can be stated in terms of the area of cross section, A, which is the area in square feet between the stream surface and the bed, measured in a vertical slice across the stream (Figure 14.4). The rate of fall in altitude of the stream surface in the downstream direction is the **gradient.**

As a stream flows under the influence of gravity, the water encounters resistance—a form of friction—with the channel walls. As a result, water close to the bed and banks moves slowly; that in the deepest and most centrally located zone flows fastest. Figure 14.4 indicates by arrows the speed of flow at various points in the stream. The single line of maximum velocity is located in midstream, where the channel is straight and symmetrical, but about one third of the distance down from surface to bed.

Our statement about velocity needs to be qualified. Actually, in all but the most sluggish streams, the water is affected by **turbulence,** a system of innumerable eddies that are continually forming and dissolving. A particular molecule of water, if we could keep track of it, would describe a highly irregular, corkscrew path as it is swept downstream. Motions include upward, downward, and sideward directions. Turbulence in streams is extremely important because of the upward elements of flow that lift and support fine particles of sediment.

The murky, turbid appearance of streams in flood is ample evidence of turbulence, without which sediment would remain near the bed. Only if we measure the water velocity at a certain fixed point for a long period of time, say several minutes, will the average motion at that point be downstream and in a line parallel with the surface and bed. Average values are shown by arrows in Figure 14.4.

Because the velocity at a given point in a stream differs

Figure 14.4 Stream flow within a channel is most rapid near the center and just below the water surface.

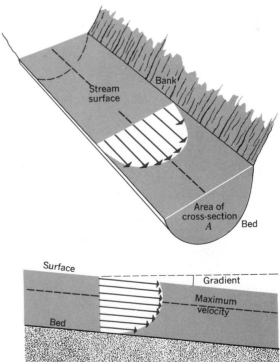

Bank
Stream surface
Area of cross-section A
Bed
Surface
Gradient
Maximum velocity
Bed

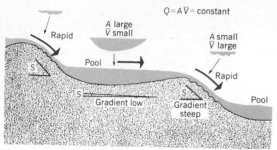

Figure 14.5 Schematic diagram of the relationships among cross-sectional area, mean velocity, and gradient. (From A. N. Strahler [1971] *The Earth Sciences,* 2nd ed., Harper & Row, New York.)

greatly according to whether it is being measured close to the banks and bed or out in the middle line, a single value, the **mean velocity,** is needed. Mean velocity is computed for the entire cross section to express the activity of the stream as a whole.

Stream Discharge

A most important measure of stream flow is **discharge, Q,** defined as the volume of water passing through a given cross section of the stream in a given unit of time. Com-

monly, discharge is stated in cubic feet per second (abbreviated to cfs). In metric units discharge is stated in cubic meters per second (cms). Discharge may be obtained by taking the mean velocity, **V,** and multiplying it by cross-sectional area, **A.** This relationship is stated by the important equation, $Q = AV$.

We realize that water will flow faster in a channel of steep gradient than one of gentle gradient, since the component of gravity acting parallel with the bed is stronger for the steeper gradient. As shown in Figure 14.5, velocity increases quickly where a stream passes from a wide pool of low gradient to a steep stretch of rapids. As velocity V increases, cross-sectional area A must decrease; otherwise their product AV, would not be held constant. In the pool, where velocity is low, cross-sectional area is correspondingly increased.

Figure 14.6 is a map showing the relative discharge of major rivers of the United States. ("River" is a popular term applied to a large stream. The word "stream" is the scientific term designating channel flow of any magnitude of discharge.) The mighty Mississippi with its tributaries dwarfs all other North America rivers, although the MacKenzie, Columbia, and Yukon rivers, as well as the Great Lakes discharge through the St. Lawrence River, are also of major proportions. The Colorado River, a much smaller stream, crosses a vast semiarid and arid region in which little tributary flow is added to the snowmelt source high in the Rocky Mountains.

Figure 14.6 This schematic map shows the relative magnitude of United States rivers. Width of the black line is proportional to mean annual discharge. (U.S. Geological Survey.)

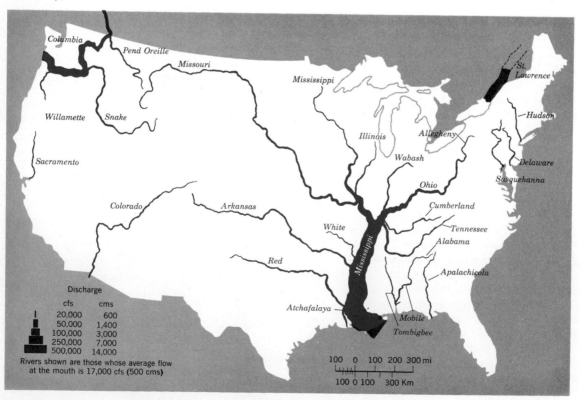

Stream Gauging

An important activity of the U.S. Geological Survey is the measurement, or **gauging,** of stream flow in the United States. In cooperation with states and municipalities this organization maintains over 6000 gauging stations on principal streams and their tributaries. Information on daily discharge and flood discharges is essential for planning the distribution and development of surface waters as well as for design of flood-protection structures and for the prediction of floods as they progress down a river system.

A stream gauging station requires a device for measuring the height of the water surface, or **stage** of the stream. Simplest to install is a staff gauge, which is simply a graduated stick permanently attached to a post or bridge pier. This must be read directly by an observer whenever the stage is to be recorded. More useful is an automatic-recording gauge, which is mounted in a stilling tower built beside the river bank (Figure 14.7). The tower is simply a hollow masonry shaft filled by water that enters through a pipe at the base. By means of a float connected by a wire to a recording mechanism above, a continuous ink-line record of the stream stage is made on a graph paper attached to a slowly rotating drum.

To measure stream discharge, we must determine both the area of cross section of the stream and the mean velocity. This requires that a **current meter** (Figure 14.8) be lowered into the stream at closely spaced intervals so that the velocity can be read at a large number of points evenly distributed in a grid pattern through the stream's cross section (Figure 14.7). A bridge often serves as a convenient means of crossing over the stream; otherwise, a cable car or small boat is used. The current meter has a set of revolving cups whose rate of turning is proportional to current velocity. As the velocities are being measured from point to point, a profile of the river bed is also made by sounding the depth. From these readings a profile is drawn and the cross-sectional area is measured from the profile. Mean

Figure 14.8 In gauging large rivers, the current meter is lowered on a cable by a power winch. Earphones, connected by wires to the meter, receive a series of clicks whose frequency indicates water velocity. (U.S. Geological Survey.)

velocity is computed by summing all individual velocity readings and dividing by the number of readings. Discharge can then be computed using the formula $Q = AV$.

Figure 14.7 Idealized diagram of a stream gauging installation. The operator rides in the cable car.

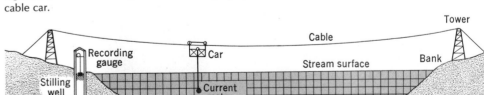

Unit 15
Ground Water–a Natural Resource

The Seventh Sense – Henry Gross and his Dowsing Rod

The title of this essay is also the title of a book by Kenneth Roberts, published in 1951. That author took as his hero a New England water diviner, Henry Gross, whose alleged feats surely border on the supernatural. Finding underground water with a divining rod, a procedure popularly known as "dowsing," has had many practitioners and still enjoys a surprisingly high level of support in rural areas. Dowsing is an attractive occupation because it needs very little capital investment—no education, no machinery, no office, and no staff. Dowsing requires only a divining rod, which can be the crotch of a small tree limb, cut to form a Y. The dowser grasps the two branches of the Y, one in each hand, and points the stem away from him horizontally. If the operator has the gift to divine a subsurface water supply, he needs only to walk across an area, letting the divining rod do its thing. Arriving at a place where water is present, the rod is drawn downward by a mysterious force, pointing to the favorable location for a well.

Henry Gross was a highly successful water dowser. He might have remained a modest practitioner throughout his life, had he not encountered author Kenneth Roberts in 1947. Throughout their remarkable association over a four-year period Roberts encouraged Henry Gross to perform feats of divining that transcended the duties of a simple dowser and touched off a major war with an outraged geology profession.

Henry soon learned that by walking backward from the point where his divining rod indicated the existence of a "vein" of water, the rod would dip at a horizontal distance equal to the precise depth of the vein. This information would be of great value to a farmer, since he could estimate the cost of drilling the well. Soon Henry's precocious dowsing rod was exploiting its talent in new fields of endeavor and even exploring new fluids. If the tip of the rod were first touched to a bottle of rye whiskey, it was thereafter able to identify other bottles of the same kind of booze by remote sensing, scrupulously avoiding bourbon and scotch. After this passing deviation, the rod got back to its major calling, the finding of underground water supplies. Henry next discovered that the rod would give him all the information he needed merely by asking it questions. Of course, the rod answered questions only as "yes," by dipping, or "no," by not dipping. Henry had to pose his ques-

Roy Goldthwaite, famous in Massachusetts as a successful "water witch," finds that his forked stick has been urged by a mysterious force to point straight down, signifying the presence of a ground water supply. (Wide World Photos.)

tions to meet this limitation, but the rod proved able to tell him not only if water were present, but its depth, rate and direction of flow and quality, as well. Heaping miracle upon miracle, the rod then proved capable of finding water from a map or air photograph alone, without requiring any field work at all. A crowning achievement was Henry's success in locating four "domes" of fresh water on the island of Bermuda, 800 miles distant, using only a map. Henry later traveled to Bermuda to pinpoint the water domes and ascertain their depths more precisely. The rod warned Henry that one of the domes was polluted; subsequent investigation turned up a privy that was causing the pollution.

Geologists, using all of the tactics at their disposal, have never been fully successful in putting down the water dowsers. A substantial body of faithful followers supports the art of dowsing. In New England, many persons believe in Henry Gross's underground "domes" and "veins" of fresh water. On Cape Cod one can find plumbers, well-drillers, and even town selectmen who still cling to the notion that a great underground vein of fresh water connects the mainland of New England with Cape Cod. The point of origin of the mysterious underground river is a sub-ject of debate; some say it derives its flow from Lake Winnipesaukee or somewhere in the White Mountains, both in the state of New Hampshire and over 150 miles distant from Cape Cod. It took a major educational campaign in the 1960s by local geologists and environmentally-conscious laymen to convince the natives of Cape Cod that their one and only source of fresh underground water is precipitation from the sky above them. Today, environmental planning on Cape Cod is moving forward through a major water-resources research program by the United States Geological Survey, funded through tax money voted by local communities.

Fresh water beneath the land surface is the subject of this study unit. Be prepared to discover some rather strange concepts about the true behavior of this underground water; it does indeed move in mysterious paths.

DATA SOURCE: *Henry Gross and His Dowsing Rod,* by Kenneth Roberts, Doubleday & Company, New York, 1951, as reviewed by J. Harlen Bretz (1952), *Journal of Geology,* vol. 60, pp. 197-200; *The Seventh Sense: A Sequel to "Henry Gross and His Dowsing Rod,"* by Kenneth Roberts, Doubleday & Company, New York, 1953, as reviewed by J. Harlen Bretz (1954), *Journal of Geology,* vol. 62, pp. 194-197.

Bedrock and Regolith

A certain proportion of precipitation that falls on the land sinks down into the soil and makes its way to great depth, moving under the force of gravity. To prepare for a study of subsurface water, we introduce some facts about materials that lie below the ground surface.

Bedrock is a geologist's term for dense, usually hard rock that has not been softened or broken up by processes of weathering and erosion since the time it was originally solidified. (We shall explain weathering and erosion processes in later units.) Overlying the bedrock in most areas is a layer of comparatively soft or loose mineral particles called **regolith** (Figure 15.1). In some cases regolith represents bedrock that has been softened and disintegrated by processes of weathering acting locally. This material is **residual regolith.** In other places we find **transported regolith,** consisting of mineral fragments carried from other areas by streams, wind, or glacial ice, or by wave and current action along a shoreline. Beaches, dunes, and river bars are examples of transported regolith composed largely of sand or gravel.

Our interest at the moment lies in the ability of bedrock and regolith to hold water and to allow water to move slowly from place to place through the mineral mass. Even without a knowledge of geology, you can appreciate the wide range in water-holding properties of bedrock and regolith. A chunk of fresh granite can be soaked in a pail of water for days, yet it will absorb no measurable amount of water—the mineral crystals of granite are simply too tightly and perfectly bonded to leave any space for water to enter. On the other hand, a pail of clean sand will quickly absorb a large quantity of water—perhaps an amount equal to one-third of its bulk volume. Dry clay also is capable of absorbing a large proportion of water, but the absorption process is very slow compared with sand. Water will drain rapidly from wet sand, but will be held by clay for long periods of time. We can predict, then, that thick layers of sand will be capable of holding water in large quantities and that water can travel along or across the sand layers quite readily. A sand layer with these properties is called an **aquifer.** (Various kinds of regolith and bedrock serve as aquifers.) In contrast, layers of clay will act as barriers to impede the subsurface movement of water.

Judging from what we have just said about granite you might suppose that a region underlain by fresh granite bedrock could not hold any subsurface water. In reality, however, bedrock of any variety or origin is almost always found to be broken by innumerable fractures, called **joints.** Joints typically occur as sets of closely spaced, parallel planes; moreover, two or three such sets of joints are usually present and intersect one another, forming **joint blocks.** Water can penetrate joint fractures and move through a mass of jointed bedrock, although very slowly in many cases. In some forms of bedrock, such as limestone, moving underground water has removed mineral matter from joint fractures, enlarging them into interconnected

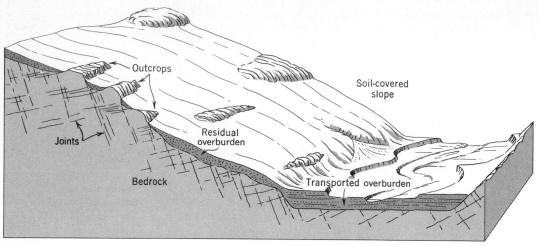

Figure 15.1   Residual regolith on the hillside is derived from bedrock beneath. Transported regolith of the valley bottom has been brought from some distance away by a stream.

passageways capable of conducting large volumes of water quite rapidly.

The point we are making in this brief geological discussion is that water can be held in storage and can move through many kinds of bedrock and regolith, but there is a wide natural range in the amount that can be stored in a given volume of those materials. There also is a wide range in the rate at which water can move from place to place in regolith and bedrock. As we continue our investigation of subsurface water, imagine the material lying beneath the surface as a uniform clean sand, which has a large capacity to hold water, and through which water can move freely—in other words, an ideal aquifer.

Ground Water

Ground water is that part of the subsurface water which fully saturates the pore spaces of the bedrock and regolith. The ground water occupies the **saturated zone** (Figure 15.2). Above it is the **unsaturated zone** in which water

does not fully saturate the pores. Water is held in the unsaturated zone by capillary force in tiny films adhering to the mineral surfaces.

Ground water is extracted from wells dug or drilled to reach the ground-water zone. In the ordinary shallow well, water rises to the same height as the **water table,** or upper boundary of the saturated zone (Figure 15.2).

Where wells are numerous in an area, the position of the water table can be mapped in detail by plotting the water heights and noting the trend of change in altitude from one well to the other. The water table is highest under the highest areas of land surface: hilltops and divides. The water table declines in altitude toward the valleys where it appears at the surface close to streams, lakes, or marshes (Figure 15.3). The reason for this water table configuration is that water percolating down through the unsaturated zone tends to raise the water table, whereas seepage into streams tends to draw off ground water and to lower its level.

Because ground water moves extremely slowly, a difference in water table level, or **hydraulic head,** is built up and maintained between high and low points on the water table. In periods of abnormally high precipitation, this head is increased by a rise in the water table under divide areas; in periods of water deficit, occasioned by drought, the water table falls (Figure 15.3).

The subsurface phase of the hydrologic cycle is completed when the ground water emerges in places where the water table intersects the ground surface. Such places are the channels of streams and the floors of marshes and lakes. By slow seepage and spring flow, the water emerges fast enough to balance the rate at which water enters the ground water table by percolation.

Figure 15.4 shows paths of flow of ground water in an ideal aquifer. Flow takes paths curved concavely upward. Water entering the hillside midway between divide and stream flows rather directly. Close to the divide point on

Figure 15.2   Zones of subsurface water.

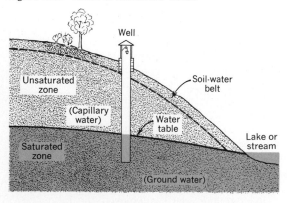

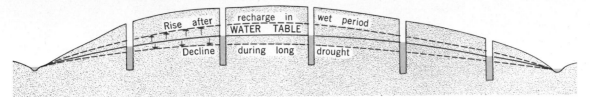

Figure 15.3 Configuration of the water-table surface conforms with the land surface above it.

the water table, however, the flow lines go almost straight down to great depths from which they recurve upward to points under the streams. Progress along these deep paths is incredibly slow; that near the surface is much faster. The most rapid flow is close to the place of discharge in the stream, where the arrows are shown to converge.

Drought and the Water Table

The northeastern United States experienced a 5-year drought, beginning in the summer of 1961 and covering a 13-state region which extended from Maine to North Carolina, an area of more than 400,000 sq mi (1,036,000 sq km). With each passing year of diminished rainfall, there occurred a reduction in yields of crops and pasture lands. Threats of forest fire were heightened and the numbers of such fires increased.

The effect of the drought upon municipal water supplies was felt in two ways: stream flow was depleted and reservoirs declined in level. Ground-water levels also declined, and in some instances the water table fell below the level of the base of supply wells.

Ground water in the Northeast is largely replenished, or **recharged,** during the late winter and early spring, at which time rains and melting snows cause the soil and regolith to become saturated. Water then percolates down through the zone that is normally unsaturated during much of the year and reaches the water table. The added quantity of ground water causes a rise in the level of the water table. Because ground water is in constant motion, flowing very slowly toward adjacent stream channels, the water

table declines when recharge is not occurring. In the Northeast a decline of water table, which normally occurs throughout the summer and fall, often lasts into early winter.

Figure 15.5 shows the seasonal rise and fall of the water table in an observation well on Cape Cod, Massachusetts. The annual cycle of rise and fall ranges through 2 to 3 feet (0.6 to 1.2 m). The drought that began in 1961 showed little effect in this area in 1962 and 1963, but thereafter the water table declined rapidly. Recharge was exceptionally small in 1965 and 1966, as the graph shows. In 1967 and 1968, a heavy recharge occurred in response to a return to normal precipitation that ended the drought.

Ponds, Lakes, and Bogs

The various events of geologic history, such as faulting, or erosion and deposition by wind and by ice sheets, have created many natural depressions with floors below the altitude of the water table. Water stands in these depressions in the form of ponds and lakes. In humid climates, water level coincides closely with the water table in the surrounding area.

Seepage of ground water, as well as direct runoff of precipitation, maintains these free water surfaces perma-

Figure 15.5 Record of an observation well on Cape Cod, Massachusetts, showing the characteristic annual cycle of rise and fall of the water table, together with the effects of a succession of drought years. (Data of U.S. Geological Survey.)

Figure 15.4 Paths of ground water movement under divides and valleys. (After M. K. Hubbert.)

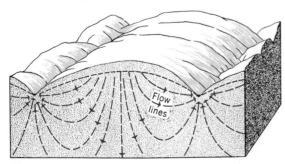

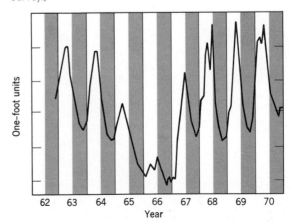

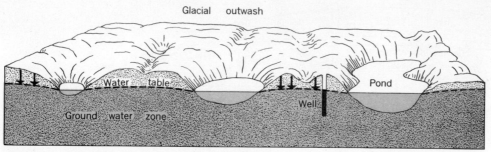

Figure 15.6 Freshwater ponds in sandy glacial deposits on Cape Cod, Massachusetts. (From *A Geologist's View of Cape Cod,* © 1966 by Arthur N. Strahler. Reproduced by permission of Doubleday & Co.)

nently throughout the year. Examples of such freshwater ponds are found widely distributed in North America and Europe where plains of glacial sand and gravel contain natural pits and hollows left by the melting of stagnant ice masses. Figure 15.6 is a block diagram showing small freshwater ponds on Cape Cod. The surface elevation of these ponds coincides closely with the level of the surrounding water table.

Many former freshwater water-table ponds have become partially or entirely filled by the organic matter from growth and decay of water-loving plants. The result is a bog with a surface close to the water table.

Ground Water as a Resource

A glance back to Figure 13.3 will show that the global volume of ground water in storage is vastly greater than the volume of fresh water temporarily stored in streams and lakes. It is not surprising, then, that ground water has been extensively developed for Man's use. The importance of ground water is especially great in arid lands, where surface streams run only on brief occasions and evaporation losses from reservoirs are high.

In later study units, we will evaluate the importance of ground-water supplies in the United States.

Unit 16
Lakes—Natural and Man-made

Long Island Sound—a Dream of a Lake

Not everyone who dreams of creating vast freshwater lakes is a civil engineer. One such dreamer was a geoscientist, Robert D. Gerard, a member of the scientific staff of the Lamont-Doherty Geological Observatory of Columbia University. His proposal, published in *Science,* August 19, 1966, called for converting Long Island Sound into a freshwater lake, to serve as a massive new water supply for the New York City region. New York City has had to reach far into the hinterland to develop upland water supplies at a rate fast enough to meet its growing demands. Long Island—New York City's unhappy neighbor—is rapidly developing almost insurmountable problems of keeping its municipal wells from being contaminated by salt and sewage. And New York City is in no mood to share its Delaware River water with Long Island.

Gerard's suggestion was to place a dam across both eastern and western ends of Long Island Sound, a body of salt water about 90 miles long, and 20 miles across at the widest portion. The western end of the Sound leads into New York Harbor by way of the East River, a narrow passage that would be easily dammed, if the problem of very swift tidal currents could be overcome. The eastern end of the Sound, opening into the Atlantic, would require a massive dam, several miles long, and strong enough to resist storm waves generated in hurricanes. Such an engineering undertaking, however, seemed to pose no inherently insuperable difficulties. Of course, the reservoir, once constructed, would have to be flushed of its salt water and replaced by fresh water. The Connecticut River could supply a large flow of fresh water, and in time the reservoir might provide a tremendous reserve of fresh water.

As soon as Gerard's proposal was published, there was a rash of communications, mostly from persons who wished they had thought of the idea first. The response came from fellow scientists as well as local politicians. Alistair W. McCrone, a fellow geoscientist, wrote a letter to *Science* proposing that the Hudson River be dammed at a point just north of Manhattan Island, providing yet another freshwater lake—hardly an exciting project compared with Gerard's proposed monster. Then a third scientist, Robert U. Ayres of the Hudson Laboratories of Columbia University, proposed that the Hudson River might be so dammed that its fresh-water flow could be diverted through the Harlem River and East River into Long Island Sound, thereby hastening the flushing out of salt water. Another reader of *Science*

Sailing on the Sound. (Ewing Galloway, New York.)

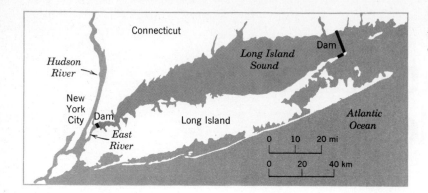

This map of Long Island Sound shows the proposed freshwater lake and the dam at each end.

wrote in to add that, if the construction of the dam at the east end of the Sound were properly planned, the removal of a great volume of earth material used to form the dam might result in a huge new harbor facility.

Now the news media took up the proposal. The *New York Daily News* indulged in a flight of fancy, envisioning the great new supply of fresh water at the city's doorstep in retrospect in 1996: "How did this miracle come about? Who made the concrete desert bloom? It was accomplished by forward-looking scientists and engineers who in the '70s and '80s planned and hammered through, over the opposition of professional scoffers, a billion-dollar scheme to dam the Hudson River and Long Island Sound. The gigantic construction job transformed these bodies of water into two of the world's largest reservoirs which, of course, were renamed Lake Lindsay and Lake Rockefeller."

Now the politicians got into the act. Representative Hugh L. Carey, a Democrat from New York City, added some touches of his own to the grandiose scheme. The dam at the eastern end of the Sound could serve as a causeway, permitting a heavy flow of highway traffic between eastern Long Island and the Connecticut mainland. A new jetport might then be developed on shallow fill in that area, using runways projecting into the water and supported on piers. Carey was quoted by the press as saying: "I think this is totally feasible. Even if we had to invest one billion dollars, the one project would solve the water, airport, and transportation problem. That's how the West got developed. The East is provincial. We need to learn what to do. I'd like to put a Western Solution to Long Island Sound. While we're talking here about the jet airport and water supply, the West goes ahead and puts up dam after dam and creates lakes that would make long Island Sound look like a cup of water. They change the course of a whole river and take it as a matter of course."

Representative Carey reputedly asked the chairman of the House Public Works Committee to have

the Corps of Engineers produce a feasibility study for the Long Island Sound project. In any case, the Corps did prepare a report in which it noted that the new freshwater reservoir could "take care of a population several times that estimated for the study area in the year 2020." The Corps report stated that dams and navigation locks would be required at both ends of the Sound. The dam at the eastern end of the Sound would need to be 7½ miles long and would be built in water reaching a maximum depth of 150 feet. There would need to be a spillway over this dam, so that high water generated in the Sound by hurricane-force winds could escape into the Atlantic. The report went on to say that some 8 to 20 years would be required to dilute the salt water of the Sound to a level that would make the water acceptable for public water supplies. However, if water of the Sound were to be pumped into the sea, that time might be substantially shortened. Then the Corps of Engineers report sounded this note of caution:

Connecticut rivers flowing into Long Island Sound carry the wastes from many communities. They disperse in the Sound rapidly and ultimately reach the Atlantic Ocean. If daily tidal flushing were eliminated, however, pollution would become intolerable unless sewage and waste treatment, much better than now available, were installed. The freshwater lake would be relatively quiescent, if not stagnant, with only wind-induced currents to spread the waste throughout the basin. Pockets of concentrated waste would be almost certain to develop in some areas. Unless the treatment included the removal of nutrients, heavy algal blooms would be inevitable.

So now we see the catch! To gain a magnificent body of fresh water, the entire surrounding region would have to give up its avenue of cheap sewage disposal. Keeping a large lake clean and pure is no small task. Look at Lake Erie and you can see what might well happen. Ecologists would look at the Long Island Sound project as a nightmare of environmental disruption. Perhaps it is for the best that New York City has had to abandon the thought of any such billion-dollar project. That dream has been destroyed by the greatest urban financial disaster ever to face the nation. Perhaps now, as Governor of New York State, trying desperately to keep a great city from collapse, Hugh Carey has changed his tune. But it was a nice dream, wasn't it?

DATA SOURCE: Robert D. Gerard (1966) Potential freshwater reservoir in the New York area, *Science,* vol. 153, pp. 870-871; R. H. Boyle, J. Graves, and T. H. Watkins (1971) *The Water Hustlers,* Sierra Club, San Francisco, pp. 231-234.

Lakes as a Resource

Lakes are integral parts of drainage systems and participate in runoff of water in the hydrologic cycle. Lakes are of major environmental importance to Man in many ways. They represent large bodies of fresh water in storage; they support ecosystems that provide food for humans. Today, the recreational value of lakes is assuming increasing importance.

Where lakes are not naturally present in the valley bottoms of drainage systems, Man creates lakes as needed by placing dams across the stream channels. Many regions that formerly had almost no natural lakes are now abundantly supplied. As you travel by airplane across such a region the glint of sunlight from hundreds of Man-made lakes will catch your eye. Some are small ponds made to serve ranches and farms; others cover thousands of acres. Obviously, an abundance of Man-made lakes represents a major environmental modification and has far-reaching consequences.

Kinds of Natural Lakes

The term **lake** includes a very wide range of kinds of water bodies. Lakes have in common only the requirement that they have an upper water surface exposed to the atmosphere and no appreciable gradient with respect to a level surface of reference. Ponds (small, usually shallow water bodies), marshes, and swamps with standing water can be included.

Lake water may be fresh or saline, and we may have some difficulty in deciding whether a body of salt water adjacent to the open ocean is to be classed as a lake or an extension of the sea. A practical criterion rules that a coastal water body is not a lake if it is subject to influx of salt water from the ocean. Lake surfaces may, however, lie below sea level, an example being the Dead Sea with surface elevation of −1300 ft. (−396 m). The largest of all lakes, the Caspian Sea, has a surface elevation of −80 ft (−25 m). Significantly, both of these large below-sea-level lakes are saline.

Basins occupied by lakes show a wide range of origins as well as a vast range in dimensions. Basins are created by geologic processes and it should not be surprising that there are lakes produced by every category of geologic process.

An important point about lakes in general is that they are for the most part short-lived features in terms of geologic time. Lakes disappear from the scene by one of two processes, or a combination of both. First, lakes that have stream channel outlets will be gradually drained as the outlet channels are eroded to lower levels. The principle is illustrated by the catastrophic breaching of landslide dams, such as that of the Madison slide described in Unit 27. Where a strong bedrock threshold underlies the outlet, erosion will be slow but nevertheless certain. Second, lakes accumulate inorganic sediment carried by streams entering the lake and organic matter produced by plants within the lake.

Lakes also disappear by excessive evaporation accompanying climatic changes. Many former lakes of the southwestern United States flourished in moister periods of glacial advance during the Pleistocene Epoch, but today are greatly shrunken or have disappeared entirely under the present arid regime. A special case of lake disappearance is that of the lowering of the water table by excessive withdrawal of ground water.

Evaporation from Lakes and Reservoirs

The water balance of a lake or reservoir is rather complicated to analyze, because water can enter or leave by a number of paths. Input of water can come from three sources: (1) stream-channel inflow and overland flow directly from land surfaces sloping down to the lake shores; (2) ground-water seepage through the lake floor; and (3) precipitation falling upon the lake surface. Output of water can occur through (1) channel outflow at the lake outlet or spillway of a dam (2) seepage of water into the ground-water zone, and (3) direct evaporation into the atmosphere.

In the case of large lakes and reservoirs in an arid climate evaporative losses can be extremely high. Evaporation from the free-water surface is not easy to measure, since it depends upon water temperature, atmospheric temperature, humidity, and pressure, and wind speed. Formulas taking into account these variables are available for estimating evaporation from lakes.

Direct measurement of evaporation from a free-water surface makes use of the **evaporating pan,** which is simply a circular container 4 to 6 ft. (1.2 to 1.8 m) in diameter and 10 in. (25 cm) or more in depth. Water is added as required and the amount of surface lowering due to evaporation measured with a gauge (Figure 16.1). Evaporation data are collected by the National Weather Service at many observing stations. The evaporation from the pan is generally greater than from a lake or reservoir, so that the

Figure 16.1   An evaporating pan with anemometer at side. Notice a thermometer immersed in the water (*upper left*). The cylindrical device at near edge of the pan is a hook gauge to measure height of water level. (NOAA, National Weather Service photograph.)

pan readings require correction by a reduction factor ranging from 60% to 80%.

Figure 16.2 is a map of the United States showing the average annual evaporation from a free-water surface as measured by the pan method. Notice the high values in the hot desert regions of the southwestern United States in contrast to low values in the cool northeastern region. Listed below are some representative figures giving annual total evaporation for actual reservoir surfaces:

	Inches	Cm
Gardiner, Maine	24	61
Birmingham, Alabama	43	109
El Paso, Texas	71	180
Tucson, Arizona	60	152
San Juan, Puerto Rico	55	140
Gatun, Canal Zone	48	122
Atbara, Sudan	124	315

Saline Lakes

Lakes with no surface outlet are characteristic of arid regions. Here, on the average year after year, the rate of water loss by evaporation balances the rate of stream inflow. If the rate of inflow should increase, the lake level will rise. At the same time the lake surface will increase in area, allowing a greater rate of evaporation. A new balance can then be achieved. Since dissolved solids are brought into the lake by streams—usually ones that head in distant highlands where a water surplus exists—and there is no surface outlet, the solids accumulate with resultant increase in salinity of the water. Salinity, or degree of "saltiness," refers to the abundance of certain common ions in the water. These dissolved solids are explained in a

Science Supplement to Unit 18. Eventually, salinity levels reach a point where salts are precipitated in the solid state, a subject we will investigate in Unit 54.

Evaporation control is a subject of major importance in conserving the water supplies in a Man-made reservoir, particularly where the reservoir is situated in a region of arid climate. This situation occurs where an exotic river is dammed. (An **exotic river** is one that is sustained in its flow across an arid region through runoff derived from a distant region of water surplus.) The Colorado River in Arizona is a good example. A large reservoir, such as Lake Mead behind Hoover Dam, presents an enormous water surface exposed to intense evaporation.

Since the input of stream water is finite, a reservoir may be designed with such a large capacity that it will never completely fill in an arid climate, because there is a point at which annual evaporation equals the annual input.

Evaporation Control

Reduction of evaporation from reservoir surfaces has been approached through the application of a synthetic chemical compound that will spread over the surface as a very thin film, cutting down on the water evaporation. Hexadecanol, a fatty alcohol, is one such compound that has been used. One problem is that the chemical must be nontoxic to plant and animal life. Another is that losses by evaporation and solution of the chemical require that it be continually replaced. On large reservoirs the film is easily broken up by winds and rain. Nevertheless, experimental applications have achieved a reduction of evaporation of about 10% on large reservoirs to as high as 25% on small ponds on the order of 0.1 to 1.0 acre (0.04 to 0.4 hectare). The saving in water must be weighed against the cost of the method.

Environmental Impact of Man on Lakes

Lakes, whether natural or Man-made, are highly susceptible to deterioration of quality in various ways under the impact of Man. One form of physical deterioration is by inflow of mineral sediment carried by streams. The accumulation of sediment is called **sedimentation.** Man's use of the land greatly increases sediment content of streams in both agricultural and urban areas. Another form of deterioration is chemical. Pollutants of various sorts, ranging from highway salts to sewage, are introduced into the lake. A third form of deterioration is organic, in which pollutants impact the ecosystem of the lake. We will find that in some cases pesticides can do damage to animal life in lakes; in other cases pollutants from sewage greatly increase the rate at which microscopic plants (algae) multiply.

We will study all of these forms of environmental quality decline in lakes in later units. Usually, it is best to treat streams and lakes together in these discussions.

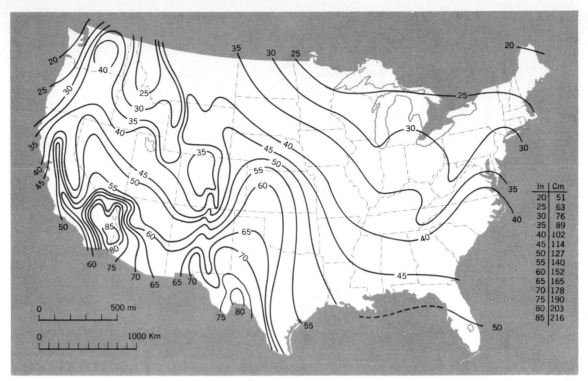

Figure 16.2 Annual evaporation from the surface of shallow lakes. The figures give water depth in inches. (Data of NOAA, National Weather Service.)

Unit 17 Freshwater Resources of the United States

Squeezing Water from Air

Schemes for obtaining large new supplies of fresh water have shown remarkable ingenuity. When a really way-out idea is proposed by scientists of impeccable qualifications, one reacts with a double take. Two schemes deserving a second look make use of the sound principle of condensation of water vapor. Their authors are from major universities: Columbia University and the Massachusetts Institute of Technology.

The Columbia proposal came in 1967 from two staff members of the Lamont-Doherty Geological Observatory. Off the record, it seems that Robert D. Gerard, a staff scientist of the Observatory, and J.

Condensation of water vapor. (Mimi Forsyth/ Monkmeyer Press Photo Service.)

Lamar Worzel, a professor of geophysics, were sitting at a bar on the island of St. Thomas, Virgin Islands, sipping cool tall glasses of liquid refreshment and basking in the everpresent trade winds that ventilate the establishment. Most persons engaged in such an intensive activity give little thought to the beads of water forming on the ice-cold glass and trickling down one by one in a constant procession to feed a small puddle on the bar. To Gerard and Worzel, the phenomenon was inspiring. Why not let the trade winds produce a steady source of fresh water? Fresh water is in very short supply on St. Thomas and many other small islands in the tropical zone. Although the tropical air masses of the trades carry enormous amounts of water vapor, there is often a long dry season on these islands and rainfall, when it comes, must be diverted from rooftops to cisterns to augment the supply.

To sweat out a large supply of water from tropical air masses a large source of cold water is needed. Refrigeration is not the answer, since a huge input of energy is needed to make ice by a mechanical process. To Gerard and Worzel, scientists whose experience with the deep ocean floor was derived from many research cruises, the answer was clear. Why not pump to the surface deep, cold ocean water that often lies close to the shore of an island or the mainland? Although the surface water of the tropical oceans is a delightful 80° F (27° C), one has only to descend to a depth of 6500 ft (2000 m) to find water at a temperature of 39° F (4° C). This frigid layer is enormously thick and the supply of cold water is limitless.

Gerard and Worzel proposed that the cold, deep water be pumped to the surface through a large-diameter pipe, then passed through a condenser with a large surface of exposed metal tubes, something like the condensing coil of an air conditioning unit. Situated on a windward hilltop, the condenser would intercept the warm, nearly-saturated air. Chilled on contact with the cold coils, the moist air could yield about two-thirds of an ounce of water for each cubic yard of air (16 gm/cu m). To produce one million gallons (4000 cu m) of fresh water per day would require pumping some 30 million gallons (110,000 cu m) of seawater through a mile-long pipe. The pump for this lift could be powered by a windmill, using energy of the constant trades.

Now comes the bonus. Water of the deep ocean is rich in nutrients, particularly nitrate and phosphate, essential to rapid growth of minute floating organisms—plankton—on which animal life of the oceans depends for its primary food source. Gerard and Worzel proposed that the used seawater be discharged into a natural lagoon that commonly lies between a coral reef and the mainland in these tropical waters. If enclosed by suitable barriers, this lagoon would form a salt lake in which to cultivate food fish on a high level of intensity. In their proposal, Gerard and Worzel suggested that the "coral corral" might harbor captive baleen whales, grazing upon the rich growth of plankton. We would probably have to veto this marine form of cattle-ranching, now that the whale has touched the hearts of an ecology-conscious public and recorded its strange songs on tape to provide us with cocktail music.

The M.I.T. proposal, presented by atmospheric scientists Victor P. Starr and David Anati, would use an enormous flexible plastic sleeve, rising into the air from ground level and serving as a chimney for rising warm air. The double-walled tube would be supported by helium gas, occupying the space between inner and outer plastic walls. The sun's heat would cause the air column to rise. Spontaneous rise of the air would result in its cooling by the adiabatic process, leading to condensation and the fall of rain through the tube back to earth. The tube would be perhaps 300 ft. (100 m) in diameter and 10,000 ft (3000 m) tall. This strange captive rainstorm would be capable of supplying irrigation water or fresh drinking water with no external power source needed to drive it.

So far, no attempt has been made to put either scheme into operation. In this study unit, we will assess the adequacy of our natural resources of surface water and ground water already condensed into liquid form by global weather processes.

DATA SOURCE: Robert D. Gerard and L. Lamar Worzel (1967) Condensation of atmospheric moisture from tropical maritime air masses as a freshwater resource, *Science,* vol. 157, pp. 1300-1302; J. P. Peixoto and M. Ali Kettani (1973) The control of the water cycle, *Scientific American,* vol. 228, no. 4, pp. 57-58.

Runoff—An Indicator of the Availability of Fresh Water

To understand the distribution of our national water resources, we can take a look at the variation in annual runoff across the United States and note areas of great water abundance in contrast to those of great water poverty. Figure 17.1 is a map on which are drawn lines to connect points of equal value of average annual runoff. The data are obtained from the great national network of stream gauges, described in Unit 14. As we explained in Unit 13, stream runoff is a measure of the excess of precipitation over evaporation (including transpiration from plants). Values of runoff given on the United States map are in inches of water—the same units as for precipitation. The map is greatly generalized, of course, and cannot show local differences that exist where narrow mountain ranges rise as moist islands from surrounding arid lowlands.

You will notice at once that a north-south line drawn through the center of the United States separates a humid eastern region from a generally arid western region. Runoff is particularly large—20 in. (50 cm) or greater—in the northeastern states, over the southern Appalachians, and along the Gulf Coast. The southwestern states are generally arid, with substantial runoff only from high mountains and plateaus. A large shaded area over much of Nevada and Utah is the Great Basin. Within this region all streams running from mountains to lowlands terminate in evaporating basins, which may be dry or may contain saline lakes, so that no runoff reaches the sea. Notice the very high values of runoff—over 80 in. (200 cm)—in the Pacific Northwest. Here coastal ranges and the lofty Cascade Mountains trap heavy orographic precipitation. The effect extends south into California in the high Sierra Nevada. (Refer back to the Science Supplement, Unit 5, for a detailed map of precipitation of California.)

With this general pattern of runoff as an indication of the availability of fresh water, we turn to the sources and uses of water in the United States.

National Water Uses

Two sets of data are used in assessing the national resources of surface water and ground water. First is **water withdrawal,** representing the quantity of water actually taken from surface-water and ground-water sources. Much of this water is returned after use to those same sources. The quantity of water actually lost to the atmosphere through evaporation and transpiration is a second quantity, the **consumptive water use.**

Figure 17.2 shows average daily United States water withdrawal for the year 1970. (These data are revised at 10-year intervals by the United States Geological Survey.)

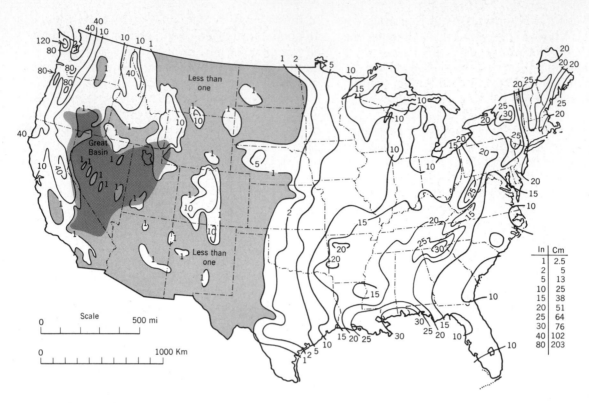

Figure 17.1   Average annual runoff (inches) over the United States. (Data of U.S. Geological Survey.)

The nation is divided up into water-use regions, named on the map. Within each region, figures give daily water withdrawal from surface-water (upper figure) and ground-water sources (lower figure). Water used for hydroelectric power is not included.

The ratio of the two figures within each region is highly revealing as to water-source differences across the nation. For the eastern states and the Pacific Northwest, where runoff is substantial, surface water is overwhelmingly the dominant source of water withdrawal. In the southwest, however, the balance shifts in favor of ground water.

Table 17.1 summarizes total United States water withdrawal and consumptive use for both public water supplies and rural supplies. Rural supplies are used for domestic and livestock needs. Irrigation use is not included, nor is self-supported industrial use (i.e., industries having their own water supplies). Public water supplies use surface water in twice the amount of ground water; of

Table 17.1   United States Water Use from Public and Rural Supplies in 1970

	Withdrawal (billion gallons per day)		Consumptive Use (billion gallons per day)	Percent of Withdrawal
Public water supplies				
Surface water	18.0	(68)		
Ground water	9.4	(36)		
Total	27.4	(104)	5.9 (22)	21.5%
Rural water supplies				
Surface water	0.9	(3)		
Ground water	3.6	(14)		
Total	4.5	(17)	3.4 (13)	75.6%

SOURCE: C. R. Murray and E. B. Reeves (1972) "Estimated Use of Water in the United States in 1970," U.S. Geological Survey Circular 676.
Note: Figures in parentheses give billions of liters per day.

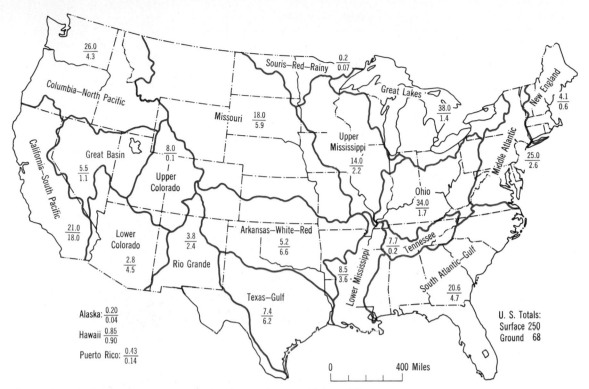

Figure 17.2 Surface-water *(upper number)* and ground-water withdrawal *(lower number)* for water-use regions of the United States in 1970. Units are billions of gallons per day. Water withdrawn for hydroelectric power is not included. (Data of C. R. Murray and E. B. Reeves [1972] U.S. Geological Survey, Circular 676, Table 17, p. 36.)

Figure 17.3 Water withdrawal for public supplies *(upper number)*, self-supplied industrial use *(middle number)*, and irrigation use *(lower number)* in the United States in 1970. Units are billions of gallons per day. (Data of C. R. Murray and E. B. Reeves [1972] U.S. Geological Survey, Circular 676.)

Table 17.2 United States Industrial and Irrigation Water Use in 1970

	Withdrawal (billion gallons per day)		Consumptive Use (billion gallons per day)		Percent of Withdrawal
Electric utilities					
Surface water	120.0	(456)			
Ground water	1.4	(5)			
Subtotal	121.4	(461)	0.8	(3)	0.6%
Other industry					
Surface water	31.0	(118)			
Ground water	8.0	(30)			
Subtotal	39.0	(148)	4.1	(16)	10.5%
Total industrial use	160.4	(609)	4.9	(19)	3.1%
Irrigation					
Surface water	81.0	(308)			
Ground water	45.0	(171)			
Total irrigation use	126.0	(479)	95.0	(361)[a]	75.4%

SOURCE: Same data source as Table 17.1.
Note: Figures in parentheses give billions of liters per day.
[a]Includes conveyance losses by evapotranspiration.

the total only about 20% is lost in consumptive use. Rural supplies use ground water in ratio of four times as much as surface water and the consumptive use is proportionately very high—about 75%.

When we turn to examine water use by industry and irrigation, we find that the total United States rates of withdrawal in both categories are much greater than that for public supplies. Figure 17.3 shows withdrawals for public supplies (upper number), self-supplied industrial use (middle number), and irrigation (lower number), by the same water-use regions as in Figure 17.2. As we would expect, irrigation withdrawal is very small in the humid eastern half of the nation, but large in the western states.

Of the self-supplied industrial withdrawal of fresh water, by far the greatest amount is used by electric utilities. Table 17.2 shows industrial withdrawal and consumptive use of fresh water in 1970. Since most of this water is used for driving turbines and for cooling, the proportion of return to source is very large, and the total consumptive use is only about 3% of withdrawal.

Future Water Needs

Figure 17.4 shows estimated future withdrawal for 1980 and 2000 as compared with 1960. We can expect withdrawals to increase only moderately for public supplies and for combined irrigation and rural use, in contrast to an enormous increase in the industrial requirement.

Figure 17.5 shows consumptive use projected to 1980 and 2000 in the same use categories as in Figure 17.4. Public supplies will hold to a constant percentage of consumptive use while that use is about doubled in the year 2000. Industrial consumptive use will increase enor-

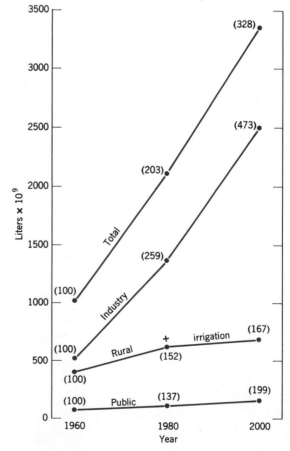

Figure 17.4 Estimated future water withdrawal in the United States. The figures in parentheses give percentage increase over 1960 values. (Data of C. R. Murray [1968] U.S. Geological Survey, Circular 556; A. M. Piper [1965] U.S. Geological Survey Water-Supply Paper 1797.)

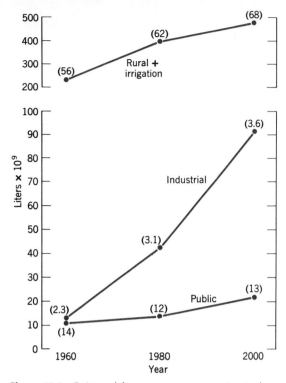

Figure 17.5 Estimated future water consumption in the United States. Figures in parentheses give percentage of estimated withdrawal. (Same data sources as Figure 17.4).

about 1400 billion gallons (b.g.) (5300 billion liters) per day. Compare this figure with the total estimated water withdrawal in the year 2000, which is about 900 b.g. (3400 b.l.) per day. Assuming that the consumptive use in 2000 will average 20% of the total withdrawal, we will be actually consuming (losing to the atmosphere) 180 b.g. (580 b.l.) per day, which is only a small fraction of the runoff. Recycling procedures can be developed to reduce even further the percentage of runoff required to be withdrawn.

This analysis suggests that for the nation as a whole there is an adequate total freshwater supply for the foreseeable future. For individual regions of the country, however, we can anticipate severe shortages. One remedy, already extensively developed, is the transfer of water from region of surplus to regions in need. The enormous concentration of persons and industry into a small area, as for example Los Angeles County and the New York City region, requires development of surface water facilities in distant uplands, but it is only by continual and costly expansion of these facilities that shortages can be avoided. In other words, the real problem of supply is not in the total quantity of fresh water available but in its distribution.

Compounding distribution problems are those of water pollution. If we continue to degrade the quality of our freshwater supplies, we will need to resort increasingly to expensive water-treatment procedures necessary to keep the water usable.

What Alternatives Exist?

For those areas experiencing or anticipating water shortages, certain alternatives exist to going farther afield in search of new supplies. One is to reduce per-capita water use by increasing the water cost to the consumer, with the anticipation that wasteful uses will be curtailed. Another means of saving water is to reduce leakage from municipal distribution systems. Leakage is estimated to run from 10 to 30% in many city water systems.

For arid and semiarid lands the maintenance of existing irrigation systems and their further expansion by reaching out to new and more distant runoff sources has been questioned in recent years. The grounds for such questioning are that most of the crops grown on these irrigated lands are low-value types (such as feed grains and forage crops) and can be grown in humid regions at less cost. As already stated, consumptive water use is extremely high in crop irrigation in hot, dry climates. For example, according to one estimate, 90% of the water use in Arizona is for irrigation, yet agriculture accounts for only about 10% of the total value of that state's economic production.

We have only touched upon a number of alternatives to increasing the transport of water in meeting increasing demands, it should be obvious that water management involves a broad spectrum of economic, political, and cultural factors.

mously, but the percentage with respect to withdrawal will remain small—under 4%.

Consumptive use in the rural and irrigation category (mostly irrigation) is so much larger than the other two categories that it requires a different scale on the graph. Consumptive use in irrigation is a very large percentage of withdrawal, as we would expect, and this percentage will rise to nearly 70% by the year 2000 as consumptive use is about doubled over the 1960 figure.

Will We Have Enough Fresh Water?

Assuming that the above estimates are fairly accurate, will we have enough fresh water to meet future demands? To get at the answer, we need to calculate the mean annual runoff leaving the boundaries of the United States. One assumption will be that we cannot count on removing any ground water from storage. Consequently all ground-water withdrawal must be the same as annual ground-water recharge. When this condition is satisfied, the amount of water annually added to surface water by seepage from the water table into streams and lakes will equal the annual recharge. This being the case, we need to deal only with the annual runoff.

Total United States annual runoff is estimated to be 480 cu mi (2000 cu km) per year. This figure converts to

Unit 18
Pollution of Streams and Lakes

Small Company Town versus a Big City—Who Cares about Some Little Specks of Asbestos?

Silver Bay, Minnesota, is a company-built town on the shore of Lake Superior. The working people among its 3000 residents are mostly employees of the Reserve Mining Company. From iron-bearing rock some 50 miles to the northwest, Reserve brings low-grade ore to its $350 million Silver Bay Plant. Here the ore is pulverized and the iron-rich particles extracted by magnets to be formed into pellets, which are then baked and transformed into high-grade iron ore. For every ton of ore pellets produced, two tons of waste sludge, called tailings, are generated. The tailings are washed to the lake shore in sluiceways and dumped into the lake. The larger, gravel-sized grains in the sludge accumulate near shore in a Man-made delta, but the fine particles travel down the lake bottom to a deeper resting place. But there are also present myriads of tiny fibrous particles—looking like microscopic toothpicks—of a mineral called asbestos. The fibers drift with the current, which heads toward the city of Duluth, located 50 miles distant at the western end of Lake Superior. Here the city water supply is withdrawn from the lake. Lake Superior's water is considered exceptionally pure—pure as any freshwater lakes of similar bulk are likely to be found in this industrial age.

Now, asbestos is a bad actor. Workers who inhale tiny asbestos fibers for many years in the course of their jobs in asbestos mining and processing plants are prone to asbestosis, a lung disease that seems to lead in many cases to a rare form of lung cancer. Construction workers who use asbestos products are also likely to suffer from asbestosis.

The Reserve Mining Company's taconite plant at Silver Bay, Minnesota, is shown here discharging tailings into Lake Superior (lower left). The company town can be seen in the upper right-hand corner. (Wide World Photos.)

Cartons of pure drinking water ready for public distribution in a food store in Duluth. This free water was being supplied to residents under a court order, because the city water supply was contaminated by asbestos particles from the Silver Bay taconite plant. (Wide World Photos.)

The dumping of tailings into Lake Superior by the Reserve Mining Company has gone on since the Silver Bay plant was built in 1947. For many years little thought was given to the addition of 67,000 tons of sludge per day to the lake's pristine waters. Then came the dawn of environmentalism, and with it a surge of investigative activity that scrutinized the impacts of waste disposal into streams and lakes. Resistance to further input of tailings into the lake began to be felt in 1968, when state and federal officials made a decision that the dumping should be stopped. When the Environmental Protection Agency (EPA) was set up in 1970, its staff began sampling of Lake Superior waters between Silver Bay and Duluth.

About this time (1972) Joseph Mengel, a geologist from the University of Wisconsin, called attention to the fact that asbestos fibers had been suspected of causing a high incidence of stomach cancers among Japanese people whose diet included talc-dusted rice. This discovery had been published in 1971 in the journal, *Science*. Talc is a soft mineral that for decades has been used to make talcum powder. In the Japanese talc are asbestos fibers of the same mineral composition as those released at Silver Bay. The Wisconsin geologist's suggestion was made public by a Duluth environmental activist, Arlene Letho; it brought an immediate response. The EPA's National Water Quality Laboratory in Duluth began a search for asbestos fibers in the lake waters and in the city air. In June 1973, they announced the finding of large numbers of asbestos fibers in Duluth's drinking water. Fibers were also found in the air at Silver Bay, presumably discharged from stacks of the ore-baking furnaces.

Citizen reactions to these discoveries reflected two very diverse points of view. In Silver Bay, where nearly all of the citizens owe their livelihood to the mining company, the EPA findings were greeted with some skepticism. The town mayor, Frank H. Scheruing, was quoted in the *New York Times* (7 August, 1973) as saying: "We feel it (asbestos) will be proven harmless just like everything else that's come up." The mayor explained that previous scares of pollutants, such as mercury, arsenic, lead, and copper in the tailings, had not been substantiated. The mayor said that, in the week the report came out, only a single half-gallon of bottled water had been sold in Silver Bay . . . "and that was to a lady who used it in her steam iron." Silver Bay residents continued to drink untreated lake waters. Some took a defiant attitude, others were simply skeptical of the EPA findings. One citizen was quoted by the *New York Times* as saying, "I've drunk it for 17 years now and nothing's happened to me yet."

The response of Duluth's citizens was quite different in tone. Their mayor, Ben Boo, was quoted by the *New York Times* as saying: "It doesn't matter whether the tailings are proven harmful or not, we just want them to stop the dumping." He explained that a poll of state residents had shown that 67% of those questioned were against dumping. Plans were then made to install a filtration system in the Duluth water supply to remove the asbestos fibers.

A court suit brought by government agencies against the Reserve Mining Company resulted in a 1974 order by a U.S. District Court judge to shut down plant operations. The judge's decision was quickly stayed by a three-judge panel of the U.S. Circuit Court, and plant operations resumed immediately. Although the U.S. Supreme Court later refused to vacate the stay, the battle to close dumping operations continued with more court actions. Perhaps the environmentalists will ultimately achieve their goal. In June 1975, the Reserve Mining Company began formal presentations to the State of Minnesota of plans to dispose of the tailings on land, where asbestos fibers could be contained and prevented from entering the lake. Several possible dumping sites are being studied. Meantime, the mining company faces fines totaling $41 million.

Jane E. Brody, a correspondent for the *New York Times,* commented on the Silver Bay controversy:

Regardless of the outcome of the present case, it is clear that it will have little effect on the allegiance of Silver Bay area residents to the Reserve Mining Company. Through the years, Reserve has been a benevolent employer operating a company town without the negative connotations that usually accompany that phrase. Indeed, it now appears that the Government, and particularly the Environmental Protection Agency, has been dubbed 'an enemy of the people' here. In Henrik Ibsen's play of that title, written nearly a century ago, a physician discovers that the local baths, the town's major source of livelihood, contain contaminated water that is killing those who come to be refreshed in the supposedly healthful spa. As thanks for his revelations, the physician is ostracized as an enemy of the people and all those who try to remain his friends are similarly scorned.

In this study unit, we will investigate the pollution of streams and lakes. Because the evidences of such environmental degradation are so easily seen by all who care to look, the elimination of surface-water pollution took an early lead in the great new campaign to clean up the environment.

Data Source: Jane E. Brody (1973) *The New York Times,* 8 August, 1973 (all quotations are from the *Times* article); (1974) Pollution and Public Health: Taconite case poses major test, *Science,* vol. 186, pp. 31-35; Karen Townsend Carlson (1975) The People's lake, *Environment,* vol. 17, no. 2, pp. 16-20, 25-26; (1976) Reserve Mining Company; still dumping on Duluth, *National Parks & Conservation Magazine,* vol. 50, no. 4, pp. 28-29.

Dissolved Substances in Surface Waters

Runoff from the lands to the oceans carries important quantities of dissolved inorganic matter in the form of ions. An **ion** is an atom or group of atoms bearing an electrical charge. When certain compounds are dissolved in water, the atoms become separated as ions. For example, ordinary table salt is the compound sodium chloride, consisting of one atom of sodium (Na) and one atom of chlorine (Cl). Thus the chemical formula for sodium chloride is NaCl. In its solid state, sodium chloride is a crystalline substance formed of atoms of sodium bonded tightly to adjacent atoms of chlorine in a one-to-one ratio. When placed in water, NaCl dissolves, meaning that the Na and Cl atoms separate and move freely among the water molecules. Separation from the crystal structure results in a sodium atom having a single positive electrical charge; it is now an ion, indicated by the symbol Na^+. A chlorine atom assumes a negative charge, becoming a chlorine ion: Cl^-.

Chemists refer to a positively charged ion as a **cation;** to a negatively charged ion as an **anion.** Some kinds of ions consist of two different kinds of atoms joined together. For example, the *ammonium ion* consists of one atom of nitrogen (N) joined with four atoms of hydrogen (H) with the formula NH_4^+; it is a cation. The *sulfate ion* is another example, with one atom of sulfur (S) joined to four atoms of oxygen (O), with the formula SO_4^{--}; it is an anion. Notice that the sulfate ion has two negative charges. Some kinds of ions have a single charge, others a double charge, and others a triple charge. Our discussion of ions will not go into chemical reactions, so that we will not make use of the various charges borne by ions. We will use the correct chemical formulas of the ions as shorthand for the names of the ions.

All surface water and all ground water, no matter how "pure" it seems to us as drinking water, contains a variety of ions in solution. An exception would be distilled water, sold in stores for use in steam irons and automobile batteries. Distilled water is condensed steam. When water is evaporated, as in boiling, the water vapor or steam that rises into the air over the water does not carry ions of dissolved solids; these remain behind in the water. You would probably judge the taste of distilled water to be rather flat. You are accustomed to a certain content of ions, as these impart a mild taste to drinking water. Manufacturers of "pure" bottled drinking water produced by distillation will add some salts to that water before marketing it, for otherwise the customers might find the taste unacceptable. Natural water ranges from that with a very low ion content to water too saline to drink, meaning that the concentration of ions from dissolved salts is very high.

Before investigating the subject of water pollution, we need to study the kinds of ions normally present in natural surface and ground water, as well as their natural sources.

The ions naturally present in fresh water of the lands are mostly of the inorganic class, meaning that they are all originally derived from non-living sources. Inorganic sources are (1) the atmosphere, (2) ocean water, and (3) soil, regolith, and bedrock. Ions move through rather complex pathways following the hydrologic cycle. We will begin with precipitation, which arrives at the ground as rain or snow. This water is referred to as rainwater.

Ions in Rainwater

We may like to think of rain that falls in sparsely settled humid regions, far from urban sources of pollution and desert sources of dust, as being "pure" water. In fact, however, all rainfall, wherever it occurs, carries down with it a variety of ions, some introduced into the atmosphere from the sea surface, some from land surfaces undisturbed by Man, and some from Man-made sources.

Sea salts enter the atmosphere as minute droplets detached from wave crests. These droplets evaporate, leaving salt residues which are carried upward in turbulent winds.

Sea salts are distributed throughout the entire troposphere and are a major form of nuclei of condensation (Unit 5).

When carried down to earth as rain, sea salts contribute all of the ions that are present in sea water. Most of the ions contributed are chlorine (Cl^-) and sodium (Na^+). Ions of magnesium (Mg^{++}), sulfate (SO_4^{--}), calcium (Ca^{++}), and potassium (K^+), are contributed in minor amounts.

Mineral dusts lifted from the ground into the atmosphere and carried upward in turbulent wind account for many of the potassium, calcium, and magnesium ions found in rainwater.

Sulfate ions (SO_4^{--}) are usually present in rainwater. They come largely from sulfate particles and gaseous sulfur compounds injected into the atmosphere by fossil fuel combustion, forest fires, volcanoes, and biological activity. Also present are nitrate ions (NO_3^-) and ammonium ions (NH_4^+) produced from gaseous forms of nitrogen introduced into the atmosphere from a variety of sources, including combustion of fuels, decay of organic matter, and fertilizers. Phosphate ions (PO_4^{---}) are also present in rainwater, but in much smaller amounts than ammonium and nitrate.

Ions in Runoff

After arriving at the ground surface, rainwater comes into contact with the soil. Here certain of the ions present in rainwater are removed while others remain in the water that eventually reaches streams and lakes. Ions are also added from mineral matter of the soil, regolith, and bedrock as the rainwater percolates downward to the ground-water zone. Examples of ions commonly released from mineral matter are sodium (Na^+), potassium (K^+), calcium (Ca^{++}), and magnesium (Mg^{++}).

Chemical analysis of water in streams is made on a regular basis by the United States Geological Survey. The concentrations of ions in all major rivers is known in considerable detail.

Across the United States, rivers vary widely in relative abundance of the kinds of ions present and in the total concentration of dissolved solids in the water. These data have environmental significance. Ions furnish nutrients to aquatic plants and are required for tissues of aquatic animals as well, yet excess quantities of certain ions,—nitrate, for example, when introduced by Man's activities—may provide an abnormally large nutrient supply. Also, downstream changes in ion concentrations allow scientists to calculate the input of various chemical pollutants produced by industrial processes in urbanized areas.

How Urbanization Affects Water Quality

Studies in the New York City region have shown that urbanization has a strong impact upon water quality. Ions are introduced into surface water from a number of sources. Rainwater over the urban area has excessive amounts of the sulfate ion (SO_4^{--}) and the nitrate ion (NO_3^-), representing washout of air pollutants produced by fuel combustion. (Refer back to Units 7 and 8 for discussion of urban air pollutants.) A small excess of the chlorine ion (Cl^-) has also been observed, and at least a part of this is thought to come from crystals of deicing salts lifted from city streets by winds.

Once the rainwater has come in contact with the soil, some important new pollutants are added. A large new input of both chlorine ions (Cl^-) and sodium ions (Na^+) comes from deicing salts spread on streets and highways in winter. Melting snow and rain carry these ions into the runoff system. Care of suburban lawns involves both the use of lime and fertilizers. Lawn lime is usually a finely pulverized limestone, with the composition of calcium carbonate ($CaCO_3$); it releases calcium ions (Ca^+) as well as bicarbonate ions (HCO_3^-) into stream runoff. Fertilizers release substantial amounts of the sulfate ion (SO_4^{--}) and the nitrate ion (NO_3^-), along with lesser amounts of the potassium ion (K^+) and the magnesium ion (Mg^{++}).

Sewage collected by sewer systems in urban areas is given treatment before being released into nearby streams and lakes (or into the ocean). As we shall find in Unit 45, treatment does not usually include removal of the ions we have already listed. Where septic tanks are used, household sewage is released into the soil and sinks down to the water table, but eventually this water also reaches streams and lakes. Sewage effluent contains all of the ions we have listed in earlier paragraphs. Particularly significant in sewage effluent are nitrate ions (NO_3^-) and phosphate ions (PO_4^{---}). (The latter was not mentioned above.) Both nitrate and phosphate ions are contributed by body wastes of humans and animals; both are nutrients to aquatic plants. The impact of these nutrients upon plant and animal communities in streams and lakes is a major topic in environmental pollution; we will return to the subject in Part V, following a study of the way in which ecosystems operate.

Other Chemical Forms of Water Pollution

Many other pollutant chemicals enter surface water and ground water. One class of pollutants consists of pesticides used to control a wide variety of weeds, plant diseases, and predatory insects. Pesticides are for the most part synthetic chemical compounds. Another class of pollutants includes certain potentially harmful organic chemical compounds synthesized for industrial purposes, such as for the manufacture of plastics. We shall discuss the impact of synthetic chemical compounds upon ecosystems in Part V.

Another class of chemical pollutants consists of toxic metals, among them lead, mercury, and cadmium, released into the environment by industrial activities and from solid-waste disposal systems. Radioactive wastes, released from activities related to the processing and use of nuclear fuels comprise still another category of water pollutants; these are discussed in Unit 63.

Acid Mine Drainage

A particularly insidious form of pollution of surface water and ground water goes under the name of **acid mine drainage.** It is an important form of environmental degradation in parts of Appalachia where abandoned coal mines and strip mine workings are concentrated.

Ground water emerging from abandoned mines, as well as soil water percolating through strip-mine spoil banks, is charged with sulfuric acid and various salts of metals, particularly of iron. The sulfuric acid is formed by reaction of water with iron sulfides, particularly the mineral pyrite (Fe_2S), which is a common constituent of coal seams.

Acid of this origin in stream waters can have adverse effects upon animal life. In sufficient concentrations it is lethal to certain species of fish and has at times caused massive fish kills. The acid waters also cause corrosion to boats and piers. Government sources have estimated that nearly 6000 mi (10,000 km) of streams in this country, together with almost 40 sq mi (100 sq km) of reservoirs and lakes are seriously affected by acid mine drainage. The acid may be gradually neutralized by reaction with carbonate rocks, but other chemical pollutants may persist. One particularly undesirable by-product of acid mine drainage is precipitation of iron to form slimy red and yellow deposits in stream channels.

Sulfuric acid may also be produced from drainage of mines from which sulfide ores are being extracted, and from tailings produced in plants where the ores are processed. Such chemical pollution also includes salts of various toxic metals, among them zinc, lead, arsenic, copper, and aluminum.

Thermal Pollution

Thermal pollution is a term applied generally to the discharge of heat into the environment from combustion of fuels and from nuclear energy conversion into electric power. In Unit 9 we covered thermal pollution of the atmosphere and its effects on the urban environment. Thermal pollution of water is different in its environmental effects because it takes the form of heavy discharges of heated water locally into streams, estuaries, and lakes. The thermal environmental impact may thus be quite drastic in a small area.

Nuclear power plants require the flow of large quantities of water for cooling. Other industrial processes also rely upon water as a coolant. Large air-conditioning plants also use water to cool the condensing coils. A cooling system may be designed to recycle the coolant, causing heat to be dissipated into the atmosphere; the principle is the same as that of the water-cooled automobile engine and most small air-conditioners. In this case, the heat load is placed on the atmosphere by radiation and conduction. Evaporation of water may be used as a means of cooling in recycling systems, but this requires an input of water to replace that lost by evaporation. A third method is to withdraw cold water from a lake or stream, or from the ground-water body, pass it through the cooling system, and discharge the heated water into the same source. For example, a large air-conditioning plant may use cold ground water and dispose of the heated water into recharge wells. In many localities, disposal by well recharge is required by law to conserve ground water.

The impact of discharges of heated water into streams and lakes upon the environments of aquatic plant and animal life is a subject we will investigate in Part V.

In this unit, we have begun the study of water pollution by evaluating some of the physical and chemical aspects of the process as it applies to streams and lakes. In the next unit we will take up some further aspects of ground-water pollution. The full environmental impact of water pollution remains to be evaluated in Part V, after we have gained some understanding of life processes within natural ecosystems. Various forms of chemical pollutants make severe impacts on ecosystems.

SCIENCE
SUPPLEMENT

Acid Rain—An Ominous Increase

What is acid rain? As we explained in Unit 7, sulfur dioxide gas (SO_2), released into the air by combustion of fossil fuels, readily forms sulfuric acid (H_2SO_4) in the minute water films of suspended droplets in the air over cities. Washout of sulfuric acid by precipitation results in rainwater with an abnormally high content of the sulfate ion, a condition known as **acid rain.** Nitric acid, formed by reactions involving pollutant nitrogen oxides, may also contribute to the acidity of rainwater.

When tested for degree of acidity, measured in terms of the pH of the rainwater, acid rain shows pH values well below a pH of 5 to 6 typical of rainwater falling in unpolluted regions. (Rainwater is normally slightly acid because of the presence of carbon dioxide in solution, forming a weak concentration of carbonic acid.)

In recent years, water chemists have noted a significant lowering of the pH of rain in northwestern Europe. Values have been reduced to between pH 3 and 5. Because pH numbers are on a logarithmic scale, these values mean that rain in these areas is now often 100 to 1000 times more acid than previously.

The accompanying four maps show pH values for rainwater in northwestern Europe for the years 1956, 1959, 1961, and 1966 (Figure 18.1). The maps show both a dramatic lowering of pH levels and a widespread increase of areas receiving significantly acid precipitation.

In 1974, American scientists studying the chemical quality of rainwater reported that for about the past 20 years rainwater over the northeastern United States has had an average pH of about 4; they have observed pH values as low as 2.1 in rainwater of individual storms at certain localities. Other observations show that values less than pH 4 occur at times over many heavily industrialized United States cities, among them Boston, New York, Philadelphia, Birmingham, Chicago, Los Angeles, and San Francisco. Values between 4 and 5 have been observed near such urbanized areas as Tucson, Arizona, Helena, Montana, and Duluth, Minnesota—localities we do not usually associate with heavy air pollution.

Some of the possible bad environmental effects of acid rain are these: excessive leaching of nutrients from plant foliage and the soil, disturbances of the balances of predators and prey in aquatic ecosystems, various metabolic disturbances to organisms, acidification of lakes and streams, and the corrosion of structures. One possible instance of the effect of acidification of stream water, observed in Norway, has been the elimination of salmon runs by inhibition of egg development. Increased fish mortality, observed in Canadian lakes, has also been attributed to acidification.

Scientists who study acid rain warn that the inevitable increase in combustion of fossil fuels will intensify the trend toward acidification, particularly if emission control standards are relaxed to permit burning of fuels of high sulfur content. They foresee some very serious consequences of the spread in extent and intensity of acidification—consequences affecting both natural ecosystems and Man-made structures.

Figure 18.1 Rainwater acidity in northern Europe in the years 1956, 1959, 1961, and 1966. Figures give pH values. (Data of S. Odén, 1972; after G. E. Likens, et al., *Environment*, vol. 14, no. 2, p. 36, Figure 1.)

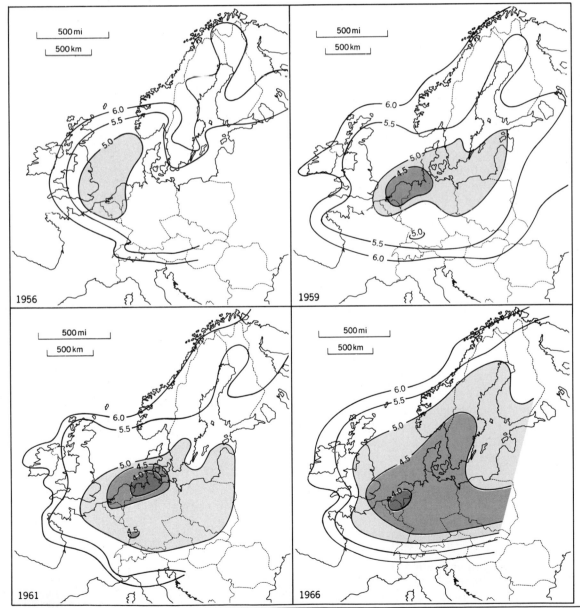

Unit 19
Environmental Impacts of Ground-water Withdrawal

The Great Hole Beneath Brooklyn

Secretly, the citizens of Brooklyn, New York, had been excavating an enormous hole beneath their city. That was going on steadily during the first three decades of the 1900s. By the year 1936 the huge excavation was over five miles in diameter and reached to a depth of 35 feet below sea level at its deepest point. This extracurricular activity was so cleverly executed that no streets caved in and no buildings toppled. What the Brooklynites had removed was water, not rock; they had mined a freshwater resource beneath the city and nearly brought a disaster upon themselves.

In these early years, Brooklyn's water supply came from wells drilled deep below the city. By the early 1930s, ground-water withdrawals were averaging more than 75 million gallons per day. Now, all fresh ground water comes from precipitation, and if it is withdrawn at an annual rate greater than it is replenished by rainfall and snowmelt, the water table will decline in elevation. Not only were the annual Brooklyn water withdrawals much greater than the annual replenishment from natural sources, but the process of urbanization had to a large extent sealed off the ground surface. Runoff from city streets and sidewalks, from parking lots and building roofs, was diverted into storm drains leading the water directly to the nearby ocean. Sanitary sewers were also carrying used water to the ocean.

Disaster came in the form of contamination of the ground water by salt water from the harbor. As wells became salty, they were closed down. Then Brooklyn was bailed out by hooking into the New York City water-supply system. Pumping was reduced to 10 million gallons per year and the used water was

returned to the ground-water table by means of recharge wells. The water table began a slow rise, filling the great hole. By 1965, not only was the hole filled, but a mound of ground water a few feet high took its place, as nature intended. The accompanying maps show three stages of ground-water levels in Kings County, the county essentially identical with the Borough of Brooklyn. Queens County also went in for water mining, and in 1965 had a sizeable hole of its own, as the map shows.

During the long period of lowered ground-water level, many Brooklynites converted cellars and basements into living and working spaces. New buildings made use of subsurface space. But by the mid-1970s, because pumping of ground water had

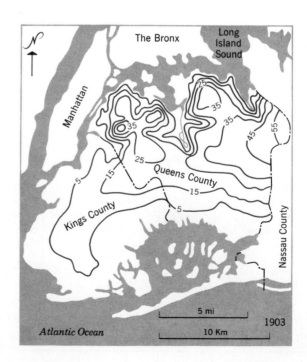

124

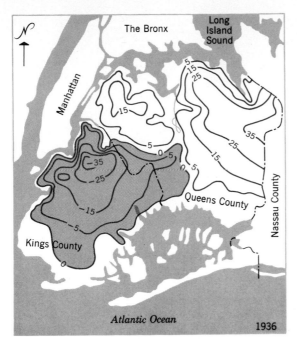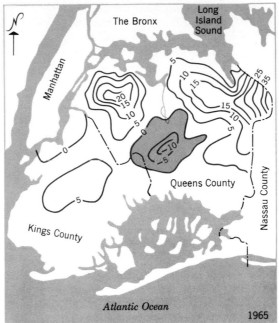

Three maps show the elevation of the ground-water surface in the area of Brooklyn and Queens in three different years. The numbers on the lines give water-table elevation in feet. Areas in color have water table below sea level. (U.S. Geological Survey.)

largely stopped, the ground water table had risen to the level of building foundations. Then, a three-year period of unusually great precipitation caused a further drastic rise in the water level and many basements experienced flooding. So Man's intervention with nature has finally run a full cycle.

Brooklyn was indeed fortunate that the city streets did not sink and buildings did not lean. Rock beneath Brooklyn is very strong and can easily support a city even when the rock is dehydrated. Other cities have not been so fortunate. We will find out in this study unit what happened to Mexico City, Mexico,

and Venice, Italy, as a result of long-continued ground-water mining.

In this study unit, we will examine science principles relating to ground-water withdrawal and to the encroachment of salt ground water, which replaces it in coastal zones.

DATA SOURCES: P. Cohen, and others (1970) *Water for the future of Long Island, New York,* Division of Water Resources, State of New York, pp. 20-21, R. C. Heath, and others (1966) The changing pattern of ground-water development on Long Island, New York, U.S. Geol. Survey, *Circular 524,* pp. 5-6.

Water Wells

Since before the dawn of civilization, Man has dug shallow wells to reach the water table and withdraw ground water for domestic and agricultural purposes. Prior to the Industrial Revolution, however, energy resources were limited to power provided by human muscles or those of draft animals, or by windmills. The amount of ground water that could be diverted from natural recharge was usually of little consequence to the operation of the natural groundwater system. Discharge of ground water through surface seepages was sufficient to maintain the flow of streams in the summer and to sustain the water levels of ponds, marshes, and bogs.

With the invention of powerful pumps utilizing electricity generated from the combustion of fossil fuels, Man's industrial society could meet heavy water demands of an expanding population. Enormous quantities of ground water were pumped for irrigation to increase food production. Not only has Man seriously depleted this natural resource, but related disturbances to the ground water system have also had a number of harmful effects on the environment.

In agricultural lands of the semiarid and desert climates, heavy dependence is placed upon irrigation water from pumped wells. Wells can be drilled within the limits of a given agricultural or industrial property; wells can provide immediate supplies of water without need to construct expensive canals or aqueducts. A few of the hydraulic principles of water wells are treated here to aid you in understanding the basis of complex economic, legal, and environmental problems arising from ground-water development and use.

Formerly the small well needed to supply domestic and livestock needs of a home or farmstead was actually dug by hand as a large cylindrical hole, lined with masonry where required. By contrast, the modern well put down to supply irrigation and industrial water is drilled by powerful machinery which may bore a hole 12 to 16 in. (30 to 40 cm) or more in diameter to depths of 1000 ft (300 m) or more, although much smaller-scaled wells and well-boring machines suffice for domestic purposes. Drilled wells, often called **tube wells,** are sealed off by metal casings which exclude impure near-surface water and prevent clogging of the tube by caving of the walls. Near the lower end of the hole, where it enters the aquifer, the casing is perforated so as to admit the water through a considerable surface area.

Rate of flow of a well or spring is stated in units of gallons (liters) per minute or per day. The yields of single wells range from as low as a few gallons per day in a domestic well to many millions of gallons per day for deep, large-bore, industrial or irrigation wells.

High-capacity pumps can easily bring water to the surface more rapidly than it can enter the well, so that the delivery of ground water is limited by the properties of the aquifer rather than by the mechanical equipment. The rate at which water can enter the well depends on the quality of the aquifer, which limits the rate of flow of water through the surrounding material.

Flow of ground water is extremely slow compared to flow of streams. It is estimated that ground water may move at a speed of 5 ft (1.5 m) per day through a sandy aquifer in which wells of good yield are developed, that in exceptional cases of coarse gravels the speed may reach 30 to 60 ft (10 to 20 m) per day. In dense clays the rate may be immeasurably slow.

Drawdown

When rate of pumping of the well exceeds the rate at which water can enter, the level of water in the well drops and the surrounding water table is lowered in the shape of a conical surface, termed the **cone of depression.** The height of the cone is the **drawdown** (Figure 19.1). By producing a steeper gradient of the water table, the flow of ground water toward the well is also increased, so that the well will yield more water. This effect holds only for a limited amount of drawdown, beyond which the yield fails to increase. The cone of depression may extend as far out as 10 mi (16 km) or more from a large well where very heavy pumping is continued. Where many wells are in operation, their intersecting cones produce a general lowering of the water table.

Depletion often greatly exceeds the rate at which the ground water of the area is recharged by percolation from

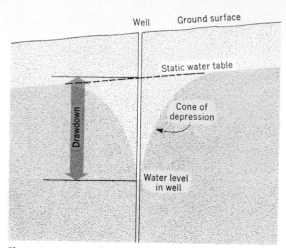

Figure 19.1   Drawdown of water table and cone of depression produced by pumping of a well.

precipitation or from the beds of streams. In an arid region, much of the ground water for irrigation is from wells driven into thick sands and gravels that are lowland deposits of transported regolith of a type termed alluvium. (These features are described in Unit 33). Recharge of such deposits depends on the seasonal flows of water from streams heading high in adjacent mountain ranges. Here, the extraction of ground water by pumping can greatly exceed the recharge by stream flow. Cones of depression deepen and widen; deeper wells and more powerful pumps are then required. Overdrafts of water accumulate and the result is exhaustion of a natural resource not renewable except by long lapses of time.

In humid areas where annual rainfall is copious—from 30 to 50 in. (75 to 125 cm) annually—natural recharge is by general percolation over the ground area surrounding the well. Here the prospects of achieving a balance of recharge and withdrawal are highly favorable through the control of pumping and the return of waste waters or stream waters to the ground-water table by means of **recharge wells** in which water flows down, rather than up.

Environmental Effects of Overdraft of Ground Water

Sustained withdrawal of ground water at a rate substantially greater than the natural recharge rate produces a number of undesirable side effects upon the environment. Sometimes these effects are slow in coming, but by the time they are recognized it may be too late to correct the damage. Because the drawdown from a well spreads toward the limits of an aquifer, a general lowering of the water table will be felt over a large area after many wells have been in operation for a period of years.

You may wonder what is harmful about a decline in water-table levels. After all, you may say, the ground water is far below the surface and is not used by plants. One harmful effect will be upon ponds, lakes, and bogs that normally stand at the level of the surrounding water table. These water bodies can be thought of as surface exposures of the water table itself (see Figure 15.6). Thousands of such water-table ponds and bogs exist in the northern United States within the area formerly covered by the Pleistocene ice sheets. Although the pond water levels rise in the spring and decline in late summer and fall, along with the water table itself, the pond level remains on the average more or less constant from year to year and from decade to decade. As a result, these aquatic habitats have come to sustain stable communities of plants and animals. If the water table is severely lowered by pumping of ground water, as shown in Figure 19.2, these water bodies will cease to exist and the ecosystems within them will be destroyed. There will, of course, be esthetic losses as well and these cannot easily be measured.

Water-table decline also affects stream flow adversely. In humid regions the year-around flow of many smaller streams is sustained by ground-water seepage. If the water table falls permanently below stream level, the stream will contain water only following heavy rain or rapid snow-melt, when water reaches the stream directly by overland flow. Again, as in the case of the ponds, the ecosystem of the permanent stream is destroyed.

Reduced stream flow has other undesirable effects farther downvalley. One effect is to allow pollutants in stream water to be more heavily concentrated; another is to permit the water of estuaries, into which streams discharge fresh water, to become more saline. The upstream invasion of salt water may be enough to reach and contaminate municipal water supply intakes.

Land Subsidence from Ground-water Withdrawal

Another serious environmental effect of excessive ground-water withdrawal is that of subsidence of the ground surface. Several localities have been affected in California, where ground water has been pumped from basins filled with alluvial (stream and lake-deposited) sediments. Water-table levels in these basins have dropped over 100 ft (30 m), with a maximum drop of 400 to 500 ft (120 to 150 m) being recorded in one locality in the San Joaquin Valley. Here the maximum ground subsidence has been about 10 ft (3 m) in a 35-year period, and has caused damage to wells in the area.

Another important area of ground subsidence accompanying water withdrawal is beneath Houston, Texas, where the ground surface has subsided from 1 to 3 ft (0.3 to 1.0 m) in a metropolitan area 30 mi (50 km) across. Damage has resulted to buildings, pavements, airport runways, and flood-control works.

Perhaps the most celebrated case of ground subsidence is that affecting Mexico City. Carefully measured ground subsidence between 1891 and 1959 ranged from 13 to 23 ft (4 to 7 m) (Figure 19.3). Subsidence began at a much

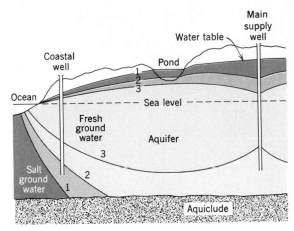

Figure 19.2 Schematic cross section showing lowering of water table and pond levels, and intrusion of salt ground water, as a result of ground-water withdrawal. (Vertical scale is greatly exaggerated above sea level.)

earlier date as a result of withdrawal of ground water from an aquifer system beneath the city and has caused many serious engineering problems. Clay beds overlying the aquifer have contracted greatly in volume as water has been drained out. To combat the ground subsidence, recharge wells have been drilled to inject water into the aquifer. In addition, new water supplies from sources outside the city area have been developed to replace local ground-water use.

Venice, Italy, has suffered severe damage to ancient buildings as a result of flooding during times of storms on the adjacent Adriatic Sea (Figure 19.4). Flooding results because the land on which Venice was built has been gradually subsiding. Venice was built in the 11th Century

Figure 19.3 Land subsidence in the old central area of Mexico City, 1900-1956, is shown by elevation graphs of four survey markers. (After J. F. Poland and G. H. Davis [1969] *Reviews in engineering geology*, Vol. II, Geological Society of America, Denver, Colo., p. 225.)

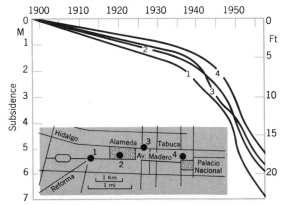

Figure 19.4 Flooding in St. Mark's Square, Venice, on November 18, 1975, during an Adriatic storm. (Wide World Photos.)

A.D. on low-lying islands in a coastal lagoon, sheltered from the ocean by a barrier beach. The area is underlain by some 3000 ft (1000 m) of layers of sand, gravel, clay, and silt, with some layers of peat. Compaction of the soft layers has been going on gradually for centuries under the heavy load of city buildings. However, ground-water withdrawal, greatly accelerated in recent decades, has aggravated the condition.

In the period 1930 to 1973, during which precise surveys have been available, the amount of sinking has amounted to about 6 in. (15 cm). While this last figure does not seem large, the total effect has been to greatly increase the frequency of flooding during winter storms. Sea level is normally raised by the effects of coastal storms, and high tides occurring at the same time may add to the rise in water level. The problem of flooding during storms is aggravated by the fact that the canals of Venice receive raw sewage, so that the flood water is contaminated.

Most of the subsidence in recent decades is attributed to withdrawals of large amounts of ground water from industrial wells at Porto Marghera, the modern port of Venice, located a few miles distant on the mainland shore. One large well is operated in Venice. Recent engineering studies indicate that if all pumping in both areas is held constant in the future, Venice will sink only about another inch (3 cm) and then subsidence will stop. If all wells were shut down, sinking would be halted and there would be a small rise—nearly an inch (2 cm) in the next 25 years. Thus, flooding and the attendant damage to churches and other buildings of great historical value seems destined to continue.

Land subsidence also occurs when large volumes of petroleum are withdrawn from oil pools beneath the surface. The principle is essentially the same as in the case of ground-water withdrawal.

Salt Water Intrusion

In coastal regions, fresh ground-water supplies are vulnerable to contamination by **salt water intrusion.** As shown in Figure 19.2, pumping of a well has not only caused the water table to decline, but has also caused the interface between salt ground-water and fresh ground-water to move inland as an invading wedge. (Salt ground water is explained in our Science Supplement.) Ultimately, the salt water is drawn into the well and the water is no longer fit for consumption. Notice that in Figure 19.2 a small coastal well also suffered salt contamination. In the case of an island or narrow peninsula, where salt ground water lies beneath a freshwater lens, salt water is easily drawn directly upward to contaminate a well. A case in point is the town water supply of Provincetown, Massachusetts, at the tip of Cape Cod. The water has become brackish during summer periods of heavy pumping. If pumping is stopped after salt contamination has occurred the salt water will be gradually pushed back to its original limits. To hasten this process and to prevent further salt intrusion, fresh water can be pumped down into recharge wells located between the contaminated well and the shore.

A sea-level canal, such as that which was planned to cut across Florida and since abandoned, poses problems of salt-water contamination of adjacent aquifers. The denser salt water enters the ground-water zone beneath the canal, forming a salt ground-water wedge that moves out beneath fresh groundwater. Contamination of nearby wells follows. Use of a system of locks that shut out salt water in damaging quantities and maintain fresh water in the canal is one possible answer to the problems of a sea-level canal. If the freshwater level is maintained several feet above sea level, the hydraulic pressure will prevent salt water from moving inland.

Relation of Fresh Ground Water to Salt Ground Water

Rock beneath the ocean floors is saturated with salt water. This zone of salt ground water comes in contact with the fresh ground-water body beneath coastlines, where an equilibrium relationship is developed. The principles are illustrated by conditions beneath an island or a narrow peninsula jutting into the sea. Figure 19.5 shows the relationships in a schematic way. The body of fresh ground water takes the shape of a gigantic lens with convex faces, except that the upper surface has only a broad curvature whereas the lower surface, in contact with the salt ground water, bulges deeply downward.

Because fresh water is less dense than salt water, we can think of this freshwater lens as floating upon the salt water, pushing it down much as the hull of an ocean liner pushes aside the surrounding water. The ratio of densities of fresh water to salt water is about as 40 to 41, so, if the water table is, say, 10 feet above sea level, the bottom of the fresh water lens will be located 400 feet below sea level, or forty times as deep as the water table is high with respect to sea level.

The fresh ground water extends seaward some distance beyond the shoreline. Although the salt ground water is stagnant, the fresh water travels in the curved paths shown by arrows in the figure. Ground water is discharged by seepage through the ocean bottom close to shore. The effect of this discharge in bays and tidal estuaries is to cause some measure of natural dilution of the salt water, creating a favorable environment for certain forms of marine life.

Figure 19.5   A lens of fresh ground water displacing salt ground water on an island or peninsula. (After G. Parker.)

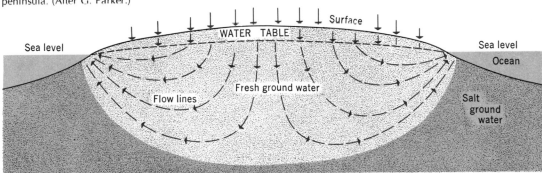

Unit 20
Pollution of
Ground Water

Good Coffee Water Needs Body*

"Crosby is a small village, formerly a railhead center, in the northwestern part of North Dakota and a few miles south of the International Boundary. As in many places in North Dakota, water is not in abundant supply. When Crosby was first established, surface water was unavailable, and dug wells were used to supply homesteaders and the community at large. Most of these hand-dug wells, commonly several feet in diameter, were relatively shallow. They were replaced in recent years with a municipal water system supplied by two drilled wells more than 150 feet deep.

In the central part of the town, however, there remains an old large-diameter dug well, about 38 feet deep, covered by boards and concrete. Water was formerly withdrawn from the well by a hand-pump and used by a great number of people who did not like the taste of the water from the city's deep-well supply. Water from the dug well was used specifically in making coffee; it reportedly produced 'the best coffee in the state.' During a ground-water investigation of the Crosby area by the United States Geological Survey in the early 1960s, a sample of water was collected from the dug well and analyzed.

The well water proved to have a high content of sulfate, chloride, and nitrate. The highly mineralized water contained more than four times the limit of dissolved solids recommended by the Public Health Service for drinking water. The local people referred to the well water as having 'body.'

Actually, the water had more body than these people realized. The high concentration of nitrate, which far exceeds the Public Health Service limit . . . , coupled with the higher-than-normal concentration of chloride, suggested that the well was contaminated by sewage wastes. The apparent contamination was brought to the attention of the local city health official, who declared the well unsafe and removed the pump handle. Immediately many people became angry because their supply of good coffee water had been terminated, apparently for no good reason. After all, they had been drinking the water for years, and no one had ever died from it, or even gotten sick—as far as they knew. Nevertheless, the pump handle was not reinstalled.

Some of the old timers reported that this ancient well had been dug near the site of a former livery stable, which had been built sometime in the late 1800s and had been operated until about 1930. Waste products from the horses evidently contaminated the ground-water supply. These wastes also provided the 'body' that patrons of Crosby's dug well prized so highly."

Doing chores on the Maine farm, ca. 1942. (U.S. Department of Agriculture.)

130

Body wastes are an unpleasant subject to discuss publicly, but apparently many people have not been too concerned about ingesting wastes that are derived from the family privy; at least, they may resent such an implication. The author from whose article we have just quoted goes on to tell about the efforts of a local physician, Dr. B. F. Higley, to thwart the pollution of homeowners' water supplies from their adjacent outdoor toilets. The incident occurred near Delaware, Ohio, where the water table is close to the surface and a sandy aquifer allows subsurface water to move freely from place to place. One homeowner, in particular, had built his privy within a few feet of his shallow well. Dr. Higley's most eloquent arguments failed to convince the homeowner of the very real possibility of polluting his own water supply. To make the point, Dr. Higley poured several pounds of salt into the privy. "Within two weeks the well water began to taste salty and the homeowner threatened to sue the good doctor for contaminating his well. Ultimately, a new well was drilled on the other side of the house."

Although the pollution of ground water by Man's wastes brings out many humorous anecdotes, it is not a funny topic. Spread of highly contagious diseases—such as infectious hepatitis, amoebic dysentery, and cholera—in surface water and ground water is a major health problem the world over. Epidemics of this nature were numerous at one time in the United States. For example, a cholera epidemic, spread through contaminated drinking water, killed 3500 New York City residents in 1832. We may think of ourselves as well-protected today from such epidemics, but now there are new, more subtle threats to health facing us through the pollution of our water supplies by industrial chemicals capable of producing cancer and birth-defects. In this study unit, we will investigate the hydraulic principles behind the pollution of ground-water supplies.

*Quoted portions of this essay are taken from a chapter of the same title, written by Wayne A. Pettyjohn in *Water quality in a stressed environment; Readings in Environmental Hydrology*, Wayne A. Pettyjohn, Ed. (1972) Burgess Publ. Co., Minneapolis, Minn., pp. 194-199. Reproduced by permission of the author and publisher.

Pollution from Solid Wastes

Disposal of solid wastes poses a major environmental problem in the United States because our advanced industrial economy is an endless source of garbage and trash. In many communities little or no effort is being made to reclaim and recycle such materials as glass, metals, paper, and wood. Durable goods of metallic construction add great bulk to the waste, as do scrapped construction materials. Traditionally, these waste products have been trucked to the town or city dump, and there burned in continually smoldering fires that emit foul smoke and gases. The partially consumed residual waste is then burried under earth.

In recent years, a major effort has been made to improve solid-waste disposal methods. One method is high-temperature incineration. Another is the **sanitary land-fill** method in which waste is not allowed to burn. Instead, it is continually covered by protective overburden, usually sand, silt, or clay available on the land-fill site. The waste is thus buried in the unsaturated zone and is subject to reaction with percolating rainwater entering the ground surface. This water picks up a wide variety of ions from the waste body and carries these down as **leachate** to the water table. Once in the water table, the leachate follows the flow paths of the ground water.

As shown in Figure 20.1, a **mound** may develop on the water table beneath the disposal site. Loose soil of the disposal area facilitates infiltration of precipitation, while lack of vegetation reduces the transpiration that might otherwise occur. Consequently, the recharge here is greater than elsewhere and the mound is maintained.

After leachate has moved vertically down by gravity percolation to the water-table mound, it moves radially outward from the mound to surrounding lower points on the water table. As shown in Figure 20.1, a supply well with its cone of depression draws ground water from the surrounding area. Linkage between outward flow from the waste disposal site and inward flow to the well can bring leachate into the well, polluting the ground-water supply.

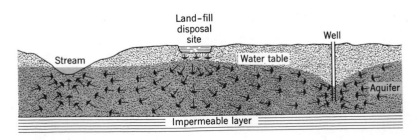

Figure 20.1 Leachate from a waste disposal site moving toward a supply well *(right)* and a stream *(left)*. (From A. N. Strahler [1972] *Planet Earth*, Harper & Row, New York.)

An important step in guarding against this form of pollution is to place a **monitor well** (or several monitor wells) on a line between the disposal site and the well. Chemical tests for presence of leachate are made regularly, while the slope of the water table can also be determined. Movement of leachate toward the supply well may be blocked by placement of a recharge well (or wells), building a freshwater accumulation (actually an inverted cone), which will oppose the movement of the leachate.

Pollution of supply wells by partially treated effluent infiltrating the ground at sewage disposal plants can occur in a basically similar manner.

Pollution Plumes

It is not necessary for a ground-water mound to be present for pollutants to travel to distant points. Where the water table has a pronounced slope, as it generally does everywhere except near the summit of a broad ground-water divide, leachate or any pollutant introduced at a given point migrates as a **pollution plume** along the flow paths of the ground water. Figure 20.2 is a map on which are drawn lines of equal elevation of the water table, labeled in feet above sea level. As the numbers on these lines show, the water table is sloping from north to south across the area of the map. An ocean or lake shoreline lies to the south. Flow of the ground water, as seen from above, is along the direction of the arrows, which cross the ground-water contour lines at right angles.

On the left side of the map we find that a municipal well, W, is located at an inland position high on the water table. The municipal sewage or solid-waste disposal site, D, is located to shoreward at lower elevation on the water table. The pollution plume from the disposal site will move shoreward away from the well to be discharged by seep-

age into water offshore. Although the well is safely situated, there may be a problem of pollution in coastal waters immediately offshore.

On the right side of the diagram we see that the disposal site, D, is located at an inland position high on the water table. A municipal well has been placed at a shoreward position and at a lower level on the water table, along the line of flow of ground water from the point D. A pollution plume from the disposal site will travel along the indicated flow path and may in time enter the field of influence of the well. Monitor wells (M), placed along the line of ground-water movement could detect the presence of pollutants in the ground water long in advance of arrival at the well. Because of the very slow rate of movement of ground water, some years might elapse before these substances would reach the well.

Pollution in Limestone Regions

Pollution of ground-water supplies can take place rapidly in limestone regions where extensive cavern systems are below the water table. (Caverns are explained in our Science Supplement.) Movement of ground water is rapid through large passageways, so that liquid wastes discharged into sinkholes can travel freely to distant points where water is being withdrawn from water-table ponds or supply wells. The peninsula of Florida, which has large areas underlain by cavernous limestone and a high water table, has presented a number of problem localities of this type. Detailed studies by ground-water geologists can reveal the presence of such pollution hazards. Such studies are essential in planning for water resource development and waste disposal systems.

Pollution from Highways

Yet another potential source of pollution of ground-water supplies is from highways and streets, through spillage of chemicals and from deicing salt applied during the winter months. Spillage of large volumes of liquids from tank trucks and tank cars as a result of highway traffic and railroad accidents poses a serious threat because a large slug of pollutant can be injected into the ground-water recharge system. The commonest pollutants to be feared are automobile fuel and heating oil, but many toxic industrial chemicals are also transported in tank trucks and cars. Leakage of fuels from underground storage tanks, used in all gasoline stations, is a related source of possible pollution.

One scientist, specializing in engineering aspects of ground water, evaluates the problem as follows:

The potential danger of releasing large volumes of these materials in surface-water or ground-water reservoirs used for drinking purposes is obvious. When released into surface-water reservoirs, chemicals derived from accidental spills may be adequately diluted in some cases or monitored as they are carried away from the region. Where they enter the ground-water reservoir,

Figure 20.2 This idealized map shows contours on the water table and ground-water flow paths leading toward a shoreline. Pollution plumes follow the flow paths.

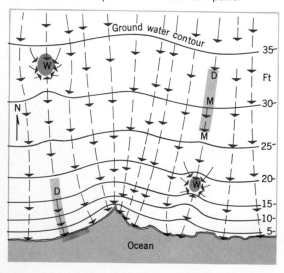

their presence may not be known in advance of damaging a water supply, the rate and direction of movement may not be known, and they may not be flushed from or diluted within aquifers to tolerable limits for years to come.*

*R. P. Parizek (1971) "Impact of Highways on the Hydrogeologic Environment," *Environmental Geomorphology*, D. R. Coates, ed., Publications in Geomorphology, State University of New York, Binghamton, N.Y., p. 188.

In recent years, the great increase in use of sodium chloride and calcium chloride as deicing salts on roads and highways has led to an increasing incidence of contamination of ground-water supplies. In some cases, wells have had to be drilled deeper and cased to greater depth to reach uncontaminated ground water. In other cases, new wells have had to be drilled at greater distance from highways, and at state expense. Obviously, planning for future water-supply development should take into account the possibility of highway pollution.

SCIENCE
SUPPLEMENT

Limestone Caverns and Karst Landscapes

Ground-water activity creates special environmental problems in regions underlain by limestone, a kind of rock easily dissolved and removed by subsurface water. Pure limestone consists of the mineral **calcite;** its chemical composition is calcium carbonate ($CaCO_3$). This mineral is acted upon by weak acids normally present in all subsurface water. The most common acid involved in limestone solution is carbonic acid.

Limestone caverns consist of interconnected subterranean cavities in the form of passageways and rooms. Within a single cavern system the total length of such openings can aggregate many miles. Figure 20.3 is a map showing details of passageways in a portion of one cavern. The rectangular pattern suggests control of passageways by sets of joints in the limestone.

The consensus of opinion among geologists is that most cavern systems were opened out in the ground-water zone. The diagrams in Figure 20.4 suggest how caverns develop. The upper diagram shows that the action of carbonic acid is particularly concentrated just below the water table. Products of solution are carried along the ground-water flow paths to emerge in streams and leave the region in stream flow. In a later stage, shown in the lower diagram, the stream has deepened its valley and the water table has been correspondingly lowered to a new position. The cavern system previously excavated is now in the unsaturated zone.

Evaporation of percolating water on exposed rock surfaces in the caverns now begins the deposition of carbonate matter, known as travertine. Encrustations of travertine take many beautiful forms that make many caverns tourist attractions.

Where limestone solution is very active, we find a landscape with many unique features. This is especially true along the Dalmatian coastal area of Yugoslavia, where the

Figure 20.3 Map of a part of Anvil Cave, Alabama. Passageways (white) show control by intersecting sets of joints in the rock layer. (By courtesy of W. W. Varnedoe and the Huntsville Grotto of the National Speleological Society.)

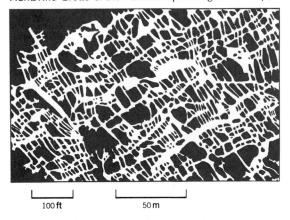

100 ft   50 m

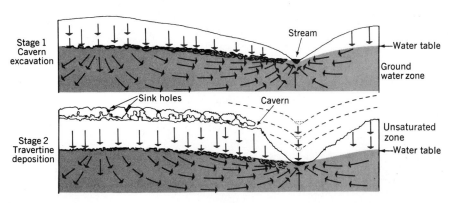

Stage 1
Cavern
excavation

Stream
Water table
Ground
water zone

Sink holes   Cavern

Stage 2
Travertine
deposition

Unsaturated
zone
Water table

Figure 20.4 Cavern development in the ground-water zone, followed by deposition in unsaturated zone. (From A. N. Strahler [1971] *The Earth Sciences,* 2nd ed., Harper & Row, New York.)

Figure 20.5 Limestone strata show in the walls of this deep sinkhole on the Kaibab Plateau of northern Arizona. (A. N. Strahler.)

Figure 20.6 Features of a karst landscape. *(A)* Rainfall enters the cavern system through sinkholes in the limestone. *(B)* Extensive collapse of caverns reveals surface streams. (Drawn by E. Raisz.)

landscape is called **karst.** The term is now applied to the topography of any limestone area where sinkholes are numerous and small surface streams are nonexistent. A **sinkhole** is a surface depression in limestone of a cavernous region. Some sinkholes are filled with soil washed

from nearby hillsides, as Figure 20.5 shows. Other sinkholes are steep-sided, deep holes.

Development of a karst landscape is shown in two block diagrams (Figure 20.6). In an early stage, funnellike sinkholes are numerous. Later, the caverns collapse, leaving open, flat-floored valleys. Some important regions of karst or karstlike topography are the Mammoth Cave region of Kentucky, the Yucatan Peninsula, and parts of Cuba and Puerto Rico.

Drillers at work on the ore space. Free State Gehuld gold mine, South Africa. (Courtesy of the Anglo-American Corporation of South Africa, Limited.)

PART III **Man and the Lithosphere**

Unit 21
Materials of the Lithosphere

The Lithosphere — Model 1830

If you had taken a course in geology in the year 1830, your textbook might well have been written by Amos Eaton, a graduate of Williams College. At the age of 40, Eaton abandoned his law practice and took up geology with consuming fervor. The first edition of his *Geological Textbook* was published in 1830, and he perpetrated it upon innocent students of Rensselaer Institute, where he taught. Clinging to the discredited and dying doctrines of the European neptunists, formulated by their late German leader, Abraham Werner, Eaton accounted for the creation of all earthly rocks and their enclosed fossils in a single fantastic episode identified as one and the same with the Creation as described in the Bible. As Bishop Ussher made clear in 1650, the Creation occurred in a six-day period in the year 4004 B.C.

Your introduction to geology, Eaton-style, would have included his textbook diagrams, reproduced on this page. In a deep world ocean, all rocks of the earth's crust were rapidly deposited from chemical solution in concentric layers, seen in the first diagram. Granite and other related rocks were deposited first as a thick paste. Later deposits formed more watery sediment layers, and these began to contain the new animals—fishes for example—as they were being created. A short time later, the human race was created. However, internal heat of the earth was beginning to build up in some deep pockets, numbered 1 through 6 in the first figure. Evidently some large stores of combustible materials existed at those points. Eaton wrote, "At length the force of the more highly rarefied steam became too great to be any longer confined within the coat of granite. It burst through at the weakest part and shot forth its craggy broken edges above the muddy waters which surrounded it." The second diagram shows these fantastic eruptions, which bent up the rock layers, or strata, around the sides of the vents.

Even in the year 1830, Amos Eaton was sadly out of date in his geological thinking. In Scotland and England, keen observers of nature were then well on the way to establishing geology as a science. And in North America Eaton's contemporaries were already adopting the new geology and would soon make great forward strides in unraveling the geological history of their continent as we understand it today.

Even as the American War of Independence was

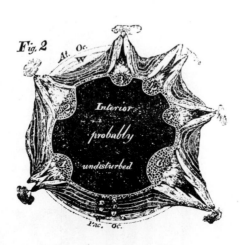

Internal fires deformed the earth's rock layers, according to Professor Amos Eaton. Down-sunken areas became the ocean basins.

being successfully concluded, two geologists of Scotland—James Hall and James Hutton—were spearheading the first revolution in geologic thought. These keen observers of nature were close friends; together they studied rocks exposed on the rugged coast of their native land. What they found spurred them into undertaking a two-man war against the totalitarian German system of geology headed by their archenemy, Professor Abraham Werner of Freiberg. That powerful figure of European geology preached a theory that all rocks, whatever their compositions and properties, came into existence quite suddenly by precipitation from the waters of a single great world ocean. Werner's schedule of events fitted the doctrine of the Christian Church regarding Creation and was widely accepted. Werner and his followers were called *neptunists*. The infectious theory even spread into Scotland where it was upheld by a professor on the faculty of the University of Edinburgh.

The revolutionary theory evolved by James Hall and James Hutton stated that enormous spans of time were required to produce the rocks of the earth's crust. *Uniformitarianism*, as their doctrine came to be called, held that processes of nature seen in action today—stream floods, breaking surf, earth-quakes, and volcanoes—can account for all past formations of rock and all present features of scenery. This principle of uniformity ruled out any supernatural events that would contradict physical laws acting today.

Ultimately, uniformitarianism was fully accepted by geologists in North America. By 1850, important strides were being made in classifying and mapping the varied rocks of the continent. Among the clergy, however, neptunism remained the theory of choice, along with other theories of the earth's origin which harmonized with Bishop Ussher's Christian calendar. Indeed, the Creation scenario was still going strong in 1925, when a biology teacher, John T. Scopes, was tried in Dayton, Tennessee, for teaching the Darwinian theory of organic evolution. The prosecutor in that famed "Monkey Trial" was William Jennings Bryan. The Biblical doctrine of Creation espoused by Bryan was upheld by a conviction of Scopes; it continues to be upheld by a few religious groups, even today.

DATA SOURCE: Archibald Geikie (1905) *The Founders of Geology*, Macmillan Co., London, 486 pp.; Geoge P. Merrill (1924) *The First One Hundred Years of American Geology*, Yale Univ. Press, New Haven, Conn., 773 pp.

Man and Inorganic Earth Materials

Our first unit on the lithosphere deals with inorganic earth materials. All life forms, which taken together comprise the biosphere, require inorganic earth materials. Certain elements derived from rock and mineral soil are essential nutrients used in the building of living cells, whether of plants or animals. A knowledge of these nutrient mineral elements and their sources is essential to an understanding of the ecosystems to be covered in Part V. We also realize that inorganic earth materials are essential to Man in an industrial society; they are used as construction materials, as sources of all industrial metals, and for manufacture of many kinds of chemicals. In this study unit we will take a broad look at minerals and rocks.

Composition of the Earth's Crust

From the standpoint of the environment of Man, the really significant zone of the solid earth is the thin outermost layer—the earth's crust. This mineral skin, averaging about 10 mi (17 km) thickness for the globe as a whole, contains the continents and ocean basins and is the source of soil and other sediment vital to life, of salts of the sea, of gases of the atmosphere, and of all free water of the oceans, atmosphere, and lands.

Figure 21.1 displays in order the eight most abundant elements of the earth's crust in terms of percentage by weight. Oxygen, the predominant element, accounts for about half the total weight. It occurs in combination with silicon, the second most abundant element.

Aluminum and iron are third and fourth on the list. These metals are of primary importance in Man's industrial civilization, and it is most fortunate that they are comparatively abundant elements. Four metallic elements follow that are important plant nutrients in soils: calcium, sodium, potassium, and magnesium. All four are on the same order of abundance (2 to 4%). Their importance in soil fertility will be stressed in a later study unit.

If we were to extend the list, the ninth-place element would be titanium, followed in order by hydrogen, phosphorus, barium, and strontium. Phosphorus is one of the essential elements in plant growth.

Rocks and Minerals

The elements of the earth's crust are organized into compounds that we recognize as minerals. **Rock** is broadly defined as any aggregate of minerals in the solid state. Rock comes in a very wide range of compositions, physical characteristics, and ages. A given rock is usually composed of two or more minerals, and usually many minerals are present; however, a few rock varieties consist almost entirely of one mineral. Most rock of the earth's crust is extremely old in terms of human standards, the times of

137

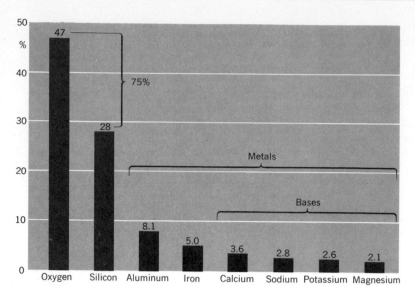

Figure 21.1 The average composition of the earth's crust is given here in terms of the percentage by weight of the eight most abundant elements.

formation ranging back many millions of years. But rock is also being formed at this very hour as a volcano emits lava that solidifies on contact with the atmosphere.

A mineral is perhaps easier to define than a rock. A **mineral** is a naturally occurring, inorganic substance, usually possessing a definite chemical composition and characteristic atomic structure. A vast number of minerals exist, together with a great number of their combinations into rocks. We must generalize and simplify this topic so as to refer to rocks and minerals meaningfully in terms both of their environmental properties and their value as natural resources.

Rocks of the earth's crust fall into three major classes. (1) **Igneous rocks** are solidified from mineral matter in a high-temperature molten state. (2) **Sedimentary rocks** are layered accumulations of mineral particles derived in various ways from preexisting rocks. (3) **Metamorphic rocks** are igneous or sedimentary rocks that have been physically and chemically changed by application of heat and pressure during mountain-making activities. Although we have listed these classes in a conventional sequence, no one class has first place in terms of origin. Instead, they form a continuous circuit through which the crustal minerals have been recycled during many millions of years of geologic time. We begin with igneous rock for simplicity, not because it is the original class of rock.

Silicate Minerals and Igneous Rocks

Igneous rocks make up the vast bulk of the earth's crust. Practically all igneous rock (over 90% by weight) consists of **silicate minerals,** which are compounds containing silicon atoms in combination with oxygen atoms in close linkage. In the crystal structure of silicate minerals, one atom of silicon is linked with four atoms of oxygen as the unit building block of the compound. Most silicate minerals also have one, two, or more of the metallic elements listed in Figure 21.1 (i.e., aluminum, iron, calcium, so-

dium, potassium, and magnesium). Further details of silicate minerals are given in our Science Supplement.

The silicate minerals occur in a high-temperature molten state as **magma.** From pockets at least several miles beneath the earth's surface, magma makes its way upward through older solid rock and eventually solidifies as igneous rock.

We can classify all igneous rocks into three great groups, based upon their general chemical composition. First is **felsic igneous rock,** characterized by an abundance of aluminum, potassium, and sodium, but with relatively little iron and magnesium. Silicate minerals most common in the felsic igneous rocks are quartz (silicon dioxide, SiO_2) and feldspar (silicate of aluminum with potassium, sodium, or calcium). (The word "felsic" was coined with two syllables: *fel* from feldspar; *si* from silica.) A good example of a felsic igneous rock is granite, familiar as a building stone and for its use in various kinds of monuments (Figure 21.2). Granite is pale in color—usually gray or salmon pink.

An important property of the felsic igneous rocks is their comparatively low density. **Density** is a measure of the mass of matter within a given volume of space. Density is stated in units of grams of mass per cubic centimeter of volume (gm/cc). Pure water, with a density of 1 gm/cc, is the standard of reference. By comparison, felsic igneous rock such as granite has a density of 2.7 gm/cc.

The second major group of igneous rocks consists of the **mafic igneous rocks;** they are lacking in silica but are rich in magnesium and iron. Minerals rich in magnesium and iron are dark in color and comparatively high in density. (The word "mafic" was coined with two syllables: *ma* is from magnesium; the letter *f* in *fic* represents iron, with the chemical symbol Fe.) Density of mafic igneous rocks is fairly great, about 3.0 gm/cc. Mafic rocks are dark in color—dark gray or black. A good example is gabbro, sometimes used as an ornamental stone in buildings and in monuments. The dark lava making up volcanic islands such as Hawaii is another common type of mafic rock; it is called basalt.

Figure 21.2 Seen close up, this coarse-grained granite rock proves to be made of tightly interlocking crystals of a few kinds of minerals. (A. N. Strahler.)

The third igneous rock group consists of the **ultramafic igneous rocks.** They lack aluminum and have large proportions of magnesium and iron; their density is high, about 3.3 gm/cc. Ultramafic rocks are comparatively rare in occurrence in surface rocks, but they comprise the great bulk of the earth below the crust.

Sedimentary Rocks

The second great class of rock is sedimentary rock. Its substance is derived both from preexisting rock of any origin and from newly formed organic matter. Igneous rock is the most important source of the inorganic mineral matter that goes to make up sedimentary rock.

Silicate minerals of igneous rock undergo chemical changes when exposed to the atmosphere. The solid rock is softened and fragmented, yielding particles of many sizes. When transported in a fluid medium—air, water, or ice—these particles are known collectively as **sediment.** Used in its broadest sense, sediment includes both inorganic and organic matter. Dissolved mineral matter in the form of ions in solution is also included.

Streams carry sediment to lower levels and to locations where accumulation is possible. Wind and glacial ice also transport sediment, but not necessarily to lower elevations or to places suitable for accumulation. Usually the most favorable sites of sediment accumulation are in shallow seas bordering the continent, but they may also be inland seas and large lakes. Thick accumulations of sediment may become deeply buried under newer sediments. Over long spans of time, the sediments undergo physical or chemical changes; they become compacted and hardened, forming sedimentary rock.

There are many different kinds of sedimentary rocks. One common class is made up of mineral particles derived by breakage from a parent rock source. Examples are the materials in a sand bar on a river bed or beach. When cemented to form a rock, the product is a common rock called **sandstone** (Figure 21.3). Layers of clay, when compacted and hardened, make another common sedimentary rock called **shale.** Another important group of sedimentary rocks consists of chemical compounds precipitated from solution in water of lakes or the ocean. An example is **limestone,** formed of calcium carbonate ($CaCO_3$).

Despite their great variety, the sedimentary rocks share some physical features in common. The sediment accumulates in nearly horizontal layers, called **strata** (or simply "beds"). Strata are separated by stratification planes or "bedding planes," which allow one layer to be easily removed from the next. Strata of widely different compositions can occur one above the next, so that the eroded strata of a great accumulation of sediments show a diversity of bands and ledges. A fine example is seen in the upper walls of the Grand Canyon, in Arizona (Figure 21.4).

Metamorphic Rocks

Any of the igneous or sedimentary rocks may be altered by the tremendous pressures and high temperatures that accompany mountain-building movements of the earth's crust. The resulting metamorphic rock is greatly changed in appearance and composition. Metamorphic rocks are harder and more compact than their parent types, except when the latter are igneous rocks. Also, the kneading action and heating that metamorphic rocks have undergone produce new structures and even new minerals. Each sedimentary and igneous rock has an equivalent metamorphic rock.

An example of a common metamorphic rock is slate, produced from shale by mountain-making forces. This gray

Figure 21.3 Rounded quartz grains from an ancient sandstone. Formerly these sand grains were part of a vast field of sand dunes in an ancient desert. The grains average about 1 mm (0.04 in.) in diameter. (Andrew McIntyre, Columbia University.)

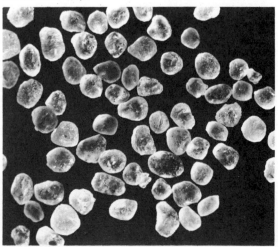

Figure 21.4   Horizontal strata exposed in the walls of Grand Canyon, Arizona. (A. N. Strahler.)

or brick-red rock splits neatly into thin plates so familiar as roofing shingles and as flagstones of patios and walks. Also familiar to most persons is marble, a metamorphic rock produced by recrystallization of limestone. The calcite mineral of the original limestone had been reformed into new crystals and the bedding planes are obscured. Impurities are drawn out into swirling streaks and bands that give marble its ornamental beauty. Perhaps the most important metamorphic rock is gneiss, often a banded rock, with light and dark bands alternating and often contorted into wavy folds (Figure 21.5).

The Rock Cycle

We can now bring together the formative processes of rocks into a single unified concept of recycling of matter through geologic time. The cycle is illustrated very simply in Figure 21.6. Two sources of energy power the cycle. From deep within the earth comes heat generated by radioactivity; it is called **radiogenic heat.** Where radiogenic heat accumulates in pockets, previously existing rock is melted and becomes magma. The magma rises and eventually reaches the surface. Here a second source of energy, solar energy, is applied. Solar energy is responsible for the breakup and chemical change of rock to form sediment, which in turn is compacted into sedimentary rock. Later deep burial and strong compression during mountain-making activity change the sedimentary rock into metamorphic rock, and this may in turn be melted to form new igneous rock. There are other loops in the rock cycle, not shown here. For example, metamorphic rock can be altered into sediment, to produce sedimentary rock.

Throughout hundreds of millions of years the rock cycle

has been in operation, constantly recycling mineral matter of the earth's crust. Rocks of all three classes are exposed at the earth's surface and are the material from which the soil layer is formed.

In this study unit we have given a very general description of the major forms of inorganic matter that comprise the solid earth, or lithosphere. This information will be used in later study units relating to a variety of environmental topics.

Figure 21.5   An exposure of ancient banded gneiss on the east coast of Hudson Bay, Quebec. (Geological Survey of Canada.)

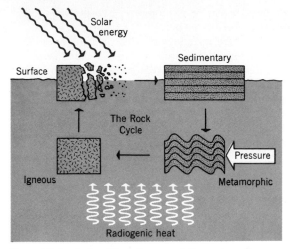

Figure 21.6 A simplified diagram of the rock cycle.

Table 21.2 The Cenozoic Era

(Epoch)		(Years before Present)
Recent		0
		10,000
Pleistocene	(Glaciation of North America and Europe)	
		2 million
Pliocene	(Cascades and Sierras formed)	
Miocene		
Oligocene		
Eocene		
		65 million

The Geologic Time Scale

To place crustal rocks and structures in their positions in time, we need to refer to some major units in the scale of geologic time. Table 21.1 is a greatly abbreviated list of the major time divisions and their ages. All time older than 600 million years (m.y.) is Precambrian time. Three **eras** of geologic time follow: Paleozoic, Mesozoic, and Cenozoic. These eras saw the evolution of life forms in the oceans and on the lands. The eras are subdivided into a number of **periods,** named in Table 21.1. The last era, the Cenozoic, is divided into five epochs, of which the youngest is the Pleistocene Epoch, known popularly as the "Ice Age." Table 21.2 lists the epochs of the Cenozoic Era. Most landforms of the continental surfaces were shaped by processes of erosion and deposition during late Cenozoic time. Man, as the genus *Homo*, evolved during the late Pliocene Epoch and throughout the Pleistocene Epoch. As you can see, Man's time on earth has been an insignificant moment in the vast duration of geologic history.

Table 21.1 Table of Geologic Time

	Period	Duration (m.y.)	Age (m.y.)	
Cenozoic Era (65)	(See separate table)			
			65	
Mesozoic Era (160)	Cretaceous	71		(Rocky Mountains formed)
			136	
	Jurassic	54		
			190	
	Triassic	35		
			225	
Paleozoic Era (345)	Permian	55		(Appalachian Mountains formed)
			280	
	Carboniferous	65		
			345	
	Devonian	50		
			395	
	Silurian	35		
			430	
	Ordovician	70		
			500	
	Cambrian	70		
			570	
Precambrian time	(Canadian Shield rocks, 1 to 3 billions years)			
Oldest dated rocks			3.5 billion	
Earth accretion completed			4.6 billion	
Age of universe			17-18 billion	

SCIENCE
SUPPLEMENT

Silicate Minerals and Igneous Rocks

Figure 21.7 gives the names and chemical compositions of seven major silicate minerals, or groups of silicate minerals. The large bulk of all igneous rocks consists of two or more of these silicate minerals in varying proportions. The table shows a subdivision of the silicate minerals into two major groups: felsic and mafic.

Among the commonest minerals of all rock types is **quartz;** its composition is silicon dioxide (SiO_2). There follow five mineral groups, collectively forming the **aluminosilicates** because all contain aluminum. Two groups of **feldspars** are set apart: the **potash feldspars** contain potassium (K) as the dominant metallic ion, but sodium (Na) is commonly present in various proportions. The **plagioclase feldspars** form a continuous series, beginning with the **sodic,** or sodium-rich varieties, and grading through with increasing proportions of calcium to the **calcic,** or calcium-rich varieties.

Belonging to the **mica group,** which is familiar because of its property of splitting into very thin, flexible layers, is **biotite,** a dark-colored mica with a complex chemical formula. Potassium, magnesium, and iron are present in biotite, along with some water. The **amphibole group,** of which the common black mineral **hornblende** is a common representative, is a complex aluminosilicate containing calcium, magnesium, iron, and water. Similar in outward appearance and having essentially the same component elements (except for water) is the **pyroxene group,** with the mineral **augite** as a representative. Last on the list is **olivine,** a dense greenish mineral which is a silicate of magnesium and iron, but without aluminum.

Generally speaking, very gradual cooling of a magma that lies deep within the crust results in formation of large mineral crystals and results in a rock with **coarse-grained texture.** Huge masses of coarse-grained igneous rock, sol-

Figure 21.7 Simplified chart of common silicate minerals and abundant igneous rocks.

SILICATE MINERALS			IGNEOUS ROCKS				
Mineral name	Composition	Density (gm/cc)	PLUTONIC: Granite / EXTRUSIVE: Rhyolite (gm/cc) 2.7	Diorite / Andesite 2.8	Gabbro / Basalt 3.0	Peridotite 3.3	Dunite 3.3
Quartz	SiO_2	2.6	27%	2%			
Potash feldspar (orthoclase)	$(K, Na) AlSi_3O_8$	2.6	40%	1%			
Plagioclase feldspars: Sodic (sodium-rich) (Na 100%, Ca 0%)	$NaAlSi_3O_8$	2.6	15%				
Plagioclase feldspars: Intermediate				61%			
Plagioclase feldspars: Calcic (calcium-rich) (Na 0%, Ca 100%)	$CaAl_2Si_2O_8$	2.8			43%		
Biotite (mica group)	Complex aluminosilicates of K, Mg, and Fe, with water	2.9	12%	2%			
Amphibole group (hornblende)	Complex aluminosilicates of Ca, Mg, and Fe	3.2	6%	17%			
Pyroxene group (augite)	Complex aluminosilicates of Ca, Mg, and Fe	3.3		18%	57%	40% ULTRAMAFIC	
Olivine	$(Mg, Fe)_2SiO_4$	3.3				60%	100%

FELSIC — MAFIC — Aluminosilicates — FELSIC — MAFIC

idifying at depth in the crust are described by the adjective **plutonic.** Granite is a typical coarse-grained plutonic rock. In contrast, rapid cooling of magma as it comes close to the surface or pours out as **lava** gives very small mineral crystals, or **fine-grained texture.** The lavas are classed as **extrusive** in contrast to the **intrusive** rocks solidified beneath the surface. Typically, lavas are formed of crystals too small to be distinguished with the unaided eye.

To simplify rock classification, we recognize five rock varieties according to mineral composition, and for each of these classes there will be coarse-grained plutonic varieties as well as fine-grained extrusive varieties. As shown in the right half of the table, there are five named plutonic varieties and three extrusive varieties (the extrusive varieties of the last two on the list are unimportant).

Bars of varying width, with attached percentage figures, show the typical mineral compositions of these igneous rocks. Note that granite and its extrusive equivalent, **rhyolite,** are rich in quartz and potash feldspar, with lesser amounts of sodic plagioclase, biotite, and amphibole. **Diorite** and its extrusive equivalent, **andesite,** are almost totally lacking in quartz and potash feldspar, but consist dominantly of intermediate plagioclase and lesser amounts of the mafic minerals. Going progressively in the direction of domination by mafic minerals, we come to **gabbro,** and its lava equivalent, **basalt.** Here the plagioclase feldspar is of the calcic type, making up about half the rock, while pyroxene makes up the other half. In a common variety of gabbro and basalt, olivine is also present. The next rock, **peridotite,** is not abundant in the crust, but probably makes up the bulk of rock below the crust. It is composed mostly of pyroxene and olivine. Finally, we list **dunite,** a rare rock of nearly 100% olivine, as an example of the ultramafic end of the series.

The Earth's Interior Structure

Figure 21.8 is a cutaway diagram of the earth to show its major parts. The earth is an almost spherical body approximately 4000 mi (6400 km) in radius. The center is occupied by the **core,** a spherical zone about 2200 mi (3500 km) in radius. Because of the sudden change in behavior of earthquake waves upon reaching this zone, it has been concluded that the outer core has the properties of a liquid, in abrupt contrast to a solid mass that surrounds it. However, the innermost part of the core is probably in the solid state.

Outside of the core lies the **mantle,** a layer about 1800 mi (2895 km) thick, composed of mineral matter in a solid state. Judging from the behavior of earthquake waves, the mantle is probably composed largely of the mineral olivine and consists of the ultramafic igneous rocks peridotite and dunite.

Outermost and thinnest of the earth zones is the **crust,** a layer about 5 to 25 mi (8 to 40 km) thick, formed largely of igneous rocks. Figure 21.9 shows details of the earth's crust. The base of the crust, where it contacts the mantle, is sharply defined. This contact is established from the way in which earthquake waves change velocity abruptly at that level. The surface of separation between the crust and

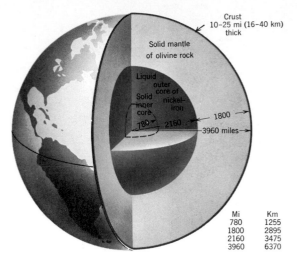

Figure 21.8 Structure of the earth's interior.

mantle is called the **Moho,** a simplification of the name of the seismologist who discovered it.

From a study of earthquake waves it is concluded that the crust of the continents consists of two layers: (1) a lower, continuous layer of basaltic (mafic) rock; (2) an upper layer of granitic (felsic) rock, which constitutes the bulk of continents. There is no sharply defined surface of separation between the granitic and basaltic layers. The granitic layer is absent beneath the ocean basins. The figure shows schematically a small part of the crust near the margin of a continent.

The crust of the continents is much thicker than the crust under the ocean basins. You can visualize the continents as vast icebergs floating in the sea with only a small part visible above the water and a great bulk deeply submerged.

Figure 21.9 The earth's crust and mantle.

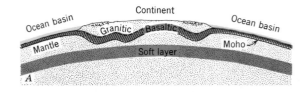

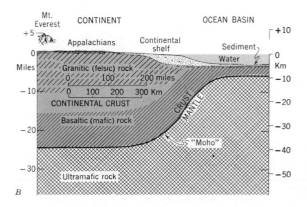

Unit 22
Volcanic Eruption
– Threat to Man

The Glowing Cloud of Death

The place was St. Pierre on Martinique Island in the West Indies. The date was May 8, 1902. The eyewitness was Assistant Purser Thompson, aboard his ship, the *Roraima*. Shortly after mooring was completed, Thompson surveyed the colorful city of 25,000 inhabitants. Behind the city rose the conical slopes of Mount Pelée, an active volcano reaching a summit elevation of nearly 4000 feet. For some days ashes had rained down upon the city and the smell of sulfur was heavy in the streets. Muffled explosions had been heard from time to time, coming from high on the volcano. There had been some panic, and many inhabitants had fled the city, but they were replaced by even larger numbers of refugees crowding in from the countryside. Then, at 7:50 in the morning, it happened. Four deafening explosions were followed by rise of a black cloud from the crater of Mount Pelée. Another black cloud shot horizontally outward, moving down the mountain slopes with express-train speed, headed directly for the city. Here is how Thompson described the events that swiftly followed:

I saw St. Pierre destroyed. It was blotted out by one great flash of fire. Nearly 40,000 people were killed at once. Of eighteen vessels lying in the Roads only one, the British steamship *Roddam* escaped and she, I hear, lost more than half on board. It was a dying crew that took her out. . . . The mountain was blown to pieces. There was no warning. The side of the volcano was ripped out, and there hurled straight toward us a solid wall of flame. It sounded like a thousand cannon. The wave of fire was on us and over us like a lightning flash. It was like a hurricane of fire, which rolled in mass straight down on St. Pierre and the shipping.

The remains of St. Pierre, photographed not long after its destruction by the death cloud. (A. Lacroix.)

The town vanished before our eyes, and then the air grew stifling hot and we were in the thick of it. Wherever the mass of fire struck the sea, the water boiled and sent up great clouds of steam. I saved my life by running to my stateroom and burying myself in the bedding. The blast of fire from the volcano lasted only for a few minutes. It shriveled and set fire to everything it touched. Burning rum ran in streams down every street and out into the sea. Before the volcano burst, the landings at St. Pierre were crowded with people. After the explosion, not one living being was seen on land. . . . The fire swept off the ship's mast and smoke stack as if they had been cut by a knife.*

Only two persons are known to have survived the catastrophe at St. Pierre. One of these was a prisoner in an underground dungeon at the time. Even so, he was badly burned by the hot gas which penetrated into every open space. The type of eruption that destroyed St. Pierre has been given the name of *nuée ardente,* or "glowing cloud." A similar event occurred in December of the same year and was photographed by a French scientist who had come to study the earlier eruption (photograph on opposite page). He also took the accompanying photograph of the devastated city.

Volcanic activity is one of the subjects we will investigate in this chapter. Volcanoes have posed a threat to Man since the earliest recorded history. The buildup of heat in rock beneath the surface is going

This cloud of heated gases and dust is the type of cloud that destroyed St. Pierre. The top of the cloud rises to an altitude of 13,000 feet. (A. Lacroix.)

on today in many places—there will be many more disasters before science can predict volcanic events accurately and people can learn to cope with this form of environmental hazard.

*From Thompson's account, as quoted by L. Don Leet (1948) Causes of Catastrophe, *Whittlesey House, New York.*

Intrusive and Extrusive Igneous Rocks

Magma that solidifies below the earth's surface and is surrounded by older, preexisting rock is called **intrusive igneous rock.** Where magma reaches the surface, it emerges as **lava,** which solidifies to form **extrusive igneous rock.** Intrusive igneous rock typically accumulates in enormous subterranean bodies, called **batholiths.** Figure 22.1 shows the relationship of a batholith to the overlying rock. As it made its way upward, the magma made room for its bulk by dissolving and incorporating the older rock above it. Batholiths are several miles in depth and may extend beneath an area of several thousand square miles.

In this unit our interest is centered upon the extrusion of igneous rock to form lava flows and volcanoes. Magma, emerging as lava, cools very quickly in contact with the air or water at the earth's surface (Figure 22.2). Quick cooling gives lava a very fine-grained texture and sometimes even

a glassy texture. Figure 22.3 shows two kinds of extrusive texture. One is a frothy, bubble-filled lava, called scoria (or sometimes pumice). The other is a natural volcanic glass. Most lava solidifies simply as a dense uniform rock of dull surface appearance in which the mineral grains are too small to be distinguished with the unaided eye.

Lava ranges in composition from felsic rock to mafic rock. An example of a common felsic lava is **andesite,** usually pale grayish in color. In contrast, **basalt** is a mafic rock and is black in color. An important difference in the two types of lava is that lavas of felsic composition are highly charged with gases under great pressure, so that when felsic lava reaches the surface it is extremely explosive. Basalt, the most common mafic magma, is highly fluid and is not explosive; it usually pours out upon the land surface in fast-moving streams and travels long distances before cooling and congealing. We will find that these contrasts in behavior of felsic and mafic magmas result in the building of very different volcanic structures.

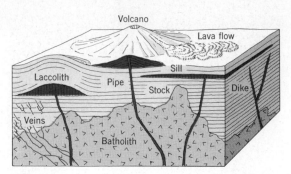

Figure 22.1 Intrusive igneous rock forms large subterranean masses of plutonic rock, called batholiths. Extrusive igneous rock pours out as lava flows and builds volcanoes.

Figure 22.3 A frothy, gaseous lava solidifies into a light, porous scoria (*left*). Rapidly cooled lava may form a dark volcanic glass (*right*). (A. N. Strahler.)

Volcanoes

Volcanism is the general term for the extrusion of magma to produce lava flows and volcanoes. Volcanism is one of the two major geologic activities by which mountains are built; the other being dislocation of the earth's crust (tectonic activity).

Volcanoes are conical or dome-shaped structures built by the emission of lava and its contained gases from a restricted vent in the earth's surface (Figure 22.4). The magma rises in a narrow, pipelike conduit from a magma reservoir far below. Reaching the surface, igneous material may pour out in tonguelike lava flows or may be ejected under pressure of confined gases as solid fragments. Ejected solid fragments ranging in size from gravel and sand down to fine silt size are collectively called **tephra.**

Figure 22.2 A freshly solidified basalt lava flow with ropy surface texture. Craters of the Moon National Monument, Idaho. (George A. Grant, U.S. Dept. of Interior.)

Form and dimensions of a volcano are quite varied, depending on the type of lava and the presence or absence of tephra. As we have already explained, the nature of volcanic eruption, whether explosive or quiet, depends on the type of magma.

Tall, steep-sided volcanic cones are produced by felsic lavas. These cones usually steepen toward the summit, where a depression, the crater, is located. Tephra in these volcanic eruptions takes the form of fine particles, described as volcanic ash, which falls on the area surrounding the crater and contributes to the structure of the cone (Figure 22.4). The interlayering of ash layers and lava streams produces a **composite volcano.** The world's lofty conical volcanoes, well known for their scenic beauty, are of the composite type. Examples are Mt. Hood in the Cascade Range, Fujiyama in Japan, Mt. Mayon in the Philippines, and Mt. Shishaldin in the Aleutian Islands (Figure 22.5). Tephra also includes volcanic bombs, solidified masses of lava ranging up to the size of large boulders, that fall close to the crater and roll down the steep slopes (Figure 22.6). Very fine volcanic dust rises high into the troposphere and stratosphere, where it remains suspended for years.

Another important form of emission from the explosive types of volcanoes is a cloud of incandescent gases and fine ash. This intensely hot cloud travels rapidly down the

Figure 22.4 An idealized cross section through a composite volcano and the magma chamber beneath. (From A. N. Strahler, [1972] *Planet Earth*, Harper & Row, New York.)

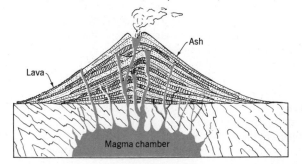

flank of the volcanic cone, searing everything in its path. As explained in opening paragraphs of this unit, a glowing cloud issued without warning from Mt. Pelée and swept down on St. Pierre, Martinique, in 1902, destroying the city and killing all but two of its 30,000 inhabitants.

Many of the world's active composite volcanoes lie in the circum-Pacific ring extending from the Andes in South America, through the Cascades and the Aleutians, into Japan; then south into the East Indies and New Zealand (see Figure 23.4). There is also an important Mediterranean group, which includes active volcanoes of Italy. Otherwise, Europe has no active volcanoes.

Calderas

One of the most catastrophic of natural phenomena is a volcanic explosion so violent that it destroys the entire central portion of the volcano. There remains only a great central depression named a **caldera.** Although some of the upper part of the volcano is blown outward in fragments, most of it subsides into the ground beneath the volcano. Vast quantities of ash and dust are emitted and fill the atmosphere for many hundreds of square miles.

Figure 22.5 Mount Shishaldin, an active composite volcano on Unimak Island in the Aleutian Islands, rises to an elevation just over 9300 ft (2800 m). A plume of condensed steam marks the summit crater. (U.S. Navy Dept., from The National Archives.)

Figure 22.6 Sakurajima, a Japanese volcano, erupted violently in 1914. These pictures show various scenes from the eruption (T. Nakasa.)

(Above) This distant view of Sakurajima shows the great cauliflower cloud of condensed stream.

(Below) Reaching the sea, the hot lava makes clouds of steam.

(Above) A blocky lava flow is advancing slowly over a ground surface littered with volcanic bombs and ash.

(Below) Volcanic ash has buried this village.

Krakatoa, a volcanic island in Indonesia, exploded in 1883, leaving a huge caldera. It is estimated that 18 cu mi (75 cu km) of rock disappeared during the explosion. Great seismic sea waves generated by the explosion killed many thousands of persons living on low coastal areas of Sumatra and Java.

Flood Basalts and Shield Volcanoes

Magma reaching the surface through rock fractures, called fissures, spreads out in thin tongues of lava. In some regions, basalt lava has welled up in enormous volumes, accumulating layer upon layer to make a total thickness of thousands of feet and covering several thousand square miles. These accumulations are called **flood basalts.** An example is the Columbia Plateau of Washington and Oregon (Figure 22.7).

The quietly erupting, highly fluid basaltic lavas give rise to a second major group of volcanoes, known as **shield volcanoes.** The best examples are from the Hawaiian Islands, which consist entirely of lava domes (Figure 22.8). Shield volcanoes are characterized by gently rising, smooth slopes that flatten near the top, producing a broad-topped volcano. The Hawaiian domes range to elevations up to 13,000 ft (4000 m) above sea level but, including the basal portion lying below sea level, they are more than twice that high. In width they range from 10 to 50 mi (16 to 80 km) at sea level and up to 100 mi (160 km) wide at the submerged base.

Shield volcanoes are built by repeated outpourings of lava. Explosive behavior and emission of tephra from shield volcanoes are not so important as they are for composite cones, which are built of felsic magmas. The lava in the Hawaiian lava domes is of a dark basaltic type. It is highly fluid and travels far down the gentle slopes.

Instead of the explosion crater, lava domes have a wide, steep-sided central depression that may be 2 mi (3.2 km) or more wide and several hundred feet deep (Figure 22.8). These large depressions are a type of caldera produced by subsidence accompanying the removal of molten lava from beneath. Molten basalt is actually seen in the floors of deep pit craters on the floor of the caldera or elsewhere over the surface of the lava dome. Most lava flows issue from fissures on the sides of the volcano.

Environmental Impact of Volcanic Activity

The eruptions of volcanoes and lava flows are environmental hazards of the severest sort, often taking a heavy toll of plant and animal life and the works of Man. What natural phenomenon can compare with the Mt. Pelée disaster in which thousands of lives were snuffed out in seconds? Perhaps only an earthquake or storm surge of a tropical cyclone is equally disastrous—you can take your choice. Wholesale loss of life and destruction of towns and cities are frequent in the history of peoples who live near active volcanoes. Loss occurs principally from sweeping clouds of incandescent gases that descend the volcano slopes like great avalanches; from lava flows whose relentless advance engulfs whole cities; from the descent of showers of ash, cinders, and bombs; from violent earthquakes associated with volcanic activity; and from mudflows of volcanic ash saturated by heavy rain. For habitations along low-lying coasts, an additional peril is the great seismic sea wave, generated elsewhere by the explosive destruction of volcanoes.

Figure 22.7 Flood basalts of the Columbia Plateau region. The basalt layers have been eroded to produce steep cliffs, rimming broad, flat-topped mesas. Dry Falls, Grand Coulee, central Washington. (John S. Shelton.)

Figure 22.8   This air view of Mauna Loa, Hawaii, shows a chain of pit craters leading up to the great central depression at the summit. (U.S. Army Air Force.)

Predicting Volcanic Eruptions

Predicting the occurrence of a devastating volcanic eruption is an important aspect of environmental protection in those places where a dense population lies near an active volcano. For many years, volcanologists stationed on the rim of Kilauea volcano on the island of Hawaii, have forecast periods of activity of Kilauea and Mauna Loa. Minor earthquakes are monitored, along with changes in ground level that signal the upwelling of lava in underlying magma chambers. Hazards to Man are not great on Hawaii, however, aside from occasional property destruction in the path of a lava flow.

Mount Baker in the Cascade Range in Washington has been showing signs of renewed eruptive activity and is being closely observed. This composite volcano is potentially dangerous because it is of the highly explosive type, capable of throwing out a great quantity of tephra, including much fine ash. The last known eruption of Mount

Baker was in the 1840s. It was reported that volcanic ash killed large numbers of fish in the Baker River and started a large forest fire. Since 1975, a crater on Mount Baker has been emitting hot gases from a small vent, suggesting that an eruption may be in the offing. Geophysical studies are being made to detect changes that may be associated with rising magma. The Soviets claim that one of their volcanologists, using geophysical methods, predicted the eruption of a new volcano in the Kamchatka Peninsula taking place in July 1975. The new eruption plume was plainly visible on satellite photographs.

The present state of the art of predicting volcanic eruptions is not very far advanced, despite the application of many geophysical techniques. One scientist active in this field of research recommends that the best course of action at present is to discourage or prevent the occupation of hazardous areas close to volcanoes with a history of previous activity. In the meantime, much fundamental research remains to be done on the internal workings of volcanoes.

Unit 23
Plate Tectonics

A Preposterous Theory

The most preposterous notion presented to the geological community in the twentieth century came from a scientist who should have known better than to deal in such nonsense. The scientist was Alfred Wegener, a German meteorologist with impeccable training and sound accomplishments in the field of atmospheric science. Born in Berlin in 1880, the son of an evangelical preacher, Wegener attended the most prestigious universities—Heidelberg, Innsbruck, and Berlin. His interest in geology must have started in 1906 when he traveled to northeast Greenland as a meteorologist with a Danish scientific expedition. An academic life followed, and in 1924 Wegener was appointed to a professorship in meteorology and geophysics at the University of Graz in Austria. His career ended tragically in 1930 during his third expedition to Greenland, where he lost his life at a remote field station high on the Greenland Ice Sheet.

Wegener's preposterous idea was that there existed until some 150 million years ago but a single continent on earth; he named it *Pangaea*. This supercontinent then ruptured into several fragments, which began to drift apart. As the American fragments pulled away from Africa and Eurasia, a narrow ocean basin appeared. It was to become the Atlantic Ocean basin. Wegener visualized Antarctica, Australia, Madagascar, and peninsular India as having been parts of Pangaea, neatly nested together close to the southern tip of Africa. These fragments also drifted apart, opening up the Indian Ocean as they separated. The accompanying illustration is Wegener's own concept of the fragmentation of Pangaea; it was published shortly before his death.

To the English-speaking geologists, Wegener's scenario was known as *continental drift,* and for the most part they had little use for the idea. But Wegener gained a few strong supporters on both sides of the Atlantic. These ''drifters'' were a source of annoyance through their perseverance in marshalling evidence that the continents had once been joined together. True, the evidence was in many ways strong, but nevertheless the mechanics of continental drift as Wegener described it was judged physically impossible. Wegener visualized each continental fragment as a raft of less-dense felsic (granitic) rock drifting through a sea of more-dense mafic (basaltic) rock. Where continents were drifting apart, an ocean basin of basaltic rock opened up between them. The leading (western) edge of the American continental raft was deformed by impact to produce the existing alpine mountain chains that are now the Andes in South America and the Cordilleran ranges of North America.

Geophysicists found Wegener's continental rafting

Wegener's concept of the drifting apart of the continents. (From Alfred Wegener *The Origin of the Continents and Ocean Basins,* Methuen and Co., London, 1924.)

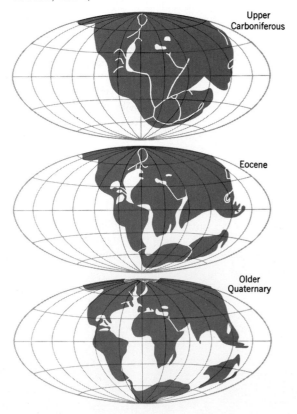

Upper Carboniferous

Eocene

Older Quaternary

completely unacceptable under known laws of physics; it simply could not happen that way. Of course these scientists were right; it did not happen that way. Yet today, all but a few earth scientists accept as fact the geographical separation of continents on a schedule in fairly close agreement with Wegener's early model. A plausible mechanism has been discovered and is now documented by convincing evidence—largely obtained by the dissenting geophysicists themselves.

The new revolution in geology was made possible by discoveries about the nature of the ocean basin floors. This knowledge began to emerge only after World War II. The 1950s were a decade of oceanic exploration unprecedented in the history of natural science. In the decade of the 1960s, the geologic revolution itself took place. Gathering momentum slowly at first, it reached a crescendo late in the decade as the last odd pieces in the puzzle quickly fitted into place.

In this study unit, we will review major concepts of modern geology to form a unified theory of the earth's major crustal features and their interactions. In so doing, we will be placing Man in the setting of the major environmental features of the globe—the continents and ocean basins.

Tectonic Activity

Tectonic activity is the geologist's term for the bending and breaking of crustal rocks under internal earth forces. Along with volcanism, tectonic activity is responsible for the growth of mountain ranges and their internal structure.

Tectonic activity takes two basic forms in the active mountain-making belts. Figure 23.1 illustrates the principles. Starting with a crustal block of a given width, **crustal compression** may occur, causing **folding.** Folding produces a series of wavelike undulations in sedimentary strata, called **folds.** Elsewhere, the crust may be pulled apart; this activity is called **crustal spreading.** Being brittle, the crustal rock near the surface fractures into blocks, which slide past one another in the process of **faulting.** The break itself is called a **fault.** A **fault block,** a single crustal mass bounded by two faults, settles down to form a depression. Faulting accompanying crustal spreading can be called **rifting.**

Global Pattern of Rifting

Although many examples of rifting with fault features can be found on the continents, by far the most important global rifting occurs on the floor of the deep ocean. Much of the floor of the ocean basins lies at a depth of 10,000 to 20,000 ft (3 to 6 km) below the ocean surface. Largely flat, these deep floors are called **abyssal plains.** However, in a central position in the ocean basins there is a belt of higher ocean floor called the **mid-oceanic ridge.** Figure 23.2 is a schematic block diagram showing the mid-oceanic ridge flanked by abyssal plains. At the continental margins, the seafloor slopes upward in a gentle rise, which steepens upward as the continental slope, forming the edge of the shallow continental shelf. The mid-oceanic ridge is characterized by a narrow troughlike **axial rift,** shown in idealized form in Figure 23.2.

The mid-oceanic ridge and its axial rift can be traced through the ocean basins for a total distance of about 40,000 mi (64,000 km). Figure 23.3 shows the extent of the ridge. From the South Atlantic, the ridge turns east and enters the Indian Ocean. Here, one branch penetrates Africa, while the other continues east between Australia and Antarctica, then swings across the South Pacific. Nearing South America, it turns north and penetrates North America at the head of the Gulf of California.

The axial rift of the mid-oceanic ridge is the origin of numerous earthquakes, indicating continued tectonic activity. Now unmistakable evidence has been accumulated to show that the crust is spreading apart along the rift. The rate of separation is from 1 to 2 in. (2.5 to 5 cm) per year. As this **seafloor spreading** occurs, basaltic lava rises from beneath the rift, solidifying and forming new oceanic crust. The axial rift is broken across at right angles by numerous fractures, which are a type of fault. Segments of the rift are offset along these fractures, as shown on the map (Figure 23.3).

Figure 23.1 Folding occurs under compression; rifting occurs where the crust is pulled apart.

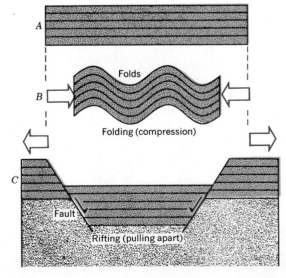

151

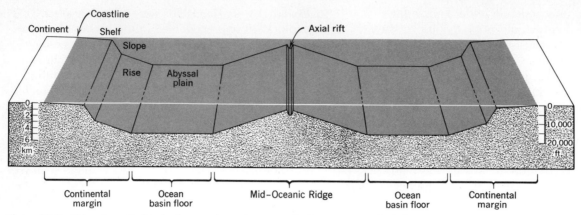

Figure 23.2 This schematic block diagram shows the ocean basins as symmetrical elements on a central axis. The model applies particularly well to the North and South Atlantic oceans.

Global Belts of Crustal Compression

Crustal compression, resulting in folding, occurs largely along narrow belts; most lie along the continental margins. These belts are sometimes referred to as **alpine chains,** because they are characterized by high, rugged mountains such as the Alps of central Europe. These mountain belts were formed quite recently in the geologic time scale, in the Cenozoic Era. The compressional activity has continued in many parts to the present day.

The mountain belts are characterized by broadly curved patterns on the map (Figure 23.3). Each curved section of an alpine chain is referred to as a **mountain arc;** the arcs are linked in sequence to form the earth's principal mountain belts. One is the **circum-Pacific belt;** it rings the

Pacific Ocean basin (Figure 23.4). In North and South America, this belt is largely on the continents and includes the Andes and Cordilleran ranges. In the western part of the Pacific basin the mountain arcs mostly lie well offshore from the continents and take the form of **island arcs,** running through the Aleutians, Kuriles, Japan, the Philippines, and many lesser islands. Between the large islands these arcs are represented by volcanoes rising above the sea as small, isolated islands.

The second chain of major mountain arcs forms the **Eurasian-Melanesian belt,** starting in the west at the Atlas Mountains of North Africa and running through the Near East and Iran to join the Himalayas. The belt then continues through Southeast Asia into Indonesia, where it joins the circum-Pacific belt.

Figure 23.3 A generalized world map of major crustal features. Major mountain arcs are shown on the continents. The mid-oceanic ridge divides the ocean basins.

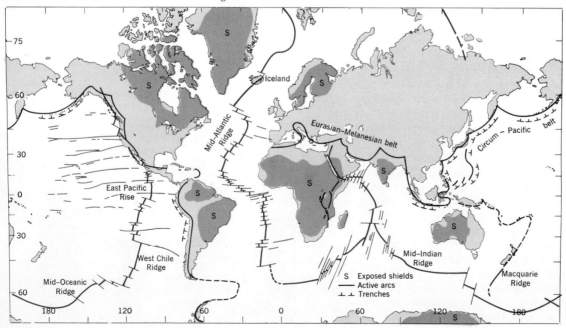

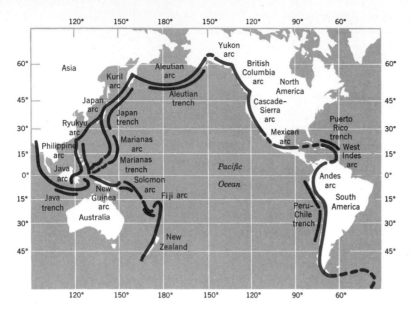

Figure 23.4 The circum-Pacific ring of mountain arcs and island arcs. Deep trenches lie offshore in many parts of the ring.

Oceanic Trenches

The circum-Pacific belt is characterized by a chain of deep **oceanic trenches** lying offshore from the mountain arcs and running close to the island arcs. The positions of these trenches are shown in Figure 23.4. Floors of the narrow trenches reach depths of 24,000 ft (7.5 km) and even more (Figure 23.5). Many lines of evidence show that the oceanic crust is sharply downbent to form these trenches. Numerous earthquakes, many of them very intense, occur in the trenches and adjacent mountain arcs, attesting to continuing tectonic activity.

Lithospheric Plates

Crustal spreading along the axial rift and downbending of the crust in the oceanic trenches involves more than just the earth's crust. Motion extends into the upper mantle, so that both the crust and upper mantle move as a single rigid layer, called the **lithosphere** (Figure 23.6). (This use of the word "lithosphere" is somewhat more restricted than its meaning as the entire solid earth.) Immediately below the lithosphere is a soft layer, called the **asthenosphere.** In this layer the mantle rock is heated close to its melting point. The soft layer yields by flowage, allowing the lithosphere

Figure 23.5 The Peru-Chile Trench, off the west coast of South America. (Portion of *Physiographic Diagram of the South Atlantic Ocean* [1961] by B. C. Heezen and M. Tharp, Boulder, Colo., Geological Society of America, reproduced by permission.)

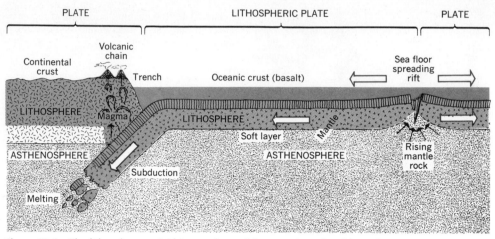

Figure 23.6   The lithosphere, a rigid upper plate, glides over the soft asthenosphere.
While one edge of a lithospheric plate is being formed during seafloor spreading on an
axial rift, the opposite edge is disappearing into the mantle by subduction.

above to glide slowly over the globe, much as pack ice of
the Arctic Ocean drifts slowly under the force of currents
and winds. In certain places, temperatures in the asthenosphere rise above the melting point, so that local pockets
of magma are produced.

The rigid lithosphere, which is approximately 50 mi (80
km) thick, is broken into a number of enormous segments,
called **lithospheric plates** (Figure 23.6). Sea-floor spreading at the axial rift of the mid-oceanic ridge represents a
line along which two lithospheric plates are moving apart.
In contrast, a trench represents a line along which two
lithospheric plates are colliding. In this case, one plate is
forced to plunge down into the mantle, a process called
subduction. Figure 23.7 is a three-dimensional representation of lithospheric plates and their relative motions.

The principal chains of active volcanoes are explained
by the rise of magma in the subduction zone, where the
downplunging plate is subjected to melting, as shown in
Figure 23.6. The association of volcanic arcs adjacent to
oceanic trenches is now clear.

Besides coming in contact along lines of seafloor spreading and subduction, lithospheric plates can slide past one
another along simple faults, called **transform faults.** Mo-

tion on a transform fault is horizontal and always in the
same direction as the fault line. Consequently, on a transform fault, the plates do not separate, nor does one plate
pass beneath the other. On the seafloor, transform faults
appear as long, straight walls or narrow trenches. Many of
the faults offsetting the mid-oceanic ridge are transform
faults (Figure 23.4).

The recent discoveries of lithospheric plates and their
motions have evolved into a new branch of geology,
called **plate tectonics.** Let us continue our investigation of
plate tectonics to seek an explanation of alpine mountain
chains.

Continental Collision

Recent discoveries of lithospheric plates and their motions
enable us to interpret mountain arcs in a new light. The
process is called **continental collision;** Figure 23.8 shows
how it works. In stage A, subduction is in progress. The
lithospheric plate on the right is moving toward the left,
bringing the two continents closer together, while the
ocean basin is being reduced in width. Sediment is accumulating both on the deep ocean floor and at the conti-

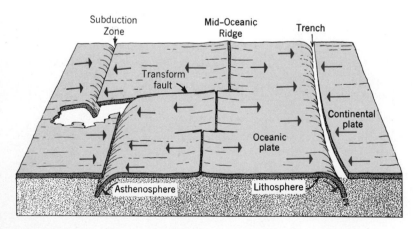

Figure 23.7   Schematic diagram showing major
features of plate tectonics. Earth-curvature has
been removed. (From A. N. Strahler, [1971] *The
Earth Sciences,* 2nd ed., Harper & Row, New
York.)

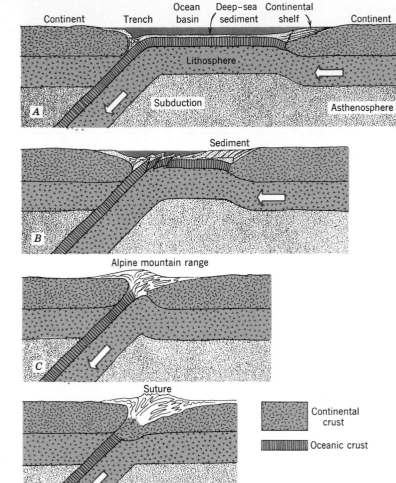

Continent   Trench   Ocean   Deep-sea   Continental
                     basin   sediment   shelf   Continent

Lithosphere

Subduction   Asthenosphere

A

Sediment

B

Alpine mountain range

C

Suture

D

Continental
crust

Oceanic crust

Figure 23.8 Stages in continental colli- sion, leading to formation of an alpine mountain range by suturing. (Based on data of J. F. Dewey and J. M. Bird.)

nental margin, under the continental shelf. In stage B, nar- rowing of the ocean basin continues. Sediment is being scraped off the descending plate margin and is becoming crumpled and faulted in the trench. In stage C the two continents have collided, squeezing the sediment mass strongly, and throwing it into complicated folds. Now the ocean basin has disappeared entirely and a high alpine mountain range has come into existence. In stage D the oceanic crust has been eliminated entirely from the crust. The alpine zone remaining is called a **suture;** the process by which it is produced is called **continental suturing.**

Examples of alpine mountain ranges that have been formed by continental suturing in the Cenozoic Era are the European Alps and Himalaya Range of southern Asia.

Continental Shields

Volcanic chains and recent alpine ranges account for only a small portion of the continental crust. The remainder consists of inactive regions of older rock. Within these inactive regions we recognize two structural types of crust: (1) shields; (2) roots of older mountain belts. **Shields** are low-lying continental surfaces beneath which lie igneous and metamorphic rocks in a complex arrangement (Figure 23.9). The rocks are very old, mostly of Precambrian age, but some are of Paleozoic age. They have had a very involved goelogic history. For the most part, the shields are regions of low hills and low plateaus, although there are some exceptions where large crustal blocks have been up- lifted. Many thousands of feet of rock have been eroded from the shields during their exposure throughout a half- billion years.

Large areas of the continental shields are under a cover of younger sedimentary layers. Accumulated at times when the shields subsided and were inundated by shallow seas, these strata may belong to the Paleozoic, Mesozoic, or Cenozoic eras. Marine sediments, laid down on the ancient shield rocks, range in thickness from hundreds to thousands of feet. These shield areas were then arched up and again became land surfaces. Running water has since eroded large amounts of the sedimentary cover but the cover remains intact over vast areas. We refer to such areas as **covered shields,** to distinguish them from the **ex- posed shields** in which the ancient rocks lie bare. Figure 23.9 shows the covered and exposed shields in relation

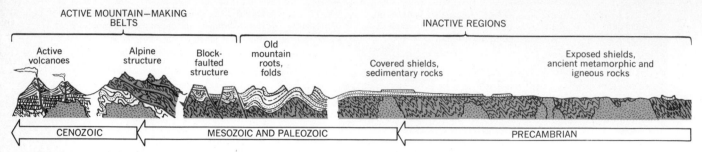

ACTIVE MOUNTAIN—MAKING BELTS

INACTIVE REGIONS

Active volcanoes

Alpine structure

Block-faulted structure

Old mountain roots, folds

Covered shields, sedimentary rocks

Exposed shields, ancient metamorphic and igneous rocks

CENOZOIC

MESOZOIC AND PALEOZOIC

PRECAMBRIAN

Figure 23.9 A schematic cross section through the upper continental crust showing rocks and structures of the active belts and inactive regions. In general, the geologic age becomes younger from right to left.

to the older mountain belts and the various kinds of structures in the active tectonic belts. An example of an exposed shield is the Canadian Shield of North America. Exposed shields are also extensive in Scandinavia, South America, Africa, peninsular India, and Australia (Figure 23.3).

Roots of older mountain belts occur within the shields in many places. These **mountain roots** are ancient continental sutures. They are mostly formed of sedimentary rocks

that have been intensely deformed and locally changed into metamorphic rocks. The Appalachian Mountains of eastern North America are an example. They were formed by suturing in the Paleozoic Era. The Highlands of Scotland offer another example. Thousands of feet of overlying rocks have been removed from these old tectonic belts, so that only root structures remain. Roots appear as chains of long, narrow ridges, rarely rising over a few thousand feet above sea level.

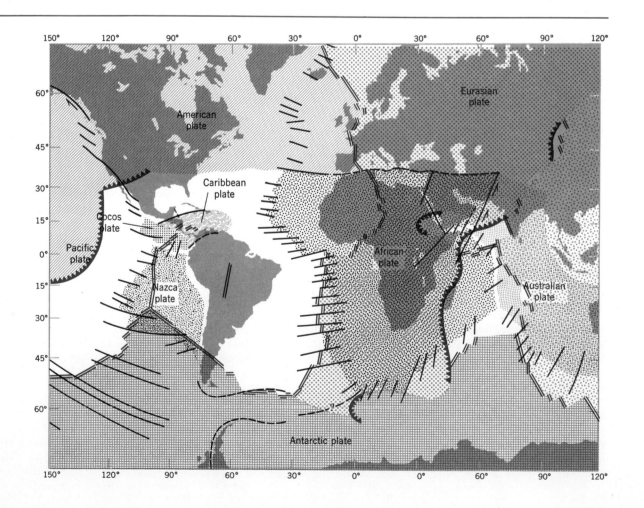

Plate Tectonics and Man

Plate tectonics has deep environmental implications on many scales of magnitude. First, of course, is that the existing features of the continents and ocean basins comprise the solid framework of Man's environment. Continents, with their mountain arcs and shields are the rock platform on which all terrestrial ecosystems rest. These major crustal features are explained by plate tectonics. Second, plate tectonics explains the global patterns of two major environmental hazards: volcanic eruptions and earthquakes. We have already investigated volcanic activity as a threat to Man. In the next study unit, we turn to earthquakes as a threat to Man.

SCIENCE
SUPPLEMENT

The Global System of Lithospheric Plates

The accompanying map, Figure 23.10, shows the major plates of the globe. The American plate includes the North American and South American continental crust and all of the oceanic crust as far east as the Mid-Atlantic Ridge. The Pacific plate is the only unit bearing only oceanic crust. It occupies all of the Pacific region west and north of the mid-oceanic ridge. It undergoes subduction beneath the American plate along the Alaskan-British Columbia coastal zone. The Antarctic plate occupies the globe south of the mid-oceanic ridge system. The African plate consists of the African continental crust and a zone of surrounding oceanic crust limited by the mid-oceanic ridge. A single Eurasian plate, which consists largely of continental crust, is bounded on the east and south by subduction zones of the great alpine mountain chains and island arcs. The Australian plate consists of continental crust of India and Australia, as well as oceanic crust of the Indian Ocean and a part of the southwestern Pacific. Other smaller plates are shown and named on the map.

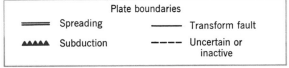

Plate boundaries

═══	Spreading	─────	Transform fault
▲▲▲▲	Subduction	‑ ‑ ‑ ‑	Uncertain or inactive

Figure 23.10 World map of lithospheric plates.

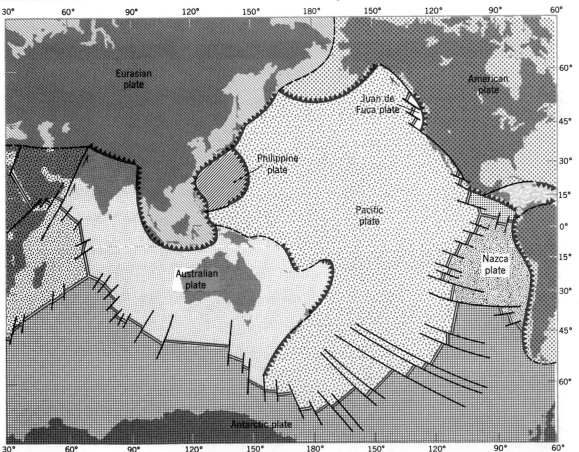

Unit 24
Earthquakes–
Threat to Man

A Deadly Tsunami

Disaster was on its way to the shores of Hawaii during the early morning hours of April 1, 1946, but no one there knew it was coming. Among its potential victims was a noted geologist, Professor Francis Shepard, an authority on the geological features of the oceans. Together with his wife, Shepard was staying at a remote coastal locality on the north shore of the island of Oahu. Here he was working on a new textbook of submarine geology. The disaster was to be the dreaded tsunami, or seismic sea wave, which many times before had brought death and destruction to island and continental shores of the Pacific Ocean. Set off at 2 A.M. by a major earthquake close to the Aleutian Islands the tsunami was moving southward at a speed of nearly 500 miles an hour, headed directly for the Hawaiian Islands. Five hours later, as the wave came ashore on Oahu, the Shepards had to run for their lives to escape the rising seawater and its angry surf.

The tsunami made itself felt as a rise and fall of sea level, repeated several times at 12-minute intervals. During the first rise, the ocean surface easily overtopped the protective barrier reef of coral lying offshore. Advancing as a surging water mass tossed by breaking surf, the first wave inundated the coastal land up to a height of 13 feet above tide level. The water then retreated, but was followed minutes later by an even higher landward surge, this time reaching 17 feet above tide level. Professor Shepard was able to photograph this second surge from a position of safety. A third, even higher surge followed the second.

The tsunami of April 1, 1946, proved a serious disaster for the city of Hilo, on the northern shore of the island of Hawaii. Here the rising water inundated a large stretch of low-lying coast, with breaking waves reaching to a height of 30 feet above sea level. A large section of the city was destroyed as houses were floated from their foundations and swept inland. Some buildings were crushed into

A tsunami off the coast of Japan as depicted by the nineteenth-century printmaker, Hokusai. The crest of a great wave towers over the terrified fishermen in their open boats. Far in the distance is a familiar landmark — Fujiyama. (Metropolitan Museum of Art, bequest of Mrs. H. O. Havemeyer, 1929. The H. O. Havemeyer Collection.)

tangled masses of debris, others floated almost intact to new locations. The tsunami breached the protective breakwater of Hilo Bay, lifting and dropping blocks of rock weighing more than 8 tons. Many small boats were carried inland and damaged. The force of the incoming water was particularly strong in the channel of the Wailuku River, a stream entering Hilo Bay. Here an entire steel span of a railroad bridge was ripped loose and carried 750 feet upstream.

The sudden rise of water and its pounding surf caught many of Hawaii's coastal inhabitants by surprise, and many were drowned. In Hilo alone 83 persons died, while the total for the islands was over 170 dead. Hundreds of homes were demolished or damaged and the total loss came to $10 million.

In the words of a U.S. Government account of the disaster, "the tsunami of April 1946 is distinguished from the rest: it was the worst natural disaster in Hawaii's history; and the last destructive tsunami to surprise those islands." In 1948 the Seismic Sea-Wave Warning System (SSWWS) was put into operation with headquarters at Honolulu. Because most tsunamis are generated by distant earthquakes, advance warning is given by the earthquake waves sent out at the time the earthquake takes place. These waves travel swiftly through rock of the crust and mantle, and are picked up by sensitive recording instruments at the warning system observatories. Ample time is available to alert people living on low ground close to the shore. How did the system pay off? In 1952 a major tsunami, generated near the Kamchatka Peninsula, reached Hawaii. The damage it inflicted came to $800,000, the death toll was

This raging surf was set up by the arrival of the second wave of the 1946 tsunami at Kawela Bay on the north coast of Oahu, Hawaii. Normally the body of water in this view is a quiet lagoon behind a sheltering coral reef. (F. P. Shepard, Scripps Institution of Oceanography.)

zero. The SSWWS had paid its way. The warning system was not entirely successful in eliminating casualties in later tsunamis. A tsunami in 1960 resulted in 61 deaths in Hawaii.

In this study unit, we investigate earthquakes, stressing their role as major hazards to Man.

DATA SOURCE: Francis P. Shepard (1963) *Submarine Geology,* 2nd ed., Harper & Row, New York, pp. 82-89; *Tsunami! The Story of the Seismic Sea-Wave Warning System* (1965), Coast & Geodetic Survey, U.S. Dept. of Commerce, U.S. Govt. Printing Office, Washington, D.C., 46 pp.

Surface Features of Faulting

Faulting is always accompanied by a slippage or displacement along the plane of breakage. Faults are often of great horizontal extent, so that the surface trace of a fault, or **fault line,** may run along the ground for many miles. Faulting occurs in sudden slippage movements that generate earthquakes. A particular fault movement may result in a slippage of as little as an inch or as much as 25 ft (8 m). Successive movements may occur many years apart, but can accumulate total displacements of hundreds or thousands of feet.

One common type of fault is the **normal fault.** The plane of slippage, or **fault plane,** is steep or nearly vertical. One side is raised or upthrown relative to the other, which is downthrown. A normal fault results in a steep, straight, clifflike feature called a **fault scarp** (Figure 24.1A). Fault scarps range in height from a few feet to a few thousand feet (Figure 24.2). Their length is measurable in miles; often they attain lengths of 200 mi (320 km).

In a **transcurrent fault** the movement is predominantly in a horizontal direction (Figure 24.1B). No scarp, or a very low one at most, results. Instead, only a thin fault line is traceable across the surface. Streams in some cases turn and follow the fault line for a short distance. In some places a narrow trench, or rift, marks the fault.

Earthquakes

Everyone has read many news accounts about disastrous earthquakes and has seen pictures of their destructive effects. Californians know about severe earthquakes from firsthand experience, but many other areas in North America have experienced earthquakes, and a few of these have been severe. An **earthquake** is a motion of the ground surface, ranging from a faint tremor to a wild motion capable of shaking buildings apart and causing gaping fissures to open up in the ground.

The earthquake is a form of energy of wave motion transmitted through the surface layer of the earth in widen-

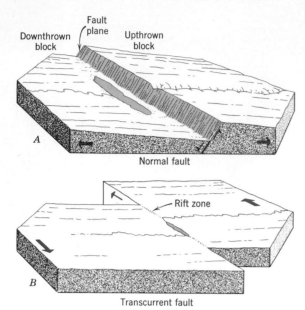

Figure 24.1   Normal and transcurrent faults.

Figure 24.3 Evidences of lateral earth movement accompanying the San Francisco Earthquake of 1906, Marin County, California. (G. K. Gilbert, U.S. Geological Survey.) *Above.* A fence offset 8 ft (2.4 m) along the main fault near Woodville. *Below:* A road offset 20 ft (6 m) along the main fault near Point Reyes Station. The shear zone is 60 ft (18 m) wide.

ing circles from a point of sudden energy release—the **focus.** Like ripples produced when a pebble is thrown into a quiet pond, these **seismic waves** travel outward in all directions, gradually losing energy.

As we already noted, earthquakes are produced by sudden movements along faults; commonly these are normal faults or transcurrent faults. Through the San Francisco Bay

Figure 24.2 This fresh fault scarp in alluvial materials formed during the Hebgen Lake earthquake of August 17, 1959, in Gallatin County, Montana. Displacement was about 19 ft (6 m) at the maximum point. Vehicle stands on the upthrown side of the fault. (U.S. Geological Survey.)

area passes the famed **San Andreas fault.** The devastating earthquake of 1906 resulted from slippage along this fault, which is of the transcurrent type (Figure 24.3). The fault is 600 mi (965 km) long and extends into southern California, passing about 40 mi (60 km) inland of the Los Angeles metropolitan area. In places the fault is expressed as a rift valley (Figure 24.4). Associated with the San Andreas fault are several important transcurrent branch faults, all capable of generating severe earthquakes.

We shall not go into the details of mechanics of faults and how they produce earthquakes. It must be enough to say that rock on both sides of the fault is slowly deformed over many years as horizontal forces are applied in the movement of lithospheric plates. Potential energy accumulates in the bent rock, just as it does in a bent crossbow. When a critical point is reached, the strain is relieved by slippage on the fault and a large quantity of kinetic energy is instantaneously released in the form of seismic waves.

Figure 24.5 shows that slow deformation of the rock takes place over many decades. Its release then causes

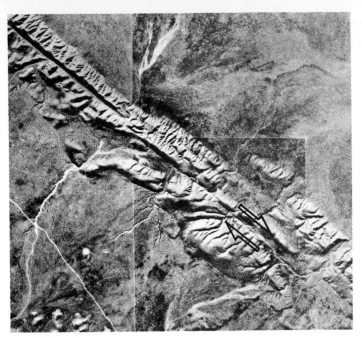

Figure 24.4 In this vertical air view, the nearly straight trace of the San Andreas fault contrasts sharply with the sinuous lines of stream channels. San Bernardino County, California. (Aero Service Division, Western Geophysical Company of America.)

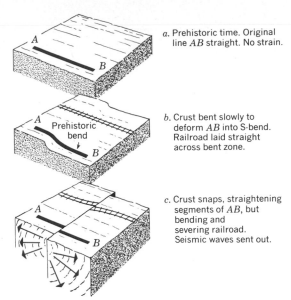

a. Prehistoric time. Original line *AB* straight. No strain.

b. Crust bent slowly to deform *AB* into S-bend. Railroad laid straight across bent zone.

c. Crust snaps, straightening segments of *AB*, but bending and severing railroad. Seismic waves sent out.

Figure 24.5 Sudden release of elastic strain accumulated by slow bending of rock along a fault. (From A. N. Strahler [1971] *The Earth Sciences,* 2nd ed., Harper & Row, New York.)

offsetting of features that formerly crossed the fault in straight lines, e.g., a roadway or fence. Faults of this type also show a slow, steady displacement known as **fault creep,** which tends to reduce the accumulation of stored strain.

Earthquake waves travel rapidly through the earth's interior and are received at distant points by delicate sensing instruments (seismographs). Our interest, however, lies in the energy of **surface waves** that travel much as do the bow-waves of a ship moving through calm water. From the environmental standpoint, it is the energy level of the earthquake that counts. We shall be interested in two measures of earthquake energy; first is the quantity of energy released at the focus; second is the intensity of the effect as measured at a given point on the earth's surface at some finite distance from the source. Whereas the earthquake focus lies at varying distances beneath the surface—down to depths as great as 400 mi (650 km)—the source point for measurement of intensity effects is the **epicenter** that lies on the surface directly above the focus.

The Richter and Mercalli Scales

The **Richter scale** of earthquake magnitudes was devised in 1935 by the distinguished seismologist, Charles F. Richter, to indicate the quantity of energy released by a single earthquake. Scale numbers range from 0 to 9, but since it is a logarithmic scale there is no upper limit of energy release. A value of 8.6 was the largest observed between 1900 and 1950. The data in Table 24.1 suggest

the quantities of energy associated with the various numbers of the scale.

It is estimated that the total annual energy release by all earthquakes is about 10^{25} ergs, and most of this is from a small number of earthquakes of magnitude over 7.

To measure the ground-shaking effects of an earthquake an **intensity scale** is used. In the United States the **modified Mercalli scale** is used, as prepared by Richter in 1956. It recognizes 12 levels of intensity, each designated by a Roman numeral. For each level there are certain

Figure 24.6 Destruction by earthquake and fire, San Francisco, California, 1906. View is southwest from the corner of Geary and Mason streets. (W. C. Mendenhall, U.S. Geological Survey.)

Table 24.1 The Richter Scale

Magnitude	Description
0	Smallest quake detectable. Energy released: 3×10^{12} ergs.
2.5–3	If nearby, the quake can be felt. Each year there are about 100,000 quakes of this magnitude.
4.5	Quakes of this magnitude can cause local damage.
5	About equal in quantity of energy to the first atomic bomb, Alamogordo, New Mexico, 1945. (Hiroshima bomb: magnitude 5.7; energy released, 8×10^{20} ergs)
6	Destructive within a limited area. About 100 per year of this magnitude in shallow-focus quakes.
7	Above this magnitude it is a major earthquake and can be recorded over entire earth; 14 per year this great and greater.
7.8	1906 San Francisco Earthquake.
8.4	Close to maximum observed. Examples are Honshu, 1933; Assam, 1950; Alaska, 1964. Energy released: 3×10^{24} ergs.
8.6	Maximum observed between 1900 and 1950. Energy released is 3 million times that of first atomic bomb (see magnitude 5).

criteria that can be readily observed by persons experiencing the earthquake. At intensity level IV, for example, hanging objects swing, a vibration like that of a passing truck is felt, standing automobiles rock, and windows and dishes rattle. Degrees of damage to various classes of masonry structures serve as criteria for identifying higher intensity levels (Figure 24.6). For example, at intensity XII, the highest number, damage to man-made structures is nearly total and large masses of rock are displaced.

One of the great earthquakes of recent times was the Good Friday Earthquake of March 27, 1964, with an epicenter located about 75 mi (120 km) from Anchorage, Alaska. Its magnitude was 8.4 to 8.6 on the Richter scale, approaching the maximum known. In Anchorage itself, the intensity was judged as VII to VIII on the modified Mercalli scale.

The San Fernando Earthquake of 1971

At about 6 A.M., on February 9, 1971, a violent earthquake shook the San Fernando valley area, lying northwest of the city of Los Angeles. The quake lasted only about 60 seconds, but during this single minute 64 persons lost their lives. The toll in human lives and the severe structural effects of the San Fernando earthquake shocked the entire Los Angeles community into renewed awareness of the need for urban planning to minimize or forestall the damaging effects of a major earthquake.

Although the earthquake was not in the really severe category by the Richter scale (it measured 6.6, which is moderate in severity), local areas experienced a ground motion of acceleration as high as, or higher than any previously measured in an earthquake. Fortunately, the

Figure 24.7 Severe structural damage and collapse of buildings of the Veterans Administration Hospital, Sylmar, Los Angeles County, California, caused by the San Fernando earthquake of February, 1971. (Wide World Photos.)

Figure 24.8 Collapsed pavement and overpass on the Golden State Freeway at the northern end of the San Fernando Valley. (Wide World Photos.)

ground shaking was of brief duration; had it persisted for a longer time the structural damage would have been much more severe than it was. Particularly disconcerting was the collapse of the Olive View Hospital in Sylmar, a new structure supposedly conforming with earthquake-resistant standards. The Veterans Hospital in Sylmar also suffered severe damage; several buildings collapsed and 42 persons were killed (Figure 24.7).

A crack produced in the Van Norman Dam caused authorities to drain that reservoir to prevent dam collapse and disastrous flooding of a densely built-up area. The Sylmar Converter Station, one of the key elements in the electrical power transmission system of the Los Angeles area, was severely damaged. Collapse of a freeway overpass blocked the highway beneath, and freeway pavements were cracked and dislocated (Figure 24.8). Fortunately, the time of the quake was early morning when most persons were at home and few were traveling the major arteries.

Yet the fault movement that set off the San Fernando earthquake was not on the great San Andreas fault but rather from an epicenter some 15 mi (25 km) from that fault, along a system of relatively minor faults. The San Andreas fault is capable of producing an earthquake of far greater intensity than the 1971 San Fernando earthquake, and although the year of this event is not predictable, the progress of urbanization may have greatly expanded the structures and population subject to devastation.

Soon after the San Fernando disaster, the National Academy of Sciences and the National Academy of Engineering set up a joint panel of experts to study the earthquake's effects and to draw up recommendations. The panel concluded: "It is clear that existing building codes do not provide adequate damage control features. Such

codes should be revised." The panel further recommended that public buildings, such as hospitals, schools, and buildings housing police and fire departments and other emergency services should be so constructed as to withstand the most severe shaking to be anticipated. Fortunately, most school buildings that were built after the severe Long Beach earthquake of the 1930s showed no structural damage. Many older school buildings, however, were rendered unfit for use.

Damage from the San Fernando earthquake of 1971 has been estimated at $500 million, but experts think that an earthquake as severe as that of 1906 at San Francisco would cause damage on the order of $20 billion, if it occurred now in a large metropolitan area. Perhaps, then, one beneficial effect of the San Fernando earthquake will be appropriation of adequate funds for research on many important aspects of earthquakes and their effects in an urban environment.

Seismic Sea Waves

An important secondary effect of a major earthquake, nicely illustrated by the Good Friday Earthquake, is the **seismic sea wave,** or **tsunami,** as it is known to the Japanese. A train of these waves is often generated in the ocean at a point near the earthquake's epicenter by a sudden movement of the sea floor. The waves travel over the ocean in ever-widening circles, as shown by the map of wave fronts (Figure 24.9). Notice, for example, that the first waves reached the California coast about 9 hours after the time of origin and were impinging upon the coast of Chile some 21 hours later. Average speed of travel was on the order of 300 mi (500 km) per hour.

Seismic sea waves are of very great wavelength—60 to

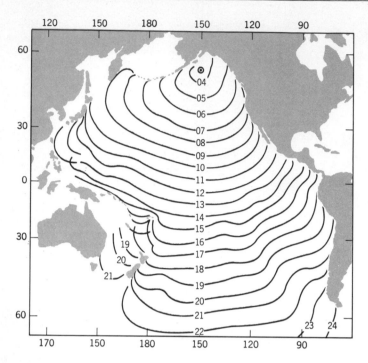

Figure 24.9 Successive hourly positions of a tsunami wave front, originating in the Gulf of Alaska as a result of the Anchorage, Alaska, earthquake of 1964. Figures give Greenwich Mean Time. (After B. W. Wilson and A. Torum, U.S. Army Corps of Engineers.)

120 mi (100 to 200 km)—and of very low height—1 to 2 ft (0.3 to 0.6 m). Consequently, they are not perceptible in deep water. When a wave arrives at a distant coastline, however, the effect is to cause a slow rise of water level over a period of 10 to 15 minutes. This rise is reinforced by a favorable configuration of the bottom offshore. Wind-driven waves, superimposed upon the heightened water level allow the surf to attack places inland that are normally above the reach of waves. For example, the particularly destructive seismic sea wave of 1933 in the Pacific Ocean caused waves to attack ground as high as 30 ft (9 m) above normal tide level and to inflict widespread destruction and many deaths by drowning in low-lying coastal areas. The catastrophic coastal flooding that occurred in Japan in 1703, with an estimated life loss of 100,000 persons, was probably caused by seismic sea waves.

Because of the far-ranging devastation that seismic sea waves can wreak, a tsunami warning system has been established for the Pacific Ocean. When a severe earthquake is recorded by seismographs and its center and time of occurrence are established, warnings are sent to distant coastal points. Arrival times are calculated on the basis of distances and water depths.

Earthquake Prediction

We now come to the interesting question of Man's ability (1) to predict the time and place of occurrence of earthquakes, and (2) to reduce the severity of earthquakes. The latter question is also tied in with a third environmental question: Does Man's activity set off earthquakes?

Earthquake prediction is still in its early stages of development, but research shows promise of leading to use-

ful methods. One line of approach uses sensitive instruments located along the fault lines where past earth movements have occurred and new earthquakes are considered likely. For example, such instruments can measure the degree of strain building up in the rock. Through experience with the relationship of past earthquakes to the degree of strain and its rate of buildup, it may be possible to anticipate when an earthquake is imminent. Measurements of changes in tilt of the ground may also prove to be indicators of an impending earthquake. A different line of research being explored is that of changes in the earth's magnetic field as indicators of coming earthquakes.

By far the most important advance in earthquake prediction has been made very recently; it deals with changes in the speed of earthquake waves immediately prior to a major earthquake. Most active faults produce large numbers of very weak earthquakes, and these can be monitored by means of seismographs placed close to the fault. It has been observed that in a period preceding a moderate or large earthquake, the speed of one type of earthquake wave gradually becomes less over a span of many weeks. Then, immediately before the major event, the wave speed rapidly increases.

To explain these changes, seismologists postulate that the reduction in wave speed results from the opening of pores in the rock adjacent to the fault, as that rock undergoes strain. Opening of pores is referred to as **dilatancy.** Next, ground water moves in to fill the pores, causing an increase in wave speed. The break follows shortly. Although some successes have been scored in earthquake prediction, by use of this **dilatancy theory,** the process is being debated and the effectiveness of the theory is under challenge. All the same, earthquake prediction is moving ahead rapidly, not only in the United States but also in the U.S.S.R. and the People's Republic of China.

Another approach to earthquake prediction is based on historical analysis of the seismic activity along an active fault. We will go into detail on this method in our Science Supplement.

Man-induced Earthquakes

Turning next to earthquake control, we must first see if any activities of Man have set off earthquakes. A case that is now almost a classic is that of the Denver, Colorado, region. Here, near the Rocky Mountain Arsenal, hundreds of earthquakes have been recorded since 1962; they seem to be correlated with pumping of fluids under pressure into a disposal well penetrating to a depth of 12,000 ft (3600 m). As an explanation, it has been proposed that the increased fluid pressure within the rock caused the release of strain already present within the rock; i.e., it had a triggering effect.

Naturally, this hypothesis leads us to wonder if it might not be possible to use engineering methods, such as fluid injections, to induce small fault movements, and thus to prevent strain buildup to dangerous levels. This possibility has attracted the attention of scientists and they are working on the theoretical concepts.

One might also be led to reason that if fluids (natural ground water or petroleum in rock pores) were to be pumped out of the rock near a major fault zone, the tendency for the fault to become locked would be increased, and seismic inactivity be induced. To investigate these possibilities, scientists of the United States Geological Survey undertook a study beginning in 1969 in which the Rangely Oil Field of western Colorado was the guinea pig. They found that the injection of water into deep oil wells (to induce more oil flow) had raised the fluid pressure by as much as 60% above normal. During this period earthquakes were being generated at the rate of 15 to 20 per week from a fault system passing through the oil field. The fluid pressure was then lowered by pumping water out of the same wells for a 6-month period. A dramatic drop in earthquake frequency resulted generally; the number fell to none at all near the wells. Pumping of fluid back into the ground has been resumed to find out if earthquakes will then increase.

It is now suspected that the pumping of fluids into the Inglewood Oil Field to raise the hydrostatic pressure and increase oil recovery was responsible for setting off the earthquake of 1963 which fractured a wall of the Baldwin Hills Reservoir. Water spilling from the reservoir brought an inundation of mud to homes in a 1-square-mile area below the reservoir and resulted in five deaths. The correlation between fluid pumpage and fault movements in this Los Angeles, California, locality is now considered to have been demonstrated. Increased fluid pressure reduces the frictional force across the contact surface of a fault, allowing slippage to occur.

Another situation in which Man may have been responsible for setting off earthquakes is in connection with the building of large dams on major rivers. The load of water from new lakes impounded behind these dams is thought to be responsible for triggering earthquakes. In a 10-year period following the filling of Lake Mead, behind Hoover Dam in Arizona and Nevada, hundreds of minor earth tremors were observed emanating from the area; they are attributed to loading of the crust by lake water. Another case in point is Lake Kariba, behind the Zambezi River in Zambia, which has been generating earthquakes of even greater magnitude.

Several scientists have been concerned with the possibility that underground nuclear explosions can set off significant earthquakes, and that a hazard may exist in this testing activity. Research thus far has shown that an underground blast does set off a large number of small earthquakes close to the site of the blast. Seismic energy of the blast triggers the release of strain along faults in the vicinity, but the radius of the known effects is on the order of 6 to 12 mi (10 to 20 km). These observations have led to the suggestion that underground nuclear blasts can be placed where they will induce strain release and thus prevent buildup of strain to dangerous levels.

SCIENCE
SUPPLEMENT

Seismic Activity on the San Andreas Fault

The historical approach to earthquake prediction is based upon the time elapsed since an earthquake-generating slip has occurred along a known active fault. The case of the San Andreas fault of California is interesting in this respect. This fault is of the transcurrent type and runs for some 600 mi (950 km) from the Salton Basin in southern California in a northwesterly direction to the San Francisco Bay region, beyond which it passes out to sea (Figure 24.10). In terms of plate tectonics, this fault is thought to represent a transverse fracture zone in which the lithospheric plate on the western side is moving to the northwest (oceanward), with respect to the eastern plate (Figure 23.11). Average movement of one plate with respect to the other is estimated to be on the order of 2 in. (5 cm) per year. Obviously, where a section of the San Andreas fault has shown no movement for a century, the potentiality for earthquake is great (2 in. × 100 years = 200 in.) since movement must occur from time to time. These sections of no known movement are described as **locked sections** and show no history of seismic activity. They are judged to be the most likely places for major earthquakes.

Sections that are seismically active are considered less of a hazard, since strain has been recently relieved or is being relieved either by small fault movements or by slow fault creep. Figure 24.11 shows the active and locked sections of the San Andreas fault. Of course, this type of prediction cannot set the time of an earthquake, even within very wide limits.

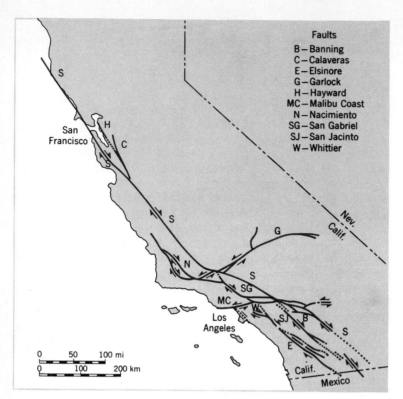

Figure 24.10 Sketch map of the San Andreas fault and associated major faults of California. (Based on data of R. H. Jahns and C. G. Higgins.)

Faults

B — Banning
C — Calaveras
E — Elsinore
G — Garlock
H — Hayward
MC — Malibu Coast
N — Nacimiento
SG — San Gabriel
SJ — San Jacinto
W — Whittier

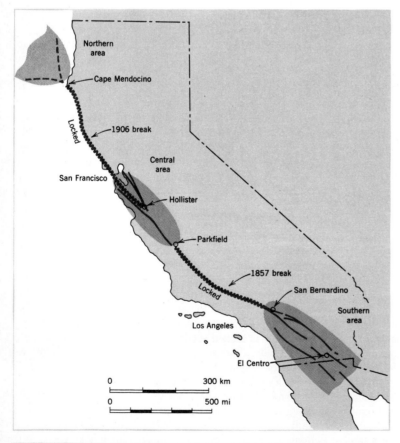

Figure 24.11 Active areas (color) and locked sections of the San Andreas fault. (After C. R. Allen [1968] in Proc., *Conference on the Geologic Problems of the San Andreas Fault System,* Stanford Univ. Publ., University Service in Geological Science, No. 11. p. 70.)

Unit 25
Mineral Resources

The Ridge of White Waters

In spite of an old saying, gold is not where you find it—at least, not much of the world's gold is waiting to be picked up. Instead, you have to go to the Witwatersrand, or "Ridge of White Waters," in the Transvaal of South Africa. Here, and in the adjoining Orange Free State, lies the modern source of about two-thirds of the world's gold production. Leave behind any romantic ideas about nuggets and flakes of pure gold glistening in the bottom of a prospector's pan. Gold of the Witwatersrand Basin—or Rand—is highly dispersed into minute particles embedded in an extremely hard conglomerate. This rock is one of the hardest found in the earth's crust.

Gold mines of the Rand are among the deepest openings Man has yet driven into the crust. Already, shafts have penetrated to a depth of 10,000 feet below the surface and are being carried even deeper. Rock temperatures at this depth often exceed 120° F, and men can work there only with the aid of powerful air-conditioning systems. Air is cooled by refrigeration in rock chambers deep beneath the surface, then pumped down further to the working levels. It is said that each year, 10 billion tons of air are pumped through the gold mines of South Africa.

No single elevator can efficiently be run from bottom to top of the deep gold mines, for the weight of the cables alone would be too great. Instead, three separate lift systems are used, one beneath the next. Rising at speeds of up to 35 miles per hour, one of these elevators can lift 100 men or 22 tons of ore at

Surface complex at the Western Deep Levels gold mine, southwest of Johannesburg, South Africa. Dumps of rock waste rise as prominent landmarks. Shaft headgears, housed in square towers, show where the mine shafts are located. (Anglo American Corporation of South Africa, Ltd.)

a time through a vertical distance as great as 4500 feet. In one mine a new shaft is being driven to reach the Carbon Leader Reef, at depths to 12,000 feet, and eventually it may go to 14,000 feet. The enormous cavity created to house the hoisting gear for this new shaft could hold a seven-story building.

Gold of the Witwatersrand Basin was deposited some 2½ billion years ago by water currents spreading sand and gravel over an ancient surface, perhaps a floodplain or delta, or even a shallow sea. In many ways, these accumulations may have then resembled the gold-bearing gravels of the Sacramento River, where Sutter first discovered California gold. African strata were then deeply buried and solidified, and finally warped into a basin-shaped structure. The gold-bearing pebble beds, called reefs, are only a few feet thick, but they extend for miles. The ore runs in long, thin "pay streaks" within the reefs. The Main Reef has been mined continuously for more than 20 miles. Since gold makes up only about 10 parts per million of the reef ore, enormous quantities of rock have to be brought to the surface. Indeed, some 100 million tons of rock are excavated annually to yield only about 10 grams of gold per ton. Altogether, the South African mines have produced over a billion ounces of gold. At today's price of about $130 per ounce, the entire haul comes to $130 billion worth of the precious metal.

Extraction of Rand gold so finely divided and so thinly diffused through the reef rock would not have been possible without a major advance in technology. In the 1890s, a process was perfected in which cyanide solutions dissolve the gold. Up to that time, the standard method of using mercury to form an amalgam with the gold had come to failure, because of the hugh quantities of mercury that were required.

This little essay about South African gold carries two messages we will repeat in this study unit on mineral resources. First, the gold of the Witwatersrand Basin took millions of years to accumulate in the reefs; no more will be produced there by nature

A seven-story building would fit into this excavation 10,000 ft (3000 m) below the surface. It will house the hoisting gear for a new shaft to reach a rich ore layer 12,000 ft (3700 m) below the surface. This is the world's deepest mine. (Anglo American Corporation of South Africa, Ltd.)

when the mining is over. Like practically all of our metallic ores, and all of our mineral fuels, the resouce is nonrenewable, but we are taking it out of the ground as if there is no tomorrow. Second, we must in future decades turn to ores of such low grade that they can be mined only by processing enormous quantities of rock and by application of increasingly expensive, energy-consuming technologies.

DATA SOURCE: Michael I. Brittan (1974) Gold recovery in South Africa, American Scientist, vol. 62, pp. 402-409.

Nonrenewable Earth Resources

Man is rapidly consuming earth resources that required geologic spans of time to be created and stored. So slowly do the geological processes operate that rates of replenishment are infinitesimally small in comparison with the present rates of consumption. The geological resources are therefore finite, and once we know approximately the world extent of a particular resource, we can predict its expiration according to any number of use schedules.*

In the formation of a mineral resource, matter has been concentrated by geologic processes. When these resources

are consumed by Man, just the reverse usually occurs—the matter is transformed from a concentrated state to a dispersed state. This pervasive principle—that resource consumption produces dispersion—is a universal fact with which Man will have to deal, sooner or later. For example, coal represents an extremely dense concentration of hydrocarbons in large quantities. Combustion of coal dis-

*Much of the text of this unit is taken from Planet Earth; Its Physical Systems Through Geologic Time, Harper & Row, Publishers, New York. © 1972 by Arthur N. Strahler. Used by permission of the publisher.

perses this matter into atmospheric constitutents and the stored energy is transformed into heat and dissipated into outer space as longwave radiation. We have no way to reverse this process without expending an even larger amount of energy. In the case of one comparatively rare metal—lead—geologic processes have concentrated the element into rich ores. We have been dispersing it into the atmosphere through combustion of leaded gasoline.

On the other hand, a great deal of used lead is recovered and used again—a process known as **recycling.** Aluminum provides an example of a metal of which only a small proportion (about one twelfth) is recycled; the remainder is widely dispersed, as witness the ubiquitous aluminum beer can. Other metals are dispersed in ways we do not see. For example, tungsten, vanadium, and chromium added in small quantities to steel as alloy metals, cannot be recovered without expenditure of considerable additional energy. Another example is silver, dispersed in electronic equipment and in photographic film in such ways that it cannot generally be recycled.

Actually, Man usually must carry out the final stages of mineral concentration, as in the case of nuclear fuels, copper ores, or most iron ores. While those deposits as mined represent an extraordinary degree of concentration when compared with their average distribution in the earth's crust, they must be concentrated further before they can be used industrially, for example, uranium, copper, or iron.

What connection is there between resource consumption and environment of the life layer? As long as humans existed in a highly dispersed population in preagricultural times, they used only renewable resources—and those in sufficiently small quantities that most ecosystems remained essentially intact. Thus Man's food came from the hunting of other animals and from plants in the natural state; water came from surface streams and lakes; fuel was wood of forest trees; and clothing was made of plant fibers, fur, and feathers. These resources were renewed seasonally and there was no measurable depletion. As agriculture evolved and animals were domesticated, plant and animal life systems were radically altered in many parts of the continents. One of the first of the nonrenewable resources to be drained was the fertile soil layer, eroded and carried away by streams in areas denuded of protective forest or grass cover. However, a primitive agrarian culture used little in the way of mineral resources.

The Roman and earlier civilizations of the Mediterranean lands exploited nonrenewable metallic resources. Important in the expansion of the Roman Empire was the control and extraction of lead, copper, tin, silver, and gold from mines around the Mediterranean Sea and throughout Europe. The depletion of many of these deposits through continuous working coincided with, and may have been to some degree a cause of, economic bankruptcy that followed the fall of the Roman Empire.

The coming of the modern industrial era brought major changes that began to impact the environment in new ways. We have already seen how the burning of hydrocarbon fuels has brought on serious air pollution problems and may be in the process of causing long-term climatic changes. The very process of mining fossil fuels and minerals defaces the land with great scars and pits, destroys ecosystems, and brings on many undesirable side effects such as water pollution and the disturbance of hydrologic systems. As nuclear energy comes into increased use, a new set of environmental problems arises to replace or add to the old ones. Contamination of water and atmosphere by radioactive wastes and excess heat and the threat of accidents within nuclear reactors are already coming to the forefront as environmental problems. Many of the substances produced in industrial processes are rare metals capable of serious environmental pollution, among them compounds of lead and mercury derived from metallic ores and ultimately dispersed into the atmosphere and hydrosphere where they are picked up and concentrated in food chains. As the richer deposits of certain scarce minerals become depleted, poorer grades of deposits are mined and these are removed and processed in much greater volumes. As a result, the devastation of mining extends over increasingly large areas. The impact of consumption of natural resources upon environment is a very real phenomenon, and the magnitude of the impact increases sharply as the expenditure of resources increases.

Nonrenewable earth resources can be grouped about as follows:

1. Soils
2. Ground water (renewable in regions of water surplus)
3. Metalliferous deposits (examples: ores of iron, copper, tin)
4. Nonmetallic deposits, including
   a. Structural materials (examples: building stone, gravel, sand)
   b. Materials used chemically (examples: sulfur, salts)
5. Fossil fuels (coal, petroleum, natural gas)
6. Nuclear fuels (uranium, thorium)

Notice that the last two groups represent sources of energy, in distinction to the preceding two groups, which are sources of industrial materials.

Soil as a resource will be covered in later study units; ground water resources have been covered in Units 15 and 17. Energy resources will be the topic of our final group of units in Part VIII. In this unit we will concentrate upon the metalliferous mineral deposits.

Metalliferous Deposits

Metals occur in economically adequate concentrations as ores. An **ore** is a mineral accumulation that can be extracted at a profit for refinement and industrial use. A number of important metallic elements are listed in Table 25.1, together with their abundance in percent by weight in average crustal rock. Whereas aluminum and iron are relatively abundant, most of the essential metals of our industrial civilization are present in extremely small proportions—witness mercury and silver with abundances of only 0.000008 and 0.000007, respectively.

In a classification of metals by uses, iron stands by itself in the quantities used in production of iron and steel. Related to iron is a group of **ferro-alloy metals,** which are used principally as alloys with iron to create steels with

Table 25.1 Average abundance of metals in crustal rock

Element	Percent by Weight
Aluminum	8.1
Iron	5.0
Magnesium	2.1
Titanium	0.44
Manganese	0.10
Vanadium	0.014
Chromium	0.010
Nickel	0.0075
Zinc	0.0070
Copper	0.0055
Cobalt	0.0025
Lead	0.0013
Tin	0.00020
Uranium	0.00018
Molybdenum	0.00015
Tungsten	0.00015
Antimony	0.00002
Mercury	0.000008
Silver	0.000007
Platinum	0.000001
Gold	0.0000004

A few metals, among them gold, silver, platinum, and copper, occur as individual elements, called **native metals.** However, most metals occur as chemical compounds. Oxides and sulfides are the most common of these compounds.

To qualify as an ore a given metal must occur in a greater concentration than the average values given in Table 25.1. The factor of concentration required for a metalliferous mineral deposit to be an ore is given for several metals in Table 25.2. For example, manganese must occur in an abundance 350 times greater than its crustal average; lead must occur in an abundance 2500 times greater than the average. The important concept is that many metals essential to our industrial society are extractable only because geologic processes acting over enormous spans of time have greatly concentrated them in rock that is now near the surface.

A notable trend in mineral extraction has been a shift from ores of simple composition to ores of complex composition. Certain ores yield a principal commodity plus one or more by-products; for example, in silver-bearing galena lead is the principal metal. In certain complex ores each of the constituents is necessary to make the operation profitable.

special properties. The ferro-alloys include titanium, manganese, vanadium, chromium, nickel, cobalt, molybdenum, and tungsten, as listed in order of appearance in Table 25.1. Other important metals, called **nonferrous metals,** stand apart individually with respect to industrial uses: aluminum, magnesium, zinc, copper, lead, and tin. A minor group listed in Table 25.1 includes antimony, silver, platinum, and gold. Finally, there are metals that are radioactive, including uranium (listed in Table 25.1), thorium, and radium.

Kinds of Ore Deposits

We offer here a brief sketch of the origin of a number of important kinds of metalliferous mineral deposits. An important concept is that magma is the primary source of metallic ore minerals. Therefore, many ores are directly associated with igneous rocks.

One major class of ore deposits has been formed within magmas by direct segregation; that is, mineral grains of greater density sank through the fluid magma while crystallization was still in progress. Masses or layers of a single

Table 25.2 Concentration of Certain Metals in Ore bodies

Metal	Clarke (percent by weight)	Concentration Clarke Required for Ore Body	Approximate Percent of Metal in Ore Needed for Profitable Extraction
Aluminum	8.13	4	20
Iron	5.00	6	30 (lower possible)
Manganese	0.10	350	35–27
Chromium	0.02	1500	30
Copper	0.007	140	0.8–0.5
Nickel	0.008	175	1.5
Zinc	0.013	300	4[a]
Tin	0.004	250	1
Lead	0.0016	2500	4
Uranium	0.0002	500	0.1

SOURCE: Brian Mason, 1966, *Principles of Geochemistry,* 3rd ed., New York, John Wiley & Sons, p. 50, Table 3.5.
[a] Percent in a multiple-element ore.

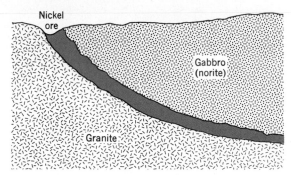

Figure 25.1 Cross section through a nickel ore deposit lying at the base of a body of gabbro and overlying a basement of older granite. (After A. P. Coleman [1913] Canada Dept. of Mines, *Monograph 170*, p. 34.)

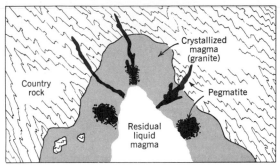

Figure 25.3 This schematic cross section shows the relationship of pegmatite bodies to an intrusive igneous body and its surrounding country rock. (From A. N. Strahler [1972] *Planet Earth,* Harper & Row, New York.)

mineral have accumulated in this way. One example is chromite, the principal ore of chromium with a density of about 4.4 gm/cc. Bands of chromite ore are sometimes found near the base of the igneous body. Another example is seen in the nickel ores of Sudbury, Ontario. These sulfides of nickel were apparently segregated from a saucer-shaped magma body and concentrated in a basal layer (Figure 25.1). Magnetite, an oxide of iron, is another ore mineral that has been segregated from a magma to result in ore bodies of major importance.

An important process associated with igneous intrusion is **contact metamorphism,** in which the invading magma and the highly active chemical solutions it contains have altered the surrounding rock (country rock). In this process, ore minerals were introduced into the country rock in exchange for existing components in the rock. For example, a limestone layer may have been replaced by iron ore consisting of magnetite (Figure 25.2). Ores of copper, zinc, and lead have also been produced in this manner.

Another type of ore deposit is also associated with igneous intrusion. In one of the final stages of the crystallization of granite from magma, there remains a watery magma rich in silica. Under high pressure, this solution left the main body of solidifying magma and penetrated the surrounding rock mass in small chambers and narrow passageways to crystallize in the form of **pegmatite** bodies.

Pegmatite consists mostly of large mineral crystals. Pegmatite bodies take the form of irregular masses within the parent plutonic rock, and occur as dikes (wall-like bodies), and as veins (Figure 25.3).

While the bulk of all pegmatites consists of the common minerals of granite, there occur unusual concentrations of rarer minerals, both metallic and nonmetallic. For example, in certain pegmatites of the Black Hills of South Dakota there occur enormous crystals of the mineral spodumene, an aluminosilicate of lithium (Figure 25.4). Several of these crystals weighed over 30 tons apiece. This and other pegmatite localities are a principal source of the light metal, lithium, which has many important uses in industry. Another metal, beryllium, is found in pegmatites in the form of the mineral beryl, an aluminosilicate of beryllium. Beryllium is an important component in high-

Figure 25.4 Large spodumene crystals in the Etta pegmatite, Pennington County, South Dakota. The hammer rests upon a single large spodumene crystal. (U.S. Geological Survey.)

Figure 25.2 Schematic cross section through an intrusive igneous body and the overlying country rock, showing veins and contact metamorphic deposits. (From A. N. Strahler [1972] *Planet Earth,* Harper & Row, New York.)

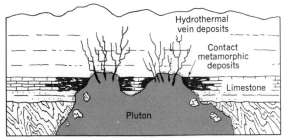

strength alloys of copper, cobalt, nickel, and aluminum. Two other metals found in pegmatites, both very rare but essential in industry, are tantalum and columbium. Because of the large size of pegmatite crystals—from several inches to as much as a few feet in diameter—they are important commercial sources of certain common nonmetallic minerals, principally the feldspars, used in manufacture of pottery, tile, porcelain, and glass. Another example is muscovite mica, needed in large sheets and plates for electrical insulation and related uses; it occurs as large sheets only in pegmatites.

Another type of ore deposit was produced by the effects of high-temperature solutions, known as **hydrothermal solutions,** that emanated from a magma during the final stages of its crystallization and were deposited in fractures to produce mineral **veins** (Figure 25.2). Some veins are sharply defined and evidently represent the filling of open cracks with layers of minerals. Other veins seem to be the result of replacement of the country rock by the hydrothermal solution. Where veins occur in exceptional thicknesses, they may consitute a **lode.**

Hydrothermal solutions have produced yet another important type of ore accumulation, the **disseminated deposit,** in which the ore is found distributed throughout a very large mass of rock. Certain great copper deposits of this type are referred to as **porphyry copper** deposits because the ore has in some cases entered a large body of igneous rocks of a texture class known as a ''porphyry,'' which had in some manner been shattered into small joint blocks that permitted entry of the solutions. One of the most celebrated of these deposits is at Bingham Canyon, Utah (Figure 25.5).

Hydrothermal solutions have risen toward the surface, making vein deposits in a shallow zone and even emerging as hot springs. Many valuable ores of gold and silver are deposits of the shallow type. Particularly interesting as a shallow hydrothermal deposit is the occurrence of mercury ore in the form of the mineral cinnabar. Most renowned are the deposits of the Almaden district in Spain, where mercury has been mined for centuries and has provided most of the world's supply of that metal.

A quite different category of ore deposits embodies the effects of downward moving solutions in the unsaturated zone and the ground-water zone (see Unit 15). Enrichment of mineral deposits in this manner has been a secondary process; the ores are classed as **secondary ores.** Consider first a vein containing primary minerals of magma origin (Figure 25.6). These minerals, mostly sulfides of copper, lead, zinc, and silver, along with native gold, were originally disseminated through the vein rock and did not exist in concentrations sufficient to qualify as ores. Through long continued erosion of the region, the ground surface truncated the vein, which was formerly deeply buried. Assuming a humid climate, there existed a water table and a ground water zone, above which lay the unsaturated zone. Water, arriving as rain or snowmelt, moved down through the unsaturated zone. The geologist refers to this water as **meteoric,** which is perfectly acceptable from the

Figure 25.5   Open-pit copper mine at Bingham Canyon, Utah. (Kennecott Copper Corporation.)

standpoint of atmospheric science. The meteoric water became a weak acid, since it contained dissolved carbon dioxide (carbonic acid) and also gained sulfuric acid by reactions involving iron sulfide.

The result of downward percolation of meteoric water has been to cause three forms of enrichment and thus to yield ore bodies. First, in the zone closest to the surface, as soluble waste minerals were removed, there accumulated certain insoluble minerals, among them gold and compounds of silver or lead, in sufficient concentration to form an ore. This type of ore deposit is known as a **gossan** (Figure 25.6). Iron oxide and quartz have also accumulated in the gossan. In colonial times, iron-rich gossans constituted minable iron ores, but they have been exhausted. Leaching of other minerals carried them down

Figure 25.6   Schematic cross section showing secondary ore deposits formed by enrichment of minerals of a vein. (From A. N. Strahler [1972] *Planet Earth,* Harper & Row, New York.)

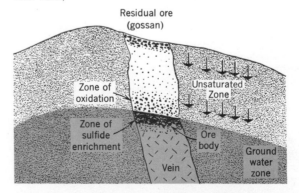

into a **zone of oxidation.** In this second zone there accumulated a number of oxides of zinc, copper, iron, and lead, along with native silver, copper, and gold. A third zone is that of **sulfide enrichment** within the upper part of the ground-water zone, just beneath the water table (Figure 25.6). Sulfides of iron, copper, lead, and zinc have been heavily concentrated in this zone. Sulfide enrichment also affected large primary ore bodies of the disseminated type, such as the porphyry copper of Bingham Canyon, Utah, referred to previously. There, the enriched layer has already been removed and mining has progressed into low-grade primary ore beneath.

Also in the category of secondary ores is bauxite. This principal ore of aluminum has accumulated as a near-surface deposit in warm, wet, low-latitude zones. Bauxite, a mixture of hydrous oxides of aluminum derived from the alteration of aluminosilicate minerals, is practically insoluble under the prevailing climatic conditions. For this reason it accumulated as the lowering of the land surface progressed. Produced under similar environmental conditions are residual ores of manganese (mineral: manganite), and of iron (mineral: limonite). The geologist applies the term **laterite ores** to these residual deposits.

Another category of ore deposit is that in which concentration has occurred through fluid agents of transportation: streams and waves. Certain insoluble heavy minerals derived from weathering of rock were swept as small fragments into stream channels and carried downvalley with the sand and gravel as bed materials. Because of their greater density, these heavy minerals were concentrated in layers and lenses of gravel to become **placer deposits** (Figure 25.7). Native gold is one of the minerals extensively

extracted from placer deposits; platinum is another. A third is an oxide of tin, the mineral cassiterite, which forms important placer deposits. Diamonds, too, are found concentrated in placer deposits, as are certain other gem stones. Transported by streams to the ocean, gravels bearing the heavy mineral were spread along the coast in beaches, forming a second type of placer deposits, the **marine placers.**

Finally, we can recognize a group of ore deposits in the category of sediments. For the most part, sediment deposition has been the principal source of nonmetallic mineral deposits, but some important metalliferous deposits are of this origin. Iron, particularly, occurs as sedimentary ores in enormous quantities. Sedimentary iron ores are oxides of iron—usually the mineral hematite. A particularly striking example is iron ore of the Clinton formation of Silurian age, widespread in the Appalachian region. For reasons not well understood, unusually large quantities of iron oxides, derived by weathering of mafic minerals in rocks exposed in bordering lands, were brought to the sea floor and were precipitated as hematite. Another metal, manganese, has been concentrated by depositional processes into important sedimentary ores.

U.S. Metal Demands and the World Supply

As we enter the last quarter-century of the 1900s, our demands for essential industrial metals will increase greatly. For a number of important metals—iron, manganese, zinc, cobalt, lead, antimony, mercury, and silver—the demand will double by the year 2000. For other metals the increase in demand will be even greater. These increased demands cannot be met from known reserves within the United States. For example, metallic titanium demands are expected to increase by a factor of about 12, but none is now produced in the United States. Aluminum demand will be up sevenfold but we produce only one-tenth of our primary aluminum. A similar situation holds for chromium, nickel, cobalt, and platinum. Our dependence is strong upon foreign supplies of iron, manganese, zinc, lead, tungsten, antimony, silver, and gold. Actually, the only metals that the United States has produced in substantial surplus relative to demand in recent years are uranium and molybdenum.

A bar graph, Figure 25.8, shows the apportionment of known recoverable reserves of ores of five metals between the Sino-Soviet bloc and the United States in comparison with total world resources. Consider the case of mercury, an essential industrial metal for which there is no known substitute in many uses. Most of the mercury reserves lie in Spain, Italy, and the Sino-Soviet bloc. It is obvious that the U.S. is heavily dependent upon foreign sources for a long list of metals. International tensions are bound to arise where mineral resources lie in the developing nations and in nations with politically unstable or unfriendly governments.

Figure 25.7 Placer mining beside the Yukon River, Alaska. A gold dredge scoops up gravel from the river floodplain, washes the gravel to secure gold particles, then dumps the waste to form curious piles like fallen stacks of poker chips. (Bradford Washburn.)

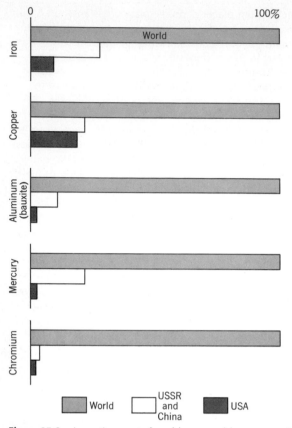

Figure 25.8 Apportionment of world recoverable reserves of ores of iron, copper, aluminum, mercury, and chromium between the Sino-Soviet nations and the United States.

Of increasing importance in manufacturing today is the secondary production of metals through reprocessing of durable metal goods manufactured in the past one to ten decades. We are not here referring to new scrap metal, derived as cuttings during initial manufacture, but to the old materials from discarded products. Metals can be reclaimed from old scrap by processes of distillation, electrometallurgy, mechanical separation, and chemical processes. As the total output of manufactured goods increases through time, the input of metals from secondary sources will also rise in volume. Recycling of metals is rising in importance as national mineral resources are being depleted at increasing rates and as the grade of ores being mined progressively declines.

Sea Bed Resources

If the prospect of eventually running out of vital mineral resources from the lands seems all too real, we may want to turn to consider possible substitutions of mineral resources from the sea. Seawater has always been available as a resource, and it has long provided the bulk of the world's supply of magnesium and bromine, as well as much of the sodium chloride. The list of elements present in seawater includes most of the known elements and, despite their small concentrations, the potential supplies are promising for future development. Sodium, sulfur, potassium, and iodine lie in the category of recoverable elements. Beyond hope of extraction, however, are the ferrous metals (principally iron) and the ferro-alloy metals in quantities sufficient to provide substitutes for the ore deposits of the continents.

Exploration of the deep ocean floor as a source of minerals is still in an early stage, but already the layer of manganese nodules found in parts of all of the oceans is regarded by some as a major future source of manganese, along with a number of metals in lesser quantities. However, prospects of substantial mineral contributions from the deep ocean floor are rather poor at this time. In the light of these conclusions, the need for conservation and careful planning for the use of mineral resources of the lands becomes all the more evident.

Mineral Resource Depletion

The impact of Man on all forms of mineral resources of the continents is admirably summarized in a statement written by a distinguished economic geologist, Thomas S. Lovering, in a report by the *Committee on Resources and Man* of the National Academy of Sciences—National Research Council:

The total volume of workable mineral deposits is an insignificant fraction of 1 percent of the earth's crust, and each deposit represents some geological accident in the remote past. Deposits must be mined where they occur—often far from centers of consumption. Each deposit also has its limits; if worked long enough it must sooner or later be exhausted. No second crop will materialize. Rich mineral deposits are a nation's most valuable but ephemeral material possession—its quick assets. Continued extraction of ore, moreover, leads, eventually, to increasing costs as the material mined comes from greater and greater depths or as grade decreases, although improved technology and economics of scale sometimes allow deposits to be worked, temporarily, at decreased costs. Yet industry requires increasing tonnage and variety of mineral raw materials; and although many substances now deemed essential have understudies that can play their parts adequately, technology has found no satisfactory substitutes for others.*

*From T. S. Lovering, "Mineral Resources from the Land," Chapter 6, p. 110, of *Resources and Man,* copyright © 1969 by the National Academy of Sciences, W. H. Freeman and Company, Publishers. Reproduced by permission of the National Academy of Sciences.

Nonmetallic Mineral Deposits

Nonmetallic mineral deposits (not including fossil and nuclear fuels) include a large and diverse assemblage of substances, and a wide range of uses. In outline form, we offer some examples of these mineral deposits classified by use categories:

Structural materials:

1. Clay: For use in brick, tile, pipe, chinaware, stoneware, porcelain, paper filler, and cement. Examples: kaolin (for china manufacture) from residual deposits produced by weathering of felsic rock; shales, marine and glacial-lake clays for brick and tile.
2. Portland cement: Made by fusion of limestone with clay or blast-furnace slag. Suitable limestone formations and clay sources are widely distributed and are of many geologic ages.
3. Building stone: Many rock varieties are used, including granite, marble, limestone, sandstone. Slate was used widely as a roofing material.
4. Crushed stone: Limestone and trap rock (gabbro, basalt) are crushed and graded for aggregate in concrete and in macadam pavements.
5. Sand and gravel: Used in building and paving materials such as mortar and concrete, asphaltic pavements, and base courses under pavements. Sources lie in fluvial and glacial deposits and in beaches and dunes. Specialized sand uses include molding sands for metal casting, glass sand for manufacture of glass, and filter sand for filtering water supplies.
6. Gypsum: (Hydrous calcium sulfate, $CaSO_4 \cdot 2H_2O$) Major use is in calcined form for wallboard and as plaster, and as a retarder in portland cement. Source is largely in gypsum or anhydrite ($CaSO_4$) beds in sedimentary strata.
7. Lime: Calcium oxide (CaO) obtained by heating of limestone, has uses in mortar and plaster, in smelting operations, in paper, and in many chemical processes.
8. Pigments: Compounds of lead, zinc, barium, titanium, and carbon, both manufactured and of natural mineral origin, are widely used in paints.
9. Asphalt: Asphalt occurs naturally, but most is derived from refining of petroleum. It is used in paving, and in roofing materials.
10. Asbestos: Fibrous forms of four silicate minerals, used in manufacture of various fireproofing materials.

Mineral deposits used chemically and in other industrial uses:

1. Sulfur: A major source is free sulfur occurring as beds in sedimentary strata, but most sulfur is supplied as a by-product of ore refining and smelting operations. Chief use is for manufacture of sulfuric acid.
2. Salt: Naturally occurring rock salt, or halite, is largely sodium chloride (NaCl), but includes small amounts of calcium, magnesium, and sulfate. It occurs in salt beds in sedimentary strata, and in salt domes. Major uses include manufacture of sodium salts, chlorine, and hydrochloric acid.
3. Fertilizers: Some natural mineral fertilizers are phosphate rock, of sedimentary origin, potash derived from rock-salt deposits and by treatment of brines, and nitrates, occurring as sodium nitrate in deserts (Atacama Desert of Chile).
4. Sodium salts: Found in dry lake beds (playas) of the western United States are various salts of sodium, such as borax (sodium borate). These have a wide range of chemical uses. Also important are sodium carbonate and sodium sulfate, found in other dry lake accumulations.
5. Fluorite: The mineral fluorite is calcium fluoride (CaF_2). It is found in veins in both sedimentary and igneous rocks. Uses are metallurgical and chemical, e.g., to make hydrofluoric acid.
6. Barite: Barite is barium sulfate ($BaSO_4$) and occurs as a mineral in sedimentary and other rocks. It is used as a filler in many manufactured substances, and as a source of barium salts required in chemical manufacture.
7. Abrasives: A wide variety of minerals and rocks have been used as abrasives and polishing agents. Examples are seen in garnet, used in abrasive paper or cloth, and diamond, for facing many kinds of drilling, cutting, and grinding tools.

The above list is by no means complete, and it can serve only to give an appreciation of the strong dependence of industry and agriculture upon mineral deposits and the substances manufactured from them.

PART IV

Man and Geomorphic Processes

Unit 26
Rock Weathering

Sic Transit Gloria Mundi — Stone Treasures in Jeopardy

In the summer of 1975, some 150 scientists and craftsmen held a conference in Bologna, Italy, to pool their ideas on how to preserve exterior stone of treasured buildings and statuary, threatened with disfigurement and destruction by exposure to the weather. Air pollution has insidious impacts upon many substances living and inert, and building stones are among the substances seriously affected. Recall from our Supplement in Unit 18 that acidity of rainwater is becoming increasingly severe. Sulfuric and nitric acid react readily with many common ornamental stone materials, particularly the carbonate rocks—limestone and marble. You have only to walk through a New England graveyard to find that the inscriptions on many marble tombstones have been nearly obliterated by acid action in the two centuries since our nation gained its independence.

One scientist, who was a specialist in natural limestone caverns, became keenly aware of the deterioration of art objects exposed to weather. Professor Herdman F. Cleland, a geologist on the faculty of Williams College, described as early as 1922 his archaeological observations in European caves inhabited thousands of years ago:

During the past summer the writer visited a number of paleolithic caves of southern France and northern Spain, and there had an opportunity to study the effects of weathering upon rocks and upon the works of man where conditions have apparently remained unchanged during a time which is variously estimated at from 18,000 to 30,000 years.

Every geologist from his own observations and reading can give many examples of rapid weathering, such as that on the western front of the Amiens Cathedral probably not an original stone placed there by builders in the fifteenth century can be found; that the outside stones of Westminster Abbey have been renewed five times over; that the stone of which the British Houses of Parlia-

The Temple of Castor and Pollux in the ancient Greek city of Acragas (now Agrigento) on the island of Sicily. The city was destroyed by Carthage in 406 B.C. and later fell into Roman hands. The temple was built about the same time as the Temple of Apollo in Delphi, Greece. (Charles Phelps Cushing.)

ment are built has crumbled so rapidly that already it has been necessary to replace many of the stone ornaments with cast iron.

The professor then commented on the well-known fact that artifacts taken from Egyptian tombs as old as 4000 years are as nearly perfect as the day they were made, a fact attributed quite reasonably to the extreme dryness of the air in the desert climate of Egypt. Cleland then went on to say:

It is perhaps because of the many archeological discoveries in arid countries that we have become accustomed to think of the agents of the weather as working slowly only where there is little or no moisture, but the wonderfully preserved paintings, engravings and clay models which are to be seen in the moist caves of southern France and northern Spain, and which antedate the works of the Egyptians by thousands of years, compel a modification of these views . . .

When the polychrome paintings on the ceilings of the great chamber of the cave of Altamira, near Santander, Spain, were discovered, careful observers doubted their authenticity because they showed so little evidence of great antiquity: the paint is so fresh that it can easily be rubbed off with the finger: the colors are probably nearly as bright as when first laid on; and there is no conspicuous flaking of the surface. Notwithstanding their modern appearance, it is generally agreed that the paintings were made by paleolithic artists thousands of years before the pyramids were built or Babylon founded.

In the caverns of Tuc D'Audoubert on the estate of Count de Begouen, near St. Girons, in the Pyrenees, is an even more remarkable example of lack of disintegration. In this cave are the clay models of bison which are in nearly as perfect condition as when made. A clay model is almost a synonym for the ephemeral for the reason that a short exposure to ordinary air causes it to dry and crack, and excessive moisture causes it to collapse. These models of bison are in fact slightly cracked but with this exception are unchanged. It is possible that the cracks were formed within the first few weeks after the figures were modeled and that none has developed in the 18,000 to 30,000 years that have followed. This seems incredible, but the proof of very great age appears to be well established.

The conditions under which the art of paleolithic man has been preserved almost unchanged for thousands of years are to be found in the uniform temperature, lack of sunlight, and absence of circulating ground water. Although the rock in the Altamira cave is saturated, there has been slight movement of the ground water and consequently little solution or deposition has been possible.

Professor Cleland's conclusion was that the constancy of temperature in the cave environment permitted the artifacts to be preserved, since they would not be subject to the continued expansion and contraction with temperature changes experienced on surfaces exposed to the outside air.

In years that followed, Professor Cleland traveled to many archaeological sites around the Mediterranean shores. He became highly indignant when he saw that the excavation of many buildings and art works was leading to their rapid decay. In 1932 he wrote: "Most archaeologists in their desire to display their discoveries to the world fail to realize that exposure to the weather soon utterly destroys the works of man. They also fail to take into account the fact that, in general, destruction takes place at an increasingly rapid rate as checks and cracks are opened in weathering, so that a column, for example, which may show little evidence of weathering at the end of a hundred years may be greatly disintegrated at the end of a second century."

Among the examples given by Professor Cleland is that of the Temple of Apollo in the Greek city of Delphi, dating to the Fourth Century B.C.: "When Delphi was excavated the archaeologists did a splendid piece of work, judged by their standards. They uncovered every column, every inscription, every carving and foundation stone that nature had so carefully preserved. Everything, in fact, is exposed, and the destructive work of the weather is at a maximum. The interesting notices in small Greek characters which tell of the freeing of slaves are in walls where they must inevitably rapidly become illegible."

Even today, efforts to preserve ancient stone surfaces from ravages of exposure to the weather are not meeting with a high level of success. The 150 experts who met in Bologna in 1975 expressed much frustration, not only with the inadequacy of their techniques, but perhaps even more so with the meager financial support given to restoration and stabilization programs.

In this study unit, we will investigate the processes by which hard rock is disintegrated and decomposed.

DATA SOURCE: Herdman F. Cleland (1922), Weathering under constant conditions, Science, vol. 56, pp. 660-661; (1932) The crime of archeology—a study of weathering, Scientific Monthly, vol. 35, pp. 169-173; Debra S. Knopman (1975), Conservation of stone artworks: Barely a role for science, Science, vol. 190, pp. 1187-1188.

The Life Layer

Now that we have completed a review of the earth's crust, its mineral composition, and its tectonic and volcanic landforms, we can focus on the shallow life layer itself. By **life layer** we mean the shallow surface zone of the lands—the environment of terrestrial life forms. The life layer is an interface at which the externally acting, solar-driven energy systems of the atmosphere and oceans mesh with the internally driven geologic system that has created and raised the continental masses. Geologic processes have caused varied rock types to become exposed to the surface environment. Our study of the interaction of these two great planetary systems began in Unit 21 with a brief mention of the breakup of rock to produce sediment. This is a process essential to the rock transformation cycle and to growth of the continental crust. In the study units of Part IV we will investigate geologic processes that shape the surface of the lands.

Landforms and Geomorphology

Landforms are the distinctive configurations of the land surface: mountains, hills, valleys, plains, and the like. Landforms are environmentally significant because they influence the place-to-place variation in ecological factors such as water availability and exposure to radiant solar energy. Through varying height and degrees of inclination of the ground surface, landforms directly influence hydrologic and soil-forming processes; these, in turn, act as direct controls on ecosystems.

Study of the life layer of the continents brings together two major branches of the earth sciences: geomorphology and hydrology. **Geomorphology** is the study of landforms, including their history and processes of origin. Geomorphology deals largely with the action of **fluid agents** that erode, transport, and deposit mineral and organic matter. The four fluid agents are: running water in surface and underground flow systems; waves, acting with currents in oceans and lakes; glacial ice, moving sluggishly in great masses; and wind, blowing over the ground.

Of the four agents, three are forms of water. Consequently, the science of hydrology is inseparably interwoven with geomorphology. One might be not far wrong in saying simply that the hydrologist is preoccupied with "where water goes," the geomorphologist with "what water does." Hydrology concerns itself with the hydrologic cycle in an attempt to calculate the water balance and to measure rates of flow of water in all parts of that cycle (Unit 13). Geomorphology concerns itself with geologic work that the water in motion performs on the land.

Denudation of the Land Surface

Denudation is a useful term for the total action of all processes by which the exposed rocks of the continents are worn away and the resulting sediments are transported to the sea by the fluid agents. Denudation is an overall lowering of the land surface. Denudation tends toward reducing the continents to nearly featureless sea-level surfaces and, ultimately, through wave action, to submarine surfaces. If it had not been repeatedly counteracted by tectonic activity throughout geologic time, denudation would have eliminated all terrestrial environments.

The important point that emerges as we look back through geologic time is that terrestrial life environments have been in constant change, even as plants and animals have undergone their evolutionary development. The varied denudation processes have produced, maintained, and changed a wide variety of landforms, which have been the habitats for evolving life forms. In turn, the life forms have become adapted to those habitats and have diversified to a degree that matches the diversity of the landforms themselves.

Geomorphic and hydrologic systems operating in the life layer have long been subjected to quite radical modification by the works of Man. Agriculture has for centuries altered the surface properties of areas of subcontinental size. Agriculture has modified the action of running water and the water balance, to say nothing of radically changing the character of the soil. Urbanization is an even more radical alteration, seriously upsetting hydrologic processes. Engineering and mining activities, such as strip mining and the construction of highways, dams, and canals, not only upset hydrologic systems but can completely destroy or submerge entire assemblages of landforms. Of the four fluid agents of landform sculpture, only glaciers of ice have so far successfully resisted changes of activity imposed by Man.

Invariably, Man's attempts to control the action of running water, waves, and currents produce unpredicted and undesirable side effects, some of which are physical, others ecological. An important reason to study geomorphology is to predict the consequences of Man-made changes and so to plan wisely for management of the environment.

Denudation is made possible by certain processes by which rock is physically disintegrated and chemically decomposed during exposure to atmospheric influences. These activities are referred to collectively as **weathering processes.** In addition to the physical and chemical changes in mineral matter that result from weathering, there is a continued agitation in the soil and regolith because of changes in temperature and water content. These daily and seasonal rhythms of change continue endlessly.

Regolith and the Mineral Soil

Figure 26.1 shows a typical exposure of soil, residual regolith, and bedrock. (Residual regolith and bedrock were explained in Unit 15.) Soil scientists and geographers use the word **soil** to mean a surface layer having distinctive zones, called **soil horizons,** and a set of physical, chemical, and organic properties enabling it to support plant growth. In this strict sense, the surface layer of large expanses of the continents cannot be called soil. For exam-

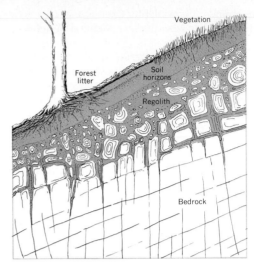

Figure 26.1 The true soil is characterized by distinct horizons and the capability to support plants. Below is infertile regolith, derived from the underlying bedrock.

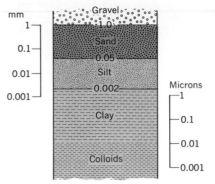

Figure 26.2 A system of particle-size grades used in soil science.

ple, dunes of moving sand, bare rock surfaces of deserts and high mountains, and surfaces of fresh lava near active volcanoes do not have a soil layer. In time these areas may develop true soils but, in that process, the surface layers will be greatly altered.

Mineral particles of regolith and soil span a very wide range of particle sizes. Sediment particles generally are described in terms of grade sizes, ranging from **gravel** and larger fragments, down through **sand, silt,** and **clay.** These grades are defined in terms of grain diameters, as shown in Figure 26.2. Millimeters are the standard units down to 0.001 mm, when the scale shifts to microns. Each unit on the scale represents a power of ten, so that clay particles of 0.001 microns diameter are one ten-millionth as large as sand grains 1 mm in diameter.

Physical Weathering

Breakup of rock through mechanical processes, without chemical change occurring, is referred to as **physical weathering.** One of the most important physical weathering processes in cold climates is **frost action,** the repeated growth and melting of ice crystals in the pore spaces of soil and in rock fractures. As water in joints freezes, it forms needlelike ice crystals extending across the openings. As these ice needles grow, they exert a powerful force against the confining walls and can easily pry apart the joint blocks.

Freezing water strongly affects soil and rock in all mid-latitude and high-latitude regions having a cold winter season, but its effects are most striking in high mountains, above the timberline, and in arctic regions. Here the separation and shattering of joint blocks produces surfaces littered with angular blocks.

Closely related to the growth of ice crystals is the

weathering process of rock disintegration by growth of salt crystals. This process operates extensively in dry climates and is responsible for many of the niches, shallow caves, rock arches, and pits seen in sandstone formations (Figure 26.3). During long drought periods, ground water is drawn to the surface of the rocks by capillary force. As evaporation of the water takes place in the porous outer zone of the sandstone, tiny crystals of salts are left behind. The growth force of these crystals is capable of producing grain-by-grain breakup of the sandstone, which crumbles into a sand and is swept away by wind and rain.

Salt crystallization also acts adversely on masonry buildings and highways. Brick and concrete in contact with moist soil are highly susceptible to grain-by-grain disintegration from this cause. The salt crystals can be seen as

Figure 26.3 White House Ruin occupies a deep niche in the sandstone wall of Canyon de Chelly, Arizona. (Ray Atkeson.)

Figure 26.4 Spheroidal weathering, shown here, has produced many thin concentric shells in a basaltic igneous rock. Lucchetti Dam, Puerto Rico. (U.S. Geological Survey.)

a soft, white, fibrous layer on basement floors and walls. Man has added to these destructive effects by spreading deicing salts on streets and highways. Sodium chloride (rock salt), widely used for this purpose, is particularly destructive to concrete pavements and walks, curbstones, and other exposed masonry structures.

Most rock-forming minerals expand when heated and contract when cooled. Where rock surfaces are exposed daily to the intense heating of the sun alternating with nightly cooling, the resulting expansion and contraction exerts powerful disruptive forces on the rock. Although firsthand evidence is lacking, it seems likely that temperature changes cause breakup of rock already weakened by other agents of weathering.

The wedging of plant roots also deserves consideration as a mechanism causing joint blocks to be separated. You may have seen a tree whose lower trunk and roots are firmly wedged between two great joint blocks of massive rock. Whether the tree has actually been able to spread the blocks farther apart or has merely occupied the available space is open to question. However, it is certain that pressure exerted by growth of tiny rootlets in joint fractures causes the loosening of countless small rock scales and grains.

Chemical Weathering

The surface environment of the lands is poorly suited to the preservation of igneous and metamorphic rocks formed under conditions of high pressure and high temperature. Most silicate minerals do not last long, geologically speaking, in the low temperatures and pressures of atmospheric exposure, particularly since free oxygen, carbon dioxide,

and water are abundantly available. Chemical change in a response to the changed environment is called **mineral alteration.**

The presence of dissolved oxygen in water in contact with mineral surfaces leads to oxidation beneath the soil surface. **Oxidation** is the combination of oxygen with the metallic elements, such as calcium, magnesium, and iron, abundant in the silicate minerals. At the same time, carbon dioxide in solution forms carbonic acid, a weak acid in soil water. **Carbonic acid action** is capable of dissolving certain minerals, especially calcium carbonate. In addition, where decaying vegetation is present, soil water contains complex organic acids, capable of reacting with mineral compounds. Certain common minerals, such as rock salt (sodium chloride), dissolve directly in water.

Water itself combines with silicate mineral compounds in a reaction known as **hydrolysis.** This process is not merely a soaking or wetting of the mineral, but a true chemical change producing a different compound and a different mineral. The reaction is not readily reversible under atmospheric conditions, so that the products of hydrolysis are stable and long lasting, as are the products of oxidation. In other words, these changes represent a permanent adjustment of mineral matter to a new surface environment of low pressures and temperatures.

Figure 26.5 Egg-shaped granite boulders are produced from joint blocks by granular disintegration in a semiarid climate near Prescott, Arizona. (A. N. Strahler.)

Figure 26.6   Solution rills in limestone, west of Las Vegas, Nevada. Scale is indicated by a pocket knife in center. (John S. Shelton.)

Results of Chemical Weathering

As chemical alteration penetrates the bedrock, joint blocks are attacked from all sides. Decay progresses inward to make concentric shells of soft rock (Figure 26.4). This form of change is called **spheroidal weathering** and produces onionlike bodies from which thin layers can be peeled away from a spherical core. Decomposition by hydrolysis and oxidation changes strong rock into very weak regolith. This change allows erosion to operate with great effectiveness wherever the regolith is exposed. Weakness of the regolith also makes it susceptible to natural forms of slippage and flowage.

In warm, humid climates of the equatorial, tropical, and subtropical zones hydrolysis and oxidation often result in

the decay of igneous and metamorphic rocks to depths as much as 300 ft (90 m). Geologists who first studied this deep rock decay in the southern Appalachians named the rotted layer **saprolite** (literally "rotten rock"). To the civil engineer, deeply weathered rock is of major importance in constructing highways, dams, or other heavy structures. Although the saprolite is soft and can be removed by power shovels with little blasting, there is serious danger of failure of foundations under heavy loads. This regolith also has undesirable plastic properties because of a high content of clay minerals.

The hydrolysis of granite is accompanied by **granular disintegration,** the grain-by-grain breakup of the rock. This process creates many interesting boulder and pinnacle forms by rounding of angular joint blocks (Figure 26.5). These forms are particularly conspicuous in arid regions. There is ample moisture in most deserts for hydrolysis to act, given sufficient time. The products of grain-by-grain breakup form a coarse desert gravel.

Carbonic acid reaction with limestone produces many interesting surface forms, mostly of small dimensions. Outcrops of limestone typically show cupping, rilling, grooving, and fluting in intricate designs (Figure 26.6).

Weathering Processes and the Biosphere

The environmental importance of weathering processes is felt in diverse ways. For example, weathering processes release vital plant nutrients into the soil. We shall investigate these nutrients in a later study unit devoted to soil-forming processes. Chemical weathering of silicate minerals produces clay minerals that, when moist, have low strength and often move spontaneously downhill to lower levels, sometimes with disastrous results for Man and Man-made structures. Our next study unit deals with these effects.

SCIENCE
SUPPLEMENT

Clay Minerals and Oxides in the Soil

An understanding of soil-forming processes and the engineering properties of soil and regolith requires a knowledge of two common mineral groups: clay minerals and mineral oxides.

Hydrolysis typically produces minerals that are soft and plastic when moistened; these are known collectively as **clay minerals.** Particles of clay are thin flakes of colloidal dimensions. **Colloids** are particles smaller than 0.01 micron (Figure 26.2). (We will explain the active role of colloids in soil processes in Unit 48.) Potash feldspar, an

abundant mineral in granite, is changed by hydrolysis to yield a clay mineral known as **kaolinite.** This soft, white mineral becomes plastic and exudes a distinctive clay odor when moistened. In pure form it is widely used in the manufacture of chinaware and porcelain.

Feldspars are commonly altered by hydrolysis to yield another clay mineral, **illite,** an abundant constituent of fine sediments. Figure 26.7 shows illite particles highly magnified under the electron microscope. A third important clay mineral produced by hydrolysis is **montmorillonite,** also shown in Figure 26.7; it is derived from several kinds of igneous rocks. An important physical property of montmorillonite is that when it becomes saturated, it swells greatly in volume, at the same time losing much of its strength.

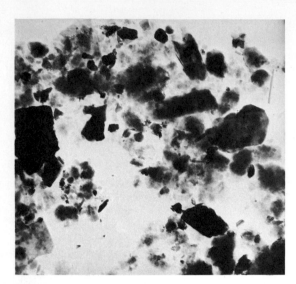

Figure 26.7   Seen here enlarged about 20,000 times are tiny flakes of the clay minerals of colloidal dimensions. The minerals are illite (sharp outlines) and montmorillonite (fuzzy outlines). These particles have settled from suspension in San Francisco Bay. (San Francisco District, U.S. Army Corps of Engineers.)

When hydrolysis occurs, ions of certain metallic elements are released into solution. Commonly, these are positively charged ions of potassium, sodium, iron, and magnesium, which are abundant in the silicate minerals. These ions are free to unite with oxygen molecules dissolved in the soil water. Union of metallic ions with oxygen is one form of a chemical process called **oxidation.**

Oxidation of iron produces a common iron-oxide mineral known as **hematite;** it is an important ore of iron where it is found concentrated in large masses. Hematite readily unites with water to form limonite, another very common iron-oxide mineral. Limonite is an earthy substance of brown to yellowish color. Both hematite and limonite, when present in thin coatings, contribute the reddish and yellowish stains seen commonly on exposed rock surfaces and in soils.

Aluminum released by chemical decay of the feldspars is oxidized and combines with water to form **bauxite,** an earthy substance abundant in soils of warm, wet climates. Where bauxite occurs in large masses, it can be mined as an ore of aluminum. Manganese, which is released during the hydrolysis of the mafic silicate minerals, also unites with oxygen and water to form a stable soil mineral (manganite) in warm, wet climates.

Unit 27
Mass Wasting and Man

Disaster in the Darkness

For some two hundred vacationers camping near the Madison River in a deep canyon not far west of Yellowstone Park, the night of August 17, 1959, began quietly, with most everyone safely bedded down in their tents or house trailers. Up to a certain point it was everything a great vacation should be—that point in time was 11:37 P.M., mountain standard time. At precisely that instant not one but four terrifying forms of disaster were set loose upon the sleeping vacationers—earthquake, landslide, hurricane-force wind, and raging flood. The earthquake was the primary cause of it all; it measured 7.1 on the Richter scale, which is about as big as they come. The first shock, lasting several minutes, rocked the campers violently in their trailers and tents. Those who struggled to go outside could scarcely stand, let alone run for safety.

Then came the landslide. A dentist and his wife watched through the window of their trailer as a mountain seemed to move across the canyon in front of them, trees flying from its surface like toothpicks in a gale. Then, as rocks began to bang into the roof and sides of the trailer, they got out and raced for safer ground. Later they found that the slide had stopped only 75 feet from the trailer. Pushed by the moving mountain came a vicious blast of wind. It swept upriver, tumbling trailers end over end.

Then came the flood. Two women schoolteachers, sleeping in their car only fifteen feet from the river bank, awoke to the violent shaking of the earthquake. Like other campers, they first thought they had a marauding bear on their hands. They turned on the headlights, and there was no bear. Starting the engine, they headed the car for higher ground, and as they did so were greeted by a great roar coming from the mountainside above them. An instant later the car was completely engulfed by a wall of water that surged up the river bank, then quickly drained back. With the screams of drowning campers in their ears, the two women managed to drive the car to safe ground, high above the river. After the first surge of water, generated as the landslide mass hit the river, the river began a rapid rise. This rise was aided by great surges of water topping the Hebgen Dam, located upstream, as earthquake aftershocks rocked the water of Hebgen Lake back and forth along its 30-mile length. But of course, in the darkness of night, the terrified victims of the flood had no idea what was happening. In the panic that ensued, a 71-year-old man performed an almost unbelievable act of heroism to save his wife and himself from drowning. As the water rose inside their house trailer, he forced open the door, pulled his wife with him to the trailer roof, then carried her up on the branches of a nearby pine tree. Here they were finally able to reach safety. The water had risen 30 feet above ground level in just minutes.

A reporter examines a camper's automobile that was first crushed by the landslide, then swept along the riverbed by the flood wave. Of the family who owned this vehicle, both parents and three of their four children perished in the slide. The debris which buried the campground forms a small mountain in the background. (UPI Telephoto.)

Seen from the air, the Madison Slide forms a great dam of rubble across the Madison River Canyon. (U.S. Geological Survey.)

The Madison Slide, as the huge earth movement was later named, had a bulk of 37 million cubic yards of rock. It consisted of a chunk of the south wall of the canyon, measuring over 2000 feet in length and 1000 feet in height. The mass descended over a third of a mile to the Madison River, its speed estimated at 100 miles per hour. Pulverized into bouldery debris, the slide crossed the canyon floor, the momentum carrying it over 400 feet in vertical distance up the opposite canyon wall. At least 26 persons died beneath the slide and their bodies have never been recovered. Acting as a huge dam, the slide caused the Madison River to back up, forming a new lake. In three weeks' time the lake was nearly 200 feet deep. Today it is a permanent feature, named (you guessed it!) Earthquake Lake.

Landslides are a topic of this study unit. Rare as they are, and usually occurring in rather sparsely settled mountains, great landslides have caused some notable disasters.

Mass Wasting

Everywhere on the earth's surface, gravity pulls continually downward on all materials. Bedrock is usually so strong and well supported that it remains fixed in place. A mountain slope, however, may become too steep in certain places through removal of rock at its base. As a result, bedrock masses may break free and fall or slide to new positions of rest. In cases where huge masses of bedrock are involved, the result may be catastrophic in loss to life and property in towns and villages in the path of the slide. As such, the phenomenon is a major form of environmental hazard in mountainous regions. Since soil and regolith are poorly held together, they are much more susceptible to the force of gravity than bedrock. Abundant evidence shows that on most slopes at least a small amount of downhill movement is going on at all times. Although this motion is imperceptible, the regolith sometimes slides or flows rapidly.

Taken altogether, the various kinds of downslope movements occurring under the pull of gravity are collectively termed **mass wasting.** They play an important part in denudation of the continental surfaces. Man's activities in moving enormous volumes of rock and soil on construction sites of dams, canals, highways, and buildings has added to the natural forms of mass wasting.

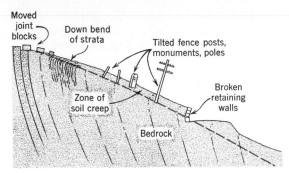

Figure 27.1 Evidences of the slow, downhill creep of soil and regolith. (After C. F. S. Sharpe.)

Soil Creep

On almost any moderately steep, soil-covered slope, some evidence may be found of extremely slow downslope movement of soil and regolith, a process called **soil creep.** Figure 27.1 shows some of the evidence that the process is going on. Joint blocks of distinctive rock types are found moved far downslope from the outcrop. In some layered rocks, such as shales or slates, edges of the strata seem to bend in the downhill direction. This is not true plastic bending, but is the result of slight movement on many small joint cracks (Figure 27.2). Fence posts and telephone poles lean downslope and even shift measurably out of line. Retaining walls of road cuts lean and break outward under pressure of soil creep from above.

What causes soil creep? Heating and cooling of the soil, growth of frost needles, alternate drying and wetting of the soil, trampling and burrowing by animals, and shaking by earthquakes all produce some disturbance of the soil and regolith. Gravity exerts a downhill pull on every such rearrangement that takes place. Each time that the particles are regrouped, they have been moved a very short distance down the hillslope.

Figure 27.2 Slow creep has caused this downhill bending of steeply dipping sandstone layers. (Ward's Natural Science Establishment.)

Earthflow and Mudflow

In humid climate regions, where slopes are steep, a mass of water-saturated soil, regolith, or weak clay or shale layers may slide downslope during a period of a few hours in the form of an **earthflow.** Figure 27.3 is a sketch of an earthflow showing how the material slumps away from the top, leaving a steplike terrace bounded by curved, wall-like scarp. The saturated material flows down to form a bulging toe.

Shallow earthflows, affecting only the soil and regolith, are common on sod-covered and forested slopes that have been saturated by heavy rains (Figure 27.4). An earthflow may affect a few square yards, or it may cover an area of several acres (Figure 27.5). If the bedrock of a mountainous region is rich in clay (shale or deeply weathered igneous rocks), earthflow sometimes involves millions of tons of bedrock, moving by plastic flowage like a great mass of thick mud.

Earthflows are a common cause of blockage of highways and railroad lines, usually during periods of heavy rains. Usually the rate of flowage is slow, so that the flows are not often a threat to life. Property damage to buildings, pavements, and utility lines, however, is often large where construction has taken place on unstable soil slopes.

One of the most spectacular forms of mass wasting and one that is potentially a serious environmental hazard, is the **mudflow,** a mud stream that pours down canyons in mountainous regions (Figure 27.6). In deserts, where vege-

Figure 27.3 An earthflow with well-developed slumping in the upper portion.

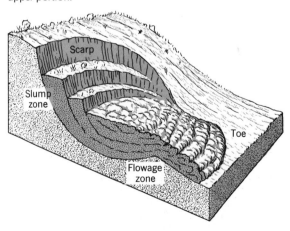

Figure 27.4 Earthflows in a mountainous region (After W. M. Davis.)

Figure 27.5   This earthflow near Snowmass, Colorado, involved the rapid movement of clay-rich glacial moraine, weakened by water saturation. (Mark A. Melton.)

tation does not protect the mountain soils, local thunderstorms produce rain much faster than it can be absorbed by the soil. As the water runs down the slopes it forms a thin mud, which flows down to the canyon floors. Following stream courses, the mud continues to flow until it becomes so thickened that it must stop. Large boulders, buoyed up in the mud, are carried with the flow. Roads, bridges, and houses in the canyon floor are engulfed and destroyed.

Where a mudflow emerges from the canyon and spreads across a plain, property damage and loss of life can result. In desert regions, the plains lie close to the mountain ranges that supply irrigation water. These favored land surfaces are often densely populated and are sites of urban

Figure 27.6   Thin streamlike mudflows occasionally issue from canyon mouths in arid regions and spread out upon the piedmont alluvial fan slopes.

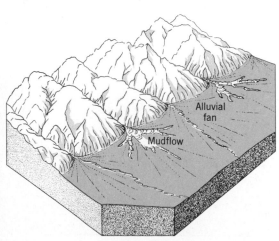

development, as well as of intensive agriculture.

Mudflows also occur on the slopes of erupting volcanoes. Heavy rains can turn freshly fallen volcanic ash and dust into mud, which then flows down the volcano slopes. Herculaneum, a city at the base of Mt. Vesuvius, was destroyed by such a mudflow during the eruption of 79 A.D. while the neighboring city of Pompeii was being buried under volcanic ash.

Mudflows show varying degrees of consistency, from a mixture about like the concrete that emerges from a mixing truck to thinner consistencies that are little different than in turbid stream floods. The watery type of mudflow is commonly called a **debris flood** in the western United States, and particularly in southern California, where it occurs commonly and with disastrous effects.

Landslides

The term **landslide** is widely used in a very general sense to mean any downslope movement of a mass of regolith or bedrock under the influence of gravity. Many geologists and engineers refer to earthflows as landslides. We shall limit our use of the term "landslide" to mean the rapid sliding of large rock masses beginning their descent as unit blocks, without internal flowage. Softening of clay minerals to produce a plastic mass, as in the case of an earthflow, is not involved in the behavior of a typical landslide. A landslide mass is rigid, rather than plastic in its behavior, traveling like a massive sled over a plane of slippage. In most cases, however, the sliding block breaks up into many smaller blocks, and these in turn may disintegrate into rubble. In its final stages, the mass of rubble often shows a gross flowage motion.

Two basic forms of landslides are (1) rockslides and (2) slump blocks. A **rockslide** consists of a bedrock mass slipping on a relatively flat rock surface, as shown in the left-hand diagram of Figure 27.7. The plane of slippage is usually a fault plane, joint plane, or bedding plane. A **slump block** is a bedrock mass that moves down on a curved slip surface, as shown in the right-hand diagram of Figure 27.7. As a slump block moves down, it also rotates on a horizontal axis, so that the upper surface of the block becomes tilted toward the cliff that remains. A rockslide can travel a long distance down a mountainside, far from its original position, whereas a slump block remains close to its original position

Figure 27.7   A rockslide *(left)* begins its motion as a block moving on a natural plane of parting in the bedrock. A slump block *(right)* moves on a curved fracture surface.

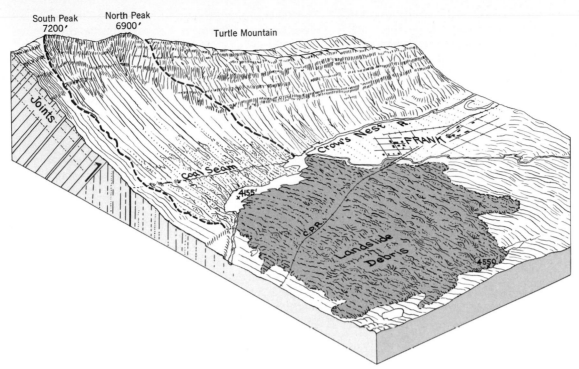

Figure 27.8 A classic example of a great, disastrous landslide is the Turtle Mountain slide, which took place at Frank, Alberta, in 1903. A huge mass of limestone slid from the face of Turtle Mountain between South and North peaks, descended to the valley, then continued up the low slope of the opposite valley side until it came to rest as a great sheet of bouldery rock debris. (After Canadian Geological Survey, Dept. of Mines.)

Rockslides

Wherever steep mountain slopes occur, there is a possibility of large, disastrous rockslides. In Switzerland, Norway, or the Canadian Rockies, for example, villages built on the floors of steep-sided valleys have been destroyed and their inhabitants killed by the sliding of millions of cubic yards of rock, set loose without any warning.

The Turtle Mountain landslide of 1903 in Alberta, shown in Figure 27.8 involved the sliding of an enormous mass of limestone, its volume estimated at 35 million cu yds (27 million cu m), through a descent of 3000 ft (900 m). The debris buried a part of the town of Frank, with a loss of 70 persons.

A similar disaster was the Madison landslide of 1959, which we described in opening paragraphs of this study unit. Oversteepening of the mountainside was caused by slow downcutting by the Madison River of a period of many centuries, so that gradually support was removed from the high rock mass. A severe earthquake was the triggering effect, releasing the slide.

Many of the world's great rockslides have occurred in mountains deeply carved by glacial action in the Pleistocene Epoch. The U-shaped trough is the dominant landform in heavily glaciated mountains such as the European Alps, the Cordilleran Range of North America, the Andes Range of South America, and the Himalayas of southern Asia (Figure 27.9).

Glacial troughs in coastal locations are typically inundated by the ocean, becoming steep-walled fiords (see Figure 56.7). The environmental hazard of rockslides is extremely high for towns and cities located on the floors of glacial troughs and at the heads of fiords. A rockslide entering the deep water of a fiord generates an enormous wave of water that runs quickly to the head of the fiord, inundating and destroying habitations located on the low-lying trough floor.

In many places glacial troughs are occupied by deep trough lakes, which may be many miles long. A rockslide entering a trough lake sets off a great wave, traveling to both ends of the lake and riding some distance up the trough floor. In the Vaiont Reservoir disaster of 1963 in

Figure 27.9 A great rockslide at S has formed a dam, D, in the floor of a glacial trough and has produced a lake L. (After W. M. Davis.)

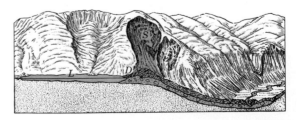

Italy, a Man-made reservoir occupied a glacial trough. A huge wave produced by a large rockslide destroyed the high concrete dam, releasing an enormous volume of flood water that quickly created enormous havoc in towns located at lower valley levels. Within a short time, 2600 lives were lost.

Closely related to the phenomenon of rockslide is **rockfall,** the free falling or rolling of single masses of rock from a steep cliff. Individual fragments may be as small as a boulder, or as large as a city block, depending upon the overall scale of the cliff and the manner in which the rock breaks up. Large blocks disintegrate upon falling, strewing the slope below with rubble and leaving a conspicuous scar on the upper cliff face.

A similar phenomenon, the **alpine debris avalanche,** occurs in high, alpine mountain chains. There, glacial erosion has produced valleys with extremely steep gradients and left large quantities of glacial rock rubble (moraine) and relict glaciers perched precariously in high positions. This kind of avalanche, a sudden rolling of a mixture of rock waste and glacial ice, can produce a tongue of debris traveling downvalley at a speed that is little less than that of a freely falling body.

Slump Blocks

Slump blocks may involve great masses of bedrock sliding downward from a high cliff and, at the same time, rotating backward on a horizontal axis (Figure 27.10). Wherever massive sedimentary strata, usually sandstones or limestones, or lava beds, rest upon weak clay or shale formations, a steep cliff tends to be formed by erosion. As the weak rock is eroded from the cliff base, the cap rock is undermined. When a point of failure is reached, a large block breaks off, slides down, and tilts back along a curving plane of slip. Slump blocks may be as much as 1 to 2 mi (1.5 to 3 km) long and 500 ft (800 m) thick. A single block appears as a ridge at the base of the cliff. A closed depression or lake basin may lie between the block and the cliff.

The slump form of mass wasting can also be seen in

Figure 27.10   Large slump blocks of bedrock rotate backwards as they slide down from a cliff.

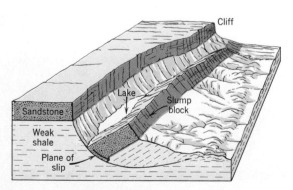

earthflows, which we previously described. In many cases, the upper part of the mass of an earthflow has rigid properties and behaves as a block, or group of blocks. Flowage occurs at some depth under this upper blocklike mass. Figure 27.3 illustrates an earthflow showing well-developed slump blocks in the upper portion, but with plastic flowage in the middle and lower portions. A step-like arrangement of slump scarps has been produced at the top of the affected area.

Slumping of large bedrock masses is rarely a threat to human life because of the slow rate of movement and the limited distance of travel. The environmental importance of slumping, both in bedrock and in regolith, lies in the potential for disruption of Man-made structures such as buildings and highways. Where a house happens to lie over the upper part of an active earthflow, where slump scarps are forming, the building can be sheared into two sections. Because slumping is difficult to stabilize, abandonment of the property may be the only economically feasible solution. Large bedrock slump blocks located along the base of a cliff should be identified and avoided in the construction of highways, dams, and power plants. Even though the slump block may appear to be stabilized and immobile, excavation of material at the base of the block may lead to reactivation of the block. The recognition of ancient earthflows and slump blocks is an important aspect of environmental protection since serious future economic losses can often be avoided in the planning stages of engineering projects.

Man as an Agent of Mass Wasting

Man's activities induce mass wasting in such forms as mudflow and earthflow. These activities include (1) piling up of waste soil and rock into unstable accumulations that fail spontaneously, and (2) removal of support by undermining natural masses of soil, regolith, and rock. Strip mining produces a spoil bank that is unstable and a constant threat to the lower slope and valley bottom below. When saturated by heavy rains and melting snows, the spoil generates earthflows and mudflows that descend upon houses, roads, and forest. (Strip mining is described in Unit 61.)

At Aberfan, Wales, a major disaster occurred when a hill 600 ft (180 m) high, built of rock waste (culm) from a nearby coal mine spontaneously began to move as an earthflow. The pile had been constructed on a steep hillslope and upon a spring line, as well, making a potentially unstable configuration. The debris tongue overwhelmed part of the town below, destroying a school and taking over 150 lives (Figure 27.11). Phenomena of this type are often called "mudslides" in the news media.

Some large earthflows have been induced by removal of supporting rock and steepening of unstable slopes during excavation for canals and dams. A classic example is from the digging of the Panama Canal, which suffered from large earthflows of clay-rich rock. These flows filled the canal at certain points and continued to move long after

Figure 27.11 Debris flow at Aberfan, Wales, sketched from a photograph. (From A. N. Strahler [1972] *Planet Earth*, Harper & Row, New York.)

the initial masses of debris were removed. In connection with the excavation of Coulee Dam on the Columbia River, deposits of older river silts moved as earthflows into excavations made for the base of the dam. To stabilize these mass movements, elaborate water drainage systems and even freezing of the entrapped water were required.

Examples of both large and small earthflows, induced or aggravated by Man's activities, are found in the Palos Verdes Hills of Los Angeles County, California. These movements occur in shales that tend to become plastic when water is added. The upper part of the earthflow

undergoes a subsiding motion with backward rotation of the downsinking mass, as illustrated in Figure 27.3. The interior and lower parts of the mass move by slow flowage and a toe of extruded flowage material may be formed.

Largest of the earthflows in this area is the Portuguese Bend "landslide" which affected an area of about 400 acres (160 hectares). The total motion over a three-year period was about 70 ft (20 m). Damage to residential and other structures totaled some $10 million. The most interesting observation, from our point of view in assessing the impact of Man on the environment, is that the slide has been attributed by geologists to infiltration of water from cesspools and from irrigation water applied to lawns and gardens. A discharge of over 30,000 gallons (115,000 liters) of water per day from some 150 homes is believed to have sufficiently weakened the shale beneath to start and sustain the flowage.

Mass Wasting in Review

The various forms of mass wasting we have described illustrate very nicely the two faces of the environmental coin. One face is the impact of the natural environmental processes upon Man. An aspect of that impact is the threat to human life when large masses of earth materials are suddenly set in swift motion as mudflows, rockslides, and avalanches. Another aspect is that of economic losses through slow mass movements, such as earthflows, which in many cases cannot be stabilized without spending very large sums of money.

The opposite face of the environmental coin is the activity of Man in inducing mass wasting. We have seen that urbanization activates various forms of mass wasting by disturbing and altering the natural land surface. In particular, highways have suffered repeatedly from severe disruption because the removal of regolith and bedrock to prepare the highway grade produces unstable slopes that were not present under natural conditions.

SCIENCE
SUPPLEMENT
Earthflows Involving Quick Clays

One special form of earthflow has proved to be a major environmental hazard in parts of Norway and Sweden and along the St. Lawrence River and its tributaries in Quebec Province of Canada. In both areas the flowage involves horizontally layered clays, sands, and silts of Pleistocene age that form low, flat-topped terraces adjacent to rivers or lakes. Over a large area, that may be 2000 to 3000 ft (600 to 900 m) across, a layer of silt and sand 20 to 40 ft (6 to 12 m) thick begins to move toward the river, sliding on a layer of soft clay that has spontaneously turned into a near-liquid state. The moving mass also settles downward

and breaks into steplike masses. Carrying along houses or farms, the layer ultimately reaches the river, into which it pours as a great, disordered mass of mud.

The accompanying block diagram, Figure 27.12, shows an earthflow of this type that occurred in 1898 in Quebec, along the Rivière Blanche. Beyond is the scar of a much older earthflow of the same type. The Rivière Blanche earthflow involved about 3.5 million cu yds (3 million cu m) of material and required three to four hours to move into the river through a narrow, bottleneck passage.

Disastrous earthflows have occurred a number of times since the occupation of Quebec by Europeans. A particularly spectacular example was the Nicolet earthflow of 1955 which carried a large chunk of the town into the Nicolet River (Figure 27.13). Fortunately, only three lives

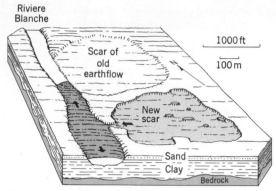

Figure 27.12 Block diagram of the 1898 earthflow near St. Thuribe, Quebec. (After C. F. S. Sharpe [1938] *Landslides and Related Phenomena*, Columbia Univ. Press, New York, p. 51, Figure 7.)

were lost, but the damage to buildings and a bridge ran into the millions of dollars.

Clays that spontaneously change from a solid condition to a near-liquid condition are called **quick clays.** The process is called **spontaneous liquefaction.** A sudden shock or disturbance will often cause a layer of quick clay to begin to liquefy; once begun, the process cannot be stopped. A good example comes from the city of Anchorage, Alaska. Severe ground shaking by the Good Friday Earthquake of 1964 set off the liquefaction of quick clay underlying an extensive flat area, or terrace, that was the site of a housing development. As figure 27.14 shows, clay flowage allowed the overlying sediment layer to subside and to break into blocks, a phenomenon called slumping.

A study of quick clays in North America and Europe has led to an explanation of their strange behavior. The clays are marine glacial deposits, that is, they are sediments laid down in shallow salt-water estuaries during the Pleistocene Epoch. The thin, platelike particles of clay accumulated in a heterogeneous arrangement, often described as a "house-of-cards" structure. There is a very large proportion of water-filled void spaces between clay particles. It is thought that the original salt water saturating the clay acted as an electrolyte to bind the particles together, giving the clay layer strength. Areas where quick clays occur have experienced a crustal uplift since they were laid down, so that the sediment deposit has been raised from immersion in salt water. The salt solution has been gradually replaced by fresh ground water. Now the clay is no longer bound by the electrolyte action and becomes sensitive. A mechanical shock causes the "house-of-cards" structure to collapse. Because a very large volume of water is present (from 45 to 80% water content by volume), the mixture behaves as a liquid, with almost no strength remaining.

Quick clays have been a source of many disastrous earthflows in Norway and Sweden. For example, in 1950, a single earthflow near Gothenburg, Sweden, involved over 100 million cu ft (3 million cu m) of clay. The flowage occurred on level ground, with a grade of only 1% (1 ft drop in 100 ft horizontal distance). Some 30 houses were moved a distance of 450 ft (140 m). The earthflow broke a railroad line, wrecked a highway, and dammed a nearby river. Yet the entire event took less than three minutes! An earlier disaster of record proportions occurred in 1893 near Trondheim, Norway; it involved about 3½ sq mi (9 sq km) of land and moved a distance of about 10 mi (16 km). In a half-hour's time sixteen farms disappeared entirely and 112 persons died.

Because many towns, cities, and farms presently occupy land underlain by quick clays, an environmental hazard exists locally. These areas require identification and mapping, so that urban planning can avoid them, limiting the land use to farming with a dispersed resident population.

Figure 27.13 A portion of the city of Nicolet, Quebec, was carried into the channel of the Nicolet River by an earthflow that occurred in November 1955. The flow moved downvalley *(right),* passing beneath the bridge. (Raymond Drouin.)

Figure 27.14 Slumping and flowage of quick clays resulted in this property destruction at Anchorage, Alaska, Good Friday earthquake of March 27, 1964. (U.S. Army Corps of Engineers.)

Unit 28
Urbanization and Stream Flow

Suburban Flooding — Ripoff of the American Homeowner

The great escape to Suburbia has ended up with entrapment, not freedom, for many American home-owners. After World War II ended, a flood of returning GIs launched the greatest home building boom of all time, lubricated by large, long-term construction loans at low interest rates. Young parents could turn into reality the dream of escaping with their children from the inner city to the countryside, far from decaying slums, deteriorating schools, and street crime. Land developers and building contractors, as always, were eager to oblige, and the carpet of tract houses spread rapidly over farm and forest, hill and dale. The "dale" part is the subject of this essay. Dales are the habitats of small harmless-looking streams, often meandering through a lush belt of green meadow, pleasingly accented by a sprinkling of contented dairy cows. Lush meadow grass needs lots of water, and that fact should have been ample warning to home builders to skip over the valley floors and locate on higher ground. But the land developer buys land where he can, builds houses, sells them, and moves on. Those who move in to stay must reckon with more water than they bargained for.

By the 1960's, environmental impact was catching up with suburban America in many parts of the country. The trouble was that local flooding was inundating streets and homes to an extent never before known. A typical case was Salt Creek, one of those pleasant little streams that once meandered through rich prairie farmlands west of the city of Chicago. On a summer day in 1972, a heavy rainstorm deluged the area, dumping 7 inches of rain in a 24-hour period upon the watershed of Salt Creek. Within hours Salt Creek became a raging torrent, rising over its banks and flooding highways, shop-

ping centers, and hundreds of new homes. Damages were estimated at $25 million.

As this and many other local floodings made their appearance in many widely separated suburban areas of the country, city engineers began to analyze the causes. Studies of storm rainfalls in earlier decades showed that stream flooding was much less severe prior to suburban development. Today, the same magnitude of storm causes the flood peak not only to be much higher than previously but also to arrive more quickly following a rainstorm. The reason for this change is not difficult to discern. Urbanization has profoundly changed the hydrologic characteristics of the land. Street pavements, sidewalks, parking lots, and building roofs—all impervious to rainfall—have replaced an absorbent soil surface. With the aid of storm drains that carry water swiftly and directly to the nearest stream channel, the new watershed is delivering its flow in one great surge. Previously, much of that rainwater was ab-

A resident of an Atlanta, Georgia, suburb retrieves her errant sailboat. It had floated out of the garage during a sudden flood, caused by a five-inch downpour. (Wide World Photos.)

sorbed and temporarily retained by the soil, then passed on gently to the stream over many days' time.

Take the case of the town of Bound Brook, New Jersey. The mayor of Bound Brook, Samuel Patullo, told a *New York Times* reporter that a three-inch rainstorm will now cause flooding in his town at a level that used to require a five-inch rainstorm or larger. An engineer who makes studies for the Army Corps of Engineers in the Philadelphia area told the *Times* reporter: "You're creating flood-prone areas that weren't subject to flooding before. This has happened with Trout Creek near Valley Forge and alongside Chester Creek just outside Chester. Just in the past few years we've had flood problems in both places."

"Land-use planning" is an expression we hear a great deal today. Good land-use planning identifies flood-prone areas and shows them on maps. Using the experience of the past, flood-prone areas are being zoned for uses that can tolerate occasional inundations—for example, a picnic area, a communal vegetable garden, or a playing field. But what of those flood-prone areas already built over in housing tracts? One anonymous planner in northeastern Illinois told the *Times* reporter: "You can't compress water. No matter how good the storm drains and levees are, the water has to go somewhere. We may have reached the point in some places where it will be cheaper, in the long run, to buy out the residents and bulldoze down the houses on the flood plains and let nature have another chance of taking care of herself."

In this study unit, we delve into the hydraulic principles behind sudden floods on on small streams.

Data Source: Seth S. King (1972) Flood perils rise as land is covered by developers, *The New York Times,* October 14.

Interception and Infiltration

To understand how urbanization leads to changes in stream flow, we must investigate certain basic concepts of hydrology. First, we need to understand what happens to precipitation after it reaches the land surface.

Imagine a hillside slope, which has been thoroughly drained of moisture in a period of drought, now subjected to a period of rain. If dense vegetation such as forest is present, much of the rain at the beginning is held in droplets on the leaves and plant stems, a process termed **interception** (Figure 28.1). This water may later be returned directly to the atmosphere by evaporation, and, if the rainfall is brief, little water will reach the ground.

When rain continues to fall beyond the limits of interception and reaches the soil surface, it enters the soil as **infiltration.** Most soil surfaces in their undisturbed, natural states are capable of absorbing completely by infiltration the water from light or moderate rains. Such soils have natural passageways between poorly fitting soil particles as well as larger openings such as earth cracks resulting from soil drying, borings of worms and animals, cavities left from decay of plant roots, or openings made by heaving and collapse of soil as frost crystals alternately grow and melt. A mat of decaying leaves and stems breaks the force of falling drops and helps to keep these openings clear.

Eventually, however, as the soil passages are sealed or obstructed, the infiltration rate drops to a low value. Any excess precipitation now remains on the ground surface, first accumulating in small puddles or pools that occupy natural hollows in the rough ground surface or form behind tiny check dams made by fallen leaves and twigs (Figure 28.1). **Surface detention** is the term applied to the holding of water on a slope by such small natural containers. If the rain continues to fall with sufficient intensity, water then overflows from hollow to hollow to become overland flow, a form of runoff.

Our Science Supplement goes into further detail on the process of infiltration and the factors that cause the rate of infiltration to differ from one region to another.

Stream Flow and Precipitation

By studying the records of stream discharge in relation to precipitation on a given watershed, the hydrologist has developed a set of basic principles applying to the variations in stream discharge with different lengths and intensities of storms and with different sizes of watersheds. (Refer to Unit 14 for explanation of stream flow and watersheds.)

Consider first a very small watershed, just over one acre (0.4 hectare) in area, upon which a heavy rain fell in a

Figure 28.1 Interception, detention, and overland flow.

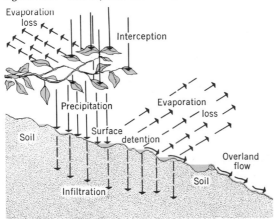

195

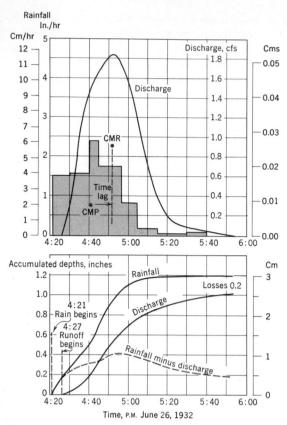

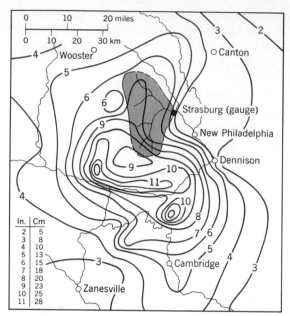

Figure 28.4 Total rainfall in inches from the rainstorm of August 6-7 on the Sugar Creek, Ohio, watershed. (Same data source as Figure 28.3.)

Figure 28.2 Hydrograph of a very small drainage area, about one acre (0.4 hectare), near Hays, Kansas, during a rainstorm in June. (Data of E. E. Foster [1949] *Rainfall and Runoff,* Macmillan, New York, p. 306, Figure 114.)

total period of about an hour. Figure 28.2 is a graph showing what happened to the water from beginning to end of the storm. Rainfall was measured with a rain gauge and is shown in terms of the intensity of rainfall, or quantity falling in each 5 or 10-minute period. Rain began at 4:21 P.M. and was extremely heavy for nearly 40 minutes, after which it let up rapidly and ceased entirely by 5:40. Discharge, measured at the outlet point of the small watershed, is shown in Figure 28.2 by a smooth curve scaled in

cubic feet per second. All of the rain was at first absorbed by the soil or was detained in surface irregularities. About 6 minutes after the rain began, discharge set in and rose rapidly for a half hour, reached the peak just after 4:50, then declined and became zero by 5:50 P.M.

The lower part of Figure 28.2 shows the quantities of rainfall and runoff accumulated from beginning to end. Here both discharge and rainfall are scaled in terms of inches of water depth, so that the values can be directly subtracted. At the end of the storm, about 5:40 P.M., a total of 1.2 in. (3 cm) of rain had fallen, but only about 1 in. (2.5 cm) of water had been disposed of by runoff. This leaves 0.2 in. (0.5 cm) of loss through combined evaporation and infiltration.

An important principle of this water graph, or **hydrograph,** as it is generally called, is that for a small water-

Figure 28.3 Hydrograph of Sugar Creek, Ohio, for four days during and after a heavy rainstorm. (Data from W. G. Hoyt and W. R. Langbein [1955] *Floods,* Princeton Univ. Press, Princeton, N.J., p. 45, Figure 13.)

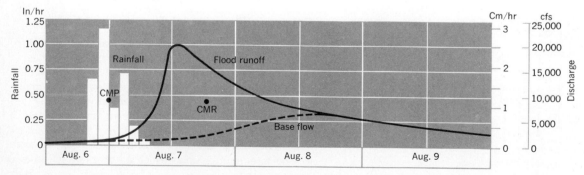

shed, the response of runoff is rapid. Response of runoff to precipitation is stated in terms of the **lag time,** measured as time difference between center of mass of precipitation and center of mass of runoff. In Figure 28.2 these centers of mass are labeled CMP and CMR respectively; the lag time is about 12 minutes. Let us now look at the hydrographs of larger areas over longer periods of time to see the effect of watershed size and storm duration on stream flow.

Figure 28.3 shows the hydrograph of Sugar Creek, Ohio, with a watershed area of 310 sq mi (805 sq km). Sugar Creek basin, a part of the much larger Muskingum River watershed, is outlined in Figure 28.4, a map showing the rainfall during the 12-hour storm of August 6 and 7, 1935, for which the hydrograph was constructed. (The lines on the map are **isohyets.** A single isohyet connects all points having the same depth of rainfall.) Over the area of Sugar Creek, the average total rainfall was 6.3 in. (16 cm) for the entire storm, but the total quantity discharged by Sugar Creek was only 3 in. (7.5 cm). Thus, 3.3 in. (8.5 cm), or more than half of the rainfall, did not leave the watershed as runoff but either percolated down to become part of the soil and ground water or evaporated.

Base Flow

Studying the rainfall and runoff graphs in Figure 28.3, we see that prior to the onset of the storm, Sugar Creek was carrying a small discharge. This was being supplied by the seepage of ground water into the channel and is termed **base flow.** After the heavy rainfall began, several hours elapsed before the stream gauge at the basin mouth began to show a rise in discharge. This time lag indicates that the branching system of channels was acting as a temporary reservoir, receiving inflow more rapidly than it could be passed down the channel system to the stream gauge. The term **channel storage** is applied to runoff delayed in this manner during the early period of a storm.

The peak of flow in Sugar Creek was reached almost 18 hours after the rain began, or about 6 hours after the cessation of rainfall—a vastly greater delay than we observed in the 1-acre plot (Figure 28.2). Lag time, as previously defined, is approximately 18 hrs. (Center of mass of runoff is based on area under runoff curve minus base-flow area.) Observe also that the rate of decline in discharge was much slower than the rate of rise. In general, then, the larger a watershed, the larger is the lag time. Because much rainfall had entered the ground and had reached the water table, a slow but distinct rise is seen in the amount of discharge contributed by base flow.

Flood Stage

The increase in discharge of a stream is accompanied by a rise in level of the water surface against the banks of the channel. The upper limit of the channel can usually be recognized by an abrupt change in the slope of the bank, where it gives way to flat ground of the adjacent **floodplain.** Although the term "flood" is not easy to define, we can say that a **flood** occurs when the rising stream surface overtops the banks and spreads out upon the floodplain. In regions of humid climate a flood occurs about once a year, or every other year, at the season when abundant supplies of water combine with the effects of a high water table to supply more runoff than can be accommodated within the heavily scoured, troughlike channel. Such annual or biennial inundation is considered a flood, even though its occurrence is expected and does not prevent the cultivation of crops after the flood has subsided, nor does it interfere with the growth of dense forests which are widely distributed over low, marshy floodplains in all humid regions of the world.

Still higher discharges of water, those rare and disastrous floods that may occur as infrequently as several decades or longer, inundate ground lying above the floodplain to affect broad steplike expanses of ground known as terraces.

For practical purposes, the National Weather Service, which provides a flood-warning service, designates a particular stage or gauge height at a given place as the **flood stage.** The term implies that a critical level has been reached above which overbank flooding may be expected to set in. Immediately at or below flood stage, the river is described as being in the **bankfull stage,** the flow being contained entirely within the limits of the heavily scoured channel.

The highest elevation reached by the water surface during a flood is called the **flood crest;** it is described both in terms of the surface elevation, or stage, and the time of occurrence at a given gauge location.

Crest-stage Gauging

Stream gauging was described in the Science Supplement of Unit 14. To monitor floods on small streams in suburban areas, large numbers of gauges are needed in a dense network. The gauges must be simple and inexpensive; their purpose is merely to record the highest level of the water surface in a particular flood. The **crest-stage gauge** fulfills these requirements. It consists of a length of pipe containing a wooden staff, as shown in Figure 28.5 The gauge is mounted on the pier of a highway bridge or is anchored in concrete along the stream bank. During a flood, the rising water enters the base of the gauge. Finely ground cork has previously been placed in the bottom of the pipe. As the water rises, it lifts the cork particles. When the water recedes, the particles adhere to the wooden staff, marking the highest point, or maximum stage of the flood. The gauge is opened and examined after the flood is over. The stage height is recorded and the gauge prepared for the next flood.

Flood-frequency Data

Data collected over many years from a crest-stage gauge can be analyzed to determine the probable frequency of flooding of any given height. Figure 28.6 shows a flood-frequency graph for a particular gauge on Salt Creek, west of Chicago, Illinois. The vertical scale on the graph gives

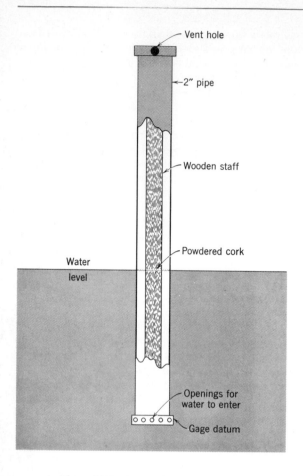

Figure 28.5   A typical crest-stage gauge.

elevation (about 671.5 ft) the recurrence interval is about 8 years. This means that, over a long period of time, floods can be expected to reach or exceed the indicated elevation on an average of once every 8 years. Reading up the sloping line, you will find that the recurrence interval of a flood reaching 672.5 ft is 30 years.

Flood-frequency data indicate the measure of risk of flooding in areas adjacent to a stream. They indicate only the probability, or odds, of flooding at a given elevation, but this information can provide a basis for making decisions as to the use of a given tract of land near the stream.

Hydrologic Effects of Urbanization

Hydrologic characteristics of a watershed are altered in two ways by urbanization. First, an increasing percentage of the surface is rendered impervious to infiltration by construction of roofs, driveways, walks, pavements, and parking lots. It has been estimated that in residential areas, for a lot size of 15,000 sq ft (0.34 acre; 1400 sq m) the impervious area amounts to about 25%, whereas for a lot size of 6000 sq ft it rises to about 80%. As you would anticipate, an increase in proportion of impervious surface reduces infiltration and increases overland flow generally from the urbanized area. In addition to increasing flood peaks during heavy storms, there is a reduction of recharge to the ground water body beneath, and this reduction in turn decreases the base-flow contribution to channels in the area. Thus the full range of stream discharges, from low stages in dry periods to flood stages, is made much greater by urbanization.

A second change caused by urbanization is the introduction of storm sewers that allow storm runoff from paved areas to be taken directly to stream channels for discharge. Runoff travel time to channels is thus shortened at the same time that the proportion of runoff is increased by expansion of impervious surfaces. The two changes together conspire to reduce the lag time, as shown by the schematic hydrographs in Figure 28.7. Figure 28.8 shows

elevation of the flood crest in feet above mean sea level. The horizontal scale gives the **recurrence interval** in years; it represents the probable interval between flood crests of any selected elevation.

The sloping line on the graph is marked to show the elevation of a flood that occurred in October 1954. Reading down to the recurrence scale, you will find that for this

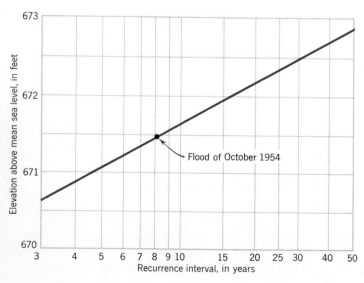

Figure 28.6   Flood-frequency graph for a single gauge on Salt Creek, Illinois.

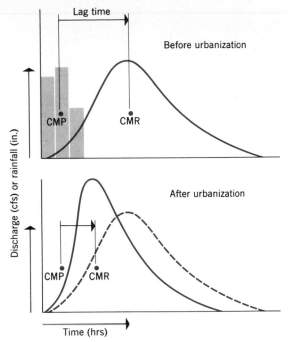

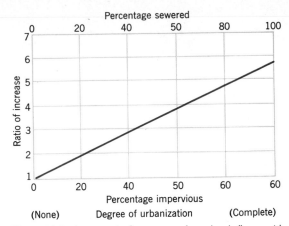

Figure 28.8 Increase in frequency of overbank flows with increase in degree of urbanization. Data are adjusted to a drainage area of 1 square mile. (After L. B. Leopold [1968] U.S. Geological Survey, Circular 554.)

Figure 28.7 Schematic hydrographs showing effect of urbanization as reducing lag time and increasing peak discharge. Points CMP and CMR are centers of mass of rainfall and runoff, respectively, as in Figure 28.3. (After L. B. Leopold [1968] U.S. Geological Survey, Circular 554.)

how combined effect of increase in sewered area and impervious area is to increase the frequency of occurrence of overbank floods as compared with frequency that existed prior to urbanization. The ratio given on the vertical axis is the increase in yearly number of overbank flows based on a drainage area of 1 square mile. Thus, for 50% impervious area and 50% sewered area the number of overbank flows yearly has increased by a factor of about 3½ times.

Increase in flood peaks results in inundation of areas previously above flood limits except during rare flood events. Serious water damage occurs with increased frequency to properties adjacent to the channel. If the stream should be free to adjust its dimensions by deepening and widening its channel to accommodate higher flood peaks there would be a serious problem arising from the resulting load of sediment.

One partial solution to the problem created by storm sewering is to return storm runoff to the ground water body by means of infiltrating basins. This program has been adopted on Long Island, where infiltration rates are high in sandy glacial materials. Another method of disposal of storm runoff is by recharge wells. At Orlando, Florida, storm runoff enters wells that penetrate cavernous limestone. The capacity of the system to absorb runoff without clogging appears to be adequate. In Fresno, California, a large number of gravel-packed wells of 30-in. (76-cm) diameter receive runoff from streets. The system has proved successful in disposing of storm drainage.

SCIENCE SUPPLEMENT

Infiltration Capacity and Land Use

Relationships among precipitation, infiltration, and runoff for a unit area of ground surface are shown in Figure 28.9. We can imagine the soil surface to be a fine sieve that receives rainfall of a given intensity and is capable of transmitting water downward at a given rate. Rainfall intensity is usually stated for short time periods, for example, in./hr, or in./10-min. Infiltration is also stated as depth per unit of time. When rainfall intensity exceeds infiltration rate, the excess water leaves the surface as overland flow.

Overland flow may also be stated in intensity units, as water depth per unit of time. The following equation then applies:

$$P - I = R_o$$
where P is precipitation rate (intensity),
I is infiltration rate,
and R_o is overland flow,

all stated as in./hr, or cm/hr. Evaporation is assumed to be zero during the rainfall period. Obviously infiltration rate will equal precipitation rate until the limit of the infiltration rate, or **infiltration capacity,** is reached.

Now, at the start of a rain that follows a dry spell, the

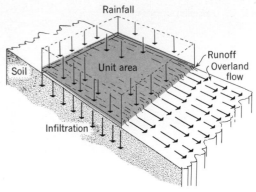

Figure 28.9 Rainfall on a unit area of ground surface is disposed of by infiltration and by runoff as overland flow. (From A. N. Strahler [1971] *The Earth Sciences,* 2nd ed., Harper & Row, New York.)

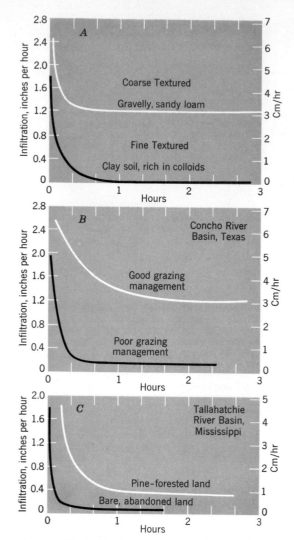

Figure 28.10 Infiltration rates vary greatly according to soil texture and land use. (Data from Sherman and Musgrave; Foster.)

infiltration capacity of a given soil is usually great, but drops rapidly as the rain continues to fall and to soak into the soil. After several hours, the soil's infiltration capacity becomes almost constant. One reason for the high starting value and its rapid drop is that soil openings become clogged rapidly by particles brought from above, or they tend to close up as colloidal clays take up water and swell. From this effect, we can easily reason that a sandy soil with little or no clay will not suffer so great a drop in infiltration capacity but continue to let water through indefinitely at a generous rate. In contrast, a clay-rich soil is quickly sealed to the point that it allows only a very slow rate of infiltration. This principle is illustrated by the graph in Figure 28.10*A*, which shows the infiltration curves of two soils, one sandy, one rich in clay.

A sandy soil may be able to infiltrate even a heavy, long-continued rain without any surface runoff occurring, whereas the clay soil must divert much of the rain into overland flow. Many forms of artificial disturbance of soils tend to decrease the infiltration capacity and to increase the amount of surface runoff (Figure 28.10*B,C*). Cultivation tends to leave the soil exposed so that raindrop impact quickly seals the soil pores. Fires also expose the soil to raindrop impact by destroying the protective vegetation and surface litter. Trampling by livestock will tamp the porous soil into a dense, hard layer. Through farming and

grazing practices, Man has thus radically changed the original proportions of infiltration to runoff. As a result of reduced infiltration, severe erosion damage has occurred in many areas. (More on this subject in Unit 31.)

Unit 29
Floods of Alluvial Rivers–Threat to Man

The Floods of Hurricane Agnes

Disastrous stream floods followed in the wake of a 1972 summer hurricane, Agnes. The storm hit the Florida panhandle with full force on June 19, then progressed northward through Georgia and the Carolinas, becoming greatly weakened. Veering out over the Atlantic Coast off New Jersey on June 22, the storm increased greatly in intensity and then abruptly headed due west into Pennsylvania. Throughout June 23, 24, and 25, Agnes remained in that general area but shifted gradually north into New York State and Ontario before finally moving rapidly out over the North Atlantic on June 27. The storm exhibited amazing rain-making prowess, deluging the northeast in heavy rains that produced flooding on streams large and small. The head of the National Oceanic and Atmospheric Administration termed this event "the most extensive flooding in the country's history."

Rainfall from Hurricane Agnes totaled from 6 to 9 inches over the southern states, but farther north, where the storm's forward motion came almost to a halt for three days, rainfall totals were much greater: Virginia, Maryland, and Delaware received about 14 inches; Pennsylvania and New York received 12 to 18 inches.

At Harrisburg, Pennsylvania's capital, the Susquehanna River crested at 33 feet on the river gauge, which was nearly 16 feet above flood stage. The Ohio River at Pittsburgh reached 11 feet above flood stage. Particularly hard hit were the Susquehanna, Juniata, and Schuylkill rivers and their tributaries. Particularly striking was the flooding of downtown Harrisburg, built on low ground some 20 feet above the normal bank line of the Susquehanna River. The Governor's Mansion (shown in the photograph) and a number of public buildings on the river front were inundated. In the Pennsylvania disaster area alone the losses were estimated as follows:

50 persons dead
250,000 persons driven from their homes
$2 billion in total damages
$1.4 billion to businesses and industry
$120 million in crop losses
$500 million in roadway damages
$50 million losses to schools
150 bridges washed out or made impassable

The lessons of Agnes have been clearly pointed out. Many of the structures damaged or destroyed

Flood water of Hurricane Agnes rose almost to the windowsills of the Governor's Mansion in Harrisburg, Pennsylvania, forcing Governor Shapp to move out. (Wide World Photos.)

were built on strips of flat land adjacent to the stream channels; these areas are known as floodplains. Flood containment structures were not adequate for a flood of this magnitude. These facts were acknowledged by spokesmen of both the U.S. Army Corps of Engineers and the U.S. Geological Survey.

In two study units we will analyze the problem of flooding of rivers that occupy broad, low flood-plains. In this study unit, we will look into river floods as hydrologic events; in the following unit, we will review engineering measures taken in efforts to contain floods on large rivers.

DATA SOURCE: State climatologists (1972) Hurricane Agnes: the most costly storm, *Weatherwise*, vol. 25, pp. 174-184; The hard-earned lessons of Agnes (1972) *Science News*, vol. 102, pp. 5-6.

River Floods

In our modern day, everyone has seen news-media pictures of major floods on large rivers. Besides loss of life by drowning and property damage by immersion, major floods cause damage by current erosion and by leaving deposits of silt and clay in the flooded areas.

Our topic in this study unit is the nature of floods on large alluvial rivers. An **alluvial river** flows on a very gentle downvalley gradient. The typical alluvial river has sinuous (snakelike) bends, called **alluvial meanders,** and occupies a floodplain. As we explained in the previous unit, the floodplain is a belt of flat land, present on one or both sides of the river channel, and subjected to inundation by overbank flooding annually or biennially.

Landforms of Alluvial River Floodplains

Before launching into an investigation of the hydrology of river floods, it is helpful to know about the surface configuration and landforms of a typical alluvial river floodplain. A block diagram, Figure 29.1 shows these features in exaggerated form.

An alluvial river flows on a thick accumulation of alluvial deposits constructed by the river itself in earlier stages of its activity. These sedimentary deposits, called **alluvium,** consist of clay, silt, sand, or gravel in various layered arrangements. The floodplain is bounded on either side by rising slopes, called **bluffs.**

Dominating the floodplain are the meandering river channel itself and also the abandoned reaches of former channels. An air photograph, Figure 29.2, shows these features nicely. Meanders develop narrow necks, which are cut through, shortening the river course and leaving a meander loop abandoned. This event is called a **cutoff.** It is quickly followed by deposition of silt and sand across the ends of the abandoned channel, producing an **oxbow lake.** The oxbow lake is gradually filled with fine sediment brought in during high floods and with organic matter produced by aquatic plants. Eventually the oxbows are converted into swamps, but they retain their identity indefinitely.

During periods of overbank flooding, when the entire floodplain is inundated, water spreads from the main channel over adjacent floodplain deposits. As the current rapidly slackens, sand and silt are deposited in a zone adjacent to the channel. The result is an accumulation known as a **natural levee.** Between the levees and the bluffs is lower ground, the **backswamp.** Because deposition is heavier closest to the channel and decreases away from the channel, the levee surface slopes away from the channel. Figure 29.3 is a profile across a river channel and its flanking levees. Figure 29.4 shows a river in flood. Notice that the higher ground of the natural levees is revealed by a line of trees on either side of the channel.

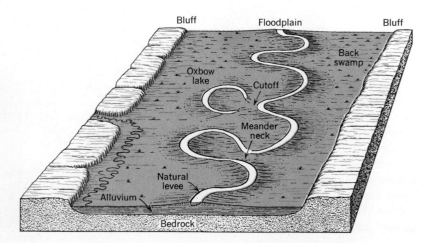

Figure 29.1   Floodplain landforms of an alluvial river.

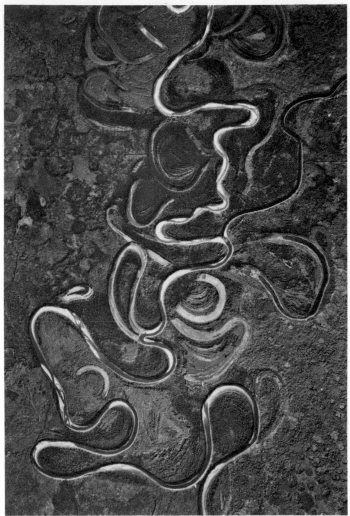

Figure 29.2 This vertical air photograph, taken from an altitude of about 20,000 ft (6100 m), shows meanders, cutoffs, oxbow lakes and swamps, and floodplain of the Hay River, Alberta. (Dept. of Energy, Mines and Resources, Canada.)

Figure 29.4 The Wabash River in flood near Delphi, Indiana, February 1954. An ice dam clogs the river channel, while lines of trees mark the crest of the bordering natural levees. The floodplain itself is inundated on both sides of the channel and reaches to the base of the bluff, at left. (U.P.I. Telephoto.)

River Hydrographs

Building upon the hydrologic concepts from Unit 28, we now examine the hydrograph of a large stream, or river, following the changes in discharge throughout a typical year. Figure 29.5 is a hydrograph of the Chattahoochee River, Georgia, a large river draining a watershed of some 3350 sq mi (8700 sq km), much of it in the humid southern Appalachian Mountains. The sharp, abrupt fluctuations in discharge are produced by surface flow following rain periods one to three days in duration. These are each similar to the hydrograph of Figure 28.3, except that they are here shown much compressed by the time scale.

After each rain period, the discharge falls off rapidly, but if another storm occurs within a few days, the discharge rises to another peak. The enlarged inset graph, showing details of the month of January, shows how this effect occurs. Where a long period intervenes between storms,

Figure 29.3 Profile across the Mississippi River showing the natural levees flanking the channel. Notice the great vertical exaggeration of the profile. (From A. N. Strahler [1971] *The Earth Sciences,* 2nd ed., Harper & Row, New York.)

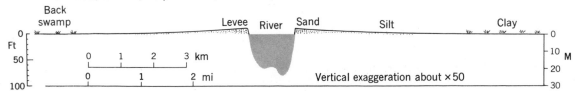

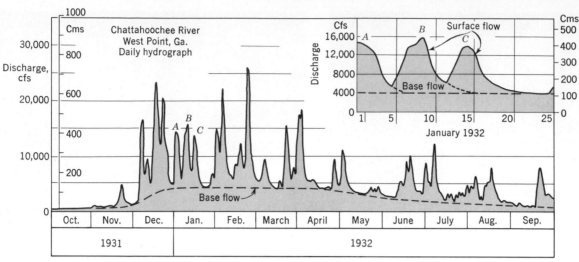

Figure 29.5 Flow peaks of the Chattahoochee River, Georgia. (After E. E. Foster [1949] *Rainfall and Runoff,* Macmillan, New York, p. 303, Figure 111, p. 304, Figure 112.)

the discharge falls to a low value, the base flow, where it levels off. Throughout the year, the base flow, which represents ground-water seepage into the stream, undergoes a marked annual cycle.

During the period of ground-water recharge (winter and early spring), water-table levels are raised and the rate of inflow into streams is increased. For the Chattahoochee River, the rate of base flow during January, February, March, and April holds uniform at about 4000 cfs (110 cms). By early summer the recharge of ground water by downward percolation has largely stopped and the base flow falls steadily. The decline continues through the summer, reaching by the end of October a low of about 1000 cfs (30 cms) supplied entirely from base flow.

Next, examine the hydrograph of the Missouri River at Omaha, Nebraska, from October 1940, to September 1942 (Figure 29.6). This great river, draining 322,800 sq mi (836,000 sq km) of watershed, is a major tributary of the Mississippi River. Notice that the discharge, ranging from 10,000 to over 100,000 cfs (280 to over 3000 cms), is several times greater than the discharge of the Chattahoochee River. High rates of flow are chiefly from snowmelt, which occurs on the High Plains in spring and in the Rocky Mountains headwater areas in early summer.

This source explains flood discharges that may occur from April through June. During midwinter, when soil moisture is frozen and total precipitation is small over the watershed as a whole, the discharge rises little above the base flow. Ground-water recharge occurring in the spring raises summer levels of base flow to about 20,000 cfs (570 cms), or two to three times the winter base flow.

Downstream Progress of a Flood Wave

The rise of a river stage to its maximum height, or crest, followed by a gradual lowering of stage, is termed the **flood wave.** The flood wave is simply a large-sized rise and fall of river discharge of the type we have already analyzed and follows the same principles.

Figure 29.7A shows the downstream progress of a flood on the Chattooga-Savannah river system. In the Chattooga River near Clayton, Georgia, the flood crest was quickly reached—one day after the storm—and quickly subsided. On the Savannah River, 65 mi (105 km) downstream at Calhoun Falls, South Carolina, the flood crest arrived a day later, but the discharge was very much larger because of the larger area of watershed involved. Downstream

Figure 29.6 Hydrograph of the Missouri River at Omaha, Nebraska. (After E. E. Foster [1949] *Rainfall and Runoff,* Macmillan, New York, p. 301.)

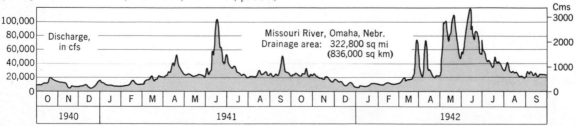

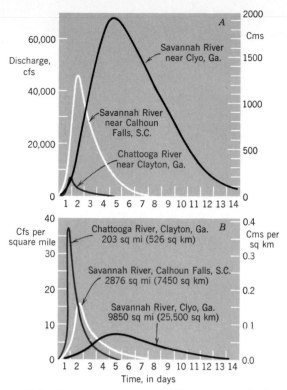

Figure 29.7 Downstream progress of a flood wave on the Savannah River in South Carolina and Georgia. (Data from W. G. Hoyt and W. B. Langbein [1955] *Floods,* Princeton Univ. Press, Princeton, N.J., p. 39, Figure 8.)

another 95 mi (153 km), near Clyo, Georgia, the Savannah River crested five days after the initial storm with a discharge of over 60,000 cfs (170 cms).

This set of three hydrographs shows that (1) the lag time in occurrence of the crest increases downstream, (2) the entire period of rise and fall of flood wave becomes longer downstream, and (3) the discharge increases greatly downstream as watershed area increases.

Figure 29.7B is a somewhat different presentation of the same flood data, in that the discharge is given in terms of a common unit of area, the square mile. This treatment eliminates the effect of increase in discharge downstream and shows us only the shape or form of the flood crest. In other words, the lag time and sharpness of peaking of the flood wave are emphasized without respect to the total discharges involved.

Flood Prediction

The National Weather Service operates a River and Flood Forecasting Service through 85 selected offices located at strategic points along major river systems of the United States. Each office issues river and flood forecasts to the communities within the associated district, which is laid out to cover one or more large watersheds. Flood warnings are publicized by every possible means. Close cooperation is maintained with such agencies as the American Red Cross, the U.S. Army Corps of Engineers, and the U.S. Coast Guard, in order to plan evacuation of threatened areas, and the removal or protection of vulnerable property.

SCIENCE
SUPPLEMENT
Flood-expectancy Graphs

Long and intensive study of river discharge data enables the National Weather Service to prepare graphs of flood stages telling the likelihood of occurrence of given stages of high water for each month of the year. Figure 29.8 shows expectancy graphs for four selected stations. The meaning of the strange-looking bar symbols is explained in the key.

The Mississippi River at Vicksburg illustrates a great river responding largely to spring floods so as to yield a simple annual cycle. The Colorado River at Austin, Texas, is chosen to illustrate a river draining largely semiarid plains. Here, summer floods are produced directly by torrential rains from invading moist tropical air masses. Floods of the late summer and fall are often attributable to tropical

storms (hurricanes) moving inland from the Gulf of Mexico.

The Sacramento River at Red Bluff, California, has a winter flood season when rains are heavy, but a sharp dip to low stages in late summer, which is the very dry period for the California coastal belt.

The flood expectancy graph for the Connecticut River at Hartford shows two seasons of floods. The more reliable is that of early spring, when snowmelt is rapid over the mountainous New England terrain. The great flood of March 1936, which is pictured in Figure 29.9, shows as a sharp peak on the graph. The second season is the fall, when rare but heavy rainstorms, some of hurricane origin, bring exceptional high stages. Thus the exceptional maximum flood stage for the month of September was set by the hurricane of September 21 to 23, 1938, which added an enormous quantity of runoff to channels already carrying bankful flow from heavy rains of September 18 to 20. Note that the data for this graph do not include the June 1972 flood caused by Hurricane Agnes.

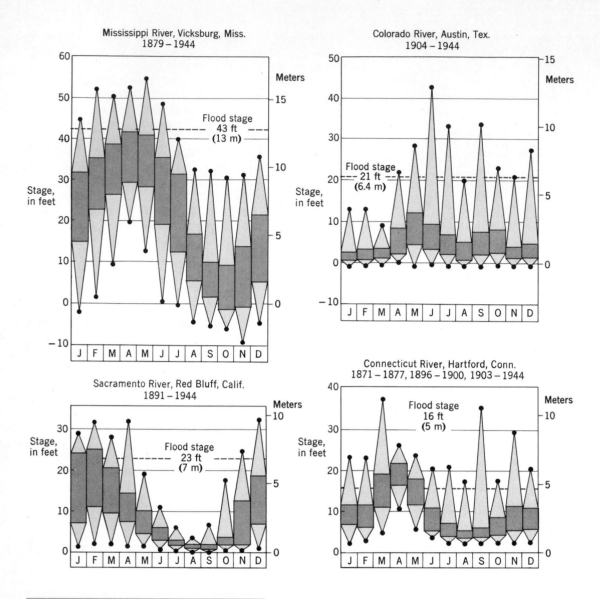

Mississippi River, Vicksburg, Miss.
1879 – 1944

Flood stage
43 ft
(13 m)

Stage, in feet

Colorado River, Austin, Tex.
1904 – 1944

Flood stage
21 ft
(6.4 m)

Stage, in feet

Sacramento River, Red Bluff, Calif.
1891 – 1944

Flood stage
23 ft
(7 m)

Stage, in feet

Connecticut River, Hartford, Conn.
1871 – 1877, 1896 – 1900, 1903 – 1944

Flood stage
16 ft
(5 m)

Stage, in feet

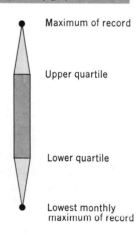

Key to flood expectancy graphs

During 25% of the years of record the maximum monthly stage fell in this range

Maximum of record

Upper quartile

During 50% of the years of record the maximum monthly stage fell in this range

Lower quartile

During 25% of the years of record the maximum monthly stage fell in this range

Lowest monthly maximum of record

Figure 29.8 Flood expectancy graphs for four United States rivers. (After National Weather Service.)

Figure 29.9   The city of Hartford was partly inundated by the great Connecticut River flood of March 1936. The river channel is to the left, its banks marked by a line of trees. (Official Photograph, 8th Photo Section, A.C., U.S. Army.)

Unit 30
River Regulation and Flood Control

Man Against the Mighty Mississippi

Thanks to Mark Twain, the mighty Mississippi River is a golden legend to those of us who spend our lives far from its broad floodplain. For those who live on its banks and floodplain, the Mississippi River is often a vengeful monster, taking particular delight in thwarting the efforts of myriads of humans to keep the water of its great floods within prescribed limits.

The Mississippi River draws its flow from a vast watershed covering or encroaching upon 30 states and with a total area comprising 40% of the contiguous 48 United States. From Cape Girardeau, Missouri, near its junction with the Ohio River, you would travel 1700 miles by riverboat to reach the Gulf of Mexico, but for an airplane the shortest distance would be 600 miles. The sweeping meanders that triple the river's airline distance give the Missis-

sippi much of its character—and many of its problems. In its lower reaches, the river channel averages about one-half mile wide and its average depth is some 40 to 50 feet. But there are many deeply scoured pools, located at the outside of the meander bends, where the bottom lies as much as 100 feet below the river surface, even in its low stages. As a matter of fact, parts of the bed are at an elevation below sea level as far upstream as 460 miles. This phenomenon results in part because the gradient of the river is so very gentle. Even as far upstream as Cairo, Illinois, where the Ohio makes its junction, the surface elevation of the Mississippi is only about 300 feet above sea level. If you divide this figure by the length we mentioned—1700 miles—it appears that the river falls only about two inches per mile, on the average, in that distance.

Both the sinuous course and low gradient of the Mississippi River so conspire to delay the passage of floods down its length that on occasion the river tops its banks and spreads in a broad sheet across the

Men and materials are brought by river steamers to a low point in the levee.

208

Workmen install planks as well as sandbags to hold back the water at low points on the levee.

Too late! The levee has been breached by a great crevasse.

floodplain to inundate backswamps in a belt several miles wide.

The answer to a flooding river seems obvious enough: along both banks, build a wall high enough to retain the highest floods. The building of such embankments—called "levees"—began as early as 1717 in the New Orleans area, then under control of the French. By about 1850, a continuous line of levees followed the river as far upstream as Memphis, Tennessee. As you learned in our last study unit, the Mississippi has natural levees—strips of land higher than the backswamps of the floodplain and parallel to the channel banks. Towns are located on these broad natural levees and the main roads run along them from one landing point to the next. The Man-made levees are merely an upward extension of the natural levees.

When the Mississippi River was in a stage of high water, but not so high as to break through its artificial levees, travelers on board a riverboat at a landing could enjoy the eerie experience of looking across the levee to dry ground many feet lower than the level of the surface of the river on which their boat was floating. Those poor folk living in shanties at the outer base of the levee experienced the even more eerie sensation of having the enormous river bulk lying above the level of their rooftops and only a stone's throw away.

Unhappily, as the Man-made levees grew in height, the confined river reached higher and higher flood crests. The levees never proved to be a total barrier. Here and there, in flood, the river broke out a deep gap in the levee—a crevasse—through which the water rushed in an incredible boiling torrent, quickly flooding the land for miles in all directions.

Undaunted by these mishaps, river engineers continued to raise the levees still higher. In a single year (1882), the river broke through the levee in 284 crevasses to destroy 59 miles of levee by erosion. By 1900 the tide of battle did seem, however, to be turning in favor of the engineers, for the number of crevasses per flood was somewhat reduced. Even so, in the great flood of 1903, shown in the accompanying photographs, the levee crest proved to be too low over much of its length. In Louisiana the levees had to be raised by means of planks and sandbags for a distance of 71 miles to prevent wash-over. River steamers were ordered to run at low speed, for even their bow waves could easily cause the levee to be overtopped. As you can easily appreciate from the photograph, it was nip and tuck all the way. Even so, there were nine crevasses in the 1903 flood.

Looking across boiling current of the wide crevasse to the remaining levee in the distance.

Control of the river engineering program had been in the hands of the Mississippi River Commission since 1879; it was a seven-man body appointed by the President of the United States. The Commission's program eventually became bankrupt, for in 1927 the most disastrous of all Mississippi River floods wreaked havoc with the levee system.

In March 1927, the Mississippi River rose to the highest flood crest on record. Inundation affected 18 million acres of land; thousands of families had to be evacuated from their homes. Deaths attributed to the flood numbered 313 persons; the damage in 1927-dollars was $300 million. At that time, Herbert Hoover was Secretary of Commerce; he was placed in charge of rescue and rehabilitation. In his *Memoirs,* President Hoover described his role in these words:

> For rescue work we took over some 40 river steamers and attached to each of them a flotilla of small boats under the direction of Coast Guardsmen. As the motor boats we could assemble proved insufficient, the sawmills up and down the river made me 1,000 rough boats in ten days. I rented 1,000 outboard motors from the manufacturers which we were to return. . . . We established great towns of tents on the high ground. We built wooden platforms for the tents, laid sewers, put in electric lights, and installed huge kitchens and feeding halls. And each tent-town had a hospital. As the flood receded we rehabilitated the people on their farms and homes, providing tents to the needy and building material, tools, seed, animals, furniture, and what not to start them

going again. We established sanitary measures to put down malaria, typhoid, pellegra and generally prevention of contagious disease, all of which we continued after the flood.

As at this time we all believed in self-help, I financed the operation by three actions. We put on a Red Cross drive by radio from the flood area, and raised $15,000,000. I secured $1,000,000 from the Rockefeller Foundation to finance the after-flood campaign of sanitation to be matched by equal contributions from the counties. We organized a non-profit organization through the United States Chamber of Commerce to provide $10,000,000 of loans at low rates, for rehabilitation, every cent of which was paid back. But those were days when citizens expected to take care of one another in time of disaster and it had not occurred to them that the Federal Government should do it.

Following the 1927 flood, control of the Mississippi River was transferred by Congress into the hands of the U.S. Army Corps of Engineers, where it remains today. In this study unit, we will describe the new program of river control put into practice by the Corps of Engineers.

DATA SOURCE: Robert M. Brown (1906) The protection of the alluvial basin of the Mississippi, *Popular Science Monthly,* September; W. G. Hoyt and W. B. Langbein (1955) *Floods,* Princeton Univ. Press, pp. 370-371; Herbert Hoover (1952) *The Memoirs of Herbert Hoover: 1920–1933,* Macmillan Co., New York. Hoover's statement is reproduced by permission of The Herbert Hoover Foundation.

Man's Use of Floodplains

In the face of repeated disastrous floods along major alluvial rivers, vast sums of money have been spent on a wide variety of engineering measures intended to reduce flood crests and to restrain flood waters within certain specified bounds. In this study unit we will examine the various engineering practices that have been used in attempts to achieve flood control.

In the United States, throughout the past 40 years or so, our policy of flood control has consisted of two phases. One is the **land phase,** based on the concept of retarding runoff over the surfaces of watersheds. This land phase is closely tied in with soil erosion control, the subject of Unit 31. The second aspect of flood control is the **channel phase,** which consists of storage of flood water behind dams and the confinement of flood water to channels or designated sections of floodplain, between dikes and flood walls.

Protection of human life and valuable property has

necessitated engineering measures of floodplain management for many decades. The channel phase, as we have already seen, began well over a century ago and was highly advanced on the lower Mississippi River by the early 1900s. The land phase, on the other hand, gained strength about the time of the Great Depression, in the early and middle 1930s, when soil conservation came to the fore in widespread efforts to save our agricultural soils from destruction.

Both phases of flood control together constitute a **structural approach** to the problem of preventing or alleviating flood damage. An alternative is seen in a **nonstructural approach** to the problem. The nonstructural approach recognizes that floods are a natural phenomenon and that even the most elaborate and costly engineering structures may not prevent flood damage. Nonstructural approaches include zoning the floodplain for uses that can accommodate occasional floods—for example, agricultural use and recreational use—without exorbitant financial loss and danger to human life. Under wise floodplain zoning new urban housing and industry are kept out of flood-prone areas.

Unfortunately, the history of settlement of our nation has been such that flood-prone areas have attracted towns and cities and the industrial plants and highways that go with them. Cheap river transport was, of course, a potent factor in encouraging the early growth of these urban concentrations close to river banks on low floodplain sites. A river not only supplies large amounts of water needed for domestic use and industry, but also serves as a convenient flow system by means of which sewage and industrial wastes can be cheaply disposed of.

Continued urban and industrial development on floodplains of major rivers began to be questioned in the 1930s. In 1937 the *Engineering News-Record* posed this question: "Is it sound economics to let such property be damaged year after year, to rescue and take care of the occupants, to spend millions for their local protection, when a slight shift of location would assure safety?" A new, broader outlook upon the relationship of Man to floods was presented in 1945 by Gilbert White in a treatise titled *Human Adjustment to Floods*. Since that time, geographers have played a leading role in analyzing problems of flood hazards and in suggesting broad policies for Man's adaptation to floods.

The Land-treatment Approach

The land-treatment approach to flood abatement attempts to detain and delay runoff on ground surfaces of watersheds and in the smaller tributary streams. This approach was strongly promoted in connection with soil conservation. Advocates of the approach claimed that floods could be prevented by retaining precipitation on the watershed and allowing it to infiltrate into the soil to be released slowly as base flow to streams. At the time when the land-treatment approach was being promoted, large areas of once-forested watersheds of the eastern United States had been laid bare as cultivated farmland, much of it in steep slopes. Unquestionably, this condition produced high volumes of overland flow from rainstorms with sharply peaked flow curves. In comparison, the same land in its naturally forested state would have yielded its storm runoff on a delayed schedule, with much lower flood peaks.

Experiments conducted by the Tennessee Valley Authority in the 1930s and 1940s showed that reforestation of bare watersheds did indeed greatly reduce the peak discharge of rainstorms and greatly delay the release of water from the watersheds. There was little if any reduction, however, in the total storm discharge. In the judgment of hydrologists who have studied the land-treatment approach, reforestation is ineffective in reducing the large downstream floods that the method was intended to alleviate. This conclusion in no way questions the benefits of land treatment methods in controlling erosion of soil. Major river floods occur when soil is saturated from prolonged, heavy rains or periods of snowmelt. Under these conditions, the small delay achieved by land-treatment methods has little or no effect on the progress of the flood wave or the height of its crest.

Flood-control Reservoirs

The land phase of flood control includes construction of dams to create **flood-control reservoirs.** These structures range greatly in size, from very small dams forming small ponds in the upper reaches of the stream network, to large dams capable of impounding enormous quantities of water. These large dams have gates, which are kept open during times of normal stream flow. When a flood begins to form, the gates are closed and the flood water is stored. The water is gradually released over an extended period of time. Figure 30.1 shows how a flood-storage reservoir in Massachusetts was able to accommodate an entire flood, releasing the flow over a 12-day period at a rate about 12% of the flood peak.

The construction of large flood-control reservoirs began in the United States in the Miami River basin in Ohio, after the occurrence of the disastrous Dayton flood of 1913. A series of storage reservoirs was completed in 1921, and thereafter the construction of flood-control reservoirs became widespread in the United States. Large-capacity reservoirs give substantial protection to downriver floodplains by "decapitating" the flood peak. Large numbers of small, upstream reservoirs also gave an important measure of protection.

In the case of large reservoirs, an extensive area of valley bottom is inundated each time the reservoir is filled. As a result, farm homes and even entire towns must be relocated to safe sites. This disruption in many cases met with strong local opposition. Those who resisted being relocated claimed that a large number of small, upstream reservoirs would be equally useful in flood control, and thus a serious controversy developed.

Flood-storage reservoirs can provide valuable accumulations of water that can be used for urban water supplies as well as for irrigation. Thus many reservoirs are multipurpose in design. Many reservoirs that have been built to provide hydropower and municipal water supplies also provide a substantial benefit in reducing downstream flood peaks.

Figure 30.1 Curves of inflow and outflow from the Knightsville Reservoir, Massachusetts, during a flood in 1948. (After W. G. Hoyt and W. B. Langbein [1955] *Floods*, Princeton Univ. Press, Princeton, N.J., Figure 31, p. 146.)

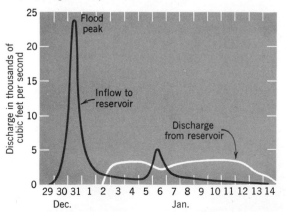

Dikes and Flood Walls

Under the channel phase of flood control, one leading engineering method is the building of embankments to confine a flood within a narrow channel. These structures are called **artificial levees** in the central United States, or **dikes** more generally the world over. Concrete **flood walls** are used in certain urban locations where the river channel is immediately adjacent to a densely built-up area.

Dikes protect the remainder of a floodplain from inundation. Dike-building was practiced for centuries in the Far East, but with a record of repeated failures and the death by drowning and ensuing starvation of uncounted thousands of farmers. For example, dike failures in a great flood on the Hwang Ho River in China in 1887 brought inundation to an area of 50,000 sq mi (130,000 sq km) and death by drowning to approximately one million persons.

Artificial levees of American river floodplains are broad embankments of earth with flat tops and gently sloping sides. In opening paragraphs of this study unit, we described the breaching of an artificial levee to form a **crevasse.** The result is rapid flooding of the low backswamp portion of the floodplain between the natural levees and the bluffs (Figure 30.2). Once flooding has occurred, the levees farther downvalley prevent the water from returning to the main channel after the flood has subsided.

In its natural state, an alluvial river floodplain experiences general flooding approximately annually, when the water in the main channel rises above the natural levee crest. After the flood wave has passed, the water from the backswamps drains back into the river by means of smaller streams that flow downvalley, parallel with the main channel. These parallel streams are prevented from joining the large stream because of the natural levees. At some downvalley point where the main channel is undercutting

the floodplain bluffs, the parallel tributary is forced into a junction with the main channel.

A famous example is the Tallahatchie-Yazoo River system in Mississippi. For a distance of about 175 mi (280 km), this stream flows parallel with the Mississippi River, to make its junction at Vicksburg, where the big river is cutting into the eastern bluffs of the floodplain. Many years ago, a leading geographer selected the Tallahatchie-Yazoo as the typical example of a floodplain stream with its junction deferred far downvalley by the presence of a natural levee; he named it a **yazoo stream.** This quaint term is still widely used. (A yazoo stream is shown in Figure 29.1.)

Flood-diversion Systems

Another means of achieving channel control is to divert part of the flood crest through a prepared sill, or threshold, in an artificial levee. The overflow fills a portion of floodplain set aside for that purpose and limited by a surrounding levee. An example is the New Madrid Floodway, located just south of the junction of the Mississippi and Ohio rivers. In other cases, the diverted water passes between two parallel levees to reach the sea. This latter system is an artificial form of a natural phenomenon of most large alluvial rivers—a **distributary system** of channels that radiate across a fan-shaped alluvial deposit called the **delta.** On the lower Mississippi River, an ancient distributary, now occupied by the Atchafalaya River, has been converted into a flood diversion system. Above New Orleans is the Bonnet Carré Spillway, a broad channel constructed to pass flood water directly into the nearby Lake Pontchartrain. Flow through this spillway protects the city downstream.

Channel improvements

A third means of river regulation is to alter the river channel in such a way that the flood discharge moves downstream more rapidly. In the case of a meandering channel (as most are), the path of the river is straightened by performing artificial cutoffs of individual bends, or of a series of bends. Figure 30.3 shows how this operation was carried out near Greenville, Mississippi. When the channel is straightened in this manner, the length of the channel is also reduced and the average gradient of the river is correspondingly steepened. A steeper gradient results in a higher average velocity of flow, and the river does not rise so high in flood stage as it would if it were following the longer meandering course.

A program of straightening the lower Mississippi River was carried out by the U.S. Army Corps of Engineers between 1933 and 1936. The natural river length of 331 miles was reduced by 116 miles. After straightening, flood crests were not so high as they had been for floods of the same magnitude previous to the program. Meander growth however, is a natural river process and is extremely difficult to prevent. Much of the benefit achieved by straightening operations has since been lost by growth of new bends.

Figure 30.2   This air view, taken in April 1952, shows a break in the artificial levee adjacent to the Missouri River in western Iowa. Water is spilling from the high river level at right to the lower floodplain level at left. (U.S. Dept. of Agriculture.)

Figure 30.3 In the oblique air photograph, looking north, we see three artificial meander cutoffs of the Mississippi River. The photograph was taken in 1937. The diagram below gives the names and dates of each cutoff. White patches in the photograph are sediment plugs blocking the ends of Batchelor Bend, in which the river formerly flowed past the city of Greenville, Mississippi *(lower right)*. (Photograph by War Dept., U.S. Army Corps of Engineers. Diagram from A. N. Strahler [1971] *The Earth Sciences*, 2nd ed., Harper & Row, New York.)

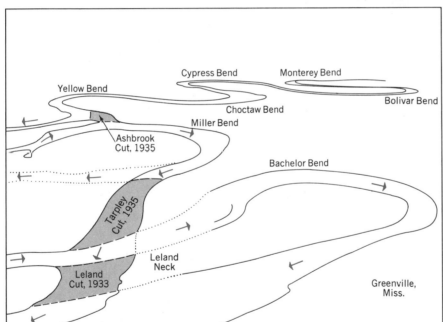

Stream Channelization

Related to flood-regulation as practiced on large alluvial rivers—but on a much reduced scale—is a form of environmental modification applied to smaller streams and their floodplains. Under the general term of **stream channelization,** modification consists of the straightening, widening, and deepening of channels in order to prevent seasonal overbank flooding and to provide permanent drainage to water-saturated bog soils of the floodplain. Meanders are eliminated in the process. Forest is cleared from the floodplain and channel banks. The land thus drained is placed in cultivation.

Stream channelization carried out by the U.S. Depart-

ment of Agriculture, Soil Conservation Service, largely since the mid-1950s, has altered more than 8000 mi (13,000 km) of channelways of smaller streams not affected by flood-regulation activities of the U.S. Army Corps of Engineers. A large area of land has thus been brought under cultivation. On the other hand, economic benefits of increased crop production have been offset in part by economic losses through reductions in local populations of fish and waterfowl. Severe damage or even total destruction of the ecosystem of the natural channel and its adjacent wetlands results from channelization. Increasing awareness of the environmental degradation that accompanies channelization has brought increasing opposition.

Unit 31
Man-induced Soil Erosion

Sheep, Goats, and Fire — Degradation of the Mediterranean Landscape

Lands rimming the Mediterranean Sea draw pilgrims by the thousands to view the wonders of antiquity—or what is left of them. Unwittingly, they are paying homage to those Romans, Carthaginians, Greeks, and Moors who for century after century denuded and degraded the Mediterranean hillsides. The ruined landscape is now a fitting shambles in which to display their ruined temples and baths.

It has not been easy for geographers and historians to reconstruct the Mediterranean landscape of 4000 B.C., a time before the spread of farming cultures westward from the Fertile Crescent to Iberia. The summer-dry Mediterranean climate lends itself to a native vegetation of woodland—an open forest—and grassland. You can see this kind of landscape today in the coastal hills of southern California, where parklike woodlands of evergreen oak with grasses clothe dark brown residual soils. You can also see hillsides and mountainsides clothed in woody shrubs—the chaparral. Forests of oak, often quite dense, favor the north-facing hill slopes that retain moisture; chaparral favors the south-facing hill slopes that become bone-dry under months of the summer sun's direct rays. A surprisingly complete cover of topsoil mantles the lower foothills. Increasingly, irrigated groves of avocados and citrus are now replacing the native chaparral and woodland on these hill slopes.

In contrast to southern California, the hill slopes you will see around you in Italy, Greece, Sicily, Turkey, Lebanon, and Israel seem extraordinarily rocky. Ledges of bedrock and a litter of boulders seem to be everywhere, often marked off into sterile plots by disrupted stone walls. Woody shrubs grow in places; elsewhere, gnarled but productive olive trees sprinkle the hillsides. In a few sheltered spots, groves of Aleppo pines rise sharply above the other plants. In many areas, vineyards cover more favorable hillsides. Moving nimbly over the rocky terrain, goats browse off the miserable patches of shrub. In contrast, many of the valley bottoms have thick accumulations of fine-grained soil, and here one finds the agricultural land of the Mediterranean region. Under irrigation these bottom lands are richly productive of cereal crops—wheat, corn, oats and barley—and citrus fruits.

The impression one receives, by and large, is that whatever soil the Mediterranean hill slopes may once have had is now mostly deposited in the valley bottoms. Those who study the region through history seem generally agreed that extensive deforestation, accompanied by severe soil erosion, has been the history of this landscape from very early times of human occupancy. They point to a number of fac-

Only a goat could find nourishment on this rock-strewn Lebanese hillside. (United Nations.)

214

tors contributing to this prolonged environmental degradation.

The need for wood as fuel seems to have been a potent force in the deforestation of Mediterranean lands. The Romans, wherever they formed colonies throughout their empire, needed wood to heat their baths. Some scholars have attributed severe deforestation directly to this need for large amounts of firewood. (Today we affluent Americans follow a not-so-different course of action, as we consume natural gas and fuel oil in prodigious quantities to heat our swimming pools, spas, and hot tubs.) Also, the Romans mined metals extensively in the Mediterranean lands; their ore smelters needed large supplies of charcoal since coal was not then in use.

As to the grasses and woody shrubs of the Mediterranean lands, sheep and goats seem to have been the principal machines of destruction, aided and abetted by their herders. The story of the sheep is a particularly interesting one in Spain, where sheepraising for wool assumed major importance in the economy from the 13th to the 18th centuries. Organized sheep owners of Spain forced the opening of vast areas of Spain to grazing by herds of Merino sheep. Their activity is said to have been a major factor in destroying the forest and reducing the shrub cover by repeated burning to improve pasture conditions. A similarly destructive role seems to have been played elsewhere by herds of goats and their managers. Annual burning of the shrub cover was carried out to encourage the growth of succulent new vegetation.

Whatever the factors and forces may have been, and in what order and intensity they acted, prolonged destruction of the plant cover by human agencies led to severe soil erosion. While Man-induced soil erosion was also a major form of environmental degradation in other parts of the civilized world—perhaps most strikingly in China—the Mediterranean region stands as a salient example.

Those settlers from western Europe who colonized the eastern fringe of the North American continent did not receive the benefit of any lesson from their neighbors in the Mediterranean lands, for that lesson had not yet been interpreted by students of history and geography. So, in a highly vulnerable environment, the American colonists put on a full-scale, repeat performance of the Mediterranean scenario, compressing the degradation of the forested land of the Piedmont upland into scarcely more than two centuries of intensive cultivation. In this study unit, we investigate the nature of Man-induced soil erosion and its consequences. Both in the United States and the Mediterranean lands, the past few decades have seen major programs of reforestation and erosion control. Much of that is too late, for soil is a nonrenewable natural resource in terms of the life span of a civilization.

DATA SOURCE: Ralph Zon (1920) Forests and human progress, *Geographical Review,* vol. 10, pp. 139-166; Sheldon Judson (1963) Erosion and deposition of Italian stream valleys during historic time, *Science,* vol. 140, pp. 898-899; Charles F. Bennett, Jr., (1975) *Man and Earth Ecosystems,* John Wiley & Sons, New York, Chapter 4.

Fluvial Processes and Landforms

Landforms created by running water are conveniently described as **fluvial landforms** to distinguish them from landforms made by weathering, mass wasting, glacial ice, wind, and waves. Fluvial landforms are shaped by the **fluvial processes** of overland flow and channel flow. Fluvial landforms and fluvial processes dominate the continental land surfaces the world over. Under what are typically prevailing environmental conditions, glacial ice is present only in comparatively small global areas located in the polar zones and in high mountains. Landforms made by wind action occupy only trivially small parts of the continental surfaces; while landforms made by waves and currents must necessarily be restricted to a very narrow contact zone between oceans and continents.

The last statement is not intended to underplay the importance of specialized life habitats of dunes, shorelines, and estuaries. It simply emphasizes the predominance of fluvial landforms as the environment of most terrestrial life and as the major source of Man's food through the practice of agriculture. Almost all lands in crop cultivation and almost all grazing lands have been shaped by fluvial processes. True, those parts of our continent recently emerged from beneath glacial ice—or shaped into active sand dunes in Pleistocene time—may derive their landform shapes from nonfluvial processes, but now they are under the fluvial regime and are undergoing change by fluvial processes.

Volcanic landforms, such as the vast lava fields of the Snake River Plain of Idaho, are also examples of landforms of nonfluvial origin, but, again, they are now being changed by fluvial processes. A good example is the erosional action of the Snake River in its great winding gorge. Fluvial processes carry on the geological activities of erosion, transportation, and deposition. Consequently, there are two major groups of fluvial landforms: erosional landforms and depositional landforms (Figure 31.1). Where rock is eroded away by fluvial agents, valleys are

215

Figure 31.1   Some examples of erosional and depositional landforms.

formed. Between the valleys are ridges, hills, or mountain summits representing unconsumed parts of the landmass. All such landforms shaped by progressive removal of the bedrock mass are designated **erosional landforms.**

Rock and soil fragments that are removed from the parent mass are transported by flowing water and deposited elsewhere to make an entirely different set of surface features, the **depositional landforms.** Figure 31.1 illustrates the two groups of landforms. The ravine, canyon, peak, spur, and col are erosional landforms; the fan, built of rock fragments below the mouth of the ravine, is a depositional landform. The floodplain, built of material transported by a stream, is also a depositional landform.

A depositional landform, once created, may in turn be eroded, with the result that a new generation of erosional landforms is created. An example is shown in Figure 31.1 where the floodplain bluff, an erosional landform, has been carved out of the fan, a depositional landform. Second generation erosional landforms are abundant in regions of fluvial denudation, since fluvial activity tends to proceed in cycles. Typically, a depositional phase alternates with an erosional phase at the same site.

Normal and Accelerated Land Erosion

Fluvial processes begin their action at the divides of drainage basins. Here the input of water into the system is derived from excess precipitation unable to infiltrate the soil surface as fast as it arrives. Overland flow exerts a dragging force over the soil surface. The flowing water picks up particles of mineral matter ranging in size from fine colloidal clay to coarse sand or gravel, depending on the speed of the flow and the degree to which the particles are bound by plant rootlets or held down by a mat of leaves. Added to this solid matter is dissolved mineral matter in the form of ions produced by acid reactions or direct solution. (These substances were explained in Unit 18.)

Slow removal of soil is part of the natural geological process of denudation and is both inevitable and universal. Under stable, natural conditions, the erosion rate in a humid climate is slow enough that a soil with distinct horizons is formed and maintained. This gradual process enables plant communities to maintain themselves in a stable equilibrium. Soil scientists refer to this state of activity as the **geologic norm.**

By contrast, through Man's activities or by rare natural events, the rate of soil erosion may be enormously speeded up to result in a state of **accelerated erosion** in which the fertile upper soil horizons are removed much faster than they can be formed. This rapid erosion comes about most commonly from a forced change in the plant cover and physical state of the ground surface and uppermost soil horizons. Destruction of vegetation by clearing of land for cultivation, or by forest fires, directly causes great changes in the relative proportions of infiltration to runoff. Interception of rain by foliage is ended; protection afforded by a ground cover of fallen leaves and stems is removed. Consequently, the rain falls directly upon the mineral soil.

Direct force of falling drops (Figure 31.2) causes a geyserlike splashing in which soil particles are lifted and then dropped into new positions, a process termed **splash erosion.** A violent rainstorm has the ability to disturb as much as 100 tons of soil per acre (225 metric tons per hectare). On a sloping ground surface, splash erosion tends to shift the soil slowly downhill. A more important effect is to cause the soil surface to become much less able to infiltrate water because the natural soil openings become sealed by particles shifted by raindrop splash. Re-

Figure 31.2   A large raindrop *(above)* lands on a wet soil surface, producing a miniature crater *(below)*. Grains of clay and silt are thrown into the air and the soil surface is disturbed. (Official U.S. Navy photograph.)

*Eroding ability
equation.

duced infiltration permits a much greater proportion of overland flow to occur from rain of given intensity and duration. The depth and velocity of overland flow then increase greatly, intensifying the rate of soil removal.

Another effect of destruction of vegetation is to reduce greatly the resistance of the ground surface to the force of erosion under overland flow. On a slope covered by grass sod, even a deep layer of overland flow causes little soil erosion because the energy of the moving water is dissipated in friction with the grass stems, which are tough and elastic. On a heavily forested slope, countless check dams made by leaves, twigs, roots, and fallen tree trunks take up the force of overland flow. Without such vegetative cover the eroding force is applied directly to the bare soil surface, easily dislodging the grains and sweeping them downslope.

Summarizing these things, we note that the eroding ability of overland flow is directly proportional to the rate of precipitation and length of slope, but inversely proportional to both the infiltration capacity of the soil and the resistance of the surface. (In the Science Supplement of Unit 28, we investigated factors controlling infiltration capacity of various land surfaces.) To complete this equation, we need only to add the effect of the steepness of ground slope. Obviously, the steeper the slope of the ground surface, the faster is the flow and the more intense the erosion. As the slope angle approaches the vertical, however, erosion will become less intense from overland flow because the ground surface intercepts much less of the vertically falling rain.

Sediment Yield

We can get an appreciation of the contrast between normal and accelerated erosion rates by comparing the quantity of sediment derived from cultivated surfaces with that derived from naturally forested or reforested surfaces within a given region in which climate, soil, and topography are fairly uniform.

Sediment yield is a technical term for the quantity of sediment removed by overland flow from a unit area of ground surface in a given unit of time. Sediment yield is usually stated in tons per acre, or metric tons per hectare. Sediment concentration is first determined for water samples of the storm runoff. Then, since the amount of water discharge is also known, the amount of sediment leaving the entire watershed is estimated. Finally, this total quantity can be divided by the surface area to give sediment yield, which is a measure of erosion intensity.

Figure 31.3 gives data of annual average runoff and sediment yield from several types of upland surface in northern Mississippi. Notice that both surface runoff and sediment yield decrease greatly with increasing effectiveness of the protective vegetative cover. Sediment yield from cultivated land undergoing accelerated erosion is over twenty times greater than from pasture and about one thousand times greater than from pine plantation land. The reforested land has a sediment yield rate representing the geologic norm of soil erosion for this region; it is about the same as for mature pine and hardwood forests that have not previously experienced cultivation.

The distinction between normal and accelerated slope erosion applies to regions of humid climate in which forest or prairie grassland are the normal type of plant cover. Even in a semiarid climate the natural plant cover, though sparse and providing rather poor ground cover of plant litter, is strong enough that the geologic norm of erosion can be sustained. In such semiarid environments, however, the sparse grasses and scattered shrubs or trees provide only minimal protection to the soil surface. In these regions the natural equilibrium is highly sensitive to being upset by depletion of the plant cover by fires or by grazing of herds of domesticated animals. These sensitive, marginal environments require cautious use since they lack the potential to recover rapidly from accelerated erosion, once it has set in.

Erosion at a very high rate by overland flow is actually a natural geological process in certain favorable localities in semiarid and arid lands; it takes the form of **badlands.** Two well-known areas of badlands are the Big Badlands of South Dakota, along the White River (Figure 31.4), and the Painted Desert and related areas of northern Arizona (Figure 31.5). These localities are underlain by clay formations that are almost impervious to infiltration of precipitation when in the moist state and are also easily eroded by over-

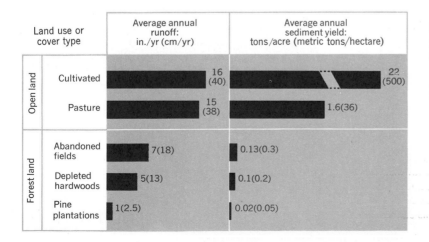

Land use or cover type		Average annual runoff: in./yr (cm/yr)	Average annual sediment yield: tons/acre (metric tons/hectare)
Open land	Cultivated	16 (40)	22 (500)
	Pasture	15 (38)	1.6 (36)
Forest land	Abandoned fields	7 (18)	0.13 (0.3)
	Depleted hardwoods	5 (13)	0.1 (0.2)
	Pine plantations	1 (2.5)	0.02 (0.05)

Figure 31.3 The bar graphs show that both runoff and sediment yield are much greater for open land than for land covered by shrubs and forest. Cultivated land has an enormous sediment yield, as compared with any of the other types. (Data of S. J. Ursic, 1965, Dept. of Agriculture.)

Figure 31.4　Vertical air photograph of an area of one square mile in the Big Badlands of South Dakota. (U.S. Dept. of Agriculture.)

land flow. Erosion rates are too fast to permit plants to take hold and no true soil can develop. A maze of small stream channels is developed and valleyside slopes are very steep. Badlands such as these are self-sustaining and have been in existence at one place or another on continents throughout much of geologic time.

Figure 31.5　Badlands, such as these in the Petrified Forest National Mounument, Arizona, are like miniature mountain topography on bare clay formations. (B. Mears, Jr.)

Forms of Accelerated Soil Erosion

Regions of humid climate—in which the natural plant cover is forest or prairie grasslands—experience accelerated soil erosion when Man expends enough energy to remove the plant cover and keep the land barren by annual cultivation or allows intensive overgrazing and trampling by livestock. With fossil fuels to power machines of plant and soil destruction, Man has easily overwhelmed the restorative forces of nature over vast expanses of continental surfaces. We now turn to consider the consequences of these activities.

When a plot of ground is first cleared of forest and plowed for cultivation, little erosion will occur until the action of rain splash has broken down the soil aggregates and sealed the larger openings. Following this change, overland flow begins to pick up and carry soil particles, a process called **entrainment.** At first the soil is removed in rather uniform thin layers, a process termed **sheet erosion.** Because of seasonal cultivation, the effects of sheet erosion are often little noticed until the upper horizons of the soil are removed or greatly thinned.

Reaching the base of the land slope, where the angle of surface is rapidly reduced to meet the valley bottom, soil particles come to rest and accumulate in a thickening layer of sediment. This type of material is called **colluvium,** or simply **slope wash.** This deposit has a sheetlike distribution and may be little noticed, except where it can be seen that fence posts or tree trunks are being slowly buried.

Material that continues to be carried by overland flow to reach a stream in the valley axis is then carried farther down the valley and may be built up into layers on the valley floor, where it becomes **alluvium,** a word applied generally to any stream-laid deposits.

As used by the agricultural soil scientist, the process of accumulation of colluvium and alluvium constitutes **valley sedimentation.** In many ways, sedimentation at the base of slopes and in valley bottoms is a process equally serious to erosion from the agricultural standpoint, because it often results in burial of soil horizons under relatively infertile, sandy layers and may choke the valleys of small streams, causing the water to flood broadly over the valley bottoms.

Where land slopes are exceptionally steep and runoff from storms is exceptionally heavy, sheet erosion progresses into a more intense activity, that of **rill erosion,** or **rilling** (Figure 31.6), in which innumerable, closely spaced channels, called **shoestring rills,** are scored into the soil and subsoil. If these rills are not destroyed by soil tillage, they may soon begin to integrate into still larger channels, termed **gullies.** This transformation comes about as the more active rills deepen more rapidly than their neighbors and incorporate the adjacent drainage areas. Erosive action thus is concentrated into a few large channels that can deepen into steep-walled, canyonlike trenches whose upper ends grow progressively upslope (Figure 31.7).

Ultimately, a rugged, barren topography, resembling the badland forms of the arid climates, may result from accel-

Figure 31.6 Shoestring rills on a barren slope. (Soil Conservation Service.)

erated soil erosion allowed to proceed unchecked.

The natural soil with its organic matter, nutrients, and its well-developed horizons is a nonrenewable natural resource. The rate of soil formation is extremely slow in comparison with the rate of its destruction when accelerated erosion has set in and is allowed to go unchecked. As a potentially disastrous form of environmental degradation, soil erosion was brought to public attention in the United States decades ago.

Soil-conservation Measures

Major efforts to affect soil-conservation measures were initiated in the late 1920s, in large part through the effective crusading of H. H. Bennett, a pioneer figure in the study of soil erosion. Congress in 1930 established ten erosion experiment stations in which research was begun on ways to control accelerated erosion. By 1933, the Soil Erosion Service had been established as an agency under the Department of the Interior and began demostration projects in erosion control. Then in 1935 the Soil Conservation Service was set up as a permanent bureau under the Department of Agriculture, and an era of revolutionary developments in soil management followed. Although tremendous progress has been made in introducing better land management methods and in creating a general awareness of the need for soil and water conservation practices, a great deal remains to be done to reduce soil losses to the minimum practicable level.

A first step in implementing soil conservation practices is the classification of agricultural and forest lands according to **land capabilities.** The Soil Conservation Service recognizes eight classes of land, ranging from land so nearly level as to be largely immune from excessive erosion (Class I) to land so steep and vulnerable to erosion as to be unsuited to any productive agricultural use. Such surfaces are relegated to wildlife and recreational purposes (Figure 31.8). For intermediate classes, the degree of susceptibility

to erosion is stated in terms of management practices that are a requirement of agricultural use.

A number of common practices effective in soil erosion control are the following: **Contouring** is a general term for plowing, planting, cultivating, and furrowing along the natural contour lines of sloping ground (Figure 31.9). The crop rows or belts, and the minor ridges their cultivation produces, are oriented at right angles to the downslope lines on which overland flow would normally move. Thus, the effect of contouring is to provide increased surface detention that allows greater infiltration. Contouring also creates obstacles that greatly reduce the velocity of downhill flow, which would otherwise be rapid on a smooth slope.

A second practice in soil conservation is that of **crop rotation,** in which a given soil belt is planted in a different crop in each year of a cycle of rotation that includes legumes to increase nitrogen content of the soil, a grass crop to improve tilth (ease of cultivation), and a clean-cultivated crop such as corn or tobacco.

Strip cropping is the planting of different crops side by side in narrow, parallel belts. When practiced as contouring, strip cropping allows the close-growing crops to catch soil particles picked up by runoff from upslope strips of clean-cultivated crops. Strip cropping is also practiced to inhibit soil loss through wind action. **Stubble mulching** is the practice of leaving the base of the plant with its root system intact and allowing plant leaves and stems to remain on the ground. As a result, erosion and soil-moisture evaporation are reduced in the season following harvest.

Terracing, a form of contour development, is the construction of a system of ditches and embankments along the contour so as to direct overland flow on a low-gradient

Figure 31.7 This great gully, eroded into deeply weathered overburden, was typical of certain parts of the Piedmont region of South Carolina and Georgia before remedial measures were applied. (Soil Conservation Service.)

Figure 31.8 Seven out of the eight land capability classes are seen in this single photograph. Class I presents practically no erosion hazard. Classes VII and VIII are steep slopes highly susceptible to damaging erosion. (Soil Conservation Service.)

Figure 31.9 Contour cultivation near Edson, Kansas. Crops are grown in broad contour belts. Shallow terrace channels between crop belts conduct the overland flow on a gentle gradient. Slopes are in Classes II and III. (Soil Conservation Service.)

path to the edges of the field, where it is drained off in controlled runoff channels. Terracing is an ancient agricultural practice that has been carried to elaborate levels of effectiveness in mountain and hill lands of steep slopes throughout southern and eastern Asia. The terraces are nearly flat and are bounded by perpendicular steps constructed as retaining walls. Figure 31.10 shows terracing in a region of China underlain by highly erodible windblown silt (loess). The area had been deeply gullied prior to being reclaimed by terracing.

Gully control follows various practices. Immediate measures consist of construction of check dams that trap sediment. Plantings of vines, grasses, and shrubs can quickly provide a protective cover over the bare gully walls and bottom. A system of permanent dams may be installed and the gully walls and head graded to a lower slope that can be stabilized by grass or other dense-growing plants.

Soil erosion control by the practices listed above also provides an important measure of water conservation (by increased infiltration) and local flood control (by reducing and delaying flow peaks). For this reason, the conservation districts that were laid out by the Department of Agriculture combine soil and water conservation. In our next study unit, we will return to the relationship between these watershed controls and the regulation of stream channels that must receive the water and sediment entrained by overland flow.

Figure 31.10 Deeply eroded wind-blown silt (loess) in Shansi Province, China (lat. 38°N, long. 112°W). Steep slopes have been terraced for cultivation, thereby arresting the extension of gully heads. Nevertheless, this region leads the world in sediment yield. (U.S. Geological Survey.)

Unit 32
Man's Impact on Sediment Load of Rivers

Soil on the Loose in the American Piedmont

Many years ago, a visiting geographer from England, Professor F. Grave Morris, visited the southeastern United States to observe at firsthand the phenomenon of soil erosion he had read about. In 1936, in the company of Professor Carl Sauer, a geographer on the faculty of the University of California at Berkeley, Morris spent about five weeks touring the Piedmont region. The Great Depression was still in full swing and the Civilian Conservation Corps (CCC) was hard at work building check dams and other engineering structures to halt the growth of huge canyonlike gullies that could be seen rending the red soil and regolith of the Piedmont hill slopes. After his return to England, Professor Morris introduced a published account of his findings with these words:

> William Byrd, the Virginian, who helped to run the dividing line between his native state and North Carolina in 1728, gives a vivid description of the River Roanoke at the point where it crosses the state boundary on its way to the sea. "In that place," he writes, "the river is 49 poles wide, and rolls down a crystal stream of very sweet water, insomuch that when there comes to be a great monarch in this part of the world he will cause all the water for his own table to be brought from Roanoke, as the great kings of Persia did theirs from the Nile and Choaspis because the waters of those rivers were light, and not apt to corrupt." Twenty-four years later, in 1752, Bishop Spangenburg, canny and observant German, who was prospecting for the intended settlement of Moravians in North Carolina, entered in his diary concerning some of the upper streams of the Catawba River, "They are crystal clear, so that one can see

the stones on the bottom even where the water is deep." Of the Yadkin he wrote, "The water is clear and delicious." In such terms two observant men describe the rivers of the Piedmont of Virginia and North Carolina in the eighteenth century, before the white man had cleared the forests that then clothed the surface of the land. None could so write of them to-day, unless it were of the tiny head-streams that rise in the Blue Ridge or the Great Smoky Mountains, for, from the moment they enter into settled and cultivated land, they begin to assume a dirty, reddish-brown colour which increases every mile of their course towards the sea until, laden with the precious soil which thus discolours their waters, they deposit their burden upon the ocean floor. Not one stream in all the south-east flows "crystal clear" nor would any king seek to drink their waters.

What Professor Morris was seeing in the turbid stream waters was soil on its way to lower levels. Some of the finest of this sediment reaches the sea, and in times past accumulated in coastal harbors with disastrous effect. For example, Joppatowne and Elk Ridge, both colonial ports along Chesapeake Bay in Maryland, became so choked with sediment that they had to be abandoned.

Studies of soil erosion on the Piedmont upland of Maryland, Virginia, the Carolinas, and Georgia, suggest that since the initial clearing of forests in the 1600s and 1700s, a layer of soil ranging in thickness from 3 to 12 in. (8 to 30 cm) has been eroded from the hill slopes. Locally the thickness has been much greater. There is also clear evidence that much of this sediment has accumulated on valley bottoms and floodplains. Colonial artifacts buried under silt and sand can be seen exposed in many places in the banks of streams. A recent estimate is that about two-thirds of the sediment eroded from hill slopes

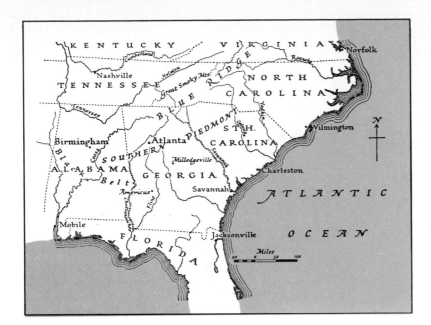

Map of the southern Piedmont upland. (From F. Grave Morris [1937] *Geographical Journal,* vol. 90, p. 370.)

has not yet reached the sea. Instead it is held in valley bottoms. But now that the hillsides are becoming reforested and the sediment supply is diminishing over the region as a whole, the streams are beginning to scour the alluvial deposits, carving new channels and carrying the sediment to coastal estuaries.

In this study unit, we will investigate the way in which streams perform their geological work, and in what ways Man has upset the precarious balances of stream activity.

DATA SOURCE: F. Grave Morris (1937) Soil erosion in southeastern United States, *Geographical Journal,* vol. 90, no. 4, pp. 363-370; John E. Costa (1975) Effects of agriculture on erosion and sedimentation in the Piedmont Province, Maryland, *Geological Society of America, Bulletin,* vol. 86, pp. 1281-1286.

Stream Erosion

Sediment entrained from hill slopes by overland flow eventually reaches a stream channel. We traced the flow paths of water from hill slopes to stream channels in Unit 14, recognizing the converging mechanism of a stream network within a drainage basin. We also investigated the nature of fluid flow within a channel. From purely hydrologic analysis, we now turn to the geological work of streams in erosion, transportation, and deposition.

Stream erosion is the progressive removal of mineral material from the floor and sides of the channel, whether carved in bedrock or alluvium. Streams erode in various ways, depending on the nature of the channel materials and the tools with which the current is armed.

The force of the flowing water alone, exerting impact and a dragging action upon the bed, can erode poorly consolidated alluvial materials such as gravel, sand, silt, and clay, a process termed **hydraulic action.**

Where rock particles carried by the swift current strike against bedrock channel walls, mineral grains and chips of rock are detached. The rolling of cobbles and boulders over the stream bed will further crush and grind smaller grains to produce an assortment of grain sizes. These processes of mechanical wear are combined under the term **abrasion,** which is the principal means of erosion in bedrock too strong to be affected by simple hydraulic action.

Finally, the chemical processes of rock weathering—acid reactions and solutions—are effective in removal of rock from the stream channel; a process called **corrosion.** Effects of corrosion are most marked in limestone, which is a hard rock not easily carved by abrasion, but yielding readily to the action of carbonic acid in solution in the stream water.

The hydraulic action of flood waters is capable of excavating enormous quantities of unconsolidated materials in a short time (Figure 32.1). Not only is the channel greatly deepened in flood, but also the banks are undermined so that large masses of alluvium slump into the river where the particles are quickly separated. This process, known as **bank caving,** is an important source of sediment during high river stages. Bank caving is associated with rapid sidewise shifts in channel position on the outsides of river bends. Typically, an alluvial river occupies a channel carved in alluvium deposited by the river itself in earlier phases of activity. Thus most bank caving represents a recycling of stream-transported materials.

Figure 32.1   This 1898 photograph of the Mississippi River shows bank caving during high water stage near Carruthersville, Missouri. In an attempt to halt bank erosion a large crew of workmen is assembling a mat woven of tree trunks and tied together. When completed, the mat will sink under the weight of boulders. This remarkable activity was largely an exercise in futility. (Photographer not known.)

Stream Transportation and Load

Mineral matter carried by a stream constitutes the **load.** We have already investigated in Unit 18 the load of dissolved solids, consisting of ions in solution which are present in all natural streams. Although the dissolved solids give a slightly increased density to the stream water, their physical effect upon the stream is negligible.

Clay, silt, and sometimes fine sand are carried in **suspension,** that is, held up in the water by the upward elements of flow in turbulent eddies in the stream. This fraction of the transported matter is the **suspended load.** Sand, gravel, and still larger fragments move as **bed load** close to the channel floor by rolling or sliding and an occasional low leap.

The load carried by a stream varies enormously in the total quantity present and the size of the fragments, depending on the discharge and stage of the river. In flood, when high flow velocities are produced in large rivers, the water is turbid with suspended load. Even boulders may be moving over the stream bed, if the channel gradient is steep.

How Channels Change in Flood

We tend to think of a river in flood as changing largely through increase in height of water surface, which causes channel overflow and inundation of the adjoining floodplain. Because of the turbidity of the water we cannot see the changes taking place on the stream bed, but these can be determined by sounding the river depth during stream-gauging measurements (Unit 14).

Figure 32.2 shows how a river channel changes its configuration with rising and falling stages. At first the bed

Figure 32.2   Changes in channel form of the San Juan River near Bluff, Utah, during the progress of a flood. (Based on data of L. B. Leopold and T. Maddock, 1953, U.S. Geological Survey, Professional Paper 252, p. 32, Figure 22.)

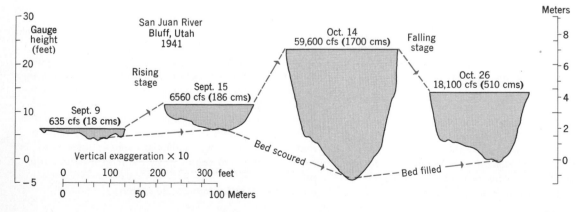
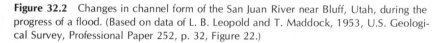

may be built up by large amounts of bed load supplied in the stream during the first phase of heavy runoff. This phase is soon reversed, however, and the bed is actively deepened by scour as stream stage rises. Thus, in the period of highest stage, the river bed is typically at its lowest elevation. When the discharge then starts to decline, the level of the stream surface drops and the bed is built back up by the deposition of bed load. In the example shown in Figure 32.2, about 10 ft (3 m) of thickness of alluvium was **reworked,** that is, moved about in the complete cycle of rising and falling stages. Obviously, each cycle of reworking involves a long distance of downstream transportation of the alluvial material.

Alternate deepening by scour and shallowing by deposition of load are responses to changes in the ability of a stream to transport its load. The maximum load of debris that can be carried by a stream at a given discharge is referred to as the **capacity.** Our Science Supplement develops this concept in detail.

Capacity for bed load increases sharply with the velocity, because the swifter the current the more intense is the turbulence and the stronger is the dragging force upon the bed. Bed-load capacity goes up about as the third to fourth power of the velocity. Thus, if stream velocity is doubled in flood, the capacity to transport bed load is increased from eight to sixteen times. It is small wonder, then, that most of the conspicuous changes in the channel of a stream, such as sidewise shifting of the course, occur in flood stage, with very few important changes occurring in low-water stages.

When the flood crest has passed and the discharge begins to decrease, the capacity of a stream to transport load also declines. Some of the particles that are in motion must thus come to rest on the bed in the form of sand and gravel bars. First the largest boulders and cobblestones will cease to roll, then the pebbles and gravel, then the sand. At even lower velocities, fine sand and silt carried in suspension can no longer be sustained, and settle to the bed. Clay particles continue far downstream with the flood wave. In this way, the stream adjusts to its falling capacity. When restored to low stage, the water may become quite clear, with only a few grains of sand rolling along the bed where the current threads are fastest.

Suspended Sediment Load of Large Rivers

The great rivers of the world show an enormous range in the quantity of suspended sediment load and in sediment yield. Data for seven selected major rivers (Table 32.1) reveal some interesting relationships among load, climate, and land-surface properties.

The Yellow River (Hwang Ho) of China heads the world list in annual suspended sediment load, while its sediment yield is one of the highest known for a large river basin. The explanation lies in a high soil-erosion rate on intensively cultivated upland surfaces of wind-deposited silt (loess) in Shensi and Shansi provinces (see Figure 31.10). Much of the drainage area is in a semiarid climate with dry

TABLE 32.1 Suspended Sediment Loads and Sediment Yields of Selected Large Rivers

River	Drainage Area (thousands of sq mi)	Average Discharge (thousands of cu ft/sec)	Average Annual Sediment Load (thousands of tons)	Average Annual Sediment Yields (tons/sq mi)
Yellow (Hwang Ho), China	280	53	2,100,000	7,500
Ganges, India	370	410	1,600,000	4,000
Colorado, U.S.A.	250	5.5	150,000	1,100
Mississippi, U.S.A.	1,200	630	340,000	280
Amazon, Brazil	2,400	6,400	400,000	170
Congo, Congo	1,500	1,400	71,000	46
Yenisei, U.S.S.R.	950	600	12,000	12
	(sq km × 10³)	(cu m/sec)	(metric tons × 10³)	(metric tons/sq km)
Yellow (Hwang Ho), China	715	1.6	1,900,000	2,600
Ganges, India	960	12	1,500,000	1,400
Colorado, U.S.A.	640	0.17	140,000	380
Mississippi, U.S.A.	3,200	19	310,000	97
Amazon, Brazil	6,100	190	360,000	60
Congo, Congo	4,000	42	65,000	16
Yenisei, U.S.S.R.	2,500	18	11,000	4

SOURCE: J. N. Holeman (1968) ''The Sediment Yield of Major Rivers of the World,'' *Water Resources Research,* vol. 4, no. 4, pp. 737-747.

NOTE: Data rounded to two digits.

winters; vegetation is sparse and the runoff from heavy summer rains entrains a large amount of sediment.

The Ganges River derives its heavy sediment load from steep mountain slopes of the Himalayas and from intensively cultivated lowlands, all subjected to torrential rains of the tropical wet monsoon season. The Colorado River represents an exotic stream, deriving its runoff largely from snowmelt and precipitation on high mountain watersheds of the Rockies, but most of its suspended sediment is from tributaries in the semiarid plateau land through which it passes.

The sediment load of the Mississippi River comes largely from subhumid and semiarid grassland watersheds of its great western tributary, the Missouri River. The Amazon River, a colossus in discharge and basin area, has a very low sediment yield because, like the Congo River, much of its basin lies within a wet equatorial climate where the land surface bears a highly protective rainforest. The Yenisei River of Siberia has a remarkably low sediment load and sediment yield for its vast drainage area, most of which is in the needleleaf forest, or taiga, of the subarctic and high midlatitude zones.

Although it is difficult to assess the importance of Man-induced soil disturbance upon the sediment load of major rivers, most investigators are generally agreed that cultivation has greatly increased the sediment load of rivers of eastern and southeastern Asia, Europe, and North America. The increase due to Man's activities is thought to be greater by a factor of 2½ than the geologic norm for the entire world land area. For the more strongly affected river basins, the factor may be ten or more times larger than the geologic norm.

The sediment load carried by a large river is of considerable importance in planning for construction of large storage dams and in the construction of canal systems for irrigation. Sediment will be trapped in the reservoir behind a dam, eventually filling the entire basin and ending the useful life of the reservoir as a storage body. At the same time, depriving the river of its sediment in the lower course below the dam may cause serious upsets in river activity. Resulting deep scour of the bed and lowering of river level may render irrigation systems inoperable. In designing for canal systems, the forms of artificial channels must be adjusted to the size and quantity of sediment carried by the water, otherwise obstruction by deposition or abnormal scour may follow.

Concept of Equilibrium and the Graded Stream

A stream system, fully developed within its drainage basin of contributing valley-side slopes, has undergone a long period of adjustment of its geometry so that it discharges through the trunk exit not only the surplus water produced by the basin but also the solid load with which the channels are supplied. A purely hydraulic system can operate without a gradient, because accumulated surplus water generates its own surface slope and is capable of flowage on a horizontal surface. The transport of bed load however, requires a gradient. In response to this requirement, a stream channel system has adjusted its gradient to achieve an average steady state of operation, year in and year out, and from decade to decade. In this condition, the stream is referred to as a **graded stream** and is considered to have achieved an **equilibrium** in its state of operation.

As an idealized concept, "an equilibrium condition" means the supply of load furnished a stream from its watershed exactly matches the capacity of the stream for transport. In nature, the balance between stream capacity and load exists only as an average condition over periods of many years. As already explained, streams scour their

Figure 32.3   Longitudinal profiles of the Arkansas and Canadian rivers. The middle and lower parts of the profiles are for the most part smoothly graded, whereas the poorly graded upper parts reflect rock inequalities and glacial modifications within the Rocky Mountains. (From Gannett, U.S. Geological Survey.)

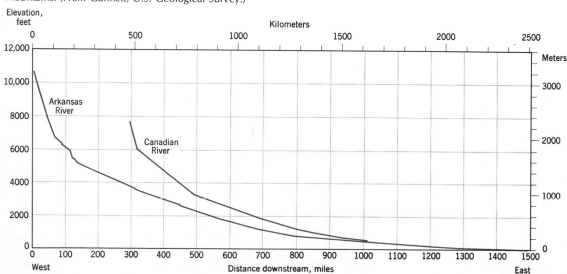

channels in flood and deposit load when in falling stage. Thus, in terms of conditions of the moment, a stream is rarely in equilibrium; but over long periods of time, the graded stream maintains its level by restoring those channel deposits temporarily removed by the excessive energy of flood flows.

Profile of a Graded Stream

The profile of a graded stream, which can also be referred to as an equilibrium profile, can be plotted on a graph of elevation versus distance. When this is done, the profile appears as upwardly concave so that the gradient diminishes from head to mouth (Figure 32.3). The gradient diminishes in the downstream direction because stream efficiency increases as the cross section becomes larger. Given two channels of identical cross-sectional form, the larger channel has proportionately less contact surface in relation to its cross-sectional area than does the smaller stream. As a result, the larger stream expends a smaller proportion of its total energy in friction with the channel. In compensation, the larger stream has adjusted its gradient to a lower value and is able to perform its function of transport of water and load on that lower gradient.

We should not expect the profile of the graded stream to be a smooth curve, since the joining of large tributaries causes abrupt increases in discharge and load from point to point along the main stream. Ideally, at each major junction the profile should show an abrupt decrease in gradient, reflecting the abrupt increase in stream efficiency. In actuality, then, the profile of a graded stream is segmented, with the segments forming a general upward concavity of the total profile.

Another factor tending to a downstream decrease in stream gradient is average particle size of the bed load. When particle size decreases in the downstream direction (as has been measured in many streams), a gentler gradient suffices to carry the finer particles as bed load than is required by an equivalent load of larger particles.

Figure 32.4 The braided stream in the foreground is aggrading the floor of a glacial trough. A shrunken glacier in the distance provides the meltwater and debris, Peters Creek, Chugach Mountains, Alaska. (Photograph by Steve McCutcheon, Alaska Pictorial Service.)

Readjustments of Stream Grade

A graded stream, delicately adjusted to its environment of supply of water and rock waste from upstream sources, is highly sensitive to changes in those controls. Changes in climate and in land surface of the watershed bring changes in discharge and load at downstream points, and these changes in turn require channel readjustments.

Consider first the effect of an increase in bed load beyond the capacity of the stream. At the point on a channel where the excess load is introduced, the coarse sediment accumulates on the stream bed in the form of bars of sand, gravel, and pebbles. These deposits of alluvium raise the elevation of the stream bed, a process called **aggradation.** As more bed materials accumulate the stream channel gradient is increased, and the increased flow velocity enables bed materials to be dragged downstream and spread over the channel floor at progressively more distant downstream reaches. But the building up of the channel

also reduces the channel gradient upstream from the place where excess load is entering, decreasing the stream capacity in that reach. As a result, bed materials accumulate in the upstream direction, as well, and the effects of aggradation progress headward in the system.

Aggradation typically changes the channel cross section from one of narrow and deep form to a wide, shallow cross section. Because bars are continually being formed, the flow is divided into multiple threads and these rejoin and subdivide repeatedly to give a typically **braided channel** (Figure 32.4). The coarse channel deposits spread across the former floodplain, burying fine-textured alluvium with coarse material.

Next, consider the effect of a decrease in bed load upon a graded stream. This change can come about in a number of ways. For example, the reforestation of a region of abandoned farmland would result in less sediment being carried into stream channels. Another example would be the building of a dam, trapping sediment in the reservoir

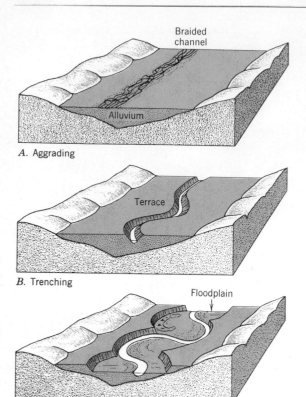

A. Aggrading

B. Trenching

C. Floodplain development

Figure 32.5   Stages in stream trenching and terrace formation. (A) Aggradation by a braided stream has partly filled a valley with alluvium. (B) Trenching leaves a wide alluvial terrace. (C) The graded stream forms a new floodplain by undercutting the terrace.

Aggradation and Sedimentation Induced by Man

With an understanding of the principles of stream aggradation and degradation, it is possible to interpret and predict the impact of Man's activities upon stream channels. The most common and obvious consequence of land disturbance is channel aggradation; it is induced by a variety of activities.

Accelerated soil erosion following cultivation, lumbering, and forest fires is the most widespread source of sediment for valley aggradation. On the other hand, this form of aggradation may be less conspicuous than other forms, since the land disturbance involves only the uppermost soil horizons. The results are typically seen in a gradual accumulation of sandy colluvium and alluvium in the smaller valleys, burying the finer-textured soils and lowering the agricultural quality of the valley bottoms. The silts, clays, and organic particles (humus) suspended in the runoff are carried far down valley to distant sites of deposition. In localities of particularly severe soil erosion, such as that which affected the Piedmont Upland of the southeastern states and was manifested in deep gullying, aggradation was rapid in valley bottoms, inundating the surface with sediment and destroying the surface for productive use (Figure 32.6). Filling of reservoirs by sediment is a major consequence of this type of accelerated valley sedimentation.

Mining operations have been the cause of extreme aggradation of channels in many places. One particularly important example was the consequence of hydraulic mining of gold-bearing gravels in the Sierra Nevada range of California. Along the walls of valleys high in the range are

above the dam and cutting off the supply of load to the stream below the dam. Deprived of much of its bed load, a previously graded stream is no longer in equilibrium. Instead, the stream scours its channel, trenching into the alluvium and lowering the stream profile. This process of profile adjustment, which is the opposite of aggradation, is called **degradation.**

Degradation causes the stream channel to assume a narrow cross section and to develop steep, wall-like banks of alluvium. The process is often referred to as **channel trenching.** After channel trenching has occurred, the former floodplain is no longer subject to annual flooding and becomes a **stream terrace** (Figure 32.5).

After degradation has taken place, the stream will normally attain a new and lower profile of equilibrium. When the new equilibrium is established, the stream channel will usually develop meanders and will shift laterally to carve a new floodplain. As shown in Figure 32.5, the terrace will then be cut away, being replaced by the widening floodplain. Most alluvial valleys show some features of terrace development. In many cases cycles of alternate aggradation and degradation have produced a very complex series of terraces. These reflect the changing response of the stream to climatic changes, often extending back many tens of thousands of years into the Pleistocene Epoch.

Figure 32.6   This thick layer of alluvium has choked the floor of a small valley. The silt and sand were carried by a stream in flood, draining cultivated fields highly susceptible to soil erosion. (Soil Conservation Service, U.S. Dept. of Agriculture.)

thick gravels containing the gold particles. These gravels were carved out by mine operators using powerful water jets. The gravel was passed through sluices to trap the gold. The gravel was then swept into the nearest stream channel and carried downstream. As aggradation extended to channels in the lowlands of the Great Valley, flooding of agricultural lands began to set in and rapidly reached a point that required preventative action. As a result, legislation was passed to regulate hydraulic mining, requiring that the gravel be trapped and retained at the site.

Aggradation of channels has also been a serious form of environmental degradation in coal-mining regions, along with water pollution (acid mine drainage) described in Unit 18. Throughout the Appalachian coal fields, channel aggradation is widespread because of the huge supplies of coarse sediment from mine wastes (Figure 32.7). Strip mining has enormously increased the aggradation of valley bottoms because of the vast surfaces of broken rock available to entrainment by runoff.

Urbanization and highway construction are also major sources of excessive sediment, causing channel aggradation. Major earth-moving projects are involved in creating highway grades and preparing sites for industrial plants and housing developments. While these surfaces are eventually stabilized, they are vulnerable to erosion for periods ranging from months to years. The regrading involved in these projects often diverts overland flow into different flow paths, further upsetting the regimen of streams in the area.

Mining, urbanization, and highway construction not only cause drastic increases in bed load, which cause channel aggradation close to the source, but also increase the suspended load of the same streams. Suspended load travels downstream and is eventually deposited in lakes, reservoirs, and estuaries far from the source areas. This sediment is particularly damaging to the bottom environments of aquatic life. The accumulation of fine sediment reduces the capacity of reservoirs. Sediment fills tidal estuaries so that channels need dredging increasingly.

The yield of sediment from a given strip-mined area is estimated to be, for example, as much as one thousand times larger than from that same land surface left in its natural condition. This ratio is seen in an estimate that in strip-mined areas of Kentucky spoil banks have yielded some 27,000 tons of sediment per square mile in a 4-year period while in the same state undisturbed forested areas have yielded only 25 tons per square mile for a comparable period.

The effect of urbanization upon suspended sediment yield is well illustrated by data from the Baltimore-Washington region, where expanding suburbs are replacing agricultural lands or lands that were previously in agricultural use but have lain abandoned for decades. Portions of the developing area that lie within the Piedmont region are rolling surfaces underlain by thick residual soils and saprolite. The climate is one of ample rainfall (42 in./yr; 110 cm/yr) well-distributed throughout the year, but with high-intensity rains more common in the summer. In wooded rural areas the sediment yield is on the order of 200 to 300 tons/sq mi/yr, while for areas being farmed the

Figure 32.7 A valley bottom in Kentucky choked with coarse debris from a strip mine area. The natural channel has been completely buried under the rising alluvium. (W. M. Spaulding, Jr., Fisheries and Wildlife, U.S. Dept. of the Interior.)

yield is on the order of 500 tons. On abandoned farm lands, the yield has dropped well below the level of cultivated land. In contrast, sediment yield from construction sites for housing developments and industrial parks has been measured as ranging from 1000 to over 100,000 tons/sq mi/yr. The lower figures apply to larger watersheds for which the proportion of disturbed area is small; the high figures to small watersheds largely occupied by the construction site. Sediment concentrations are high in streams throughout the year in this region.

Suspended sediment is a form of water pollution and may make water unfit for use in municipal water supplies and for certain industrial uses. Turbidity of reservoirs and lakes also represents a deterioration of aesthetic qualities of those water bodies with resultant loss of recreational value.

While accelerated sediment production will always be associated with urbanization, much can be done to reduce the concentrations and effects. Regulation includes limitation of duration of bare surfaces to exposure and the immediate application of erosion reduction measures, such as mulching and planting of graded surfaces, and the construction of sedimentation basins to trap coarser sediment.

Effects of Dams on Rivers

Large dams on rivers introduce major side effects into the river channel far upstream and downstream from the dam and its reservoir.

Let us take up first the upstream changes brought about by a large dam. Bed load and most, if not all, of the suspended load brought into the reservoir comes to rest in

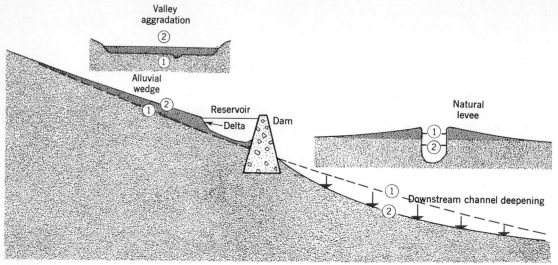

Figure 32.8 Schematic profile and cross sections of a river showing upstream and downstream effects of a dam and reservoir. (From A. N. Strahler [1972] *Planet Earth,* Harper & Row, New York.)

the standing water. This activity is a form of delta-building as explained in Unit 36. The delta surface constitutes a horizontal extension of the graded stream channel, as illustrated in Figure 32.8. However, because a gradient is required to move bed load across the deposit, aggradation accompanies lengthening of the channel. The aggradation is propagated upstream as a thickening wedge of coarse alluvium, which buries fine-grained floodplain deposits.

A possible example is the valley of the Rio Grande, upstream from the Elephant Butte Reservoir in New Mexico. In a 30-year period after completion of the reservoir aggradation had reached a thickness of 10 ft (3 m) at the head of the reservoir. The village of San Marcial was literally buried in these deposits. At the city of Albuquerque, 100 mi (160 km) upstream from the reservoir, aggradation in the same period had reached a depth of 4 ft (1.2 m). The process can be expected to continue indefinitely, since the delta deposit in the reservoir will continue to be extended. Continual upbuilding of the channel must accompany this extension in order to maintain a gradient on which to transport the load. Not all experts agree that aggradation of the Rio Grande is entirely the result of dams; for, aggradation of the channel was in progress at San Marcial for two decades prior to the filling of the reservoir. This sediment came in large part from tributaries heading in areas then experiencing accelerated erosion. The stated effects of the dam are thus not clearly established.

In the downstream direction, another set of changes takes place. Below a large storage dam, water without load is released in a large, but controlled discharge. This clear water flows out over a channel previously adjusted for the transport of a large quantity of coarse bed load. To satisfy its capacity for bed material, the stream scours its bed and lowers the channel to a new gradient.

Changes on the lower Colorado River, following construction of Hoover Dam, illustrate the kinds of changes that can be anticipated. Since the dam was completed in 1936, flow has been regulated so that a substantial flow occurs throughout the winter, which is normally a period of low flow, but flood flows are eliminated. Changes quickly began to occur along a 100-mi (160-km) stretch of channel between Hoover Dam and Parker Dam. Scour of the channel was vigorous, removing bed material and lowering the channel until there remained only a layer of boulders too large to be moved. This phenomenon is known to engineers as **armoring.**

As the small diagram in Figure 32.8 shows, one effect of lowering of the channel is to cause channel trenching where a floodplain is present. Because the Colorado River surface is now well below the top of its natural levees, an irrigation system previously using gravity flow was rendered unworkable and required that a costly pumping system be installed to lift the water over the levees.

The cutting off of suspended load from the lower Colorado had a marked effect as far downstream as Yuma, some 350 mi (560 km) below Hoover Dam. River depth was increased from 1 to 5 ft (0.3 to 1.5 m), while the stream bed elevation was lowered by about 10 ft (3 m). Width of the channel decreased substantially after dam construction. The decrease in width and increase in depth have been attributed to the fact that no flood stages have been permitted to occur since the dam was put in operation.

Channel degradation below dams has been documented for many streams, with average lowering of the bed on the order of 1 to 2 ft (0.3 to 0.6 m) for such rivers as the Missouri, Red, Canadian, Platte, and Rio Grande.

Capacity, Suspended Load, and Discharge

Stream load is measured in units of mass carried through a given cross section per unit of time. Thus load is stated in terms of tons (English or metric) per day or per year. The maximum load of sediment that can be carried by a stream at a given discharge is referred to as **capacity for load.** Because the stream load is carried both as bed load and as suspended load, two measures of stream capacity can be recognized: **bed-load capacity** and **suspended-load capacity.** In an alluvial river, there is an abundant source of both forms of load in the channel floor and banks. As river stage rises, flow velocity increases, and more sediment is entrained by channel scour and bank caving. Thus the capacity of the river to transport load can usually be fulfilled in all stages.

Because both velocity and turbulence of a stream increase greatly as its depth and discharge increase in flood stage, most of the sediment transport takes place in high stages. Figure 32.9 gives an example of the increase in suspended load with discharge, as measured at a single gauging station. The scales are logarithmic and show that the load in flood stage may be over 10,000 times as great as in the lowest stages. The line fitted to the plotted points shows that a 10-fold increase in discharge brings a 100-fold increase in suspended load. This load may be derived from overland flow on the watershed surfaces during heavy rains, or from bank erosion.

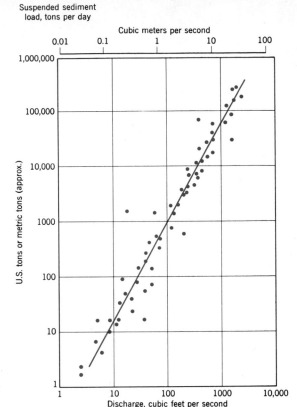

Figure 32.9 Increase of suspended sediment load with increase in discharge. Data are for the Powder River, Arvada, Wyoming. (After L. B. Leopold and T. Maddock [1953] U.S. Geological Survey, Professional Paper 252.)

Unit 33
Alluvial Fans and Ground Water

The Qanats of Iran

Most of the great wonders of antiquity are huge masses of masonry built high above the ground—the Pyramids of Egypt, the Tower of Babel, the Colosseum of Rome, and the like. Almost as fantastic are ancient irrigation systems of shafts and tunnels burrowed deep into the ground by human moles. These features are the *qanats* of Iran, and they are still in use today.

A qanat is essentially an underground aqueduct, ingeniously devised and executed so as to conduct water under many miles of sloping plain from a high ground-water source to distant fields and towns. The setting for the system is a sloping body of alluvium called an alluvial fan. It is a wedge of gravel and sand lying at the foot of a mountain slope. The alluvial wedge has been built over tens of thousands of years by a mountain stream emerging from a canyon mouth. The wedge consists of the load of debris carried by the stream in flood and spread out upon the land surface at the foot of the mountain range.

Stream flow from winter rainfall and snowmelt percolates into the coarse debris at the head of the alluvial wedge, or fan, and recharges a ground-water aquifer in the sand and gravel beneath. Typically, in the structure of such fans, a silt layer lies beneath the aquifer, impeding the downward flow of ground water, which instead moves slowly toward lower levels away from the mountain area.

The qanat features a tunnel, pitched on a very low gradient, tapping the ground water aquifer near its upper limit, or head. Ground water seeps into the upper end of the tunnel and is conducted to the lower end, where it emerges in an irrigation canal. Qanats are constructed entirely with hand labor, using methods little changed for perhaps as long as three thousand years. The project begins with digging of a head well. Using a mattock and a spade, two men excavate a shaft about three feet in diameter. The earth is lifted to the surface in leather buckets by a primitive windlass. When the shaft has reached a point where an adequate water seepage occurs, tunnel excavation is begun, starting at the lower end, or exit, and working up a gradual grade toward the head well. At intervals of perhaps 50 yards, a vertical ventilation shaft is dug. If weak earth is encountered and threatens to cause a tunnel collapse, elliptical sections of tile are installed to form a lined tunnel. Otherwise, there is no artificial support to the tunnel ceilings and walls, which are evidently quite stable in hard clay or well-packed coarse gravels. A single tunnel is typically from one to 10 miles long.

Using a crude windlass and leather buckets, a work crew lifts accumulated silt from the water conduit of the qanat below. The child, at right, is needed on this job because the ventilation shaft is too small to admit a grown man. (Photograph by Lockland.)

232

This line of earth-rimmed holes marks the position of a subterranean qanat. Each hole is a shaft by means of which the water-conducting tunnel can be cleaned of debris. (Patrick Morin, FAO.)

The chain of ventilation shafts makes a curious pattern when seen from the air—something like a chain of bomb craters. Rims of earth built around the openings serve to keep out surface water and sediment during times of local flooding. These shafts are used to clean and maintain the tunnel.

Statistics about the Iranian qanats seem almost unbelievable. There are about 22,000 qanats in the country, their total length is about 170,000 miles. They deliver a total volume of flow of about 20,000 cubic feet per second, which is about 75% as large as the flow of the lower Euphrates River. The total water flow of the qanats of Iran is capable of irrigating 3 million acres of land. Until recently, the qanats furnished about 75% of the Iranian water supply. Even the city of Tehran, with one million inhabitants, formerly depended upon a qanat system fed by runoff from the high Elbruz Mountains.

Perhaps the most remarkable feature of the qanats is their antiquity. The system first began to be developed 3000 years ago. Records show that an Assyrian king, Sargon II, while campaigning in Persia in the seventh century B.C., came upon a qanat system. The Persians donated the idea to Egypt about 500 B.C. and a qanat system was later built in Egypt. Use of qanats spread into the Indus valley, Turkestan, Iraq, Syria, Arabia, and Yemen, then was carried by the Arabs westward across North Africa and even into Spain and Sicily. None of these systems persisted into the modern era.

In this study unit, we will investigate the alluvial fans of arid regions. Today, ground water derived from alluvial fans is a major source of water in the southwestern United States.

DATA SOURCE: H. E. Wulff (1968) The qanats of Iran, *Scientific American*, vol. 218, no. 4.

Fluvial Processes in Arid Environments

Much of the world's land surface lies in an arid climate. Here, annual evaporation greatly outweighs precipitation. Surplus water is generally not available over upland surfaces for percolation to a ground-water body, and consequently streams are not fed by base flow. Stream channels are therefore normally dry except when fed by direct surface flow immediately following high-intensity rainstorms. (These streams are described as **ephemeral**.) Yet, on such occasions overland flow can entrain much debris and can fill channels to bankfull stage with a raging torrent. On steep gradients these desert floods perform a great deal of erosion and transportation in a short period of flow.

Furthermore, desert precipitation, being largely from convection cells, is highly localized. A torrential rain in one small watershed may be entirely lacking in another watershed a mile or two distant. Added to this localization of precipitation is the orographic effect, in which mountain ranges promote convection and trap copious rainfall in contrast to low-lying, intermontane basins and plains.

Channel flow derived from mountain watersheds typically decreases downstream through direct evaporation and the infiltration of water into highly permeable beds of coarse alluvium.

The desert stream is typically **influent,** losing discharge by percolation; whereas the stream of humid lands is typically **effluent,** gaining discharge by base flow (Figure 33.1). In alluvial basins of arid lands, a ground-water body is built up and recharged by influent streams deriving flow from mountain watershed. A water-table mound forms beneath the channel. Ground-water reserves of alluvial basins of California and Arizona, referred to in Unit 19, are of this type.

Alluvial Fans

The combination of stream flow issuing from mountain canyons and carrying a heavy load of coarse debris, together with the loss of discharge through evaporation and influent seepage, causes the growth of a distinctive landform, the **alluvial fan** (Figure 33.2). As stream capacity is reduced by diminishing discharge, the stream aggrades its

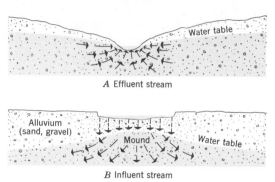

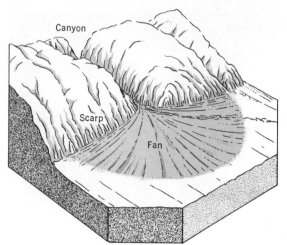

Figure 33.1 Effluent and influent streams. (From A. N. Strahler [1971] *The Earth Sciences,* 2nd ed., Harper & Row, New York.)

Figure 33.2 A simple alluvial fan.

Figure 33.3 A great alluvial fan in Death Valley, built of debris swept out of a large canyon. Notice that the main stream issuing from the canyon has regraded its profile to a lower gradient, trenched the head of the fan, and begun simultaneously to build newer alluvial deposits *(lower left).* Older remnant fan surfaces are being eroded by many narrow, subparallel streams. (Spence Air Photos.)

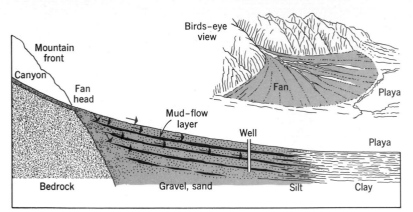

Figure 33.4 Idealized cross section of a complex alluvial fan showing the movement of ground water from fan head through aquifers of gravel and sand. (From A. N. Strahler [1972] *Planet Earth*, Harper & Row, New York.)

channel after it emerges from the canyon. Aggradation in turn causes sidewise shifting of the braided channel, but the narrow canyon mouth, lined with resistant bedrock, acts as a fixed point on the channel. As a result, the shifting braided stream sweeps in a radial manner and builds a conical deposit of alluvium.

Because the larger particles of the bed load come to rest first, while the finer ones travel further, the fan shows a size gradation from coarse to fine, and a decrease in gradient, from the fan apex to its outer periphery. Over long periods of time, where great mountain blocks rise high above low basins, large and complex alluvial fans have accumulated and may have radii several miles long (Figure 33.3).

Complex desert fans also include **mudflows,** mud

streams which are interbedded with the channel deposits (Figure 27.6). As a result, the structure of such a fan is favorable to the accumulation of ground water under artesian pressure (Figure 33.4). Water infiltrating the fan apex makes its way down the inclined alluvial beds, which are the aquifers in the system, and is held under pressure under mudflow layers, which are the aquicludes.

Alluvial fans are the dominant class of ground-water reservoirs in the southwestern United States. Sustained heavy pumping of these reserves for irrigation has lowered the water table severely in many fan areas (Unit 19). Rate of recharge is extremely slow in comparison. Efforts are being made, however, to increase this recharge by means of waterspreading structures and infiltrating basins on the fan surfaces.

Unit 34
Wave Action and Coastal Change

The Highland Light of Cape Cod

Henry David Thoreau, the naturalist, described it in 1855 in these words: "This light-house, known to mariners as the Cape Cod or Highland Light, is one of our primary sea-coast lights, . . . and is usually the first seen by those approaching the entrance of Massachusetts Bay from Europe. It stands about twenty rods from the edge of the bank, which is here formed of clay." The bank to which Thoreau refers rises about 130 feet above the ocean level. He goes on to say, "The mixed sand and clay lay at an angle of forty-degrees with the horizon, where I measured it, but the clay is generally much steeper. No cow or hen ever gets down it."

Thoreau's account of the rapid wearing back of the great bank on which the Highland Light is built is one of the first of which we have a written record. These are Thoreau's words:*

According to the light-house keeper, the Cape is wasting here on both sides, though most on the eastern. In some places it had lost many rods within the last year, and, erelong, the light-house must be moved. We calculated, *from his data,* how soon the Cape would be quite worn away at this point, "for," said he, "I can remember sixty years back." We were even more surprised at this last announcement,—that is, at the slow waste of life and energy in our informant, for we had taken him to be not more than forty,—than at the rapid wasting of the Cape, and we thought that he stood a fair chance to outlive the former. Between this October and June of the next year I found that the bank had lost about forty feet in one place, opposite the light-house, and it was cracked more than forty feet farther from the edge at the last date, the shore being strewn with the recent rubbish. I judged that generally it was not wearing away here at the rate of more than six feet annually. One old inhabitant told us that when the light-house was built, in 1789, it was calculated that it would stand forty-five years, allowing the bank to waste one length of fence each year, "but," said

The Highland Light of Cape Cod.
(A. N. Strahler.)

236

The Nauset Light *(far right),* and parking lot *(far left).* (Harold L. R. Cooper, Cape Cod Photos.)

he, "there it is (or rather another near the same site) about twenty rods from the edge of the bank."

In 1889, an investigator for the U.S. Coast and Geodetic Survey undertook to measure the rate at which the outer coastline of Cape Cod is being eroded back. Over a 40-year period the average distance of retreat was about 3½ feet per year along a coastline some 15 miles long. The report stated that about 32 million cubic yards of sand and clay had disappeared: "This volume can best be understood by supposing it deposited on the 55 acres included within the Capitol Grounds in Washington, D.C., which it would cover to a depth of 375 feet—in other words, the statue of Freedom on the dome of the Capitol would be buried to a depth of 67 feet."

*From Henry D. Thoreau, *Cape Cod,* © 1961 by Thomas Y. Crowell Company, New York, pp. 174-176.

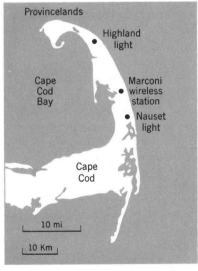

The forearm of Cape Cod.

An April nor'easter eating away the arm of Cape Cod. Coast Guard Beach, Eastham. (Harold L. R. Cooper, Cape Cod Photos.)

Another Cape Cod lighthouse has fared equally poorly in contest with the hungry waves of Atlantic nor'easters. It is the Nauset Light, some 14 miles south of the Highland Light. The bank here is made up mostly of loose sand and is about 70 feet high. The accompanying photograph shows the present lighthouse. Three previous lighthouses in succession were dismantled as the eroding bank moved relentlessly inland. It is said that the construction materials of those threatened wooden towers were pulled apart by residents and incorporated into nearby summer homes. The parking lot that you see in the photograph is now more than half gone; slabs of asphalt paving can now be seen sliding down the sand slope into the sea.

If you go to visit the site of Marconi's first transatlantic wireless station (midway between the two lighthouses), you will find remaining only two of the four massive concrete blocks on which the four corners of his steel tower rested. The outer two blocks have long since slid down the steep sandbank to the beach below.

Today, all of the high outer bank of Cape Cod lies within the Cape Cod National Seashore. For several years, National Park Service managers tried to halt erosion of the bank where it was threatening to undermine parking lots and buildings. They tried dumping over the bank blocks of concrete from old gun platforms at nearby abandoned Camp Wellfleet. Even streetsweepers from nearby towns emptied their contents at low points near the bank. The program was an exercise in futility. After due consideration, based upon a study by the Corps of Engineers, park officials decided to let the waves have their way. The park would simply have to abandon or move back its buildings and parking lots. This is now the official National Parks policy on shore properties. After all, shouldn't nature be allowed to do what comes naturally in parklands dedicated to the preservation of a natural environment?

DATA SOURCE: Barbara B. Chamberlain (1964) *These Fragile Outposts,* The Natural History Press, Garden City, New York, pp. 259–263; Arthur N. Strahler (1966) *A Geologist's View of Cape Cod,* The Natural History Press, Garden City, N.Y., pp. 39–45.

Shorelines and Coasts

As in the case of the fluvial systems on the lands, Man is a potent agent of change in coastal environments maintained by action of waves, currents, and tides. Armed with powerful machines run by fossil fuels, Man can make radical alterations in the landforms of shorelines and estuaries. Certain of these natural environments are maintained in a stable state by a very delicate balance of forces and can easily be disrupted, with severe impact upon their ecosystems. We shall want to investigate these sensitive areas where environmental changes have occurred. Yet Man's role in implementing changes must be distinguished clearly from similar natural changes that have taken place repeatedly in the past as responses to fluctuations in climatic and hydrologic controls. To make such assessment, we need a good working knowledge of fundamental principles of wave action and tides.

First, however, let us agree on the meaning of two important terms: shoreline and coast. The **shoreline** is the line of contact of water surface with the land. Because this line fluctuates constantly with the changing water level of breaking waves and tides, we need to expand the term

to include the entire surface over which the water line sweeps; this surface is the **shore** or **shore zone.** The **coast** is a zone that includes not only the shore, but also a shallow water zone adjoining it and a belt of land above the limit of water action that is influenced by marine processes. Consequently, cliffs and dunes bordering the shore are part of the coast.

Waves in Deep Water

Waves of the ocean and lakes are generated by winds. Energy is transferred from the atmosphere to the water surface by a rather complex mechanism involving both friction of the moving air on the water surface and direct wind pressure.

Figure 34.2 Orbital motion in deep-water waves of relatively low height.

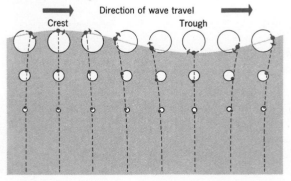

Figure 34.1 Terminology of water waves.

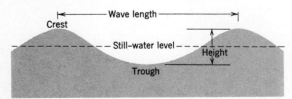

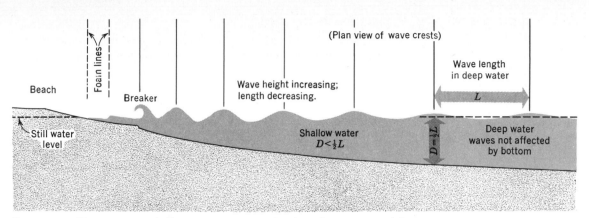

Figure 34.3 Waves entering shallow water increase in height and steepness until the breaking point is reached.

Wind-generated ocean waves belong to a type known as **oscillatory waves,** because the wave form travels through the water and causes an oscillatory water motion. A simple terminology applied to waves is illustrated in Figure 34.1. **Wave height** is the vertical distance between **trough** and **crest. Wavelength** is the horizontal distance from trough to trough, or crest to crest.

In the oscillatory wave, a tiny particle, such as a drop of water or a small floating object, completes one vertical circle, or **orbit,** with the passage of each wave length (Figure 34.2). Particles move forward on the wave crest, backward in the wave trough. At the sea surface, the orbit is of the same diameter as the wave height, but dies out rapidly with depth. The water particles return to the same starting point at the completion of each orbit. In ideal waves of this type there is no net motion of water in the direction of the wind.

Shoaling Waves and Breakers

Most shore zones have a fairly smooth, sloping bottom extending offshore into deeper water. As a train of waves enters progressively shallower water depths, there comes a point at which the orbital motion of the waves encounters interference with the bottom. As a general rule, this critical depth is about equal to one half of the wave length (Figure 34.3).

As the waves continue to travel shoreward, the wavelength decreases, while the wave height increases, as shown in Figure 34.3 Consequently, the wave is steepened, and becomes unstable. Rather suddenly the

crest of the wave moves forward, and the wave is transformed into a **breaker,** which then collapses (Figure 34.4). The turbulent water mass then rides up the beach as the **swash,** or **uprush.** This powerful surge causes a landward movement of sand and gravel on the beach. When the force of the swash has been spent against the slope of the beach, the return flow, or **backwash,** pours down the beach, but much of the water disappears by infiltration into the porous beach sand. Sand and gravel are swept seaward by the backwash.

Marine Erosion

The forward thrust of water produced by storm breakers is a powerful eroding agent along those coasts where high land is close to the shore. The swash of storm waves carves a steep wall, or marine cliff, into a bedrock mass. We shall investigate the evolution of marine cliffs of rock in Unit 57, which deals with the scenery of mountainous coasts. Since wave erosion is extremely slow in hard bedrock, however, environmental changes by natural processes are comparatively unimportant along rocky coasts. On the other hand, wave erosion is an important environmental concern along coasts made up of soft sedimentary strata or of unconsolidated regolith, such as alluvium, glacial deposits, or sand dunes.

In a few places along the coasts of North America and northern Europe, marine cliffs are being rapidly eroded back in weak glacial deposits. For example, the Atlantic Ocean (eastern) shore of Cape Cod has a 15-mile (24-km) stretch of marine cliff ranging in height from 60 to 170 ft

Figure 34.4 A breaking wave.

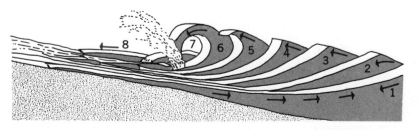

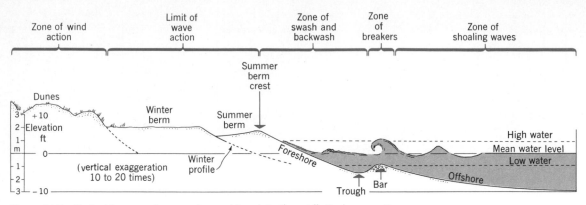

Figure 34.5 Typical forms and zones of a sand beach in the midlatitude zone. (From
A. N. Strahler [1971] *The Earth Sciences,* 2nd ed., Harper & Row, New York.)

(18 to 52 m) and carved into unconsolidated glacial sands
and gravels. This feature is better described as a **marine
scarp,** since the loose sand holds a slope angle of about
30° to 35° from the horizontal and is by no means a sheer
wall. Here the rate of shoreline retreat has averaged nearly
3 ft (1 m) per year for the past century, and a single winter
storm will cut the scarp back a distance of several feet.

Beaches

Sediment enters the shore zone of breaking waves from a
number of possible sources. Sediment may be derived directly from a marine cliff or scarp that is being actively
eroded. Sediment entering the ocean or a lake from the
mouth of a stream is another major source of supply.
Storm waves may scour the offshore zone and drag sand
and gravel landward to reach the breaker zone.

Whatever the origin of the sediment, it is shaped by
swash and backwash into a sediment deposit, familiar to

everyone as a **beach.** Sediment composing beaches ranges
from fine sand to cobblestones several inches in diameter.
Within a given stretch of beach the sediment is usually
quite well sorted into a particular size grade. Thus there
are beaches of fine sand, or of coarse sand, or of gravel, or
of cobbles. As a rule, beaches composed of fine sand are
broad and have a very gently seaward slope, whereas
beaches of coarse sand or gravel are quite steep. Beaches
formed of cobblestones are very steep and show a high
crest, or ridge form. Particles of silt and clay do not form
beaches, but instead are easily carried away from the
shoreline in suspension in currents, to settle out in
deep water.

The Beach Profile

A sand beach with its bordering shallow-water zone of
breaking waves, on the one side, and a zone of wind
action with dune development forming a border on the

Figure 34.6 Low tide on the outer beach of Sandy Hook, New Jersey. The crest of the
summer berm bears vehicle tracks. Swash at high tide swept just over the berm to reach its
limit at point A. The next high-water swash reached only to point B. The foreshore lies at
the right, a broad winter berm belt is at the left. Sand dunes form the ridge on the skyline.
(A. N. Strahler.)

landward side, represents a succession of unique life habitats in which each assemblage of plant and animal forms is adapted to a different environment.

Figure 34.5 is an idealized profile across a typical beach developed by exposure to waves of the open ocean in a midlatitude location experiencing a strong contrast between wave action of summer and winter seasons. The profile shows summer conditions in which waves are of low height and comparatively low levels of energy.

During the summer, accumulation of sand takes place, building a **summer berm,** which is a benchlike structure (Figure 34.6). A higher **winter berm** lies behind the summer berm. The winter berm can be cut back deeply by a storm, but is rebuilt following the storm. The **foreshore** is the sloping beach face in the zone of swash and backwash. Beneath the breaker zone is a low underwater bar, called an **offshore bar.** It lies in the **offshore** region of the beach, in the zone of shoaling waves and below the level of low tide. Actually, there are many variations in beach-profile forms from place to place and season to season, depending upon wave form and wave energy and upon the composition of the beach.

Beaches can experience a widening, or out-building process called **progradation,** as shown in Figure 34.7A. The sand that is added to the beach may come from deeper water, or it may be brought along the shore from another part of the coast. A common indication of progradation is the presence of numerous parallel **beach ridges,** each of which represents a former berm crest. Beaches can also experience a narrowing, or back-cutting process known as **retrogradation,** shown in Figure 34.7B. In this case, the sand may be moved to deeper water in the offshore zone, or it may be transported along the shoreline to another part of the coast.

Littoral Drift

In an idealized situation in which waves approach a straight shoreline, their crests parallel with that line, the wave breaks at the same instant at all points and the swash rides up the beach at right angles to the shoreline. The backwash returns along the same line. Consequently, particles move up and down the beach slope along a fixed line.

However, along most shorelines, most of the time, waves approach the coast at an oblique angle, as shown in Figure 34.8. As these waves travel toward a shoreline over a gently shoaling ocean bottom, they undergo a gradual decrease in velocity of forward travel. As a result, the wave crests become curved in plan, and the crests tend to become more nearly parallel with the shoreline. This wave-bending phenomenon is called **wave refraction** (Figure 34.8).

Despite some refraction, however, the wave crest arrives in the breaker zone with an oblique approach to the shoreline. The swash of the breaker then rides obliquely up the foreshore, as shown in Figure 34.9. As a result, the sand, pebbles, and cobbles are moved obliquely up the slope. After the swash has spent its energy, the backwash flows

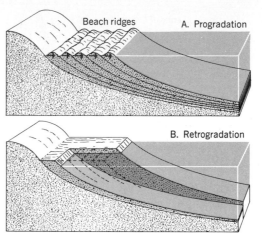

Figure 34.7 Progradation and retrogradation. (From A. N. Strahler [1971] *The Earth Sciences,* 2nd ed., Harper & Row, New York.)

down the slope of the beach, being controlled by the pull of gravity which moves it in the most direct downhill direction. Now the particles are dragged directly seaward and come to rest at positions to one side of the starting points. Because wave fronts approach consistently from

Figure 34.8 Wave refraction along a straight shoreline.

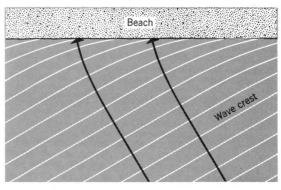

Figure 34.9 Beach drift of sediment caused by swash of obliquely approaching waves.

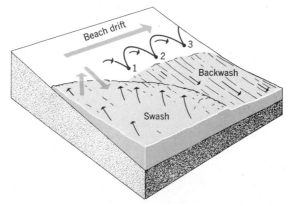

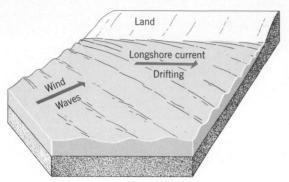

Figure 34.10 Longshore current drifting.

the same direction on a particular day, this movement is repeated many times. Individual rock particles thus travel a considerable distance along the shore. Multiplied many thousands of times to include the numberless particles of the beach, this form of mass transport, called **beach drift,** is a major process in shoreline development.

Rarely is beach drift not taking place, in one direction or the other, along a marine shoreline. Usually, a given stretch of shoreline is subjected to a dominant direction of wave approach throughout a given season of the year or throughout the entire year. Consequently, beach drift can be assigned a single direction of net transport as the seasonal or yearly average.

A process related to beach drifting is **longshore drift.** When waves approach a shoreline under the influence of strong winds, the water level is slightly raised near shore by a slow shoreward drift of water. An excess of water, which must escape, is thus pushed shoreward. A **longshore current** is set up parallel to shore in a direction away from the wind (Figure 34.10). When wave and wind conditions are favorable, this current is capable of moving sand along the bottom in the breaker zone in a direction parallel to the shore.

Both beach drifting and longshore drifting move particles in the same direction for a given set of onshore winds and oblique wave fronts and therefore supplement each other's influence in sediment transportation. The combined transport by beach and longshore drift is termed **littoral drift.** Let us now apply the principle to the evolution of beach deposits.

Littoral drift along a straight section of shore is illustrated in Figure 34.11. Where an embayment occurs, drift continues along the line of the straight shore, with the result that an embankment of sediment is constructed along that line. This narrow beach deposit, extending out into open waters, is called a **sandspit,** or simply a **spit.** Through wave refraction sediment is carried around the spit end, which develops a landward curvature (Figure 34.11).

Littoral drift is an important cause of both progradation and retrogradation along a shoreline. When more sediment is arriving at a particular section of beach at a rate more rapidly than it is leaving, progradation occurs. When sediment is leaving a given section of beach more rapidly than it is arriving, retrogradation occurs. We now turn to consider how Man's interference with the natural processes of littoral drift can bring about either progradation or retrogradation.

Shore Protection

We have already noted that marine scarps, carved into unconsolidated materials, yield rapidly under the impact of storm waves. Consider the case already cited—that of the outer shore of Cape Cod—in which measured retreat has averaged close to 3 ft (1 m) per year over more than a century. Loss of 300 ft (100m) of land in a century is perhaps not in itself a large amount, even along some 20 mi (32 km) of coast. However, coasts of this type are usually favored with excellent bathing beaches because of the abundant quantities of loose sediment available to waves.

As a result, along many such coasts, resort communities have grown up at the very brink of the marine scarp. Costly homes, beach clubs, restaurants, and hotels are crowded together, as close as possible to the sea. Here, even a few yards of retrogradation threaten property destruction, and if it is not prevented, the threat is realized. A lesser problem is the loss of recreational usage which occurs as a sand beach is depleted to leave only a narrow zone of pebbles and cobbles.

Engineering structures designed to meet wave attack head on are not only extremely expensive, but also prone to failure. The impacting pressure of breaking storm waves upon a vertical wall runs up into the thousands of pounds per square foot.

Figure 34.11 Littoral drift along a straight shoreline is building a curved sandspit into a bay. (From A. N. Strahler [1971] *The Earth Sciences,* 2nd ed., Harper & Row, New York.)

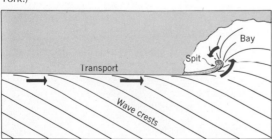

Figure 34.12 Effects of groin construction upon a sand beach. (From A. N. Strahler [1972] *Planet Earth,* Harper & Row, New York.)

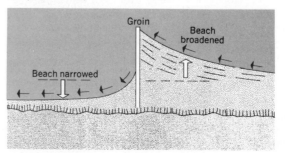

Figure 34.13   A system of groins for trapping of beach sand, Willoughby Spit, Virginia. Littoral drift is from lower left to upper right. (Photograph by Dept. of the Army, Corps of Engineers.)

If direct resistance to frontal attack is not always the best answer to coastal erosion, what else can be done? In some circumstances a successful strategy is to install structures that will cause progradation and thus build a broad beach with an ample berm. The principle here is that the excess energy of storm waves will be dissipated in reworking the beach deposits. Cutting back of the berm in a single storm will be restored by berm-building between storms.

Induced progradation requires that sediment moving by littoral drift be trapped by the placement of baffles across the path of sediment transport. To accomplish this result, groins are installed at close intervals along the beach. A **groin** is simply a wall or embankment built at right angles to the shoreline (Figure 34.12); it may be constructed of huge rock masses, or of concrete, or of wooden pilings. Figure 34.13 shows the shoreline changes induced by groins. Sand accumulates on the updrift side of the groin, developing a curved shoreline. On the downdrift side of the groin the beach will be depleted because of the cutting off of the normal supply of drift sand. The result may be harmful retrogradation and cutting back of the scarp. For this reason groins must be closely spaced so that the trapping effect of one groin will extend to the next. Ideally, when the groins have trapped the maximum quantity of sediment, beach drift will be restored to its original rate for the shoreline as a whole. However, there have been many instances of damaging retrogradation induced by groin construction on the updrift side of an unprotected shoreline.

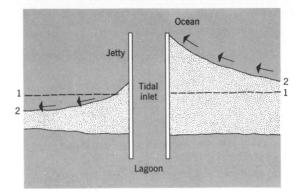

Figure 34.14   Effects of twin jetties upon beach on either side of an inlet. (1) Original shoreline; (2) modified shoreline. (From A. N. Strahler [1972] *Planet Earth,* Harper & Row, New York.)

More serious and permanent effects often accompany the construction of long **jetties** to maintain a navigable inlet in a bar connecting a bay with the open sea (Figure 34.14). Tidal currents then maintain a deep channel. These jetties, which are walls similar in plan to groins, cause sediment to accumulate on the updrift side, but result in serious beach depletion on the downdrift side. The effects of a long jetty can extend far along the shoreline (Figure 34.15).

In some instances the source of beach sand is from the mouth of a river. Construction of dams on the river may drastically reduce the sediment load and therefore also cut off the source of sand for littoral drift. Retrogradation may then occur on a long stretch of shoreline.

Figure 34.15   Jetties at Cold Spring Inlet, New Jersey, mark the entrance to Cape May Harbor. Beach sand has accumulated on the updrift side *(right)* of the inlet, but the beach has been depleted on the downdrift side *(left)*. (Dept. of the Army, Corps of Engineers.)

Man's Adjustment to Coastal Hazards

In our study of river floods, we took note of a new outlook upon the problem of human adjustment to natural hazards. Geographers have pointed out that human occupancy of high-hazard floodplains needs to be reexamined. Instead of using vulnerable floodplains for continued growth of housing developments and industrial plants, would it not be wiser to zone that land for uses that can absorb an occasional inundation? Much the same approach is now being taken with regard to human occupancy of those coastal zones where there is a high risk of severe retrogradation—undermining and destroying buildings, streets and boardwalks—or the danger of flooding by swash of storm waves reaching far inland when the ocean level is raised by strong onshore winds and high tides.

The coastal zone can profit as much from land-use planning through zoning ordinances as can areas prone to river flooding. Should the building of new vacation homes and motels, and the roadways needed to serve them, be allowed close to a shoreline vulnerable to being cut back many yards in a single storm? Should vast sums of money be spent in attempting to build groins to preserve a retro-grading beach? Should massive seawalls be erected to prevent further property losses along shore zones that have already been built up? (Figure 34.16.) We noted in opening

Figure 34.16   Storm waves breaking against a coast underlain by weak sand quickly undermined this shore home at Seabright, New Jersey. The barrier of wooden pilings *(right)* proved ineffective in preventing cutting back of the cliff. (Douglas Johnson.)

this study unit that the National Park Service has adopted a policy of letting nature take its course along coastlines under its control. This is a topic we will investigate further in the next study unit, which is concerned with problems of barrier-island coasts.

Unit 35
Impact of Man on Sandy Coasts

Provincetown's Ordeal by Sand

Provincetown, Massachusetts, was once a city with sand troubles. A famous fishing port on Cape Cod, thriving since colonial days, Provincetown is safely nestled in a quiet harbor within the curved fist of Cape Cod. A fingerlike sandspit encloses the harbor, while the wrist and forearm of the Cape protect it from vicious Atlantic storms attacking from the north and east. It was these same gale-force winds that brought the sand into the streets of Provincetown.

The northern tip of Cape Cod, called the Provincelands, is almost completely covered with sand dunes. Shaped into wavelike ridges, many of the dune summits rise to heights over 80 feet above sea level. At the time the first colonists settled here a forest of pitch pines kept the dunes pretty well in check, while beachgrass protected the higher dune surfaces.

The first settlers rapidly destroyed the protective plant cover of the Provincelands. Pine trees were cut for fuel and for pitch and turpentine needed for the fishing fleet. Sheep and cattle grazed the dune summits, destroying the beachgrass. Now winds from the north and east began to carry the loose sand south toward Provincetown Harbor. Early in the 1700s, legislation was enacted to forbid grazing and tree-cutting, but the laws were poorly enforced or simply ignored.

The invasion of Provincetown by sand began in earnest about 1725. Steep dune slopes began to bank up against houses. Driving sand frosted the

The Great Beach of the Provincelands during a winter storm. Snow covers the first dune ridge. Older dunes in the background are largely forested. (Harold L. R. Cooper, Cape Cod Photos.)

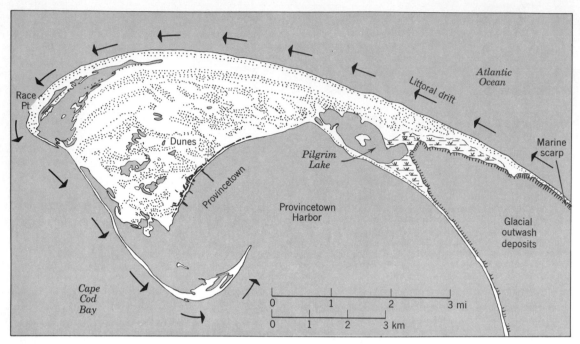

The Provincelands of Cape Cod. The dunes are nourished by beach sand carried by littoral drift in the direction shown by color arrows.

window panes. Sand drifts accumulated in the streets. Only the constant removal of sand by carts kept the streets open. By the late 1700s and early 1800s, the dune ridges were advancing upon Provincetown Harbor along a front over 4 miles long. Commissioners appointed by the Commonwealth reported upon the situation in 1825, recommending protective legislation and the extensive planting of beachgrass. Their advice was heeded, and beachgrass grown from seed imported from Holland was set out in rows. Brush was piled between the rows to make a baffle for trapping the moving sand.

When Henry David Thoreau, the naturalist, visited Provincetown in 1849, he was told by natives that the sand had made no progress in the previous 10 years, but evidence of its invasion was still about. This is what Thoreau observed:

The sand is the great enemy here . . . The sand drifts like snow, and sometimes the lower story of a house is concealed by it, though it is kept off by a wall. The houses were formerly built on piles, in order that the driving sand might pass under them. . . . There was a school-house just under the hill on which we sat, filled with sand up to the tops of the desks, and of course the master and scholars had fled. Perhaps they had imprudently left the windows open one day, or neglected to mend a broken pane. . . . In some pictures of Provincetown the persons of the inhabitants are not drawn below the ankles, so much being supposed to buried in the sand. . . . I saw a baby's wagon with tires six inches wide to keep it near the surface. The more tired the wheels, the less tired the horses.*

Invasion by coastal dunes is an old story in Europe. In the Landes region of western France, bordering the Bay of Biscay, deforestation set off the landward migration of great dunes; their speed was clocked at from 60 to 80 feet per year. One village was twice moved back from the advancing wave. Plantings of dunegrass and pines were made in the late 1700s and halted the sand invasion. To this day, it is forbidden even to cross the dunes on foot, so sensitive are the grasses to any disturbance.

Perhaps a new era of coastal sand invasions is at hand, now that the dune buggy is riding rough-shod over our coastal dunes, senselessly churning the sensitive roots of the beachgrass. In this study unit, we investigate the interplay between waves and wind along broad, sandy beaches, highly vulnerable to rapid changes when Man interferes with the natural processes of give and take.

*From Henry D. Thoreau, Cape Cod, © 1961 by Thomas Y. Crowell Company, New York, pp. 256-258.

DATA SOURCE: Barbara B. Chamberlain (1964) These Fragile Outposts, Natural History Press, Garden City, N.Y., pp. 174-176, 180-181; Arthur N. Strahler (1966) A Geologist's View of Cape Cod, Natural History Press, Garden City, N.Y., pp. 79-89.

Continental Shelves

Recall from Unit 23 that the stable continental margins on both sides of the Atlantic Ocean have a continental shelf. Along these continental margins, the continental lithosphere and the oceanic lithosphere do not meet in an active plate boundary; instead, they are geologically inactive. Since the Cretaceous period, beginning about 130 million years ago, these stable continental margins have been receiving layers of sediment brought from the continental interiors. As Figure 35.1 shows, the sediment has accumulated in wedgelike layers, thickening toward the ocean and forming the continental shelf. As the sediment accumulated, the crust gradually subsided. Today there exists a thick **continental shelf wedge.** For many millions of years the continental shelves have been shallow and broad. Sediment carried by underwater currents down the steep continental slope have accumulated upon the continental rise, forming another thick sediment wedge, labeled "deep-sea sediments" in Figure 35.1. The continental shelf wedge is of great importance today as a possible source of new petroleum accumulations.

Because of minor changes in ocean level, and slight upward and downward movements of the continental crust, shelf sediments have been alternately deposited and exposed over the continental margin. Where the gently inclined strata are exposed today, they comprise a **coastal plain,** labeled in Figure 35.1.

Barrier Island Coasts

The broad continental shelf of North America, which borders the Atlantic and Gulf coasts, is characterized by a wide, low coastal plain and a wide zone of shallow water offshore. Here the action of waves, currents, and winds forms a narrow offshore strip of land, called a **barrier island,** or **barrier beach** (Figure 35.2). Behind the barrier island lies a **lagoon,** which is a broad expanse of shallow

water, often several miles wide, and in places largely filled with tidal desposits. A characteristic feature of most barrier islands is the presence of gaps, known as **tidal inlets.** Through these gaps, strong currents flow alternately seaward and landward as the tide rises and falls. In heavy storms, the barrier may be breached by new inlets (Figure 35.3). Tidal currents will subsequently tend to keep a new inlet open, but it may be closed by shore drifting of sand.

Shallow water results in generally poor natural harbors along barrier-island shorelines. The lagoon itself may serve as a harbor if channels and dock areas are dredged to sufficient depths. Ships enter and leave through one of the passes in the barrier island, but artificial sea walls and jetties are required to confine the current and keep sufficient channel depth. Many of the major port cities are located where a large river empties into the lagoon. The lower courses of large rivers provide tidal channels that may be dredged to accommodate large vessels and thus make seaports of cities many miles inland.

One of the finest examples of a barrier island and lagoon is along the Gulf Coast of Texas (Figure 35.4). Here the island is unbroken for as much as 100 mi (160 km) at a stretch, and passes are few. The lagoon is 5 to 10 mi (8 to 16 km) wide. Galveston is built on the barrier island adjacent to an inlet connecting Galveston Bay with the sea. Most other Texas ports, however, are located on the mainland shore. Corpus Christi, Rockport, Texas City, Lavaca, and other ports are located along the shores of river embayments.

Littoral Drift on Barrier-Island Shorelines

Because barrier-island shorelines are very simple in plan, with long stretches that are nearly straight or broadly curved, littoral drift is an important activity. In many cases the littoral drift moves almost entirely in one direction

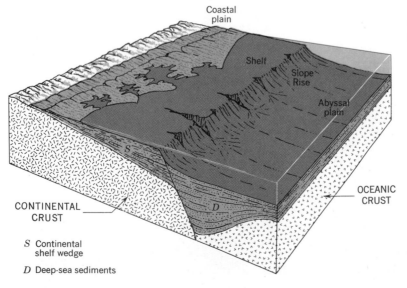

Figure 35.1 This block diagram shows an inner wedge of sediments beneath the continental shelf and an outer wedge of deep-sea sediments beneath the continental rise and abyssal plain.

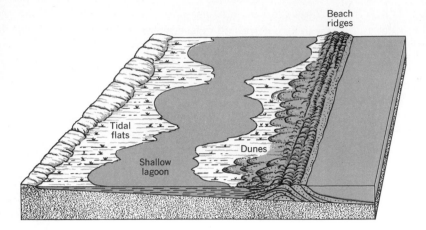

Figure 35.2 A barrier island is separated from the mainland by a wide lagoon. Sediments fill the lagoon, while dune ridges advance over the tidal flats.

throughout one season of the year, so that large amounts of beach sediment travel in one direction along the coast.

Littoral drift causes important changes in the form of a tidal inlet in a barrier island or barrier beach. Figure 35.5 illustrates the typical change. Littoral drift builds out the barrier beach on the updrift side of the inlet. Here the beach takes the form of a lengthening sandspit (see Figure 34.11). In time this beach overlaps the end of the beach on the opposite side of the inlet. The beach on the downdrift side of the inlet is depleted and tends to be pushed landward. Over a long period of time, the inlet migrates slowly along the coast in the downdrift direction.

Under favorable conditions, littoral drift gradually builds out a barrier-island shoreline, broadening the island. The island now shows multiple **beach ridges,** which are constructed in periods of storm, when the swash heaps up

Figure 35.3 East Moriches Inlet was cut through Fire Island, a barrier island off the Long Island shoreline, during a severe storm in March 1931. This aerial photograph, taken a few days after the breach occurred, shows the underwater tidal delta being built out into the lagoon *(right)* by currents. The entire area shown is about 1 mi (1.6 km) long. North is to the right; the open Atlantic Ocean on the left. (U.S. Army Air Forces Photograph.)

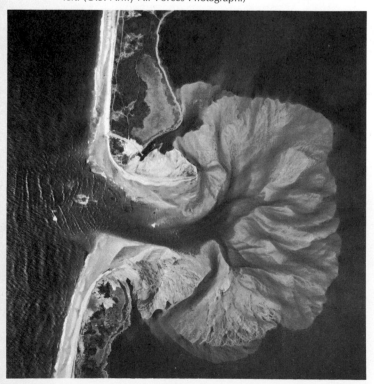

Figure 35.4 The Gulf Coast of Texas is dominated by its offshore barrier island.

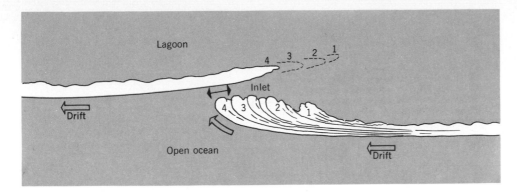

Figure 35.5 Because of littoral drift, right to left, an inlet in a barrier beach has migrated toward the left. (From A. N. Strahler [1971] *The Earth Sciences,* 2nd ed., Harper & Row, New York.)

sand into high berms (Figure 35.2). At certain points on a barrier island coast, littoral drift coming from opposite directions along the shoreline builds out an accumulation of beach ridges into the shape of a pointed foreland, or cape. Because of its toothlike shape, this feature is called a **cuspate foreland** (Figure 35.6).

Figure 35.6 Sketch map of Cape Canaveral (renamed Cape Kennedy), Florida, as it was in 1910, before Man-induced modification. Ridges near the shore *(right)* are beach ridges; those farther inland are dune ridges built upon older beach ridges. (After Douglas Johnson, 1919.)

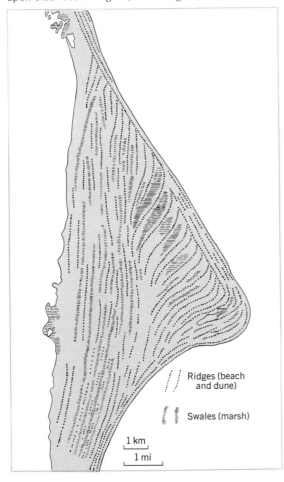

Ridges (beach and dune)

Swales (marsh)

1 km
1 mi

Coastal Sand Dunes

Along most barrier beaches wind action shares with waves the task of building up the barrier. **Dunes** are sand accumulations built by wind. Transportation occurs when wind speed is great enough to cause sand grains to make long, low leaps into the air, rebounding repeatedly in impacts with surface grains. This process is called **saltation** (Figure 35.7).

Wind can easily move sand in an upslope direction to higher levels. When strong onshore winds are blowing across the dry berm of a beach, large amounts of sand are carried landward and heaped up into dunes. These can easily be built to levels of 20 to 50 ft (6 to 15 m) above the highest limits of the swash. In this way, the barrier beach grows in height as its breadth is increased by progradation.

Plants of various species can grow on a dune surface, even while sand is accumulating. Where dune growth is carried out in the presence of vegetation, the dunes are referred to as **phytogenic dunes.** Phytogenic dunes formed immediately landward of a beach are referred to as **foredunes.** They comprise a ridge of irregularly shaped hills and hollows. The plant cover is typically **beachgrass,** which serves as a baffle to slow wind speed and trap sand grains (Figure 35.8).

Coastal dunes are only partially protected by a natural plant cover. Here and there the wind excavates a deep depression, called a **blowout,** and heaps the sand into a high, horseshoe-shaped dune ridge on the landward side. This feature is called a **coastal blowout dune** (Figure 35.9A). On the landward side of this dune ridge, free sand falls upon a steep lee slope, where it slides to the base of the dune. In this way, a coastal blowout dune advances upon forest, killing trees, and in some cases covering roads and buildings that lie in its path (Figure 35.10).

Coastal blowout dunes in some cases continue to advance slowly landward, becoming drawn out into highly elongate forms with nearly parallel sides. In this extreme state, they are called **hairpin dunes** (Figure 35.9B). Figure 35.11 shows old hairpin dunes that have been stabilized by a shrub cover and are no longer moving. Where very large supplies of sand are present, coastal dunes may accumulate so fast that they remain free of plant cover. Called **transverse dunes,** they form a belt of sharp-crested ridges and deep depressions resembling a storm-tossed sea frozen into immobility (Figure 35.11).

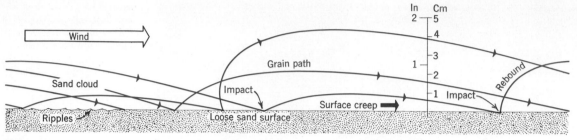

Figure 35.7   Sand particles travel in a series of long, low leaps. Impact by leaping grains causes surface creep. (After R. A. Bagnold.)

Figure 35.8   Foredunes protected by beachgrass, Provincelands of Cape Cod, Massachusetts. (A. N. Strahler.)

Figure 35.10   The advancing face of a coastal blowout dune is burying a forest. Cape Henry, Virginia. (Douglas Johnson.)

Dune Stabilization

Opening paragraphs of this chapter told the story of dune activation brought on by deforestation and overgrazing of coastal dunes of the Provincelands of Cape Cod. Control of dune advance was achieved by plantings of beachgrass and by strict control measures.

Another example of effective dune control is that of the Warrenton dune locality situated at the mouth of the Columbia River in Oregon. Active dunes were threatening to overwhelm agricultural lands, military installations, highways, towns, and expensive resort homes. Sand reaching the mouth of the Columbia River was accumulating in

Figure 35.9   (A) Coastal blowout dunes. (B) Hairpin dunes formed by the landward extension of blowout dunes.

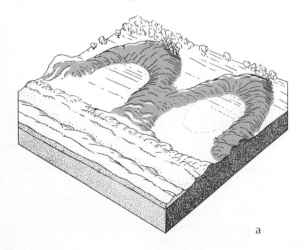

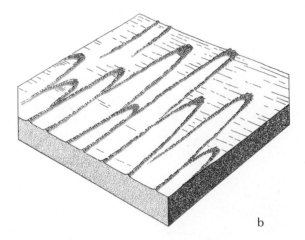

a   b

Figure 35.11 The arrows on this photograph point to elongate blowout dunes of hairpin form, which once advanced from the beach and have since become stabilized by vegetation. Active transverse dunes are overriding the blowout dunes in a fresh wave, San Luis Obispo Bay, California. (Spence Air Photos.)

such a way as to threaten to prevent movement of ocean-going vessels through the river mouth. Dune-control work, started in 1935, consisted of plantings made in two stages. The first stage consisted of plantings of permanent plant species, including grasses, hairy vetch, and purple beachpea. Careful maintenance of the cover has since kept the dunes stabilized.

Man and Barrier Islands

Coastal dunes can play an important role in holding back the swash of storm waves. Unquestionably, the dune barrier in many cases prevents storm swash from surging across a barrier island and pouring into the lagoon beyond. Waves of a single storm may eat away a large part of the dune ridge, but this sand will be restored by wind during long periods between storms. Along some barrier beaches, however, the dunes are low. Here the storm swash can spread across the entire barrier island in broad sheets, a process called **overwash** (Figure 35.12). The role that Man plays in interfering with natural overwash is presently being debated.

The weight of opinion as to the best way to manage barrier islands seems to be swinging toward a policy of "hands off." Where barrier beaches remain undeveloped, they should be protected from future invasions by highways and resort facilities. Recognizing that these low-lying coasts are high-hazard zones from the standpoint of coastal flooding by storms is analogous to the recognition of river floodplains as high-hazard zones with respect to river floods.

Figure 35.12 Storm swash is surging across the barrier beach at Cape Hatteras. (Robie Ray, *The Virginian-Pilot.*)

Unit 36
Reclamation of
Tidal Lands

The Great Iron Post in Denton Fen

There is a curious iron post in Denton Fen, a mile or so from the village of Holme, in the English Fens of Huntingdonshire. As you can see from the accompanying photograph, it is rather too ornate a column to be found in such a rural scene. Records show that the iron post came from the old Crystal Palace in London, at the time that structure was dismantled. In 1848, a civil engineer named John Lawrence drove the iron post into the ground of the fenland, a coastal region of flat, marshy ground underlain by peat. The post passed through 22 feet of peat into an underlying layer of blue clay. The top of the iron post was driven down just enough that its top was flush with the ground surface. The purpose of this operation

was to make a benchmark by means of which the amount of subsidence of the land surface could be measured in later years. You see, the owner of the land planned to drain the marshland so that it could be developed into farmland. His engineer knew from experience that the spongy peat would compact greatly after it was drained, and that much of the peat layer would then oxidize and disappear on exposure to the atmosphere. Also, the peat might be destroyed by burning when dry.

White marks on the photograph show the ground levels in later years. Because the post was firmly anchored in the clay bed below, it remained immovable while the peat layer subsided. By 1932, the year the photograph was taken, the total subsidence was 10.7 feet. There remained a layer of peat 11 feet thick.

The Fens from which the iron post protrudes are found in southeast England, landward of a broad coastal embayment known as the Wash. After the disappearance of the glacial ice that covered this part of England in the Pleistocene Epoch, the low area that is now the Fens became a shallow tidal estuary and was gradually filled by clay and, finally, by peat formed from dense growth of water-loving plants. Today the peat land is separated from the North Sea by a broad, low belt of beach gravels.

Now that the surface of the peat Fens has subsided, it lies several feet below sea level and is threatened with flooding on a grand scale, both from the rivers that flow across it between dikes, and from the North Sea. Many other parts of the North Sea coast of England and Holland have drained coastal marshes lying below sea level. Many of these have suffered heavily from flooding during great storms that have breached the coastal defenses.

Ground level — 1848

Shrinkage:
ft (m)
— 1860 4.8 (1.5)

— 1870 7.7 (2.3)
— 1875 8.2 (2.5)

— 1892 10.0 (3.0)
— 1932 10.7 (3.3)

Depth of peat in 1932 11 ft. 4 ins

DATA SOURCE: Major Gordon Fowler (1933) Shrinkage of the peat-covered fenlands, *Geographical Journal*, vol. 80, pp. 149-150; Kenneth Thompson (1957) Origin and use of the English peat Fens, *Scientific Monthly*, August, pp. 68-76. (Photograph at left by Major Gordon Fowler.)

Man and Tidal Lands

Tidal lands (or **tidelands**) are low coastal lands protected from wave action by barrier beaches or other protective landforms, but subject to flooding by salt water as the sea level rises to high tide. To understand tidal lands, we need to know how these land surfaces originate as geologic features and how the tides operate.

Tidal lands are of major importance environmentally because of a conflict of interest between Man and nature. On the one hand, tidal lands are unique environments of complex and sensitive ecosystems made up of both terrestrial (land) and aquatic (water) plants and animals. For example, tidal waters are the spawning grounds of many species of ocean fishes. If Man should destroy these spawning grounds, the marine food resource will be gravely depleted. On the other hand, there are strong pressures upon Man to modify the tidal lands for agricultural uses and to expand cities.

Tidal lands can be extremely productive of food crops and forage. We will learn how the Dutch people, in a great effort to feed their growing population, transformed large areas of tidal lands into agricultural lands. But if Holland's population then continues to grow and there is no more tidal land to reclaim, what has been gained in the long run? We can more easily answer the question of what has been lost: the habitats of shellfish and finfish, of waterfowl and mammals, and in total, of one of the most highly productive ecosystems on earth.

Coastal Submergence and Sedimentation

To be formed, tidal lands require shallow water protected from wave action, but open to the inflow and outflow of salt water with the tide. Bodies of water of this type are referred to generally as **estuaries.** Shallow estuaries are gradually filled with fine-textured sediment and organic matter to become tidal land. Several geological processes and events can produce shallow estuaries. The lagoons behind barrier islands are an important type of estuary. We investigated barrier islands and their lagoons in Unit 35.

Another process of estuary formation is related to a rise of sea level. Recall from Unit 6 that, as the Pleistocene ice sheets melted, the stored water was returned to the oceans and sea level rose to reach nearly to its present level about 5000 years ago. The rising sea level submerged the continental coasts to produce a variety of bays.

Any stream-carved valley, when partially submerged becomes a bay. Wave action and littoral drift soon builds a **baymouth bar** cutting off the bay from the open ocean and creating a form of estuary (Figure 36.1). A **bar** is simply a low, narrow ridge of coarse sediment built by littoral drift. The sandspit is one form of bar. Along some rugged coasts, the rise of sea level also produced many offshore islands. As waves attack an island, the sediment produced from cliffs is built by littoral drift into bars connecting the island with the mainland. These bars, called **tombolos,** create a bay between the island and the mainland (Figure 36.2).

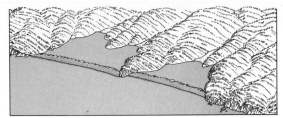

Figure 36.1 Baymouth bars, sealing off two bays. (After W. M. Davis.)

A quite different kind of estuary is formed where the rise of sea level has drowned the lower reaches of a large river. The river floodplain now becomes the shallow floor of the estuary, while the former floodplain bluffs become the shoreline. Although there may be no protective bar across the mouth of the estuary, it is sheltered from ocean waves by reason of its narrowness and length.

Tidal Currents

Most marine coastlines are influenced by the **ocean tide,** a rhythmic rise and fall of sea level under the influence of changing attractive forces of moon and sun on the rotating earth. Where tides are great, the effects of changing water level and the currents set in motion are of major importance in shaping coastal landforms.

The tidal rise and fall of water level is graphically represented by the **tide curve.** We can make half-hourly observations of the position of water level against a measuring stick attached to a pier or sea wall. We then plot the changes of water level and draw the tide curve. Figure 36.3 is a tide curve for Boston Harbor covering a day's time. The water reached its maximum height, or high water, at the 12-ft (3.7-m) mark on the tide staff, then fell to its minimum height, or low water, occurring about 6¼ hours later. A second high water occurred about 12½ hours after the previous high water, completing a single tidal cycle. In this example, the range of tide, or difference

Figure 36.2 Two tombolos connecting an island to the mainland. (After W. M. Davis.)

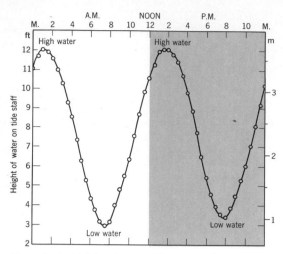

Figure 36.3 Height of water at Boston Harbor measured every half hour.

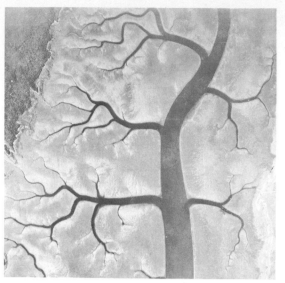

Figure 36.5 Viewed from the air at low tide, these tidal mud flats near Yarmouth, Nova Scotia, show a well-adjusted branching system of tidal streams. The area shown is 1.5 mi (2.4 km) wide. (Canadian Armed Forces Photograph.)

between heights of successive high and low waters, is 9 ft (2.7 m).

The rising tide sets in motion in bays and estuaries currents of water known as **tidal currents.** The relationships between tidal currents and the tide curve are shown in Figure 36.4. When the tide begins to fall, an ebb current sets in. This flow ceases about the time when the tide is at its lowest point. As the tide begins to rise, a landward current, the flood current, begins to flow.

Tidal Sediment

Once a protected coastal bay or estuary has been formed, it begins to fill with fine-textured sediment—silt and clay. Sediment is either carried in suspension by streams emptying into the estuary or transported by tidal currents from points where waves are actively eroding clay-rich sediments. The flow of tidal currents in and out of inlets

in the protecting barrier island or bar circulates the suspended sediment within the entire estuary. The coarser silt particles settle out rapidly when the current slackens. Clay particles, brought by freshwater streams from the land, clot together into silt-sized bodies when salt water mixes with the fresh water. This process is called **flocculation.** The clots of clay formed by flocculation sink to the bottom. The sediment accumulates in layers and gradually fills the estuary. A high proportion of locally derived organic matter is normally present in such sediments, and they can be called **organic-rich muds.**

Figure 36.6 Salt marsh at South Wellfleet, Massachusetts. Late winter stubble and dead leaves of salt-marsh grass cover the peat layer. A small tidal channel lies drained empty at low tide. (A. N. Strahler.)

Figure 36.4 The ebb current flows seaward as the tide level falls; the flood current flows landward as the tide level rises.

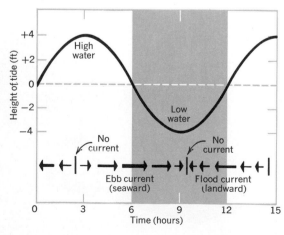

Tidal Mud Flats and Salt Marshes

In time, tidal sediments fill bays and estuaries to produce **mud flats,** which are barren expanses of mud exposed at low tide but covered at high tide (Figure 36.5). Next, there takes hold upon the mud flat a growth of salt-tolerant plants (such as the genus *Spartina*). The plant stems entrap more sediment and the flat is built up to approximately the level of high tide, becoming a **salt marsh** (Figure 36.6).

The uppermost layer of the salt marsh is composed largely of organic matter and is one of the forms of **peat.** Salt-marsh peat is resilient and tough in structure, capable of effectively resisting wave and current action. Tidal currents maintain their flow through the salt marsh by means of a highly complex network of sinuous **tidal streams** in which the water alternately flows seaward and landward (Figure 36.7).

Salt Marsh of Deltaic Plains

In addition to the bays and estuaries we have already described, tidal lands are formed as deltaic plains. A **deltaic plain** is a coastal lowland consisting of ancient and modern delta deposits. A good example is the deltaic plain of

Figure 36.7 This broad tidal salt-marsh along the east coast of Florida is laced with serpentine tidal channels. (Laurence Lowry.)

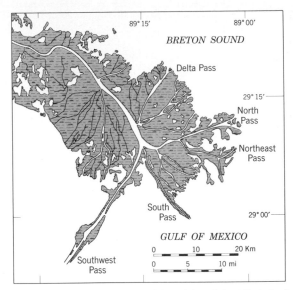

Figure 36.8 The modern bird-foot delta of the Mississippi River. Much of the land is salt marsh.

the Mississippi River, including the active delta of the present river mouth.

The active delta of the Mississippi River is of a type known as a **bird-foot delta** (Figure 36.8). Narrow, finger-like distributaries are built out into the shallow waters of the Gulf of Mexico. Natural levees border the river channel. At the end of each finger is a **pass.** Certain passes are kept open for river navigation by means of jetties. A block diagram, Figure 36.9, shows the structure of the bird-foot delta. Beneath each distributary is a **bar finger** of sand, surrounded by clay. As the clay layer compacts under its own load, there is a subsidence of the delta surface between the distributaries. Salt marsh fills the subsided areas between the natural levees.

The Mississippi River deltaic plain consists of the abandoned distributaries of a number of earlier-formed deltas (Figure 36.10). These waterways are referred to as **bayous.** Extensive areas of salt marsh lie between the bayous.

Salt Marshes and Rising Sea Level

Salt marshes began to form along the coasts of North America and Europe shortly after the final disappearance of the Pleistocene ice sheets, roughly 10,000 years ago. In the intervening postglacial period, sea level rose slowly in tidal estuaries along the coast. One layer of salt marsh was added upon another. Today, beneath large areas of tidal lands, we find salt-marsh peat with layers of organic-rich tidal muds as thick as 20 to 30 ft (6 to 9 m) and even greater. These thick accumulations are of great environmental importance because, when drained of their water, the porous material undergoes compaction and there is a subsidence of the land surface. Lands that have subsided below sea level are in danger of serious flooding by ocean water during storms. This phenomenon was the subject of our opening paragraphs.

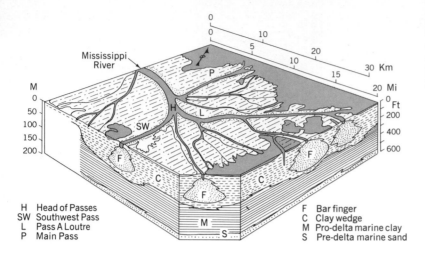

Figure 36.9 Idealized diagram of structure and composition of the modern bird-foot delta of the Mississippi River. (Simplified from H. N. Fisk, E. McFarlan, Jr., C. R. Kolb, and L. J. Wibert, Jr., [1954] *Journal of Sedimentary Petrology,* vol. 24, p. 77, Figure 1.)

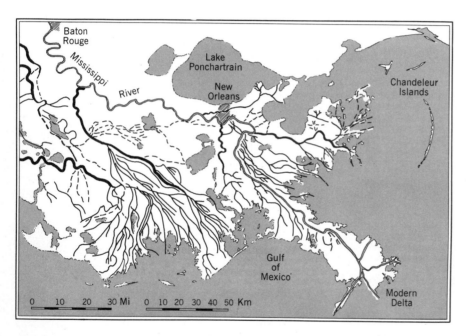

Figure 36.10 Deltaic plain of the Mississippi River, formed during the last 5000 years, has a large number of abandoned distributary channels, shown in bold lines on this map. (Redrawn and simplified from a map by C. R. Kolb and J. R. Van Lopik [1966] in *Deltas in Their Geologic Framework,* M. L. Shirley, ed., Houston Geological Society, Houston, Texas, p. 22, Figure 2.)

Reclamation of Tidal Lands

Under pressures of expanding populations in need of more food, agricultural lands in Europe, the British Isles, and to a lesser degree the New World, have been expanded at the expense of the sea by **reclamation**—literally the reclaiming of shallow tidal lands that had fallen victim to the rising postglacial sea levels and to gradual crustal subsidence.

In general, reclamation applies to two types of estuarine environments. First is the mud-flat environment—shallow, but open water in which expanses of mud are exposed at low tide. These sediments are largely inorganic silts, brought by streams emptying into broad estuaries (e.g., deltaic sediments). The second environment is that of the salt marsh, with its peat layer, already filling to a greater or lesser degree what were previously open tidal estuaries.

The greatest reclamation region has been that of the Low Countries along the North Sea, where extensive areas have been reclaimed in Belgium and the Netherlands. (Figure 36.11).

A large area of coastal tidelands, ranging in width from 25 to 40 mi (40 to 65 km) and bordered by a belt of coastal sand dunes, occupies the North Sea coast of the Netherlands. Reclamation began as early as 900 A.D. by the building of dikes, earth embankments made of indigenous sediment. With exclusion of sea water, many large lakes were formed, and removal of peat led to their enlargement. In the seventeenth century, these lake basins were drained by pumpage. The method was to cut off a small area by dikes and pump out the water through use of windmills. The area of drained land, much of it lying more than 8 ft (2.5 m) below sea level, consists of diked land parcels, called **polders,** within an elaborate network of drainage canals. Development of this period reclaimed over 90 sq mi (235 sq km) of land. By 1920, the country had some 1000 mi (1600 km) of sea dikes, and the reclaimed area then totaled about 330 sq mi (860 sq km).

The Low Countries are protected from the North Sea by a sand barrier built in postglacial time by northeastward

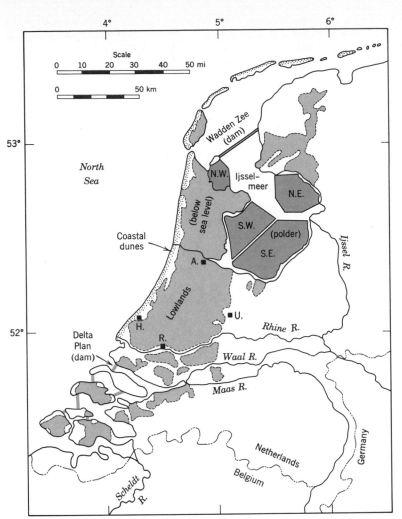

Figure 36.11 Map of Netherlands coastal low-lands and deltaic plains. Areas below sea level are shaded. Zuider Zee and Delta Plain reclamation works, including dams and polders, are shown in color. (Data of Zuider Zee Board and Geological Survey of Netherlands.)

littoral drift from a point near Calais, France, where the marine cliff of chalk ends. Building of dune ridges progressed concomitantly with the lengthening and widening of the beach-sand barrier. Older dune ridges, those lying nearest the mainland, have bases now situated 10 to 12 ft (3 to 4 m) below mean sea level, which shows that coastal submergence has been in progress as the barrier has been built up. A cross section, Figure 36.12, shows the dune barrier north of Haarlem (refer also to Figure 36.11).

The sand barrier thus protects polder lands that lie below sea level. The dune surfaces are stabilized with forest and beachgrass.

The Zuider Zee, a large shallow estuary lying east and north of Amsterdam was converted into a fresh-water body by construction of a 20-mi (32-km) dam, completed in 1932. Salinity in this water body dropped rapidly and by 1937 all salinity was excluded except near the locks by which the new lake, Lake Ijssel, (Ijsselmeer) is drained into

Figure 36.12 Cross section through the great dune barrier of the Netherlands coast in vicinity of Haarlem. Notice that the surface of the polderland is somewhat below mean tide level. (After P. Tesch, Geological Survey of Netherlands.)

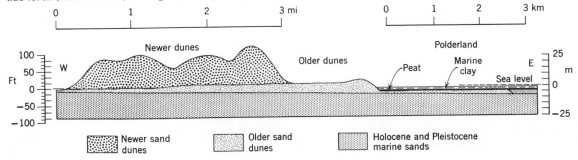

the Wadden Zee. Salt-water organisms rapidly died out in the new lake and were replaced by fresh-water forms, save for the eel, which thrives in the new lake. Reclamation of Lake Ijssel is taking place in sections, as Figure 36.13 shows. When complete, the new land will total about 860 sq mi (2300 sq km), leaving a much smaller lake for drainage of water from the Ijssel River (a distributary of the lower Rhine).

A second area of new reclamation in the Netherlands, affects four estuaries lying to the southwest of Rotterdam. These elongate coastal-water bodies are the drowned mouths of the Rhine, Maas (Meuse), and Scheldt rivers, and the land itself represents deltaic deposits of these rivers. Under the name of the Delta Plan, reclamation has begun with the construction of three large primary dams across the mouths of the estuaries (see map) and a number of secondary dams. The dammed areas will become fresh-water lakes, and these in turn will be reclaimed by dike-building and pumping. As in the case of the Zuider Zee project, the change from saline to fresh water will

Figure 36.13   The Zuider Zee reclamation project, Netherlands. (Photographs by courtesy of Netherlands Information Service.) Left: Construction of an enclosing dike within Lake Ijssel, the first step in creating the Southern Flevoland Polder. Below: New polder land adjacent to the city of Medemblick, in the northwestern part of Lake Ijssel. A large pumping station, adjacent to the enclosing dike at the right, removes water from canals draining the diked area.

eliminate salt-water organisms and these will be replaced by fresh-water organisms. Economic losses to the mussel and oyster industry will be large.

A second area of major reclamation is along the east coast of England. The largest single area is that of the Fens, a marshy lowland lying inland of the Wash, a conspicuous coastal embayment between Lincolnshire and Norfolk. In postglacial time, the interior portion of the Fens accumulated peat up to thicknesses of 20 ft (6 m), while the seaward portion accumulated silty sediment. Reclamation was accomplished in the 17th century by extensive ditching and construction of embankments. Since then, the surface of peat lands has been lowered many feet in places by a combination of removal and burning of the peat, by its natural oxidation under exposure to the atmosphere, and by shrinkage from dehydration.

Reclaimed tidal marshes, or **fenlands,** occupy many localities of the English coast from the Humber River estuary on the north to the Thames estuary on the south. These lands lie below sea level and are highly susceptible to inundation by salt water during storms that allow the ocean level to overtop the various dune ridges, beach ridges, and embankments separating the reclaimed land from the sea. A particularly devastating North Sea storm, which also severely damaged reclaimed areas of the Netherlands, occurred in January 1953. A combination of extremely high winds, a spring tide, and a storm surge resulted in flooding of over 300 sq mi (780 sq km) of fenlands and a loss of over 300 lives.

Flooding of fenlands and polders with salt water does serious damage to croplands. The sodium ion of sea salt (NaCl) replaces the calcium ion in the soil, with a resulting deterioration in the physical state of the soil (the tilth, or ease of cultivation is destroyed). Because the salt itself is toxic to most crops, a flushing out of the salts is required. Exclusion of salts by normal rains takes place in time, but from 1 to 5 years may elapse before crops can be grown. Applications of gypsum (calcium sulfate) accelerate the replacement of sodium with calcium.

Flooding of the fenlands and polders by winter storms is a long-standing environmental problem bringing together processes and principles of many sciences, including meteorology, oceanography, geomorphology, civil engineering, and soil science. The subject makes a good example of the interdisciplinary nature of environmental geography. The cases we have described show that Man, in the drive for more food to meet the needs of an increasing population has radically altered the natural environment and ecosystems of large areas, and at the same time has aggravated the natural hazards of coastal flooding.

Ultimately, the limits of land reclamation will be reached, while at the same time a sizeable fraction of the estuarine environment will be permanently destroyed, with consequent losses in food resources of the sea. Careful planning will be required if reclamation is to provide more gain than it loses in terms of natural resources.

Fortunately, reclamation of tidal lands in North America, while long practiced, never reached the proportions found in the Old World. Tidal lands are now being increasingly protected by strict legislation governing the uses of wetlands generally. In the United States, pressures upon tidal lands are predominantly from urbanization and industry, rather than from agriculture. In all urban seaboard areas, tidal mud flats and salt marshes are disappearing under expanding earth fills upon which industrial installations, housing developments, highways, and airfields are built. Although the organic content of these sediments poses difficulties in terms of foundation engineering (the runways of La Guardia Airport in New York have been subsiding continuously for years), these problems can be met in a number of ways and are not a limiting factor in use of tidal lands.

Unit 37
Landforms of Continental Glaciation

Louis Agassiz and the Glacial Theory

Conversions are often spectacular, the convert becoming a zealous apostle of his new viewpoint. One such convert was Jean Louis Rodolphe Agassiz, a leading nineteenth-century zoologist. Born in Switzerland in 1807, Agassiz' early preoccupation was with research on fossil fishes. While amassing enough information on the fishes to fill a five-volume treatise, Agassiz' interest became diverted to the glaciers of the Alps.

To understand what was going on, we must look back some decades and pick up the threads of a controversy. The objects of speculation in this controversy were boulders out of place, or erratics. Over many parts of the British Isles and northern Europe,

boulders were observed to consist of rock different from that comprising the bedrock on which they rest. In many cases the boulder could be identified as having a source many miles away. Early in the 1800s, the view was widely held by geologists that erratics were carried by icebergs drifting in a sea that once covered the lands. Upon melting, the bergs dropped their boulders at odd places. Erratic boulders and layers of finer sediment associated with them came to be known as drift, an expression quite appropriate if they were truly of iceberg origin. To this day, we refer to such deposits as drift. In his younger years, Charles Darwin adhered to the iceberg hypothesis.

Getting back to the Alps, there are countless erratics over the Swiss upland meadows and in the deeply carved valleys. Many of these bear scratches and grooves. Upon seeing these, James Hutton, the

Physical geography field trips, *circa* 1916. Led by Professor Armin Lobeck, the Physiographers Club of New York City visits an enormous glacial erratic on Long Island. This erratic was carried by the ice sheet from what is now the mainland of New England.

260

Scottish geologist mentioned in Unit 21, concluded that the erratics had been carried by glaciers, which he said were formerly much longer and thicker than we find them today, and that the marks were produced during transport.

Thus the germ of a new theory of erratics had its beginning. Others took up the idea, and during the 1820s and 1830s the glacial theory, as it was to become known, was debated in sessions of the Helvetic Society, a prestigious science forum. It was here, in 1834, that Louis Agassiz entered the picture. He had attended a meeting of that society at which a Swiss colleague, Jean de Charpentier, read a paper strongly supporting the glacial theory, even going so far as to argue in favor of a former great polar ice cap as the bearer of erratics now found spread over the British Isles and northern Europe. Agassiz felt sure that Charpentier was wrong, and in the summer of 1836 he examined for himself some glaciers and the valley deposits associated with them in hope of finding evidence against the glacial theory. Instead, after weeks of study, Agassiz became a convert. Waxing enthusiastic, he addressed the Helvetic Society the following year, arguing for Charpentier's view.

Three years later, Agassiz published his views in a book entitled *Étude sur les glaciers,* and it received widespread publicity. Unfortunately, Agassiz did not give much credit to Charpentier, who had priority in the matter, and the latter felt miffed. The iceberg theory of erratics, however, lingered on well after Agassiz' exposition, and it was not until the 1860s that it was put to rest by leading geologists.

Agassiz came to America in 1846, and became a professor of zoology and geology at Harvard University. He was well received, particularly by Edward Hitchcock, state geologist of Massachusetts, who had already espoused the glacial theory. Even so, as in Europe, the glacial theory was not fully accepted in the United States until the 1860s. Exploration of the Greenland Ice Sheet in the 1850s helped to sell

Members of a Columbia class scramble up the sandy wall of a glacial kame. Few such deposits of sand and gravel remain in the New York metropolitan area; they have been consumed as concrete aggregate to create highrise buildings and highway overpasses. (A. K. Lobeck.)

the glacial theory, since it proved that a vast ice sheet can exist and that glacial drift is being formed today.

The great ice sheets of North America left an environmental legacy through their profound influence upon the landforms and soils of primeval lands, which settlers from the Old World encountered as they moved westward. Our study units deal with landforms left by glacial ice. Along with action of the ice was a subtle but profound action by prevailing winds, which left a blanket of silt over the freshly deposited glacial landforms. This layer of silt was to prove an agricultural resource of inestimable value to those pioneers who reached the prairie plains of the Middle West.

Erosion by Ice Sheets

Unit 6 described the extent of Pleistocene ice sheets in North America and Europe. As the ice spread outward from centers of accumulation over Labrador and Hudson Bay, it possessed strong powers of erosion. Because soil and regolith were easily incorporated into the moving ice, hard bedrock of the Canadian Shield was exposed. As joint blocks of bedrock were pried free, they served in turn as tools of abrasion for the moving ice. The abrasive action is now recorded in countless scratches, called **striations,** and fracture marks on bedrock surfaces.

A common landform shaped by ice abrasion is a knob of solid bedrock that has been shaped by the moving ice (Figure 37.1). One side, that from which the ice was approaching, is characteristically smoothly rounded and shows a striated and grooved surface. This is termed the stoss side. The other, or lee side, where the ice plucked out angular joint blocks, is irregular, blocky, and steeper than the stoss side.

Vastly more important than the minor abrasion forms are enormous excavations that the ice sheets made in some localities where the bedrock is weak and the ice current was accentuated by the presence of a valley paralleling the

Figure 37.1   A glacially abraded rock knob. (From A. N. Strahler [1971] *The Earth Sciences,* 2nd ed., Harper & Row, New York.)

Figure 37.3   Seen from the air, this esker in the Canadian shield area appears as a narrow embankment crossing the terrain of glacially eroded lake basins. (Canadian Department of Mines, Geological Survey.)

direction of ice flow. Under such conditions the ice sheet behaved much as a valley glacier, scooping out a deep, U-shaped trough. The Finger Lakes of western New York State are fine examples. Here a set of former stream valleys lay parallel to southward spread of the ice, which scooped out a series of deep troughs. Blocked at the north ends by glacial debris the basins now hold elongated lakes (Figure 37.2). Many hundreds of lake basins were created by ice action all over the glaciated portions of North America and Europe. Countless small lakes of Minnesota, Canada, and Finland occupy rock basins scooped out by ice action (Figure 37.3).

Glacial Drift

The term **glacial drift** has long been applied to include all varieties of rock debris deposited in close association with glaciers. Drift is of two major types: (1) **Stratified drift** consists of layers of sorted and stratified clays, silts, sands, or gravels deposited by meltwater streams or in bodies of standing water adjacent to the ice. (2) **Till** is a heterogeneous mixture of rock fragments ranging in size from clay to boulders and is deposited directly from the ice without water transport.

Over those parts of the United States formerly covered by Pleistocene ice sheets, glacial drift averages from 20 ft

(6 m) thick over mountainous terrain such as New England, to 50 ft (15 m) and more over the lowlands of the north-central United States. Over Iowa, drift is from 150 to 200 ft (45 to 60 m) thick; over Illinois, it averages more than 100 ft (30 m) thick. Locally, where deep stream valleys existed prior to glacial advance, as in Ohio, drift may be several hundred feet thick.

Landforms Left by Ice Sheets

To understand the form and composition of deposits left by ice sheets, we need first to consider the conditions prevailing at the time of existence of the ice, as shown in Figure 37.4. Block A shows a region partly covered by an ice sheet with a stationary front edge. This condition occurs

Figure 37.2   Seen from an altitude of 10,000 ft (3000 m), Canandaigua Lake occupies a glacially-deepened trough within the northern fringe of the Appalachian Plateau in New York. In this infrared photograph, the green vegetation of fields and forests is almost white in contrast to the lake water, which appears black. Lake Ontario lies in the distance. (Wahl's Photographic Service, Inc., Pittsford, N. Y.)

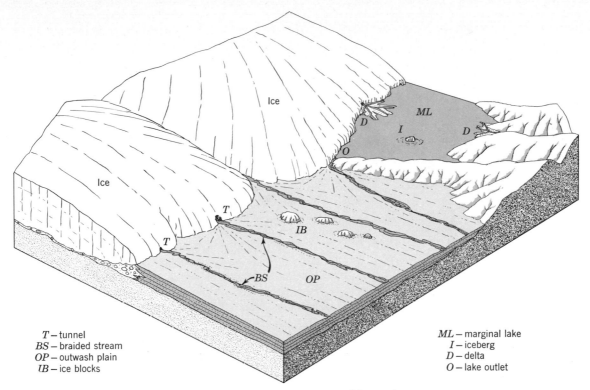

T — tunnel
BS — braided stream
OP — outwash plain
IB — ice blocks

ML — marginal lake
I — iceberg
D — delta
O — lake outlet

A. With the ice front stabilized and the ice in a wasting, stagnant condition, various depositional features are built by meltwater.

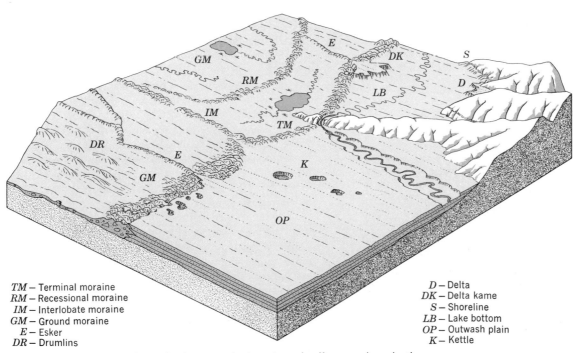

TM — Terminal moraine
RM — Recessional moraine
IM — Interlobate moraine
GM — Ground moraine
E — Esker
DR — Drumlins

D — Delta
DK — Delta kame
S — Shoreline
LB — Lake bottom
OP — Outwash plain
K — Kettle

B. After the ice has wasted completely away, a variety of new landforms made under the ice is exposed to view.

Figure 37.4 Marginal landforms of continental glaciers.

Figure 37.5   Rugged topography of small knobs and kettles characterizes this interlobate moraine northeast of Elkhart Lake, Sheboygan County, Wisconsin. (W. C. Alden, U.S. Geological Survey.)

when the rate of ice ablation balances the amount of ice brought forward by spreading of the ice sheet. Any increase in ice movement would cause the ice to shove forward to cover more ground: an increase in the rate of wasting would cause the edge to recede and the ice surface to become lowered. Although the Pleistocene ice fronts did advance and recede in many minor and major fluctuations, there were long periods when the front was essentially stable. This condition is represented in Block A.

Figure 37.6   Moraine belts of the north-central United States have a festooned pattern left by ice lobes. (After R. F. Flint and others [1945] *Glacial Map of North America.*)

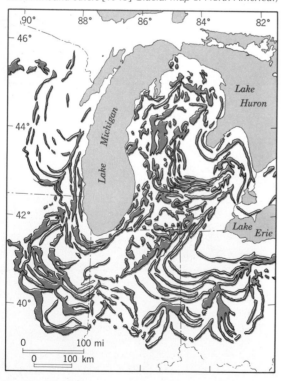

The transportational work of an ice sheet resembles that of a great conveyor belt. Anything carried on the belt is dumped off at the end and if not constantly removed will pile up in increasing quantity. Rock fragments brought within the ice are deposited at the forward margin as the ice evaporates or melts. There is no possibility of return transportation.

Glacial till that accumulates at the immediate ice edge forms a rubbly heap of irregular thickness, the **terminal moraine.** After the ice has disappeared, as in diagram B, the moraine appears as a belt of knobby hills interspersed with basinlike hollows, some of which hold small lakes. The term **knob-and-kettle** is often applied to such morainal belts (Figure 37.5). Terminal moraines tend to form curving patterns, the convex form of curvature directed southward and indicating that the ice advanced as a series of **lobes** (Figure 37.6). Where two lobes came together, the moraines curved back and fused together into a single moraine pointed northward. This is termed an **interlobate moraine** (Figure 37.4, block B). In its general recession accompanying deglaciation, the ice front paused for some time along a number of lines, causing morainal belts similar to the terminal moraine belt to be formed. These belts, known as **recessional moraines** (Figures 37.5 and 37.6), run roughly parallel with the terminal moraine but are often thin and discontinuous.

Block A of Figure 37.4 shows a smooth, sloping plain lying in front of the ice margin. This is the **outwash plain,** formed of stratified drift left by aggrading streams issuing from the ice. Their deposits are broad alluvial fans upon which were spread layer upon layer of sands and gravels. The adjective **glaciofluvial** is applied to stream-laid stratified drift. Where outwash accumulated around isolated ice blocks left behind in a previous episode of ice advance and recession, the blocks later melted away, leaving kettles. The outwash plain is then described as a **pitted plain.**

Large streams issue from tunnels in the ice, particularly when the ice for many miles back from the front has become stagnant, without forward movement. Tunnels then develop throughout the ice mass, serving to carry off the meltwater. After the ice has gone (Figure 37.4, block B) the outwash plain remains in its original form, but may be bounded on the iceward side by a steep slope which is the mold of the ice against which the outwash was built. Such a slope is called an **ice-contact slope.** Farther back, behind the terminal moraine, the position of a former ice tunnel is marked by a long, sinuous ridge known as an **esker.** The esker is the deposit of sand, pebbles, and cobbles formerly laid upon the floor of the ice tunnel. Because ice formed the sides and roof of the tunnel, its disappearance left merely the stream-bed deposit, which now forms a ridge (Figure 37.3). Eskers are often many miles long.

Another common glacial landform is the **drumlin,** a smoothly rounded, oval hill resembling the bowl of an inverted teaspoon. It consists of glacial till (Figure 37.4, block B). Drumlins invariably lie in a zone behind the terminal or recessional moraine. They commonly occur in groups or swarms, which may number in the hundreds. The long axis of each drumlin parallels the direction of ice movement so that the drumlins point toward the terminal moraines and serve as indicators of direction of ice movement.

Between moraines, the surface left by the ice is usually overspread by a cover of glacial till known as **ground moraine.** This cover is often inconspicuous because it forms no prominent or recognizable topographic features. Even so, the ground moraine may be thick and can obscure or entirely bury hills and valleys that existed before glaciation. Where smoothly spread, the ground moraine forms a level **till plain,** but this feature is likely to be found only in regions already fairly flat to start with. In more hilly and mountainous regions, such as New England, the preglacial valleys and hills retain their same general outlines despite glaciation.

Deposits Built into Standing Water

Where the general land slope is toward the front of an ice sheet, a natural topographic basin is formed between the ice front and the rising ground. Valleys that may have opened out northward are blocked by ice. Under such conditions, **marginal glacial lakes** form along the ice front (Figure 37.4, block A). These lakes overflow along the lowest available channel, which lies between the ice and the ground slope or over some low pass along a divide. Into marginal lakes, streams of meltwater from the ice build **glacial deltas,** similar in most respects to deltas formed by any stream flowing into a lake. Streams from the land also build deltas into the lake. When the ice has disappeared the lake drains away, exposing the bottom upon which layers of fine clay and silt have been laid. These fine-grained sediments, which have settled out from

Figure 37.8 Dust clouds raised by strong winds blowing over vegetation-free bars of the braided channel of the Delta River, central Alaska. Silt carried in this way builds modern loess deposits upon adjacent upland surfaces. (U.S. Navy photograph, from T. L. Péwé [1951] *Journal of Geology,* vol. 59, p. 400.)

suspension in turbid lake waters, are called **glaciolacustrine sediments** and are a variety of stratified drift. Glacial lake plains are extremely flat, with meandering streams and extensive areas of marshland.

Deltas, built with a flat top at what was formerly the lake level, are now curiously isolated, flat-topped landforms known as **delta kames.** Built of very well-washed and sorted sands and gravels, delta kames commonly show the steep sand layers characteristic of deltas (Figure 37.7).

Loess

In various parts of the world throughout midlatitude zones, the parent matter of rich agricultural soils is a layer of wind-transported sediment called **loess.** Usually unstratified, loess commonly exhibits natural vertical parting (cleavage) that allows it to stand in vertical faces, prisms, and pillars, even though the material is soft enough to be cut with a knife or shovel. In color, loess is usually yellowish or tawny orange, and sometimes brown. Particles composing loess fall mostly in the size range of silt. Five to ten percent of the particles may fall into the coarse clay grade; about the same proportion may be very fine sand. Most upland loess deposits are considered to have been transported in suspension by wind.

Strong evidence favors the source of North American and European loess in partially dry, braided stream channels and aggrading floodplains. These channels carried meltwater from the margins of stagnant and wasting ice sheets. During the summer, strong winds deflated the alluvial surfaces and carried the silt in suspension to be deposited over the uplands between valleys. This process can l

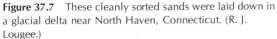

Figure 37.7 These cleanly sorted sands were laid down in a glacial delta near North Haven, Connecticut. (R. J. Lougee.)

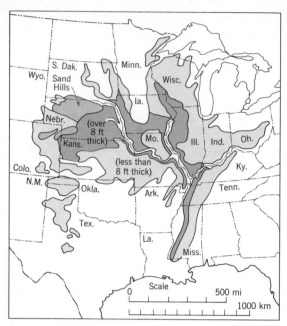

Figure 37.9 Map of loess distribution in the central United States. (Data from Map of Pleistocene Eolian Deposits of the United States, Geological Society of America, 1952.)

seen in action today in summer in alluvial valleys in Alaska (Figure 37.8).

A map of distribution of loess over the central United States (Figure 37.9) shows a general correspondence with the Mississippi, Missouri, and Platte rivers and their tributaries.

While the loess of the central states attains a maximum thickness of about 100 ft (30 m) in Kansas, thicknesses up to 200 ft (60 m) are measured in central Alaska. Loess of

Figure 37.10 Road sunken deeply into loess, Shensi, China. (Frederick G. Clapp, courtesy of The American Geographical Society.)

northern China is commonly over 100 ft (30 m) thick and reaches a maximum depth of around 300 ft (90 m).

Because loess forms vertical walls along valley sides and is able to resist sliding or flowage, but at the same time is easily dug into, it has been widely used for cave dwellings both in China and in Central Europe. In China, old trails and roads in the loess have become deeply sunken into the ground as a result of the pulverization of the loess of the road bed and its removal by wind and water (Figure 37.10).

Environmental and Resource Aspects of Glacial Deposits and Loess

Because much of Europe and North America was glaciated by the Pleistocene ice sheets, landforms associated with the ice are of fundamental environmental importance, and the deposits constitute a natural resource as well. Agricultural influences of glaciation are both favorable and unfavorable, depending on preglacial topography and whether the ice eroded or deposited heavily.

In hilly or mountainous regions, such as New England, the glacial till is thinly distributed and extremely stony. Soils that developed on glacial deposits of the northern United States and Canada are generally of low fertility. Extensive bogs, unsuited to agriculture unless transformed by water drainage systems, are another unfavorable element. Early settlers found cultivation difficult because of countless boulders and cobbles in the soil.

Till accumulations on steep mountain slopes are subject to mass movements in the form of earth flows and debris avalanches. Clays in the till become weakened upon absorbing water from melting snows and spring rains. Where slopes have been oversteepened by excavation for highways, movement of till is a common phenomenon.

Along morainal belts the steep slopes, irregularity of knob-and-kettle topography, and abundance of boulders conspired to prevent crop cultivation but invited use as pasture. These same features, however, make morainal belts extremely desirable as suburban residential areas. Pleasing landscapes of hills, depressions, and small lakes make ideal locations for large estates.

Extensive till plains, outwash plains, and lake plains, on the other hand, comprise some of the most productive agricultural land in the world. In this class belong the prairie lands of Indiana, Illinois, Iowa, Nebraska, and Minnesota. We must not lose sight of the fact that in these areas upland loess forms a blanket over clay-rich till and sandy outwash. Exposed glacial drift would be a poor parent base for soil.

Glaciofluvial deposits are of great economic value. The sands and gravels of outwash plains, kames, and eskers provide the aggregate necessary for concrete and the base courses beneath highway pavements. The purest sands may be used for molds needed for metal castings.

Glaciofluvial deposits, where they are thick, form excellent aquifers and are a major source of ground-water supplies. Deep accumulations of stratified sands in preglacial bedrock valleys are capable of yielding ground water in quantities sufficient for municipal and industrial uses. Water development of this type is widespread in Ohio, Pennsylvania, and New York.

Man and Geomorphic Processes

We have concluded our twelve study units of Part IV dealing with geomorphic processes and landforms. Because geomorphic processes are continually at work over the lands of the globe, their interaction with Man is particularly intense, as compared with internal geologic processes such as tectonics and volcanism. Human activity cannot stop a volcano from erupting, and it seems even doubtful if there is any way to stop a moving lava flow. Although scientists are speculating on ways to turn a single future disastrous earthquake into a series of harmless minor quakes, success in achieving that goal lies a very long way off—if it is ever to be reached at all.

On the other hand, the natural transport of water and sediment in streams and along coasts is readily altered by Man's engineering activities. This group of study units has shown many ways in which Man has interfered with geomorphic processes. Looking back upon the various attempts to regulate floods—river floods and coastal floods—an important change in human outlook emerges as a significant trend. Less than a half-century ago, we were dedicated to controlling river floods and to keeping back the sea, protecting our vested interests by sheer force of machine power. Today, there is a move afoot to cease these futile efforts to achieve 100% protection from natural hazards. Instead, the goal is increasingly to look for ways to avoid the impacts of those hazards and to leave natural processes to act as they have acted over countless thousands of centuries in the past.

In terms of water resources, a similar change of outlook is occurring. In place of planning new and grandiose schemes of water transfer to make the desert bloom, we are suggesting that the desert be left to its natural state of operation. Let agriculture, industry, and urban development be redirected to regions with naturally ample water surpluses. The environmentalist forces that now militate against the dam builders, the levee builders, and seawall builders are not the only forces seeking to preserve our natural scenery; economic forces are perhaps equally strong.

Can we really afford the billions of dollars it will take to construct the Central Arizona Project to bring water to the desert? Can we really afford the billions of dollars that will be required to protect all of our floodplains from 100-year floods? Perhaps resistance to funding enormous new engineering projects is not merely a temporary expression of economic recession, inflation, and high interest rates. Perhaps resistance reflects a new set of national priorities. Should not these huge expenditures be used to reduce environmental pollution, to reverse urban decay, to improve education, to give better health care, to improve the lot of minority citizen groups, and to reduce crime?

In Part V, we turn to the interaction of Man and natural ecosystems. Here, too, we will be dealing with natural systems that are extremely vulnerable to disturbance and damage by human activities.

SCIENCE
SUPPLEMENT
Origin of the Great Lakes

The Great Lakes of the United States and Canada are truly remarkable environmental features. By an accident of nature—the Pleistocene glaciation—these huge freshwater bodies happen to lie in a midlatitude continental area that has proved enormously productive both agriculturally and industrially. Taken together, the surface area of the Great Lakes is about 95,000 sq mi (246,000 sq km), much greater than any single freshwater lake in the world. Other large freshwater lakes of the world lie in less favorable environments from the human standpoint: Great Bear and Great Slave lakes in the far north of Canada; Lakes Victoria and Tanganyika in equatorial Africa; Lake Baikal in Siberia.

Many serious environmental problems beset the Great Lakes. One reason is that the water supplies for a large number of industrial cities are drawn from the same lakes into which are fed in return enormous quantities of pollutant wastes. We shall discuss certain environmental problems of the Great Lakes in Unit 44. At this point, a brief account of the origin of the Great Lakes will develop the natural-science background for those problem studies.

In preglacial times, lowlands existed where the lakes now stand. These lowlands were occupied by major streams. Repeated ice advances of four glaciations extensively and deeply eroded weak rocks of the former lowlands and carried the debris south to form blocking lines of hills, called moraines, on the south.

Stages in Great Lakes evolution are shown in the series of six maps in Figure 37.11. These maps are simplified and show only a few representative stages. Map A shows the earliest lakes beginning to form as the ice front receded. Lakes Chicago and Maumee were marginal glacial lakes, ponded between the ice front and higher ground to the south. Both lakes overflowed southward by streams draining into the Mississippi River system.

Map B shows continued retreat and the diversion of one lake into another by a marginal stream following the ice front. Map C catches the action at a point when drainage was established eastward along the ice front to enter the Hudson River System, by way of the Mohawk Valley. In Map D, final ice recession was under way and part of

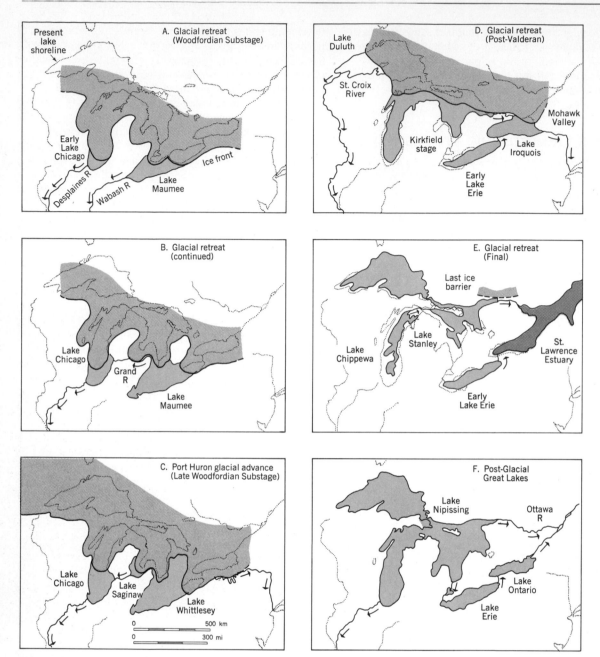

Figure 37.11 Six stages in the evolution of the Great Lakes. (After J. L. Hough [1958] *Geology of the Great Lakes,* Univ. of Illinois Press, Urbana, pp. 284-296.)

ancestral Lake Superior had opened up, draining south into the Mississippi system, while the other lakes drained east to the Hudson system.

Map F shows the very last of the ice disappearing in Ontario and opening an outlet along what is now the Ottawa River. This outlet led directly into the St. Lawrence valley, which was then an estuary of salt water. Map F shows a stage of maximum extent of the Great Lakes. Crustal tilting caused the Ottawa River outlet to be abandoned,

and lowering of lake levels caused abandonment of the drainage of Lake Michigan into the Mississippi system.

One result of this complex history of changing lake levels and areal extents is that today there are broad marginal zones of lake plains along the shores of lakes Michigan, Huron, Erie, and Ontario. These plains are intensively developed as agricultural lands and have absorbed the urban expansion of major lake cities such as Chicago, Toledo, Detroit, Cleveland, Toronto, Buffalo, and Erie.

PART V

Man and Ecosystems

Unit 38
Flow of Energy in the Biosphere

The Silent Spring of Rachel Carson

"There was once a town in the heart of America where all life seemed to live in harmony with its surroundings. The town lay in the midst of a checkerboard of prosperous farms, with fields of grain and hillsides of orchards where, in spring, white clouds of bloom drifted above the green fields. . . .

Along the roads, laurel, viburnum and alder, great ferns and wildflowers delighted the traveler's eye through much of the year. Even in winter the roadsides were places of beauty, where countless birds come to feed on the berries and on the seed heads of the dried weeds rising above the snow. The countryside was, in fact, famous for the abundance and variety of its bird life, and when the flood of migrants was pouring through in spring

A blue heron in the Blackwater Game Refuge, Cambridge, Maryland. (Richard Frear/Photo Researchers.)

and fall people traveled from great distances to observe them. Others came to fish the streams, which flowed clear and cold out of the hills and contained shady pools where trout lay. . . .

Then a strange blight crept over the area and everything began to change. Some evil spell had settled on the community: mysterious maladies swept the flocks of chickens; the cattle and sheep sickened and died. Everywhere was a shadow of death. The farmers spoke of much illness among their families. In the town the doctors had become more and more puzzled by new kinds of sickness appearing among their patients. There had been several sudden and unexplained deaths, not only among adults but even among children, who would be stricken suddenly while at play and die within a few hours.

There was a strange stillness. The birds, for example—where had they gone? Many people spoke of them, puzzled and disturbed. The feeding stations in the backyards were deserted. The few birds seen anywhere were moribund; they trembled violently and could not fly. It was a spring without voices. On the mornings that had once throbbed with the dawn chorus of robbins, catbirds, doves, jays, wrens, and scores of other bird voices there was now no sound; only silence lay over the fields and woods and marsh.

In the gutters under the eaves and between the shingles of the roofs, a white granular powder still showed a few patches; some weeks before it had fallen like snow upon the roofs and the lawns, the fields and streams.

No witchcraft, no enemy action had silenced the rebirth of new life in this stricken world. The people had done it themselves."*

With these paragraphs, Rachel Carson began

*Excerpted from *Silent Spring* by Rachel Carson, Copyright © 1962 by Rachel L. Carson, published by Houghton Mifflin Company. Used by permission.

270

her famous book *Silent Spring*—a book destined to change the attitude of a people and a nation toward the natural life around them. Rachel Carson's book was largely devoted to a single theme, that of the inadvertent poisoning of wildlife, domestic animals, and even humans by pesticides and other chemicals used for insect control. With page after page of thoroughly documented scientific observations and conclusions, Dr. Carson gathered the facts together and alerted the nation to the hazards of indiscriminate application of pesticides.

Although Dr. Carson's book was focused primarily on the impact of pesticides in the environment, a topic dealt with more fully in Unit 47, her contribution to ecology and the conservation movement was much larger. *Silent Spring* made a fundamental point about the science of ecology—that all organisms are interrelated through the vast web of nature. The chemicals dispersed to control insects are taken in by lower organisms and passed on, through the food chain, to the higher animals that feed on them, and ultimately to Man. In this way, Man's interference at one level of the ecosystem echoes and rebounds throughout the entire ecosystem, of which Man is but a part.

Thus, Rachel Carson's most lasting contribution to our welfare was probably not so much her documentation of pesticide poisoning, but the awakening of a generation to the fact that Man and all living organisms are coupled together through the pathways of energy flow and material cycling in the world ecosystem.

Ecology and Ecosystems

All living organisms of the earth, together with the environments with which those organisms interact constitute the **biosphere.** Organisms, whether belonging to the plant kingdom or to the animal kingdom, also interact with each other. Study of these interactions—in the form of exchanges of matter, energy, and stimuli of various sorts—between life forms and the environment is the science of **ecology,** very broadly defined. The total assemblage of components entering into the interactions of a group of organisms is known as an ecological system, or more simply, an **ecosystem.** The root "eco" comes from a Greek word connoting a house in the sense of household, which implies that a family lives together and interacts within a functional, physical structure.

Ecosystems have inputs of matter and energy used to build biological structures, to reproduce, and to maintain necessary internal energy levels. Matter and energy are also exported from an ecosystem. An ecosystem tends to achieve a balance of the various processes and activities within it. For the most part, these balances are quite sensitive and can be easily upset or destroyed. Physical geography meshes closely with ecology. For example, organisms and their life processes play an important role in shaping the characteristics of the soil layer.

To the geographer, ecosystems are a part of the physical composition of the life layer. A forest, for example, is not only a living community of organisms; it is also a collection of physical objects on the land surface. A forest is physically very different from an expanse of prairie grassland. Plant geographers are aware of these place-to-place differences in the physical aspect of vegetation. They attempt to categorize the varied types; they map the global distribution of vegetation forms.

Geographers also view ecosystems as natural resource systems. Food, fiber, fuel, and structural material are products of ecosystems—they represent organic compounds placed in storage by organisms through the expenditure of energy basically derived from the sun. Geographers are interested in the influence of climate on ecosystem productivity.

The Ecosystem and the Food Chain

As an example of an ecosystem, consider a salt marsh (Figure 38.1). A variety of organisms is present: algae and aquatic plants, microorganisms, insects, snails, and crayfish, as well as larger organisms such as fishes, birds, shrews, mice, and rats. Inorganic components will be found as well: water, air, clay particles and organic sediment, inorganic nutrients, trace elements, and light energy. Energy transformations in the ecosystem occur by means of a series of steps or levels, referred to as a **food chain.**

The plants and algae in this chain are the **primary producers.** They use light energy to convert carbon dioxide and water to carbohydrates (long chains of sugar molecules) and eventually to other biochemical molecules needed for the support of life. This process of energy conversion is called photosynthesis. Organisms engaged in photosynthesis form the base of the food chain.

At the next level are the **primary consumers** (the snails, insects, and fishes); they live by feeding on the producers. At a still higher level are the **secondary consumers** (the mammals and birds); they feed on the primary consumers. As in many ecosystems, still higher levels of feeding are evident: the marsh hawks and owls. The **decomposers** feed on detritus, or decaying organic matter, derived from all levels. They are mostly microscopic organisms (microorganisms) and bacteria.

The food chain is really an energy flow system, tracing the path of solar energy through the ecosystem. Solar energy is stored by one class of organisms, the primary

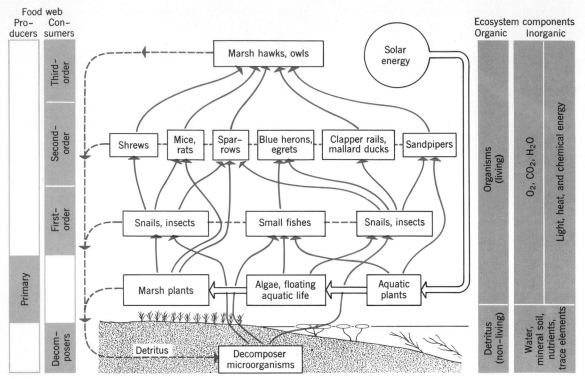

Figure 38.1 Flow diagram of a salt-marsh ecosystem in winter. Arrows show how energy flows from the sun to producers, consumers, and decomposers. (Food web after R. L. Smith [1966] *Ecology and Biology,* Harper & Row, New York, p. 30, Figure 3.1.)

producers, in the chemical products of photosynthesis. As these organisms are eaten and digested by consumers, chemical energy is released. This chemical energy is used to power new biochemical reactions, which again produce stored chemical energy in the bodies of the consumers.

At each level of energy transformation, energy is lost as waste heat. In addition, much of the energy input to each organism must be used in respiration. **Respiration** can be thought of as burning of fuel to keep the organism operating. Respiration is basically the oxidation of organic compounds, accompanied by release of heat energy. Energy expended in respiration is used for bodily maintenance and cannot be stored for use by other organisms higher up in the food web. This loss of energy to respiration means that generally both the numbers of organisms and their total amount of living tissue must decrease drastically up the food chain.

Photosynthesis and Respiration

Stated in the simplest possible terms, **photosynthesis** is the production of carbohydrate. **Carbohydrate** is a general term for a class of organic compounds consisting of the elements carbon, hydrogen, and oxygen in various proportions. Carbohydrate is formed by a series of complex biochemical reactions using water (H_2O) and carbon dioxide (CO_2) as well as light energy. We can express carbohydrate by the formula CH_2O, although carbohydrate usually consists of several or many CH_2O units. A

simplified reaction for photosynthesis can be written:

$$H_2O + CO_2 + \text{light energy} \rightarrow CH_2O + O_2$$

Oxygen as O_2 gas is a by-product.

To state respiration in the simplest possible terms, we simply reverse the above reaction:

$$CH_2O + O_2 \rightarrow H_2O + CO_2 + \text{chemical energy}$$

Neither photosynthesis nor respiration is as simple as we have made it out to be. The chemical compounds involved in respiration include many that are far more complex than simple carbohydrate, but they all represent the products of photosynthesis and subsequent synthesis of more complex organic molecules.

At this point, it is helpful to link photosynthesis and respiration in a continuous cycle involving both the primary producer and the decomposer. Figure 38.2 shows one closed loop for hydrogen (H), one for carbon (C), and two loops for oxygen (O). We are not taking into account that there are two atoms of hydrogen in each molecule of water and carbohydrate, or that there are two atoms of oxygen in each molecule of carbon dioxide and oxygen gas. Only the flow pattern counts in this representation.

A good place to start is the soil, from which water is drawn up into the body of a living plant. In the green leaves of the plant, photosynthesis takes place while light energy is absorbed by the leaf cells. Carbon dioxide is being brought in from the atmosphere at this point. Here

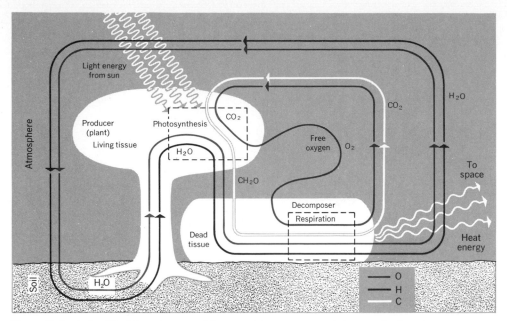

Figure 38.2 A simplified flow diagram of the essential components of photosynthesis and respiration.

oxygen is liberated and begins its atmospheric cycle. The plant tissue then dies and falls to the ground, where it is acted on by the decomposer. Through respiration, oxygen is taken out of the atmosphere or soil air and combined with the decomposing carbohydrate. Energy is now liberated. Here both carbon dixoide and water enter the atmosphere as gases.

An important concept emerges from this flow diagram. Energy passes through the system. It comes from the sun and returns eventually to outer space. On the other hand, the material components, hydrogen, oxygen, and carbon, are recycled within the total system. Of course, many other material components are recycled in the same way. These are plant nutrients; among them are the cations essential in the growth of plants. Nutrients are constantly recycled. Because the earth as a planet is a closed system, the material components never leave the total system, but they can be stored in other ways and forms where they are unavailable for use by plants for prolonged periods of geologic time. We shall develop this concept in Unit 40.

Net Photosynthesis

Because both photosynthesis and respiration go on simultaneously in a plant, the amount of new carbohydrate placed in storage is less than the total carbohydrate being synthesized. We must thus distinguish between gross photosynthesis and net photosynthesis. **Gross photosynthesis** is the total amount of carbohydrate produced by photosynthesis; **net photosynthesis** is the amount of carbohydrate remaining after respiration has broken down sufficient carbohydrate to power the plant. Stated as an equation,

Net photosynthesis = Gross photosynthesis − Respiration

Since both photosynthesis and respiration occur in the same cell, gross photosynthesis cannot be readily measured. Instead, we shall deal with net photosynthesis. In most cases, respiration will be held constant, so that use of the net instead of the gross will show the same trends.

The rate of net photosynthesis is strongly dependent on the intensity of light energy available, up to a limit. Figure 38.3 shows this principle. On the vertical axis the rate of net photosynthesis is indicated by the rate at which a plant takes up carbon dioxide. On the horizontal axis light intensity increases from left to right. At first, net photosynthesis rises rapidly as light intensity increases, but the rate then slows and reaches a maximum value shown by the plateau in the curve. Above the maximum, the rate falls off because the incoming light is also causing heating. Increased temperature, in turn, increases the rate of respiration, which offsets gross production by photosynthesis.

Figure 38.3 The curve of net photosynthesis shows a steep initial rise, then levels off as light intensity rises.

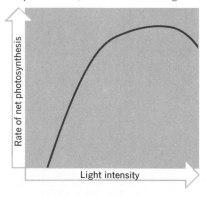

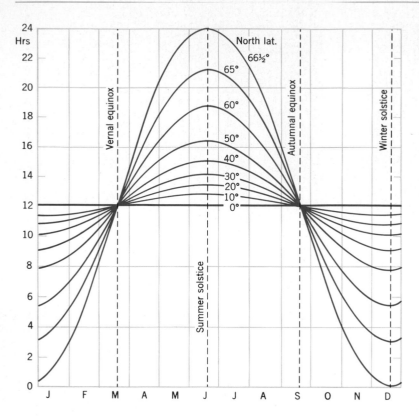

Figure 38.4   Duration of the day at various latitudes throughout the year. Vertical scale gives number of hours the sun is above the horizon.

Light intensity sufficient to allow maximum net photosynthesis is only 10 to 30% of full summer sunlight for most green plants. Additional light energy is simply ineffective. The factor of duration of daylight then becomes the important factor in the rate at which products of photosynthesis accumulate as plant tissues. On this subject, you can draw on your knowledge of the seasons and the changing angle of the sun's rays with latitude. Figure 38.4 shows the duration of the daylight period with changing seasons for a wide range of latitudes in the northern hemisphere. At low latitudes, days are not far from the average 12-hour length throughout the year, whereas at high latitudes, days are short in winter but long in summer. The seasonal contrast in day length increases with latitude. In subarctic latitudes, photosynthesis can obviously go on in summer during most of the 24 hours, and this factor can compensate partly for the shortness of the season.

Photosynthesis also increases in rate as air temperature increases, up to a limit. Figure 38.5 shows the results of a laboratory experiment in which sphagnum moss was grown under constant illumination. Gross photosynthesis increased rapidly to a maximum at about 70° F (20° C), then leveled off. Respiration increased quite steadily to the limit of the experiment. Net photosynthesis, peaked at about 65° F (18° C), then fell off rapidly.

Net Primary Production

Plant ecologists measure the accumulated net production by photosynthesis in terms of the **biomass,** which is the dry weight of the organic matter. This quantity could, of

course, be stated for a single plant or animal, but a more useful statement is made in terms of the biomass per unit of surface area within the ecosystem—the acre, square foot, or square meter. Of all ecosystems, forests have the greatest biomass; that of grasslands and croplands is very small in comparison. For freshwater bodies and the oceans the biomass is even smaller—on the order of one-hundredth that of the grasslands and croplands.

The annual rate of production of organic matter is the vital information we need, not the biomass itself. Granted

Figure 38.5   Respiration and gross and net photosynthesis vary with temperature. (Data of Stofelt, 1937, in A. C. Leopold [1964] *Plant Growth and Development,* McGraw-Hill, New York, p. 31, Figure 2.26.)

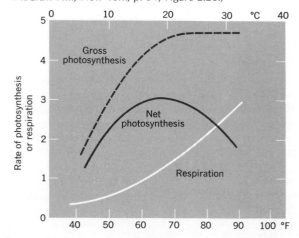

Table 38.1 Net primary production for various ecosystems

	Grams per Square Meter per Year	
	Average	Typical Range
Lands		
Rainforest of the equatorial zone	2000	1000-5000
Freshwater swamps and marshes	2000	800-4000
Midlatitude forest	1300	600-2500
Midlatitude grassland	500	150-1500
Agricultural land	650	100-4000
Lakes and streams	500	100-1500
Extreme desert	3	0-10
Oceans		
Estuaries (tidal)	2000	500-4000
Continental shelf	350	200-600
Open ocean	125	1-400

that forests have a very large biomass and grasslands very little, what we want to know is: Which ecosystem is the more productive? In other words, which ecosystem produces the greatest annual yield in terms of resources useful to Man? For the answer, we turn to figures on the **net primary production** of various ecosystems. Table 38.1 gives this information in units of grams of dry organic matter produced annually from 1 sq m of surface. The figures are only rough estimates, but they are nevertheless highly meaningful. Since we wish only to make comparisons, English units are omitted. Note that the highest values are in two quite unlike environments: equatorial rainforests and tidal estuaries. Agricultural land compares favorably with grassland, but the range is very large in agricultural land, reflecting many factors such as availability of soil water, soil fertility, and use of fertilizers and machinery.

Energy Flow along the Food Chain

The primary producers trap the energy of the sun and make it available to support consuming organisms at higher levels in the food chain. But remember that energy is lost during each upward step in the chain, so that the number of steps is limited. In general, anywhere from 10 to 50% of the energy stored in organic matter at one level can be passed up the chain to the next level. Four levels of consumers are about the normal limit.

passed up the chain when only 10% moves from one level to the next. The horizontal scale is in powers of ten. In ecosystems of the lands, the biomass also decreases with each upward step in the chain; the number of individuals of the consuming animals also decreases with each upward step. In the food chain shown in Figure 38.1, there

are only a few individuals of marsh hawks and owls in the third level of consumers, whereas there are countless individuals in the primary level. These facts serve as a clear message to Man; they tell us that when we raise beef cattle, swine, sheep, and fowl to eat, we are extremely wasteful of the world's total food resource. These animals, in storing food for humans to consume, have already wasted two-thirds or more of the energy they consumed as plant matter from the producing level. If, instead, we subsisted largely on grains and other food plants such as legumes, grown on the available farm lands, then our food resource could support a much larger population. Although this observation does not apply to sheep and cattle subsisting entirely on grazing lands that are unfit for cereal crops, it is, all the same, a potent concept.

In the next unit, we will investigate the soil-water cycle vital to plants and then turn to the study of cycling of nutrients through the primary producers. Armed with this information, we can then examine agricultural ecosystems to find out how Man has altered the patterns of flow of energy and nutrients in attempts to intensify net primary production.

Figure 38.6 Percentage of energy passed up the steps of the food chain, assuming 90% is lost energy at each step.

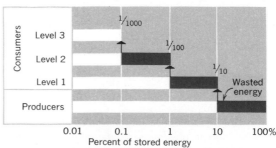

Chemical Energy Released by Oxidation

Organisms differ in the types of energy and matter needed to sustain them. In terms of these needs, we recognize two classes of organisms: autotrophs and heterotrophs. **Autotrophs** manufacture their own foods from inorganic substances by using light or chemical energy. Green plants are examples of autotrophs. (In earlier paragraphs we referred to autotrophs as primary producers.) The autotrophs require only the simplest forms of matter; these are water, carbon dioxide, and oxygen, as well as sixteen inorganic nutrients. Their biochemical systems are capable of producing the biological macromolecules needed for life entirely from these inorganic substances.

Heterotrophs, on the other hand, cannot utilize light energy, and instead depend on chemical energy in the form of reduced carbon compounds of organic origin. Thus, any organism which feeds on other organisms or their remains is a heterotroph. (In earlier paragraphs we referred to heterotrophs as consumers.) In addition to organic compounds, heterotrophs may require specific molecules that they are no longer able to synthesize for themselves—for example, most heterotrophs cannot synthesize all the amino acids and must obtain those they lack from organic sources in their diet.

We might thus divide inputs of energy and matter to organisms into two subgroups each: **inorganic inputs,** which will be more important for autotrophs, and **organic inputs,** which will be more important for heterotrophs. This same division holds, of course, for outputs as well.

All heterotrophic organisms ingest chemical energy as a power source. The energy of organic compounds is usually released by combining them with oxygen in the process of **oxidation.** You are probably most familiar with oxidation in burning, the uncontrolled reaction of substances with atmospheric oxygen. Although oxidation by organisms may produce the same products as burning, it is a controlled reaction and the energy of organic compounds is released slowly. This form of oxidation is **biological oxidation.**

Biological oxidation involves breaking the molecular bonds between atoms of organic molecules and inserting oxygen atoms until the stable end products of CO_2 and H_2O are formed. Thus, a sugar molecule, $C_6H_{12}O_6$, is oxidized until all six carbon atoms have been converted to CO_2 and all twelve hydrogen atoms have been converted to H_2O. At that point, no further energy may be derived from the end products, CO_2 and H_2O, for no more oxygen atoms may be added to them. Therefore, the fewer the oxygen atoms contained in the original compound, the greater is the energy capable of release by oxidation. Compounds with relatively few oxygen atoms are described as **reduced;** the more reduced the compound, the more energy it yields on oxidation.

The two basic types of food-source molecules are **lipids** (fats and oils) and carbohydrates. Lipids are long chains of carbon atoms with hydrogen atoms attached to the carbons. Each carbon atom in the lipid chain can yield one CO_2 and one H_2O molecule. Thus lipids are highly reduced and yield much energy in oxidation.

In contrast to the lipids are the carbohydrates, which are the products of photosynthesis. A typical carbohydrate is a six-carbon sugar molecule. Each carbon atom already has at least one oxygen atom attached, and is less reduced, therefore, than the carbon atom of a lipid molecule. As a result, carbohydrates yield less energy on complete oxidation than do lipids.

Proteins also present an energy source to organisms. Proteins are made up of a set of building blocks, the **amino acids.** There are 23 different kinds of amino acids found in living matter, and in proteins they are strung together in a linear fashion to form chains. In general, amino acids contain somewhat fewer than one oxygen per carbon atom, and so are somewhat more reduced than are carbohydrates. Proteins, then, represent an energy source intermediate in yield between carbohydrates and lipids.

Heat energy released by the oxidation of a variety of different compounds is shown below.

Substance	Composition	Heat (thousands of calories per gram)
Hydrogen gas	H_2	34
Carbon (example: anthracite coal)	C	8
Methane	CH_4	13
Petroleum	Complex hydrocarbons	10
Lipid	$C_{47}H_{104}O_6$	9.5
Protein	Complex amino acid chain	5.5
Glucose (six-carbon sugar)	$C_6H_{12}O_6$	4
Wood	Mostly carbohydrate	4
Plant tissue: terrestrial plants		4.5
Animal tissue: insects, vertebrates		5.5

The values are obtained by rapid oxidation in a closed container known as a **bomb calorimeter,** under controlled laboratory conditions. In the 1880s, Max Rubner, a German physiologist, showed that when proteins, carbohydrates, and fats are oxidized in the animal body by slow normal processes of respiration, the heat equivalents of those substances are almost identical with values obtained by the bomb calorimeter.

Among lipids, proteins, and carbohydrates, notice that lipids yield the most energy per unit of weight. Thus energy stored as body fats and oils occupies much less bulk than an equivalent quantity of energy stored in the form of either carbohydrate or protein. Fat is therefore used preferentially in energy storage by animals that must move their biomass from one place to another. The energy value shown in the table for animal tissue, which is higher than that shown for plant tissue, reflects this difference.

Unit 39
The Soil-water Balance

Where Did All Those Indians Go?

Flagstaff, Arizona, lies in the beautiful high country of northern Arizona, much of it clothed in forests of tall ponderosa pines. This is a volcanic region, with extinct volcanoes forming the San Francisco Peaks and many smaller volcanic cones and craters. Today much of the area is within the Coconino National Forest, which yields a rich timber harvest. There are also many cattle ranches and even some farms on which beans are raised. You would think that this verdant region would have supported a substantial American Indian population before the coming of the White Man, but the truth is that it was nearly uninhabited in the century in which Columbus discovered the New World. Yet there are Indian ruins to be seen in this area. When were they inhabited, and why did the Indians leave?

An archeologist who spent many years in Flagstaff may have solved the mystery of the vanished Indians. He was Dr. Harold S. Colton and he knew intimately every square mile of that region. Some 1500 prehistoric sites, once inhabited by agricultural Indians, have been recorded, and from these over 500 collections of broken pottery have been carefully studied and dated. Dr. Colton was able to estimate the resident Indian population of the region from the number and extent of the ancient dwelling sites for each historical period. His findings are

Wupatki Ruin stands as a silent reminder of a time when fertile volcanic soils supported an Indian population in the region of Sunset Crater, northern Arizona. (Fred E. Mang, Jr., National Park Service.)

shown in the accompanying bar graph. Between 600 and 900 A.D., the population was very sparse, but the number began to rise by 975, followed by a spectacular increase to a peak of over 8000 persons in 1160. There seems to have been a rapid collapse after that, with only about 600 persons remaining in the area by 1250. What caused this rise and fall of Indian population?

Dr. Colton was also a good geologist, and, having thoroughly studied the volcanic history of the Flagstaff region, he divided it into stages of eruption of the various kinds of volcanoes. The last volcanic eruption to occur was that of Sunset Crater, a small cone of loose volcanic ash about 900 feet high. Its name comes from the rosy color of the summit, which contains a cuplike crater. All of the material of the cone is loose cinder, and you sink ankle-deep in it as you try to climb the steep sides.

The eruption of Sunset Crater occurred about 900 A.D. and probably took only a few months before the explosive activity ceased. Fine black particles blown from the volcanic vent spread over the land surface for miles around to form a layer of loose black sand. The event is closely dated by studying the growth rings of trees buried and killed in the eruption. The layer of black sand covered an area of about 800 square miles, and much of it lay upon a previously barren surface of older black lava or red clay, scarcely able to support more than some bunch grasses, woody shrubs, and a few pines and junipers.

The black volcanic sand layer acted as a mulch. If you have tried vegetable gardening, you know that a mulch can be any sort of dead plant material, such as leaves or grass, that is spread over the garden soil to keep down weeds, to protect the soil from being beaten down by rains, and to reduce the loss of soil moisture by evaporation. Sand or gravel can also be used as a mulch. The volcanic sand from Sunset Crater made a dramatic improvement in the agricultural productivity of the area it covered. Soil moisture was protected from rapid evaporation during the hot summers. Crops could now be grown in the area and a much larger population supported. So, be-

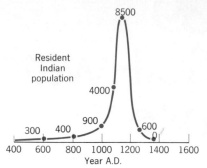

Indian population in the Flagstaff area. (Data of H. S. Colton.)

tween 1071 and 1100, there was a veritable land rush to the area, with hundreds of families taking up new homes. But then the scene changed. Strong winds blew the black sand along the ground, heaping it into moving dunes and scouring the clay and rock surface beneath it. Torrential rains, which are common during summer thunderstorms, washed much of the sand off the slopes and into stream channels, to be carried to distant canyons. The Indians, abandoning their plots and villages, moved out of the area and into the nearby Verde Valley to the south. Dramatically, the population fell to a few hundred persons, and by the year 1350 all permanent inhabitants were gone.

Our study unit deals with moisture in the soil. No topic could be more important in terms of food resources for the human race. The subject is a bit on the technical side and may be tough going in places. With the knowledge you acquire about vital soil moisture and its annual cycle, you will be well equipped to evaluate plans for increasing the world's food supply and staving off famine and starvation for millions of humans now barely subsisting on the land.

DATA SOURCE: Harold S. Colton (1932) The effect of a volcanic eruption on an ancient pueblo people, *Geographical Review*, vol. 32, p. 582; Harold S. Colton (1949) The prehistoric population of the Flagstaff area, *Plateau*, vol. 22, no. 2, pp. 21-25.

Soil Water and Ecosystems

For plants—the primary producers—water serves as the fluid medium for transporting nutrients from the soil and plant roots into all parts of the plant tissues. Ample soil water is essential for plant growth. In addition, water molecules furnish the hydrogen and oxygen used in photosynthesis of carbohydrate. In this study unit we will investigate the balance of water in the soil throughout an annual cycle of changes from surplus of water to deficit of water.

Storage Capacity of the Soil

The **soil-water balance** can be thought of as a subcycle within the hydrologic cycle. We begin this subcycle at the point at which precipitation infiltrates the soil, a process explained in Unit 28. When infiltration occurs, the water is drawn downward through the soil pores, wetting successively lower layers. This activity is called **soil-water recharge.** Eventually the soil layer holds the maximum possible quantity of water, although the larger pores remain filled with air. Water movement then continues downward through the underlying belt.

Suppose now that the rain stops and several days of dry weather follow. Excess soil water continues to drain downward under gravity but some water clings to the soil particles and effectively resists the pull of gravity because of the force of capillary tension. We are all familiar with the way in which a water droplet seems to be enclosed in a "skin" of surface molecules, which draws the droplet together into a spherical shape so that it clings to the side of a glass indefinitely without flowing down. Similarly, tiny films of water adhere to the soil grains, particularly at the points of grain contacts, and will stay until disposed of by evaporation or by absorption into plant rootlets.

When a soil has first been saturated by water, then allowed to drain under gravity until no more water moves downward, the soil is said to be holding its **storage capacity** of water. (Among soil scientists, storage capacity is referred to as **field capacity**.) Drainage takes no more than two or three days for most soils. Most excess water is drained out within one day. Storage capacity is measured in units of depth, usually inches or centimeters, just as with precipitation. This means that for a given cube of soil, say 12 in. on a side (1 cu ft), if we were to extract all of the stored water, it might form a layer of water 3 in. deep in a pan of 1 sq ft. This would be equivalent to complete absorption of a 3-in. rainfall by a completely dry 12-in. layer of soil.

Storage capacity of a given soil depends largely on its texture. To understand this relationship, it is necessary to know how soil texture is described by soil scientists.

Soil Texture

The mineral fraction of the soil usually spans a very wide range of particle sizes. The term **soil texture** refers to the proportions of particles falling into each of several size grades. The size grades and their limiting grain diameters were explained in Unit 26. (Refer to Figure 26.2 for a review of the grade scale.) In measuring soil texture, gravel and larger particles are eliminated, since these play no important part in soil processes. Only the remaining grades—sand, silt, and clay—are used in defining soil textures.

Soil texture is described by a series of names emphasizing the dominant constituent, whether sand, silt, or clay. Figure 39.1 gives examples of five soil textures with typical percentage compositions. A **loam** is a mixture containing a substantial proportion of each of the three grades. Loams are classified as sandy, silty, or clay-rich when one of the grades is dominant.

Texture is important because it largely determines the ability of the soil to retain water and to transmit water to lower levels. Figure 39.2 shows how storage capacity varies with soil texture. Pure sand holds the least water, while pure clay holds the most. Loams hold intermediate amounts. Sand transmits the water downward most rapidly, clay most slowly. When planning the quantity of irrigation water to be applied, these factors must be taken into account. Sand reaches its capacity very rapidly, and

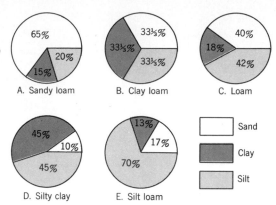

Figure 39.1 Typical compositions of five soil texture classes.

added water is wasted. Clay-rich loams take up water very slowly and, if irrigation is too rapid, water will be lost by surface runoff. By the same token, sandy soils require more frequent watering than clay-rich soils. The organic content of a soil also strongly affects its water-holding capacity.

Soil texture is largely an inherited feature of a given soil and depends on the composition of the parent regolith and underlying rock. Some rocks furnish a large spread in particle sizes, others yield mostly sand or mostly clay. The intermediate loam textures are generally best as agricultural soils because they drain well, but also have favorable water retention properties.

Figure 39.2 also shows how the wilting point is related to soil texture. **Wilting point** is a lower limiting value of soil water below which the leaves of garden crops will wilt, leading to death of the plant. Wilting point is highest in clay soils, because water molecules are tightly held to the clay particles by electrical forces and cannot be released to enter plant roots.

Figure 39.2 Storage capacity and wilting point vary according to soil texture.

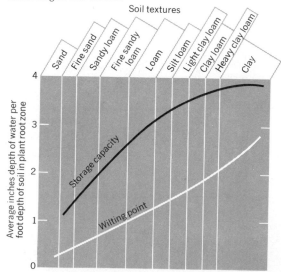

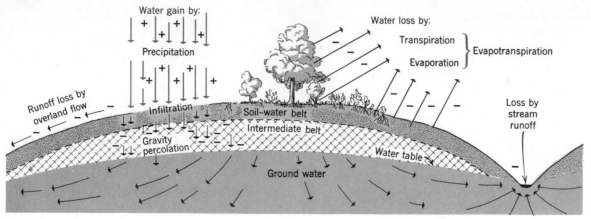

Figure 39.3   The soil-water belt occupies an important position in the hydrologic cycle.

Evaporation and Transpiration

Between periods of rain, water held in the soil is gradually given back to the atmosphere by a twofold drying process. First, direct evaporation into the open air occurs at the soil surface. Air also enters the soil freely and may actually be forced alternately in and out of the soil by atmospheric pressure changes. Even if the soil did not "breathe" in this way, there would be a slow diffusion of water vapor surfaceward through the open soil pores.

Second, plants draw the soil water into their systems through vast networks of tiny rootlets. This water, after being carried upward through the stem and branches into the leaves, is discharged through leaf pores into the atmosphere in the form of water vapor. The process is termed **transpiration.**

In studies of plant ecology and hydrology, the term **evapotranspiration** covers the combined moisture loss from direct evaporation and the transpiration of plants. The rate of evapotranspiration slows down as soil water supply becomes depleted during a dry summer period, because plants employ various devices to reduce transpiration. In general, the less water remaining, the slower is the loss through evapotranspiration.

Figure 39.3 illustrates the various terms explained up to this point and serves to give a more detailed picture of that part of the hydrologic cycle involving the soil. The soil layer from which plants can draw moisture is the **soil-water belt.** This belt gains water through precipitation and infiltration. As the minus signs show, the soil loses water through transpiration, evaporation, and overland flow. Excess water also leaves the soil by downward **gravity percolation** to the ground water zone below. Between the soil-water belt and the ground water zone is an **intermediate belt.** Beneath upland areas, water held in the intermediate belt lies too deep to be returned to the surface by evapotranspiration, since it is below the level of plant roots.

Figure 39.4   A typical annual cycle of soil-water change in the Middle West shows a short period of surplus in the spring and a long period of deficit during the summer and fall. (Data of Thornthwaite and Mather.)

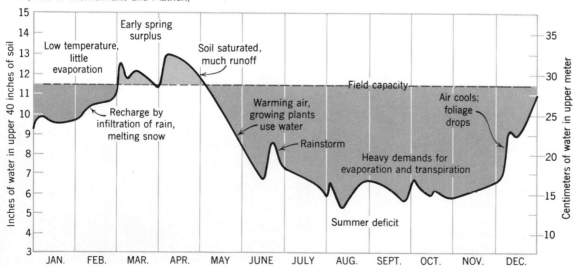

The Soil-water Cycle

We can turn next to consider the annual water budget of the soil. Figure 39.4 shows the annual cycle of soil water for a single year at an agricultural experiment station in Ohio. This example can be considered generally representative of conditions in humid, midlatitude climates where there is a strong temperature contrast between winter and summer.

Let us start with the early spring, (March). At this time the evaporation rate is low, because of low air temperatures. The abundance of melting snows and rains has restored the soil water to a surplus quantity. For two months, the quantity of water percolating through the soil and entering the ground water keeps the soil pores nearly filled with water. This is the time of year when one encounters soft, muddy ground conditions, whether driving on dirt roads or walking across country. This, too, is the season when runoff is heavy, and major floods may be expected on larger streams and rivers. In terms of the soil-water budget, a **water surplus** exists.

By May, the rising air temperatures, increasing evaporation, and full growth of plant foliage bring on heavy evapotranspiration. Now the soil water falls below the storage capacity, although it may be restored temporarily by unusually heavy rains in some years. By midsummer, a large **water deficit** exists in the water budget. Even the occasional heavy thunderstorm rains of summer cannot restore the water lost by heavy evapotranspiration. Small springs and streams dry up, and the soil becomes firm and dry. By November (and sometimes in September), however, the soil water again begins to increase. At this time the plants go into a dormant state, sharply reducing transpiration losses. At the same time, falling air temperatures reduce evaporation. By late winter, usually in February at this location, the storage capacity of the soil is again fully restored.

The Soil-water Budget

From the example of soil-water change in a single year, we move forward to a more generalized concept. The gain, loss, and storage of soil water are accounted for in the **soil-water budget.** Figure 39.5 is a flow diagram to illustrate the budget. Water held in storage in the soil-water zone is increased by recharge during precipitation, but decreased by use through evapotranspiration. Surplus water is disposed of by downward percolation or by overland flow.

To proceed, we must recognize two ways to define evapotranspiration. First is **actual evapotranspiration,** which is the true or real rate of water vapor return to the atmosphere from the ground and its plant cover. Second is **potential evapotranspiration,** representing the water vapor return under an ideal set of conditions. One condition is that there be present a complete (or closed) cover of uniform vegetation consisting of fresh green leaves, and no bare ground exposed through that cover.

The leaf cover is assumed to have a uniform height above ground—whether the plants be trees, shrubs, or

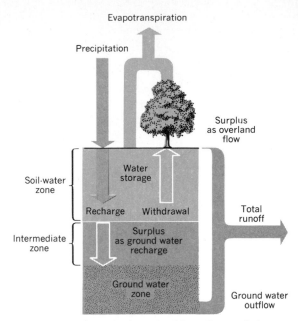

Figure 39.5   Schematic diagram of the soil-water balance in a soil column.

grasses. A second condition is that there be an adequate water supply, such that the storage capacity of the soil is maintained at all times. This condition can be fulfilled naturally by abundant and frequent precipitation, or artificially by irrigation. To simplify the ponderous terms we have just defined, they may be transformed as follows:

> actual evapotranspiration is **water use**
>
> potential evapotranspiration is **water need**

The word "need" signifies the quantity of soil water needed if plant growth is to be maximized for the given conditions of solar radiation and air temperature and the available supply of nutrients.

The difference between water use and water need is the **soil-water shortage.** This is the quantity of water that must be furnished by irrigation to achieve maximum crop growth within an agricultural system. All of the terms in the soil-water budget can be stated in inches or centimeters of water depth, the same as for precipitation. A particular value of field capacity of the soil is established in advance. In the soil-water budgets presented here, the soil layer is assumed to have a storage capacity of 12 in. (30 cm).

A simplified soil-water budget is shown in Figure 39.6, a graph on which average monthly values are plotted as points and connected by smooth lines. In this example, precipitation is much the same in all months, with no strong yearly cycle. In contrast, water need shows a strong seasonal cycle: low values in winter and a high summer peak. For midlatitudes in a humid climate, this model is about right.

At the start of the year, a large water surplus exists, and this is being disposed of by runoff. By May, conditions have switched over to a water deficit. In this month, plants

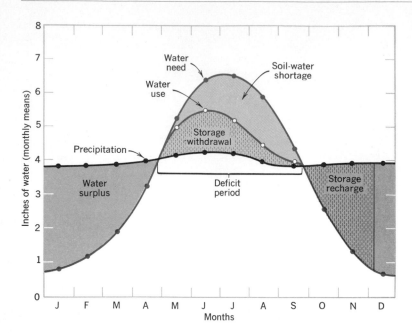

Figure 39.6   A simplified soil-water budget typical of a humid midlatitude climate.

begin to withdraw soil water from storage. **Storage withdrawal** is represented by the difference between the water-use curve and the precipitation curve. As storage withdrawal continues, the plants reduce their water use to less than the optimum quantity, so that without irrigation the water-use curve departs from the water-need curve. Storage withdrawal continues throughout the summer. The deficit period lasts through September. The area labeled "soil-water shortage" represents the total quantity of water needed by irrigation to insure maximum growth throughout the deficit period.

In October, precipitation again exceeds water need, but the soil must first absorb an amount equal to the summer storage withdrawal. So we have a period of **storage recharge,** and it lasts through November. In December the soil has reached its full storage capacity, and a water surplus again sets in, lasting through the winter.

C. Warren Thornthwaite, a distinguished climatologist who was concerned with practical problems of crop irrigation, developed these concepts of a soil-water balance and proposed a system of classification of world climates based on these principles. Associates and students of Thornthwaite extended his work and collected hydrologic data for a vast network of observing stations on all land areas of the globe. Water need was calculated for thousands of stations by means of a formula using air temperature, precipitation, and latitude. Water need (potential evapotranspiration) is a difficult quantity to measure, and several methods have been developed to estimate its true value.

United States Water Need

In Unit 16, we discussed the average annual evaporation of water from shallow lakes. Figure 16.2 is a map of the United States showing the wide range in annual evaporation, from very high values in the deserts of the Southwest to low values in the cool humid Northeast and Pacific Northwest coast. As you might expect, water need is related to evaporation from lake surfaces, but the two quantities are by no means identical. Water need is calculated on the basis of a complete canopy of green vegetation, whereas evaporation from lake surfaces is based upon direct measurement of the water loss from small lakes or from evaporating pans.

Figure 39.7 is a map showing average annual water need (potential evapotranspiration) for the United States. Notice that the highest values occur over the desert basins of the Southwest; this maximum is also seen in the evaporation map (Figure 16.2). High values of water need also prevail over a belt bordering the Gulf Coast from Texas to Florida. Values fall steadily as one progresses northward because of the reduced total annual solar radiation and colder mean annual air temperatures.

A Comparison of Two Water Budgets

To extend your working knowledge of the soil-water budget, you may examine data for two stations. They are located on opposite sides of the North American continent.

Pittsburgh, Pennsylvania, represents the humid continental climate with strongly developed winter and summer seasons (Figure 39.8). The seasonal pattern of changing soil-water storage at this station is very much like that described for the experiment station in Ohio (Figure 39.4). At Pittsburgh precipitation runs quite uniformly through the year, while water need has a strong annual cycle. Three cold winter months show little or no water need, because plants are dormant and soil water is frozen. In

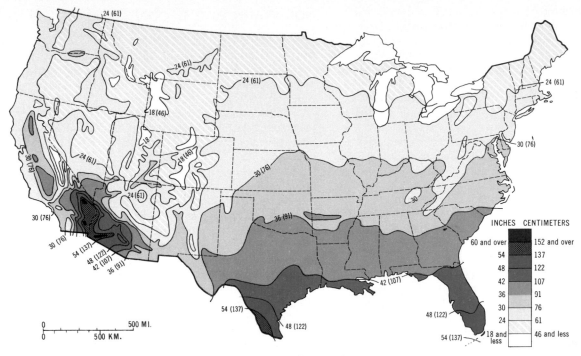

Figure 39.7 Average annual potential evapotranspiration in the United States. (Courtesy of *The Geographical Review* [1948] vol. 38. Copyrighted by the American Geographical Society, New York.)

summer the water need exceeds precipitation by a moderate amount, but the accumulated soil-water shortage is not severe. A substantial water surplus occurs in winter and spring, and the larger streams flow throughout the year. Some water is held in reserve as snow, to be released rapidly in early spring. River floods occur at this season.

Forests thrive in this climate, drawing the necessary soil water from storage during the summer. Irrigation is not generally required for field crops such as corn and for pasture land. This soil-water budget is well suited to diversified farming and dairying.

The second example is the soil-water budget for Los Angeles, California, located on the west coast of the United States, a few degrees of latitude more southerly than Pittsburgh (Figure 39.9). Los Angeles is located in a semiarid coastal zone strongly influenced by a persistent

Figure 39.8 The soil-water budget for Pittsburgh shows only a small water shortage during the summer and a large water surplus in winter and spring. (Data of C. W. Thornthwaite Associates, Laboratory of Climatology, Centerton, N.J.)

Figure 39.9 The soil-water budget for Los Angeles shows a large soil-water shortage in summer. No water surplus is developed in winter. (Same data source as Figure 39.8).

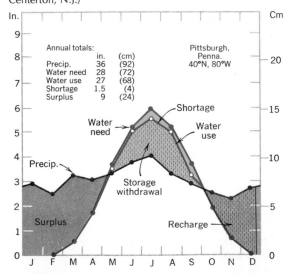

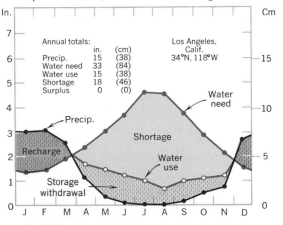

subtropical high-pressure cell and a cool current just off-shore. The climate of this area is referred to as a Mediterranean climate, because it resembles that of lands surrounding the Mediterranean Sea. Summers are very dry while winters are rainy. Both precipitation and water need show strong annual cycles, but they are exactly out of phase. As a result, the summer peak of water need develops at just that season when precipitation drops close to zero for four consecutive months.

The withdrawal of soil water from storage begins in spring and extends over an eight-month period. The soil-water shortage is severe during this time. Here is a region of summer-dry climate in which irrigation will be extremely valuable; in fact, summer crop cultivation will not be possible here without irrigation. The native plants are adapted to a long, warm summer with little or no rainfall. The winter is a period of soil-water recharge, but it is insufficient to generate a surplus.

Permanent streams do not originate in the area with this soil-water budget, but stream flow occurs in the winter following periods of heavy rain. The soil-water budget is quite different in mountains bordering the Los Angeles basin. As we explained in Unit 5, the orographic effect is strong on mountain ranges of California; hence, these mountain summits generate a water surplus.

Soil Water and Global Food Resources

In a world beset by severe and prolonged food shortages, the Thornthwaite concepts and calculations are of great value in assessing the benefits to be gained by increased irrigation. Only in a few parts of the tropical and mid-latitude zones is precipitation ample to fulfill the water need during the growing season. In contrast, the equatorial zone generally has a large water surplus throughout the year.

In later study units, dealing with Man, soils, and climate at a number of widely separated global localities, we will present other representative soil-water budgets. We will be asking this question: Can the developing nations increase their food production fast enough to stave off mass starvation? This is a grave problem in our times, and the answers given by well-informed specialists span the range from extreme pessimism to extreme optimism. Another question we hear is, "Will there be enough fresh water to supply the rapidly increasing demands of the energy-consuming industrial nations?" Your appreciation of current problems of agriculture and fresh-water supply over the lands of the globe can be greatly increased by an understanding of soil-water budgets.

SCIENCE
SUPPLEMENT

Calculating a Model Soil-water Budget

The basic equation for the soil-water budget is as follows:

$$P = E + G + R$$

where

P is precipitation
E is evapotranspiration
G is change in soil-water storage
R is runoff (by overland flow or by infiltration to the ground-water zone)

The equation applies to a unit column of soil, such as that represented in Figure 39.5. Units of measure are millimeters of water per day or per month, depending upon the time-span of the data.

Table 39.1 gives simplified data for a station of Mediterranean climate, similar in some respects to the climate of Los Angeles (Figure 39.8), but with larger total annual precipitation, so that a substantial water surplus is generated. Additional terms used in the table are defined as follows:

E_a actual evapotranspiration (water use)
E_p potential evapotranspiration (water need)
D soil-water shortage

The basic equation has been changed in Table 39.1 to use E_a instead of E. The data of Table 39.1 are presented in graph form in Figure 39.10. Each month is represented by two vertical bars. The height of each bar is proportional to units of millimeters per month. Each bar is divided up into segments showing the several terms of the water-budget equation. The left-hand bar shows P, part of which matches an equal quantity of water lost by evapotranspiration, and part of which may represent recharge ($+G$) or surplus (R). The right-hand bar shows E_p, part of which may represent water deficiency (D) or soil-water utilization ($-G$).

We have assigned numerical values to each term of the water-budget equation for each month, as shown in Table 39.1 (all values in this example are multiples of 5 mm).

By means of simple arithmetic, we have calculated the water balance for each month singly and for the year as a whole. Tallied separately at the right are the monthly differences between E_p and E_a, giving a total soil-water deficiency, D, of 115 mm for the year. This is the quantity of water that would have to be supplied by irrigation to sustain the full value of E_p.

The importance of the water-budget calculation in estimating the need for irrigation of crops should be obvious. We have also been able to calculate the annual runoff, 330 mm, and can use this information to estimate the recharge of ground water and the runoff into streams. In this way, an assessment of the water resource potential of a region can be made. The information is invaluable when planning regional economic development and resource management.

TABLE 39.1 A Model Soil-Moisture Budget

Equation:	P	=	E_a	+G	+R	E_p	$(E_p - E_a) = D$
January	110	=	10		+100	10	0
February	90	=	20		+ 70	20	0
March	60	=	35		+ 25	35	0
April	30	=	60	−30		60	5
May	25	=	70	−45		85	15
June	20	=	60	−40		95	40
July	25	=	50	−25		90	40
August	40	=	45	− 5		70	25
September	70	=	45	+25		45	0
October	90	=	30	+60		30	0
November	105	=	15	+60	+ 30	15	0
December	120	=	15		+105	15	0
Totals	785	=	455	−145 +145	+330	570	125
	785	=	785				

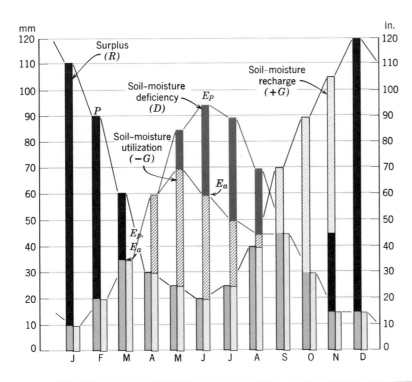

mm

In.

Figure 39.10 A model soil-water budget.

Unit 40
Cycling of Materials in Ecosystems

Killer Plants with Garlic Breath

Across a broad band of western states from Montana to New Mexico, ranges an unusual menace to the health and well-being of livestock and humans— killer plants with garlic breath. These plants are responsible for two dreaded diseases of sheep and cattle: alkali disease, and blind staggers.

Throughout the years, the toll has been heavy. In 1907 and 1908, more than 15,000 sheep were poisoned in a region south of Casper, Wyoming, by eating two kinds of toxic plants, woody aster and two-grooved vetch. The year 1930 saw two episodes of acute sheep poisoning. About 340 sheep, grazing near Elk Mountain, Wyoming, died within 24 hours after eating the deadly two-grooved vetch. Near Rock River, Wyoming, 75 sheep in a flock of 125 died in a single night. A year later, a flock of 200 sheep grazed overnight in a small valley near Pueblo, Colorado. By morning, 197 of the sheep were dead. All had succumbed to the virulent disease, blind staggers.

After a number of years of careful research, the true culprit was identified. The poisonings were produced by ingestion of large quantities of the element selenium, which occurs in low but significant concentrations in soils derived from certain limestones and shales found from Montana to Arizona and east to Nebraska and Kansas. The livestock were killed by grazing on a few particular species of plants which tend to absorb selenium from the soil and concentrate it in their tissues. Some 28 species of vetch are known to absorb selenium from the soil in large amounts. Other concentrators of selenium include the woody aster, prince's plume, and a plant closely related to goldenrod. Many of these plants are among the most handsome and conspicuous of wildflowers in the western United States.

Ordinarily, selenium is toxic to plants in low concentrations. But for the plants mentioned above, selenium usually has the opposite effect—it stimulates their growth. When ordinary crop plants are grown in the greenhouse, and watered with a solution containing selenium, even in very small concentrations, injury or death results. In the case of the

Sheep graze a rich valley pasture in Montana. (U.S. Forest Service.)

species mentioned above, however, even fairly high concentrations will stimulate their growth. Most of these species are restricted to areas where soil selenium concentrations are high.

Many selenium compounds are aromatic. The selenium-indicator plants usually have an unpleasant garlicky odor, with the strength of the smell increasing as selenium is concentrated in the tissues. The odor can be strong enough to be highly offensive to persons driving through selenium-rich areas.

Another disease of livestock, the alkali disease, is also produced by selenium poisoning, but by very low concentrations. This chronic low-level poisoning produces emaciation and stunted growth, as well as some loss of hair. A striking symptom is deformity of the hoofs, which become long and curved, and are sometimes sloughed off. Alkali disease in chickens causes them to lay eggs which do not hatch or else produce chicks with a greasy or wiry down; these live only a short time.

The case of the killer plants with garlic breath is actually an example of a natural material cycle which has direct importance for Man. Although the normal movement of the selenium is from the weathered rock to the ocean, selenium-concentrating plants have evolved a new pathway in the cycle, one that allows them to grow successfully on selenium-containing soils. Unfortunately, it also allows the selenium to enter the food chain on which Man is ultimately dependent. The object of our study unit is to trace the normal cycles of nutrients and other important materials on which the biosphere and Man are dependent.

Data Source: S. F. Trelease (1942) Bad earth, *Scientific Monthly,* vol. 54, pp. 12-28.

The Material Cycle in Ecosystems

Matter in organisms and ecosystems serves two functions: First, matter can serve to store chemical energy as carbohydrate. Second, matter can serve to make up physical structures that support the biochemical activities of life. Life is only possible with molecules that intercept and transform energy from one form to another. Life also requires molecules that contain and provide the physical and chemical environment necessary for those energy-transforming processes. As molecules are formed and re-formed by chemical and biochemical reactions within an ecosystem, the atoms that compose them are not changed or lost. Matter can thus be conserved within an ecosystem, and atoms and molecules can be used and reused, or cycled, within ecosystems.

Atoms and molecules move through ecosystems under the influence of both physical and biological processes. The pathways of a particular type of matter through the earth's ecosystem comprise a **material cycle** (sometimes referred to as a **biogeochemical cycle,** or **nutrient cycle**).

Ecologists recognize two types of material cycles—gaseous and sedimentary. In the **sedimentary cycle,** the compound or element is released from rock by weathering, then follows the movement of running water either in solution or as sediment to the sea. Eventually, by precipitation and sedimentation, these materials are converted into rock. When the rock is uplifted and exposed to weathering, the cycle is completed.

In the **gaseous cycle,** a shortcut is provided—the element or compound can be converted to a gaseous form, diffuse through the atmosphere, and thus arrive over land or sea, to be reused by the biosphere, in a much shorter time. The primary constituents of living matter—carbon, hydrogen, oxygen, and nitrogen—all move through gaseous cycles.

The major features of a material cycle are diagrammed in Figure 40.1. Any area or location of concentration of a material is a **pool.** There are two types of pools: **active pools,** where materials are in forms and places easily accessible to life processes, and **storage pools,** where materials are more or less inaccessible to life. A system of pathways of material flows connects the various active and storage pools within the cycle. Pathways between active pools are usually controlled by life processes, whereas

Figure 40.1 Materials of the biosphere are continually cycled and recycled by both life processes and physical processes.

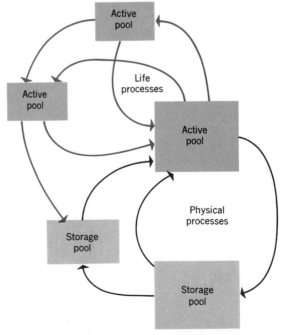

pathways between storage pools are usually controlled by physical processes.

The magnitudes of the total storage and total active pools can be very different. In many cases, the active pools are much smaller than storage pools, and materials move more rapidly between active pools than between storage pools or in and out of storage. Taking an example from the carbon cycle, photosynthesis and respiration will cycle all the carbon dioxide in the atmosphere (active pool) through plants in about 10 years, but it may be many millions of years before the carbonate sediments (storage pool) now forming as rock will be uplifted and decomposed to release carbon dioxide.

Nutrient Elements in the Biosphere

We will take the fifteen most abundant elements in living matter as a whole and designate their total mass as 100%. Percentages of each of the elements are given in Table 40.1. The three principal components of carbohydrate—hydrogen, carbon, and oxygen—account for almost all living matter and are called **macronutrients.** The remaining one-half percent is divided among 12 elements. Six of these are also macronutrients: nitrogen; calcium; potassium; magnesium; sulfur; and phosphorus. The macronutrients are all required in substantial quantities for organic life to thrive. The first three macronutrients—

Table 40.1 Elements comprising global living matter, taking 100 percent as the total of the 15 most abundant elements.

Basic carbohydrate	
Hydrogen (M)	49.74
Carbon (M)	24.90
Oxygen (M)	24.83
	Subtotal 99.47

Other nutrients	
Nitrogen (M)	0.272
Calcium (M)	0.072
Potassium (M)	0.044
Silicon	0.033
Magnesium (M)	0.031
Sulfur (M)	0.017
Aluminum	0.016
Phosphorus (M)	0.013
Chlorine	0.011
Sodium	0.006
Iron	0.005
Manganese	0.003

M - macronutrient

Data of E. S. Deevey, Jr. (1970) *Scientific American,* Vol. 223

hydrogen, carbon, and oxygen—are materials whose pathways we have already followed in the photosynthesis-respiration circuits (Figure 38.2). We will undertake a more detailed analysis of the gaseous cycles of carbon and oxygen, because of their involvement with atmospheric changes induced by Man through the combustion of hydrocarbon compounds. We will also give special attention to nitrogen, the fourth most abundant element in the composition of living matter; it also moves in a gaseous cycle. Of the remaining macronutrients, you will recognize three—calcium, potassium, and magnesium—as cations derived from rocks through mineral weathering. (Unit 18 explained the role of these ions in runoff.) Two other macronutrients derived from rock weathering are sulfur and phosphorus.

Quite a number of additional elements, not among the nine macronutrients, are also vital to life processes. Their presence is needed in mere traces and, for this reason, they are called **micronutrients.** The micronutrient list includes iron, copper, zinc, boron, molybdenum, manganese, and chlorine.

The Carbon Cycle

Some details of the carbon cycle are shown in a schematic diagram, Figure 40.2. Both gaseous and sedimentary cycles are found in the total picture of carbon in the environment. In its gaseous cycle, carbon moves as carbon dioxide (CO_2) which occurs as a free gas in the atmosphere and as a gas dissolved in freshwater of the lands and in salt water of the oceans. In its sedimentary, or nongaseous cycle, carbon resides in carbohydrate molecules in organic matter (CH_2O), as hydrocarbon compounds in rock (petroleum, coal), and as mineral carbonate compounds such as calcium carbonate ($CaCO_3$). The world supply of atmospheric carbon dioxide is represented in Figure 40.2 by a box. This atmospheric pool is supplied by respiration from plant and animal tissues in the oceans and on the lands. Under natural conditions, some new carbon enters the atmosphere each year from volcanoes by outgassing in the form of CO_2 and carbon monoxide (CO). Man's industrial role is to inject substantial amounts of carbon into the atmosphere through combustion of fossil fuels. This Man-made increment and its probable effects on global air temperatures were discussed in Unit 4.

Carbon dioxide leaves the atmospheric storage pool to enter the oceans, where it is used in photosynthesis by minute marine plants, the phytoplankton. These organisms are primary producers in the ocean ecosystem and are consumed by marine animals in the food chain. Phytoplankton also build skeletal structures of calcium carbonate. This mineral matter settles to the ocean floor to accumulate as sedimentary strata, an enormous storage pool not available to organisms until released later by rock weathering. Organic compounds synthesized by phytoplankton also settle to the ocean floor and eventually are transformed into the hydrocarbon compounds making up petroleum and natural gas. On the lands, accumulating plant matter has, under geologically favorable circum-

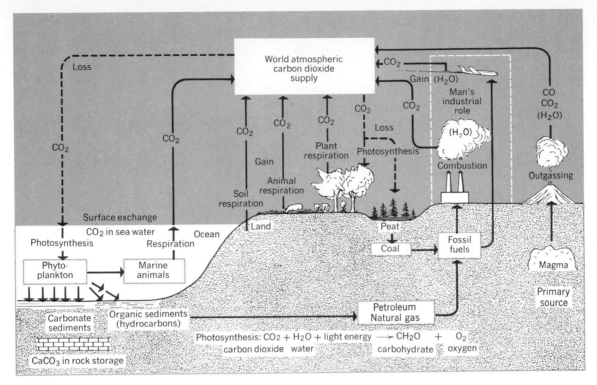

Figure 40.2 The carbon cycle. (After A. N. Strahler [1972] *Planet Earth,* Harper & Row, New York.)

stances, formed massive layers of peat, which were transformed into coal. Petroleum, natural gas, and coal comprise the fossil fuels, and these represent huge storage pools of carbon.

The Oxygen Cycle

Details of the oxygen cycle are shown in schematic form in Figure 40.3. Shown here is a gaseous cycle in which oxygen is in the molecular form as a gas (O_2). The complete picture of cycling of oxygen also includes its movements and storages when combined with carbon in carbon dioxide and in organic and inorganic compounds. These we have covered in the carbon cycle.

The world supply of free atmospheric oxygen is shown in Figure 40.3 by a box at the top of the diagram. Oxygen enters this storage pool through release in photosynthesis, both in the oceans and on the lands. Each year a small amount of new oxygen comes from volcanoes through outgassing, principally as CO_2 and H_2O (shown in Figure 40.2). Balancing the input to the atmospheric storage pool is loss through organic respiration and mineral oxidation. Adding to the withdrawal from the atmospheric oxygen pool is Man's industrial activity through the combustion (oxidation) of wood and fossil fuels. Forest fires and grass fires (not shown) are another means of oxygen consumption. The oceans serve as a major storage pool for dissolved gaseous oxygen. Some oxygen is continuously placed in storage in mineral carbonate form in ocean-floor sediments.

The Nitrogen Cycle

Nitrogen moves through the biosphere in a gaseous cycle in which the atmosphere, containing 78% nitrogen by volume, is a vast storage pool available to organisms. Nitrogen is an abundant macronutrient, since it is contained within each amino acid building block of protein.

Almost all the nitrogen available to living organisms is obtained from the atmosphere through the efforts of nitrogen-fixing bacteria. These bacteria have a biochemical system that can convert nitrogen from its inert atmospheric form, molecular nitrogen, to other forms, such as ammonia and nitrate, which can be used directly by plants. The plants assimilate these forms of nitrogen and convert them to organic forms, which are consumed by animals grazing on the plants. In this way, nitrogen is passed up the food chain.

The conversion of molecular nitrogen (N_2) into usable forms is called **nitrogen fixation.** Only microorganisms possess the ability to fix nitrogen. One class of such microorganisms are certain species of free-living soil bacteria. Some blue-green algae can also fix nitrogen. Another class consists of the symbiotic nitrogen fixers. In a symbiotic relationship, two species of organisms live in close physical contact, each contributing to the life processes or structures of the other. Symbiotic nitrogen fixers are bacteria of the genus *Rhizobium;* they are associated with some 190 species of trees and shrubs as well as almost all members of the legume family. Legumes important as agricultural crops are clover, alfalfa, soybeans, peas, beans, and

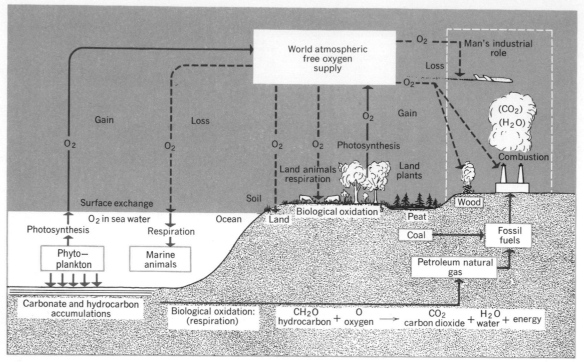

Figure 40.3   The oxygen cycle. (After A. N. Strahler [1972] *Planet Earth,* Harper & Row, New York.)

peanuts. *Rhizobium* bacteria infect the root cells of these plants in root nodules produced jointly by action of the plant and the bacteria (Figure 40.4). The bacteria supply the nitrogen to the plant in the form of ammonium or amino acids, while the plant supplies nutrients and organic compounds needed by the bacteria. Crops of legumes are planted in seasonal rotation with other food crops to ensure an adequate nitrogen supply in the soil.

Certain bacteria can return nitrogen to its inert atmospheric form. This function completes the nitrogen cycle, by which nitrogen moves from the atmosphere to organisms in the life layer and back again to the atmosphere.

The Material Cycle in Review

To summarize the material cycle in the biosphere, we can use a schematic flow diagram, Figure 40.5. It relates to the nongaseous components only, since we have already given special attention to the gaseous components. The diagram shows the pathways taken by the more important elements from the inorganic realms of the lithosphere and hydrosphere through the realm of living tissues, or biosphere, and returning to the inorganic realm. Within the large box representing the lithosphere are smaller compartments representing the parent matter of the soil and the soil itself. In the soil, nutrients are held as ions on the surfaces of soil colloids and are readily available to plants. (This subject will be explained in Unit 48).

The nutrient elements are also held in enormous storage pools where they are unavailable to organisms. These stor-

age pools include seawater (unavailable to land organisms), sediments on the sea floor, and enormous accumulations of sedimentary rock beneath both lands and oceans. Eventually, elements held in the geologic storage

Figure 40.4   Root nodules on the soybean. The nodules contain bacteria of the genus *Rhizobium,* and convert atmospheric nitrogen to forms usable by the plant. (Courtesy of the Nitragin Co., Inc.)

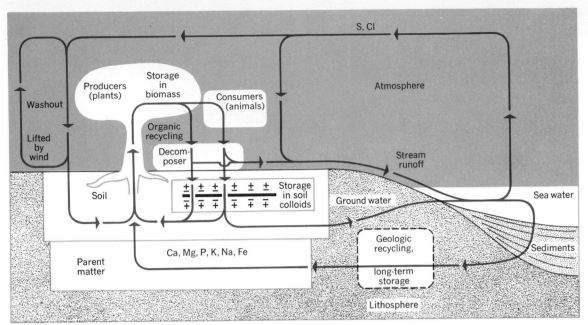

Figure 40.5 Flow diagram of the mineral portion of a materials cycle in and out of the biosphere and within the inorganic realm of the lithosphere, hydrosphere, and atmosphere. The four macronutrients of atmospheric origin—hydrogen, carbon, oxygen, and nitrogen—are omitted.

pools are released into the soil by weathering. Soil particles are lifted into the atmosphere by winds and fall back to earth or are washed down by precipitation. Chlorine and sulfur are shown as passing from the ocean into the atmosphere and entering the soil by the same mechanisms of fallout and washout.

The organic realm, or biosphere, is shown in three compartments: producers, consumers, and decomposers. Considerable element recycling occurs between organisms of these three classes and the soil. The elements used in the biosphere, however, are continually escaping to the sea as ions dissolved in stream runoff and ground-water flow.

Unit 41
Adaption of Plants to the Environment

Darwin Ascends Mount Banks

Sir Charles Darwin is often regarded as the founder of modern biology. With the publication of his book, *The Origin of Species,* Darwin introduced in 1859 the theory of evolution by means of natural selection, that is, species vary constantly from one generation to the next, and the environment acts to select those members of a generation most able to survive. This theory, now universally accepted by science, shows that plants and animals are adapted to their environments through the mechanism of evolution. The distribution pattern of plants and animals is thus related directly to the distribution of environments to which they are adapted. Darwin developed much of his theory as a naturalist on board the *H.M.S. Beagle,* a Royal Navy vessel that took five years (1831-1836) to sail around the world on a surveying mission for the British Admiralty. You might find it of interest to join the young Charles on his way to a mountain-top in Tierra del Fuego, that rugged land at the southern tip of South America. What follows is his own description of making his way through what we now call the southern beech forest, a type of broadleaf evergreen forest found on the cool, wet, west and south coasts of South America:

The next day I attempted to penetrate some way into the country. Tierra del Fuego may be described as a mountainous land, partly submerged in the sea, so that deep inlets and bays occupy the place where valleys should exist. The mountain sides, except on the exposed western coast, are covered from the water's edge upwards by one great forest. The trees reach to an elevation of between 1000 and 1500 feet, and are succeeded by a band of peat, with minute alpine plants; and this again is succeeded by the line of perpetual snow, which, according to Captain King, in the Strait of Magellan descends to between 3000 and 4000 feet. To find an acre of level land in any part of the country is most rare. I recollect only one little flat piece near Port Famine, and another of rather larger extent near Goeree Road. In both places, and everywhere else, the surface is covered by a thick bed of swampy peat. Even within the forest, the ground is concealed by a mass of slowly putrefying vegetable matter, which, from being soaked with water, yields to the foot.

Finding it nearly hopeless to push my way through the wood, I followed the course of a mountain torrent. At first, from the waterfalls and number of dead trees, I could hardly crawl along; but the bed of the stream soon became a little more open, from the floods having swept the sides. I continued slowly to advance for an hour along the broken and rocky banks, and was amply repaid by the grandeur of the scene. The gloomy depth of the ravine well accorded with the universal signs of violence. On every side were lying irregular masses of rock and torn-up trees; other trees, though still erect, were decayed to the heart and ready to fall. The entangled mass of the thriving and the fallen reminded me of the forests within the tropics—yet there was a difference: for in these still solitudes, Death, instead of Life, seemed the predominant spirit. I followed the watercourse till I came to a spot, where a great slip had cleared a straight space down the mountain side. By this road I ascended to a considerable elevation, and obtained a good view of the surrounding woods. The trees all belong to one kind, the Fagus betuloides; for the number of the other species of Fagus and of the Winter's Bark, is quite inconsiderable. This beech keeps its leaves throughout the year; but its foliage is of a peculiar brownish-green colour, with a tinge of yellow. As the whole landscape is thus coloured, it has a sombre, dull appearance; nor is it often enlivened by the rays of the sun.

This serene watercolor by Owen Stanley shows Darwin's ship H.M.S. *Beagle,* being prepared for the start of her world cruise in 1831. The ship, a 10-gun brig displacing only 235 tons, pitched fearfully in a wild storm as it left Plymouth Harbor and the seasick young naturalist had good reason to question the wisdom of his decision to take part in the expedition. (Reproduced by permission of The Trustees of the National Maritime Museum.)

December 20th.—One side of the harbour is formed by a hill about 1500 feet high, which Captain FitzRoy has called after Sir J. Banks. . . . I was anxious to reach the summit of this mountain to collect alpine plants; for flowers of any kind in the lower parts are few in number. We followed the same watercourse as on the previous day, till it dwindled away, and we were then compelled to crawl blindly among the trees. These, from the effects of the elevation and of the impetuous winds, were low, thick, and crooked. At length we reached that which from a distance appeared like a carpet of fine green turf, but which, to our vexation, turned out to be a compact mass of little beech-trees about four or five feet high. They were as thick together as box in the border of a garden, and we were obliged to struggle over the flat but treacherous surface. After a little more trouble we gained the peat, and then the bare slate rock.

A ridge connected this hill with another, distant some miles, and more lofty, so that patches of snow were lying on it. As the day was not far advanced, I determined to walk there and collect plants along the road. It would have been very hard work, had it not been for a well-beaten and straight path made by the guanacos; for these animals, like sheep, always follow the same line.

When we reached the hill we found it the highest in the immediate neighborhood, and the waters flowed to the sea in opposite directions. We obtained a wide view over the surrounding country: to the north a swampy moorland extended, but to the south we had a scene of savage magnificence, well becoming Tierra del Fuego. There was a degree of mysterious grandeur in mountain behind mountain, with the deep intervening valleys, all covered by one thick, dusky mass of forest. The atmosphere, likewise, in this climate, where gale succeeds gale, with rain, hail, and sleet, seems blacker than anywhere else. In the Strait of Magellan, looking due southward from Port Famine, the distant channels between the mountains appeared from their gloominess to lead beyond the confines of this world.

The object of this study unit is to explore how plant life forms are adjusted to the climatic factors of moisture and temperature, and how they vary from one area to another.

DATA SOURCE: Charles Darwin (1879) *A Naturalist's Voyage: Journal of Researches into the Natural History and Geology of the Countries visited During the Voyage of H.M.S. Beagle Round the World, under the Command of Capt. FitzRoy, R.N.,* John Murray, London.

Plants and Man

In this study unit we continue to investigate the biosphere, but with our focus on vegetation of the lands. Thinking of plants as stationary objects on the landscape places them in much the same frame as other physical elements of that landscape such as landforms, soils, streams, and lakes.

Plants are also consumable and renewable sources of food, medicinals, fuel, clothing, shelter, and a host of other life essentials. The ways in which humans have used this plant resource to their advantage—or have been hindered by plants in their progress—have been persistent themes in the writings of geographers.

Structure and Life Form of Plants

The plant geographer classifies plants in terms of the **life form,** which is the physical structure, size, and shape of the plant. Botanical associations are not necessarily related to life form. Although the life forms go by common names and are well understood by almost everyone, we shall review them to establish a uniform set of meanings.

Both trees and shrubs are erect, woody plants (Figure 41.1). They are perennial, meaning that the woody tissues endure from year to year, and most have life spans of many years. **Trees** are large, woody perennial plants having a single upright main trunk, often with few branches in the lower part, but branching in the upper part to form a

Figure 41.1 This forest of mature beech and hemlock trees has a lower layer of scattered shrubs and seedling trees and a basal layer of herbs. Allegheny National Forest, Pennsylvania. (U.S. Forest Service.)

crown. **Shrubs** are woody perennial plants having several stems branching from a base near the soil surface, so as to place the mass of foliage close to ground level.

Lianas are also woody plants, but they take the form of vines supported on trees and shrubs. Lianas include not only the tall heavy vines of the wet equatorial and tropical rainforests (see Figure 41.4A), but also woody vines of midlatitude forests.

Herbs comprise a major class of plant life forms. **Herbs** are tender plants, lacking woody stems, and are usually small. They occur in a wide range of shapes and leaf types. Some are annuals, others are perennials. Some are broad leaved, others are grasses. Herbs as a class share few characteristics in common except that they form a low layer as compared with shrubs and trees.

Forest is a vegetation structure in which trees grow close together with crowns in contact so their foliage largely shades the ground. In most forests of the humid climates the life forms are arranged in distinct layers, and the vegetation is said to be stratified (Figure 41.2). Tree crowns form the uppermost layer, shrubs an intermediate layer, and herbs a lower layer. The lowermost layer consists of mosses and related small plants. In **woodland,** crowns of trees are mostly separated by open areas, usually having a low herb or shrub layer.

Lichens represent yet another life form seen in a layer close to the ground. Lichens are plant forms in which algae and fungi live together to form a single plant structure. In some alpine and arctic environments lichens grow in profusion and dominate the vegetation.

Plant Habitats

As we travel through a hilly wooded area, we observe that the vegetation is strongly influenced by landform and soil. Landform refers to the configuration of the land surface, including features such as hills, valleys, ridges, or cliffs. Vegetation on an upland—relatively high ground with thick soil and good drainage—is quite different from that on an adjacent valley floor, where water lies near the surface much of the time. Vegetation is often different in form on rocky ridges and on steep cliffs, where water drains away rapidly and soil is thin or largely absent.

The total vegetation cover is actually a mosaic of small units which reflects the inequalities in conditions of slope, drainage, and soil type. Such subdivisions of the plant environment are described as **habitats.** In the example shown in Figure 41.3, the Canadian forest actually comprises at least six habitats: upland; bog; bottomland; ridge; cliff; and active dune. Just where each habitat is located and how large an area it occupies depends largely on the geologic history of the region and on processes of erosion and deposition that have acted in the past to shape the landforms.

Closely tied in with the effect of landform on habitat is the distribution of water in the soil and rock. Finally, each habitat has its own set of soil properties, determined not only by the conditions of slope and water but, in part, by the plants themselves.

In establishing the larger units of vegetation for generalized maps, the plant geographer usually bases the map

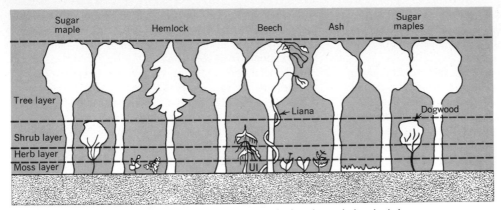

Figure 41.2 This schematic diagram shows the layers of a beech-maple-hemlock forest, similar to that pictured in Figure 41.1. The vertical dimensions of the lower layers are greatly exaggerated. (Modified from Pierre Dansereau [1951] *Ecology*, Vol. 32.)

classes upon the life-forms of the upland habitat, because it is here that a middle range of environmental conditions prevails.

Awareness that varied habitats present a wide spectrum of controls over plants leads us to look further into the role of soil-water availability in favoring certain forms of plants.

Plants and Water Need

We will now investigate the response of plants to the degree of availability of water. The green plants, or leaf-bearing plants, give off large quantities of water to the atmosphere through transpiration. This water loss takes the form of evaporation from water films on exposed surfaces of certain leaf cells. (Only a very small proportion of the water consumed by plants is used directly in photosynthesis.) Most plants derive their water through roots in the soil zone. These plants must have mechanisms by which to control the excessive loss of water by transpiration at times when stored soil water is depleted and a shortage becomes severe.

The adaptation of plant structures to water budgets with large water shortages is of particular interest to the plant geographer. Transpiration occurs largely from specialized leaf pores, which provide openings in the outer cell layer. These pores allow water vapor and other gases to pass into and out of the leaf. Surrounding these openings are cells that can open and close the openings and thus, to some extent, regulate the flow of water vapor and other gases. Water vapor may also pass through the cuticle, or outermost protective layer of the leaf. This form of water loss is reduced in some plants by thickening of the outer layers of cells or by the deposition of wax or waxlike material on the leaf surface. Many desert plants have thickened cuticle or wax-coated leaves, stems, or branches.

A plant may also adapt to a desert environment by greatly reducing the leaf area or by bearing no leaves at all. Needleleaves and spines representing leaves greatly reduce loss from transpiration. In cactus plants the foliage leaf is not present, and transpiration is limited to fleshy stems.

In addition to developing leaf structures that reduce water loss by transpiration, plants in a water-scarce environment improve their means of obtaining water and of storing it. Roots become greatly extended to reach soil moisture at increased depth. In cases where the roots reach to the ground-water table, a steady supply of water is assured. Plants drawing from such a source may be found along dry stream channels and valley floors in desert regions. Other desert plants produce a widespread but shallow root system enabling them to absorb the maximum quantity of water from sporadic desert downpours that saturate only the uppermost soil layer. Stems of desert plants are commonly greatly thickened by a spongy tissue in which much water can be stored.

A quite different adaptation to extreme aridity is seen in many small desert plants that complete a very short cycle of germination, leafing, flowering, fruiting, and seed dispersal immediately following a desert downpour.

Plants may be classified according to their water requirements. Terms associated with the water factor are built on three simple prefixes of Greek roots: *xero-*, dry; *hygro-*, wet, and *meso-*, intermediate. Plants that grow in

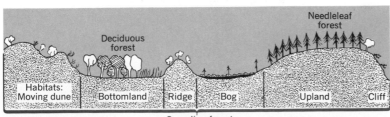

Figure 41.3 Habitats within the Canadian forest. (Modified from Pierre Dansereau [1951] *Ecology*, Vol. 32.)

dry habitats are **xerophytes;** those that grow in water or in wet habitats are **hygrophytes;** those of habitats of an intermediate degree of wetness and relatively uniform soil-water availability are **mesophytes.**

The xerophytes are highly tolerant of drought and can survive in habitats that dry quickly following rapid drainage of precipitation (e.g., on sand dunes, beaches, and bare rock surfaces). The plants typical of dry climates are also xerophytes; cactus is an example (see Figure 41.4l). The hygrophytes are tolerant of excessive water and may be found in shallow streams, lakes, marshes, swamps, and bogs; an example is the water lily. The mesophytes are found in upland habitats in regions of ample rainfall. Here the drainage of soil water is good, and moisture penetrates deeply where it can later be used by the plants.

Plants and Seasons

Certain climates have a yearly cycle with one season in which water is unavailable to plants because of lack of precipitation or because the soil water is frozen. This season alternates with one in which there is abundant water. Plants adapted to such regimes are called **tropophytes,** from the Greek word *trophos,* meaning change, or turn. Tropophytes meet the impact of the season of unavailable water by dropping their leaves and becoming dormant. When water is again available, they leaf out and grow at a rapid rate. Trees and shrubs that seasonally shed their leaves are **deciduous plants;** in distinction, **evergreen plants** retain most of their leaves in a green state through the year.

The Mediterranean climate found in lands surrounding the Mediterranean Sea and in coastal southern California, also has a strong seasonal wet-dry alternation, the summers being dry and the winters wet. Plants in this climate adopt the habit of xerophytic plants and characteristically have hard, thick leathery leaves. An example is the live oak, which holds most of its leaves through the dry season. Such hard-leaved evergreen trees and woody shrubs are called **sclerophylls.** The prefix *sclero-* is from the Greek word for "hard." Plants that hold their leaves through a dry or cold season have the advantage of being able to resume photosynthesis immediately when growing conditions become favorable, whereas the deciduous plants must grow a new set of leaves.

Plants and Temperature

Temperature, another of the important climatic factors in plant ecology, acts directly on plants through its influence on the rates at which the physiological processes take place. In general, we can say that each plant species has an optimum temperature associated with each of its functions, such as photosynthesis, flowering, fruiting, or seed germination. Some overall optimum yearly temperature conditions exist for its growth in terms of size and numbers of individuals. There are also limiting lower and upper temperatures for the individual functions of the plant and for its total survival.

Temperature also acts as an indirect factor. Higher air temperatures increase the water vapor capacity of the air, inducing greater transpiration as well as faster rates of direct evaporation of soil water.

In general, the colder the climate, the fewer are the species that are capable of surviving. A large number of tropical plant species cannot survive below-freezing temperatures. In the severely cold arctic and alpine environments of high latitudes and high altitudes, only a few species can survive. This principle explains why a forest in the equatorial zone has many species of trees, whereas a forest of the subarctic zone may be dominated by just a few. Tolerance to cold is closely tied up with the ability of the plant to withstand the physical disruption that accompanies the freezing of water. If the plant has no means of disposing of the excess water in its tissues, the freezing of that water will damage the cell tissue.

Plant geographers recognize that there is a critical level of climatic stress beyond which a plant species cannot survive and that a geographical boundary will exist to mark the limits of its distribution. Such a boundary is sometimes referred to as a frontier. Although the frontier is determined by a complex of climatic elements, one climate element related to soil water or to temperature, can sometimes be singled out as coinciding with the plant frontier.

Terrestrial Ecosystems — The Biomes

Ecosystems fall into two major groups: aquatic and terrestrial. The **aquatic ecosystems** include life forms of the marine environments and the freshwater environments of the lands. Marine ecosystems include the open ocean, coastal estuaries, and coral reefs. Freshwater ecosystems include lakes, ponds, streams, marshes, and bogs. The **terrestrial ecosystems** comprise the assemblages of land plants and animals spread widely over the upland surfaces of the continents. The terrestrial ecosystems are largely determined by climate and soil and, in this way, are closely woven into the fabric of physical geography.

Within terrestrial ecosystems, the largest recognizable subdivision is the **biome.** Although the biome includes the total assemblage of plant and animal life interacting within the life layer, the green plants dominate the biome physically because of their enormous biomass, as compared with that of other organisms. The plant geographer concentrates on the characteristic life form of the green plants within the biome. As we have already seen, these life forms are principally trees, shrubs, lianas, and herbs, but other life forms are important in certain biomes.

The following are the principal biomes, listed in order of availability of soil water and heat.

Forest	(ample soil water and heat)
Savanna	(transitional between forest and grassland)
Grassland	(moderate shortage of soil water; adequate heat)
Desert	(extreme shortage of soil water; adequate heat)
Tundra	(insufficient heat)

Formation Classes

Plant geographers subdivide the biomes into smaller vegetation units, called **formation classes,** which concentrate on the life form of the plants. For example, at least four and perhaps as many as six kinds of forests are easily recognizable within the forest biome. At least three kinds of grasslands are easily recognizable. Deserts, too, span a wide range in terms of the abundance and life form of plants.

Table 41.1 lists a number of the most important plant formation classes with brief notes on the character of the vegetation and the associated latitude zones and climates.

A number of these formation classes will be explored in more detail in study units of Part VI.

Figure 41.4 shows photographs of ten of the formation classes. Figure 41.5 consists of three schematic profiles showing how one formation class grades into another along a north-south profile from the equatorial zone to the arctic zone, and along an east-west profile across the United States.

Large areas of the earth's land surfaces have been strongly impacted by Man through intensive agriculture, grazing, and timber cutting. In the next study unit, we will investigate the nature of these disturbances, which modify or destroy the natural vegetation of the biomes and formation classes.

Table 41.1 The Formation Classes

FOREST BIOME

Equatorial rainforest (Tropical rainforest)	Tall, smooth-barked, evergreen, broadleaf trees with high crowns. Warm, wet equatorial and tropical climates with large water surplus.
Monsoon forest	Open forest of tropical lands with dry, cool season and wet monsoon season. Many trees are deciduous; shed leaves in low-sun season.
Midlatitude deciduous forest	Broadleaf, deciduous trees shed leaves in winter. Substantial soil-water surplus.
Needleleaf forest	Needleleaf, evergreen trees forming dense forest in high latitudes. Long, very cold winters.
Sclerophyll forest	Open forest of hard-leaved, evergreen trees. Midlatitude regions with very dry summer and moist winter.

SAVANNA BIOME

Tropical savanna woodland	Scattered trees with grassland. Tropical climate with long, dry season and short, wet monsoon season.

GRASSLAND BIOME

Tall-grass prairie	Dense growth of tall grasses and herbs. Midlatitude regions of subhumid climate.
Short-grass prairie (steppe)	Short, sparse grasses. Semiarid plains in midlatitudes. Moderate soil-water deficit.

DESERT BIOME

Semidesert	Woody shrubs and grasses. Semiarid climate in midlatitudes. Much bare soil. Large soil-water deficit.
Dry desert	Widely scattered desert shrubs with bare ground intervening. Dry desert climate in tropical and midlatitude zones. Large annual soil-water deficit.

TUNDRA BIOME

Arctic grassy tundra	Treeless landscape with sedges, grasses, mosses, flowering herbs. Severely cold climate of subarctic zone. Permanently frozen ground below soil (permafrost).
Alpine tundra	Similar to arctic tundra. Occurs at high altitudes, above tree-line, in wide range of latitudes.

A. Equatorial rainforest of the Amazon lowland in Brazil. This forest of tall broad-leaved evergreen trees has numerous lianas. (Otto Penner, Instituto Agronómico do Norte.)

Figure 41.4   Examples of formation classes.

B. Monsoon forest in Chieng Mai Province, northern Thailand. Scale is indicated by a line of people crossing the clearing. (Robert L. Pendleton, American Geographical Society.)

C. Needleleaf forest of spruce trees in Quebec, Canada. (Pierre Dansereau.)

D. Sclerophyll woodland of oak and grassland, Monterey County, California. (U.S. Forest Service.)

E. Tropical savanna, in Kenya. (Richard U. Light, American Geographical Society.)

F. Tall-grass prairie. Kalsow Prairie, Iowa, has been set aside as an example of virgin prairie. (State Conservation Commission of Iowa.)

H. Semidesert of sage-brush, Vermilion Cliffs, near Kanab, Utah, 1906. (Douglas Johnson.)

J. Arctic tundra. Cotton-grass meadows on the coastal plain of Alaska. (William R. Farrand.)

G. *(left)* Short-grass prairie. Short-crested wheatgrass in Montana. (U.S. Forest Service.)

I. Dry desert, Sonoran Desert, southwestern Arizona. Ocotillo plant in the left foregound; saguaro cactus plants ın left distance. (A. N. Strahler.)

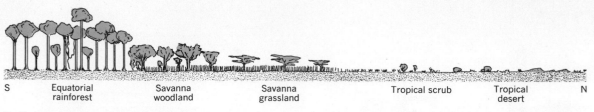

S   Equatorial   Savanna   Savanna   Tropical scrub   Tropical   N
         rainforest   woodland   grassland   desert

Profile from equator to tropic of cancer, Africa

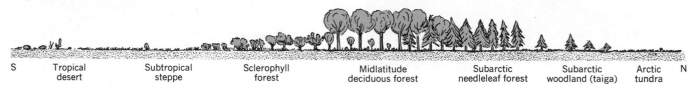

S   Tropical   Subtropical   Sclerophyll   Midlatitude   Subarctic   Subarctic   Arctic   N
         desert   steppe   forest   deciduous forest   needleleaf forest woodland (taiga) tundra

Profile from tropic of cancer to Arctic circle, Africa-Eurasia

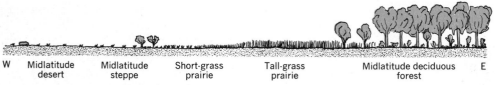

W   Midlatitude   Midlatitude   Short-grass   Tall-grass   Midlatitude deciduous   E
       desert   steppe   prairie   prairie   forest

Profile across United States, 40°N, Nevada to Ohio

Figure 41.5   Three schematic profiles showing the succession of plant formation classes across climatic gradients.

Unit 42
Man's Impact on Terrestrial Ecosystems

"Juggernaut Out of Control"

None of Man's activities is more destructive of ecosystems than war. With the increasing dependence of modern warfare on technology, Man's capacity to destroy the living world both deliberately and inadvertently also increases. The Vietnam War provides numerous examples of wanton ecological destruction achieving little in the way of military gains. Ecological destruction is only one phase of an American military operation, referred to by one newswriter as a "juggernaut out of control." The riders of this ponderous vehicle inflicted incalculable damage upon the land of the very people they were trying to save from communist domination.

Herbicides—poisons that kill unwanted plants—became weapons of war in Vietnam as early as 1962, when military spraying operations began in earnest. In the nine-year period that followed, approximately one-seventh of the surface area of South Vietnam was treated with herbicides, mostly sprayed from lowflying C-123 cargo planes. Some 19,000 individual spraying flights were made. Altogether, the area treated is about equal to the area of the state of Massachusetts. Most of the herbicide (90%) was applied to forest land to cause defoliation (leafdropping) and reduce enemy concealment. The remainder was applied to cropland in an attempt to deprive the enemy of food supplies.

The herbicide used to cause defoliation of forests was designated Agent Orange; it is the same type of weed and brush killer used widely in the United States. Agent Blue, used to kill crops, is an arsenic compound (cacodylic acid). Its application in Vietnam destroyed enough food to sustain 600,000 persons for one year, according to an estimate made by the U.S. Department of Agriculture. Crop spraying was also used widely in the hardwood forests of the Central Highlands of Vietnam. Here the inhabitants are mostly Montagnards, a tribe of about one million persons, living in comparative isolation from the lowland Vietnamese. Many areas of the delta region, south and east of Saigon, were sprayed with herbicides, killing mangrove forests covering thousands of acres. These forests harbored Vietcong terrorists, but also supported a large civilian population through cultivation of rice.

Following press reports of severe ecological damage by the military spraying program, the American Association for the Advancement of Science at its 1969 annual meeting in Boston appointed a Herbicide Assessment Commission to prepare a report on the controversial program. The commission was headed by Harvard biologist Matthew S. Meselson.

A flight of four U.S. Air Force C-123 aircraft sprays a defoliating chemical on tropical rainforest in Vietnam, 1967. Each plane covered a swath about 1000 feet wide. (U.S. Air Force Photo.)

In addition to pointing out the shocking deficiencies in the precautions taken by the military to protect innocent civilian populations from needless crop destruction, Meselson and his committee also released evidence of severe ecological damage produced by the defoliation program.

According to the committee's report, somewhere between 20 and 50% of South Vietnam's mangrove forests were utterly destroyed, showing almost no signs of new life after years of spraying. In addition, about half the mature trees in hardwood forests north and west of Saigon were killed by spraying. Following destruction of the hardwood forest, worthless bamboo invaded many areas, threatening to dominate the local vegetation for decades in the future.

Another problem with the defoliation program arose from the fact that the defoliants used contained the chemical dioxin as an impurity. Laboratory studies have shown that dioxin is a very potent compound that produces genetic deformity and birth defects in unborn human infants. The committee found an increase in two specific types of birth defects reported at a large Saigon hospital that was coincident with widespread spraying. They also noted that one heavily sprayed province showed a very high rate of stillbirths among Vietnamese women. Although this evidence suggested that there might be an effect of dioxin on the Vietnamese population, the data were insufficient to prove that conclusion.

The Vietnam defoliation program provides a dramatic example of how Man can impact terrestrial ecosystems. In a global context, however, the normal human activities of farming, grazing, and using

Taken in 1970, this picture shows the total destruction of a South Vietnam mangrove forest, sprayed with herbicide in 1967. Little if any regeneration had occurred following the spraying. (Herbicide Assessment Commission of the American Association for the Advancement of Science.)

land for other agricultural purposes through many centuries have provided a greater and more lasting impact on the landscape. The purpose of this unit is to describe how these activities affect ecosystems and how ecosystems respond through natural processes of slow change.

DATA SOURCE: Philip M. Boffey (1971) Herbicides in Vietnam: AAAS study finds widespread devastation, *Science*, vol. 171, pp. 43–47; Deborah Shapley (1974) Herbicides: Academy finds damage in Vietnam after a fight of its own, *Science*, vol. 183, pp. 1177–1180.

Man's Interference with Natural Vegetation

Two concepts of the geography of vegetation stand opposed but inseparable, like the two sides of a coin. One is the concept of **natural vegetation** (or native vegetation), a plant cover that attains its development without appreciable interference by Man and that is subject to natural forces of modification and destruction, such as storms or fires. This concept is represented by the biomes and formation classes described in Unit 41. The other concept is that of vegetation sustained in a modified state by Man's activities. Extremes of both cases are found over the world.

Natural vegetation can still be seen over vast areas of the wet equatorial climate where rainforests are as yet scarcely touched by Man. Much of the arctic tundra and the needleleaf forest of the subarctic zones is in a natural state. In contrast, much of the continental surface in midlatitudes is almost totally under Man's control through intensive agriculture, grazing, or urbanization. You can drive across an entire state, such as Ohio or Iowa, without seeing a vestige of the plant cover it bore before the coming of the white people. Only if you know where to look for them, can you find a few small plots of virgin prairie or virgin forest.

Some areas of natural vegetation appear to be untouched but are dominated by Man in a subtle manner. Some of our national parks and national forests have been protected from fire for many decades and have thus been put in an unnatural condition in comparison with their original state as a natural ecosystem. When lightning starts a forest fire, the smoke-eaters parachute down and put out the flames as fast as possible. But we realize that periodic burning of forests and grasslands must be a natural phenomenon, and it must perform some vital function in the ecosystem. One vital function is to release nutrients from storage in the biomass so that the soil can be revitalized. Already those who manage our parks and forests are experimenting with a "hands-off" policy in fire control.

Man has influenced vegetation in yet another way—by

moving plant species from their indigenous habitats to foreign lands and foreign environments. The eucalyptus tree is a striking example. From Australia the various species of eucalypts have been transplanted to such far-off lands as California, North Africa, and India. Sometimes these exported plants thrive like weeds, forcing out natural species and becoming major nuisances. Scarcely one of the kinds of grasses on the coast ranges of California is a native species, yet for the casual observer these plants represent the native vegetation. Even so, all plants have limits of tolerance to the environmental conditions of soil water, soil nutrients, and temperature range. Consequently, the structure and outward appearance of the plant cover conforms to the basic environmental controls, and each formation class of vegetation type stays within a characteristic geographical region, whether this be forest, grassland, or desert.

Ecological Succession

In Unit 41 we introduced the concept of habitat of an ecosystem. Within a given habitat will be found a smaller unit of ecosystem, the **plant community,** composed of a number of species which are usually found growing together. These species use the resources of their habitat in such a way as to either maintain the habitat or modify it. No particular dimensions and boundary limits can be set for plant communities; these properties depend on the changing patterns in the habitat. Within a given plant community, we can recognize a structure of vegetation which is distinctive. We will also find a certain species composition that may seem more or less fixed, or that may be gradually changing with time.

The phenomenon of change in ecosystems through time is familiar to us all. A drive in the country reveals patches of vegetation in many stages of development—from open, cultivated fields through grassy shrublands to forests. Clear lakes gradually fill in with sediment from the rivers that drain into them and become bogs. These kinds of changes, in which plant and animal communities succeed one another on the way to a stable end point, are referred to as **ecological succession.**

In general, succession leads to formation of the most complex community of organisms possible in an area, given its physical controlling factors of climate, soil, and water. The series of communities that follow one another on the way to the stable stage is called a **sere.** Each of the temporary communities is referred to as a **seral stage.** The stable community, which is the end point of succession, is the **climax.**

If succession begins on a newly constructed mineral deposit such as a sand dune or river bar, it is termed **primary succession.** If succession occurs on a previously vegetated area that has been recently disturbed by such agents as fire, flood, windstorm, or Man, it is referred to as **secondary succession.**

The colonization of a sand dune provides an example of primary succession. Growing foredunes bordering the ocean or lake shore present a sterile habitat. The dune sand—usually largely quartz, feldspar, and other common rock-forming minerals—lacks such important nutrients as nitrogen, calcium, and phosphorus, and its water-holding ability is very low. Under the intense solar radiation of the day, the dune surface is a hot, drying environment. At night, radiation cooling in the absence of moisture produces low surface temperatures. One of the first colonizers, or **pioneers,** of this extreme environment is beachgrass (Figure 42.1A). This plant reproduces vegetatively by sending out rhizomes (creeping underground stems), and the plant thus slowly spreads over the dune. Beachgrass is well adapted to the eolian (wind-dominated) environment; when buried by moving sand, it does not die, but instead puts up shoots to reach the new surface (see Figure 35.8).

After colonization, the shoots of beachgrass act to form a baffle that suppresses movement of sand, and thus the dune becomes more stable. With increasing stabilization, plants that are adapted to the dry, extreme environment but cannot withstand much burial begin to colonize the dune. Typically, these are low, matlike woody shrubs such as beach wormwood or false heather (Figure 42.1B).

On older beach and dune ridges of the central Atlantic coastal plain, the species that follow matlike shrubs are typically larger woody plants and trees such as beach plum, bayberry, poison ivy, and choke cherry (Figure 42.1C). These species all have one thing in common—their fruits are berries eaten by birds. The seeds from the berries are excreted as the birds forage among the low dune shrubs, thereby sowing the next stage of succession. As the scrubby bushes and small trees spread, they shade out the matlike shrubs and any remaining beachgrass. Pines may also enter at this stage.

At this point, the soil begins to accumulate a significant amount of organic matter. No longer dry and sterile, it now possesses organic compounds and nutrients, and has accumulated enough colloids to hold water for longer intervals. These soil conditions encourage the growth of such broadleaf species as red maple, hackberry, holly, and oaks, which shade out the existing shrubs and small trees (Figure 42.1D). Once the forest is established, it tends to reproduce itself—the species of which it is composed are tolerant to shade and their seeds can germinate on the organic forest floor. Thus, the stable stage—the climax—is reached. The stages through which the ecosystem has developed constitute the sere, progressing from beachgrass to low shrubs to higher shrubs and small trees to forest. Although this example has stressed the changes in plant cover, animal species are also changing as succession proceeds.

Old-Field Succession

Where disturbance alters an existing community, secondary succession can occur. **Old-field succession,** taking place on abandoned farmland, is a good example of secondary succession. In the eastern United States, the first stages of the sere often depend on the last use of the land before abandonment. If row crops were last cultivated, one set of pioneers, usually annuals and biennials, will appear; if small grain crops were cultivated, the pioneers are often perennial herbs and grasses. If pasture is abandoned, those

A. Beachgrass is a pioneer on beach dunes and helps stabilize the dune against wind erosion.

B. The low, matlike shrubs in the center of the photo replace beachgrass in the better stabilized areas.

C. This beach thicket of poison ivy, bayberry, and wild cherry paves the way for the development of the forest climax.

D. The climax forest on dunes at Sandy Hook, New Jersey. The holly tree (background at left) is an important plant of the climax forest. Notice the abundance of leaves and organic matter on the forest floor.

Figure 42.1   Stages in beach dune succession. (A. H. Strahler.)

pioneers that were not grazed will have a head start. Where mineral soil was freshly exposed by plowing, pines are often important following the first stages of succession, because pine seeds favor disturbed soil and strong sun for germination. Although slower growing than other pioneers, the pines eventually shade the others out and become dominant. Their dominance is only temporary, however, for their seeds cannot germinate in shade and litter on the forest floor. Seeds of hardwoods such as maples and oaks, however, can germinate under these conditions, and as the pines die, hardwood seedlings grow quickly to fill the holes produced in the canopy. The climax, then, is the hardwood forest, which can reproduce itself. Figure 42.2 shows an example.

All changes of the sere result from the action of the plants and animals themselves—one inhabitant paves the way for the next. As long as nearby populations provide colonizers, the changes lead in an automatic fashion from sand dune or old field to forest. This type of succession is often termed an **autogenic** (self-producing) **succession.**

In many cases, however, autogenic succession does not run its full course. Environmental disturbances, such as wind, fire, flood, or clearing by Man, may occur often enough to permanently alter or divert the course of succession. In addition, conditions such as site exposure, unusual bedrock, impeded drainage, and the like can hold back the course of succession so successfully that the climax is never reached—instead, an earlier stage of the sere becomes more or less permanent and is as stable at that site as the climax may be on more favorable sites. Some investigators thus see more than one climax as often being valid in a particular area—this is the **polyclimax theory.** Whether succession in a particular area can have one or many stable end points is not as important for us here,

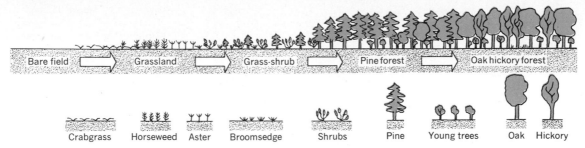

Bare field ⟹ Grassland ⟹ Grass-shrub ⟹ Pine forest ⟹ Oak hickory forest

Crabgrass — Horseweed — Aster — Broomsedge — Shrubs — Pine — Young trees — Oak — Hickory

Figure 42.2 Old-field succession in the Piedmont region of the southeastern United States, following abandonment of corn fields and cotton fields. This is a pictorial graph of continuously changing plant composition spanning about 150 years. (After E. P. Odum [1973] *Fundamentals of Ecology,* 3rd ed., W. B. Saunders Co., Philadelphia.)

however, as the nature of the process of succession itself.

Cutting and clearing of forest trees brings a Man-made demise to the forest climax. Inadvertent introduction of a plant disease from a foreign continent can cause the extinction of a particular plant species. An example is the chestnut blight, which eliminated the American chestnut from the forests of the eastern United States. Accidentally imported insects may also wipe out most of the mature individuals of a plant species when there is no native predator available to combat the invasion. These are just a few of the ways in which Man interferes with natural vegetation.

Our next study unit deals with agricultural ecosystems, in which Man completely dominates the land surface, not only by physical means but also by chemical means through use of fertilizers and pesticides.

SCIENCE SUPPLEMENT
Bog Succession

Extensive land areas of North America and Europe have innumerable **bogs,** former glacial lake basins now filled with partially decomposed plant matter which we recognize as **freshwater peat.** (Salt-marsh peat was explained in Unit 36.) Decay of plant matter is slow in these cold climates. Plant matter that accumulates below the water level of a lake is in a continually saturated condition, with little oxygen available to promote the activity of decomposers.

Figure 42.3 (see p. 306) shows by diagrams the stages in filling of lakes during autogenic bog succession. At the water's edge is a zone of sedges, followed by rushes. These construct a floating layer that encroaches upon the open water. There follows a zone of sphagnum (peat moss), which eventually completely fills the lake. Now the peat deposit supports hygrophytic trees (largely spruce) which produce a woody peat (Figure 42.4). This community may in turn be replaced by mesophytic trees, marking the climax stage. In the shallower upland ponds, shown on either side of the profile, the mesophytic growth is achieved much earlier than over the larger water body.

Figure 42.4 Bog succession in Emmet County, Michigan. A bog mat lies at the edge of the lake, a black spruce forest in background. (Pierre Dansereau.)

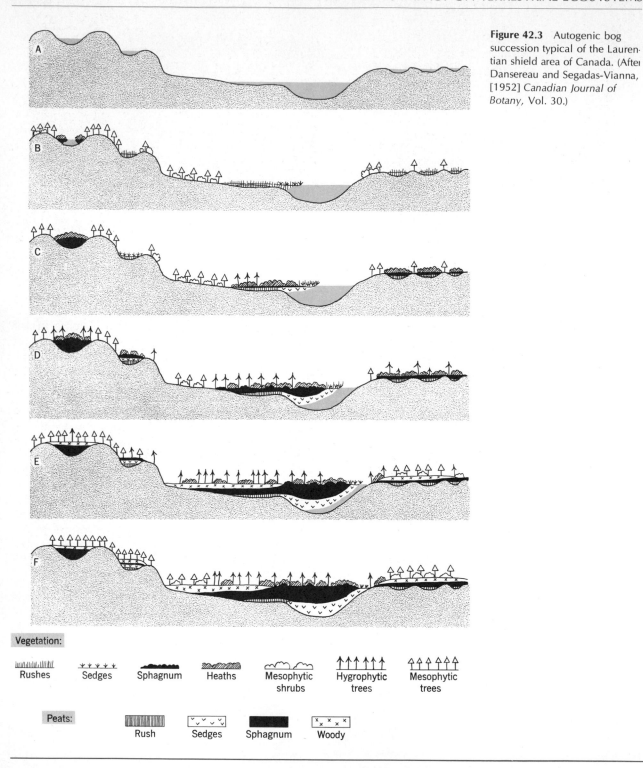

Figure 42.3 Autogenic bog succession typical of the Laurentian shield area of Canada. (After Dansereau and Segadas-Vianna, [1952] *Canadian Journal of Botany*, Vol. 30.)

Vegetation:

Rushes   Sedges   Sphagnum   Heaths   Mesophytic shrubs   Hygrophytic trees   Mesophytic trees

Peats: Rush   Sedges   Sphagnum   Woody

Unit 43
Agricultural Ecosystems

Dr. Borlaug and the Green Revolution

A 1970 report in *Science News* opened with this statement:

> The 1968-69 crop year on the Gangetic and Indus plains in India and West Pakistan ordinarily would have produced a famine. The monsoon was shorter than normal and winter rains were nearly nil; temperatures during March, when grain was filling, were five to eight degrees above normal. But there was no famine. Instead, the Pakistani wheat crop was about 14 percent higher than in the preceding year and the Indian crop eight percent. With or without drought and bad growing weather, wheat yields have been increasing comparably in Mexico, Turkey, and Afghanistan. A pessimistic 1967 report on world hunger by the President's Science Advisory Committee is a happily outdated document as its Malthusian predictions fail to come true and the specter of mass famine is averted—temporarily, at least.[1]

The occasion for this triumphant announcement was the awarding of the Nobel Peace Prize to Norman Ernest Borlaug, leader in the Green Revolution. Dr. Borlaug and his co-workers had succeeded in bringing to fruition a broad, complex program of agriculture improvement for the developing nations. Dr. Borlaug began his work with the Rockefeller Foundation in 1943 by experimenting in Mexico with varieties of wheat in an effort to improve various qualities of that cereal. Improvements included its yield per acre, its resistance to fungus disease, its protein content, its adaptation to various growing seasons, and its ability to take in large amounts of fertilizer to mature a heavy ear of grain on a short stem without falling over. Borlaug and his Mexican colleagues collected wheat varieties from many parts of the world and began to interbreed them to produce new strains of wheat. The result was a dwarf variety with strong stems. After an initial crop failure, in which most of the new seed wheat was lost to rust disease, the strain was further improved and a successful product emerged.

The new wheat moved Mexico into the ranks of a wheat-exporting country. Tried out in Pakistan and India, the new wheat increased yields from a miserable 7 to 8 bushels per year per acre to 60 to 70 bushels per acre. In India the success was so astounding that armed guards had to be posted around fields at experiment stations to prevent theft of the new seed grain.

The Green Revolution spread next into improvement of rice yields, carried out at the International Rice Research Institute in the Philippines. Drawing upon more than 20,000 varieties of rice, new highly productive strains were developed and passed on to rice farmers. By 1970, Philippine President Ferdinand E. Marcos announced: "The rice revolution has been permanently won."

Dr. Norman Borlaug explains the advantages of a new strain of wheat. (The Rockefeller Foundation.)

Here in the Punjab province of north India, wheat sheaves are being loaded on a wagon for transport to the threshing site. The tractor, a European import, symbolizes the technology and input of fossil fuels required to gain full benefits of the green revolution. (Jehangir Gazdar © Woodfin Camp.)

By 1973, a disturbing theme in a minor key began to be heard. Was the Green Revolution really working? There had been many problems. The new strains of wheat and rice required substantial and dependable supplies of water, fertilizer, pesticides, and financial credit. To a great number of poor farmers these inputs were simply not available. By 1973, rice production in the Philippines had risen only from 20 to 25 percent for the nation as a whole, and had leveled off. Then came the energy crunch, as the OPEC countries imposed oil embargoes and raised the price of oil. With an increase in oil prices came a

major increase in the price of fertilizers. In north India, for example, the fuel shortage severely curtailed irrigation by pumping from tube wells.

Meantime, human populations were increasing steadily in the developing nations. Tens of millions more mouths had appeared to consume the added production brought about by the Green Revolution. This population increase was no surprise to Dr. Borlaug; in 1970 he was quoted as saying that the Green Revolution "offers the possibility of buying 20 to 30 years of time . . . in which to bring population into balance with food production." In 1974, *Science News* reported Dr. Borlaug as concluding that time bought by the Green Revolution has been "largely wasted." He went on to say that only full cooperation among the industrialized nations can prevent chaos in world food supplies. He added: "The stage is set for real trouble."[2]

Meantime, a majority of persons in the United States has been enjoying high-protein food on an undiminished scale, despite minor inflation and a general rise in food prices. In this study unit we will investigate the nature and functioning of agricultural ecosystems. To go even further, we will add some details on how we use massive quantities of energy from fossil fuels to produce our huge output of food. Professor Howard T. Odum, an ecologist, used a nice phrase to describe our agricultural output: "potatoes partly made of oil." He explained: "A whole generation of citizens thought that the carrying capacity of the earth was proportional to the amount of land under cultivation and that higher efficiencies in using the energy of the sun had arrived. This is a sad hoax, for industrial man no longer eats potatoes made from solar energy; now he eats potatoes partly made of oil."[3]

[1]*Science News* (1970) vol. 98, p. 347.
[2]*Science News* (1974) vol. 106, p. 218.
[3]Howard T. Odum (1971) *Environment, Power, and Society*, Wiley Interscience, New York, pp. 115-116.

Fossil Fuels and Modern Agriculture

The principles of energy use and flow in natural ecosystems also apply to agricultural ecosystems. Important differences exist, however, between natural ecosystems and those that are highly managed for agriculture. The first major difference is the reliance of agricultural ecosystems on inputs of energy that are ultimately derived from fossil fuels. The most obvious of these inputs is the fuel that runs the machinery used to plant, cultivate, and harvest the crops. Another is application of fertilizers and pesticides

which have required large expenditures of fuel to extract or synthesize and to transport. Fossil fuels also power activities such as the breeding of plants, which have higher yields and are resistant to disease, and developing new chemicals to combat insect pests. Fuel is expended in transporting crops to distant sources of consumption, thus enabling large areas of similar climate and soils to be used for the same crop. In these and many other ways, the high yields obtained today are brought about only at the cost of a large energy input derived from fossil fuels. Fuel costs are thus a major share of food costs.

Functioning of Agricultural Ecosystems

In terms of ecosystem structure and function, agricultural ecosystems are very simple. They usually consist of one genetic strain of one species. Such ecosystems are overly sensitive to attacks by one or two well-adapted insects that can multiply very rapidly to take advantage of an abundant food source. Thus, pesticides are constantly needed to reduce insect populations. Weeds, too, are a problem, adapted as they are to rapid growth on disturbed soil in sunny environments. Weeds can divert much of the productivity to undesirable forms. Herbicides are often the immediate solution to these problems.

Application of agricultural chemicals is one of the ways in which Man uses energy inputs to increase net primary productivity. Large increases in productivity are achieved by application of nutrient elements and compounds—usually of nitrogen and phosphorus—which are in short supply in most soils. In natural ecosystems, these elements are returned to the soil following the death of the plants that concentrate them. In agricultural ecosystems, this recycling is interrupted by harvesting the crop for consumption at a distant location. Nutrients must be added each year in the form of fertilizers, and these are synthesized or mined only with considerable energy input from fossil fuels.

Agricultural Production and Energy Resources

The inputs of energy that Man adds to managed ecosystems in the form of agricultural chemicals and fertilizers, as well as those in the form of the work of farm machinery, have acted to boost greatly the net primary productivity of the land. Table 43.1 gives some examples of how agricultural yields have responded to these inputs. (Units used in the table are the energy equivalents of the biomass.) The table shows that Man has acted to raise the net primary productivity of agricultural ecosystems more than five times over through the use of energy contained in fossil fuels.

As the United States, in company with other nations, enters a period of apprehension over the future adequacy of energy resources to meet growing demands, we can do well to evaluate the level of efficiency of our agricultural system in delivering food energy in return for the energy we expend upon that production.

The total U.S. energy consumption in 1974 is estimated to have amounted to $18,900 \times 10^{12}$ kilocalories per year (kcal/yr). Table 43.2 gives a breakdown of the proportions of the total energy consumed by U.S. agriculture. The total agricultural energy use of 498 kcal/yr represented 2.6% of the total U.S. energy consumption. This agricultural energy use is about 10% as much as was expended in fuel for transportation and about 14% as much as was expended for heating of buildings.

Energy consumed in agriculture is subdivided in the table into two major categories: (1) petroleum and electricity expended on farms; (2) energy represented by materials expended and equipment used on farms. Petroleum expended as fuel on the farm amounted to 51% of the total agricultural expenditure. (Petroleum consumption listed under purchased inputs represents fuel consumed in the manufacture of those input materials.) Fertilizer accounted for about 28% of the total agricultural energy used, whereas pesticides used a very small proportion, about 0.6%.

The schematic flow diagram, Figure 43.1, shows how the fuel energy input enters into both the purchased inputs and the operations performed on the farm to raise and harvest crops. Solar energy of photosynthesis is, of course, a "free" input. But, in order to be delivered to the humans or animals who consume it, the raw food or feed product of this flow system requires expenditure of fossil fuel energy.

Excluding the solar energy of photosynthesis, the energy expended upon production of a raw food or feed crop is referred to as **cultural energy.** Let us examine the cultural energy input needed to produce various feed and food crops. The upper graph in Figure 43.2 shows the relative efficiency of food production of 24 crops. The horizontal scale shows cultural energy expended in terms of thousands of megacalories per acre per year (mcal/acre/yr). The vertical scale shows the ratio of food energy produced

Table 43.1 Crop Productivity and Efficiency with and without Fossil Fuel Energy Subsidy

Crop	Net Productivity, as Harvested (kcal/m²/day)	Efficiency of Primary Production (percent)
Without fossil fuel energy inputs		
Grain, Africa, 1936	0.72	0.02
All U.S. farms, 1880	1.28	0.03
With fossil fuel energy inputs		
Grain, North American average, 1960	5	0.12
Rice, U.S., 1964	10	0.25

SOURCE: Data of several sources, compiled in H. T. Odum (1971), *Environment, Power and Society,* Wiley-Interscience, New York, p. 116, Table 4.1.

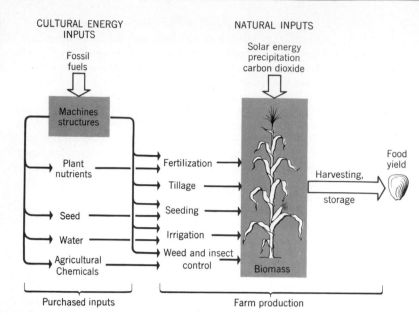

CULTURAL ENERGY
INPUTS

NATURAL INPUTS

Figure 43.1   A schematic diagram of the inputs of cultural energy into various stages in the agricultural production system. (After G. H. Heichel [1976] Agricultural production and energy resources, *Amer. Scientist,* vol. 64, p. 65.)

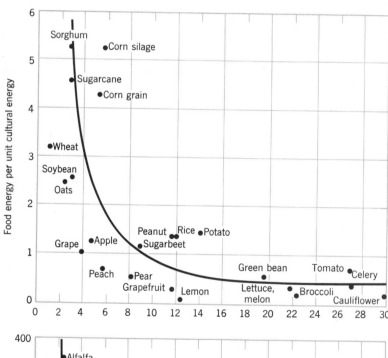

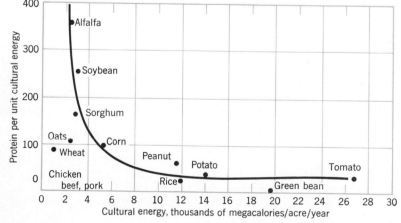

Figure 43.2   *(upper graph)* Cultural energy used to produce certain food crops in relation to yield of food energy. *(lower graph)* Protein yield in relation to cultural energy for several kinds of crops. (After G. H. Heichel [1976] Agricultural production and energy resources, *Amer. Scientist,* vol. 64, p. 66.)

Table 43.2 Energy Consumed by Agriculture in the United States

	kcal 10¹²	Percent of Total U.S. Energy Budget
Farm production		
Crops		
Petroleum	189	1.0
Electricity	3	0.02
Livestock		
Petroleum	63	0.3
Electricity	9	0.05
Purchased inputs		
Fertilizer	140	0.7
Petroleum	49	
Feeds and additives	25	
Animal and marine oils	9	0.5
Farm machinery	8	
Pesticides	3	
Total	498	2.6

SOURCE: Data of Economic Research Service, 1974, as presented by G. H. Heichel (1976) *American Scientist,* vol. 64, p. 64.

to input of cultural energy; the higher the ratio, the greater is the efficiency (and the lower is the cultural input required). Notice that field crops, such as sorghum and corn, used largely as animal feeds, have the highest levels of efficiency, whereas foods consumed directly by humans have relatively low efficiencies. Garden crops require a very high cultural energy input per unit area of land and also have very low efficiencies.

The lower graph in Figure 43.3 shows on the vertical scale the protein derived from each unit of cultural energy. Alfalfa and soybeans rate very high on this scale. (Soybean protein is presently being processed in various forms for human diet as a meat substitute.) Notice that oats, wheat, and corn have intermediate values of protein yield, but that rice ranks very low. (Protein deficiency is a serious health problem for peoples subsisting largely on rice.) A small area of the graph at the lower left is labeled "chicken, beef, pork." This insertion serves to show that protein obtained from meat has an energy efficiency only about one-tenth as great as from soybeans. Indeed, the energy available from edible meat represents only about 10–30% of the energy expended in animal feed, a fact previously pointed out in our discussion of energy flow in the food chain (Unit 38).

The data thus indicate clearly that our food production system is not a very efficient one in terms of cultural energy expended to furnish food to humans. The most highly coveted parts of the American diet, meat and garden vegetables, are extremely wasteful of cultural energy as compared with, say, diets based largely on grain foods (bread, breakfast cereals) and soybean products.

DATA SOURCE: G. H. Heichel (1976) Agricultural production and energy resources, *American Scientist,* vol. 64, pp. 64-72.

Unit 44
Lakes and
Eutrophication

Lake Washington — An Environmental Success Story

If all you ever hear about pollution is horror stories, here's a change of pace for you—the story of Lake Washington, which was stricken with a bad case of premature aging but was then brought back to youth through the efforts of concerned citizens.

Lake Washington is a freshwater lake located to the east of Seattle, Washington. A long narrow body of water, the lake is oriented in a north-south direction, and its entire western shore, some 18 miles long, is occupied by the city. A number of smaller communities occupy the east shore, which is served by bridges across the narrow lake.

The degradation of Lake Washington began in the late 1880s, as Seattle and the surrounding communities began dumping raw sewage into the lake. As the years went by, it became obvious that raw

sewage effluent was creating a health hazard. As a result, Seattle and the surrounding communities built secondary treatment plants to process the sewage before it entered the lake. By 1955, some 10 treatment plants were in operation, pumping about six and a half million gallons of treated sewage into the lake each day.

The lake soon began to show signs of a serious decline in quality. Although the sewage entering the lake was treated, nitrates and phosphates were not removed, and these compounds encouraged the growth of algae. By 1963, the algae count was so high that visibility in the lake water was reduced to about one meter.

As the lake's beauty declined and it became less and less suitable for recreation, the citizens of Seattle became increasingly concerned. Spurred on by the League of Women Voters, the residents of the area formed a government corporation, the Municipality of Metropolitan Seattle, and passed a $121 million bond issue enabling the corporation to build an en-

The Corinthian Yacht Club holds a regatta on Lake Washington. Mt. Rainier looms faintly in the distance. (Monkmeyer Press Photo Service.)

tirely new sewage system. Instead of releasing treated sewage into Lake Washington, the new system intercepted the effluent of the treatment plants, pumping it into nearby Puget Sound. In this way the nitrogen and phosphorus from the effluent, which had stimulated the algae growth, were released to a much larger body of water where its impact would not be readily felt.

The recovery of Lake Washington was rapid and dramatic. In 1970, Dr. W. T. Edmondson of the University of Washington, observed "The lake is back to its condition in 1950 now. Prompt action headed off trouble before it really got bad." Much of the rapid recovery was due to the fact that the lake is fed by particularly pure snowmelt streams. Although only one-third of the lake's volume is flushed each year, the purity of the inflowing water was sufficient to rapidly lower phosphate levels and reduce the number of algae. Underwater visibility increased,

and light penetration had nearly tripled by 1970. Once again, the citizens of the greater Seattle area were able to enjoy many forms of recreation on their now-restored lake.

The case of Lake Washington is a success story showing how Man can create a pollution problem and then solve it. Unfortunately, cases in which Man has created the problem, but not solved it, are far more numerous. The purpose of this unit is to help you more fully understand the natural behavior of lake ecosystems and how they respond to Man's activities.

DATA SOURCE: W. T. Edmondson (1970) "Phosphorus, nitrogen, and algae in Lake Washington after diversion of sewage," *Science,* vol. 169, pp. 690-691; R. H. Gilluly (1970) "Eutrophication speeded by Man," *Science News,* vol. 98, pp. 17-19; J. Crossland and J. McCaull (1972) "Overfed," *Environment,* vol. 14, no. 9, pp. 30-37.

Lakes and Ponds

Lakes and ponds are still-water habitats. From an ecological viewpoint, a **pond** is a body of water shallow enough for sunlight to reach its bottom everywhere. A **lake,** on the other hand, is deep enough to have an area where sunlight does not reach the bottom in amounts sufficient for photosynthesis to proceed. Although lakes and ponds may seem at first to be fairly uniform habitats, there is actually a great deal of environmental variation within them.

As physical features of the environment, lakes were explained in Unit 16. Because lake basins are so diverse in their geologic origins, the dimensions and bottom materials of lakes show a very wide range of differences. Unit 16 also discussed the water balance of lakes. The relationship of lake and pond levels to the ground water table was discussed in Unit 15. A review of these subjects will supply a helpful background of information upon which to begin an investigation of the ecosystems of lakes and ponds.

Temperature Layers in a Lake

Temperature and oxygen content are both highly important environmental factors in lakes and ponds. For a typical lake in summer in midlatitudes, if we were to take a series of temperature readings from the surface downward, the temperature profile would look like that in Figure 44.1. Because the upper warm layer, known as the **epilimnion,** has a uniform temperature throughout, it is called an **isothermal layer.** Below the epilimnion, temperatures drop rapidly. This zone is named the **thermocline.** An important property of the thermocline is that water does not easily rise or sink through this layer, the reason being that water density changes with water temperature. Below the ther-

mocline, temperatures again become uniform with depth, constituting the **hypolimnion,** a cold layer close to 39° F (4° C).

During the late autumn, the epilimnion becomes progressively colder and the thermocline is thus destroyed. The water of the lake is mixed by vertical currents in an overturning motion, after which the lake freezes over and all motion ceases. During the winter, water temperature is

Figure 44.1 Summer temperature profile of a small lake in the midlatitude zone. (From A. N. Strahler [1971] *The Earth Sciences,* 2nd ed., Harper & Row, New York.)

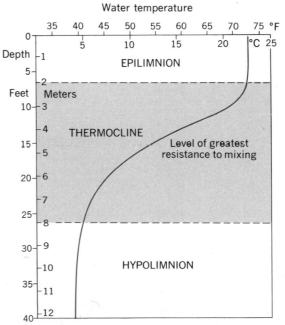

at a uniform 39° F (4° C) except at the frozen surface. (Details of these seasonal changes are given in the science supplement.)

Figure 44.2 shows both summer and winter temperature profiles for a typical small lake in the northeastern United States. Also shown are profiles of dissolved oxygen content for both summer and winter. In summer, the epilimnion, thermocline, and hypolimnion are well developed. Dissolved oxygen is greatest in the epilimnion, where constant mixing and the photosynthetic activity of tiny floating aquatic plants is greatest. Dissolved oxygen is low in the hypolimnion, for the thermocline prevents mixing with the water above, and the darkness creates an environment in which oxygen is consumed by decomposers and by consumers that feed upon dead tissues.

In winter, temperature and dissolved oxygen values are quite different. Temperature is at a uniform 39° F (4° C) except for the ice layer and the water nearest it. Oxygen levels are high for several reasons. First, recent mixing has increased the oxygen content. Second, oxygen is more soluble in cold water than in warm water. Third, the cold temperatures depress the activity of oxygen-consuming decomposers. Their abundance near the bottom, however, does produce a slight drop in oxygen in the bottom layer.

Biological Divisions of a Lake

A lake may also be divided into layers from a biological viewpoint. Three zones can be recognized, each with a different set of ecological characteristics and a different group of organisms (Figure 44.3). These zones are defined by the position of the **compensation level,** the depth at which light energy is just sufficient for photosynthesis to balance the respiratory needs of primary producers. The compensation level is approximately located at the depth to which 1% of the incoming solar radiation penetrates. Above the compensation level, in the **euphotic zone,** primary producers dominate, whereas below the compensation level, in the **profundal zone,** only consumers find nutrition. Within the euphotic zone are two subdivisions: the shallow **littoral zone,** where light reaches the lake bottom, and the deep water **limnetic zone,** where the bottom is below the compensation level. Ponds, by definition, lack substantial limnetic or profundal zones.

Figure 44.2   Temperature and dissolved oxygen variation with depth in summer and winter, Linsley Pond, Connecticut. (After E. S. Deevey, Jr. [1951] *Scientific American,* vol. 185, no. 4, pp. 70-71.)

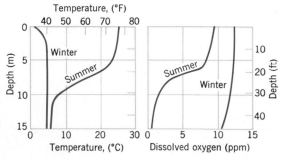

In the shallow waters of the littoral zone, light and oxygen are abundant. Nutrient levels are normally high, for decomposition of nutrient-containing organic matter brought in by streams is rapid where oxygen is ample. Here waves and currents keep sediment agitated. The primary producers of the littoral zone are the aquatic flowering plants and the algae. The flowering plants are rooted to the lake bottom.

Phytoplankton, floating organisms which dominate the limnetic zone, as well as being abundant in the littoral zone, are of three major groups: The **diatoms** are a class of the free-floating golden-brown algae with siliceous shells. The **green algae** are present in a variety of forms. The **blue-green algae,** which occur in both one-celled and colonial forms, are important from both ecological and environmental viewpoints. They respond readily to increased nutrient concentrations and tend to **bloom** (to grow to a large population) when stimulated by organic inputs, such as sewage. Many of the blue-green algae produce toxic compounds which can build up to lethal concentrations during blooms, and thus destroy other organisms. Such toxic compounds can also present a water-quality problem if the lake or pond is tied into a public water supply.

Dependent on the phytoplankton as a food source are the minute floating and weakly swimming animals, the grazing **zooplankton.** Also present in, but not restricted to the limnetic zone, are the **nekton,** or swimming organisms—the fishes and some invertebrates. The distribution of fishes throughout the water column is usually dependent on temperature, oxygen, and food content of the water, with each species occupying different suitable environments. For example, bass, pike, and sunfish often occupy the warm epilimnion, whereas the lake trout is more likely to be found in the deeper, colder waters near and below the thermocline.

The profundal zone, by definition, lacks sufficient light for photosynthesis; it is therefore dominated by consumers. The profundal environment is greatly influenced by activities in the limnetic zone above. In lakes in which productivity is high, large quantities of organic debris will fall through the thermocline and hypolimnion to settle on the bottom. The degradation of this debris by the decomposing bacteria and microorganisms, however, requires oxygen. For this reason highly productive lakes are likely to present anoxic (without oxygen) or nearly anoxic environments near the profundal bottom. Lakes with small littoral zones and low primary production, on the other hand, will have higher oxygen levels in bottom waters and will therefore usually support a greater diversity of bottom life.

The organic ooze that accumulates on the bottom of the lake in the profundal zone is a stratum of great biological activity. Most plentiful are the anaerobic bacteria (bacteria that do not require oxygen). These bacteria reduce sulfur, nitrogen, and organic compounds in order to degrade organic matter. Because these reduced end products can be toxic to other organisms, the bottom zone of highly productive lakes, where anaerobic bacteria are most active, usually shows fewer species and less activity of higher life forms than the bottom dwellers of less productive lakes. Typical bottom organisms are small crustaceans, mollusks (such as freshwater clams), and a variety of scavenging

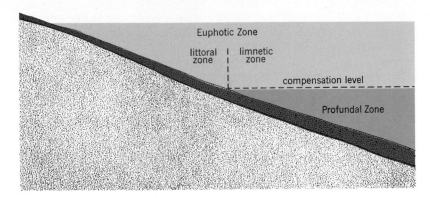

Figure 44.3 Biological zones of a lake.

protozoa, which are often found encased in shells. Annelid worms such as bloodworms and wormlike larval forms are also typical. Most of these higher organisms are resistant to low oxygen levels and can endure severe stagnation, but none can survive indefinitely without oxygen.

The most productive lakes are those with a large littoral zone in relation to their volume. Here, sunlight reaches most of the lake's waters, providing an energy source for the primary producers in addition to significant warming during the growing season. Shallowness of the water allows the development of a large biomass of highly produc-

tive, rooted aquatic plants. Phytoplankton blooms are characteristic because of high inorganic nutrient concentrations produced as bottom microorganisms degrade large volumes of organic matter. Since profundal waters have low oxygen concentrations, stagnation of bottom water is relatively frequent. Such shallow, highly productive lakes are termed **eutrophic lakes.**

In contrast are **oligotrophic lakes,** which are much less productive. An oligotrophic lake is usually deep and steep-sided, with a narrow littoral zone. Concentrations of inorganic nutrients are low, and so is phytoplankton den-

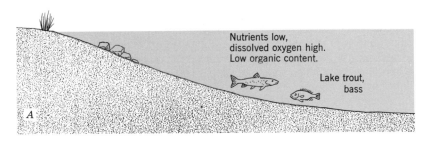

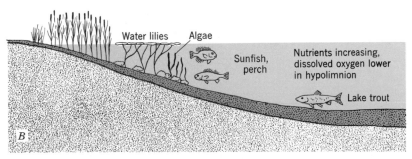

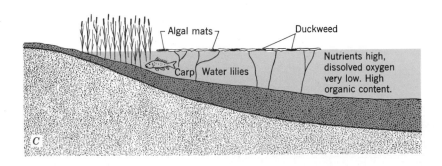

Figure 44.4 Eutrophication. A. Oligotrophic lake. Typically clear, cold, and deep, the lake contains few nutrients. B. As nutrients are washed into the lake and as sediment and organic matter increase, productivity builds. Plant life is abundant. C. Eutrophic lake. Sediment fills in the deep portions of the lake; abundant nutrients encourage algae and duckweed blooms. Few fish can survive the low oxygen levels. Portions of the bottom are anaerobic.

sity. Blooms are rare, for the intense competition for nutrients keeps population levels low. Dissolved oxygen is high in the hypolimnion; its large volume, low temperatures, and low input of organic matter serve to keep oxygen-depleting microorganisms in check. Cold-water bottom fishes such as lake trout or landlocked salmon find suitable habitats in the profundal zone.

Eutrophication

On the geologic time scale, oligotrophic lakes tend to become eutrophic. Constant inputs of sediment and dissolved nutrients from streams tend to make oligotrophic lakes more shallow and more productive. Eutrophic lakes, in turn, are being filled by stream inputs as well as accumulations of their own organic debris, and will eventually form bogs if deposition continues. The normal course of events is thus a succession, called **eutrophication,** from a deep, clear lake to a wet bog, produced by both geological and biological processes acting through geologic time. Figure 44.4 shows three stages in the proccess of eutrophication.

Eutrophication is thus a slow, natural process, but Man has inadvertently speeded up this change in many cases. Clearing for farmland and residential construction greatly increases the sediment loads of rivers draining into lakes, enlarging their littoral zones and decreasing their profundal volumes. Inputs of inorganic nutrients to lakes may also be greatly increased. Agricultural runoff contributes nitrates and phosphates; sewage treatment plants contribute nitrates, phosphates, and organic matter. Logging and burning act to release from terrestrial cycles other nutrients, among them sulfur, magnesium, and potassium. Runoff then conveys these nutrients into rivers and then into lakes. Toxic chemicals and compounds from industrial wastes enter lakes and are concentrated in second- and third-order consumers. As a result, lake populations are diminished, and the collection of organisms present

changes from that of a grazing food chain to that of a detritus-feeding chain. Taken together, these processes can accomplish in a span as short as a human life changes that normally take thousands of years. The result is **cultural eutrophication,** a by-product of Man's exploitation of the earth's surface.

Eutrophication of the Great Lakes

As we explained in Unit 37, the Great Lakes are relatively young, geologically speaking. They date from the final retreat of the Pleistocene ice sheets in Wisconsin time (Figure 44.5). Listed below are the five Great Lakes in order of surface area:

	sq mi	sq km
Superior	31,800	82,400
Huron	23,000	59,600
Michigan	22,400	58,000
Erie	9,900	26,000
Ontario	7,500	19,400

Figure 44.6 is a schematic profile and cross section of the lakes giving surface elevations and depths. Four of the five lakes have bottom depths well below sea level. In contrast, Erie is shallow—about 200 ft (60 m)—a factor that has been important in allowing its advanced pollution.

The Great Lakes have a relatively small surrounding watershed area—only about three times the area of the lakes themselves and equivalent to only about 3.5% of the total land area of the United States. (The dashed line on the map shows the watershed of each lake.) Yet this small portion of land harbors about one-seventh of the United States population and about one-third of the Canadian population. The Lake Erie shore is the most intensively developed of all the lakes, with the major population centers at Detroit, Toledo, Cleveland, Erie, Buffalo, and Windsor. Population concentrations are also heavy on the southern

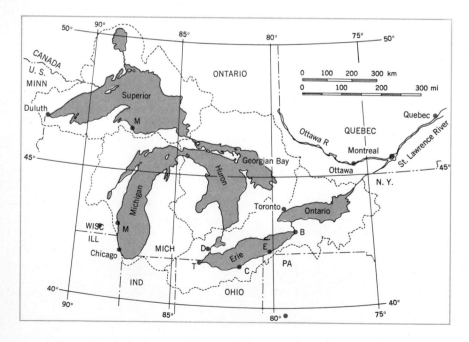

Figure 44.5 Outline map of the Great Lakes and their watersheds (dashed lines.)

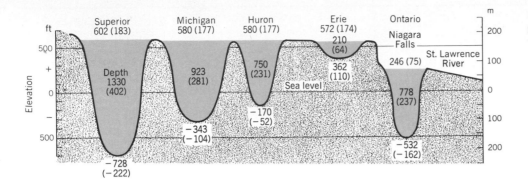

Figure 44.6 A generalized profile and cross section of the Great Lakes.

shore of Lake Michigan, where Milwaukee, Chicago, and Gary are situated.

One measure of eutrophication is the concentration of dissolved solids in the waters of a lake; for the dissolved solids are mostly inorganic nutrients. The graph in Figure 44.7 shows how these pollutants have increased in each of the five Great Lakes in the past 50 years. Lake Superior, with little surrounding development, has remained almost unchanged. Lake Huron shows an increase of only a few parts per million, produced largely by Lake Michigan water which passes through Huron. Dissolved solids have risen noticeably in Lake Michigan because of the heavy concentration of industrial activity at the southern end. Dissolved solids levels in both Lakes Erie and Ontario have risen dramatically, approaching 50 ppm in 50 years. Although its shore is less developed industrially, Lake Ontario's level of dissolved solids has increased because it receives water from Erie through the Niagara River. Additions are also important from large population centers of Toronto, Hamilton, and Rochester.

Of the five Great Lakes, Man's impact has been greatest on Erie, for it has the smallest volume of water and the greatest volume of pollutants. Oxygen depletion in the hypolimnion of Erie is now much more frequent and much more severe than in the past, and depletion now affects a significantly greater bottom area. The benthic (bottom-dwelling) fauna of the west end of the lake has changed, particularly in response to new, low oxygen levels. Mayfly larvae, indicators of a diverse, aerobic bottom environment, are now virtually absent; populations of sludge worms, which can withstand the most anoxic conditions, had increased by 1961 to values exceeding 1000 per square meter for most of the western end of the lake.

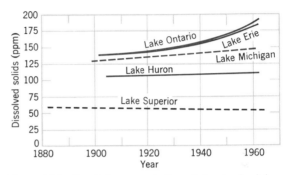

Figure 44.7 Trends in concentration of dissolved solids in the five Great Lakes. (Data of several authors, presented in A. M. Beeton [1965] *Limnology and Oceanography*, vol. 10, p. 246.

Table 44.1 shows how catches of four important species of commercial fishes have declined in Lake Erie in recent years. The decimation of these fish populations which the data reflect has been brought about largely by failure of the fish to reproduce. The sea lamprey, a blood-sucking parasite that has had a disastrous impact on fisheries of the other Great Lakes since it was introduced through the Welland Canal, has not been an important factor in Lake Erie. While the lake herring, whitefish, sauger, and walleye have declined drastically, the less desirable freshwater drum (or, sheepshead), carp, yellow perch, and smelt have increased in their place, and the total annual catch for Lake Erie has remained near 50 million pounds. Thus, heavy pollution has acted to shift the species composition of fishes in Lake Erie.

Table 44.1 Decline in Lake Erie Fish Catches

	Catch (pounds per year)		
Species	Past	Present	Percent Decline
Lake herring	20,000,000 (pre-1925)	7,000 (1962)	Over 99.9
Whitefish	2,000,000 (pre-1948)	13,000 (1962)	Over 99.3
Sauger	1,000,000 (pre-1945)	1,000–4,000 (early sixties)	99.9
Walleye	15,400,000 (1956)	1,000,000 (early sixties)	93.5

SOURCE: Data from Alfred M. Beeton (1965), *Limnology and Oceanography*, vol. 10, no. 2, p. 250.

SCIENCE SUPPLEMENT

Heating and Cooling of Lakes

The environmental properties of freshwater lakes in middle and high latitudes pass through an annual thermal cycle in response to the strong annual cycle of net radiation. In turn, this thermal cycle strongly influences the growth of aquatic plant and animal life in lakes.

Let us start with late winter or very early spring, when the lake surface is still covered with ice and the water beneath lies stagnant at a temperature not far above the freezing point (Diagram A, Figure 44.8). As solar radiation rapidly increases, the ice is melted and warming of a surface layer begins (Diagram B). Once the layer has exceeded 39° F (4.4° C), it is less dense than the colder water below and remains on top. Winds blowing over the lake surface create small waves, and these cause a mixing that results in thickening of the warm layer (Diagram C). A strong thermocline develops and moves downward.

As the summer progresses, the warm surface water layer, or epilimnion, becomes thicker and the thermocline is pushed down to greater depths (Diagram D). For a shallow lake, 50 to 75 ft (12 to 23 m) deep or less, the entire water body may be warmed, but for deeper lakes, a cold hypolimnion persists. Inflowing water of streams or springs may add to the mixing of warm and cold water.

As winter approaches and the incoming radiation declines, heat is lost from the surface layer (Diagram E). Being denser than the warmer water below, this cold surface water sinks to the bottom and sets up a general convection process called **overturning.** The thermocline is destroyed and gradually the water becomes uniformly cold throughout. Mixing ceases when the point of maximum density (39° F; 4° C) is reached. Further cooling produces a less dense surface water layer that remains on top, eventually freezing into a continuous ice layer.

In warm tropical and equatorial climates, where solar radiation is uniformly great throughout the year, lake water is comparatively warm down to the bottom. The coldest water that can sink to the lake floor can be no colder than the average surface water temperature at the coolest time of year. This seasonal cooling easily results in overturn and general mixing because the overall range of temperatures is small. For example, lakes at low elevation in Indonesia, situated near the equator, have a bottom temperature always close to 79° F (26° C), while the surface water temperature ranges annually from 49° to 84° F (26° to 29° C). When the surface water temperature is increasing, a weak thermocline develops, just as in lakes of midlatitudes, but it is destroyed when the seasonal cooling takes place. Because solar radiation at the top of the atmosphere is un-

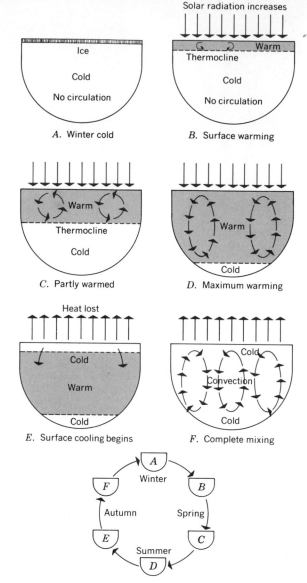

Figure 44.8 Schematic diagram of the annual cycle of heating, cooling, and mixing of lake water in the midlatitude zone. (From A. N. Strahler [1971] *The Earth Sciences,* 2nd ed., Harper & Row, New York.)

iformly great throughout the year at low latitudes, the cooling of the surface water seasonally is brought about by the occurrence of a rainy season (a rainy monsoon) in which cloud cover reduces incoming radiation and copious rains have a cooling effect. In the dry season, solar radiation again becomes intense and the surface water is warmed.

Unit 45
Stream Ecosystems and Sewage Pollution

The Tragedy of the Tiber

Here in North America, we often think we have a corner on the pollution market. What with Lake Erie "dead" and still others dying, with our murky Mississippi and ugly Ohio, we tend to see our own water pollution problems as bigger than those of others. After all, the greater the affluence, the greater the effluence. But things could be worse—a lot worse. You could live in Rome, overlooking the Tiber.

The history of Rome and the Tiber River on which it lies begins some 25 centuries ago in ancient Roman mythology. The famous Seven Hills of Rome were at first farming communities established on tiny hilltops along the banks of the Tiber. The river afforded protection for the Romans, acting as a natural moat, and also provided a vital water supply for the Romans and their agriculture. By the fifth century B.C., these early settlements had coalesced into a single community, and the Tiber served as a trade route for river traffic as well.

In the third century B.C., the Romans began to build their famous aqueducts, providing Rome and its surrounding lands with abundant water for public use. With the building of the aqueducts, however, the degradation of the Tiber began. After use, the waste water from fountains, baths, and street runoff, was channeled into a network of sewers culminating in the Cloaca Maxima, which to this day drains directly into the Tiber. No longer serving as a source for irrigation and fresh water, the Tiber was now used to carry away the waste of the imperial city.

Technicians from Rome's health department run tests on polluted water of the Tiber River, hoping to determine what chemical had suddenly killed thousands of fish. (UPI.)

The tradition of the Tiber as the sewer of Rome continues to the present. Each day, nearly 200,000 gallons of untreated sewage flows directly into the Tiber through the Cloaca Maxima and other sewers. For comparison, this quantity of effluent is more than three times greater than that reaching all rivers in England. Needless to say, no one swims in the Tiber—in fact, bathing in the river and its tributaries has been banned since 1896. More recently, however, the ban was extended to the ocean beaches where the Tiber flows into the Mediterranean Sea. As a result, severe declines in tourist income were reported from that area.

Although riverside land values traditionally decline as water quality declines, this has not been the case with the Tiber. The solution has been to zone the banks of the river and its tributaries for industrial activities. Because riverside industry does not need to bear the cost of building sewers or waste-treatment facilities, riverbank properties have actually increased in land value.

Naturally enough, Italian authorities are concerned about the infernal river of the Eternal City. Following the appearance of foaming streams and frothing fountains, the Italian government banned the sale of nonbiodegradable detergents. Efforts are now under way to curb excessive dumping of chemical waste by industry into the Tiber within the city limits of Rome. In addition, several large sewage treatment plants are now under construction to treat the waste of the Roman metropolitan region. The completion of these plants and their future operation should do much to improve the water quality of the Tiber. Enforceable water pollution laws, aimed at reducing industrial effluents, will also go a long way toward cleaning up the Tiber. With these efforts, it may be possible to reverse the degradation of 2,000 years of neglect, and the citizens of Rome will once again be able to enjoy, like their forebearer, Julius Caesar, a refreshing dip in the historic Tiber.

The Tiber is just one of many examples of rivers and streams polluted by human activities. The purpose of this unit is to describe some characteristics of the natural stream environment, how it is impacted by sewage pollution, and how that impact can be reduced through sewage treatment.

DATA SOURCE: Shari Steiner (1971) Effluence of the Eternal City, *Geographical Magazine*, vol. 43, no. 12, pp. 820-822.

The Biological Environment of Streams

The moving-water environment of a stream presents some contrasts to the still-water environment of a lake. The most obvious difference is that streams have a current, although there are pools within streams where the current is weak or absent, and zones within lakes, such as wave-washed shores, where a current is present. One of the most important effects of a current is that it serves to import nutrients and foods to the habitats of organisms. There is also a simultaneous export of waste products. For this reason, stream waters can be as many as 30 times more productive than lake waters.

The current presents some problems, however, for organisms seeking a particular environment within the stream. Unless, like the stronger fish, they can maintain their position, they will be carried downstream. Most plants maintain attachment to the channel bed by means of roots or rootlike structures. The animals, on the other hand, maintain their positions by a wide variety of adaptative structures. These include suckers and hooks for attachment to bottom objects; sticky surfaces, such as those of snails and flatworms; and streamlined and/or flattened bodies to cut water resistance and to allow the use of narrow crevices for shelter. In addition, many animals instinctively exhibit positive adaptive behavior by heading into the current or by staying very close to objects on the bottom.

A second major environmental difference between the stream and the lake is in the oxygen level. The constant mixing and agitation of the water-air interface serves to keep stream waters thoroughly oxygenated. As a result, many organisms of streams are sensitive to a drop in oxygen levels, an effect easily induced by the bacterial degradation of influent sewage.

A third important difference is that there is a great deal more energy exchange between a stream and the terrestrial environment that surrounds it than between a lake and its environs. A careful examination of the stream environment will show that consumers are much too numerous to be supported exclusively by the producers within the stream. Instead, they are maintained in large part by inputs of nutrients and detritus from the vegetation of the banks, floodplain, and surrounding surfaces that drain into the stream.

The nature of the stream bottom greatly affects the flora and fauna of the stream. Sand and silt are usually the least productive materials. Neither offers much physical support for bottom organisms. Clay bottoms or bedrock bottoms are usually more favorable. The most productive bottom is composed of cobbles or gravel. The rubble supplies a great variety of surfaces for attachment as well as many attractive pockets and crevices to shelter bottom-dwelling consumers from the swift-moving current.

Most rapidly moving streams exhibit alternations of pools and riffles. The riffles, which are shallow reaches with swift current, are the more productive of the two habitats (Figure 45.1). Plants that cling to the bottom are

Figure 45.1 This small stream presents a diversity of aquatic environments, ranging from the swiftly flowing waters of the riffle zones to the quieter pools that alternate with them. (Robert Perron.)

Width and depth of the channel increase downstream, whereas gradient decreases. The range in variation of velocity diminishes, producing a more uniform environment. The contrast between pools and riffles becomes less marked and the large trunk river appears slower and more sluggish than the small stream (Figure 45.2). Suspended sediment load increases in ratio to bed load, and bed materials become finer downstream. Typically, the bed of a stream of low gradient in a floodplain channel is composed mostly of fine silt or sand. Water temperature increases as the shade of vegetation on the banks becomes less effective and as greater turbidity increases the absorption of solar radiation.

Downstream changes in physical environment from the small headwater stream to the large trunk river are accompanied by changes in the stream community. Detritus-feeders increase in response to an increased proportion of soft mud bottom. Burrowing worms and midge larvae become dominant bottom consumers and are joined by crustaceans, snails, and other mollusks. Bottom-feeding fishes, such as carp, catfish, and suckers, are now important parts of the swimming fauna. Rooted aquatic plants and bank vegetation show zonation patterns characteristic of the littoral zone of lakes and ponds. Plankton populations are now much larger, although they are still not as great as in the lakes or ponds.

Figure 45.2 This distributary in the Amazon delta presents quite a different aquatic environment from that of the swift stream of Figure 45.1. Note the lack of obvious pools and riffles as well as the greater turbidity. (Robert Perron.)

particularly important producers. They may be diatoms, water mosses, and blue and blue-green algae that coat the stones and sticks of the stream bottom. Swift currents in the riffle zone constantly tear bits of these organisms loose, sweeping them away, providing an energy source for downstream pools as well as a source of colonizers for the riffles below. The larvae of many insects, such as blackflies, mayflies, caddisflies, and stoneflies, are important animals in the riffle zone. Most of these larvae graze the bottom-clinging plants and phytoplankton. The fishes are also sometimes found in riffles, where they obtain much of their food by grazing or predation. They rely on the pools for rest and shelter.

The pools present a contrasting environment to the riffles. Here the bottom is usually soft sediment, which encourages burrowing worms and larvae. The pool ecosystem often bears a strong resemblance to that of a shallow pond.

Traced from their headwaters to the sea, streams undergo changes in hydrology, as we have seen in Unit 14.

Response of Streams to Sewage Pollution

As we have seen in Unit 18, Man's activities have had a great impact on the quality of surface water. Industrial and urban use of water has changed the chemical composition of runoff by adding elements and compounds, some of which are beneficial and others of which are harmful to aquatic organisms. Let us, then, examine the impact of a common pollutant—sewage—on a typical stream.

Table 45.1 shows the important inorganic elements and compounds that characterize a sewage effluent. There are relatively high levels of nitrate, phosphate, and sulfate, as compared to uncontaminated water. Sodium and potassium chlorides are also abundant. The major component of raw sewage is undecomposed organic matter. The amount of this organic matter is expressed as the **biological oxygen demand** (B.O.D.) of the waste, and defined as the quantity of oxygen which microorganisms will consume in degrading the waste to carbon dioxide and water. Large numbers of bacteria and sewage fungi will also characterize the raw effluent.

Figure 45.3 shows how a stream responds to the input of raw sewage. Four zones in the stream below the outfall can be recognized. The first is the **zone of degradation**, where water quality is declining as the effluent mixes with the stream waters. The B.O.D. of the stream jumps, and dissolved oxygen levels begin to plunge. Dissolved salts and suspended solids also increase dramatically from low levels just above the outfall.

As an increasing number of decomposer organisms become active, the **zone of active decomposition**, or **septic zone,** begins. Here sewage fungi, protozoa, and bacteria reach high levels, while dissolved oxygen reaches its low

point. If the amount of effluent is large enough in relation to the size of the stream, dissolved oxygen may become totally depleted, and anaerobic conditions will prevail. The reduced forms of nitrogen and sulfur reach their highest concentrations here, as do the anaerobic bacteria that produce them. Oxygen concentrations are too low for the normal fauna of the stream, but are usually suitable for the sludge worms, which reach their peak at the end of the zone.

Eventually, much of the sewage decomposes and the activities of microorganisms are slowed. Mixing of the water surface introduces oxygen that is now not immediately consumed; dissolved oxygen levels rise somewhat. In this **zone of recovery,** a few of the members of the stream's original fauna return. Protozoa and small invertebrates multiply in response to the large numbers of bacteria, a food source they readily exploit. As recovery progresses, nitrogen, phosphorus, and sulfur are converted to their in-

Table 45.1   Typical Concentration of Ions in Urban Sewage Effluent

Ion	Symbol	Concentration, parts per million
Chlorine	Cl^-	160
Sulfate	SO_4^-	160
Bicarbonate	HCO_3^-	210
Nitrate	NO_3^-	20
Sodium	Na^+	150
Calcium	Ca^{++}	40
Magnesium	Mg^{++}	16
Phosphate	PO_4^{+++}	6–12

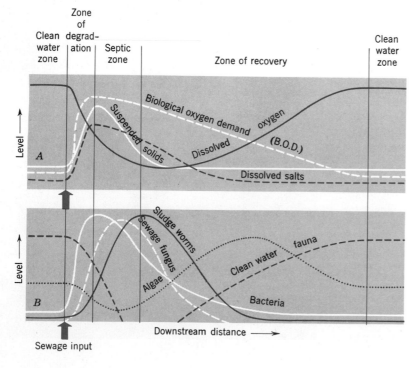

Figure 45.3   Response of a stream to an input of untreated sewage. A. Changes in chemical properties. B. Changes in physical properties. (Curves after H. B. N. Hynes [1960] *The Biology of Polluted Waters,* University of Toronto Press, Toronto and Buffalo, p. 94, Fig. 16. Division into zones after W. T. Edmondson, in W. W. Murdoch, ed. [1971] *Environment: Resources, Pollution, and Society,* Sinauer Associates, Stamford, Connecticut, p. 216.)

Figure 45.4 Sewage treatment. Upper left: An aerial view of one of New York's sewage treatment plants. The rectangular vats are settling tanks; anaerobic digestion takes place in the round tanks in the foreground. (New York Department of Water Resources.)

Lower left: A trickling filter. Wastewater is sprayed by rotating arms over the gravel bed, where bacteria oxidize the organic matter the water contains. (Environmental Protection Agency.)

cumulate in aquatic ecosystems. Organic mercury compounds are a good example. In addition, the "dead" zone near the outfall serves as a very effective barrier to the upstream and downstream movement of organisms, for it severs the biological communication between segments of the stream. Further, the affected area will obviously not be suitable for recreation or other human use, and will, in fact, provide a human health hazard.

Sewage Treatment

The impacts described above are for raw sewage rather than treated sewage. The treatment process is basically designed to reduce the B.O.D. of the sewage, and therefore reduce the impact on the stream. In **primary treatment,** the waste water is screened, then allowed to stand and separate into liquid and solid portions. The solid portion, or **sludge,** is buried or otherwise disposed of; the liquid portion is treated with chlorine to kill the bacteria and viruses and is then discharged into natural runoff systems.

In **secondary treatment,** the process is carried further by an additional step involving bacterial decomposition (Figure 45.4). The sludge goes to a digesting tank, where it remains till bacteria decompose it almost completely. The residue is then air dried and disposed of by incineration or burial. The liquid portion is sprayed onto a **trickling filter,**

organic oxidized forms, and serve to stimulate populations of algae. In turn, the algae increase oxygen levels and provide food and shelter for the typical stream organisms, which return in increasing numbers toward the end of the zone. Eventually, all the organic matter will be oxidized, excess nutrients will be stored in the biomass of the stream, and the stream will return more or less to its original condition in the **clean water zone.**

Although the sewage effluent does not seem at first to produce any permanent downstream damage to the stream, there are other impacts. Sewage wastes may contain industrial chemicals and toxic compounds which cannot be degraded by bacteria and therefore can ac-a bed of stones whose surfaces become coated with bacteria. The organic materials in the liquid are decomposed by the bacteria in the presence of abundant oxygen. In effect, secondary treatment moves the "dead" zone from the stream into the sewage plant. After an additional settling, the liquid is chlorinated and then discharged. Efficient secondary treatment can remove as much as 90% of the B.O.D. of the sewage before it is discharged.

Unfortunately, secondary treatment does not result in the removal of the simple inorganic nutrients. Thus, the effluent of a secondary sewage treatment plant may impact a stream, not by depressing the oxygen level through introduction of a large B.O.D. load, but rather by stimulating the growth of algae. If the algae are subject to blooms, their die-off can produce almost as great a B.O.D. as primary treatment, and thus create the same problem the process was designed to prevent. The solution is **tertiary treatment,** in which nitrates, phosphates, and other inorganic ions are removed from the effluent before it is released. Tertiary treatment is very costly, however, and in addition does not remove all harmful substances.

An alternative form of tertiary treatment, presently being evaluated in experimental and pilot operations, disposes of the liquid fraction from secondary treatment by spray irrigation upon forests or forage crops. As the nutrient ions enter the soil, they are held by organic and inorganic soil colloids. The nutrients then are taken up by plants and placed in storage within the biomass. Eventually, the plant matter can be removed from the area, providing commercially useful forest products or feed for animals. Thus, the ions which would otherwise pollute ground water or streams are recycled with some savings in treatment costs. The spray irrigation system of sewage treatement has been called a **living filter,** in recognition of the role that plants play in the final processing stage.

In Unit 18, we covered a number of other topics in water pollution of streams and lakes. These include the introduction of various ions into stream flow in urban areas, thermal pollution, acid mine drainage and acid rain. There remains another important area of environmental pollution which affects Man and the ecosystems of streams, lakes, and the oceans. This area includes synthetic chemicals used as insecticides and herbicides as well as other synthetic chemicals released by industrial processes into streams and lakes. We will deal with these substances in Unit 47.

Unit 46 Marine Ecosystems

Fangs

If you saw the movie *Jaws,* it may be difficult to imagine anything more terrifying than the attack of the great white shark. With incredible strength and power, this magnificent beast strikes unexpectedly, ripping apart human flesh and leaving the ocean surface boiling with blood. If you found the tale of the killer shark gripping, wait till you read the scenario below. It concerns the invasion of the blue Caribbean by a new and fearsome predator—the venomous black and yellow sea snake. For our story, we've modestly chosen the title "Fangs."

So far, the voyage has been beautiful. In the two weeks since you left Los Angeles, your sparkling new cruise ship, the *Caribbean Queen,* idly cruised down the Mexican coast, calling at Mazatlan, Manzanillo, and Acapulco, on its way to the waters of the crystal Caribbean.

A dramatic highlight of the voyage was the passage through the new Pan-American Sea-Level Canal, opened some three years ago. The impression of speed through the canal was quite exhilarating—with the swift current behind the ship adding to her five-knot headway, it was like flying through the narrow channel. The lush, green blanket of tropical vegetation which lined the steep, nuclear-carved sideslopes of the channel seemed to rush by, almost close enough to touch. Bird calls and animal cries echoed between the ship's broad white hull and the channel walls, the chatters and shrieks adding to the drama of the scene.

Your reverie is interrupted as the beachboy from the fashionable Kingston resort hotel approaches. "You like another rum collins?" he asks.

"No," you reply, "I think it's time for a swim." You stroll across the fine white sand, and step into the warm blue water. The foamy breakers caress your body as you swim through them into the gentle swells beyond.

Suddenly, a young woman not far from you screams. "Help! Help! They're biting me!" Still screaming, she thrashes the water, desperately making for shore. Then you see them. Her body is covered with yellow-and-black snakes, twined around her arms, legs, and torso.

Just as you realize that you, too, are in danger, you see undulating forms under the water approaching you. With horror and fear, you swim desperately for the shore, but it is a race you know you cannot win. You feel them now, encircling

A deadly sea snake on the beach. This venomous black and yellow predator, *Pelamis platurus,* inhabits coastal waters of the eastern Pacific Ocean, where even sharks give it a wide berth. (William A. Dunson.)

your body, like muscular hands dragging you down. You cry out with fear, choking on the bitter salt of the water. You struggle for breath as you feel the sharp, stabbing pain of the venomous bites on your legs, arms, and chest. As your mind clouds and your eyes dim, your last recollection is of the excruciating pain of your cramped muscles as the poison takes action . . .

Sound pretty far-fetched? Well, actually it is. The sea snake in question, *Pelamis platurus,* is presently found only in the eastern Pacific. It is sluggish and fairly nonaggressive, and rarely, if ever, attacks humans. A solitary swimmer, the snake stays generally well offshore, feeding on organisms found in windrows of seaweed far from the beaches.

There is some scientific basis for our tale, however. Many marine ecologists are now concerned about the prospects of a new sea-level canal through the Isthmus of Panama. Such a canal would permit free interchange between the organisms of the eastern Pacific and western Caribbean oceans. Both these areas have very rich marine faunas—that is, each area has a large number of distinctive marine organisms.

What will happen when these two faunas mix? Ecologists tell us that many of the species will be thrown into direct competition with one another. Sooner or later, some species will win the struggle for existence while others will lose. Thus, we would expect a mixing of the faunas to produce a large number of species extinctions.

Because the black and yellow sea snake has no counterpart in the Caribbean, and virtually no important predators in either area, some ecologists believe that it could become widespread in the Caribbean after introduction through a sea-level canal. Even if this migration should occur, it seems unlikely that the snake's habits would change enough to present a hazard to humans. However, that remote possibility does provide our scenario with at least a grain of truth.

Inadvertent introduction of organisms into new geographic areas is only one of many possible human impacts on marine ecosystems. This unit describes the structure and functioning of marine ecosystems as well as Man's utilization of the marine food chain.

DATA SOURCE: R. H. Gilluly (1971) "Consequences of a sea-level canal," *Science News,* vol. 99, pp. 52-53; J. C. Briggs (1972) letter entitled, "Aquatic ecosystems," *Science,* vol. 176, pp. 581-582.

Marine Environments

Marine ecosystems of the salt-water environment are extremely varied both in physical properties and in the types of life assemblages present. The marine environments include estuaries, mangrove coasts, and coral reefs, which are shallow-water littoral zones. Beyond lies the open ocean, a marine environment varied greatly in its vertical dimension from surface layer to deep bottom.

Like the terrestrial and freshwater ecosystems, marine ecosystems are productive in terms of food resources for Man; they are also sensitive to disturbance and degradation through Man's input of industrial wastes.

Estuaries

As we have seen in Unit 36, estuaries are transitional environments at the ocean's edge where fresh and salt water mix. By and large, the flora and fauna of the estuary are derived from marine forms, rather than terrestrial forms. Most estuaries are dominated by a few, rather than many, species. Because of the constant shifts in temperature, salinity, and turbidity, as well as tidal currents, estuaries present an unusual environment to which only a few species are sufficiently adapted to spend their entire life cycle. Those species that are so adapted, however, are usually present in large numbers.

As we observed in Unit 38, estuaries provide examples of ecosystems with well-developed detritus food chains (Figure 38.1). Primary production is greatest in the intertidal salt-marsh zone surrounding the estuary (Figure 46.1). Here, productivity compares favorably with the most productive of natural environments (Table 38.1). The grasses and sedges of the salt marsh are highly salt-tolerant and ecologically adapted to the transitional environment; moreover, their annual growth is very great. Algae on the marsh surface and banks of the tidal channels are also highly productive. Only about 5% of the net primary production, however, is directly consumed by grazing insects and other plant-eaters; most of it reaches the saline water and becomes detritus, rich in nutrients and energy.

A typical estuarine food chain has been presented in Figure 38.1. Bottom dwellers feeding on detritus are numerous in most estuaries. These include crabs, lobsters, and young shrimp among the crustaceans; clams, oysters, and mussels among the mollusks. The detritus, as well as some living plant matter, also supports the young of such fish as striped mullet, flounder, menhaden, and croaker. In fact, the estuary serves as a nursery for the juvenile forms of many commercially important finfish and shellfish. The estuary's low salinity protects them, for it serves as a barrier to the entrance of most predators from the open sea.

One reason for the high productivity of estuaries is that they tend to serve as **nutrient traps.** Fine particles of clay and organic material are transported to the estuary by the rivers that empty into it. These particles are rich in ad-

Figure 46.1 A tidal salt marsh in Maryland. The dominant grass is a species of cordgrass, *Spartina*. (Grant Heilman.)

nutrient concentration process by reducing the escape of vital nutrients to the open ocean. The efficiency of the estuary as a nutrient trap also makes it an excellent trap for such toxic compounds as pesticides and heavy metals.

Man exerts an impact on estuaries mainly by draining and filling (Unit 36), which often simply eliminate the estuarine environment. When a decision is made to fill a coastal tidal land, the value of the commercial fish that are dependent on it is often underestimated or not even considered. If the tidal land is thought of as a capital investment producing interest equal to the value of the annual catch of finfish and shellfish which it supports, values of from $5000 to $25,000 per acre are obtained. This figure does not include such intangibles as recreational benefits or scenic values. Clearly then, conversion of tidal land to such uses as sanitary landfills or parking lots probably represents a loss, rather than a gain, to society. Table 46.1 shows how much acreage each section of the U.S. coastline has lost to dredging and filling operations. According to the data, California has lost the largest percentage of its tidal lands, followed by the Gulf and South Atlantic coasts.

Mangrove Swamps

Mangroves are woody shrubs that are capable of growing in salt water. Together with a few other plants, they form **mangrove swamps** found at the ocean's edge in the tropical and equatorial zones. The several species of mangroves have more or less the same appearance. They are tall, and many-branched in form; they have smooth leaves, and prop or buttress roots (Figure 46.2).

The mangrove swamp exhibits a cosmopolitan flora—that is, it has more or less the same species wherever it is found throughout the world. The wide distribution of mangrove species occurs because many of the plants use the ocean waters as a method of seed dispersal. An example is the red mangrove. Its seed actually begins to germinate

sorbed nutrients and ions. When they reach salt water, the particles flocculate and settle, as described in Unit 36, concentrating nutrients in the sediments. Equipped with water filters, detritus feeders ingest the particles and remove the adsorbed nutrients and bacteria during digestion. They also extract dissolved nutrients directly from the water. Constant activity of the tides serves as an energy subsidy to bring new particles to filter-feeders and carry digested particles away. The filter-feeders, then, aid the

Table 46.1 Important Estuarine Habitat Lost from Dredging and Filling Operations, 1950–1969

Coastline Zone	Acres of Important Habitat	Acres Lost	Percent Loss
North Atlantic	271,000	2,500	0.9
Middle Atlantic	2,201,800	77,000	0.4
Chesapeake	603,300	5,000	0.9
South Atlantic	823,800	42,300	5.1
Biscayne and Florida Bay	922,200	21,100	2.4
Gulf of Mexico	8,325,000	426,700	5.1
Southwest Pacific (Calif.)	388,000	46,200	12.0
Northwest Pacific (Wash.-Oregon)	2,142,000	21,000	1.0
Alaska	593,400	1,500	0.003
Great Lakes	432,000	2,600	0.1

SOURCE: Data from *National Estuary Study,* Department of the Interior, Fish and Wildlife Service, (1970), vol. 2, p. 122.

Figure 46.2 A mangrove forest growing in a saline embayment at Harney's River, Florida. (American Museum of Natural History.)

before it falls, growing into a young seedling borne on its parent branch. Soon the seedling falls into the water, and is floated by winds and currents until it touches a suitable substrate of soft mud. Here it develops roots and branches, perhaps as a colonizer on a faraway mud flat. Other plants of the mangrove swamp possess floating seeds or other adaptations to facilitate their worldwide dispersal.

The food chain of the mangrove swamp is similar to that of the estuary. It has a detritus base—mangrove leaves—although phytoplankton and algae do make a minor contribution to the community economy. Small crustaceans, mollusks, and fish consume the detritus, and are in turn consumed by the larger fish and fish-eating birds. Like the estuary, the mangrove swamp harbors many commercially important species of fish in their juvenile stages.

Coral Reefs

Coral reefs are rocklike masses of carbonate mineral matter accumulated in the surf zone through organic processes. The reef-forming organisms are **corals,** animals that secrete lime to form their skeletons, and **algae,** plants that also make limy encrustations. Corals are colonial types of animals, that is, they occur in large colonies of individuals. As coral colonies die, new ones are built upon them, thus developing a coral limestone made up of the strongly cemented limy skeletons. Coral fragments torn free by wave attack and pulverized may be deposited to form beaches, spits, and bars, which later are cemented into a limestone.

Coral-reef coasts occur in warm, tropical and equatorial zones between the latitude limits 30° N and 25° S. Water temperatures above 68° F (20° C) are necessary for dense reef coral growth. Furthermore, reef corals live near the water surface, down to limiting depths of about 200 ft (60 m). Water must be free of suspended sediment and well aerated for vigorous coral growth. Thus, corals thrive

in positions exposed to wave attack from the open sea. Because muddy water prevents coral growth, reefs are missing opposite the mouths of turbid streams. Coral reefs are remarkably flat on top and have a surface level approximately equal to the upper one-third mark of the range of tide. Thus they are exposed at low tide and covered at high tide.

Three general types of coral reefs may be recognized: (1) fringing reefs, (2) barrier reefs, and (3) atolls. **Fringing reefs** are built as platforms attached to shore (Figure 46.3). They are widest in front of headlands where wave attack is strongest, and the corals receive clean water with abundant nutrients. Fringing reefs may be from 0.25 to 1.5 mi (0.4 to 2.5 km) wide, depending on exposure to surf and the length of time that the reef has been developing.

Barrier reefs lie out from shore and are separated from the mainland by a lagoon, which is a type of estuary (Figure 46.4). The lagoon is shallow and flat-floored, usually 120 to 240 ft (35 to 75 m) deep. There are, however, many towerlike columns of coral in the lagoon. Passes, which occur at intervals in barrier reefs, are narrow gaps through which excess water from breaking waves is returned from the lagoon to the open sea. They sometimes occur opposite deltas on the mainland shore, because of the inhibiting effect of turbid water on coral growth.

Atolls are more or less circular coral reefs enclosing a lagoon, but without any land inside. In all other respects they are similar to barrier reefs. On large atolls, parts of the reef have been built up by wave action and wind to form low island chains, connected by the reef (Figure 46.5). A cross section of an atoll shows that the lagoon is flat-floored and shallow, and that the outer slopes are steep, often descending thousands of feet to great ocean depths.

Coral reefs are exceedingly diverse life environments; they accommodate a very large number of species, many

Figure 46.3 A fringing reef on the south coast of Java forms a broad bench between surf zone (left) and a white coral-sand beach. Inland is rainforest. (Luchtvaart-Afdeeling, Bandung.)

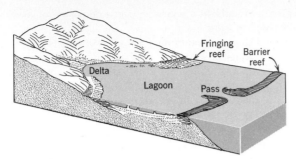

Figure 46.4 A barrier reef is separated from the mainland by a shallow lagoon. (After W. M. Davis.)

of which are uniquely adapted to this distinctive environment. From the viewpoint of productivity, coral reefs rank with estuaries as highly productive ecosystems. In contrast to estuaries, however, the ratio of production to respiration nears unity in the coral reef. The coral reef thus consumes as much energy as it fixes. This condition is characteristic of a stable, mature ecosystem.

Besides the algae and corals, other important organisms on the reef are the larger consumers. Many species of brightly colored fish graze among the algae. Crustaceans, such as lobsters, and other invertebrates as well, are common detritus-feeders. Top consumers of the food chain are sharks and the moray eels; they lurk in the deeper waters, awaiting their prey.

Open-Water Marine Ecosystems

Beyond the shallow inshore waters of such transitional environments as estuaries, mangrove swamps, and coral reefs, lie distinctive marine ecosystems of the open water. Biological oceanographers divide the open water into two regions: the **neritic zone,** which includes the water and bottom between the shoreline and the edge of the continental shelf, and the **oceanic zone** of deep water beyond (Figure 46.6).

Primary producer organisms occur in the upper layer, or **euphotic zone,** which is penetrated by sunlight. These are **phytoplankton,** small photosynthetic organisms with little

Figure 46.5 Islands of the Kwajalein Atoll in the Pacific Ocean are built of coral sand rising above the level of a broad coral reef. Open ocean lies at the left and bottom of the photo; lagoon at center and upper right. Overwash of breaking waves forms a streaked pattern across the reef. (Official U.S. Naval photograph.)

or no capacity for motion. **Zooplankton** are also minute planktonic organisms, but are animals and do not photosynthesize. **Neuston** are small organisms that live at or on the water surface. **Nekton,** which are strong swimmers, include fishes and amphibians.

Nekton of the open ocean include fishes, squid and octopus, marine mammals (whales, porpoises), and reptiles

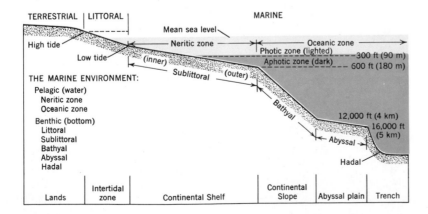

Figure 46.6 A schematic cross section of an ocean basin from the edge of a continent to a deep trench. (From A. N. Strahler [1971] *The Earth Sciences,* 2nd ed., Harper & Row, New York.)

(sea turtles). Many of the nekton are plankton feeders and possess adaptations to facilitate gathering and consuming plankton. The baleen whales are examples—their gills serve the double duty of oxygenating their blood and straining **krill,** red shrimplike crustaceans, from the water. In Antarctic waters, the marine food chain has only three levels: primary producers (phytoplankton), krill, and whales.

Bottom-dwelling organisms found on the floors of the continental shelves include most of the life forms found in estuaries. The animal forms include crustaceans (lobster, shrimp), and shellfish (clam, abalone), all of which we recognize as important food resources for Man. Deep-water and deep-bottom environments of the open ocean are only sparsely populated by organisms. These animals must be adapted to living in total darkness under enormously high confining pressures.

Upwelling and Nutrient Supply

The primary producers of the oceans, largely phytoplankton, thrive where plant nutrients are in most abundant supply. One source of nutrients is runoff from the lands. As we would expect, estuaries and the shallow waters of the continental shelves receive large amounts of nutrients from the land and can nourish large populations of primary producers (Figure 46.7). Over the deep oceans generally, the surface layer (euphotic zone) is poorly supplied with nutrients and, despite the large input of solar energy avail-

able for photosynthesis, cannot support a dense population of primary producers.

A second source of nutrients for marine waters is the deep ocean water layer, made available by a rising water motion, called **upwelling.** The deep bottom layer of the ocean receives a constant rain of detritus from upper layers; this material is a source of nutrients, particularly nitrate and phosphate. Within a few narrow zones close to the continental margins, upwelling brings these nutrients to the surface, where they nourish dense populations of phytoplankton.

Upwelling of deep, cold water can be caused by prevailing winds, forcing surface water to move away from a coast. Water rises from below to replace the water moving away from the land. The most important zones of upwelling are in tropical latitudes, as shown in Figure 46.7. They are associated with cool, equatorward moving currents off the western coasts of North and South America and Africa. Another tropical zone of upwelling lies off the east coast of Africa and the Arabian peninsula.

The Peru Current, off the west coast of Peru, in a latitude range of about 5° to 20° S, is a particularly striking example of a productive zone of upwelling. Nutrients brought to the surface sustain a dense population of primary producers and consumers. Myriads of small fish, the anchoveta, feed upon the zooplankton and in turn supply food for seabirds and for larger fish, such as tuna. For their part, the birds excrete their wastes on the mainland coast of Peru. The accumulated deposit, called guano, is a source of fertilizer rich in nitrates and phosphates.

Figure 46.7 Distribution of world fisheries. Coastal areas and upwelling areas together supply over 99 percent of world production. (Compiled by the National Science Board, National Science Foundation.)

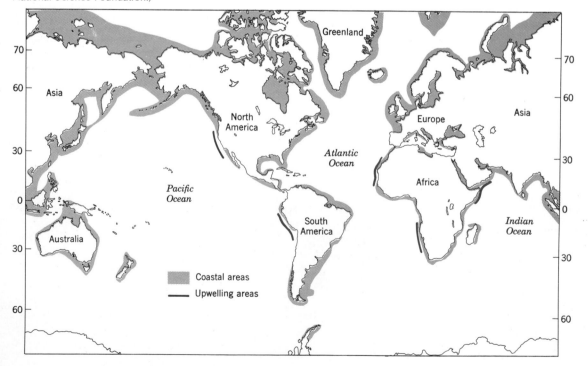

The Oceans as a Food Source for Man

Popular fancy has always leaned to the notion that the bounty of the sea is limitless; that when the lands can no longer produce enough food to support the growing human population, we can turn to marine food resources. The facts lead to a quite different conclusion.

To put the marine food resource in its proper perspective, we should be aware that at the present time the sea furnishes only about 1% of the calorie value of food consumed by the human race, and that this amounts to only about 10% of the total world protein consumption.

Table 46.2 compares primary productivity for four types of marine ecosystems. The deep-water oceanic zone is the least productive of the marine ecosystems. At the same time, however, it comprises about 90% of the world ocean area. Continental shelf areas are a good deal more productive, and, in fact, support much of the world's fishing industry at the present time (Figure 46.7). Except for the shallow-water estuarine and reef ecosystems, the upwelling zones are most productive. These limited areas constitute the world's most productive fishing grounds, and yield about one-half the world's annual harvest. For example, the Peruvian coastal fishery of the anchoveta, the small fish mentioned above which is used to produce fish meal for animal feed, is located in a narrow zone of upwelling and yields about 12 million metric tons (mmt) per year, or nearly one-fifth of the present total harvest of all marine fish.

Since the middle of the nineteenth century, fish catches have been rising at rates that have kept pace with food needs of an expanding world population. Improved technology in recent years has been a very important factor in increasing catches. This expansion cannot continue much further, however, for the total annual sustained yield of ocean fish is estimated to be between 100 and 200 mmt per year, compared with the present harvest of about 70 mmt per year. At present rates of expansion, this limit will be reached between 1980 and 2000. Beyond that time, overfishing will deplete the stock of fish. In 1949, an international fisheries conference identified some thirty major fish stocks thought to be underexploited; today, fourteen of

these are either fully exploited or overfished.

These figures show that the ocean is not a vast, untapped food resource, capable of indefinite expansion into the future. If we continue to utilize its finfish according to existing patterns and standards, the ocean food resource will soon be exploited to its limit and beyond under the press of an expanding world population.

Only a small portion of the available energy in an ecosystem can be passed from one level of a food chain to the next. Consequently, a much larger population of consumers can be supported by feeding upon plants at the producing level than upon other consumers at higher levels. From a diet of fish, taken at the highest levels of the marine food chain, we may be forced to turn to lower levels for our food supply. One step in this direction is to make use of krill as a human food resource. One expert in the field of marine fisheries has suggested that it may be possible to harvest as much as 50 to 100 mmt per year of these tiny shrimplike creatures from Antarctic waters, where they thrive in great shoal-like masses. The Soviet Union has been experimenting with conversion of krill into a paste-like food. The next step down in the food chain is to make direct use of plankton as a food. The prospect, if lacking in gustatory appeal, may offer one means of postponing the world-food crisis certain to arise if growth of the human population continues unchecked.

Table 46.2 Primary Productivity of Four Ecosystems

Ecosystem	Gross Primary Production, (kcal/m²/year)
Open ocean	1,000
Neritic zone	2,000
Upwelling zone	6,000
Estuarine and reef ecosystems	20,000

SOURCE: Data from Ryther as converted by E. P. Odum, (1971), *Fundamentals of Ecology*, W. B. Saunders Co., New York, p. 51, Table 3-7.

Unit 47
The Impact of Chemical Pollutants on Ecosystems

The Minamata Disease—An Industrial Tragedy in Japan

It was in the early 1950s that fishermen and their families in the city of Minamata, Japan, first began to show the symptoms of what was to become known as the Minamata disease. The first signs were loss of sensation at the extremities of the hands and feet and in areas around the mouth. These symptoms were followed by difficulty in walking, slurred speech, reduced vision, and hearing loss. Unfortunately, many persons fell prey to eventual paralysis, followed by coma and death.

Public health officials were at first baffled by the new disease. Then clues began to accumulate. Autopsies showed structural damage to the brains of the victims. In addition, sea birds and even cats in Minamata began showing similar symptoms. It was not until 1959, however, that the cause of the disease was pinpointed—mercury poisoning.

This poisoning of the food chain was local and quite direct. The Chisso Corporation, a plastics manufacturer, was releasing mercury-laden wastes into Minamata Bay. The mercury, in its toxic methyl form, was then concentrated in the predatory fish through the food chain of the bay ecosystem. The fisherfolk were first to suffer the effects of the disease, for they subsisted largely on fish. Sea birds and cats also fell prey to the disease since they, too, depended on a fish diet. All told, 397 persons were stricken with mercury poisoning, of whom 60 died.

Even though mercury was shown to be the culprit, the Chisso factory did not stop its flow of toxic waste products to the bay. In fact, the company continued to dump mercury wastes even after it was blamed for

Minamata Bay at sunset.
(W. Eugene Smith.)

the disease by the Japanese government in 1968. Nearly twenty years of pollution, however, finally caught up with the Chisso Corporation. In 1973, the company was ordered to pay some $3.8 million to a group of 45 of the victims and their survivors. And, this group was just one of six groups seeking financial redress from the company. Some estimates of the company's total liability run as high as $38 million—a burden that could eventually break the company. In 1975, executives of the Chisso Company were charged with "professional negligence resulting in death." By 1976, a total of nearly 900 victims of the poisoning were officially recognized, and an additional 3000 persons had applied for compensation. Estimates of the total number of victims not yet discovered run as high as 10,000.

The Minamata disease is just one example of the impact of chemical pollution on Man. The object of this unit is to describe the effects of chemical pollutants on ecosystems, and to discuss two types of chemical pollution in particular—that of marine oil, and of DDT.

DATA SOURCE: K. R. Stunkel (1974) "New hope in Japan," *Environment*, vol. 16, no. 8, pp. 18-20; L. J. Goldwater (1971) "Mercury in the environment," *Scientific American*, vol. 224, no. 5, pp. 15-21.

Pollution and Ecosystems

In a number of earlier units we introduced various forms of air and water pollution resulting from fuel combustion, urban activities of various sorts, mining, and use of fertilizers. Unit 18 showed how pollutant ions enter runoff and stream flow. Unit 20 explained how pollutant ions move in the ground-water system. The impact of raw sewage upon stream ecosystems was described in Unit 44. Now we turn to forms of chemical pollution involving complex molecules, both of natural origin in petroleum fuels, and of synthetic origin as compounds produced by chemical processes for use as pesticides and for industrial uses. Another class of pollutants strongly impacting ecosystems and Man are the toxic metals, such as mercury.

Food chains play a major role in concentrating certain chemical pollutants to dangerously high levels in consumers, so that not only may the ecosystem be damaged, but humans who eat the flesh of tainted consumers can suffer serious health effects as well.

The subjects we introduce in this study unit will bring together a number of principles of ecosystem operation, together with a variety of principles of the physical operation of environmental systems of the atmosphere and hydrosphere.

Marine Oil Pollution

Most persons are familiar with two major marine oil-pollution events of recent years. One was the *Torrey Canyon* disaster of 1967 off the coast of Cornwall, England. A huge oil tanker of that name ran aground and broke apart, releasing 100,000 metric tons of oil with lethal effects upon ecosystems of the shore zone. Another was the Santa Barbara accident, beginning in 1969, in which crude oil leakage from an offshore well produced a large oil slick that spread to the shoreline, polluting beaches and damaging marine life of the coast. Altogether some 10,000 metric tons of oil were introduced into the ocean from the Santa Barbara accident. Great as these quantities of oil may seem, they are only a very small proportion of the total quantity of oil introduced into the oceans annually from all sources, both natural and Man-made.

Evidence of widespread marine oil pollution comes from collection of floating oil-tar lumps over wide reaches of the oceans. These lumps represent the nonvolatile residues of crude oil spilled in oil transportation. Marine scientists pick up the oil-tar lumps in a type of net (neuston net) towed behind a vessel to pick up tiny floating animals from the surface water layer. On one cruise of the Woods Hole Oceanographic Institution's Research Vessel *Chain*, oil-tar lumps as large as 3 in. (5 cm) in diameter were picked up in the Sargasso Sea of the subtropical Atlantic Ocean. Within two to four hours of towing, the nets became so encrusted with tar that they had to be cleaned with solvent. Data from similar plankton tows in the northwestern Atlantic Ocean and the Mediterranean Sea showed tar concentrations of 1 milligram per square meter (mg/m^2) for the North Atlantic Ocean and 20 mg/m^2 for the Mediterranean Sea. Thor Heyerdahl reported that during his 1970 voyage across the Atlantic Ocean in the papyrus vessel, *Ra*, pollution by tarlike and asphaltlike lumps was visible during 6 of the trip's 52 days. While vast areas of the oceans remain unsampled, pollution from marine oil undoubtedly exists on a large scale.

Sources of marine oil pollution are varied (Table 47.1). A major source is that connected with oil transportation on the open ocean and in estuaries and ports where oil is transferred. In addition to major oil spills from collision and breakup of grounded tankers, there is a continual infusion of oil from tank and bilge cleaning operations and leakage of lubricating oil from propeller shaft bearings. It has been estimated that the total annual contribution of oil to the oceans from transport sources alone runs to at least 1 million metric tons and may even be double that amount. The lower value represents one-tenth of one percent (0.1%) of all oil transported by water. (About 60% of all oil produced is transported by water.)

An additional infusion of crude oil occurs through natural and accidental seepages from the ocean floor, as in the case of the Santa Barbara accident (Unit 61). Tankers sunk during World War II pose a continual threat of oil leakage. Another major source is oil released from the lands in the form of refinery wastes, unburned fuels, and used lubricants carried to the oceans by streams and by ocean-outfall sewage systems. Yet another source of

Table 47.1 Marine Oil Pollution Sources, 1969

Source	Thousands of Metric Tons per Year	Percent of Total
Tankers in normal operations		
Controlled	30	1.4
Uncontrolled	500	24.0
Other ships (bilge pumping)	500	24.0
Offshore oil production (normal operations)	100	4.8
Accidental spills		
Ships	100	4.8
Nonships	100	4.8
Refineries	300	14.4
Rivers carrying automobile and industrial hydrocarbons	450	21.6
Total	2,080	100.0

SOURCE: *Man's Impact on the Global Environment* (1970), SCEP report, The MIT Press, Cambridge, Mass., p. 267 Table 5.10.

marine oil pollution (not listed in Table 47.1) is the direct fallout of petroleum hydrocarbon particles from the atmosphere, injected by automobile exhausts and various industrial activities. Altogether the various sources listed in Table 47.1 contribute about 2 million metric tons per year of oil and oil products to the oceans, as calculated for the year 1969. This figure represents about 0.1% of the 1969 world petroleum production of 1.8 billion metric tons.

Impact of Oil Spills on Marine Ecosystems

The effects of an oil spill upon a marine ecosystem of the littoral zone occur in two phases. First is the **initial impact,** as the patches of floating oil reach the littoral zone. There follows a **recovery period,** in which both physical and biological environments are gradually restored to the initial conditions. Little detailed scientific information is available on either phase of impact, but some tentative conclusions have been drawn, using all available data on documented cases.

Intensity of the initial impact depends upon a number of physical and chemical variables related to the oil spill itself. For example, crude oil that contains low-boiling-point fractions is much more toxic than old, residual oil with little volatile content. The initial impact is likely to kill most sessile (anchored) organisms when they become coated with oil. Shore birds suffer lethal effects of immersion in the oil layer (Figure 47.1). Filter feeders on the bottom, for example, clams, will ingest hydrocarbons that

sink to the ocean bed and become incorporated in bottom sediments.

During the recovery period, natural processes gradually remove the oil from rocky surfaces, beach sands, and bottom sediments. The recovery period varies in length depending upon the physical bottom conditions. A rocky bottom may recover by natural removal of oil in as short a period as two years, whereas a bottom composed of fine sediments may require from four to ten years to become free of oil.

Organisms that were exterminated in the initial impact return as the habitat becomes tolerable, but some classes of organisms return more quickly than others. For example, barnacles disperse rapidly and can invade the recovered area with ease; whereas certain species of worms and snails invade slowly by creeping inward from the periphery. One rule-of-thumb estimate is that recovery for a given species is at least as long as the life span of an individual of that species. Because of the highly uneven restoration rates for the different species of organisms, return to a balanced ecosystem in a complex series of changes takes a long period. The time span required for a full and complete restoration of an ecosystem to its pre-spill equilibrium state has not yet been documented, but is probably not less than two to three years under favorable conditions.

DDT in the Environment

The cyclic movement of matter through ecosystems applies not only to such naturally occurring compounds as nitrates and phosphates, but also to Man-made compounds that are absorbed by organisms. DDT is an example of a synthetic compound that moves through the food chain and has produced a significant impact on the biosphere.

Figure 47.1   This oil-soaked grebe will not survive the ordeal. (Paul Fusco/© Magnum Photos.)

DDT is one of many toxic chemical compounds, some simple and some complex, classed as **pesticides,** substances used to reduce the numbers of an unwanted plant or animal population. Before the widespread advances in chemical technology accomplished during and after World War II, two types of insecticides were in use: (1) **inorganic compounds,** including compounds of arsenic, sulfur, copper, or cyanide, and (2) complex organic compounds, often referred to as **botanicals,** which were obtained from plant tissues. Use of these compounds was not widespread, and except in local areas, impact was minimal. In the postwar era, however, many new organic compounds were developed with toxic properties suitable for use as pesticides of one sort or another. One large class of pesticides thus developed is the **chlorinated hydrocarbons,** of which DDT is a member.

Besides their apparent low toxicity to humans, the chlorinated hydrocarbons have two general characteristics that make them desirable as insecticides. First, they are toxic to a large range of organisms and therefore can control many pests at once. Second, they are relatively long-lasting and therefore need to be applied less frequently. Unfortunately, these characteristics also make the chlorinated hydrocarbons all the more dangerous to natural ecosystems. The danger lies in their **biological magnification** within the food chain, a phenomenon produced by the high solubility of these compounds in fats and oils and their storage within the fatty tissues of organisms.

Table 47.2 lists some concentrations of DDT in the body tissues of organisms sampled from a salt marsh in Great South Bay, on the southern shore of Long Island, New York. DDT enters the marsh by aerial spraying for mosquito control. Because it is highly insoluble in water, most of the DDT remains in the marsh soil or settles to be incorporated in the bottom sediments of channels and pools. A very small amount, however, does dissolve in the water. The algae, phytoplankton, and decomposer bacteria of the marsh are thus exposed to very low concentrations of DDT in their environment. Because DDT is much more readily soluble in fats and oils, it tends to accumulate in the bodies of these tiny organisms and reach concentrations many times those of the water itself. When these organisms are ingested in large numbers by zooplankton or detrital feeders such as clams and tiny crustaceans, the DDT they take in also tends to be retained because of its insolubility in water. In this way, the concentration of DDT in body tissues increases by many orders of magnitude up the food chain, from fingerling fish to larger fish to predatory birds, such as the herring gull and cormorant.

Note that this buildup of DDT would not occur if there were some rapid means of breaking it down into nontoxic compounds. Physically, the DDT molecule is very stable and, unlike many other organic molecules, does not decompose under continued exposure to oxygen, sunlight, or other reagents or energy sources available at the earth's surface. From a biological viewpoint, DDT is also very stable. Only a few microorganisms seem to possess the ability to degrade DDT efficiently, and the process appears to require anaerobic conditions. In animals, DDT is metabolized very slowly by the liver into breakdown products DDE and DDD, both of which are still highly toxic. These factors combine to yield a half-life for DDT in

Table 47.2 DDT Residues from an Estuary at the Eastern End of Great South Bay, Long Island, New York.

Sample	DDT Residues (ppm)
Water	0.00005
Plankton, mostly zooplankton	0.04
Shrimp	0.16
Atlantic silverside (*Menidia menidia*)	0.23
Crickets	0.23
Mud snail (*Nassarius obsoletus*)	0.26
American eel, immature (*Anguilla rostrata*)	0.28
Flying insects	0.30
Cordgrass, shoots (*Spartina patens*)	0.33
Hard-shelled clam (*Mercenaria mercenaria*)	0.42
Chain pickerel (*Esox niger*)	1.33
Atlantic needlefish (*Strongylura marina*)	2.07
Cordgrass, roots (*Spartina patens*)	2.80
Common tern (*Sterna hirundo*)	3.15
Herring gull, brain (*Larus argentatus*)	4.56
Herring gull, immature (*Larus argentatus*)	5.43
Osprey, abandoned egg (*Pandion haliaetus*)	13.8
Double-crested cormorant, immature (*Phalacrocorax auritus*)	26.4
Ring-billed gull, immature (*Larus delawarensis*)	75.5

SOURCE: Data of G. M. Woodwell, C. F. Wurster, and P. A. Isaacson, (1967), *Science,* vol. 156, p. 822.
NOTE: Data include DDT as well as its metabolites, DDD and DDE.

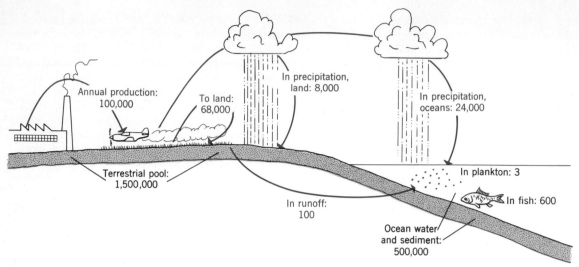

Figure 47.2   The DDT cycle. Pool capacities (black) in units of metric tons. Flows between pools (color) in units of metric tons per yr. (Data from *Man's Impact on the Global Environment*, [1970]. Report of the Study of Critical Environmental Problems SCEP, M.I.T. Press, pp. 126-136.)

the biosphere estimated at about 15 years. (In other words, the amount of DDT present will be halved in each successive 15-year period.)

The toxic effects of DDT vary from organism to organism. For example, the main impact of DDT on marine fishes has been to drastically curtail reproductive rates because DDT is concentrated in the yolk sac of the fish egg. The embryo is thus exposed to high concentrations of the poison as it draws on the food reserves in the yolk, and it succumbs. The primary effect of DDT on birds is to interfere with calcium metabolism, causing the laying of thin-shelled eggs that break easily, killing the young inside. Another effect is to upset hormonal balance, producing abnormal behavior as well as other symptoms.

Recent research on the movements of DDT in the biosphere has yielded sufficient data to sketch the broad outlines of a **DDT cycle** (Figure 47.2). At the present time, the total amount of DDT in the biosphere is estimated to be near 2 million metric tons, about three-fourths of which is in terrestrial environments, with the remaining one-fourth in marine environments. DDT enters the air largely through aerial spraying operations, but significant amounts enter the air by simply evaporating from water surfaces, plant surfaces, and soils. In this fashion, about one-fourth of the total annual production of 100,000 metric tons/year reaches the ocean. Estimates of DDT reaching the ocean in runoff are very much lower, a result of the very low solubility of DDT in water.

Note that the DDT cycle has two differences from conventional cycles: first, DDT is synthetic—there is no natural source for DDT. Second, there is no link to bring DDT from the ocean sediments back to land, and therefore the cycle is not complete. A third difference arises because DDT, though long-lasting, is not stable indefinitely. Eventually, all the DDT in the biosphere will be broken down into harmless components. Yet this pesticide has the po-

tential to create a considerable impact on ecosystems vital to Man's support before it is degraded.

Thanks to Man's ingenuity, DDT is only one of a great many new synthetic compounds that exist in the environment and move through the biosphere in complex ways. When this fact is considered in light of Man's significant impact on such natural cycles as nitrogen and carbon, we can see just how great is the potential for global alteration of natural systems.

Mercury in Ecosystems

Mercury, one of the heavy metals, is another pollutant substance passed along the food chain and concentrated in the higher levels of consumers.

Small amounts of mercury in the ocean and atmosphere are part of the natural environment. This mercury is thought to reach the earth's surface through outgassing of volcanoes; it is recycled along with other elements in the sedimentary material cycle.

Additional mercury enters the environment through industrial processes, and through the combustion of fossil fuels, which often contain traces of mercury. The quantity of mercury emitted by burning of coal is estimated to be on the order of 3000 metric tons per year. This amount is roughly the same as the amount of mercury released to the environment through industrial processes. Mercury has many important industrial uses, including uses in manufacture of chlor-alkali paints, electrical appliances, mildew-proofing compounds in paint, silver amalgam used in dentistry, mercury thermometers, catalysts in plastics manufacture, and a fungicide used to protect seed grains.

Environmental mercury becomes a hazard to humans under two quite different circumstances. First is direct poisoning by eating of foods treated with mercury compounds. An example is poisoning of persons who have inadvertently eaten seed grains treated with mercury compounds used to prevent fungus growth. Second is poisoning by eating finfish and shellfish that have accumulated high levels of toxic mercury compounds in their tissues as a result of compounds passed through the food chain in a manner comparable to the biological magnification of DDT.

Mercury in the food chain takes the chemical form of **methyl mercury** (CH_3Hg). This organic form of mercury attacks the human central nervous system with severely damaging effects. Effects include loss of vision, hearing, coordination, and intellectual ability. These effects are permanent and no cure is known.

Methyl mercury has a long residence time in animal tissues; the half-life is about 200 days in several types of fish. As a result, biological magnification is particularly effective. Organisms in the food chain assimilate some mercury directly from the environment and also ingest it as food. The primary producers—phytoplankton and other aquatic plant forms—absorb mercury from the water around them. Fish can absorb mercury directly from water passing through the gills as well as by ingesting organisms lower in the food chain. Large individuals of tuna and swordfish have been found to contain extremely high concentrations of methyl mercury, up to 1 part per million (ppm). Some seals and whales have been found to have even higher concentrations. The Food and Drug Administration has set a limit of 0.5 ppm upon fish sold for human food.

Museum specimens of fish, preserved for many decades, have recently been analyzed for mercury content. Tuna and swordfish showed levels of methyl mercury of from 0.5 to 1.5 ppm, values quite similar in range to those in living fish. These findings suggest that levels of mercury exceeding the FDA standard can be accumulated through natural environmental sources of mercury.

One possible solution to the problem of high levels of mercury found in the catches of commercial tuna is to select only smaller fish, since the level of concentration is much lower in the younger, smaller specimens. Low levels of mercury can be tolerated by humans because mercury is continually excreted from the human body (the half-life is 70 days). Unless fish forms a large part of the human diet, no health problem should be anticipated.

Special situations of extremely high methyl mercury concentrations in shellfish and finfish have arisen in local areas where industrial wastes containing mercury have been fed into marine ecosystems confined in bays. Two such incidents have been reported from Japan. In the period 1953 to 1960, hundreds of persons living near Minamata Bay were seriously poisoned by eating fish contaminated with waste methyl mercury released from industrial plants producing plastics. A similar incident occurred in Niigata, Japan. In Sweden, high concentrations of methyl mercury in birds and fish of lakes and rivers have been attributed to the transformation of mercury compounds released from wood pulp processing plants.

Man and Ecosystems in Review

The ten study units of Part V, which we have now completed, deal almost entirely with the science of ecology. In our Introduction, we emphasized that geography draws upon many disciplines, including several branches of the natural sciences, to perform its function of integrating human knowledge to focus upon the environmental qualities of the earth's inhabited land regions. Ecology, as we have seen, is one of those natural sciences essential to an understanding of the human environment.

Part V has emphasized two major areas of geographical concern. First is the understanding of natural terrestrial ecosystems and their modification by Man into agricultural ecosystems. Resource geography deals heavily in the distribution of plant formations and their transformation into food-producing systems. The second major area is the understanding of pollution of the hydrosphere and atmosphere by Man's industrial and agricultural activity. Geographers have a keen interest in analyzing the influences of humans upon the environmental quality of both urban and nonurban regions. Curbing environmental pollution is closely tied in with the broad area of land-use planning, an applied field of science with which professional geographers are closely involved.

The knowledge of Man and ecosystems you have accumulated in Part V will be most useful to you in approaching the new material in Part VI—Man, Soils, and Climate. In the seven study units of Part VI you will investigate the environmental quality of a selected number of world regions, defined in terms of the ecologist's system of biomes. A new topic of physical geography will be a major concern—the soil and its capacity to support plants. Principles of the flow of energy and the cycling of water and nutrients in ecosystems will take on new meaning as we explore soils and soil fertility in each of the biomes—forest, savanna, grassland, desert, and tundra. In this exploration, we will be well within the academic heartland of geography, viewing objectively the struggle of the human race to adapt to and modify the natural landscapes to serve human needs.

Facing page: Rice field in Sumatra. (Charles P. Cushing. From H. A. Roberts.)

PART VI Man, Soils, and Climate

Unit 48
Soil Fertility

Trouble at Mount Vernon —A Farm in Distress

As the wave of American Bicentennial celebrations recedes into the past, many romantic notions about the successes of our founding fathers remain fresh in our minds. We visualize George Washington, retired happily on his Virginia estate Mount Vernon, reaping a richly deserved bounty from expansive farmlands under his personal supervision. We picture Thomas Jefferson at Charlottesville, managing his fields from his eyrie atop Monticello, while at the same time keeping a telescopic sight on his brainchild under construction, the new campus of the University of Virginia. These romantic visions fade under reality when we learn that fertility of farmlands in the colonies was declining rapidly, even as the new nation was struggling to stay alive. Ignorance of a simple point of soil science was responsible—acid soils need lime.

Without lime to correct soil acidity, essential nutrients for healthy crop growth cannot be retained in the soil, even though natural fertilizers are added. We read that George Washington conserved animal manure to spread on his fields, and that he had his field hands bring rich mud from creeks and marshes to spread on the soil to bring in a new supply of nutrients. A modern historian, Avery Craven, an authority on the agricultural history of that region, tells us that in 1834, 35 years after Washington's death, a visitor to Mount Vernon declared that "a more widespread and perfect agricultural ruin could not be imagined."

Another American, Edmund Ruffin (1794-1865), is credited with solving the mystery of failing agricultural fertility of the eastern seaboard. Ruffin owned lands at Coggins' Point on the coastal plain of Virginia. As with others, his land was rapidly declining in crop yields in the early 1800s. He tried many experiments to stop the decline, but application of manure had little effect and clover would not grow to enrich the soil. Quite by chance, Ruffin obtained a copy of Davy's *Agricultural Chemistry,* published in 1813. Despite Ruffin's lack of formal education in science, he was quick to grasp the significance of one statement: ". . . any acid matter . . . may be ameliorated by application of quicklime."

So it came about that on a February morning in

Harrowing the soil, sowing the seed. (New York Public Library, Picture Collection.)

340

1818, Ruffin directed his field hands to haul marl from pits in low areas of his lands. (Marl is a soft lime mud that occurs widely as sedimentary strata on the eastern coastal plain.) The workers spread two hundred bushels of marl over several acres of newly cleared ridge land of poor quality. In the spring, Ruffin planted this area in corn to test the effect of the marl. In the words of historian Avery Craven, this is what happened: "Eagerly he waited. As the season advanced, he found reason for joy. From the very start the plants on marled ground showed marked superiority, and at harvest time they yielded an advantage of fully forty per cent. The carts went back to the pits. Fields took on fresh life. A new era in agricultural history of the region had dawned."* In 1832, Ruffin published his findings in

*Avery Craven (1932) Edmund Ruffin, Southerner, D. Appleton and Co., New York, p. 55.

a work titled An Essay on Calcareous Manures. His advice was outspokenly opposed, but time showed him to be right.

An interesting footnote on this anecdote is that Edmund Ruffin was an ardent supporter of states' rights and secession. He fired the first shot against Fort Sumter to set off the Civil War in fine style. But shortly after the surrender of General Robert E. Lee at Appomattox, Ruffin, aged and weary, succumbed to depression and committed suicide.

In this study unit, we will investigate the chemistry of soil fertility. Few subjects hold as much significance for the human race as world food production levels off in the face of rising populations among the developing nations.

Data Source: Emil Truog (1938) Putting soil science to work, Journal of the American Society of Agronomy, vol. 30, pp. 973-985.

Soil Processes, Organic Processes, and Climate

With this unit, we begin a series of investigations into the ways in which soil processes and organic processes are tied in with climate. Some questions we ask are these: How does climate influence the way in which soil develops a certain natural level of fertility? How is natural vegetation influenced by climate and soil fertility? How well has Man adapted to these natural conditions in terms of agricultural development?

These questions and others will be explored through a series of study units, each dealing with a distinctive environmental region of the earth. In this method of approach, we will take a few samples from the wide spectrum of global environments. We will not cover all possible climates in a systematic way, nor all possible kinds of soils, nor all possible kinds of plant formation classes. Our aim is rather to point out how various global environments present a diversity of opportunities and restraints to human occupation and agricultural development.

The Concept of Climate

Climate, always a keystone in physical geography, has formed the basis for defining environmental regions of the globe. Let us first examine the content of traditional **climatology,** the science of climate. In the broadest sense, **climate** is the characteristic condition of the atmosphere near the earth's surface at a given place or over a given region. Components that enter into the description of climate are mostly the same as weather components used to describe the state of the atmosphere at a given instant. If weather information deals with the specific event, then climate represents a generalization of weather.

The climate of a given observing station, or of a designated region, is described through the medium of weather observations accumulated over many years time. Not only are mean, or average, values taken into account, but also the departures from those means and the probabilities that such departures will occur.

We have learned in Part V that land plants require light energy, carbon dioxide, water, and nutrients. The input of these ingredients comes from two basic sources: (1) the adjacent atmosphere; and (2) the soil. Input of light energy, heat energy, and water from the atmosphere is encompassed by the concept of climate. In short, plants depend on climate and soil. Of these two sources of energy and matter, the soil is the more strongly affected by the plants it serves through the recycling of matter.

When broadly defined as a source of energy and water, climate is an independent agent of control. Climate is determined by latitude and by large-scale air motions and air-mass interactions within the troposphere. If we are to establish a pyramid of priorities and interactions, climate occupies the apex as the independent control (Figure 48.1). Below it and forming the base of the pyramid are (1) the organic process of plants and (2) the soil process. Plants and soil interact with one another at the basal level.

With this broad-based introduction to Part VI—Man, Soils, and Climate—we are prepared to investigate how soil processes interact with climate to determine the levels of fertility of various soils.

The Dynamic Soil

The soil is the very heart of the life layer on the lands. The soil layer is a place in which plant nutrients are produced and held. As we emphasized in Unit 39, the soil layer also holds water in storage for plants to use. The role of climate

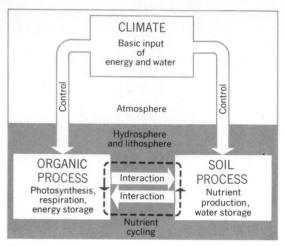

Figure 48.1   The role of climate in environmental processes of the life layer.

is to vary the input of water and heat into the soil. This same heat energy and water are responsible for the breakup and chemical change of rock to produce the parent mineral body of the soil. As we have already found, mineral matter is the source of many plant nutrients.

But climate acting on rock cannot make a soil layer capable of sustaining a rich plant cover. Plants themselves, together with many forms of animal life, play a major role in determining the qualities of the soil layer. Those qualities have evolved through centuries of time by the interaction of organic processes with physical and chemical soil processes. The organic processes include the synthesis of organic compounds, and these are eventually added to the body of the soil. Plants use the mineral nutrients to build complex organic molecules. Upon the death of plant tissues, these nutrients are released and reenter the soil, where they are reused by living plants. So the familiar concept of nutrient cycling by plants is one of the keys to understanding the development of the soil layer.

The soil is a dynamic layer in that many complex physical and chemical activities are going on simultaneously within it. These activities maintain the soil layer in a certain equilibrium condition over long periods of time. Because climate and plant cover vary greatly from place to place over the globe, the equilibrium condition of the soil is expressed very differently from place to place. Anyone can observe that the pale gray soil beneath a spruce forest in Maine is quite different in composition and structure from the dark brown soil beneath the prairie farmlands of Iowa. Yet, in each of these localities, the soil has reached an equilibrium suitable to the climate controls and organic processes prevailing there.

The geographer is keenly interested in the differences in soils from place to place over the globe. The capability of a given soil to furnish food crops largely determines which areas of the globe support the bulk of the human population. Despite changes in population distribution made possible by technology and industrialization, most of the world's inhabitants still live where the soil furnishes them food. Many of these same humans die prematurely, how-

ever, because the soil fails to furnish enough food for all.

The substance of the soil exists in all three states—solid, liquid, and gas. The solid portion consists of both inorganic (mineral) and organic substances. The liquid present in the soil is a complex solution capable of engaging in a multitude of important chemical reactions. Gases present in the open pores of the soil consist not only of the atmospheric gases, but also gases liberated by biological activity and chemical reactions within the soil. Soil science, often called **pedology,** is obviously a highly complex body of knowledge. We shall do no more than cover a few of the high points of this science.

Of the physical properties of soils, texture was explained in Unit 39 in connection with soil water and the relationship of soil texture grades to storage capacity. We turn now to the chemical properties of soils.

Soil Colloids and Cation Exchange

By far the most important constituents of the soil are the colloids, which may be of either inorganic matter (clay minerals) or organic matter (humus colloids). Silt and sand particles in the soil are largely inert and act more or less as a skeleton for the soil. The colloids make up the active fraction because of their high surface area and chemical activity. You can picture a clay particle as a thin, platelike body, shown in Figure 48.2. (See Figure 26.7 for a photograph of colloidal clay particles.) The molecular structure of clay minerals is such that oxygen atoms, which are negatively charged, are nearest the upper and lower surfaces. This condition is indicated on the diagram by minus signs on the clay particle. As a result, positive ions, or cations, will be attracted to the clay particle surface and held there by electrostatic attraction. Ions of hydrogen (H^+), aluminum (Al^{+++}), sodium (Na^+), potassium (K^+), calcium (Ca^{++}) and magnesium (Mg^{++}) are commonly present in soil solutions and all are found on clay particle surfaces. In many soil reactions, these cations replace one another in the process of **cation exchange.**

Cation exchange is governed by a replacement order, indicating which ion is capable of replacing another. This is a kind of seniority system in which the ion of a given rank can take over the position of ions of lower seniority. The aluminum ion can displace any of the other metallic ions, so it occupies the top position on the list. In order of replacement ability, there follow cations of calcium, magnesium, potassium, and sodium.

The capacity of a given quantity of soil to hold and to

Figure 48.2   A colloidal particle with negative surface charges and a layer of positively charged ions.

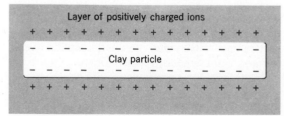

exchange cations is called the **cation-exchange capacity,** and is a general indicator of the degree of chemical activity of a soil. Capacity is indicated in a unit known as the milliequivalent, which is a measure of the ratio of weight of ions to weight of soil. The exact definition of this unit is not important here, but its relative magnitude does concern us. We find that the exchange capacities of various soil colloids are as follows:

Organic colloids (humus)	150–500
Montmorillonite	80–150
Illite	10–40
Kaolinite	3–15

The numbers tell us that humus colloids are a major contributor to total cation exchange of a given soil, and this should serve as a warning that practices which reduce the humus content of the soil will seriously decrease its chemical activity and hence also its ability to hold plant nutrients.

Soil Acidity and Alkalinity

The various soil cations capable of being readily exchanged on colloidal particles belong to two general classes. One class, already mentioned in Unit 40 as being important plant nutrients, consists of the **base cations** (or, simply, **bases**). The other class consists of **acid-generating cations.** The base cations most important in soils are the following:

Calcium	Ca^{++}
Magnesium	Mg^{++}
Potassium	K^+
Sodium	Na^+

When base cations comprise the large majority of cations held by soil colloids, the soil is in a condition described as **alkaline.**

The most important acid-generating cation in soils is the aluminum ion, Al^{+++}. The hydrogen ion (H^+) is also important as an acid-generating cation. The presence of either or both of these ions in substantial proportions results in a soil condition described as **acid.** The degree of acidity increases as the numbers of hydrogen ions or aluminum ions increase.

The range of alkalinity or acidity of a soil is measured in terms of a number known as the **pH** of the soil solution.* A pH value of 7.0 is neutral in this scale; values below 5 represent a strongly acid soil solution; values above 10 represent a strongly alkaline soil solution. Table 48.1 shows a classification of soils according to acidity and alkalinity. For agricultural soils, this quality is very important, since certain crops require near-neutral values of pH and cannot thrive on acid soils. Plants differ considerably in their preference for soil acidity or alkalinity, and this is an important factor in the distribution of plant types.

As Table 48.1 shows, agricultural soils with pH under about 6 require the application of lime for the successful cultivation of crops. **Lime,** as the word is used in agriculture, may be either calcium oxide (CaO) or calcium carbonate ($CaCO_3$). The latter is the major constituent of natural limestone, which is ground into powder and spread over fields. Calcium oxide is manufactured by heating pulverized limestone in a furnace and driving off carbon dioxide. Both forms of lime eliminate hydrogen ions from soil colloids, replacing them with calcium ions. After the soil pH has been raised to the desired level, fertilizers rich in macronutrients (nitrogen, phosphorus, potassium) must also be added to the soil, because these nutrients are deficient in most acid soils.

Base Status of Soils

As in many forms of human society, soils are stratified into "status" levels, and are classified into major groups on that basis. Status in soils is determined by the **percentage base saturation,** defined as the percentage of exchangeable base cations with respect to the total cation exchange

*The term pH is a measure of the concentration of hydrogen ions; it is the logarithm to the base 10 of the reciprocal of the weight in grams of hydrogen ions per liter of water. Consequently, the smaller the pH number, the greater is the hydrogen ion concentration.

Table 48.1 Soil Acidity and Alkalinity

pH	4.0	4.5	5.0	5.5	6.0 6.5	6.7 7.0	8.0	9.0	10.0 11.0
Acidity	Very strongly acid		Strongly acid	Moderately acid	Slightly acid	Neutral	Weakly alkaline	Alkaline	Strongly alkaline	Excessively alkaline
Lime requirements	Lime needed except for crops requiring acid soil		Lime needed for all but acid-tolerant crops		Lime generally not required	No lime needed			
Occurrence	Rare	Frequent	Very common in cultivated soils of humid climates				Common in sub-humid and arid climates	Limited areas in deserts	

SOURCE: C. E. Millar, L. M. Turk, and H. D. Foth (1958), *Fundamentals of Soil Science,* 3rd ed., John Wiley & Sons, New York, Chart 4.

capacity of the soil. A value of 35% has been used by soil scientists as a dividing number separating one class of soils of **high base status** (greater than 35%) from those of another class of **low base status** (less than 35%). Soils of high base status have high natural fertility for food crops; those of low base status are naturally low in fertility and require special treatment and the application of chemicals to correct the deficiency. Base status of soils thus has enormous impact upon Man's food resources and the possibilities for future expansion of agricultural food production into areas not now under cultivation.

Soil Orders

Soil scientists arrange all natural soils into a number of **soil orders,** of which there are ten altogether. Excluded from any soil order are mineral surfaces incapable of supporting plants. The classification system of soil orders was introduced by soil scientists of the United States in 1960 and has since gained wide acceptance. A completely new set of soil names was coined for the new classification system; these names have a strange sound to geographers accustomed to conventional soil classification systems developed over an earlier span of many decades. The new United States system is based, however, upon modern knowledge of soil physics and soil chemistry and has a high level of significance for the potential agricultural yield of soils the world over. We shall now illustrate this point by describing and comparing two of the soil orders important in the eastern United States: Alfisols and Ultisols. These soil orders are distinguished on the basis of their percentage base saturation; accordingly they differ substantially in natural fertility.

Alfisols and Ultisols

Alfisols comprise a soil order with high base status; the percentage base saturation exceeds 35%. In the central and eastern United States, Alfisols occupy large areas of fertile farmlands in Wisconsin, Michigan, Illinois, Indiana, Ohio, Kentucky, Pennsylvania, New York, and a number of other states. Figure 48.3 shows these areas of Alfisols. Much of this area was originally forested but is now intensively farmed to yield corn, soybeans, small grains, and dairy products. Much of the region of Alfisols was subjected to Pleistocene glaciation, so that the soil has developed on glacial drift with a variable cover of loess. An Alfisol belt extending south along the east side of the lower Mississippi valley is underlain by thick loess. (See map of loess distribution, Figure 37.9.)

Alfisols are characterized by well-developed soil horizons. Typically, there is a dark brown upper horizon and beneath that a pale gray horizon. In our next study unit, we will explain the significance of these horizons and the way in which they are produced. The important point here is that the Alfisols have ample supplies of clay colloids with moderate to high cation exchange capacity. These clay minerals are an inheritance from the comparatively young parent matter from which the soil has evolved,

namely, glacial drift, loess, alluvium, and lake-bed sediments. Alfisols lie in a region of humid climate in which the soil-water budget shows a water surplus in late winter and spring. This surplus water, percolating down through the soil, has carried out any carbonate matter that may have been present in the parent matter, but has not yet removed base cations to the point that base saturation is less than 35%. The soil tends to be weakly acid and may require lime applications. Because of the high base status, the Alfisols are capable of absorbing and holding nutrients supplied by fertilizers so that extremely high crop yields are possible. Even without fertilizers, the early settlers who cleared the forests of the Middle West found the Alfisols as a group to be a naturally productive soil, amply supplied with nutrients.

The **Ultisols** comprise a soil order with low base status; the percentage base saturation is less than 35%. As the map shows (Figure 48.3), Ultisols occupy much of the southeastern United States. In a rough way, they correspond with the Confederate States of the Civil War era. Much of this area originally bore a forest, which ranged from deciduous forest to pine forest. Settlers found that some parts of the area were well suited to tobacco and cotton, which became dominant cash crops in the agricultural economy. Ultisols of the southeastern United States are typically reddish or yellowish in color. They show well-developed horizons, but appear to have little humus. The parent matter of upland surfaces on which the Ultisols have developed has been exposed to weathering for many

Figure 48.3   Extent of Alfisols and Ultisols in the central and eastern United States. (Data of U.S. Department of Agriculture.)

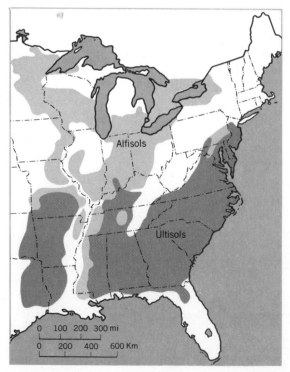

Figure 48.4 This plantation of slash pine grows on sandy soil of the Georgia coastal plain. A cup is attached to the base of each tree to catch sap exuding from a cut into the sapwood. Turpentine is distilled from the sap. (Grant Heilman)

tens of thousands of years, since this region lies south of the limit of continental glaciation. In short, these are old soils—the syllable "ulti" was chosen to signify "ultimate" of leaching. Under a warm humid climate with substantial soil-water surplus, only clay minerals of low cation exchange capacity remain (kaolinite, for example), along with oxides of iron and aluminum that have little ion-holding capacity. The Ultisols are slightly acid and need lime. Nutrient base cations are deficient in the Ultisols. The nutrients lie in a shallow surface layer and are rapidly depleted by crop farming. Even when nutrients are supplied by applications of fertilizers, the nutrients are not well retained in the soil for sustained use by plants. The low natural fertility of the Ultisols is seen in the history of abandonment of farmlands on the Piedmont Upland and a period of intense soil erosion which followed (Units 31 and 32). Nevertheless, despite their natural deficiencies, Ultisols of the United States have been made agriculturally productive by large inputs of cultural energy (see Unit 43). These soils occur widely in the tropical and equatorial zone, in less-developed countries unable to make the necessary large inputs of cultural energy without massive subsidy from the highly developed and energy-rich nations.

One direction of successful use of the Ultisols lies in tree farming. For example, pines of certain species, economically valuable as sources of pulpwood, fence posts, and turpentine, do very well in sandy Ultisols (Figure 48.4). These trees have low requirements for base cations and their deep roots are capable of recycling nutrient ions that are carried downward below the limits of use by short-rooted crops.

Unit 49
Spodosols and the Needleleaf Forest

Settler, Beware of the Pines!

Settlers who reached southern Michigan in the early 1800s found much good farmland beneath hardwood forests of beech and maple. To the north lay forests of red pine and jack pine, growing on sandy soils with many areas of flat plains. As the pines were cut away for timber it seemed only reasonable that the Jack Pine Plains would provide more good farmland. Pioneer farmers who moved into the cleared pine lands achieved only disaster. Crops of wheat, oats, corn, and even forage grasses failed dismally. True, the growing season here is shorter than in the fertile southern region of the state. But the pine region also lies at the same latitude as a fertile farming region in Wisconsin on the western side of Lake Michigan. So coldness of climate is not the explanation. If you were to spade up the soil of the Jack Pine Plains, you would find only a thin surface layer of humus, and below that several inches of pale gray sand almost devoid of clay. On chemical analysis the sand would prove to be largely mineral quartz—about as sterile a medium for plant growth as you could contrive by any means. Russian peasants from the needleleaf forests would have recognized the soil of the Jack Pine Plains; they would have called it "Podzol." In Russian this term means "ash-soil." The ashen layer is cleanly leached of plant nutrients.

The problem of infertility of the Jack Pine Plains of Michigan was studied by a noted botanist, W. J. Beal. In 1889 he published his findings in a state bulletin, titled *Experiments and Observations on the Jack Pine Plains.* His conclusion: "It would be impossible to profitably grow any forage, grain, fruit or vegetable crop in this sandy soil without the use of fertilizer." He warned, "The poor homesteader, above all others, should understand the principles of agriculture if he expects to succeed on these lands. If he has to depend for his living from the start on what he can dig out of the soil and has no other business to help him, the plains are no place for him." Only with capital at his disposal, Beal concluded, could a farmer give this soil the generous treatment needed to make it yield a good crop. Beal's advice has been heeded. The land has been returned to forest. Each summer thousands of urbanites from the cities of Detroit, Toledo, Chicago, and points south trek north to use the wooded lakelands. The pattern is a familiar one, for the soils we have described cover a vast re-

Pioneers clearing the forests of the interior lowland. (Culver Pictures.)

346

gion spanning the northern Great Lakes area and New England. "The land of abandonment," it has been called—fitting recognition of the countless European settlers who tried and failed to make the ashen soil yield up a living. The descendants of those who stayed are farming another green crop— the folding money released by that horde of summer visitors; it is a crop guaranteed not to fail.

In this study unit, we will investigate the soil processes that produce the ashen soil of the northern needleleaf forests.

DATA SOURCE: Soil Survey Division, *Soils of the United States,* in *Soils and Men,* Yearbook of Agriculture 1938, U.S. Dept. of Agriculture, U.S. Govt. Printing Office, pp. 1027-1129.

Soils and Time

Because the processes that develop and maintain a soil in equilibrium with its environment are extremely complex, we can only look into a few of the more important relationships. A characteristic set of soil horizons makes up the soil profile. Horizon development requires a long span of time, a fact of great environmental importance. Man's agricultural and industrial activities, using vast energy sources, can destroy in a short time a delicate soil profile that took centuries to form.

Starting with a new layer of parent matter—for example, the deposits of a river flood, or of a glacier—in which organic matter is lacking and no horizons exist, evolution to a stable profile configuration may take one to two centuries to develop under the most favorable of conditions, but the figure is probably better estimated in terms of thousands of years.

The important point is that the true soil is a nonrenewable resource in terms of agricultural production. Once the natural soil is degraded or destroyed, the loss in terms of useful plant production is permanent.

In this study unit, we will examine soil profile development under needleleaf forest in climates with severely cold winters. A particular set of soil-forming processes applies under these climatic conditions and produces a distinctive set of soil properties, both physically and chemically. First, however, it will be necessary to explain some basic concepts of soil description.

Concept of the Pedon

Modern soil science makes use of the concept of the **soil individual,** which is the smallest distinctive division of the soil of a given area. A unique single set of properties applies to the soil individual, and this set differs from that applying to adjacent soil individuals. The soil individual is visualized in terms of space geometry as being composed of pedons. A **pedon** is a soil column extending down from the surface to reach a lower limit in regolith or bedrock. As Figure 49.1 shows, soil scientists visualize a pedon as a six-sided (hexagonal) column. The surface area of single pedon ranges from 1 to 10 sq m. The **soil profile** is the display of horizons on one face of the pedon. Obviously, the same soil profile is displayed on all six faces of the pedon. In practice, a soil scientist digs a deep pit, exposing a soil profile in the side of the pit.

Figure 49.1 shows a number of **soil horizons,** which are distinctive, horizontal layers identified in terms of physical and chemical composition, organic content, or structure, or a combination of such properties. Most horizons are visibly set apart on the basis of color. Mineral soil horizons are designated by a set of capital letters and numeral subscripts, starting with A at the top. In Figure 49.1 we see A, B, and C horizons. An organic horizon, designated by the letter O, lies upon the A horizon.

The **soil solum** consists of the A and B horizons of the soil profile; these are the dynamic and distinctive layers of the profile. The C horizon, by contrast, is the parent matter. The soil solum occupies the zone in which living plant roots exert control on the soil horizons; the C horizon lies below that level of root activity. Of course, the C horizon is subject to inorganic processes of change, such as the physical and chemical weathering processes explained in Unit 26.

The soil individual consists of nested soil pedons, all of

Figure 49.1 Concept of the soil individual and the pedon.

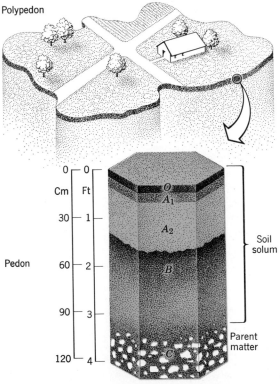

347

which are alike. As labeled in Figure 49.1, the soil individual is thus a **polypedon.** The enclosing walls of a pedon are, of course, purely imaginary. The polypedon is not, as the diagram might imply, broken into hexagonal blocks.

Spodosols and their Soil Profile

As we noted in the closing paragraph of Unit 48, soil scientists consider that all true soils fall into ten soil orders. Two of these orders, Alfisols and Ultisols, were described in some detail in Unit 48, but without a detailed analysis of their characteristic soil profiles. We will now take a close look at a soil order called the **Spodosols.** In the opening essay of this unit, Spodosols were described as characterized by a pale, ashen-gray horizon, from which they were called *podzols,* or "ash soils," by Russian peasants living in the northern needleleaf forests. Another common name for the Spodosols is "white earths." The modern name, Spodosols, is taken from the Greek word, *spodos,* meaning "wood ashes."

Characteristically (but not always), Spodosols are found on sandy parent materials from which soil water drains easily. Sandy glacial drift is one such parent material. Large parts of the glaciated regions of North America and Eurasia are underlain by such sandy parent materials and have Spodosols. Yet, Spodosols are also found in unglaciated areas at lower latitudes where sandy parent materials are exposed to a humid climate. An example is the occurrence of Spodosols in coastal belts of Florida. Practically all Spodosols, however, occur north of the 40th parallel of latitude.

The profile of a typical Spodosol is pictured in Figure 49.2. A photograph, Figure 49.3, shows the appearance of horizons in a freshly exposed Spodosol profile. The O horizon consists of dark-colored, partly decomposed organic matter. Under cover of a dense forest of pine or spruce, this horizon may be several inches thick. It contains an abundance of decomposer microorganisms, particularly the fungi. The process of decomposition produces organic acids, so that the O horizon is quite strongly acid in chemical balance.

Figure 49.3 This Spodosol profile has formed in sandy parent material in Maine. Depth scale in feet. (Soil Conservation Service.)

Below the O horizon is a thin dark A_1 horizon, consisting of a mixture of mineral matter and humus. The particles of humus have been derived from the O horizon above. Below the A_1 horizon lies a distinctive, very light-colored A_2 horizon, referred to as an **albic horizon.** In most cases, the A_2 horizon proves to be composed of porous, loosely compacted quartz sand, remarkably free of humus and finer mineral particles.

Abruptly, the A_2 horizon at its base gives way to a dense B horizon, often reddish brown in color. This is the **spodic horizon.** The spodic horizon contains densely packed sesquioxides of iron and aluminum, along with colloidal particles of humus. A **sesquioxide** is a compound consisting of oxygen atoms in combination with either iron, aluminum, or manganese in the ratio of three atoms of oxygen to two atoms of the metallic element. Sesquioxide of iron is represented by the formula Fe_2O_3; sesquioxide of aluminum by the formula Al_2O_3. Water molecules are also included in the sesquioxides. The sesquioxides can undergo no further oxidation and are extremely stable compounds in the soil. The B horizon grades downward into the parent matter of the soil, designated as the C horizon.

Eluviation and Illuviation

To understand how the Spodosol horizons are formed, and how the albic and spodic horizons in particular come into being, we must study the processes by which various

Figure 49.2 Soil horizons of a Spodosol.

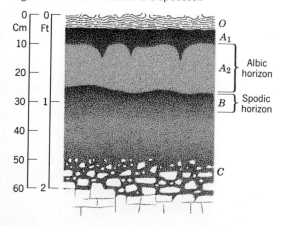

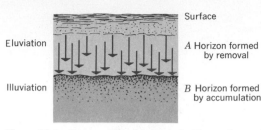

Figure 49.4 Downward migration of soil constituents is characteristic of cool, humid climates having a large water surplus.

materials are moved vertically within the soil column.

Let us focus on processes of selective removal and accumulation of soil materials. Soils formed in regions of large water surplus are subject to selective removal of matter as the excess water percolates through the soil to the ground-water zone and is eventually disposed of as stream runoff. In many cases, however, matter carried downward simply accumulates at a lower level in the soil, where it forms a distinctive horizon (Figure 49.4). The downward transport process is called **eluviation**, or more simply, **leaching.** Eluviation produces a distinct soil horizon from which the matter has been removed; in the Spodosols this is the A_2 horizon, or albic horizon. Accumulation of matter in the underlying zone is called **illuviation**; in the Spodosols this is the B, or spodic, horizon.

Leaching of Bases from Spodosols

In the cold climates in which Spodosols are largely found, the activity of decomposer bacteria is comparatively slow, with the result that the organic matter accumulates to form a thick O horizon. Organic acids generated in this organic layer are carried down into the mineral soil horizons. Here the excess hydrogen ions displace most of the base cations, which are removed from the soil and carried down to the ground-water body, then into stream channels and exported from the area. Thus a natural process of base cation depletion is in continual operation. Besides, both

quartz sand—the principal constituent of the A_2 horizon—and the sesquioxides of the B horizon have low cation exchange capacities. If clay minerals with high base-exchange capacity were originally present in the parent matter, they have already been chemically altered and destroyed. If calcium carbonate was originally present, it has been acted upon by soil acids and the calcium ions removed by leaching.

The needleleaf forests typical of Spodosol areas are conifers, for example, pine, spruce, fir, and larch. These plants have low requirements for the nutrient bases and do not recycle them in large quantities. Thus plants with high tolerance for acid conditions and limited needs for nutrient bases have come to dominate the northern areas of Spodosols. In warmer climates, such as Florida, we also find pine forest on sandy Spodosols.

Agricultural Potential of the Spodosols

As our opening essay on the Jack Pine Plains emphasized, Spodosols rate very poorly in terms of natural fertility for food crops, particularly such cereals as wheat, oats, barley, and corn. The high inputs of lime and fertilizers needed to make Spodosols agriculturally productive make farming economically unprofitable in competition with Alfisols, which enjoy a high base status. For example, productive Alfisols occur over some large parts of Wisconsin and Minnesota, at the same latitude and under the same severe winter conditions as Spodosols of Michigan and northern New England.

Forests are generally the best adapted plant resource for the Spodosol regions of North America and Eurasia. Thus the principal nonmineral economic product throughout the Spodosol regions of eastern Canada is pulpwood from the needleleaf forests. Logs are carried down the principal rivers to pulp mills and lumber mills (Figure 49.5). Forests of pine and fir in Finland and European Russia in a region of Spodosols are the primary plant resource; the products are exported in the form of paper, pulp, cellulose, and construction lumber.

Figure 49.5 This saw mill at Hudson, Ontario processes logs floated across the surface of a sprawling lake in the Canadian Shield. (Ronny Jaques Studio, Toronto, from Black Star.)

Histosols

Throughout much of the northern region of Spodosols in areas that were heavily glaciated there is much poorly drained land. These moist sites represent former shallow lake basins filled with bog accumulations, a process of succession explained in the science supplement of Unit 42 (see Figure 42.3). Soils of these poorly drained areas have a very high organic content; they belong to the soil order **Histosols.** This name is coined from the Greek word *histos,* meaning "tissue." In common language of farmers, the histosols are **peats** or **mucks.**

The upper horizon of Histosols is referred to as the **histic epipedon.** (An **epipedon** is simply an uppermost soil horizon.) The histic epipedon contains more than 20% of organic matter and is water saturated for at least 30 days at one season of the year, under natural conditions.

Histosols occur not only with Spodosols but also with Alfisols in the glaciated area. They can be made highly productive for garden crops when drained and treated to correct high acidity. In time, however, the organic matter is lost by oxidation, and in some cases by burning.

Histosols occur widely over the globe, in low latitudes as well as in high latitudes. A good example of an occurrence of Histosols in the subtropical zone is the Florida Everglades. A large area extending south from Lake Okeechobee is covered by a Histosol known as the Okeechobee muck. With drainage and other required treatments, the Okeechobee muck produces sugar cane and vegetables such as onions, cabbage, tomatoes, peppers, and beans. Many other areas of Histosols occur along the coastal plain of the Atlantic and Gulf coasts, where recent uplift has raised former shallow lagoons above sea level.

Soil-water Balance of the Cold Continental Climate

The climate under which extensive areas of spodosols have formed in North America and Eurasia is referred to by geographers as the **boreal climate,** or **continental subarctic climate.** Also included, at somewhat lower latitudes is that part of the **humid continental climate** having a cool summer. The characteristics of these climates are basically similar, with cold winters and a large annual temperature range. Followed from south to north across this belt, ranging from latitude 45° N to 65° N, the annual range of temperature increases, winters become longer, and summer temperatures cooler.

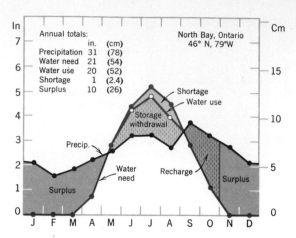

Figure 49.6   The soil-water balance of North Bay, Ontario. (Data of C. W. Thornthwaite Associates, Laboratory of Climatology, Centerton, N.J.)

Figure 49.6 shows monthly mean precipitation and components of the soil-water balance for a representative observing station at North Bay, Ontario, Canada, located at about latitude 46½° N, just north of Lake Huron in the Canadian Shield. The climate here is classified as humid continental climate with a cool summer. Mean monthly air temperatures are below freezing from November through March. Total annual precipitation averages 31 in. (78 cm). Precipitation is rather evenly distributed throughout the year, but with somewhat higher monthly amounts in summer and fall months than in winter months.

Water need (potential evapotranspiration) is effectively zero for five consecutive months (November through March) when the soil water is frozen. A very small soil-water shortage (deficiency) develops in summer, but stored soil water is ample to allow plants to use water almost to their full capacity. Recharge begins in September, and by November a surplus is developed. After winter has set in, the surplus accumulates as snow, to be released by melting in spring. The total water surplus is quite substantial—about 10 in. (26 cm)—and furnishes copious flow to streams of the area. Leaching of the soil (eluviation) is an active process during the spring, as surplus water makes its way downward through the soil.

The climate and water balance data of North Bay are also fairly representative of Spodosol areas in Minnesota, northern Michigan, and New England.

Unit 50
The Arctic Tundra

Caribou May Safely Graze?

Will caribou walk across the Trans-Alaska Pipeline? Perhaps as much as any other detail of the issues debated, this question symbolizes the intense and often emotional conflict between environmentalists and builders in the long-fought issue over the great pipeline that runs from Alaska's north shore at Prudhoe Bay to Valdez on the south. Caribou move in great herds during annual migrations along the treeless tundra of the North Slope of Alaska, between the Brooks Range and the Arctic Ocean. In the course of migration these caribou must cross the route of the new pipeline. Eskimos, native inhabitants of the tundra, depend upon caribou for much of their food. Migration serves a vital function in the survival and reproduction of the caribou herds.

To learn what he could about the possible impact of the Trans-Alaska Pipeline System (TAPS) on caribou movements, one scientist turned to Scandinavia to find out what is known about the habits of the caribou's European cousin, the reindeer. These reindeer, which number over half a million individuals, are largely located in Lapland, where they live in a semidomesticated state. Many Man-made changes in the environment have posed problems to reindeer in their seasonal migrations. Development of forestry, mining, hydropower, and the accompanying influx of new residents has increased the construction of roads, railroads, and fences. In one case in Norway, a new railroad line was found to frighten the reindeer and greatly inhibit their migration across the tracks. Finally, the animals simply stopped migrating to the winter pasture across the tracks. Because they were forced to stay in a region lacking in winter food, the reindeer had to be reduced in numbers by hunting. From an original population of 15,000 individuals, the herd is now down to about 1500 individuals, but the plant cover of the region still shows the effects of heavy overgrazing.

In one area in Sweden, inhibitions to reindeer migration became severe because of Man-made barriers. Reindeer herders then resorted to trucking the animals from summer to winter ranges. What they learned was that transport by truck disrupted the reindeers' social structure and their normal migratory behavior, perhaps because the younger animals failed to gain an orientation of the migratory pattern.

Snowmobiles, those glorious fun things that Americans love to ride over other people's private lands, are also a problem in Lapland, where the Lapp herders have adopted them as an aid in managing their reindeer herds. During migrations, the snowmobiles can cause panic among the herds. Careless use of snowmobiles during the calving season can result in losses of both the mothers and their calves. Recreational use of snowmobiles now poses a further threat to the Lapland reindeer, as Scandinavian sportsmen seek faster and surer ways to kill their quarry.

Caribou crossing the service road that parallels the Trans-Alaska Pipeline. (Don Carl Steffen, DCS.)

The oil companies building the Alaskan pipeline were quick to make all the necessary assurances that caribou-crossing facilities would be provided along the pipeline. In 1973, both houses of Congress put an end to further delays in construction of the Trans-Alaska Pipeline System. Pressed to action by the energy crunch, the Senate, by vote of 49 to 48, and the House, by vote of 221 to 198, declared that the environmental impact study on TAPS was to be accepted, and that no further review of that report was necessary. And so, TAPS was launched, and the economy of Alaska began to boom. But not all Alaskans are happy.

A new cause for concern about the tundra environment has come to the fore. Paralleling the pipeline is a service highway built on a thick gravel base and capable of handling heavy truck traffic. Several companies have petitioned the Alaska Transportation Commission for permits to operate tour buses on the highway. The Federal Bureau of Land Management is also making plans for recreational uses of lands along the pipeline. These uses include hunting and travel across the tundra by off-road vehicles.

Native residents of Alaskan villages and environmentalists see a serious threat in such uses of land along the pipeline. Game, on which the residents depend for food, is already scarce and would be rapidly depleted by recreation-seeking hunters from cities. Devastation of the tundra by vehicles would be enormous. Alyeska, the pipeline company, is not keen on having the highway used by visitors, one of the reasons being possible sabotage of the pipeline and acts of vandalism. The debate continues.

In this study unit, we will investigate the tundra lands of the far north in North America and Eurasia. This treeless belt bordering the Arctic shores, along with the cold woodland, or taiga, that lies to the south, presents a remarkable environment in terms of the adaptation of plants and animals to long, bitterly cold winters and a condition of permanently frozen ground beneath a shallow soil layer.

DATA SOURCE: David R. Klein (1971) Reaction of reindeer to obstructions and disturbances, *Science,* vol. 173, pp. 393-398; Charles J. Cicchetti (1972) *Alaskan Oil: Alternative Routes and Markets,* The Johns Hopkins press, Baltimore, see Chapter 2, pp. 31-57.

Arctic Permafrost

In arctic and subarctic lands of the northern hemisphere, winters are long and severely cold, because of a long-continued energy deficit in the radiation balance (see the net radiation curve for Yakutsk, U.S.S.R., 62° N latitude, Figure 4.3). As a result, subfreezing soil temperatures occur for six or seven consecutive months and all moisture in the soil and subsoil is solidly frozen to depths of many feet (Figure 50.1). Summer warmth is insufficient to thaw more than the upper few feet so that a condition of perennially frozen ground, or **permafrost,** prevails over large parts of lands lying poleward of the 60th parallel of latitude. Seasonal thaw penetrates from 2 to 14 ft (0.6-4 m), depending on location and nature of the ground. This shallow zone of alternate freeze and thaw is termed the **active zone.**

The distribution of permafrost in the northern hemisphere is shown in Figure 50.2. Three zones are recognized. Continuous permafrost, which extends without gaps or interruptions under all topographic features, coincides largely with the arctic tundra, but also includes a large part of the forested subarctic region known as **taiga** in Siberia. Followed north beneath the Arctic Ocean, the continuous permafrost layer disappears under the protection of the overlying ocean waters. Discontinuous permafrost, which occurs in patches separated by frost-free zones under lakes and rivers, occupies much of the forested subarctic zone of North America and Eurasia. Sporadic occurrence of permafrost in small patches extends in places as far south as the 50th parallel.

Depth of permafrost reaches 1000 to 1500 ft (300 to 450 m) in the continuous zone near latitude 70° (Figure 50.2). Perhaps much of this permanent frost is an inheritance from more severe conditions of the last ice age, but some permafrost bodies may be growing under existing climate conditions.

Figure 50.1   This vertical river-bank exposure near Livengood, Alaska, reveals a V-shaped ice wedge surrounded by layered silt of alluvial origin. (T. L. Péwé, U.S. Geological Survey.)

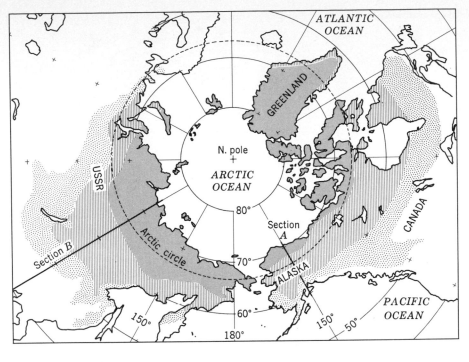

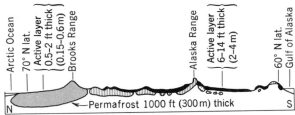

Section A: Alaska, on long. 150° W

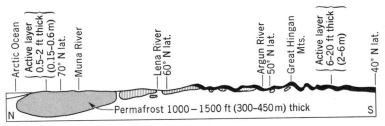

Section B: Asia, on long. 120° E
(Modified from I. V. Poiré)

Diagrammatic cross sections of permafrost

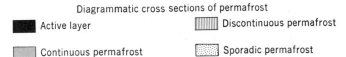

Figure 50.2 Distribution of permafrost in the northern hemisphere, and representative cross sections in Alaska and Asia. (From Robert F. Black, "Permafrost," Chapter 14, of P. D. Trask [1950] *Applied Sedimentation,* John Wiley & Sons, New York.)

Surface Processes and Forms of the Arctic Environment

Permafrost regions of the arctic land fringes of North America, Greenland, and Eurasia are subjected to a special set of physical weathering and mass wasting processes; these give rise to a unique assemblage of surface forms, mostly in the category of microrelief features. Since the arctic land surface underlain by permafrost is highly sensitive to disturbance by Man-made activities, an understand-ing of the environmental factors will go far to assure wise planning for the extended occupation and economic development of arctic regions.

A distinctive feature of the arctic lands is the development of **patterned ground,** a general term for the occurrence of a pattern of nested polygons in the soil or unconsolidated alluvium. In fine-grained material such as floodplain silts, ice has been segregated into **ice-wedges** perpendicular to the surface (Figure 50.1). Seen from above, the ice wedges form a polygonal network, which is

Figure 50.3 Ice-wedge polygons in fine-textured flood-plain silts near Barrow, Alaska. Dark areas within polygons are lakes. In the middle distance is a meandering river channel. (R. K. Haugen, U.S. Army Cold Regions Research & Engineering Laboratory.)

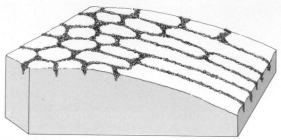

Figure 50.5 Sketch of stone polygons on upland, grading into stone stripes on adjacent slope. (After C. F. S. Sharpe. From A. N. Strahler [1971] *The Earth Sciences,* 2nd ed., Harper & Row, New York.)

one of the forms of patterned ground (Figure 50.3). Where the surface layer is composed of coarse clastic materials—pebbles, cobbles, and boulders—the larger fragments are concentrated by repeated alternations of freeze and thaw of soil ice into wedges forming a polygonal pattern. The term **stone polygons** (also **stone rings,**

stone nets) is given to these features (Figure 50.4). Where a flat upland surface grades into a marginal hillslope, the polygons are drawn out by downslope creep into elliptical forms and then into parallel **stone stripes** (Figure 50.5). Similar features will be found at high elevations in the alpine environment above timberline over a wide range of latitudes.

Because the seasonal thaw affects only a shallow layer, soil moisture reaches the saturation level and the water cannot escape through the impermeable frozen layer below. The thawed layer is then in a weakened and plastic condition and is highly susceptible to mass gravity wasting where the surface has an appreciable inclination. Under a protective sod of tundra vegetation the saturated soil moves unevenly downslope to produce bulges (Figure 50.6). The process is called **solifluction** from the Latin words for "soil" and "to flow." In addition to the **solifluction lobes** shown in Figure 50.6, there result **solifluction terraces** which give a distinctive stepped pattern to large expanses of mountainsides.

Figure 50.4 Stone rings near Thule, Greenland. Notice that a set of smaller, secondary rings has begun to form within the floor of the larger ring in the foreground. (A. E. Corte, Geology Department, Universidad Nacional del Sur, Bahia Blanca, Argentina.)

Figure 50.6 Solifluction lobes cover this Alaskan mountain slope in the tundra climate region. (P. S. Smith, U.S. Geological Survey.)

Man's Physical Impact on Permafrost Areas

Environmental degradation of permafrost regions arises from Man-made surface changes, usually related to the destruction or removal of an insulating surface cover, which may consist of a moss or peat layer in combination with living plants of the tundra or arctic forest. When this layer is scraped off, the summer thaw is extended to a greater depth, with the result that ice wedges and other ice bodies melt in the summer and waste downward. This activity is called **thermal erosion.** Meltwater mixes with silt to form mud, which is then eroded and transported by water streams, with destructive effects that are evident in Figure 50.7.

The consequences of disturbance of permafrost terrain became evident in World War II, when military bases, airfields, and highways were hurriedly constructed without regard for maintenance of the natural protective surface insulation. In extreme cases, scraped areas turned into mud-filled depressions and even into small lakes which expanded in area with successive seasons of thaw, engulfing nearby buildings. Engineering practices now call for placing buildings on piles with an insulating air space below, or for the deposition of an insulating pad of coarse gravel over the surface prior to construction. Steam and hot water lines are placed above ground to prevent thaw of the permafrost layer.

Another serious engineering problem of arctic regions is in the behavior of streams in winter. As the surfaces of streams and springs freeze over, the water beneath bursts out from place to place, freezing into huge accumulations of ice. Highways are thus made impassable.

The lessons of superimposing Man's technological ways upon a highly sensitive natural environment were learned the hard way—by encountering unpleasant and costly effects that were not anticipated.

Much of the intense debate over environmental safety of the Trans-Alaska Pipeline System (TAPS) has centered upon the impact of a steel pipe 50 in. (130 cm) in diameter carrying hot oil. If not properly insulated from the permafrost, large-scale melting of the ground ice would follow, leading to collapse and rupture of the pipe, and releasing crude oil to the adjacent tundra. Approximately the northernmost 200 mi (320 km) of the pipeline crosses continuous permafrost, while a 450-mi (725-km) central stretch runs across discontinuous permafrost. The Yukon River and 350 other streams must be crossed in safety. The region of the pipeline is highly active seismically, with many major earthquake epicenters close to the pipeline route. These epicenters are largely concentrated in the southern area of the pipeline, but some occur in the central area of discontinuous permafrost. Oil spills resulting from earthquake damage to the pipeline have thus been a major concern.

Where the Alaska pipeline passes over tundra permafrost, it rests upon a thick bed of coarse gravel, insulating the hot pipe from the frozen ground. The access road which parallels the pipeline is also built upon a thick layer of gravel. Even if these measures are adequate to protect the permafrost beneath from melting, there remains a se-

Figure 50.7 After one season of thaw this vehicular winter trail through the Alaskan arctic forest had suffered severe thermal and water erosion. (R. K. Haugen, U.S. Army Cold Regions Research & Engineering Laboratory.)

vere threat to the integrity of permafrost in a wide belt on either side of the pipeline. It is anticipated that large numbers of sightseers and hunters will use the parallel road as a highway to gain access to the remote tundra. Using off-the-road vehicles (ORV), these visitors will create permanent tracks across the tundra and these may lead to thermal erosion on a vast scale.

The Tundra Biome

Along the arctic fringes of the continental masses of North America and Eurasia lies the **tundra biome**—a vast belt of low shrubs, grasses, sedges, and mosses. Precipitation in most areas is small. For plants, much of the tundra is a cold desert, with annual total precipitation values as low as 12 in. (30 cm).

During the spring and summer, the active zone of the soil is subjected to many freeze-thaw cycles. Constant growth and shrinkage of ice within the active soil layer churns and heaves the soil to produce a highly unstable base for plants. Tussocks or hummocks, produced by the combined action of frost and vegetation, are also common. Figure 41.4J shows such features in an Alaskan cottongrass (Eriophorum) meadow. Uneven accumulations of snow and uneven melting, together with the flat nature of much of the lowland tundra, act to produce patches of bog and marsh.

Superimposed on this varied pattern of soil is a varied pattern of vegetation. Shrubs of the heath family, willows, and birches are the dominant woody plants of the tundra ecosystem. Grasses, sedges, and perennial herbs are common. Lichens and mosses are also abundant. Vegetation is usually scarcest on dry, exposed slopes and summits—the

Figure 50.8 Vegetation of the arctic fell-field. The plants grow in a small patch of soil surrounded by a ring of cobbles. (American Museum of Natural History.)

rocky pavement of these areas gives them the name of **fell-field,** from a Danish term meaning "rock desert" (Figure 50.8). In the wet lowland areas, a carpet of sphagnum moss with sedges and heaths typically covers the ground.

As is most often true in particularly dynamic environments, species in the tundra are few, but the abundance of individuals is high. Among the animals, vast herds of caribou in North America or reindeer (their Eurasian relatives) roam the tundra, lightly grazing the lichens and plants and moving constantly. A smaller number of musk-oxen are also primary consumers of the tundra vegetation. Wolves and wolverines, arctic foxes, and polar bears are predators. Among the smaller mammals, snowshoe rabbits and lemmings are important herbivores. Invertebrates are scarce in the tundra, except for a small number of insect species. Black flies, deerflies, mosquitoes, and "no-see-ums" (tiny biting midges) are all abundant and can make July on the tundra most uncomfortable for both Man and beast. Reptiles and amphibians are also rare. The boggy tundra, however, offers an ideal summer environment for many migratory birds such as waterfowl, sandpipers, and plovers.

The food chain of the tundra ecosystem is simple and direct. The important producer is "reindeer moss," a lichen (Figure 50.9). In addition to the caribou and reindeer, lemmings, ptarmigan (arctic grouse), and snowshoe rabbits are important lichen grazers. The important predators are the fox, wolf, lynx, and Man, although all these animals may feed directly on plants as well. During the summer, the abundant insects help support the migratory waterfowl populations. The directness of the tundra food web makes it particularly vulnerable to fluctuations in the populations of a few species.

Impact of the Trans-Alaska Pipeline System (TAPS) upon the tundra biome has been a subject of intense study and controversy. The problem of caribou migration has been discussed in our opening essay. Construction of broad gravel ramps and overpasses is expected to allow caribou migration across the pipeline. Underpasses may also be used. The workability of these crossings remains to be

demonstrated. The most serious threat to the tundra biome will probably come from visitors who reach the tundra along the parallel access road and invade the adjacent tundra for recreational purposes and hunting. Thus far, human hunters have lived in harmony with the tundra ecosystem, since the resident human population is very sparse and the total needs for animal food are not large. Large numbers of hunters, invading the tundra from urban centers and killing game for trophies, could bring rapid decimation to populations of caribou, moose, fox, wolf, and bear, and, at the same time, deprive the resident hunters of their food source.

Soils of the Arctic Tundra

Large expanses of upland slopes and cliffs in arctic lands fringing the Arctic Ocean have no true soil. Here, the land surface consists of bare bedrock or blocky surfaces, or of shingle beach ridges along uplifted marine shorelines. Locally, however, there is a primitive form of soil capable of supporting sparse plant life, such as the clumps of plants within stone polygons of the fell-field (see Figure 50.8). These primitive soils, which lack recognizable horizons belong to the soil order of Entisols.

Entisols, recently formed soils without horizons, are found in many places over the land surfaces of the globe. (The syllable *ent* is taken from the word "recent.") Entisols are so varied in origin, appearance, and climatic affiliation that it is almost impossible to say anything meaningful about the order collectively. This soil order is a "wastebasket" of classification, in which every item is different from the others and none of the items have much in common. For example, one class of Entisols consists of dune sands. Another occurrence can be found on alluvial fans where bed load of streams has been accumulating. Recently fallen volcanic tephra, weathered just enough to support plants, is classed with the Entisols.

Entisols of the arctic tundra belong to a subclass called **Cryorthents.** The prefix *cyro* refers to "frost" or "ice." The

Figure 50.9 Reindeer moss, the lichen *Cladonia rangifera*. (Larry West.)

mineral body of this soil is little affected by chemical weathering and is finely divided rock produced by frost action. Layers of humus and peat may also be present, accumulated by plant growth in an environment in which bacterial decay is almost inactive, except in brief periods during the short summer.

Other areas of the arctic tundra, those described as grassy tundra, are underlain by soils of the order **Inceptisols.** The name is derived from the Latin word *inceptum,* meaning "beginning." Inceptisols are immature soils with weakly developed horizons. Insufficient time has elapsed since the parent matter was exposed for other soil orders with well-developed horizons to have formed. As in the case of the Entisols, the ranges of physical properties and regions of occurrence of Inceptisols are so great that no simple general description can be given. Leaching has affected most Inceptisols to a moderate degree. These soils are found on parent materials of fairly recent geologic origin, such as glacial drift, alluvium, and volcanic materials. Inceptisols may have substantial amounts of clay minerals, and these may give a high cation-exchange capacity to the soil. Consequently, many areas of Inceptisols are highly fertile and support rich forests. Certain of the world's most productive floodplain soils are classified as Inceptisols.

Inceptisols of the tundra lands are in a subclass called **Cryaquepts. Aquepts** are Inceptisols of wet places. When the prefix *cry* is added, the name means "aquepts of cold climates." Layers of gray silt and peat layers characterize the Cryaquepts.

Cryorthents and Cryaquepts of the tundra are also found in the needleleaf woodland, or taiga, of subarctic regions. These soils extend south into the needleleaf, or boreal forests, as well. Histosols occur in patches of poorly drained bog land within the Cryorthents and Cryaquepts.

Unit 51
Man and the Midlatitude Grasslands

The Dust Bowl Years —A Lesson Forgotten?

New York Times, May 12, 1934: "A cloud of dust thousands of feet high, which came from drought-ridden states as far west as Montana, 2,500 miles away, filtered the rays of the sun for five hours yesterday. New York was obscured in a half-light similar to the light cast by the sun in a partial eclipse. A count of the dust particles in the air showed that there were 2.7 times the usual number, and much of the excess seemed to have lodged itself in the eyes and throats of weeping and coughing New Yorkers." The dust pall spread over the entire eastern seaboard and far out over the Atlantic, borne on strong west-

erly winds. Places closer to the source had a correspondingly heavier fall. The city of Chicago is estimated to have received a deposit of 20 million tons of the dust, an average of four pounds for each person living in that city.

The year 1934 saw the coming of the Dust Bowl in Kansas, eastern Colorado, and states to the north and south. With the Dust Bowl an era of plenty ended for the Great Plains. Throughout the 1920s favorable climate allowed farmers to expand wheat cultivation westward into the higher, more arid sections of the plains. Earlier droughts with crop failures had occurred in the 1890s and again in 1910, but these events were easily forgotten. Investors with eastern capital developed large, mechanized wheat farms, as well as cattle ranches. Although wheat

This swiftly moving black cloud signals the arrival of a stifling dust storm. Dust Bowl, Great Plains, *ca.* 1934. (Library of Congress.)

prices had dropped drastically after a boom during World War I, the 1920s saw the continued expansion into areas where only the good fortune of a succession of wet years staved off disaster. Then, starting 1931, a succession of drought years began. Millions of acres of wheat shriveled on the fields and remained unharvested. Cattle died in large numbers and thousands of farm families went broke, turning to the government for subsistence. So began the great exodus of farm families. Many made the westward trek to California, a story now familiar to all through John Steinbeck's novel *Grapes of Wrath*.

The spring of 1934 saw the start of a succession of episodes of blowing topsoil. As cold polar air masses swept south across the plains, severe air turbulence scoured the bare fields and raised the fine soil upward through an air layer thousands of feet deep. The arrival of such a dust storm could be seen far in advance as a great black cloud wall. Once the black wall enveloped a farmhouse or a town, daytime gave way to nighttime blackness. The choking dust penetrated every house through closed doors and windows, and there was no escape from it—no place to get a breath of clean air. It was a terribly frightening experience as well as a severe threat to health. Many persons became ill with a respiratory disease called "dust pneumonia."

As the Dust Bowl persisted into the middle 1930s, the plight of that region became a national concern. President Franklin D. Roosevelt toured the drought-stricken region and reported on it in one of his fireside chats in 1936. A leading solid conservationist, Hugh H. Bennett, worked unceasingly for a program and funds to restore the damaged Dust Bowl and protect the area from future erosion. One outcome of the disaster was the formation of the Soil Conservation Service in 1935, with Bennett at its head.

By the late 1930s, a period of rainy years had returned to the Great Plains, and with it came a return of the farmer and rancher. But by this time a program of soil conservation was in effect. Many areas that had been formerly planted in wheat were restored to pasture. New practices of cultivation were introduced to reducing the blowing of the topsoil. Tree belts were planted to break the force of the wind. Despite another drought period in the early 1950s, when conditions somewhat resembling the Dust Bowl made a brief return appearance, crop cultivation over the Great Plains continued to expand. High grain prices of the early 1970s increased the expansion of wheat cultivation into former pasture lands. In an effort to cash in on this bounty, many wheat farmers have gone back to practices that led to severe soil losses in the Dust Bowl years. Many

Moving out—start of the long trek to California. (Library of Congress.)

fields are being planted in successive years, without allowing intervening fallow years for the accumulation of soil moisture. Plowing techniques that leave the soil bare are returning to favor, while windbreaks of trees are being eliminated to increase the area of cropland. In 1975, a committee reporting to the U.S. Senate warned: "The farm community may be creating another dust bowl."

The United States can ill afford another Dust Bowl, for we stand very close to the precipice of a world food crisis. Huge grain reserves that were accumulated in the U.S. in the 1960s and early 1970s have disappeared, as foreign grain sales have mounted. The United States and Canada are today the only remaining great grain exporters. Without grain reserves, and with the possibility of a drought ahead for the Great Plains, we are courting disaster. Such, at least, is the warning we hear today.

In this study unit, we will investigate the mid-latitude grasslands, to find out what factors of climate and soil make this environmental region the breadbasket of the world, but at the same time a fragile environment sensitive to deterioration under the impact of Man's agricultural activity.

DATA SOURCE: J. B. Bennett, F. R. Kenney, and W. R. Chapline, (1938) The problem: subhumid areas, *Soils and Men,* 1938 Yearbook of American Agriculture, U.S. Dept. of Agriculture, U.S. Govt. Printing Office, Washington, D.C., pp. 68-76; Erik Eckholm (1976) Losing ground, *Environment,* vol. 18, no. 3, pp. 6-11.

Midlatitude Grasslands

Grasslands of the midlatitudes cover enormous areas in North America, Eurasia, and South America. Climates of these grasslands are best generalized by the statement that they are transitional from humid to arid. Between these two extremes lie climates ranging from subhumid to semiarid. We will need to analyze the terms "subhumid" and "semiarid" in terms of the soil-water balance.

In North America, grasslands set in to the west of a ragged boundary running roughly north-south in the middle of the continent, as shown on the map, Figure 51.1. Forest, which lies to the east, persists in narrow embayments following river floodplains, while grassland occupies the uplands. Here, on plains of low altitude under a subhumid climate, flourish the tall-grass prairies. Traveling west across these prairies and arriving at the 98th meridian of longitude (about halfway across Kansas, Nebraska, and the Dakotas), we come to the short-grass prairie and enter a semiarid climate. The transition is accompanied by a

steady rise in altitude of the land surface. Extending to the west as far as the Rocky Mountains are the High Plains, with altitudes rising from 3000 ft (900 m) in the eastern section to 5000 ft (1500 m) at the western limits. The short-grass prairie spans a great north-south distance—over 1500 mi (2400 km)—and reaches from Texas to Alberta.

The great grassland belt of the U.S.S.R. runs from the Ukraine, just north of the Black Sea, eastward for about 2500 mi (4000 km) in a narrow strip known as the Kirgiz Steppe. Most of this Asiatic midlatitude grassland is short-grass prairie. Some tall-grass prairie is found in Hungary and Rumania, where it goes by the name of the Puszta. In South America, a large expanse of tall-grass prairie, the Pampa, occupies parts of Uruguay and Argentina. Besides the common denominator of grassland vegetation in these three world regions, there is another common denominator in a distinctive class of brown soils. These soils belong to a soil order known as the Mollisols. To obtain a broad and unified understanding of the midlatitude grasslands, we will need to undertake a three-pronged investi-

Figure 51.1 Grasslands of North America.

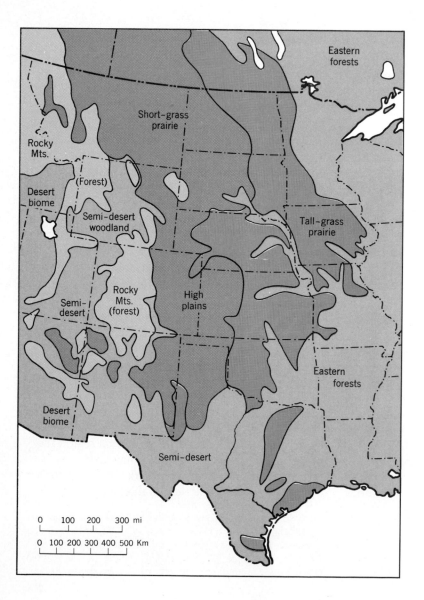

Eastern forests

Short-grass prairie

Rocky Mts.

(Forest)

Desert biome

Semi-desert woodland

Tall-grass prairie

Semi-desert

Rocky Mts. (forest)

High plains

Eastern forests

Desert biome

Semi-desert

0   100   200   300 mi

0 100 200 300 400 500 Km

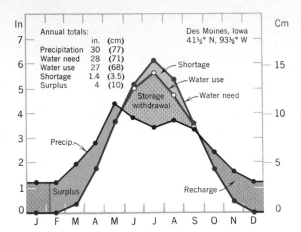

Figure 51.2 Soil-water budget for Des Moines, Iowa. (Data of Thornthwaite Associates, Laboratory of Climatology, Centerton, N.J.)

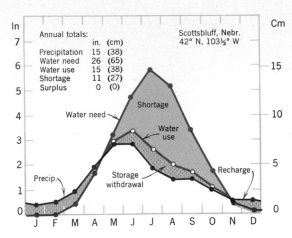

Figure 51.3 Soil-water budget for Scottsbluff, Nebraska. (Data of C. W. Thornthwaite Associates, Laboratory of Climatology, Centerton, N.J.)

gation including soil-water balance, mollisol profile development, and the grassland ecosystem. This knowledge will lead to an appreciation of the enormous grain production of these grasslands, and why they have been called by geographers "breadbaskets" of the world.

Climate of the Midlatitude Grasslands

The midlatitude grasslands are associated with the **dry continental climate,** characterized by a large annual temperature range—cold winters and hot summers. As we noted earlier, the grasslands of North America extend west from the edge of the humid continental climate, with its forests, to the semidesert and desert regions on the west. Consequently, there is from east to west a full spectrum of gradual change from humid climate, through subhumid and semiarid climates, to arid climate.

The subhumid continental climate of the tall-grass prairies is represented by the soil-water budget for Des Moines, Iowa (Figure 51.2). Precipitation has a strong annual cycle with a summer maximum. Water need also peaks strongly in the summer, but the shortage of soil water is small and occurs mostly in July and August. Soil-water recharge begins in October and quickly restores the soil water to field capacity. There is a moderate water surplus, released by melting of snow and ground ice in early spring. Comparing Des Moines with Pittsburgh (Figure 39.8), you will notice that the surplus is much smaller than at Pittsburgh, but the summer shortage is almost the same.

The semiarid continental climate is illustrated by the soil-water budget for Scottsbluff, in westernmost Nebraska, on the High Plains (Figure 51.3). Here annual precipitation is only about half that at Des Moines. The soil-water deficiency (water need) at Scottsbluff is large and extends over a six-month summer period. There is no water surplus, so that the soil water does not reach its storage capacity at

any time of the year. Streams flow intermittently, and only larger streams fed by snowmelt in the Rocky Mountains can sustain a flow across the High Plains year-around.

Mollisols

Soils of the midlatitude grasslands are represented by the soil order of **Mollisols.** These are thick, dark-colored soils rich in base cations. The name is derived from the Latin word *mollis,* meaning "soft." The Mollisols are characterized by a very dark brown to black upper horizon, or A horizon, known as the **mollic epipedon** (Figure 51.4). Clay minerals of high base-exchange capacity are abundant in

Figure 51.4 The Mollisol soil profile.

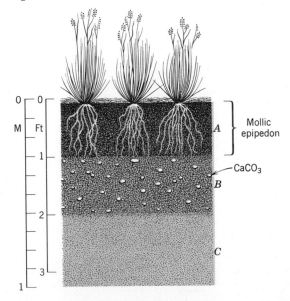

Figure 51.5 Granular structure of the mollic epipedon. The bar at upper right represents one inch. (Division of Soil Survey, U.S. Dept. of Agriculture.)

both A and B horizons, and the percentage base saturation is high (over 50%), which gives the Mollisols a high base status. The A horizon of Mollisols typically has a **granular structure** of fairly loose, small soil aggregates, (Figure 51.5). The underlying B horizon of some Mollisols is characterized by an excess amount of calcium carbonate ($CaCO_3$), which occurs as grains, nodules, and sometimes as rocklike slabs. Calcium ions are abundant in the A horizon as well.

Darkening of the A horizon of the Mollisols is the result of deep extension of plant roots into the soil and their partial decay when the roots die. Humus particles are also carried down into the soil from the surface by the eluviation process. Reworking of the A horizon by many kinds of animals (earthworms, ants, moles, rodents) distributes the humus uniformly.

The abundance of calcium carbonate in certain suborders of Mollisols can be attributed to the dryness of climate, which typically lacks a water surplus adequate to perform leaching. The soil solution is alkaline, moreover, and lacks soil acids that would otherwise rapidly attack and dissolve calcium carbonate. In many areas the parent matter of the soil, which may be loess or sedimentary strata, is rich in calcium carbonate.

Recycling of base cations by grassland plants is an important activity, serving to bring to the surface bases that might otherwise be slowly leached out in the subhumid regions of the Mollisols.

Suborders of the Mollisols

Although the soil order of Mollisols has seven suborders, we will limit our description to three of the suborders which are important in the interior grasslands of North America and which show a response to climate differences.

Borolls are Mollisols of the cold, northern grasslands. They will be found in Alberta and Saskatchewan and in the northern tier of states in the United States. They also occur in the Kirgiz Steppes of Asia. The borolls are important in the production of spring wheat, planted in spring and growing to maturity in summer by using stored soil water.

Udolls are Mollisols of the humid continental climate regions. They will be found in Iowa, eastern Nebraska, eastern Kansas, eastern Oklahoma, and Illinois (Figure 51.6). In Illinois they were formerly called **prairie soils.** Here, because of the greater precipitation and a small annual soil-water surplus, calcium carbonate is lacking in the soil profile. Udolls underlie rich farmlands in which corn and soybeans are major crops.

Ustolls are Mollisols of the subhumid and semiarid grasslands. They were formerly known as **chernozems, chestnut soils,** and **brown soils.** One feature of the Ustolls is that the B horizon sometimes shows a **prismatic structure** in which soil aggregates form elongated vertical blocks (Figure 51.7). Short-grass prairie is the natural plant cover of the Ustolls, while small grains, particularly wheat, are grown over large areas. Irrigation is extensively practiced over the region of Ustolls, as farming without irrigation is a high-risk operation. Cattle grazing is also extensive over areas of Ustolls.

Figure 51.6 A Udoll developed from glacial drift. Scale in feet. (Division of Soil Survey, U.S. Dept. of Agriculture.)

Figure 51.7 This Ustoll profile is developed on loess in Colorado. The B horizon shows prismatic structure. Scale in feet. (Division of Soil Survey, U.S. Dept. of Agriculture.)

The Grassland Biome

Grasses which constitute the dominant vegetation of the grassland biome are usually of two types: sod formers and bunch grasses. The **sod formers,** spread by rhizomes, form a tough sod mat of interlocking stems, whereas the **bunch grasses** grow in scattered clumps. In addition to the grasses there are other herbaceous plants, the forbs. **Forb** is a general term used to describe the annual and perennial herbs that do not belong to the grass family. The principal prairie

forbs are the legumes and the composites (members of the *Asteraceae,* a family including daisies, asters, and dandelions). Together the forbs may account for more species than the grasses. The grasses, however, dominate the biomass. Figure 41.4F shows one of the few remaining patches of virgin prairie in the midwest.

In terms of vegetation the plains of North America are usually divided into three areas: tall-grass prairie, mixed-grass prairie, and short-grass prairie. The area of **tall-grass prairie** formerly occupied a zone ranging from western Ohio and Indiana northward and westward to Wisconsin and Minnesota. Much of this area is actually suited to forest, but fires and grazing kept this area in tall-grass prairie in presettlement time. Now, much of the former tall-grass prairie, where not maintained in pasture of crop farming has reverted to forest, a result of Man's protection of the area from fire.

The **mixed-grass prairie** occupies a mid-continental position to the west of the tall-grass prairie, where not maintained in pasture or region and serves as a transitional area between the short-grass prairie to the west and the tall-grass prairie to the east. Because of the great seasonal variation in rainfall and evaporation experienced here, the aspect of the mixed-grass prairie changes from year to year.

The **short-grass prairie** is characteristic of the High Plains and intermountain basins of the Rocky Mountains; it grades into desert on its western and southern edge. Shallow-rooted, short species of grass dominate; sod formers are important in the short-grass prairie, and the dense sod acts to keep low the number of forbs (See Figure 41.4G)

A characteristic surface feature of the short-grass prairie is a shallow depression called a **blowout.** Blowouts are produced by the process of **deflation,** the lifting of fine soil particles by turbulent eddies in the wind. A blowout may be from a few yards to a mile or more in diameter, but it is usually only a few feet deep. Any small depression in the surface of a plain, particularly where the grass sod cover is broken through, may develop into a blowout. Rains fill the depression, creating a shallow pond. As the water evaporates, the mud bottom dries out and cracks, forming small scales or pellets of dried mud that are lifted out by the

Figure 51.8 A blowout hollow on the plains of Nebraska. The ground is well trampled by the hooves of cattle. The remnant column of the original soil provides a natural yardstick for the depth of material removed by deflation. (U.S. Geological Survey.)

wind. In grazing lands, animals trample the margins of the depressions into a mass of mud, breaking down the protective root structure and facilitating removal of the dried mud. In this way the depression is enlarged and deepened (Figure 51.8).

Droughts of the 1930s turned most of the short-grass prairie into a vast Dust Bowl ranging from New Mexico north to the western Dakotas. Undoubtedly, breaking of the sod cover and planting the short-grass prairie in wheat intensified the deflation and dust storms which accompanied the droughts. The drought converted much of the mixed-grass prairie into short-grass prairie, and the tall-grass prairie into mixed-grass prairie. Following abatement of the drought, most of the tall and mixed-grass prairie was able to revert to its normal vegetation. Soil erosion was so severe in the Dust Bowl, however, that much of the area has still not recovered, and changes seem to be permanent.

Like forest ecosystems, grassland ecosystems exhibit stratification. The three main layers are the root layer, the ground layer, and the herbaceous layer. The **root layer,** occupying the dark A soil horizon, is very much deeper and thicker than in forests—the roots of the grasses usually comprise nearly 50% of a plant's biomass and penetrate the soil to considerable depths, often as much as 6 ft (2 m) (Figure 51.9). Typically the grass roots are thickest in the upper 6 in. (15 cm) of the soil, where they are joined by roots and rhizomes of the other plants present. Undoubtedly, the deep penetration of the roots facilitates obtaining soil moisture during the long summer season of soil-water deficiency.

The **ground layer** is located at the soil surface. Here the annual increment of dead leaves and stems decays into **mulch,** the organic-rich surface litter layer of the grassland ecosystem. The quantities of mulch produced can be very large; as much as five tons per acre may be present on a climax tall-grass prairie. Inorganic nutrients are closely cycled through the mulch and its decomposer organisms; the organic content of the soil is high. Apparently, the accumulation and decay of mulch is a natural process required for the maintenance of the prairie. Where mulch accumulation is blocked by heavy grazing and mowing, the prairie can regress to weeds and to the more drought-tolerant grasses.

The **herb layer** varies during the seasons. In the spring, low plants such as strawberry, violets, mosses, and others

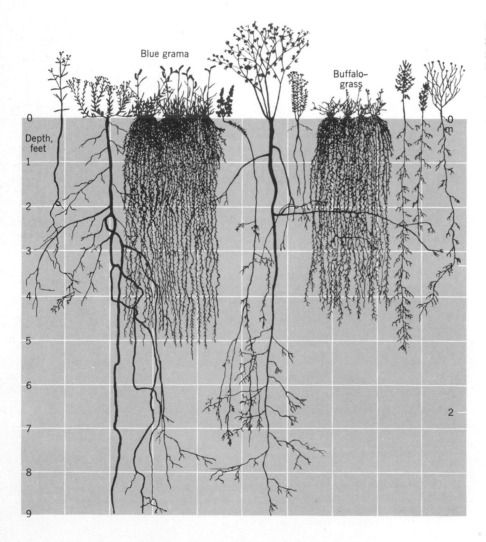

Figure 51.9 Drawings of roots of grasses (blue grama and buffalo-grass) and several kinds of forbs at Hays, Kansas. Roots at left extended to depths below 11 ft (3½ m). (From J. E. Weaver and F. W. Albertson, Drawing of Grass Roots, *Ecological Monographs* 13: 100. Copyright 1943 by Ecological Society of America.)

Figure 51.10   A family of prairie dogs. Note the large mound they have constructed. (Leonard Lee Rue III/ National Audubon Society.)

The grassland ecosystem supports some rather unique adaptations to life. A common adaptive mechanism is a jumping or leaping locomotion, assuring an unimpeded view of the surroundings. Jackrabbits and jumping mice are examples of jumping rodents. The pronghorn combines the leap with great speed, which allows it to avoid predators and fire. Burrowing is also another common life habit, for the soil provides the only shelter in the exposed grasslands. Examples are burrowing rodents, including prairie dogs, gophers, and field mice. Rabbits exploit old burrows, using them for nesting or shelter. Invertebrates also seek shelter in the soil, and many are adapted to living within the burrows of rodents, where extremes of moisture and temperature are substantially moderated.

The prairie dog is an interesting burrowing animal. Now widely hunted and poisoned, this animal competes with cattle for forage and builds undesirable dogtowns, covering much of the immediate area with mounds and undermining it with burrows (Figure 51.10). Actually, the activities of the prairie dog seem to have been beneficial to the short-grass prairie before the arrival of European Man. Selective feeding by prairie dogs on shrubs and annual plants allows perennial grasses and forbs to increase. The diggings are important as sites of colonization for species preferring disturbed soils. In short, the activities of the prairie dog favored the development of a diverse, heterogeneous short-grass prairie. The animal increased its range during the 1930s, both in response to the increase in area of the short-grass prairie during the drought years, and in response to the near extinction of its most successful predator, the black-footed ferret. After the drought, the prairie dog was able to maintain some areas in short-grass prairie where more desirable mixed-grass and in some cases tall-grass prairie had existed before. Thus, the prairie dog has been often associated with degrading range conditions.

grow rapidly. They are soon overtopped by the grasses and the taller forbs, which create a middle layer. The tallest layer is usually the flowering stems of the grasses; by the time of its development the ground layer may be almost completely hidden.

The animals of the grassland are distinctive. As would be expected, large grazing mammals are abundant. In North America, these included the pronghorn antelope and the buffalo. Now nearly extinct, the buffalo *(Bison)* once numbered 60 million and roamed the grasslands from the Rockies to the Shenandoah Valley of Virginia. By 1889, however, this herd had been reduced to 800 individuals, or approximately the same number alive today. Most of the buffalo population is now confined to Yellowstone National Park. Today, cattle, rodents, and rabbits are the major grazers in the grasslands ecosystem.

Figure 51.11   Farmlands of the corn belt in Iowa are laid out on a grid pattern. Before consolidation occurred, there were about four farms per square mile in this area. (Aero Service, Western Geophysical Co., Inc.)

Grasslands and the Global Food Resource

At several points in this study unit we have mentioned the high agricultural productivity of grassland soils. Both parent materials and climate have conspired to generate soils of high base status, ideally suited to grains and cereals needing rich supplies of the nutrient bases. Today the American tall-grass prairies are totally dominated by intensive agricultural use. From the air, we see only the endless grid of squares, based on square-mile land sections and quarter-sections (Figure 51.11). Fields of corn and soybeans stretch as far as the eye can reach, with only narrow tree belts defining the floodplains of small streams. In the region of the short-grass prairies the scene changes to one of enormous wheat fields (Figure 51.12). We would also find great expanses of wheat fields in the Argentine Pampa and across the Ukraine and Kirgiz Steppes of the U.S.S.R.

In these wheat producing areas, the human population is comparatively sparse, while the grain yields have been enormous, furnishing large surpluses for export to nations desperately short of foods.

The picture of midlatitude grasslands as the world's breadbasket needs to be tempered with a note of warning. The semiarid climate of this region has a very high level of unreliability, a fact long known to wheat farmers of North America. Climatologists are now warning of the possibility of droughts in major grain-producing areas. Recent droughts in the wheat-producing areas of the U.S.S.R. led in recent years to large purchases of U.S. wheat. From an era of large grain surpluses in storage, the U.S. has moved to a position of severely depleted grain reserves. This situation worries many agricultural scientists, who point out that world reserves of grain are becoming perilously low. More than ever, the human race is gambling on the productivity of the grasslands, gambling at the short end of unfavorable odds.

Figure 51.12   These combines are harvesting winter wheat on the High Plains of western Kansas. (Grant Heilman.)

Unit 52
Man and the Rainforest

Amazonia on the March — Downward?

"Green Hell" is a favorite writers' term for the vast rainforests of Amazonia, occupying the equatorial lowland of the Amazon River and its tributaries. Amazonia appears from the air as an endless carpet of green, laced with winding river channels. Amazonia matches roughly the same area (one-half million square miles) as the United States east of the Rockies. Yet, when you look at a world population map, Amazonia stands out as an enormous human desert along with the Sahara Desert, central Asia, and the interior of Australia: "Fewer than two persons per square mile," the map legend reads.

Today, your plane flight across eastern Amazonia would cross an ugly red scar, which you would recognize at once the fresh grade of a major highway. Oddly enough, the soil beneath the green rainforest is a rusty red color. Green on red is a worldwide symbol of the warm, wet climates; you will find it close to home in Georgia, Hawaii, and Puerto Rico.

The Trans-Amazonica Highway, as the new road is called, will eventually span Brazil from the Atlantic Ocean on the east, to the Peruvian border on the west, for a total length of 3300 miles.

Construction crews who push the new highway deeper into the rainforest face many personal discomforts in Green Hell. Survey parties penetrate the forest first, following a route laid out from study of air photographs. They are followed by forest-clearing crews using power saws to fell the tall, smooth-barked trees. Heavy earth-moving machinery then carves a highway bed from the heavy red clay soil. Finally, a base course of rocklike laterite is laid down. The work force in a given stretch of highway consists of about 600 men, living in advance stations that look like army camps. They work seven days a week and take short furloughs to civilization at intervals of 60 to 90 days. They are inoculated against yellow fever and take medication to ward off malaria. A few are disabled by forest yaws or hepatitis, and there are some cases of snakebite, since the men are invading the habitat of the bushmaster and the fer-de-lance. A handgun strapped to the hip is favored by some workers who fear chance encounter with a jaguar.

And what benefit is to be gained by the Trans-Amazonica Highway? The answers given by Brazil's promoters of economic growth must be very much like those given a century ago by builders of the transcontinental railroad in the United States: new agricultural land to be cleared, timber resources to be exported, rich ore deposits to be worked, new oil fields to be tapped, and a permanent home for millions of new settlers. Brazil's rapid population growth in the face of a low gross national product is the motivating force in the move to transform Amazonia. Economic development of Amazonia will

Grading the line of the Trans-Amazonica Highway. (Edward P. Leahy/Camera Press, London.)

This roadbed, carved for the Trans-Amazonica Highway, makes a great slash through virgin equatorial rainforest. (Edward P. Leahy/Camera Press, London.)

Ecologists fear the destruction of the rainforest ecosystem as an impending major tragedy for the biosphere.

Viewing the present course of Brazil's rapid economic expansion, a zoologist and his coauthor have sketched this word-picture of the shape of things to come in Amazonia:

> If development continues at its present pace, the remaining virgin forest, with trees up to 200 feet and more in height, will be cut, milled, and turned into timber and wood products to help fuel the economic growth of modern industrial Brazil. Once gone, the native forest will be replaced with monocultural stands of selected native species or exotics, which may prove to have limited pest resistance and will speed the depletion of already limited soil nutrients. In addition, with each shipment of wood exported, valuable soil minerals will be removed, never again to reenter the system. Agricultural practices, if based on temperate zone models, may further deplete the soil, eventually leading to crop failures and reducing farmers to lives of subsistence agriculture. Mineral development activities may destroy the forest, bare the soil to leaching, and, in time, deplete the mineral wealth of the region.
>
> After the disappearance of the native rain forest, with its unique species of birds and other animals, a secondary forest in its place may make a slow recovery. It is difficult to say how long the soil rebuilding process will take, but in many areas of severe depletion it will be many years before the nutrient supply again reaches a point capable of supporting a luxuriant vegetation.
>
> The rich will have become richer, the poor more impoverished and the native Indians, who once existed in harmony with the forest, will be gone. Where the forests stood, there may instead remain farms and some persistent cities with their surviving industries.*

In this study unit, we will investigate the equatorial rainforest, seeking basic scientific knowledge of the environmental factors that bear on the great debate over the future of Amazonia as a natural system.

*John C. Jahoda and Donna L. O'Hearn (1975) The reluctant Amazon Basin, *Environment,* vol. 17, no. 7, p. 29. Quoted by permission of the authors and the Scientists' Institute for Public Information.

DATA SOURCE: Edward P. Leahy (1973) Trans-Amazonica, the rainforest route, *Geographical Magazine,* vol. 45, pp. 298-303; Edwin Brooks (1973) Twilight of Brazilian tribes, *Geographical Magazine,* vol. 45, pp. 305-310; M. J. Eden (1975) Last stand of the tropical forest, *Geographical Magazine,* vol. 47, pp. 578-582.

tap new resources for export and will attract new capital from other nations. This, the promoters say, is the only way that Brazil can gain ground to reach the high economic status of other nations.

Those with misgivings about the development of Amazonia are also highly vocal, though most of the dissent comes from foreign specialists in agriculture, soil science, ecology, and anthropology. On the human side is the inevitable social disruption and wholesale extinction of Indian tribes incapable of adjusting to the invasion. This genocide is not a new phenomenon, but it will intensify rapidly. Soil scientists recognize the low base status of the red soil and its requirement for expensive and constant treatment if it is to be made agriculturally productive.

The Rainforest Environment

In this study unit, we travel to a part of the world unfamiliar to most Americans: the warm, wet environment of low latitudes where there is no winter. Here plants can flourish year-around with ample soil water most of the year for maximum net production by photosynthesis. Agricultural scientists and ecologists refer to this environment as the "humid tropics." More precisely, the parts of the world we have in mind are mostly in the **equatorial zone,** a belt lying astride the equator and ranging in latitude from about 10° S to 10° N. Warm, wet environments also extend into higher latitudes of the **tropical zone** along narrow eastern coastal belts within the tropical easterlies, or trade winds. Here the wet climate may be found as far poleward as 20° to 25°. Keep in mind that most of the earth's tropical zone, centered on the tropics of Cancer and Capricorn, lies under a great desert belt, which we shall investigate in Unit 54. Other parts of the tropical zone are within a climate having a very dry season alternating with a very wet season. This tropical wet-dry climate is the subject of Unit 53.

Soil-Water Balance of the Rainforest

The major regions in which a wet equatorial climate occurs are the Amazon lowland of South America, the Congo basin of equatorial Africa, and the East Indies, from Sumatra to New Guinea.

In the wet equatorial climate average monthly and annual temperatures are always close to 80°F (27°C). The seasonal range of temperature is so slight as to be imperceptible because the sun is not far from the zenith throughout the year. Rainfall is heavy during the entire year, but with considerable differences in monthly averages.

You can get some idea of the extreme monotony of the daily temperature cycle in this climate from Figure 52.1. This graph shows minimum and maximum daily temperatures for 2 months at Panama, lat. 9° N. The daily range is normally from 15 to 20 F° (8 to 11 C°), a vastly greater range than the annual range of monthly mean temperatures. In other words, daily variations far exceed seasonal variations in the wet equatorial climate.

The soil-water balance of the wet equatorial climate is well illustrated by Figure 52.2. Januarete, Brazil, is located

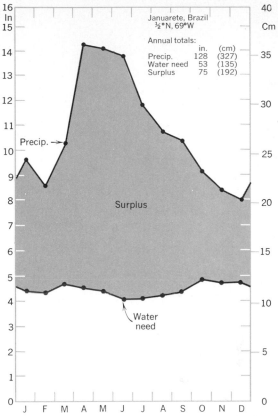

Figure 52.2 The soil-water budget for Januarete, Brazil, a rainforest station in the Amazon lowland of South America. (Data of C. W. Thornthwaite Associates, Laboratory of Climatology, Centerton, N.J.)

almost on the equator in the Amazon lowland, deep in the heart of South America. Water need is uniformly high throughout the year, because air temperatures are uniformly very warm and the sun is always high in the sky. Because precipitation is much greater than water need in every month, a water surplus exists in every month, and the annual total water surplus is thus very large. In all months, soil-water storage remains close to field capacity. Without a cold season and frost, plant growth proceeds at the maximum rate in all months; rainforest is the typical natural vegetation (Figure 52.3). Stream flow in this region is copious throughout the year.

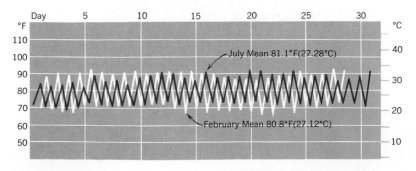

Figure 52.1 July and February temperatures at Panama, lat. 9° N. The sawtooth graph shows daily maximum and minimum readings for each day of the month. (After Mark Jefferson, *Geographical Review.*)

Figure 52.3   This air view over the rainforest of the Amazon Basin shows the Rio Negro, a tributary of the Amazon River. (Colonel Richmond, courtesy of the American Geographical Society.)

Oxisols

Soils found in regions of the wet equatorial climate fall mostly into two orders: Ultisols and Oxisols. We described Ultisols in Unit 48, in connection with their occurrence in the southeastern United States. Recall that the Ultisols are old soils, typically red to yellow in color, with large amounts of sesquioxides of iron and aluminum, and that they have low base status. The same description holds for Ultisols of the wet equatorial belt in the East Indies. In that region of the world, Ultisols are found throughout Malaysia, Indonesia, and New Guinea.

The **Oxisols** are also very old soils; they are also very rich in sesquioxides of iron and aluminum. Chemical weathering has progressed to the limit of further change and there remain only minerals of low cation exchange capacity. Consequently, the Oxisols have very low base status and are extremely poor in nutrients needed for food crops. Oxisols lack a distinctive horizon of clay accumulation (B horizon) that is found in the Ultisols. Moreover, in Oxisols we do not find the pale, leached A₂ horizon that occurs in the Ultisols just above the B horizon of clay accumulation. The Oxisols have an **oxic horizon,** at least one foot (30 cm) thick, composed almost entirely of sesquioxides.

Another distinctive feature of the Oxisols is the limited occurrence of a lower horizon known as **plinthite;** it consists of sesquioxides that can harden into a rocklike consistency when exposed to the atmosphere where repeated wetting and drying takes place. A common name for plinthite is **laterite,** derived from the Latin word *later,* meaning "brick." For centuries it has been known that plinthite can be excavated and carved into blocks for use as a building stone. Upon exposure, the material hardens into stone and is extremely durable in the warm wet climate. An example of the use of laterite as a building stone is the great temple at Angkor Wat, in Cambodia (Figure 52.4).

The poor supply of nutrient bases which the Oxisols offer to plants is almost entirely contained in the surface layer of fallen plant matter. The nutrients released by decomposers are immediately taken up by plant roots and stored in the biomass. Primitive peoples developed an agricultural system, often called **slash-and-burn,** in which a small patch of forest was cut away and the foliage and branches burned. Nutrients released in this way provided for the growth of crops for a year or two, after which the plot was abandoned.

The Rainforest Biome

The equatorial rainforest biome (often called tropical rainforest) consists of tall, smooth-trunked, broadleaved trees with crowns close together, in a close canopy almost completely shading the ground beneath (Figure 52.5). The trees retain their leaves throughout the year, except that individual species may shed their leaves at intervals. The

Figure 52.4 This Cambodian temple was built of blocks of laterite. (Georg Gerster/Rapho-Photo Researchers.)

through. The canopy trees of the tropical rainforest are often very tall and large in girth, although they do not approach the girth of the coniferous giants of the northwest American coast (see Figure 41.4A). The larger trees often show a flared base formed of flange-like buttress roots (Figure 52.7).

In contrast to midlatitude forests, animal life of the equatorial rainforest is most abundant in the upper layers of the vegetation. Above the canopy, birds and bats are important carnivores, feeding largely on insects above and within the topmost canopy. Below this level are found a wide variety of birds, mammals, reptiles, and invertebrates; they feed on the leaves, fruit, and nectar abundantly available in the main part of the canopy. Ranging between the canopy and the ground are the scansorial (climbing) mammals, which forage in both layers. At the surface are the larger ground mammals, including herbivores, which graze the low leaves and fallen fruits, and carnivores, which prey upon the abundant vertebrates and invertebrates found at the surface.

A major difference between the low-latitude rainforest and forests of higher latitudes is the great diversity of species which it possesses. The equatorial rainforest may have as many as 3,000 different plant species in a square mile area—other forests would be considered very diverse indeed with only one-tenth that number! The fauna of the rainforest is also very rich. A 6-sq mi (16-sq km) area in the Canal Zone, for example, contains about 20,000 species of insects, whereas there are only a few hundred in all of France. This large number of species occurs because the rainforest environment is so uniform and free of physical stress and because the ecosystem is so diverse that almost any mutation can survive physically and find a particular niche to which it is suited. As a result of the great number of species, the rainforest has served as a center for the origin of new species, providing both ancestral stocks and recent additions to the flora and fauna of higher-latitude zones.

forest structure often has an upper stratum of scattered, emergent crowns which project above the main canopy. Inside the rainforest, an understory layer of trees 15 to 50 ft (5 to 15 m) high is scattered throughout.

In contrast to other forest biomes, epiphytes (air plants) as well as climbing vines, or lianas, are abundant (Figure 52.6). The dense shade at the forest floor restricts the growth of many species, and thus the rainforest in its natural, undisturbed state is usually open and easy to pass

Figure 52.5 The complex layering in the tropical rainforest of canopy and understory trees, high and low shrubs. (After J. S. Beard [1946] *The Natural Vegetation of Trinidad,* Clarendon Press, Oxford.)

Figure 52.6 Lianas of the equatorial rainforest, near Belém, Brazil. (Otto Penner, Instituto Agronómico do Norte.)

Figure 52.7 Buttress roots at the base of a large tree (*Bombacopsis*) of the rainforest on Barro Colorado Island, Canal Zone. (American Museum of Natural History.)

Plant Resources of the Rainforest

Many plant products of the rainforest are of economic value. Rainforest lumber, such as mahogany, ebony, or balsawood, is an important export. Quinine, cocaine, and other drugs come from the bark and leaves of tropical plants; cocoa comes from the seed kernel of the cacao plant. Natural rubber is made from the sap of the rubber tree. The tree comes from South America, where it was first exploited. Rubber trees also are widely distributed through the rainforest of Africa. Today, the principal production is from plantations in Indonesia, Malaya, Thailand, Vietnam, and Sri Lanka (Ceylon).

An important class of food plants native to the wet low-latitude environment are starchy staples; some are root structures, others are fruits. Manioc, also known as cassava, is one of these staples. The plant has a tuberous root—something like a sweet potato—that reaches lengths over a foot and may weigh several pounds (Figure 52.8). Prepared so as to remove a poisonous cyanide compound, the roots yield a starchy food with very little (1 percent or less) protein. Used as a food in the Amazon basin of Brazil, manioc was taken to Africa in the sixteenth century where its use has increased widely. Manioc is now also important in Indonesia. Unfortunately, the food contributes

to malnutrition because it contains too little protein. Manioc is cultivated in small plantations placed in forest clearings. Like the manioc, the yam is a large underground tuber that provides another starchy staple. A major source of food in West Africa, the plant was introduced into the Caribbean region during the era of slavery and is an important food in the region today. The yam has a higher protein content than the manioc.

Taro is another starchy staple of humid low-latitude climates. The taro plant has large, elephant-ear leaves, which are edible, but the food value lies mostly in an enlarged underground portion of the plant, called a corm. Visitors to Hawaii know the taro plant through its transformation into poi, a fermented paste. Few mainland tourists eat poi a second time, but it has long been a favored food of the native Hawaiians. Taro corms consist of about 30% starch, 3% sugar, and only about 1% protein. Taro was imported into Africa from Southeast Asia and eventually reached the Caribbean region.

An important starchy staple in the form of a fruit is the breadfruit. A single breadfruit can attain a weight of 10 lb (5 kg) and is rich in carbohydrate. A native of the Pacific islands, the breadfruit has long been a staple of the diet of the Polynesians. In 1789, Captain Bligh of H.M.S. *Bounty* attempted to bring in his ship a cargo of small breadfruit trees to the West Indies to be cultivated as a food supply for African slaves.

The banana and plantain are starchy staples familiar to everyone. The banana plant lacks woody tissue and is, in fact, a perennial herb; the fruit is classed as a berry by botanists. First cultivated for food in Southeast Asia, the banana then spread to Africa. It was imported into the Americas in the sixteenth century and quickly became well established. The plantain, a coarse variety of the banana that is starchy, has little sugar and requires cooking.

Perhaps the plant most important to Man in the low latitudes is the coconut palm. Besides being a staple food,

Figure 52.8 Tuberous manioc roots, brought in dugout canoes from villages in the Brazilian rainforest, are being loaded on a river boat for transport to market. At one time manioc, in the form of tapioca, was popular in the United States as a dessert pudding. (Charles Perry Weimer.)

Future Prospects for the Rainforest

Can the wet low-latitude environment be exploited as a major new source of food for Man? Some agricultural specialists are highly optimistic; but others, specializing in ecology, are pessimistic, or at best very dubious. What we can do here is to point out restraints on such expansion, where it relates to raising staples such as rice, soybeans, corn, or sugar cane, which are field crops harvested seasonally.

First, the low content of nutrients in ultisols and oxisols will require massive and repeated applications of fertilizers. These applied nutrients are not held in storage in substantial quantities in the soil and are quickly exported from the land in runoff because of the large water surplus. Second, there is no dry season in which crops can reach maturity and be harvested under dry conditions, as is the case in the tropical wet-dry climates and the subhumid and semiarid continental climates of midlatitudes. Third, the Oxisols are capable, in a few areas, of becoming lithified—literally turning to rock—when denuded of plant cover and exposed to the atmosphere.

It is easy to say that agricultural technology can overcome these and other difficulties. Even if this conclusion is valid, no one questions the fact that the cost will be enormous in terms of cultural energy input through all parts of the agricultural system. Fertilizers, pesticides, machinery, and fuel only a part of that energy input. Large amounts of capital will also be needed to set up efficient management and marketing systems.

In view of the pending destruction of the rainforest ecosystem as a consequence of agricultural expansion, we can justifiably raise the question as to whether benefits will outweigh losses. Would not the human effort and energy expenditure be more effectively applied in those environments where many natural factors favor the increased cultivation of protein-rich food staples?

it provides a multitude of useful products in the form of fiber and structural materials. The coconut palm flourishes on low islands and coastal fringes in low latitudes (Figure 52.9). Copra, the dried meat of the coconut, is a valuable source of vegetable oil. Copra and coconut oil are major products of Indonesia, the Philippines, and New Guinea. Palm oil and palm kernels of other palm species are an important product of the equatorial zone of West Africa and the Congo River basin.

Figure 52.9 A grove of coconut palms on Bowditch Island, a small coral island near the equator and not far from Samoa. The engraving was made from a sketch by A. T. Agate, a staff artist with the Wilkes Exploring Expedition of 1838 through 1842.

Plant Succession in Disturbed Areas of Rainforest

An understanding of the successional process in the rainforest is important in understanding Man's impact. Ecologists divide the plant species of the rainforest into two groups: the **primary species,** which are characteristic of the virgin rainforest, and **secondary species,** which are adapted to disturbed sites. When disturbance occurs (produced, for example, by flood, windstorm, or the fall of a large canopy tree), both primary and secondary species compete for the new habitat. If the soil remains largely undisturbed, the primary species will usually win out with little difficulty. Seedlings and saplings of the primary species are always present in the understory, and the opening of a new area to strong sun allows them to grow so rapidly in filling the void that they easily outstrip any secondary species that may have managed to invade the new area.

When the soil as well as the vegetation is disturbed, the case is somewhat different. Primary species usually have seeds that are not able to remain dormant and thus sprout rapidly. (Rapid sprouting is actually an evolutionary advantage in the climax rainforest because fruits and seeds are readily consumed by herbivores, fungi, and bacteria.) If primary species are to return to the disturbed area, seed sources must be readily available at the time and place of disturbance. The seed sources will thus be those primary species that are nearby and happen to be in fruit. In addition, birds, monkeys, rodents, and other animals may carry seeds of primary species into the disturbed area. The secondary species, on the other hand, possess seeds that remain dormant in the soil for a considerable time; with soil agitation and exposure to light, they are triggered to germinate. In most cases, however, the secondary species are soon dominated by the primary species obtained from nearby sources, and the vegetation thus returns more or less to its former state.

In the past, Man has farmed the rainforest by the slash-and-burn method—cutting down all the vegetation in a small area, then burning it. Burning the slash on the site releases the trapped nutrients, and a portion of the nutrients is thus returned to the soil. The supply of nutrients derived from the original biomass is small, however, and the harvesting of crops rapidly depletes the nutrients. After a few seasons of cultivation, the soil thus loses much of its productivity. A new field is then cleared in another area and the old field abandoned. Primary species are able to reinvade the abandoned area because fruiting species and animal seed carriers are close by, and so the rainforest soon returns to its original state. The primitive slash-and-burn agriculture is thus compatible with the maintenance of the rainforest ecosystem.

On the other hand, modern, intensive agriculture, which uses large areas of land, is not compatible with the rainforest ecosystem. When such lands are abandoned, seed sources are so far away that the primary species cannot take hold. Instead, secondary species dominate, often accompanied by species from other vegetation types whose seeds are preadapted to long periods of dormancy. The dominance of these secondary species is permanent, at least on the human time scale. The rainforest ecosystem is, in this sense, a nonrenewable genetic resource of many, many species of plants and animals which, once displaced by large-scale cultivation, can never return to reoccupy the area. A recent appraisal of low-latitude rainforest ecosystems concluded with the following statement:

All the evidence available supports the idea that, under present intensive use of the land in tropical rainforest regions, the ecosystems are in danger of a mass extinction of most of their species. This has already happened in several areas of the tropical world, and in the near future it may be of even greater intensity. The consequences are nonpredictable, but the sole fact that thousands of species will disappear before any aspect of their biology is investigated is frightening. This would mean the loss of millions and millions of years of evolution, not only of plant and animal species, but also of the most complex biotic communities in the world.*

*A. Gómez-Pompa, C. Vázquez-Yanes, and S. Guevara, *Science,* vol. 177, p. 765. © 1972 by the American Association for the Advancement of Science.

Unit 53
Monsoon Lands of Southeast Asia

How to Live with Lions — The Gir Forest Ecosystem

When lions are mentioned, you probably think of the African savanna. There are a few Asiatic lions left in a small refuge in India, and they are the subjects of this essay. The Asiatic lions once ranged from Greece into eastern India. Now only 177 individuals remain (1976), sequestered in the Gir Forest of western India. A wildlife sanctuary covering about 500 square miles, the Gir Forest lies on the peninsula of Gujarat, about 200 miles airline distance from Bombay. The Gir Hills, in which the Gir Forest is located, has a climate rather on the dry side and, unlike the teeming rice and wheat lands of India's more humid sections, has a rather sparse population of humans. These people, who share the Gir Forest with the 177 lions, are Hindus of the Maldhari tribe. They number about 6000 and live in 136 tiny villages. The Maldhari own about 25,000 cattle, which graze in the open forest. Our story concerns an ecosystem composed of the Maldhari, their cattle and buffalo, and the 177 lions, along with a number of other wild animal species—leopards, spotted deer, sambar deer, Indian gazelle, nilgai antelope, and wild boar. There are also many intruders to cope with, for the Gir Forest is not closed off and protected like an American national park. Logging is permitted and the teak forest is being clear-cut in patches, while new stands of teak trees are being planted to reforest the bare areas. Besides the loggers there are invading herders who bring in cattle and water buffalo from surrounding areas to graze in the forest. Then there are tourists, several thousand each year, who come to see the lions. Chunks of meat put out daily attract the lions to places where they can be ogled at close range by the tourists. An effort is being made to attract more foreigners as tourists, since they are the big spenders.

The Maldhari people live very much like the cattle-owning tribes of the African savanna. Their dwellings are constructed of twigs, poles, grass, and mud. The village cluster of six or seven dwellings is surrounded by a fence of acacia thorns to protect the cattle from marauding lions. The Maldhari favor the water buffalo, which gives a milk with a very high butterfat content. From the milk the women produce butter, which they clarify into *ghee*, a cooking oil used throughout India. The ghee is sold to communities outside the forest for a meager cash income. Another Maldhari export is buffalo dung, gathered from the forest floor. Mixed with topsoil, this dung is sold to farmers outside the area, and in so doing the forest loses some of its plant nutrients and the soil is degraded.

The Gir lions live almost entirely upon Maldhari cattle and buffalo, from which they manage to make a kill at intervals. The loss of a female milk buffalo is

A family of Asiatic lions feeds on a water buffalo that has just been killed. The lioness (right) is blind in the right eye. The Maldhari herdsmen's cattle are easy prey for these protected lions, which now hunt in broad daylight. (Stephen H. Berwick.)

This small Maldhari village consists of rude shelters for the half-dozen families it houses. Buffalo (black), cattle (white), and a browsing camel (foreground) deplete the plant cover by over-grazing and trampling. (Stephen H. Berwick.)

crippling to the economy of a family, which may lose one-third of its annual income from the manufacture of ghee. However, their loss is not entirely the lion's gain. Although the Maldhari are devout Hindus and will not kill cattle, they chase the lions away from the dead cow or buffalo and stand guard while an outcast (untouchable) person is called to skin the animal for its hide and cut up the carcass for its meat.

The Maldhari cattle and buffalo, about half of which are unproductive male animals, severely deplete the grasses and shrubs of the Gir Forest. Annual grasses have been replaced by poorer species of perennial grasses. Timber cutting and insect infestations have depleted the teak forest and thorny shrubs are spreading over the degraded land. Trampling by cat-

tle has packed the soil more densely, so that less of the rainfall of the wet season enters the soil and more runs off over the soil surface to increase the intensity of soil erosion. Ecologists refer to the total process as xerification. (Xeric is the ecologists' adjective for a dry environment.) The Gir Forest, which lies in the monsoon lands of Southeast Asia, experiences a wet season and a dry season. Depletion of the plants of the Gir Forest takes place during the dry season, when there is severe competition among the cattle and buffalo for the little dried grass and browse available. In a natural environment, with only a sparse population of wild animals, these food demands would be small and the forest plants would recover in the wet season. That recovery is no longer possible.

Today, no sector of the Gir ecosystem is holding its own. The numbers of lions with doubtless diminish as pressures from outside the forest increase. The Maldhari people barely exist, while suffering from malnutrition and disease. Their average life expectancy is only 24 years, far below the 41-year average for India as a whole. Malaria is on the increase as the mosquito population becomes more resistant to DDT. Smallpox increased 38-fold in a three-year period. Deep mud during the rainy monsoon makes roads impassable, and medical aid is cut off for long periods.

The climate of Southeast Asia with its alternation of a season of severe drought with a season of heavy rains places a harsh stress on an overpopulated land. When the rains fail there is famine, and tens of thousands die; when rains are too heavy there are floods, and many more thousands perish. In this study unit we will investigate the climate, soils, and agriculture of these monsoon lands.

DATA SOURCE: Stephen Berwick (1976) The Gir Forest: An endangered ecosystem, *American Scientist,* vol. 64, pp. 28-40.

The Population of Southeast Asia

Southeast Asia, land of the monsoon, is home for hundreds of millions of humans, most of whom eke a bare subsistence from the soil. Asia's entire population, with over 2.3 billion persons, is 58% of the earth's total population. The People's Republic of China leads all Asian nations with a population upwards of 800 million, while India follows with 600 million; Bangladesh has over 70 million; Pakistan almost 70 million; Burma, Cambodia, Laos, Thailand, and Vietnam together account for another 46 million. When we examine a population density map, it appears that a large proportion of these Southeast Asians occupy alluvial lowlands, which are river floodplains and deltaic plains of those rivers. In India and Bangladesh this high-

density region is the combined floodplain and deltaic plain of the Ganges-Brahmaputra river system; in Burma the major concentration is on the lower Irrawaddy and Sittang plains; in Thailand, on the lowland of the Chao Phraya; in Cambodia and Vietnam, on the Lower Mekong floodplain and its deltaic plain. Populations of hill and mountain lands in Southeast Asia are sparse by contrast.

Evidently, there is a unique combination of physical factors that allows the floodplains and deltaic plains of Southeast Asia to support these countless millions of humans. The answer lies in two principal factors: climate and soil. The Asiatic monsoon climate provides an ample water surplus in its strongly developed rainy season. But that same climate also has led to the evolution of large upland areas of infertile Oxisols and Ultisols—soils of low base status. We might then say that the monsoon climate provides the necessary water, but works in an unfavorable direction to produce poor residual soils. Soils of the alluvial plains and deltaic plains sustain their fertility under these climatic tendencies of oxidation and leaching because of the continual import of parent materials with high cation-exchange capacity. These materials are silts and clays carried by rivers from mountainous source regions. The fertile soils belong to the order of Inceptisols. To understand the unique environment of the high-density populations of Southeast Asia, we must investigate both the monsoon climate and the varied soils.

Monsoon Winds of Southeast Asia

To understand the tropical monsoon climate, with its alternation of a very wet season with a very dry season, we need to begin with the annual cycle of surface winds. The key to understanding the surface winds lies in seasonal change in barometric pressure. In Unit 3, we idealized the global winds as forming simple east-west belts. The Hadley cell circulation produces a system of tropical easterlies converging upon the equator in the intertropical convergence zone. Beneath subsiding air of the tropical zone is the subtropical high-pressure belt in which adiabatic warming results in extreme aridity of climate. Poleward of the subtropical high-pressure belt we find the prevailing westerly winds. This belted system works quite well in the southern hemisphere, where land areas are small compared with ocean areas. However, in the northern hemisphere the vast continents of North America and Eurasia and the intervening North Atlantic and North Pacific oceans exert a powerful control over pressure conditions. As a result, the belted arrangement typical of the southern hemisphere is absent.

In winter the large, very cold land areas develop high-pressure centers. At the same time, intense low-pressure centers form over the warmer oceans. Over north central Asia in winter, we find the Siberian high, with pressure exceeding 1030 millibars. Over central North America there is a clearly defined, but much less intense, ridge of

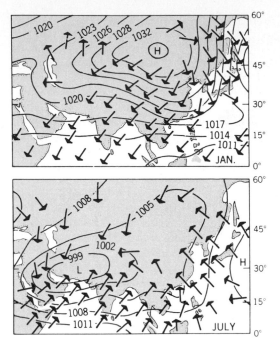

Figure 53.2 The Asiatic monsoon winds alternate in direction from January to July in response to reversals of barometric pressure over the large continent.

high pressure, called the Canadian high. Over the oceans are the Aleutian low and the Icelandic low, named for the localities over which they are centered. These two low-pressure areas have much cloudy, stormy weather in winter. Figure 53.1 shows these pressure centers as they appear grouped around the north pole. Highs and lows occupy opposite quadrants.

In summer pressure conditions are exactly the opposite of winter conditions. In summer the land areas develop low-pressure centers because at this season land-surface temperatures rise sharply above temperatures over the adjoining oceans. At the same time, the ocean areas develop strong centers of high pressure.

The powerful control exerted by the great landmass of Asia on air temperatures, pressures, and surface wind systems is shown in Figure 53.2. In summer southern Asia develops a cyclone into which there is a strong flow of air (July map). From the Indian Ocean and the southwestern Pacific warm, moist maritime air masses move northward and northwestward into Asia, passing over India, Indochina, and China. This air flow constitutes the **summer monsoon.** During this season the intertropical convergence zone shifts northward, taking up a position over southeastern Asia. Lifting of moist air masses in weak, slow-moving low-pressure systems along the convergence zone produces heavy convectional rainfall.

In winter, when Asia is dominated by a strong center of high pressure, there is an outward flow of air reversing that of the summer monsoon (January map). Blowing southward and southeastward toward the equatorial oceans, this **winter monsoon** is associated with dry weather for a period of several months.

Figure 53.1 This schematic map of the northern hemisphere in winter shows intense centers of high and low pressure occupying opposing quadrants.

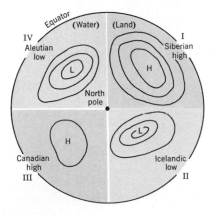

Soil-Water Budget of the Monsoon Climate

The monsoon climate of Southeast Asia is a variation of the **tropical wet-dry climate,** a climate class of global extent in low latitudes. A similar climate can be found in the tropical zone of Africa and the Americas.

The monsoon climate is illustrated by the soil-water budget for Calcutta, India, a great city located on the deltaic plain of the Ganges River (Figure 53.3). This location is close to the tropic of Cancer. The budget shows great seasonal contrasts. Precipitation is slight in the low-sun months (November to February), but rises to large values in the rainy season (June to September). The annual curve of water need also shows a strong seasonality, peaking at the onset of the rainy season. As a result, there is a large water surplus after the rains have started (July to September), but a severe soil-water shortage preceding the rains (March to May). Agriculture depends on these monsoon rains; if they do not materialize, the shortage can extend through the year, bringing crop failure. When the monsoon rains are exceptionally heavy, river floods can be an equally serious disaster, driving people from their homes and inundating their crops. This "feast-or-famine" budget is typical of those tropical countries of Asia and Africa most severely beset with food shortages and famines.

The tropical wet-dry climate shows a similar soil-water budget along east coasts of islands and continents in the belt of the tropical easterlies. We can refer to this climate as the **trade-wind coastal climate.** Here the monsoon effect is not the cause of wet and dry seasons. Instead, the wet season occurs when the intertropical convergence zone has shifted to a position over the region. At this time, rainy conditions like those of the equatorial rainforest exist for several months. Then, when the intertropical convergence zone has shifted away from the region and is replaced by the subtropical high-pressure belt, a drought sets in. We see this pattern in the Philippine Islands, the West Indies and Central America, the Ivory Coast of western Africa, the northeast coast of Brazil, and the northeast coast of Australia.

Figure 53.4 illustrates the soil-water budget for a station located in the trade-wind belt of the Philippine Islands. The precipitation cycle shows a strong annual cycle that peaks markedly following the high-sun season and drops to low values following the low-sun season. Water need also has a pronounced annual cycle, but it follows closely the solar radiation cycle with a maximum at summer solstice and a minimum at winter solstice. During the three-month period March through May, water need is greater than precipitation; hence soil water is withdrawn from storage and a small soil-water shortage is developed. This shortage is not severe, however, in its effect on forest

Figure 53.3 The soil-water budget for Calcutta, India. (Data of C. W. Thornthwaite Associates, Laboratory of Climatology, Centerton, N.J.)

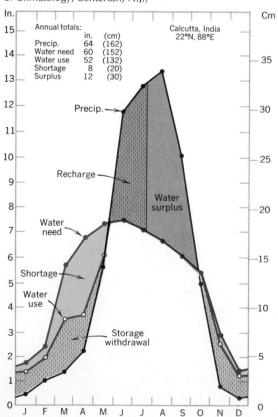

Figure 53.4 The soil-water budget for Aparri, Philippine Islands. (Data of C. W. Thornthwaite Associates, Laboratory of Climatology, Centerton, N.J.)

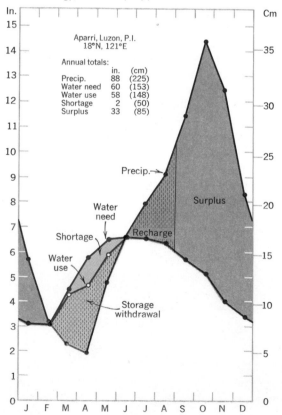

plants. Then, in June, as rainfall begins to increase, the soil-water storage is recharged and, by September, a surplus sets in. The total surplus is substantial, and during this period streams flow full to their banks. There may also be heavy flooding, particularly when a typhoon strikes. In this climate, rice is an important crop, growing during the wet season and maturing for harvest in the short dry season.

Comparing this water budget with that of Calcutta, you will notice that the dry season is much shorter and less severe than at Calcutta. In addition, the season of water surplus is much longer than at Calcutta. This Philippines example can be thought of as a transition into the equatorial rainforest climate.

Soils of the Wet-Dry Tropical Lands

Soils of the monsoon climate regions of Southeast Asia and the other global areas of tropical wet-dry climate are remarkably varied both in the soil orders represented and in the agricultural productivity of those orders. This patchwork of varied soils explains why some areas are densely populated while others are sparsely populated, even though the climate may have the same input of soil water in a rainy season.

Ultisols of low base status occupy large upland areas of Southeast Asia (Figure 53.5). These are very old, residual soils with plinthite (laterite) horizons and are agriculturally poor lands. However, they support forests and grazing lands that have some economic value.

Other upland areas in Southeast Asia have Alfisols, which, you will recall from Unit 48, are soils of high base status. Alfisols occur in large areas of northern India and Pakistan, on the eastern side of the Indian peninsula, on Sri Lanka (Ceylon), and in a large central area of Cambodia and Thailand. The Alfisols of these regions, as well as Alfisols in other wet-dry tropical climates in west Africa, east Africa, northern Australia, and northeastern Brazil, are of a suborder called **Ustalfs.** The prefix *ust* comes from the

Latin word *ustus* for "burnt," and signifies that the soil forms under high temperatures and under seasonally dry conditions. The Ustalfs are typically reddish in color and were formerly called **reddish-brown soils** and **reddish-chestnut soils.** (Alfisols of the midlatitudes belong to a different suborder, the **Udalfs,** formed under moist conditions with a cold winter.) The reasons for high base status of the tropical Alfisols are varied, but are related to a parent matter rich in the minerals that weather to yield bases and thus assure a high percentage of base saturation. Some areas of these Alfisols are underlain by alluvium, others receive a rain of dust from adjacent deserts. The dust keeps adding minerals rich in bases and thus enriching the soil. It seems likely that without this continual dust fall, leaching and oxidation would have produced Ultisols and Oxisols in these same areas.

Another important order of soils found in the wet-dry tropical climate is the order of **Vertisols.** Properties that characterize the Vertisols are these: (1) a high content of clay minerals which shrink greatly when dried out and swell greatly when water is added; (2) deep, wide cracks during the dry season of the year; (3) evidence of movement of soil blocks because of the annual shrinking and swelling of the soil. Vertisols are black soils without conspicuous horizons; they have gone under such names as **black cotton soils** and **black tropical clays.** During the long dry season of the tropical wet-dry climate, large cracks appear; these may be several inches wide and two feet or more deep (Figure 53.6). Loosened soil particles fall from the ground surface into the cracks. In popular language, the soil "swallows itself" and is continually mixed from bottom to top. When rains come, water pours into the cracks, soaking the lower zone first and causing it to swell. Swelling results in lifting of one block against its neighbor, so that the ground surface is unevenly heaved up. Fence posts and pavement blocks in Vertisols often show tilting from this soil activity.

Vertisols are rich in the clay mineral montmorillonite,

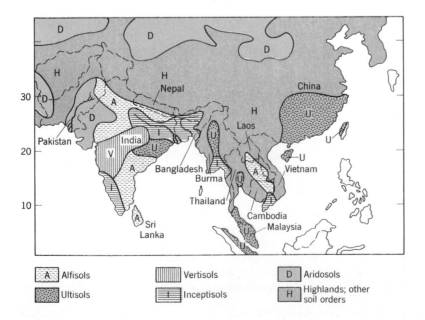

Figure 53.5 Soil orders of Southeast Asia.

A Alfisols

Ultisols

Vertisols

Inceptisols

D Aridosols

H Highlands; other soil orders

Figure 53.6   Deep soil cracks in a Texas Vertisol, the Houston black clay. The crop shown here is cotton. (Soil Conservation Service, U.S. Dept. of Agriculture.)

which is described as an "expanding clay." This mineral also has a high cation exchange capacity. There is limited leaching of bases, so that the Vertisols have a high percentage base saturation. Although they are high base status soils, the Vertisols have had little use as agricultural soils in the low latitudes because, when moist, the soil is tough and sticky. Ploughs drawn by oxen or water buffalo cannot till this soil, and it is typically left in woodland and grassland, used as forage for grazing animals. Soil scientists think that with sufficient investment in power-driven farm machinery and certain forms of treatment to improve the structure, the Vertisols hold promise for significantly adding to the food resources of these lands of perpetual food shortages and famine.

An important large area of Vertisols covers the western half of the Indian peninsula. Here the parent material consists of ancient basaltic lava flows, called the Deccan basalts. Basalt is a mafic igneous rock from which weathering produces the montmorillonite clay found in Vertisols. Rainfall during the short rainy season is insufficient in this area to allow the bases to be leached away.

Inceptisols form important lowland soils in the Ganges-Brahmaputra valley of India and Bangladesh, the lower Irrawaddy valley in Burma, the Chao Phraya Lowland of Thailand, and the lower Mekong valley and deltaic plain of Vietnam (Figure 53.5). These are densely populated areas with an intensive rice culture. The Inceptisols of these areas are within a suborder called **Aquepts.** The prefix *aqu* obviously comes from the Latin word *aqua* for "water." The Aquepts are saturated with water at some season of year. In Southeast Asia, this saturated period is the rainy monsoon. Aquepts are formed on a parent matter of silt and clay carried by rivers and deposited during river floods on floodplains and deltaic plains. Annual flooding replenishes these clays, which have a high cation exchange capacity, so that a high level of fertility is maintained, even though the warm climate and long wet season

tend to leach and oxidize the soil. Aquepts of the Asiatic monsoon climate are fully exploited for agriculture; their yields can only be increased by applying the ingredients of the Green Revolution, namely, better strains of rice, more fertilizers, and the use of petroleum-powered machinery on enlarged farm plots. Irrigation will permit growing of a dry-season crop in some areas.

Plant Formation Classes of the Wet-dry Tropical Climate

The unique climate of the Asiatic monsoon lands and other areas of a wet-dry tropical climate produces certain unique plant formation classes, ranging from grasslands to forest. Rainforest occurs in those monsoon areas with a very short dry season, because stored soil water can provide the needs of forest trees during that short period.

The forest biome is represented in Southeast Asia by **monsoon forest,** which is more open than the equatorial rainforest. Consequently, there is less competition among trees for light but a greater development of vegetation in the lower layers (see Figure 41.4B). Maximum tree heights range from 40 to 100 ft (12 to 35 m), which is less than in the equatorial rainforest. Many tree species are present and may number 30 to 40 species in a small tract. Tree trunks are massive; the bark is often thick and rough. Branching starts at comparatively low levels and produces large round crowns. Perhaps the most important feature of the monsoon forest is that most of the tree species present are deciduous. The shedding of leaves results from the stress of a long dry season which occurs at time of low sun and cooler temperatures. Thus the monsoon forest in the dry season has somewhat the dormant winter aspect of deciduous forests of midlatitudes. Some writers use the name "tropical deciduous forest" for monsoon forest, emphasizing the deciduous character rather than the climate regime. A representative example of a monsoon forest tree is the teakwood tree.

Lianas and epiphytes (air plants) are locally abundant in monsoon rainforest but are fewer and smaller than in the equatorial rainforest. Undergrowth is often a dense shrub thicket. Where second-growth vegetation has formed, it is typically jungle. Clumps of bamboo are an important part of the vegetation in climax teakwood forest. Perhaps the type regions of monsoon forest are in Burma, Thailand, and Cambodia. Large areas of deciduous tropical forest occur in west Africa and in central and South America, bordering the equatorial rainforest.

Savanna woodland is widespread in areas of tropical wet-dry climate. It occurs in semiarid areas of India. Savanna woodland consists of trees spaced rather widely apart. The intervening ground has a dense, low layer that may consist of grasses or low shrubs. This formation class is sometimes called "parkland" because of the open, parklike appearance of the vegetation. Trees are of medium height, the crowns are flattened or umbrella shaped, and the trunks have thick, rough bark. Some species of trees are xerophytic forms with small leaves and thorns. Others are deciduous, shedding their leaves in the dry season. In this respect, tropical savanna woodland is closely akin to the monsoon forest into which it grades. The trees are capable of withstanding the fires that sweep through the lower layer in dry season.

Thornbush is another tropical formation class, occurring where there is a very long dry season and only a short, but intense, rainy season. This vegetation formation consists of tall, closely spaced woody shrubs commonly bearing thorns and largely deciduous. Cactus plants may also be present. The lower layer of herbs may consist of annuals, which largely disappear in the dry season, or of grasses.

Tropical scrub is a dense growth of low woody shrubs occurring in patches or clumps separated by barren ground. Scrub may develop in stony, sandy, or gravelly sites in areas of thornbush.

Savanna grassland has widely scattered trees rising from broad expanses of grasses. This formation class might equally well be placed in the grassland biome. Although some areas of savanna grassland are found in the semiarid parts of the Indian peninsula, the major areas of these grasslands are in Africa (see Figure 41.4E). Grasses in the tropical savanna are characteristically tall, with stiff coarse blades, commonly higher than the height of a human, and even up to 12 ft (4 m) high. In the dry season these grasses form a yellowish straw mat that is highly flammable and subject to periodic burning. Many plant geographers hold the view that periodic burning of the savanna grasses is responsible for the maintenance of the grassland against the invasion of forest. Fire does not kill the underground parts of grass plants, but limits tree growth to a few individuals of fire-resistant species. The browsing of animals, which kills many young trees, is also a factor in maintaining grassland at the expense of forest. All formation classes of the wet-dry tropical climate feel the strong control of the feast-or-famine soil-water budget. In all these formations plants quickly turn green and grow vigorously at the onset of the rainy season.

Agriculture in the Monsoon Lands

Of the staple food crops grown widely in the monsoon climate of Southeast Asia, rice is perhaps the most important and the most closely linked to the wet-dry cycle. About one third of the human race subsists on rice, and most of these persons live in Asia. Most of this crop is paddy rice, grown on flat lowlands or in terraced fields. Paddy rice requires flooding at the time the seedling plants are cultivated. This activity is traditionally timed to coincide with the peak of the rainy monsoon season (Figure 53.7). After the crop matures, it is harvested in the dry season. Sugar cane is another important crop that grows rapidly during the rainy season and is harvested in the dry season.

Sorghum, which goes by other names such as kaffir corn, or guinea corn, is an important food crop of the tropical wet-dry environment in Africa and India. It is a grain capable of survival under conditions of a short wet season and a long, hot dry season.

Wheat is intensively cultivated in northern india and Pakistan, within the more arid part of the monsoon climate. This agricultural region includes the Punjab of northern Pakistan and northwestern India and the Indian state of Uttar Pradesh, the latter lying mostly within the broad lowland of the Ganges River. Much of the region is irrigated to supplement the monsoon rains, and some areas produce two crops per year.

Peanuts are another major food crop of the tropical wet-dry environment in India, and they have been introduced into a corresponding climate zone of West Africa.

While striking increases of rice and wheat yields were achieved in Southeast Asia by the green revolution, the recent sharp increases in price of fertilizers and fuel have dealt a staggering blow to the new agriculture. Because of the green revolution, wheat production in the Punjab of India was doubled in the five years between 1966 and 1971. Food experts hoped this phenomenal increase

Figure 53.7 In this scene in the northern Philippines rice seedlings are being transplanted into a paddy field flooded by monsoon rains. By the time this rice crop has been harvested, a single acre may have consumed a thousand person-hours of hand labor. (Dept. of Tourism, Philippines Board of Travel & Tourist Industry.)

would sustain the growing needs of India's population, which increases by some 17 million persons per year. But wheat production leveled off and, in 1974, was forced into sharp decline by a number of negative factors. Among them were the partial failure of rains and an enormous increase in the costs of fertilizers and fuels. Also, bore wells, drilled into the sand and gravel to reach ground water, require electricity for pumps, an energy source that was severely cut.

One hazard of the green revolution lies in the requirement that the genetic strains bred for high yields must be used to the exclusion of a variety of native strains. If the high-yield strain proves vulnerable to an epidemic disease, the entire crop of a whole nation might be wiped out in one season. A second hazard lies in the need to increase the size of fields, which demands the merging of many small plots into large ones to allow mechanized agriculture to work most efficiently. In so doing, a variety of food crops is no longer grown, and dependence for survival comes to rest on a single crop. Under traditional practices, the Asiatic farmer planted several food crops to ensure that if some failed, others would yield enough food to prevent starvation. The technique of the green revolution is being viewed more and more as a gamble with human life, one that imposes the technology of the industrial midlatitude nations on an ancient agricultural system that has developed important safeguards to insure its survival without outside aid.

Unit 54
Deserts and Their Irrigation

Death of a Civilization—Its Lesson Unheeded

What causes a civilization to collapse after it has flourished for 2000 years? For the ancient hydraulic civilizations, those that relied on irrigation of crops in a desert land, one cause of collapse was self-inflicted, although not intentionally. No doubt, you learned as a child about the Fertile Crescent, that lowland of antiquity spreading in a great arc across the Near East. The Fertile Crescent starts on the east at the head of the Persian Gulf in the lower plain of the Tigris and Euphrates rivers; it follows this broad valley to the northwest through what is now the nation of Iraq, but what was long known as Mesopotamia. Upon entering Syria, the Fertile Crescent turns west, then southward through the coastal region of Lebanon and Israel.

The Sumerian civilization evolved in the lower Tigris-Euphrates valley, where a village culture has been discovered dating to about the fifth millenium, B.C. By 3000 B.C. the Sumerian civilization was well established. The agriculture upon which that civiliza-

tion rested was dependent upon an irrigation system of canals. Supported by this agricultural base, urban culture progressed to a high level and a cuneiform system of writing was invented. Skilled craftsmen produced pottery and—using gold, silver, and copper—jewelry and ornate weapons.

Trouble set in for the Sumerians about 2400 B.C. It came in the form of a deterioration of their croplands because of the accumulation of salt in the soil. This process, today called salinization, resulted from the evaporation, century after century, of salt dissolved in the irrigation water diverted from the two great rivers. Wheat, a staple crop, is quite sensitive to salt and its yield declines sharply as the salt concentration rises in the soil water. Barley, another staple crop of that time, is somewhat less sensitive to salt, but only up to a limit.

The first indications by means of which historians can infer the onset of salinization in the Sumerian agricultural lands is a shift in the proportions of wheat and barley in their national agricultural output. It seems that around 3500 B.C. these two grains were grown in about equal amounts. By 2500 B.C., however, wheat accounted for only about one-sixth

An artist's visualization of the Ziggurat, part of a great Sumerian temple at Ur, built about 2200 B.C. A solid mass of brick, rising about 50 feet high, is all that remains today. (Joint Expedition of the British Museum and the University Museum, University of Pennsylvania.)

383

of the total grain production. Evidently the more salt-tolerant barley had, of necessity, replaced wheat over much of the area.

At this point in time, the Sumerian grain yield began to decline seriously. Records showed that in 2400 B.C., around the city of Girsu, fields were yielding an average of about 1700 pounds of grain per acre, a high rate, even by modern standards. By 2100 B.C. the grain yield had declined to 990 pounds per acre, and by 1700 B.C., to a mere 600 pounds. Cities so declined in population that they finally dwindled into mere villages. As Sumerian civilization withered in the south, Babylonia in the northern part of the valley rose to ascendency. Soon political control passed from Sumer to Babylon.

Historians chronicle an event that seems also to have played a part in the decline of the Sumerian civilization. A group of cities along the Euphrates River needed more irrigation water than they had. After a long and fruitless series of conflicts with other water-diverting cities farther upstream, the problem was solved by running a canal across the valley from the Tigris River. Now there was plenty of water, and it was used so liberally that a rise of the ground-water table set in. As the water table came closer to the ground surface, capillary force drew the ground water to the surface, where it evaporated rapidly in the hot sun. The result: an even faster accumulation of salt. When the water table came up still farther, it saturated the roots of the barley plants, devastating the crops. Unknowingly, through their greed for water, these Sumerians had sealed their own fate.

The rising civilization of Babylon was also doomed to fall in turn. Along the Tigris River, east of the modern city of Baghdad, an extremely elaborate system of irrigation canals was evolved. This system was begun in a pre-Babylonian period, 3000 to 2400 B.C. After a long history of abandonments and reconstructions, it was superseded between 200 and 500 A.D. by a final irrigation system based upon a central canal, the Nahrwan Canal. The irrigation system featured long, branching distributaries that proved to be traps for silt. Frequent cleaning out of the silt was required, and it piled up in great embankments and mounds beside the channels. Gradually, silt from the mounds was washed by rains into nearby fields to add layer upon layer to the land surface. According to one estimate, about 3 feet of silt accumulated over the fields in a 500-year period. This rise in level of the farmland by silting made its irrigation all the more difficult. Until the strong central government authority collapsed, things went along well enough. But thereafter, the entire system gradually broke down, and by the 12th century it was abandoned completely. Not long after, Mongol hordes invaded the valley, but by then there remained little of the once prosperous civilization that had held sway for over 4000 years.

Salinization, waterlogging, and silt accumulation have affected nearly every major irrigation scheme practiced on alluvial lands in a desert climate. One might almost say that failure was a built-in feature from the start. Today Pakistan struggles with salinization and waterlogging in a vast irrigation system in the Indus Valley. The lower Colorado River lands, including areas in Mexico, have suffered from salinization. Israel faces the threat of salinization of vital agricultural lands only recently placed in irrigation. Some new tricks may help. For example, soaking the ground through tubes, while keeping the soil covered under a plastic sheet, can reduce the build-up of salt.

Small wonder, then, that new proposals to increase the extent of irrigated desert soils arouse little enthusiasm. Perhaps a record of nearly 100% failure, spread over the entire span of civilization, is beginning to get its message across. In this study unit, we investigate the global deserts as a unique kind of environmental region.

DATA SOURCE: T. Jacobsen and R. M. Adams, Salt and silt in ancient Mesopotamian agriculture, *Science* (1958) vol. 128, pp. 1251-1258; Erik P. Eckholm, Salting the earth, *Environment* (1975) vol. 17, no. 7, pp. 9-15.

Man and Exotic Rivers

A world population map is a fascinating document. Why, you ask, is this area blank and that area deeply colored to show a high population density? We have already answered this question with regard to some sparsely populated areas, which proved to be rainforest, and some densely populated regions, which proved to be alluvial and deltaic plains in the monsoon lands of Southeast Asia. One place on the population map is sure to catch your eye—the Nile Valley of Egypt. From south to north a ribbon of densely populated ground follows the Nile from Ethiopia to the Mediterranean Sea. The Nile Valley, bounded on either side by desert, holds an **exotic river,** a stream that crosses a desert. An exotic river is sustained in its flow by a source region of water surplus, usually a highland area or mountain chain where orographic precipitation is concentrated. Other exotic rivers are the Tigris and Euphrates in Mesopotamia, the Jordan in Israel, the Indus in Pakistan, the Helmand in Afghanistan, and the Colorado in the southwestern United States. All of these exotic rivers have been tapped to provide irrigation for desert soils formed on alluvium of the river floodplain or its low-lying alluvial terraces. Desert soils have proved remarkably fertile under irrigation. There have been many problems, as we shall see, particularly with the buildup of salts in the soil. To understand the impact of irrigation upon the desert environment, we will need to examine the climate and soil-water budget of the desert, along with desert soils and the desert biome.

Deserts of the Globe

The world's great desert regions fall into two major classes: (1) tropical deserts and (2) midlatitude deserts. (We exclude the cold desert of the arctic zone and ice sheets).

The tropical deserts are a result of the Hadley cell circulation in which air subsides over the subtropical zone (Unit 3). Adiabatic warming of the descending air reduces its relative humidity and tends to eliminate cloudiness. The result is the formation of persistent subtropical high-pressure belts centered over the tropics of Cancer and Capricorn. As you learned in Unit 10, these high-pressure belts consist of a number of cells, within which are the source regions of tropical air masses. Cells situated over the continents are the source regions of the continental tropical air mass (see Figure 10.3).

The midlatitude deserts occupy continental interiors in the midlatitude zone. They exist because of the rain-shadow effect, which we explained in Unit 5. In this region of prevailing westerly winds, mountain ranges develop a rainshadow on the eastern, or lee side of the ranges (Figure 5.11). An example we used is the desert of California and Nevada, located to the lee of the Sierra Nevada (Figure 5.12).

The extent of the world's deserts is shown on the accompanying map, Figure 54.1. The tropical deserts occupy a latitude range of from 15° to 35° N and S. The greatest of all desert belts includes the Sahara Desert, Arabian Desert, Iranian Desert, and Thar Desert of North Africa and Asia, stretching continuously from the Atlantic Ocean to north India. In North America, there is very little land area in this latitude zone, but tropical desert occupies much of the southwestern United States, Lower (Baja) California, and western Mexico. In the southern hemisphere, the largest tropical desert is the Great Australian Desert, occupying most of that continent. Another large tropical desert area is in southern Africa—the Kalahari Desert.

A curious natural phenomenon is that tropical deserts occupy the western coastal zones and even extend out over the adjoining ocean. Even though the ocean surface is capable of supplying large amounts of water vapor for producing clouds and rainfall, the continually subsiding air mass "puts a lid on" by holding the moist marine air to a shallow layer over the water. Nearly rainless coastal deserts of this type occur in Baja California, the coast of Peru and Chile (Atacama Desert), Southwest Africa (Namib Desert), and the coasts of Morocco and Australia (Figure 54.2). Cold ocean currents flow close to shore in these west-coast desert strips, so that persistent fog banks lie offshore.

The midlatitude deserts are poleward extensions of the tropical deserts; there is no gap between them. The greatest deserts in this zone are in central Asia, where they occupy intermountain basins from the Caspian Sea to northern China. The Gobi Desert of Inner Mongolia is the largest of these deserts. In North America, dry climate extends north over the Basin and Range region, east of the Cascades and Sierras, and north over the High Plains into Canada, east of the Rockies. Little of this area is true desert. In South America there is a narrow rainshadow strip of desert to the east of the Andes Range in Patagonia.

Semiarid climate, also called **steppe climate,** borders all of the world's deserts, forming a transition zone into humid climates. On the world map, Figure 54.1, we have shown the semiarid steppes in a lighter shade of color.

Soil-Water Budget of the Desert

The true desert regions of the globe have an annual total precipitation of less than 10 in. (25 cm), while large areas have less than 4 in. (10 cm). The semiarid steppes generally show annual precipitation in the range of 10 to 30 in. (25 to 76 cm). The steppes are typically grasslands of the short-grass prairie; we have already discussed the midlatitude grasslands biome and its soils in Unit 51.

Figure 54.3 illustrates the soil-water budget for a tropical desert station in the heart of the Great Australian Desert. Notice that the sequence of months begins with July, so as to keep the cycles in the same phase as in the northern hemisphere. While rainfall averages are measurable in small amounts in all months, the values of water need are always the larger. Consequently, a soil-water deficit (shortage) prevails throughout all months of the year and racks up a very large annual total. Soil-water storage is close to zero at all times. It is easy to understand why vegetation is sparse in a desert such as this. Great quantities of irrigation water would be needed to support field crops, and much of this would be lost directly by evaporation from the soil. The cost benefits of such a program would need to be carefully weighed before launching a large water importation program.

Desert Soils

Desert soils with well-developed horizons belong to the soil order **Aridisols.** The derivation of the name is obvious. Much of the desert area, however, consists of Entisols lacking in horizons. Aridsols have a pale color—gray or reddish—which is explained by the lack of humus in the soil. Plants are so sparse and grow so slowly that little organic matter is produced to yield humus.

Many Aridisols show a horizon of clay accumulation, the **argillic horizon,** possibly produced by illuviation. However, the processes of eluviation and illuviation that produce strong clay horizons in soils of humid climates are very weak in the desert climate, because rain rarely satu-

Figure 54.1 World map of deserts. (Based on Goode Base Map. Copyright by the University of Chicago. Used by permission of the Department of Geography.)

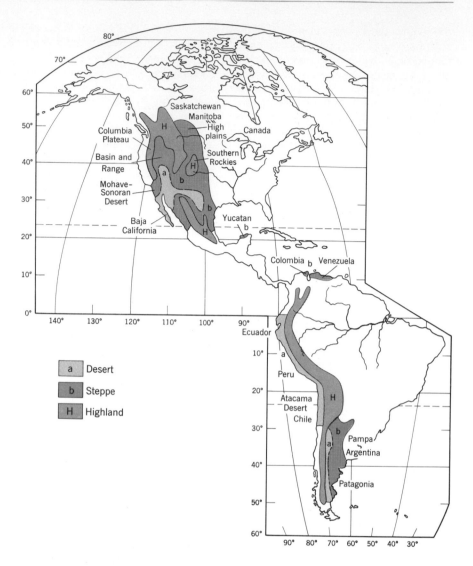

a Desert

b Steppe

H Highland

Figure 54.2 In this air view of the barren coast of Peru, a fog bank can be seen in the distance, lying over the cold Peru current. (Ministerio de Fomento, Peru.)

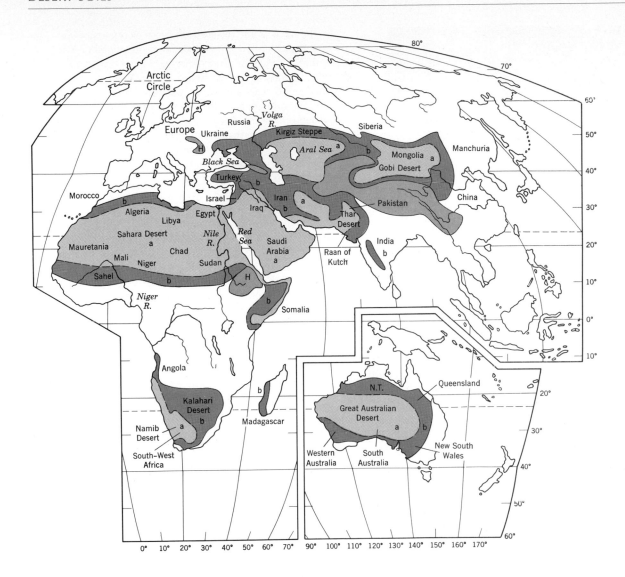

rates more than a shallow surface layer. The argillic horizons are thus considered relics of a more humid climate period, such as the pluvial period associated with the Wisconsin glacial stage.

Many Aridisols have a dense underlying horizon of calcium carbonate accumulation, called the **petrocalcic horizon.** This is a rocklike layer, known in the southwestern United States as **caliche.** It also occurs in the Mollisols of semiarid regions bordering the desert (Figure 54.4).

Aridisols are surprisingly rich in plant nutrients—the base cations and micronutrients. Sparseness of plant cover is due to lack of soil water, not to lack of nutrients. One problem from an agricultural standpoint is that the Aridisols are usually strongly alkaline, or they may contain large amounts of sodium and other salts toxic to most crops. Sodium salts may form a distinctive horizon, the **natric horizon,** in areas of poor drainage. These low, flat surfaces, called **playas,** receive occasional flooding by streams from nearby highlands and may be covered by standing water in a shallow temporary lake. Evaporation of the undrained water leaves behind soluble salts of sodium. When sodium-rich Aridisols are developed for agriculture, it is necessary to provide drainage for the soil and flush

Figure 54.3 The soil-water budget for a desert station. (Data of C. W. Thornthwaite Associates, Laboratory of Climatology, Centerton, N.J.)

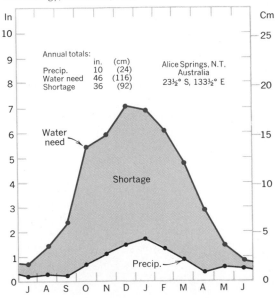

Annual totals:

	in.	(cm)
Precip.	10	(24)
Water need	46	(116)
Shortage	36	(92)

Alice Springs, N.T. Australia 23½° S, 133½° E

Figure 54.4 Caliche, consisting of slabs of rocklike calcium carbonate, lies below a brown soil (Mollisol) in New Mexico.

out the excess salts with irrigation water. Once the problems of high alkalinity and high sodium content have been solved, these fine-textured soils can prove remarkably productive for food and feed crops.

Entisols are widespread in the desert regions. One particular suborder of Entisols, the **Psamments,** occupy large areas in North Africa and the Arabian peninsula, the Kalahari Desert of southern Africa, and the Great Australian Desert. Psamments, Entisols with sandy texture, are developed on areas of sandy alluvium or stabilized sand dunes. The prefix *psamm* is taken from the Greek word *psammos,* meaning "sand." (Areas of Psamments also occur under humid climates; this suborder should not be thought of as exclusively desert soils.)

The Desert Biome

Plants that are adapted to conditions of soil-water deficiency are termed **xerophytes.** One method by which xerophytes conserve water is reduction of transpiration. For example, some xerophytes produce new leaves only after a rain; but when soil water is exhausted, the leaves are shed, and the plant enters a state of dormancy. Other xerophytes have leaves that are heavily cutinized— meaning they are covered with a thick, waxy layer that retards water loss. The shiny layer also acts to reflect sunlight and thus to lower leaf temperatures and reduce transpiration. These adaptations do not necessarily retard transpiration when water is available; in fact, maximum transpiration rates for xerophytes are often greater than those of **mesophytes,** plants adapted to abundant supplies of water. Another xerophytic adaptation is the small leaf. Although the reduced leaf size is usually compensated by an increase in the number of leaves, the small leaf has a more efficient system for supplying water to the cells in time of drought.

The cacti of the desert biome are examples of **succulents,** xerophytes that store large quantities of water within stem tissues. Succulent cacti have low transpiration rates at times of soil water deficiency because their thickened stems have a lower surface area per unit of cellular volume, and because their leaf pores (stomata) remain closed during the day to open only at night. Cacti and many other xerophytes have very extensive, very shallow root systems that allow them to utilize the water from the briefest of showers or from the condensation of dew on the soil surface on clear, still nights.

Other mechanisms are used by plants to cope with the drought periods of the desert. Some plants simply avoid the problem by having a very short life cycle and spending the drought period as dormant seeds. When a rare, soaking rain occurs, these plants not only germinate, grow, and flower rapidly but also set their seed before soil water is exhausted. Because these annual plants are so short-lived, they are referred to as **ephemeral annuals.** Also in a special category are **phreatophytes,** perennial desert plants with deep roots that draw upon ground water held in alluvium of valley floors.

To cope with shortage of water, **xeric animals,** those adapted to dry conditions, have evolved methods that are somewhat similar to those used by the plants. Many of the invertebrates exhibit the same pattern as the ephemeral annuals—evading the dry period in dormant stages. When rain falls, they emerge to take advantage of the new and short-lived vegetation. The tiny brine shrimp of the Great Basin, for example, may wait many years in dormancy until normally dry lake beds fill with water, an event that occurs perhaps three or four times a century. The shrimp then emerge and complete their life cycles before the lake evaporates. Many species of birds regulate their behavior to nest only when the rains occur, the time of most abundant food for their offspring.

By nature mammals are poorly adapted to desert environments, yet many survive there by employing a variety of mechanisms to avoid water loss. Just as plants reduce transpiration to conserve water, so many desert mammals do not sweat through skin glands; they rely instead on other methods of cooling. For example, the huge ears of the jackrabbit serve as efficient radiators of heat to the sky. Calculations have shown that a jackrabbit sitting in a shaded depression could dispose of about one-third of its metabolic heat load through longwave radiation from the uninsulated ears to the clear desert sky above. Many of the desert mammals conserve water by excreting highly concentrated urine and relatively dry feces. In addition, many are able to use to their advantage metabolic water, formed by the normal oxidation of carbohydrate. The desert mammals also evade the heat by nocturnal activity. In this respect, they are joined by most of the rest of the desert fauna, spending their days in cool burrows in the soil and their nights foraging for food.

The North American deserts are usually divided into two groups: the northern, or cool deserts of the Great Basin, which experience cold winter temperatures, and the southern, or hot deserts (Mohave, Sonoran, and Chihua-

Figure 54.5 Sagebrush semidesert near the Vermilion Cliffs, Kanab, Utah. (Douglas Johnson.)

huan), ranging from southern California and northwestern Mexico into west Texas, in which winter temperatures remain warm. The biota of the northern deserts is simpler and less diverse than that of the southern deserts. The plant formation class found here is semidesert and the climate is semiarid. Sagebrush is the dominant plant over well-drained upland and alluvial fan surfaces; it is often accompanied by such other tough woody plants as greasewood and blackbrush (Figure 54.5). The southern, hot deserts possess a much greater variety of species (see Figure 41.4l). Here are many succulents, including the giant saguaro cactus.

Desert Irrigation and Salinization

Man's interaction with the desert environment is as old as civilization itself. Two of the earliest sites of civilization—Egypt and Mesopotamia—lie in the tropical deserts. The key to Man's successful occupation of the deserts lies in availability of large supplies of water from nondesert sources. This is a concept so familiar to all that it scarcely needs to be stated. For Egypt and Mesopotamia, the water sources of ancient times were exotic rivers deriving their flow from regions having a water surplus and flowing across the desert region because of geologic events and controls having nothing to do with climate.

Irrigation of desert soils on flat alluvial surfaces involves an elaborate system of diversion dams and distributary canals. A dam or low barrier is built across the river, upstream from the area to be irrigated, and a part of the flow diverted into a canal. The canal, or a closed pipelike conduit, carries the water downvalley on a lesser gradient than the river channel, and thus arrives at the delivery area at a sufficiently high level to be distributed by gravity flow to the cultivated surfaces. Control gates are used to admit water to secondary irrigation ditches. From these the water is finally diverted into furrows that cross the fields (Figure 54.6). (Various other types of irrigation systems are used in dry climates and to supplement stored soil water in humid climates.)

Can Man increase production of food by expanding agriculture into the deserts, both in tropical and midlatitude regions? Making the desert bloom is a romantic concept fostered on the American scene for generations by bureaucrats, politicians, and land developers. Were these promoters of vast irrigation schemes working in the long-term public interest? Only in recent years have the undesirable environmental impacts of desert irrigation come to the forefront. Yet we could have read the modern scenario in the history of rise and fall of the Mesopotamian civilization. Ultimately, all major desert irrigation systems on low alluvial plains suffer from two undesirable side effects—salinization and waterlogging of the soil.

The irrigated area is subject to very heavy soil-water losses through evapotranspiration. Salts contained in the irrigation water remain in the soil and increase in concentration. This process is called **salinization.** Ultimately, when salinity of the soil reaches the limit of tolerance of the plants, the land must be abandoned. Prevention or cure of salinization may be possible by flushing the soil salts downward to lower levels by use of more water. This remedy requires greater water use than for crop growth alone.

Infiltration of large volumes of water into low, flat alluvial plains causes a rise in the water table and may, in time, bring the zone of saturation close to the surface. This phenomenon is called **waterlogging.** Crops cannot grow in perpetually saturated soils. Furthermore, when the water table rises to the point that upward movement under capillary action can bring water to the surface, evaporation is increased and salinization is intensified.

One of the largest of the modern irrigation projects affected adversely by salinization and waterlogging lies within the basin of the lower Indus River in Pakistan. Here

Figure 54.6 Irrigation of desert sandy loam, near Palm Springs, California. (N. L. Reglein.)

the annual rate of rise of the water table has averaged about 1 ft (0.3 m), while the annual increase in land area adversely affected is on the order of 50,000 acres (20,000 hectares).

The question of expanding irrigation agriculture in the southwestern United States was recently studied by the Committee on Arid Lands of the American Association for the Advancement of Science. In their 1972 report this body recommended that additional large-scale importation of irrigation water from distant sources should be made only where there are compelling reasons to do so. One such reason is to augment rapidly failing ground-water supplies in districts already under irrigation. A second is to arrest the progress of salinization in areas already under irrigation. In short, they agreed that additional water should be imported only to prevent social and economic disruption in established irrigated areas. The lesson is that the search for new regions in which to expand agriculture should be directed to other, more favorable environments where the scales are not so heavily weighted by enormous evaporative water losses.

Man and Food Resources

In this series of seven study units on the interrelationships among Man, soils, and climate we have sampled a wide range of global environments. Other environments important to Man were omitted or touched upon only lightly. Yet we have sampled the full spectrum from humid climates with a large water surplus to desert climates. We have found environments highly productive of food and others poorly endowed with the soil nutrients or soil water needed to be productive. What we have revealed should be enough to dispel the naive idea that large areas of the continents are simply awaiting agricultural expansion to supply human needs. We realize, instead, that increases in the world's food crops can only be won by spending large amounts of cultural energy on overcoming or counterting the natural disadvantages of climate and soil. This is a sobering thought when combined with the realization that the human population is continuing to grow and that our supplies of energy and chemicals from fossil fuels are limited.

Facing page: Maine coast, Mount Desert Island, Acadia National Park. (Photograph by Hylander.)

PART VII **Man and Scenery –
the Wilderness Resource**

Unit 55
River Gorges, Rapids, and Waterfalls

The Great Railroad War

The winning of the West involved a lot of shooting. One notable shooting incident took place over a deep canyon, and the rights of a railroad to use it. This was the Great Railroad War, waged between 1876 and 1880 for possession of the Royal Gorge of the Arkansas River in central Colorado. The gorge is only a few miles long, but it is over 1000 feet deep, with near-perpendicular walls of granite. The river at the bottom runs in rapids over a bouldery bed, with scarcely room for a person to stand beside it, let alone for a railroad line.

The contestants in the Great Railroad War were the Denver & Rio Grande and the Atchison, Topeka & Santa Fe, the latter an outfit of unlimited resources, financed by dudes from Boston. The Rio Grande was a local outfit, the brainchild of Gen. William G. Palmer. He planned to open up the Rocky Mountain region with a new system of railroad lines.

The Royal Gorge, or Big Canyon, as it was known locally, was to be used by General Palmer's line as a means of crossing the Colorado Front Range, a formidable barrier in the path of east-west travel. Meantime, the Santa Fe people had designs on the Royal Gorge for their own railroad. They planned a mass attack upon the gorge so as to occupy it before the Rio Grande could move and defend its property. Through the telegraph, which the Rio Grande luckily controlled, the attack plans leaked out. To forestall its attackers, the Rio Grande made plans to start grading the line through the gorge on April 20, 1878. But when the general manager of the Santa Fe got wind of this strategy, he sent his civil engineer to occupy the gorge immediately with a survey and grading party. Because the Rio Grande wouldn't let the engineer ride on their trains, he had to ride horseback to the mouth of the gorge at Canyon City.

His exhausted horse fell dead within three miles of Canyon City, and he ran the rest of the way. Once there, he recruited a force of several hundred armed men, led them to the mouth of the gorge, and fortified the position. He had popular support because the local citizenry hated the Rio Grande folks and were glad of a chance to get even.

A long period of sporadic armed conflict set in, with shootings and bloodshed. The record is not specific about engagements and casualties, so we

In this 1910 photograph, steam locomotives labor to haul a freight train up the steep grade of the Royal Gorge of the Arkansas River. (A. K. Lobeck.)

392

can't say much more. Rio Grande engineers and graders descended into the canyon by ropes, to stand waist-deep in ice-cold water as they surveyed the grade and began blasting the hard granite. Even mules and carts were lowered by rope, so that construction camps could be set up in the bottom of the gorge. With both companies trying to work at the same time in these narrow confines, it is little wonder that many hand-to-hand fights broke out and many shots were exchanged.

The Great Railroad War finally came to an end in 1880, when the Federal Supreme Court ruled in favor of the Rio Grande. We are told that the legal battles involved some of the finest lawyers of the country and that "the encounters in the field were marked by deeds of heroism and bloodshed that were worthy of a better cause."

Times have changed. The environmentalists are here! Let us rewrite in fancy the events of 1876-1880 in the context of our times:

The Denver Dispatch, April 20, 1976: Attempts to obtain approval from the Environmental Protection Agency (EPA) for construction of a high-speed monorail through the Royal Gorge were thwarted today by a coalition of environmentalist groups, including the Sierra Club, the National Audubon Society, the Friends of the Earth, and the National Parks and Conservation Association. Lawyers for this coalition testified before the EPA environmental impact hearing that the Royal Gorge is the only unspoiled canyon left in the United States and the only remaining habitat of both terrestrial and aquatic ecosystems unique to the Southern Rockies. The environmental impact report submitted by the Denver & Rio Grande was labeled a "whitewash" by a Sierra Club Spokesman, who pointed out that the report failed to take into account the effect of air pollution from engine exhausts upon delicate flora of the canyon walls.

He noted further that waste lubricating oil, dripping from the monorail cars into the river would prove toxic to sensitive detritus feeders on the bed of the channel.

The Washington Times, November 10, 1980: The Supreme Court today upheld by a vote of 7 to 2 a lower court order barring construction of the proposed monorail line through the Royal Gorge in Colorado. In delivering the majority decision, the Chief Justice remarked: "We have saved a priceless wilderness area for the spiritual renewal of countless generations of Americans to come."

The Denver Dispatch, July 8, 1982: Park officials of the Royal Gorge Wilderness Preserve reported today that the thousands of hikers, boat riders, and canoeists who descended upon the Preserve during the past Fourth of July weekend completed the total destruction of the natural ecosystems of the inner walls and channel of the Royal Gorge. One park ranger told this reporter: "The whole place is a shambles . . . every plant and bush has been trampled into the ground. . . . The river stinks with pollution . . . dead fish floating belly-up everywhere . . . and you should see the beer cans . . . and the graffiti on every rock surface in reach of a spray can!"

With this unit, we begin an investigation of the scenery of selected types of wild and rugged terrain which still remain, in part at least, a national resource upon which no value can be assessed in dollars. We will learn about the geomorphic processes and geologic structures that have produced spectacular landforms in areas set aside as national parks and monuments, and as wilderness areas.

DATA SOURCE: M. R. Campbell (1922) *Guidebook of the Western United States,* Part E, Bulletin 707, U.S. Geological Survey, U.S. Govt. Printing Office, Washington, D.C.

The Wilderness Ethic

In this group of study units we look at a number of landscape types that involve striking scenery and often a terrain so rugged that the inroads of Man's agricultural and urban impact have long been delayed. Our region of concern is primarily North America in midlatitudes, where only four centuries have seen a total wilderness partly transformed to fields, highways, and cities. Conquest of the American wilderness was never questioned so long as the frontier ethic prevailed. On the contrary, conquest of nature was the cornerstone of the frontier ethic. As plains and rolling hills were altered to suit the human population, some for-

bidding areas were bypassed. Appalachia was one of these; it was merely a mountain barrier to be leaped. Reaching the limit of the High Plains, the pioneer farmers leaped again, this time to the Pacific Coast, leaving almost untouched the Rocky Mountains, the Colorado Plateau, the Great Basin, the Sierras, and the Cascades. Human attack upon these rugged lands was then mounted by ranchers, miners, and lumbermen. Soon the scars of mining could be seen from afar on many mountainsides in the Rockies.

Quite apart from the issues of conserving natural resources for prolonged production and consumption there arose in the minds of a few western travelers the idea that certain selected scenic areas must be set aside as national parks—islands of pristine nature in a battlefield of resource exploitation. One such person who comes to mind is John Muir, the naturalist and author. We think of Muir as a leading crusader for setting aside natural parks in the Sierras—Sequoia and Yosemite, for example. Another figure in this crusade was the pioneer photographer, William Henry Jackson, who first brought back to eastern audiences photographs of the Rocky Mountain region, including the Yellowstone Park area of western Wyoming.

Through the first three decades of the 1900s, although the major national parks and numerous national monuments had been set aside throughout the West, exploitation of natural resources went forward almost unchecked. By now a new form of resource exploitation had gained momentum: the building of large dams by the U.S. Bureau of Reclamation for the purposes of diverting water to irrigation systems in intermountain valleys and of generating electric power.

The conservation movement, which was also evolving through this period, seems to have addressed itself primarily to limiting the abuses of resource use and to prolonging the life expectancy of resources. The focus remained on the economic value of forests, grazing lands, and mineral deposits, and upon the concept of national protection and regulation to counter excesses of private exploitation. The Bureau of Reclamation grew in stature as an American hero-figure, converting the "worthless" desert floors into "fruited plains."

The **wilderness ethic** seems to have gained wide popular support only in the past decade or two. The central concept is that there is intrinsic worth in large natural areas, as yet unimpacted by Man, simply because they are functioning ecosystems, and because they can revive and uplift the spirit of humans who penetrate those wild areas to observe but not to destroy. The idea that a wilderness has value to a society merely through its existence is not easily appreciated by a nation that has judged value in terms of the dollar yield of a product on the open market.

The newest dimension to be added to this already complex conflict of Man over the disposition of nature's resources is the rising pressure of recreation as an industry and as a destructive force. A new class of automotive devices forms the mechanized cavalry of an army of citizens who fan out from the cities in weekend and summer waves to infiltrate the wilderness. The recreational vehicle, or RV, may be a camper, house trailer, or a van equipped for housekeeping. The particular breed of recreational vehicle with the greatest wilderness-penetrating power is the off-the-road vehicle, or ORV; a four-wheel drive vehicle or a specialized motorcycle designed to surmount steep hillsides. The RVs have overwhelmed every state and national park facility from the ocean shore to the high mountains. No part of the barren desert is denied to them. Every accessible lake and reservoir is invaded weekly by an armada of power boats brought on trailers and rolled into the water down paved ramps provided by courtesy of the government through public funds. The phenomenal rise in skiing as a popular sport is another new form of impact upon high mountains. A ski resort also attracts a community of vacation homes, used both in winter and in summer,

as well as resort hotels popular as conference centers.

Study units in this group—Man and Scenery—present the physical geography of a number of classes of scenic regions in which we find some remaining wilderness areas, or areas only lightly impacted by Man. All are threatened in one way or another by a wide spectrum of exploitational activities. A knowledge of the geomorphology of these landscapes will broaden the range of appreciation possible by those of you who value the wilderness resource for the learning experience it can provide.

Evolution of a River Gorge

The evolution of a river gorge can be visualized in terms of a series of stages in the life history of a stream. This evolutionary concept was introduced by the American geographer, William Morris Davis. Any landscape, according to Davis, could be viewed as changing with time through a succession of stages, just as organisms pass through a life cycle of growth to reach an end stage.

The initial stage in the life history of a stream occurs as soon as a new land surface is created by uplift and dislocation of a portion of the earth's crust. We assume here for simplicity of discussion that the surface was formerly under the ocean and has now become exposed for the first time (Figure 55.1A). Runoff must flow down the initial slopes, whatever their form. Water flow will be concentrated where slight depressions exist in the slopes, causing the development of stream channels. These are quickly deepened by erosive action of the water and any loose rock particles it carries. Original depressions will fill up with water, making lakes. Overflow at the lowest points on the rims of these lake basins will serve to make a connected system of drainage from higher to lower lakes. Thus the stream system comes into existence. The initial stage is characterized by falls, rapids, and lakes along its course (Figure 55.1A).

Once formed, the stream enters upon the **young stage.** Deepening of the channel is the principal activity of a young stream, whose capacity for load exceeds the load available to it. Lake outlets are cut through, draining the lakes and extending the stream across the old lake floors. Waterfalls are cut down at the lip until they are nothing more than rapids. A deepening gorge or canyon is perhaps the most striking landform associated with a young stream. The gorge is steep-walled and has a V-shaped cross section. The stream occupies all the bottom of the gorge. From the steep walls much weathered rock material is shed into the stream. Landslides occur frequently, large fallen masses sometimes temporarily damming the stream. Steep slopes of loose rock fragments may here and there extend down into the water. Because of rapid denudation of the steep valley walls, bedrock outcrops are conspicuous, locally forming bold cliffs (Figure 55.1B).

The environmental importance of the gorge of a young river can be readily imagined. There is no room for roads or railroads between the stream and the valley sides; road beds must be cut or blasted at great expense and hazard from the valley walls. Maintenance is expensive because of undercutting by the stream and the sliding and falling of

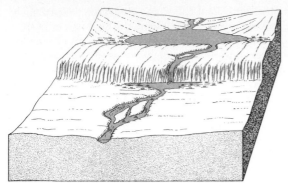

A. In the initial stage a stream has lakes, waterfalls, and rapids.

B. By middle youth the lakes are gone, but falls and rapids persist along the narrow incised gorge.

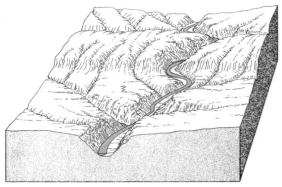

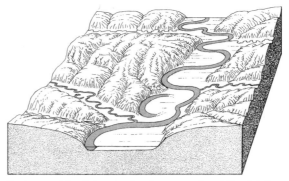

C. Early maturity brings a smoothly graded profile without rapids or falls, but with the beginnings of a floodplain.

D. Approaching full maturity, the stream has a floodplain almost wide enough to accommodate its meanders.

Figure 55.1 Stages in the life history of a stream. (After E. Raisz.)

rock, which can wipe out or damage the road bed. Yet, as we found in the opening essay of this unit, a young gorge may afford the only passage through a mountain range.

Another environmental consideration is that a young stream is not navigable, even though it might otherwise have a sufficient discharge.

The steep gradients of young streams, especially at waterfalls, make them important sources of hydroelectric power. Most large young rivers, however, do not possess abrupt drops in gradient, and so it is necessary to build high concrete dams in order to create artificially the vertical drop necessary for turbine operation. An example is the Hoover Dam, behind which lies Lake Mead, occupying the canyon of the young Colorado River.

As a stream progresses through the stage of youth it removes falls and rapids from its course, creating a smooth, even gradient. Deepening of the valley now becomes greatly retarded, allowing the canyon or gorge walls to be worn down to more moderate slopes.

The **mature stage** is reached when the stream has completed its phase of rapid downcutting and has prepared itself a smoothly graded course. It is now in a state of balance, or equilibrium, in which the average rate of supply of rock waste to the stream from all its tributaries and their

slopes is equal to the average rate at which the stream can transport the load. In other words, the stream's capacity is satisfied by the load supplied. (This concept was developed in Unit 32.)

Immediate evidence of the earliest stage of maturity is the beginning of development of a flat valley floor. During enlargement of a bend, the river channel shifts toward the outer part of the bend, leaving a strip of relatively flat land, or floodplain, on the inner side of the bend (Figure 55.1C).

As lateral cutting by the stream continues, floodplain strips grow wider and presently join to form more or less continuous belts along either side of the stream (Figure 55.1D). The stream bends are now larger and more smoothly rounded, forming meanders. As valley development progresses the floodplain becomes wide enough to accommodate the meanders without cramping their form. The stream has then reached the stage of full maturity.

Waterfalls

Waterfalls of major rivers are a comparative rarity in nature. Existence of a large waterfall usually means that a favorable geologic structure exists at the point of the falls. One favorable structure is a massive formation of hard the origin of the Great Lakes, recall that the Niagara River came into existence just following the final retreat of the Wisconsin ice sheet. Overflow of Lake Erie into Lake Ontario happened to be situated over a gently inclined layer of dolomite (calcium-magnesium carbonate), beneath which lies easily eroded shale (Figure 55.2). As the detailed diagram shows (Figure 55.3), the fall is maintained by continual undermining of the hard dolomite by erosion in the plunge-pool at the base of the fall. In this way the falls have retreated about 6.5 mi (10.4 km) since they were formed some 12,000 to 13,000 years ago at a point on the Niagara Escarpment, leaving behind a spectacular gorge. Present rate of recession of the Canadian Falls is some 4 to 6 ft (1 to 2 m) per year but has varied considerably from century to century. The height of the falls is now 170 ft (52 m) and its discharge about 200,000 cubic feet per second (17,000 cubic meters per second). The drop of Niagara Falls is utilized for the production of hydroelectric power by the Niagara Power Project, in which water is withdrawn upstream from the falls and carried in tunnels to generating plants located 4 miles downstream from the falls. Capability of this project is 2400 megawatts of power, making it the largest single producer in the western hemisphere.

The second class of larger waterfalls are those formed by recent tectonic activity. In the rift valley region of East Africa, crustal blocks have been dislocated by recent faulting, creating lake basins and sharp drops in the gradients of major rivers, and giving rise to falls and rapids. An example is Murchison Falls on the upper (White) Nile River near the north end of a down-dropped crustal block (graben) in which Lake Albert is situated. The height of this fall is 130 ft (40 m). Victoria Falls on the Zambezi River, height 355 ft (108 m), owes its drop to erosion of weak rock along a fault zone (Figure 55.4).

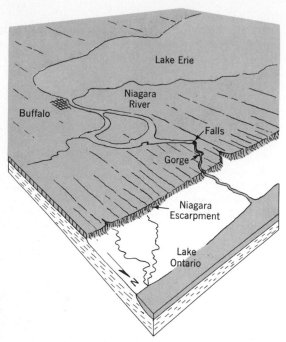

Figure 55.2   A bird's-eye view of the Niagara River with its falls and gorge carved in strata of the Niagara Escarpment. View is toward the southwest from a point over Lake Ontario. Redrawn from a sketch by G. K. Gilbert, 1896. (From A. N. Strahler) [1971]*The Earth Sciences,* 2nd ed., Harper & Row, New York.)

sedimentary rock overlying a weak shale or clay formation. Another favorable structure is a recent fault, which has uplifted one crustal block above the level of the adjoining block, producing a high fault scarp over which the river must descend.

An example of a waterfall of the first type is Niagara Falls, on the Niagara River connecting Lake Erie with Lake Ontario. Referring back to Unit 16, in which we outlined

Figure 55.4   This air view of Victoria Falls of the Zambezi River shows that the river has excavated a long cleft in the bedrock, probably along a fault zone. (Photographer not known.)

Figure 55.3   Niagara Falls is formed where the river passes over the eroded edge of a massive limestone layer. Continual undermining of weak shales at the base keeps the fall steep. (After G. K. Gilbert and E. Raisz.)

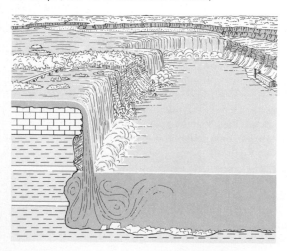

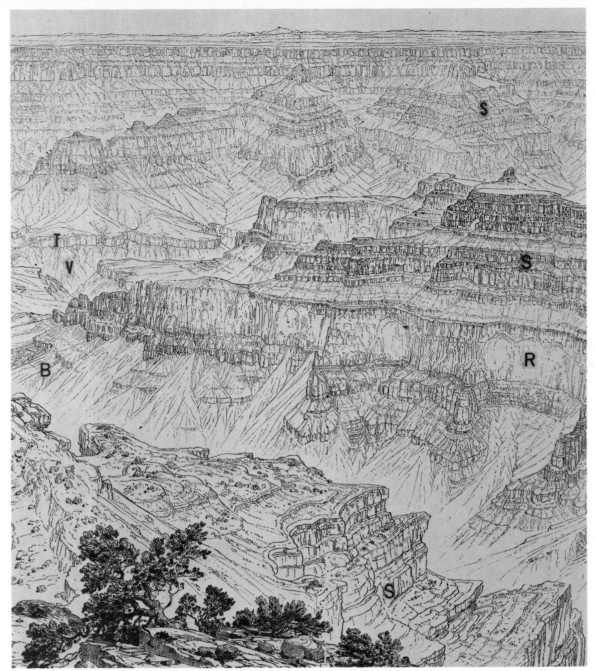

Figure 55.5 Panoramic drawing by the artist W. H. Holmes, looking south across Grand Canyon from Point Sublime. Formations are identified by letters; S, Supai; R, Redwall; B, Bright Angel; T, Tapeats; V, Vishnu. (From C. E. Dutton [1882] *Tertiary History of the Grand Canyon District,* Washington, D.C., U.S. Govt. Printing Office, Plate 29.)

The Grand Canyon of the Colorado River

The wilderness resource is epitomized in the Grand Canyon of the Colorado River, in northern Arizona. Perhaps no other natural feature in North America has been more highly celebrated in poetry and prose or more lavishly illustrated by photography and landscape painting. Many other great canyons are as deep and as long as Grand Canyon, but none can match it in the display of intricately eroded sedimentary strata which form the stepped upper walls (see Figure 21.4).

The unique character of the Grand Canyon lies in its dual structure. The upper 3000 ft (900 m) of the canyon walls are eroded in flat-lying strata of Paleozoic age (Figure 55.5), whereas the somber Inner Gorge, which holds

Figure 55.6 The Inner Gorge of Grand Canyon, looking upstream toward the Kaibab Bridge. Bouldery debris (left), swept down from a steep side-canyon in flood, forces the river against the opposite bank, undermining the steep rock wall (right). Mesas of horizontal strata loom on the skyline. (John S. Shelton.)

the youthful Colorado River, is a V-shaped trench carved in metamorphic rocks of Precambrian age (Figure 55.6). In this narrow gorge, which Major John Wesley Powell named the "Granite Gorge," fierce rapids flow over great boulder masses swept into the main channel from steep side canyons.

The outer sedimentary walls of Grand Canyon consist of formations of shale, limestone, and sandstone. The resistant formations, which are limestone and sandstone strata, form sheer cliffs, undermined continually as underlying weak shale formation are eroded by running water. The result is a succession of steps or benches. Isolated masses, detached from the canyon rim by erosion of the upper strata, form buttes, characteristic landforms of the canyon lands of the Colorado Plateau.

Man's Impact on River Gorges

The most obvious threat to wilderness areas contained in deep mountain gorges and canyons is the construction of high concrete dams for urban water supplies, irrigation, hydropower, or a combination of these functions. Inundation by a deep reservoir is, of course, the one total form of environmental destruction. In Unit 32 we explained how a dam on a large river can upset the channel equilibrium both upstream and downstream from the dam as a result of regulation of river discharge and the trapping of the sediment load within the reservoir behind the dam.

The Colorado River is impounded by the Hoover Dam downstream from the Grand Canyon National Park as well as upstream by the Glen Canyon Dam. Neither Lake Mead nor Lake Powell, the reservoirs behind these dams, actually lies within the national park, but already a profound effect upon the channel of the Colorado River has been documented within the park area. One effect of the Glen Canyon Dam is from the regulation of flow of the Colorado River through Grand Canyon. Flood stages no longer occur, so that the higher banks of the channel are no longer subjected to abrasion. A new zone of vegetation has formed at a lower level. Because the river now carries a greatly reduced load, scouring and cutting away of sandbars and beaches has occurred, making camping and mooring more difficult for parties descending the river by boat. On the other hand, large numbers of boat parties have trampled the remaining beaches, breaking down the vegetation and adding to the rate of erosion of the remaining sedimentary deposits. Under the impact of this heavy use by boat parties, rare but sensitive native species of plants along the river banks are giving way to hardier invading species.

This example from the Grand Canyon points up a persistent environmental conflict found in the management of national parks and wilderness areas. Although these areas can be effectively closed to logging, mining, grazing, and other commercial forms of degradation, they suffer environmental damage through overuse by the very public they were set aside to serve. Recreational use can have a strong adverse impact upon the physical landscape and the ecosystem, when the level of that use becomes too intense. Again, we see in population growth the seeds of yet another conflict in the making.

Unit 56
The Alpine Environment

John Muir and the Yosemite

Of all the names of those who strove to preserve the western wilderness, certainly the most widely revered is that of naturalist John Muir. For most of us, Muir's name is linked inseparably in history with the High Sierra and its parks—Yosemite, Sequoia, and Kings Canyon. Muir was a remarkable person, for he did in fact dwell in that wilderness year after year, but all the while writing profusely, preaching the concept of transcendentalism—that natural objects were "the terrestrial manifestation of God."

John Muir was born in Scotland. In later life he recalled: "When I was a boy in Scotland, I was fond of everything that was wild, and all my life I've been growing fonder and fonder of wild places and wild creatures." At the age of eleven, John emigrated with his family to central Wisconsin. In 1849 this region was a wilderness where the forest had yet to be cleared for farms. Back-breaking labor and the hazards from Indian attack filled most pioneers with a deep hatred for the forest wilderness; they sought only to change it into friendly open country as rapidly as possible. Not so with John Muir, who in later years referred to his boyhood home as "that glorious Wisconsin wilderness."

By a stroke of good fortune for all American environmentalists John Muir gravitated to a college education at the University of Wisconsin at Madison. There, in the 1860s, Muir took classes in geology and botany, but what is perhaps more significant, in classics and literature as well. He was introduced to the writings of the American transcendentalists Emerson and Thoreau, whose philosophy of nature eminently fitted his own homespun outlook. But, like so many others, Muir became a college dropout, completing only his first two years. He later wrote: "I was only leaving one University for another, the Wisconsin University for the University of the Wilderness." His first wanderings took him on a hiking trip from Indiana to the Gulf of Mexico and in 1869

he wound up in San Francisco. Upon inquiring of the local folk as to where he might find "any place that is wild," he was sent on his way to the lofty Sierra Nevada, and so began a long communion with nature that was to affect the Man-wilderness outlook of Americans for generations to follow.

Muir shunned artificial habitations; he backpacked the trails of the High Country, often alone for weeks on end. A volume of Emerson's *Essays* went with him, and from it he evolved his own brand of the wilderness ethic. We can gain some feeling for his outlook by reading a few short passages from his voluminous writings:

The clearest way into the Universe is through a forest wilderness. . . . I am often asked if I am not lonesome on my solitary excursions. It seems so self-evident that one cannot be lonesome where everything is wild and beautiful and busy and steeped with God that the question is hard to answer—seems silly. . . . Climb the mountains and get their good tidings. Nature's peace will flow

John Muir deep in the wilderness of the High Sierra. (National Park Service.)

into you as the sunshine into the trees. The winds
will blow their freshness into you, and the storms
their energy, while cares will drop off like autumn
leaves. . . . in God's wildness lies the hope of the
world—the great fresh, unblighted, unredeemed
wilderness. . . . I care to live only to entice people
to look at Nature's loveliness.

John Muir was soon involved in a great conflict
over the future of the western wilderness. On the
one hand, there were the *conservationists,* those
who sought to conserve lumber and mineral resources for extended use in the American economy,
but who failed to grasp the notion that wilderness
possessed intrinsic value in its natural undisturbed
state. Unfortunately, the conservationists proved to
be the unwitting agents of exploiters. Conservationists achieved federal legislation to conserve
the nation's forests, but in practice federal forest
management proved scarcely more than an unholy
alliance with lumber interests. Muir sided strongly
with the *preservationists,* those who sought to preserve large areas of wilderness from any exploitation.
He finally parted company entirely with the conservationists and intensified his crusade for the establishment of wilderness preserves. He wrote that
"thousands of tired, nerve-shaken, over-civilized
people are beginning to find out that going to the
mountains is going home; that wildness is a necessity; and that mountain parks and reservations are
useful not only as fountains of timber and irrigating
rivers, but as fountains of life."

On September 30, 1890, a bill setting aside the
Yosemite Valley and its mountain surroundings as a
national park passed both houses of congress with
little difficulty. President Benjamin Harrison signed
the bill.

What would John Muir find today at Yosemite National Park if he chose to go there as an ordinary
visitor? His request for a room reservation at the
Ahwahnee Lodge would have met with this reply:
"Sorry, but the entire lodge is taken that week by the
National Convention of Investment Fund Managers. I
suggest you try to get motel accommodations outside
the park." Complying with this suggestion, and later
hiking several miles to reach the park, Muir would

Yosemite National Park provides bus transport on
roads closed to private autos. (Cecil Stoughton,
National Park Service.)

have found himself in a sea of humanity, oozing
from hotels, cabins, and tent warrens, swarming
across the meadows in search of beer to drink and
bear to feed, trampling the nature trails in all directions, and climbing like so many flies up the sheer
granite face of El Capitan. He could have easily filled
his pack with plastic food wrappers on the short path
to the foot of Bridal Veil Falls. Perhaps he would
have overheard a couple talking about the conces-
sion corporation's plans for a new aerial tramway up
the side of the canyon to reach a viewing facility
(with attached fast-food service) to be perched on
the brink beside the falls. John Muir with his flowing
white mane would be just another "dirty old
man"—an anachronism, less than a century after his
great victory on behalf of the American public.

In this study unit, we will investigate the alpine
environment as a wilderness resource. Yosemite Valley is a great rock trough, carved by an alpine glacier
during the Ice Age. The distant Sierra summits that
tower above Yosemite represent a landscape
carved by glacial ice and alpine weathering
processes.

DATA SOURCE: Roderick Nash (1973) *Wilderness and the American
Mind,* revised edition, Yale University Press, New Haven. References to passages quoted from Muir's writings will be found
documented in Chapter 8, pp. 122-140.

The Alpine Zone

Of all the landforms within a day's drive from cities in the
midlatitude zone of North America and Europe, the least
impacted are the high alpine landforms produced by
glaciation and physical weathering. Here we find the alpine environment projecting above timberline as islands in
a sea of needleleaf forest. We will be dealing with both the

alpine zone and high forest zone, since our subjects are
landforms dominated by glacier erosion and deposition.

Since the end of World War II, the phenomenal rise in
skiing as a popular sport has produced an invasion of
many high, glaciated mountain areas that had previously
escaped penetration because of poor access. Ski resorts
have multiplied in numbers and size, bringing massive
support facilities in the form of hotels, restaurants, night

clubs, gas stations, police and fire departments, highway maintenance units, specialty stores, condominiums, and private vacation homes. These same facilities serve for summer recreation and convention use, with expansion of hiking and horseback trails, and the construction of new Man-made lakes.

In this unit, we will investigate the evolution of alpine scenery by geomorphic processes and then examine the vertical changes, or altitude zonation, in which one ecosystem gives way to another as the life environment becomes progressively more hostile.

Alpine Glaciers

In a science supplement in Unit 6, we explained how glaciers are nourished at high altitudes by snowfall in the zone of accumulation, and how the ice is disposed of by melting and evaporation at the lower end of an alpine glacier in the zone of ablation. In that unit we were concerned with glaciers as hydrologic systems, extremely sensitive to climate changes that upset glacier equilibrium. We now turn to the physical features of alpine glaciers and to their geomorphic activity in creating distinctive landforms.

Figure 56.1 illustrates a number of features of alpine glaciers. The center illustration is of a simple glacier occupying a sloping valley between steep rock walls.

Snow is collected at the upper end in a bowl-shaped depression, the **cirque.** The upper end lies in the zone of accumulation. Layers of snow in the process of compaction and recrystallization constitute the firn. The smooth **firn field** is slightly concave up in profile (upper right). Flowage in the glacial ice beneath carries the excess ice out of the cirque, downvalley. An abrupt steepening of the grade forms a **rock step,** over which the rate of ice flow is accelerated and produces deep **crevasses** (gaping fractures), which form an **ice fall.** The lower part of the glacier lies in the zone of ablation. Here the rate of ice wastage is rapid, and old ice is exposed at the glacier surface, which is extremely rough and deeply crevassed. The **glacier terminus** is heavily charged with rock debris. Recession of the glacier leaves a heap of rubble called the **end moraine.**

The uppermost layer of a glacier is brittle and fractures readily into crevasses, whereas the ice beneath behaves as a plastic substance and moves by slow flowage (lower left). If one were to place a line of stakes across the glacier surface, the glacier flow would gradually deform that line into a parabolic curve, indicating that rate of movement is fastest in the center and diminishes toward the sides. Rate of flowage of glaciers is very slow, indeed, amounting to a few inches per day for the more sluggish alpine glaciers, up to several feet per day for an active alpine glacier.

Glacial ice is usually heavily charged with rock fragments, ranging from pulverized rock flour to huge angular

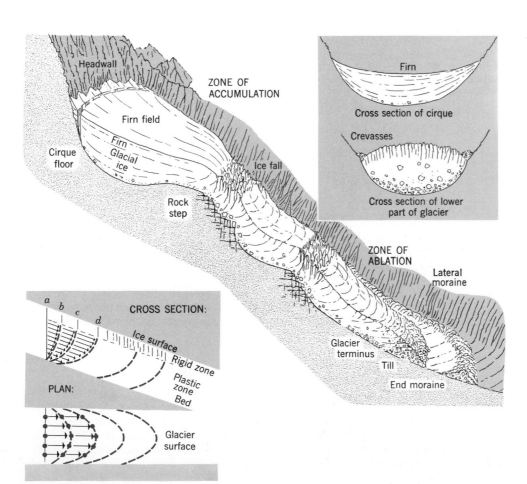

Figure 56.1   Structure and flowage of a simple alpine glacier.

Figure 56.2 The Eklutna Glacier, Chugach Mountains, Alaska, seen from the air. A deeply crevassed ablation zone *(foreground)* contrasts with the smooth-surfaced firn zone *(background)*. (Steve McCutcheon, Alaska Pictorial Service.)

boulders of fresh rock. Some of this material is derived from the rock floor on which the ice moves. In alpine glaciers, rock debris is also derived from material that slides or falls from the cirque wall and valley walls. Glaciers are capable of great erosive work. **Glacial abrasion** is erosion caused by ice-held rock fragments that scrape and grind against the bedrock. By **plucking,** the moving ice lifts out blocks of bedrock that have been loosened by freezing of water in joint fractures.

Accumulating on the edge of the glacier by sliding from the steep valley sides, rock debris is dragged along on the moving ice. Where two ice streams join, this debris is carried downvalley in a narrow band, called a **medial moraine.** Figure 56.2 shows a prominent medial moraine, which can be easily traced upvalley to its source at a point where two ice streams join.

Landforms Made by Alpine Glaciers

Landforms made by alpine glaciers are shown in a series of diagrams in Figure 56.3. Previously unglaciated mountains are attacked and modified by glaciers, after which the

glaciers disappear and the remaining landforms are exposed to view.

Diagram A shows a region sculptured entirely by weathering, mass wasting, and streams. The mountains have a smooth, full-bodied appearance, with rather rounded divides. Soil and regolith are thick. Imagine now that a climatic change results in the accummulation of snow in the heads of most of the valleys high on the mountain sides.

An early stage of glaciation is shown at the right side of Diagram B, where snow is collecting and cirques are being carved by the outward motion of the ice and by intensive frost shattering of the rock near the masses of compacted snow.

In Diagram B, glaciers have filled the valleys and are integrated into a system of tributaries that feed a trunk glacier. Tributary glaciers join the main glacier with smooth, accordant junctions. The cirques grow steadily larger. Their rough, steep walls soon replace the smooth, rounded slopes of the original mountain mass. Where two cirque walls intersect from opposite sides, a jagged, knifelike ridge is formed. In the European Alps this sharp ridge is called an **arête,** a French word meaning "ridge crest." Where three or more cirques grow together, a sharp-pointed peak is formed. The name **horn** is applied to such peaks in the Swiss Alps (Figure 56.4). One of the best known is the striking Matterhorn.

Glacier flow constantly deepens and widens its rock channel, so that after the ice has finally disappeared a deep, steep-walled **glacial trough** remains (Figure 56.3, Diagram C). The U-shape of its cross-profile is characteristic of a glacial trough. Tributary glaciers also carve U-shaped troughs, but they are smaller in cross section, with floors lying high above the floor level of the main trough; they are called **hanging troughs.** Streams, which later occupy the abandoned trough systems, form scenic waterfalls and cascades where they pass down from the lip of a hanging trough to the floor of the main trough. High up in the smaller troughs the bedrock is unevenly excavated, so that the floors of troughs and cirques contain rock basins and rock steps. The rock basins are occupied by small lakes, called **tarns.** Major troughs sometimes hold large, elongated lakes.

Depositional landforms made by alpine glaciers are the end moraines that mark the limit of downvalley extent of the glacier terminus (Figure 56.5). The curved end moraine turns upvalley at each side, and may extend for some distance up the glacial trough as a lateral moraine. A series of end moraines is often found, each marking a temporary period of glacier equilibrium during the retreat phase (Figure 56.6).

Glacial Troughs and Fiords

Many large glacial troughs now are nearly flat-floored because aggrading streams that issued from the receding ice front were heavily laden with rock fragments. Figure 56.7 shows a comparison between a trough with little or no fill and another with alluvial-filled bottom. The deposit of alluvium extending downvalley from a melting glacier is the

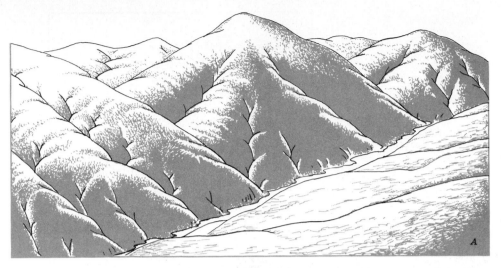

Figure 56.3 Landforms produced by alpine glaciers. (A) Before glaciation sets in, the region has smoothly rounded divides and narrow, V-shaped stream valleys. (B) After glaciation has been in progress for thousands of years, new erosional forms are developed. (C) With the disappearance of the ice a system of glacial troughs is exposed. (After A. K. Lobeck.)

Figure 56.4 The Swiss Alps appear from the air as a sea of sharp arêtes and toothlike horns. In the foreground is a cirque. (Swissair Photo.)

valley train. (Refer to Figure 32.4 showing valley-train deposition in progress by a meltwater stream.)

Where the floor of a trough open to the sea lies below sea level, the sea water enters as the ice front recedes, producing a narrow estuary known as a **fiord** (Figure 56.7D). Fiords may originate either by submergence of the coast or by glacial erosion to a depth below sea level. Fiord excavation below sea level occurs because ice is of such a density that, when floating, from three-fourths to

Figure 56.5 Thick morainal deposits at the lower end of the remnant of the Black Glacier, Bishop Range, Selkirk Mountains, British Columbia. Talus cones line the base of the trough wall. (H. Palmer, Geological Survey of Canada.)

Figure 56.6 End moraines of a former valley glacier appear as curved embankments marking successive positions of the ice margins. (After W. M. Davis.)

nine-tenths of its mass lies below water level. Therefore, a glacier several hundred feet thick can erode to considerable depth below sea level.

Fiords are observed to be opening up today along the Alaskan coast, where some glaciers are melting back rapidly and the fiord waters are being extended along the troughs. Fiords are found largely along mountainous coasts in latitudes 50° to 70° N and S, because orographic precipitation of snow was particularly heavy where maritime polar air masses, carried by the westerlies, encountered coastal mountain ranges (Figure 56.8).

U-shaped glacial troughs provide broad, accessible strips of land at relatively low levels. These are utilized for town sites, for pasture, and as arteries of transportation. In the Italian Alps several great flat-floored glacial troughs extend from the heart of the Alps southward to the plain of northern Italy. These are important environmental controls because they provide smooth and easy access into the heart of the Alps and to the principal Alpine passes. The Brenner Pass lies at the head of a magnificient trough of this type, the Adige River valley.

Frost Action in Alpine Environments

As we noted in Unit 25, one of the most important forms of physical weathering is frost action, the breakup of rock by the expansive force of growing ice crystals occupying joint fractures or pore spaces in the rock. The effects of frost action are particularly striking in high mountains, above timberline, as well as in arctic lands at low al-

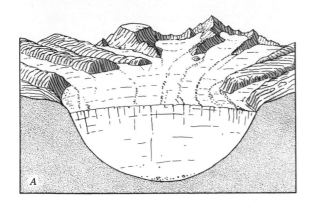

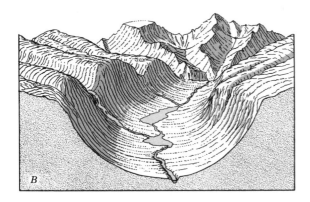

Figure 56.7 Development of a glacial trough. (After E. Raisz.)

Figure 56.8 This Norwegian fiord has the steep rock walls of a deep glacial trough. (Mittet and Co.)

titudes. Frost action superimposes its effects upon the landscape long after alpine glaciers have disappeared from the scene.

Exposed bedrock surfaces above timberline are often found littered with large angular blocks. An extensive surface of this type is called a **felsenmeer** (German for "rock sea"), or simply a **boulder field** (Figure 56.9).

Frost action on cliffs of bare rock in high mountains and in arctic regions detaches rock fragments that fall to the cliff base. Where production of fragments is rapid they accumulate to form **talus slopes** (also called **scree slopes**). Most cliffs are notched by narrow ravines that funnel the fragments into individual tracks, so as to produce conelike

Figure 56.9 A felsenmeer on the summit of Medicine Bow Peak, Snowy Range, Wyoming, at 12,000 ft (3650 m) elevation. The rock is quartzite. (A. N. Strahler.)

Figure 56.10   Talus cones at the base of a frost-shattered cirque headwall. Moraine Lake in the Canadian Rockies. (Ray Atkeson.)

ance created by walking across the slope, or dropping of a large rock fragment from the cliff above, will easily set off a sliding of the surface layer of particles. The upper limiting angle to which coarse, hard, well-sorted rock fragments will stand is termed the **angle of repose,** and is typically an angle of about 33° to 36° with respect to the horizontal.

Vegetation and Life Zones in High Mountains

When ascending a high mountain range, such as the Sierra Nevada in California or the Southern Rockies in Colorado, you will pass through a succession of distinct vegetation zones, finally reaching a tundra zone not unlike that of the arctic lands.

In midlatitudes, where steppe or desert exists at low altitudes, zonation is particularly striking. Figure 56.12 shows the vegetation zones of the Colorado Plateau region of northern Arizona. Zone names, altitudes, dominant forest trees, and annual precipitation are given in the figure. Ecologists have set up a series of **life zones,** whose names suggest the similarities of these zones with latitude zones encountered in poleward travel on a meridian. Desert vegetation of the hot, dry Inner Gorge of the Grand Canyon gives way to grassland and woodland, then to a forest of western yellow pine. Still higher is the Hudsonian zone, 9500 to 11,500 ft (2900 to 3500 m). It bears a needleleaf forest quite similar to subarctic needleleaf forest. As the upper limit of forest, or timberline, is approached, the coniferous trees take on a stunted appearance and decrease in height to low shrublike forms.

A vegetation zone of alpine tundra lies above tree line and resembles in many ways the arctic tundra (Figure 56.13). The snowline is encountered at about 12,000 to 13,000 ft (3700 to 4000 m) in these midlatitudes, which is, of course, much lower than at the equator (see Figure 6.5).

talus bodies arranged side by side along the cliff (Figure 56.10). Where a large range of sizes of particles is supplied, the larger pieces, by reason of their greater momentum and ease of rolling, travel to the base of the cone, whereas the smaller grains lodge in the apex. This mechanism tends to sort the fragments by size, progressively finer from base to apex (Figure 56.11).

Most fresh talus slopes are unstable, so that the disturb-

Figure 56.11   Idealized diagram of talus cones formed at the base of a cliff, which might be 200 to 500 ft (60 to 150 m) high.

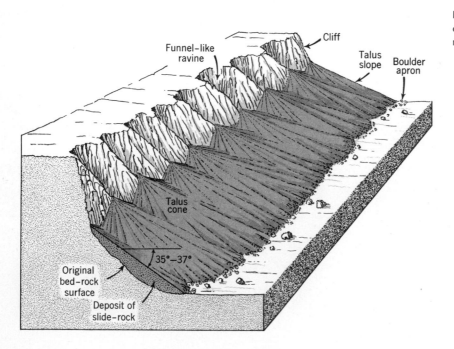

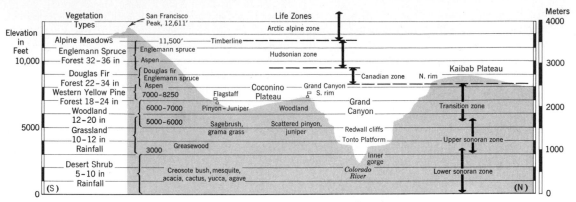

Figure 56.12 Altitude zoning of mountain and plateau climates in the arid southwestern United States. Grand Canyon-San Francisco Mountain district of northern Arizona. (Data of G. A. Pearson, C. H. Merriam, and A. N. Strahler.)

Poleward, the snowline decreases in altitude, eventually reaching sea level in the vicinity of the arctic circle.

As you might expect, soils also change their character with increasing altitude, responding to changes in climate and vegetation. In midlatitudes of the western United States, soil profiles change with life zones. From desert soils (Aridisols) in low basins, the profile changes in succession to brown soils (Mollisols), up to an altitude of about 8000 ft (2400 m). Here, under the needleleaf forest, are Spodosols like those of the subarctic climate. Still higher you would find Inceptisols, Entisols, and Histosols like those of the arctic tundra.

Man's Impact on the Alpine Environment

At first thought, the alpine environment might seem to be largely immune to Man's impact. The sheer rock walls of peaks in the High Sierra can only be conquered by a handful of extremely skilled mountain climbers, or perhaps by helicopter when weather is favorable. The rock-based landforms of alpine glaciation resist change, although they may be scarred by mineral mining and by the grades of highways rising in switchbacks to surmount high passes.

Environmental impact upon the alpine tundra is, however, a real threat. Large areas of our glaciated western

Figure 56.13 Alpine tundra in the center of this view gives way at the left to needleleaf forest at a lower altitude. The bushlike plants are dwarf willow, barely able to grow under the impact of blizzard winds and driving snow. Arapahoe National Forest, Colorado. (U.S. Forest Service.)

ranges have flattened or broadly rounded summit areas, where glaciation reached only a youthful stage and the cirque walls do not intersect in sharp arêtes. There is also much alpine tundra and alpine meadow in the floors of high glacial troughs and cirques. There are many freshwater lakes, as well. Recall from our study of the arctic tundra (Unit 50) that the tundra soil and vegetation is highly sensitive to destruction under the grinding wheels of trucks and the treads of tractors. So it is with the alpine tundra, although thermal erosion by melting permafrost is not a problem. Off-the-road vehicles (ORVs) operating in high mountain areas can wreak havoc on the plant cover of alpine tundra, exposing the soil to accelerated erosion. The tramping of alpine meadows by thousands of summer tourists is also highly destructive. In short, even massive granite ranges such as the Sierra Nevada and the Colorado Front Range have fragile ecosystems, and they must be protected in years to come, as rising urban populations exert stronger and stronger stresses upon the fringes of the wilderness environment.

SCIENCE SUPPLEMENT

Solar Radiation and Air Temperatures at High Altitudes

The rapid decrease in density of the atmosphere with increasing altitude brings with it major changes in the environments of radiation and heat at the ground surface. Recall from Unit 3 and Figure 3.3 that barometric pressure decreases by about one-thirtieth of itself for every 950 ft of altitude increase. Thus at 15,000 ft (4.6 km), an altitude representative of mountain summits in the higher ranges of the western United States, pressure is only about 570 mb, or a little over half the sea-level value. Air density is correspondingly reduced, with the result that the overlying atmosphere reflects and absorbs a much smaller portion of the incoming solar radiation than at sea level.

Measurements of solar radiation at altitude 12,000 to 14,000 ft (3.6 to 4.3 km), taken near the summit of a mountain range in the desert region along the border between California and Nevada, showed noon peak values approaching 2.0 langleys per minute (ly/min) under clear-sky conditions. Compare this value with a June maximum of about 0.7 (ly/min) typical for a sea-level station in mid-latitudes in a humid climate. At the mountain location, the peak of net all-wave radiation reached almost 1.6 langleys per minute, a value about triple that at a sea-level station. Of course, the sea-level data include days with cloud cover as well as clear days, while the mountain measurements are for clear skies only. Nevertheless, the great daytime intensity of incoming and outgoing radiation at the high altitude position is truly remarkable.

Increasing intensity of incoming solar radiation with higher altitude has a profound influence upon air and ground temperatures. Surfaces exposed to sunlight heat rapidly and intensely, shaded surfaces are quickly and severely cooled. Thus, at high mountain locations, air is heated rapidly during the day and cooled rapidly at night. This altitude effect is shown by the increasing spread between high and low air temperature readings from left to right in Figure 56.14.

The contrast between exposed and shaded surfaces is particularly noteworthy at high altitudes. It has been found that temperatures of objects in the sun and in the shade differ by as much as 40 to 50 F° (22 to 28 C°).

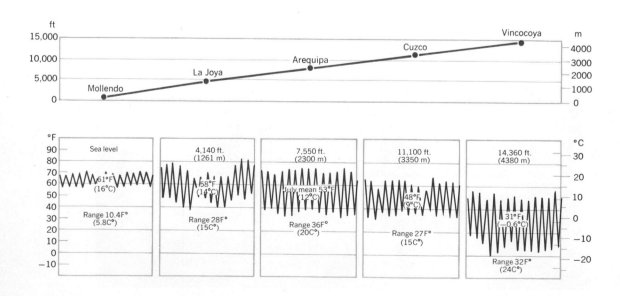

Table 56.1 Altitude and Mean Annual Air Temperature

| | Approximate Altitude | | Approximate Mean Annual Air Temperature | |
	Ft	Km	°F	°C
Belém, Brazil	0	0	80	27
Takengön, Indonesia	4000	1.2	70 (66)	21 (19)
Quito, Ecuador	9500	2.9	59 (47)	15 (9)
Jauja, Peru	11,000	3.4	54 (41)	13 (5)

Table 56.2 Altitude and the Boiling Point of Water

| Altitude | Pressure (height of mercury column) | | | Boiling Temperature | |
Ft	M	In	Cm	°F	°C
Sea level	0	29.9	76	212	100
1000	300	28.8	73	210	99
3000	900	26.8	68	206	97
5000	1500	24.9	63	203	95
10,000	3000	20.7	53	194	90

Increased intensity of solar radiation is accompanied by an increase in intensity of violet and ultraviolet rays; thus sunburn is more severe.

The general decrease in air temperature with altitude has been discussed in Unit 1. Recall that the average environmental lapse rate is about 3½F° per 1000 ft (2 C° per 300m). Using that rate, we might expect a station at an altitude of 10,000 ft (3000 m) to have a temperature about 35 F° (20 C°) below that of a nearby sea-level station. Actually the difference is somewhat less than this amount. In equatorial regions, where the average air temperature of all months of the year is almost a constant figure, the effect of increasing altitude can be seen in the sample figures of Table 56.1. Figures in parentheses are calculated by means of the normal environmental temperature lapse rate, assuming 80 °F (27 °C) to be the sea-level value. That the higher places are considerably warmer than the calculated value can be explained through the absorption and reradiation of solar energy by the ground surface.

Besides the thermal effects we have found, the high altitude environment has other physical effects important to Man and other life forms. At high altitudes, intensity of surface bombardment by cosmic particles is increased, with the result that organisms are subjected to larger doses of ionizing radiation than at sea level. For a mile-high city such as Denver, Colorado, the intensity of ionizing radiation from cosmic sources is about double that at sea level, while at an altitude of 20,000 ft (6 km) the intensity is about seven times greater.

The physiological effects of a pressure decrease on humans are well known from the experiences of flying and mountain climbing. The principal influence is through an insufficient amount of oxygen to supply the blood through the lungs, a condition known as **environmental hypoxia.** At altitudes of 10,000 to 15,000 ft (3000 to 4500 m) mountain sickness (altitude sickness) occurs, characterized by weakness, headache, nosebleed, or nausea. Persons who remain at these altitudes for a day or two normally adjust to the conditions, but physical exertion is always accompanied by shortness of breath.

At reduced pressures the boiling point of water or other liquids is reduced so that cooking time of various foods is greatly lengthened. Table 56.2 gives some data on pressure and boiling point relationships. From these figures it is obvious that the use of pressure cookers will be of great value above 5000 ft (1500 m) wherever the cooking involves boiling of water.

In summarizing the relationship of altitude to radiation and the thermal environment, the important points are that while the average air temperature falls with increasing altitude, the intensities of both incoming and outgoing radiation of energy show a strong increase. You might be tempted to say that climbing to a higher altitude near the equator is like traveling from the equator to the poles. This may be a valid analogy when restricted to average temperatures, but it does not apply at all for the daily ranges.

Unit 57
The Scenery of Rugged Coasts

Islands in Jeopardy

Juan Rodriguez Cabrillo, the Spanish explorer, found them in 1542—a chain of rocky, cliffed islands off the California coast. The Channel Islands lie from 10 to 70 miles from the California mainland shore, but there has been no safety in isolation for the communities of marine mammals and sea birds occupying the many rocky coves and narrow beaches. Under constant attack from crashing surf generated over a vast fetch of Pacific Ocean, the Channel Islands have acquired rugged marine cliffs eroded from solid rock. Surrounded by the cold waters of the California Current, the island shores are shrouded in a low fog much of the time, but little rain falls except in winter, and the island slopes support only a cover of shrubs and grasses.

Chumash Indians lived on the Channel Islands at the time the Spaniards came, for there was abundant food to be had in the rich wildlife of the rocky coasts. There were large numbers of fur seals, sea lions, elephant seals, and sea otters. Large colonies of shore birds lived on the rocky cliffs and on the beaches—pelicans, cormorants, petrels, puffins, and many others. Flocks of grebes, terns, herons, and loons stopped over in their annual migrations, for the Channel Islands are on the Pacific Flyway.

This rich supply of protein was not to pass unnoticed and unexploited by the White Man. Spanish sailors soon transformed the rocky shores into a food source, descending upon the beaches and cliffs to collect bird's eggs, and killing seals to restock the ships' meat larders. Then, in the early 1800s, came the Russians with a massive attack upon the shore mammals. To secure pelts for their fur trade, these invaders slaughtered hundreds of thousands of fur seals and nearly wiped out large herds of elephant seals and sea otters. They salted the meat of these animals to make jerky, shipping both the furs and meat to the Russian colonies in Alaska and points west as far as China.

The Americans, who next descended upon the Channel Islands, took up where the Russians left off. The taking of sea otter pelts, which brought as much as $25 apiece, led to near-extinction of that animal, while herds of elephant seals were reduced to a few hundred surviving individuals. Ranchers brought cattle, sheep, hogs, goats, and burros to the sparsely vegetated islands, with the result that the plant cover was denuded and the soil laid bare to erosion under winter rains.

Lying so close to the huge Los Angeles urban center, it is small wonder that the Channel Islands face new and more powerful impacts. Two minute fragments of the island chain have gained protection under the National Park Service as national monuments—Santa Barbara Island and the Anacapa Islands. A proposal has been made to include the three large westernmost islands—Santa Cruz, Santa Rosa, and San Miguel—under federal protection as parks or national monuments. Of these the largest is Santa Cruz Island, with 97 square miles. It is privately owned by two families, one of which sought to bring their land under commercial zoning status

The intertidal zone, Anacapa Island. (Leonard Lee Rue IV/Bruce Coleman.)

410

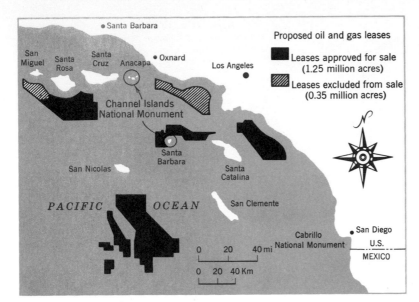

This map shows federal offshore areas along the southern California coast which were proposed for oil and gas exploration by private interests. Areas in solid color were approved for sale as leaseholds in 1975. Areas in the diagonal color were excluded from this sale. (Data from U.S. Dept. of the Interior.)

in order to build a resort community. This move brought an awakening of public interest in steps to protect the islands.

A study completed by the National Park Service in 1959 recommended that all of the Channel Islands should be preserved because of their great scientific and cultural value. Santa Catalina Island, as almost everyone knows, has already been developed as a resort facility under ownership of the Wrigley family. San Clemente and San Nicolas islands, both lying farther out from the mainland than the others, are under administration of the U.S. Navy, as is the westernmost island, San Miguel. Unbelievable as it seems, parts of these islands have been in use by the Navy as target ranges, with great damage to plants, animals, and archeological sites.

As if these multiple threats are not enough, the shore life of the Channel Islands faces what may be its worst impact through massive oil spills. The Santa Barbara Oil Spill of 1969, emanating from a drilling platform in the channel between the mainland and the westernmost islands, gave a small foretaste of what may be expected if new drilling for oil and gas is permitted on a greatly expanded scale over large

offshore areas lying close to the islands. The U.S. Department of the Interior plans to lease over 1¼ million acres of seabottom for oil exploration. Senator John Tunney called this plan "a nightmarish blueprint for disaster."

The fate of the Channel Islands remains in grave doubt. National park status is opposed by coalitions of oil companies, land developers, and ranchers, while the Navy is determined to hold on to at least one island—San Miguel. Conservation groups are strong and vocal, but the alleged need to develop all remaining national petroleum resources as quickly as possible has been a powerful force to override the protectionists' wishes.

The story of the Channel Islands is not unique; it is merely one example of the threats of destruction facing many sections of rugged coast of North America. In this study unit, we investigate the landforms of rugged coasts and the way in which they are originated by geologic processes and shaped by wave action.

DATA SOURCE: Stanley Medders, California's Channel Islands, *National Parks & Conservation Magazine* (1975) vol. 49, no. 10, pp. 11-15.

Rugged Coasts—A National Resource

Along parts of both the Atlantic and Pacific coasts of North America the sea is attacking a rugged, mountainous land. Here solid bedrock meets the impact of storm waves and gives scarcely an inch in a century's time. Low-lying coastlines of weak sand and clay, which we investigated in Unit

35, are dominated by natural changes forced by waves, tide, and winds. We learned that rapid retrogradation of those weak shorelines presents a unique set of coastal management problems. The rugged coasts of solid bedrock have management problems of a different sort. On rugged coasts Man, not the ocean, is the agent of environmental deterioration. The scenery of the rugged coasts is often spectacular, for the steep forested mountain slopes de-

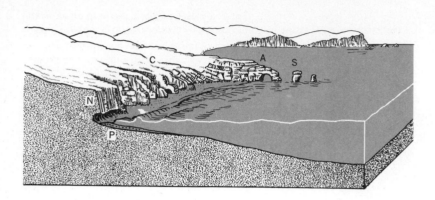

Figure 57.1 Landforms of sea cliffs. A=arch; S=stack; C=cave; N=notch; P=abrasion platform. (After E. Raisz.)

scend to the brink of a sheer rock wall, pounded at its base by surf and carved into an intricate array of promontories and clefts. What could be more satisfying than to build one's summer house on the brink of that cliff? Or perhaps to build a motel and a restaurant, so that others may share in the enjoyment?

Rugged coasts share many wave-eroded landforms in common, but there is a wide range of basic configurations of such coasts and in the succession of geologic events that brought each variety to its present condition. In this unit, we will first review the characteristic landforms of marine erosion found on almost any cliffed coast. We will then attempt to distinguish between a number of basically different coasts and interpret their special features.

Sea Cliffs

Some details of a wave-cut cliff, or **sea cliff,** are shown in Figure 57.1. A deep basal indentation, the wave-cut notch, marks the line of most intense wave erosion. The waves find points of weakness in the bedrock, penetrating deeply to form crevices and sea caves. More resistant rock masses

project seaward and are cut through to make picturesque arches. After an arch collapses the remaining rock column forms a stack, but this is ultimately leveled.

As the sea cliff retreats landward, continued wave abrasion froms an **abrasion platform** (Figure 57.2). This sloping rock floor continues to be eroded and widened by abrasion beneath the breakers. If a beach is present, it is little more than a thin layer of gravel and cobblestones.

Most rugged coastlines present a succession of promontories, or **headlands,** jutting seaward. Between these headlands are open bays, usually marking the places where natural valleys descend to sea level. At these bay heads cliffs are usually low, or may be lacking entirely. Along such a coast, erosional energy of the waves is concentrated on the exposed headlands. Here sea cliffs develop. Sediment from the eroding cliffs is carried by littoral drift along the sides of the bay, converging on the head of the bay (Figure 57.3). The result is a crescent-shaped beach, often called a **pocket beach.** A pocket beach provides a place to launch fishing boats and to beach them safely (Figure 57.4).

Common Kinds of Coastlines

There are many different kinds of coastlines, each kind unique because of the distinctive landmass against which the ocean water has come to rest. One group of coastlines

Figure 57.2 Marine cliffs bordered by a broad abrasion platform. A pocket beach lies at lower left. Pacific coast, south of Cape Flattery, Washington. (Photographer not known.)

Figure 57.3 On an embayed coast, sediment is carried from eroding headlands to the bayheads, where pocket beaches can accumulate. (From A. N. Strahler [1971] *The Earth Sciences*, 2nd ed., Harper & Row, New York.)

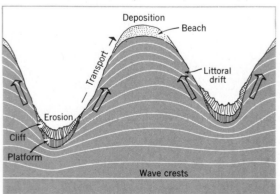

Figure 57.4 The chalk cliffs of Normandy, along the French channel coast, show stacks, arches, and sea caves. This documentary photo, taken in the early 1900s, shows a pocket beach intensively used by fishermen, vacationers, and some of France's greatest Impressionist painters. (Photographer not known.)

derives its qualities from **submergence,** the partial drowning of a coast by a rise of sea level or a sinking of the crust. Another group derives its qualities from **emergence,** the exposure of submarine landforms by a falling of sea level or a rising of the crust. Another group of coastlines results when new land is built out into the ocean by volcanoes and lava flows, by the growth of river deltas, or by the growth of coral reefs.

A few important types of coastlines are illustrated in Figure 57.5. The **ria coast** (A) is a deeply embayed coast resulting from submergence of a landmass dissected by streams. This coast is often rugged, with many offshore islands. A **fiord coast** (B) is deeply indented by steep-walled fiords, which are submerged glacial troughs (Unit 56). The **barrier-island coast** (C) is associated with a recently emerged coastal plain (Unit 35). The offshore slope is very gentle, and a barrier island of sand is usually thrown up by wave action at some distance offshore. Large rivers build elaborate deltas, producing **delta coasts** (D). (Delta coasts and deltaic plains were explained in Unit 36.) The **volcano coast** (E) is formed by eruption of volcanoes and lava

A. Ria coast.

B. Fiord coast.

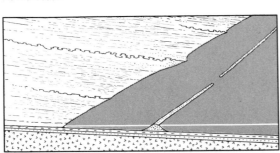

C. Barrier-island coast.

D. Delta coast.

E. Volcano coast *(left).* **F.** Coral-reef coast *(right).*

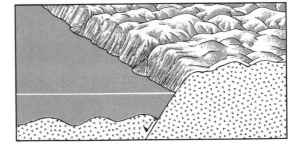

G. Fault coast.

Figure 57.5 Seven common kinds of coastlines are illustrated here. These examples have been selected to illustrate a wide range in coastal features.

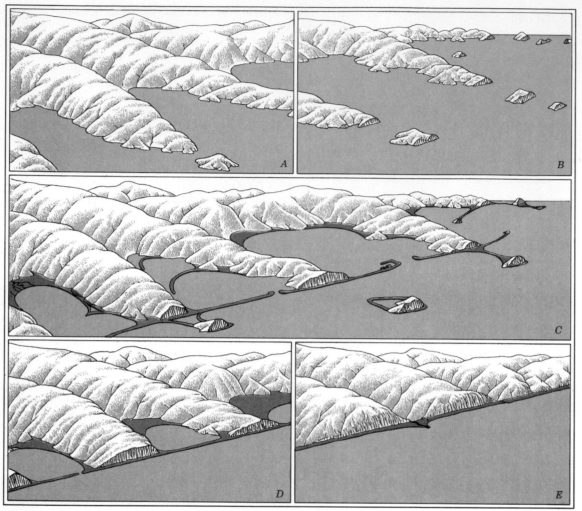

Figure 57.6   Stages in the evolution of a ria coastline.

flows, partly constructed below water level. Reef-building corals create new land and make a **coral-reef coast** (F). (Coral-reef coasts were explained in Unit 46.) Down-faulting of the coastal margin of a continent can allow the shoreline to come to rest against a fault scarp, producing a **fault coast** (G).

Development of a Ria Coast

The ria coast is formed when a rise of sea level or a crustal sinking (or both) brings the shoreline to rest against the sides of valleys previously carved by streams. This event is illustrated in Figure 57.6A. Soon wave attack forms cliffs on the exposed seaward sides of the islands and headlands (B). Sediment produced by wave action then begins to accumulate in the form of beaches along the cliffed headlands and at the heads of bays. This sediment is carried by littoral drift and is built into sandspits across the bay mouths and as connecting links between islands and mainland (C). Finally, all outlying islands are planed off by wave action and a nearly straight shoreline develops in

which the sea cliffs are fully connected by baymouth bars (D). Now the bays are sealed off from the open ocean, although narrow tidal inlets may persist, kept open by tidal currents. Frame E shows a much later stage in which the coastline has receded beyond the inner limits of the original bays.

The influence of ria coastlines on human activity has been strong down through the ages. The deep embayments of the ria shoreline make splendid natural harbors. Much of the ria coastline of Scandinavia, France, and the British Isles is provided with such harbor facilities. Consequently, these peoples have a strong tradition of fishing, shipbuilding, ocean commerce, and marine activity generally. Mountainous relief of ria and fiord coasts made agriculture difficult or impossible and forced the people to turn to the sea for a livelihood. New England and the Maritime Provinces of Canada have a ria coastline with abundant good harbors. The influence of this environment was to foster the same development of fishing, whaling, ocean commerce, and shipbuilding seen in the British Isles and Scandinavian countries.

Acadia National Park

The rocky coast of Maine is an example of a ria coast that was strongly influenced by continental glaciation. The Pleistocene ice sheet moved south over New England and spread far out on what is now the shallow continental shelf. The ice strongly abraded the bedrock of New England hill summits, somewhat modifying the preglacial topography that had been shaped by fluvial processes. Under the load of the ice sheet, the crust beneath New England was forced to sink, as it did elsewhere over North America and Europe where ice sheets were thick. Then, after the ice had disappeared, the depressed land surface was partially submerged as sea level rose to assume its present position.

One of our most famous national parks preserves the rugged coastal scenery along a stretch of the Maine coast where high hills and low mountains of granite meet the sea in a gradual descent of the land surface. Acadia National Park is mostly situated on Mount Desert Island, near Bar Harbor. Deep bays, penetrating far into the mainland, and numerous forested rock islands in the offshore zone characterize Acadia National Park (Figure 57.7). Actually, some 240 islands lie within the park limits. Ice abrasion was strong, not only over the granite hills, but also in the floors of valleys paralleling the trend of the ice motion. Some of the partly submerged valleys of Mount Desert Island thus developed the U-shape cross profile characteristic of glacial troughs. One of these troughs in particular, Somes Sound, has the appearance of a fiord. Other deeply scoured valleys on the island contain lakes that may be classed as glacial trough lakes.

Like all national parks, Acadia faces strong pressures from increasing numbers of visitors. The entire Maine coast is under extreme environmental impact from some 8 million summer visitors annually. The 4000-mi (6400-km) Maine shoreline is about 97% privately owned, so that

Acadia is merely one small spot on the total scenic coast. In 1970, a privately sponsored organization, the Maine Coast Heritage Trust, was incorporated to secure as much unspoiled coastal land as possible from future destruction by growth of private homes and commercial recreation facilities. A special effort is being made to include the spruce-covered islands and headlands close to Acadia National Park. Under the trust, a landowner can insure the protection of his land against all future development, although retaining the use of facilities already existing on the land.

Mountainous Coasts of Emergence

The Pacific Coast of the United States shows a very different type of coastline from that found in Maine. As we explained in Unit 35, the eastern coast of North America is a highly stable coast in terms of plate tectonics, for it does not lie on an active plate boundary. In contrast, the Pacific Coast of the United States and Canada lies on the boundary between the Pacific Plate and the North American Plate (see Figure 23.11). This active plate boundary includes zones of subduction as well as transform faults. One characteristic of the tectonically active coastal belt is that crustal blocks of the continental margin are moved up or down along faults. Much of the coastline shows the effects of **coastal emergence,** in which the tectonic uplift of the coastal landmass periodically exposes new land that was formerly beneath the sea.

Crustal uplift along a hilly or mountainous coast can occur very rapidly through fault movement along faults situated offshore. When there is a rapid rise of the coast, the existing shoreline may be abruptly lifted above the limits of wave action to become a **raised shoreline** (or **elevated shoreline**). The former wavecut cliff has now become a steep escarpment marking the inner edge of the

Figure 57.7 The Maine coast at Bar Harbor, viewed from Mount Cadillac on Mount Desert Island, Acadia National Park. (Runk/Schoenberger, from Grant Heilman.)

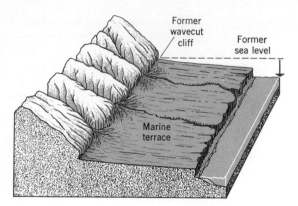

Figure 57.8 A raised shoreline becomes a cliff parallel with the newer, lower shoreline. The former abrasion platform is now a marine terrace.

Figure 57.10 The Big Sur of California is a mountainous coast with high marine cliffs and many outlying stacks. (Joe Monroe/Photo Researchers.)

former abrasion platform, which has become a **marine terrace** (Figure 57.8). Fluvial denudation begins to destroy the terrace, and it may also undergo partial burial under alluvial fan deposits.

Marine terraces are important to Man along mountainous coasts because they offer strips of flat ground extending for tens of miles parallel with the shoreline. Highways and railroads follow these terraces, and they are excellent sites for coastal towns and cities. Where the soil is good, agriculture makes use of the flat terrace surfaces.

Repeated uplifts result in a series of raised shorelines in a steplike arrangement. Fine examples of these multiple marine terraces are seen on the western slope of San Clemente Island, off the California coast (Figure 57.9).

Along some stretches of a coastline of emergence marine terraces are absent, because of the rapid uplift of a large crustal block. Here, mountains lie close to the sea,

and there is a very steep descent of the land to the water's edge. An example is the Big Sur of central California (Figure 57.10). This 60-mi (95-km) stretch of coast remained forested and largely undeveloped because it was separated from interior agricultural valleys by the massive Santa Lucia range. Public access is limited to the coastal highway, which winds tortuously along the mountain face and in places dips low to reach the sea at the heads of bays.

The Fiord Coast of Alaska

The wilderness scenic resource of a mountainous coastline reaches its wildest aspect along the fiord coast of southern Alaska and British Columbia. Glacier Bay National Monument, covering an area of 4400 sq mi (11,000 sq km), is dedicated to the preservation of a coast where active glaciers reach the sea at the heads of long inlets (Figure 57.11). As recently as the year 1700, during the cold climate period known as the Little Ice Age (Unit 6), glacial ice covered the entire bay area. Rapid glacier recession set in soon thereafter. In 1794 Captain George Vancouver found here only the beginnings of a fiord. Since then, ice recession has reached as far as 65 mi (105 km) into the land, opening up branching fiords with such names as Muir Inlet and Johns Hopkins Inlet, designating the glaciers that still feed into them. The calving of icebergs from the receding glacier fronts is an awe-inspiring sight and is witnessed by many tourists each summer from cruise ships that enter the bay. Today, Glacier Bay National Monument faces the threat of serious disfigurement by mineral exploration and mining, a practice permitted within national monuments. To prevent this fate, a move is under way to designate the monument as a national park and thus make possible its removal from mineral exploration activities.

Figure 57.9 Marine terraces on the western slope of San Clemente Island, off the southern California coast. More than twenty terraces have been identified in this series; the highest has an elevation of about 1300 ft (400 m). (John S. Shelton.)

Figure 57.11 Icebergs, carved from tidewater glaciers, are a special feature of Glacier Bay National Monument, Alaska. This view shows Muir Inlet, a fiord of Muir Glacier. (National Park Service.)

The Volcano Coastline of Hawaii

Spectacular volcano coastlines comprise much of the Island of Hawaii, largest of the islands and the only major island of the Hawaiian group on which active volcanoes are found today. The other islands are, of course, formed of volcanic rock, but their coastlines were shaped by later nonvolcanic activities, including stream erosion, submergence, and emergence.

Young lava flows dominate the coast of the southern two-thirds of Hawaii. These flows have come from the great shield volcano, Mauna Loa, and its smaller companion, Kilauea. Along the western side of Hawaii, on a stretch known as the Kona Coast, lava flows have descended the flank of Mauna Loa in a steady slope from the volcano summit to the sea. Wave action has produced marine cliffs all along the Kona Coast, and it has only a few small indentations that can be used as harbors. Several times in the past decades, lava flows have descended to the sea, building new land and stretches of volcano shoreline. The flow of 1950 from Mauna Loa into the ocean at three points along the Kona Coast was a spectacular display as plumes of steam rose from the boiling sea water (Figure 57.12).

Much of the volcano coastline of the Island of Hawaii has so far escaped massive disfiguration because of its remoteness and because the fresh lava flows offer little attraction to tourism. However, the Kona Coast is undergoing rapid real estate development in the form of grossly incongruent hotels and condominium complexes. The phase of exploitation of coastal wilderness for economic gain is in the ascendency on this island, as on other islands of Hawaii.

Coastal Zone Management

Coastlines of any description, whether low, sandy barrier islands or rugged cliffed coasts, and whether subdued by urban ports or remaining as wilderness, are being studied and treated under a modern broad-based program known generally as **coastal zone management.** Under new laws

Figure 57.12 An enormous cloud of condensed steam forms over the place where a basaltic lava flow from Mauna Loa enters the ocean. South Kona Coast, Hawaii, 1950. (Camera Hawaii.)

and newly appointed coastal zone commissions, the conflicts between those who would change the coastal zone environment for economic gain and those who would protect the coastal zone and its ecosystems as a natural resource, are being arbitrated to one degree or another.

The frontier ethic and the wilderness ethic meet head on in the deliberations of coastal-zone management bodies. Many regard as unalienable the right to build a new marina or a new resort hotel complex on coastal land that is privately owned. Those who oppose such development point out that preservation of coastal scenery and coastal ecosystems is an unalienable right of the public at large and its future generations. Most recent of the major areas of conflict is the construction of terminal and port facilities at which to bring ashore petroleum and liquified gas and to process these fuels. Equally controversial is the construction of nuclear power plants at coastal sites. These are issues and dilemmas we will focus upon in our final study units. What you have learned about coastlines, coastal processes, and marine ecosystems in this and earlier units will form a broad scientific base of information to assist you in evaluating problems of coastal zone management.

SCIENCE SUPPLEMENT

Wave Refraction Along an Embayed Coast

Change in direction of travel of water waves in response to change in bottom configuration is referred to as **wave refraction** (Unit 34). When undergoing refraction, the wave crest appears to become bent as seen from above. Figure 57.13 shows a train of uniform waves approaching a shoreline with bays and promontories. Successive positions of a wave are indicated by the lines numbered 1, 2, 3, etc. In deep water the wave fronts are parallel. As the shore is neared, the retarding influence of shallow water is felt first in the areas in front of the promontories. Shallowing of water reduces speed of wave travel at those places, but in the deeper water in front of the bays the retarding action has not yet occurred. Consequently, the wave front is bent, or refracted, in rough conformity with the shoreline. The wave will break first upon the promontory and on the bay head last.

Particularly important in understanding the development of embayed shorelines is the distribution of wave energy along the shore. On Figure 57.13, dashed lines (lettered a, b, c, d, etc.) divide the wave at position 1 into equal parts, which may be taken to include equal amounts of kinetic energy traveling forward with the wave. Along the headlands, the energy becomes concentrated into a short piece of shoreline; along the bays, it is spread over a much greater length of shoreline. Consequently, the breaking waves act as powerful erosional agents on the promontories, but are relatively weak and ineffective at the bay heads.

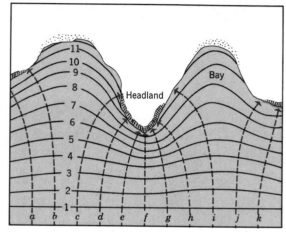

Figure 57.13 Wave refraction along an embayed coastline.

The important principle is that promontories are rapidly eroded back, whereas the bays experience little or no erosion. Thus in time wave action acts to produce a simple shoreline as an ultimate form. Over short distances this simplified shoreline may be nearly a straight line, but more typically shows a curvature in an arc of large radius.

Simplification of the shoreline minimizes the extent of wave refraction and tends to equalize the distribution of wave energy along the shoreline. In some respects, this evolutionary process is analogous to the gradation of a stream profile, in which a nearly uniform gradient is attained by elimination of rapids.

Unit 58
The Mountainous Desert

The Great Motorcycle Race

What a sight! Forming a line as far as the eye can see, 3000 motorcycle riders are poised for a gigantic mechanized assault upon the desert. The scene is laid near Barstow in the Mojave Desert; it is repeated each year in the Thanksgiving weekend. It is the start of a race across the desert floor to Las Vegas, Nevada, a distance of 160 miles. Thousands of spectators and well-wishers mass behind the thin line of latter-day cavalry, urging them to show no mercy on their deadly errand. Beware, you lumbering desert tortoises who may happen to lie on the track of these roaring demons! Beware, you lowly creosote bushes who dare to stand your ground!

In this drama of Man and nature the actors have strange labels: ORV stands for off-road-vehicle—anything capable of making mechanical progress over rough ground; 4WD is a four-wheel drive version of the ORV—it applies powerful gears to four churning wheels and is guaranteed to go just about anywhere, through sand and mud and over boulders, BLM is the Bureau of Land Management, a fed-eral organization supposed to protect the desert from the ORVs, but close to impotent in performance because of its minuscule police staff.

Another example: in April 1973, 700 riders mounted on two-wheeled ORVs converged upon an area of the desert in which the vanishing desert tortoise still survives. By the end of the day their motorbikes had destroyed all vegetation along a strip of ground three miles long and 3 to 6 feet wide. Scientists from the University of California who later viewed this area reported that the scar of destruction of this single race will persist for more than a century; they referred to this form of racing as a "Frankenstein monster." Too late: BLM has declared the area closed to ORVs and has designated it as a tortoise preserve.

The 4WDs are another breed of desert cavalry. Gregarious drivers, equipped with families and all the comforts of home, form safaris of as many as 500 vehicles parading down the desert roads. When they stay on the designated roads, the damage is minimal—perhaps a few hundred cactus plants and other desert shrubs uprooted to take home to Los

The Barstow-to-Las Vegas motorcycle race, Thanksgiving weekend, 1970. (U.S. Department of the Interior, Bureau of Land Management.)

Angeles, and perhaps a few tortoises left turned on their backs to die slowly in the burning sun. There may also be a few Joshua trees set on fire, and a few more bullet scars on some ancient Indian rock drawings (petroglyphs). There will certainly be a trail of beer cans and plastic food wrappers to document their visit.

But after all, has not the Old Testament set a precedent for these goings-on? No less an authority than the Lord of Israel is quoted by the Prophet Isaiah as declaring: "I will make waste mountains and hills, and dry up all their herbs . . ." (Isaiah 42:15). How can the children of the Lord be held to blame if they follow this example and get a lot of enjoyment out of it besides?

While on the subject of the ancient Hebrews, it is interesting to consider how these desert-dwellers viewed their environment. Whereas, for the northern Europeans the concept of wilderness was associated with dark and forbidding forests, the Hebrews thought of wilderness in terms of a dry, hot, barren desert. Drought was viewed as God's punishment when He was displeased with Man's behavior: "I will make the rivers islands, and I will dry up the pools." (Isaiah 42:15). "I will also command the clouds that they rain no rain upon it [the vineyard]." (Isaiah 4:6). God could also be benevolent. To those who repented their evil ways He promised "in the wilderness shall waters break out, and streams in the desert" (Isaiah 35:6).

We cannot blame BLM for the continuing destruction of the desert environment of the Southwest. Even if new, more stringent laws were passed to pro-

tect the desert, and even if more large areas were set aside as off-limits to ORVs, BLM with 11 million acres of desert to administer has far too small a staff to begin to enforce new laws and new limits. Pressure groups seek to have even more land opened to ORVs. The California Association of Four-Wheel Drive Clubs, Inc., has brought legal suit against the government to increase the area of desert open to their travel. So the outlook is not encouraging for protection of desert lands. By the year 2000, according to one estimate, there will be 50 million visitor-days of "recreational" desert use, as compared with 5 million visitor-days in 1968, and 13 million in 1973. In his 1973 report on the progress of destruction of the desert environment, Stanley Medders commented on the prospect: "Such an increase could mean only one thing in terms of desert use under today's conditions: total ecological disaster for an already overtaxed land."*

In this study unit, we will investigate the landforms of mountainous deserts which occupy much of the southwestern United States. We will emphasize an understanding of the origin of this desert scenery and the geologic processes by which the scenery has evolved.

*Stanley Medders, Crisis in a ravaged land; the California Desert, *National Parks & Conservation Magazine* (1973) vol. 47, no. 12, p. 15.

DATA SOURCE: AAAS Committee on Arid Lands, Off-road vehicle use, *Science* (1974) vol. 184, pp. 500-501; Luther J. Carter, Off-road vehicles: A compromise plan for the California desert, *Science* (1974) vol. 183, pp. 396-399.

The Basin and Range Province

Mountainous deserts of North America are the subject of this study unit; they lie within a region known to geographers as the **Basin and Range Province.** Figure 58.1 shows the limits of this geomorphic province. The pictorial representation suggests the nature of the landscape as well. Innumerable long, narrow mountain ranges lie side by side in a roughly north-south alignment. Between the ranges are open valleys, or basins, with rather smooth floors but quite lacking in any systematic drainage pattern of major rivers.

The Basin and Range Province covers all of Nevada and extends westward to the foot of the Sierra Nevada as well as eastward to the Colorado Plateau and Wasatch Mountains in Utah. This part of the province, which is roughly 400 mi (650 km) in east-west extent is known as the **Great Basin,** because it is completely lacking in any river outflow to the ocean. All streams within the Great Basin end in evaporating flats or shallow lakes. The Basin and Range Province extends south into southeastern California, then

eastward across the southern halves of Arizona and New Mexico, ending in westernmost Texas. An extension of the province runs far south along the western side of Mexico.

The Basin and Range Province owes its distinctive character to a remarkable coincidence of two natural factors: (1) a block-faulted crust and (2) a desert climate. In terms of plate tectonics, this region seems to represent a broad belt of extension (pulling-apart) of the North American lithospheric plate. The brittle crust of the earth has responded by fracturing into a multitude of fault blocks and these have moved up or down with respect to one another in a jostling motion. (The concept of faulting was explained in Unit 23.)

The desert climate with its desert soils and desert biome were covered in Unit 54. Our concern now is with the landforms and scenery of the mountainous desert of the western United States and with the plight of a wilderness region invaded and modified by Man.

In the Basin and Range Province sparseness of population goes hand in hand with sparseness of vegetation. In 1977, the state of Nevada, which lies wholly within this

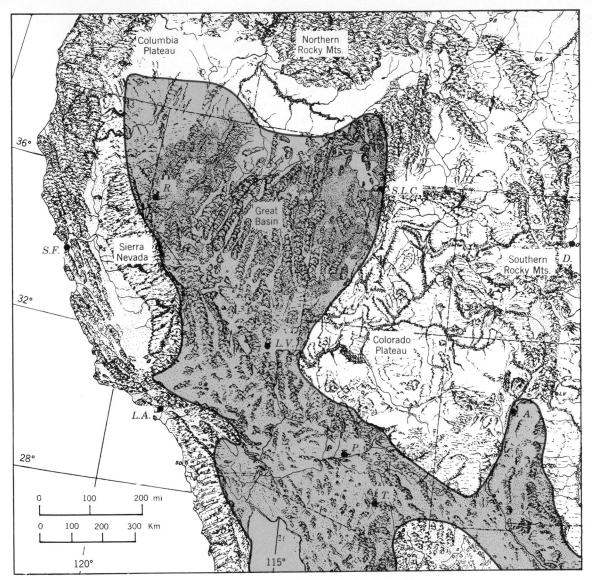

Figure 58.1 The Basin and Range Province. (From A. K. Lobeck [1948] *Physiographic Diagram of North America,* Hammond Incorporated, New York. Reproduced by permission of Hammond Incorporated.)

region, had only about 600,000 inhabitants in its 110,000 sq mi (286,000 sq km). Contrast this with Pennsylvania, whose 45,000 sq mi (117,000 sq km) contain nearly 12,000,000 persons. The vastness of waste land in this region can be appreciated when we realize that the explosion of the first test atom bomb was kept a secret within a single intermountain basin in New Mexico.

Block Mountains

Most mountain ranges of the Basin and Range Province are **block mountains.** Each is a single crustal mass bounded by normal faults (Unit 24). A typical arrangement of normal faults in pairs facing in opposite directions gives rise to an alternation of uplifted and down-dropped blocks. The up-

lifted block is called a **horst;** the down-dropped block is a **graben** (Figure 58.2).

Block mountains may be horsts, lifted between two opposite-facing normal faults, or of a tilted type in which one side is faulted up while the other side is faulted down (Figure 58.3). A tilted block has one steep face, the fault scarp, and one gently sloping side. The initial divide lies near the top of the fault scarp and is situated far over to one side of the block. A lifted block is bounded by steep mountain faces on both sides and has a broad, relatively flat, summit.

Figure 58.4 shows some erosional features of a large, tilted fault block. The freshly uplifted block has a steep mountain face, but this is rapidly dissected into deep canyons. The upper mountain face reclines in angle as it is

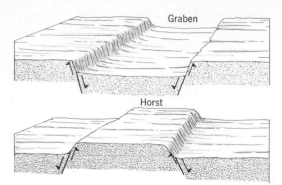

Figure 58.2   Graben and horst.

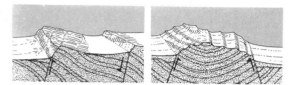

Figure 58.3   Fault block mountains may be of tilted type *(left)* or lifted type *(right).* (After W. M. Davis.)

removed, while rock debris accumulates in the form of alluvial fans adjacent to the fault block. Vestiges of the fault plane are preserved as **triangular facets,** the snubbed ends of ridges between canyon mouths.

The Denudation Cycle in Mountainous Deserts

Landscape of the Basin and Range Province is not everywhere the same. In the northernmost portion, in southern Oregon and Idaho, fault blocks are fresh in appearance and basins are narrow. Farther south, in central Nevada, the ranges are high and rugged, with intervening basins of about equal width. In southern Arizona, however, the ranges are low, narrow, and ragged in appearance, whereas the basins are very broad. Evidently there is a progression of landforms—a **denudation cycle**—that begins when fault blocks are rapidly uplifted.

A denudation cycle for the mountainous desert is pic-

tured in three block diagrams in Figure 58.5. Block A shows the initial stage with a freshly formed block mountain and an adjoining down-faulted basin. In this early stage, numerous large tectonic depressions exist between uplifted blocks. These depressions do not fill up with water to form lakes, as they would in a humid climate, but remain dry because of excessive evaporation in the dry climate. The flat central parts of such depressions provide the beds of temporary lakes and are known as **playas.** Playa lakes are shallow and fluctuate considerably in level, often disappearing entirely for long periods. Because they have no outlets, playa lakes contain salt water often more strongly saline than ocean water.

Throughout the denudation cycle, the intermountain depressions become filled with rock waste as alluvial fans are built out from the adjoining mountain masses (Figure 58.6). In the southwestern United States and Mexico the fan surface is called a **bajada.** This is a term of Spanish origin meaning "descent" or "slope" and is pronounced *ba-ha-da.*

When the basins are filled with alluvium and the mountain masses are cut up into an intricate set of canyons, divides, and peaks, the region is said to be in the mature stage (Block B). As maturity progresses, the mountains are worn lower, at the same time shrinking in size as the alluvium of the fans (bajadas) encroaches progressively farther inward upon the mountain base.

When the old stage is reached, mountains are represented by small islandlike remnants (Block C). Eventually even these remnants are eroded away and a vast undulating plain remains. It contains shallow depressions occupied by playas. Wind action in the dry climate is effective in eroding shallow depressions and in building dunes of shifting sand.

Pediments and Pediplains

Throughout most of the Basin and Range Province, the sloping surfaces of boulders, gravel, and sand which extend from the abrupt base of steep mountain faces to the flat ground of the playas are alluvial fans, underlain by thick deposits of alluvium shed by the mountains. These slopes are true bajadas. In some places, however, the alluvium, although outwardly taking the form of alluvial

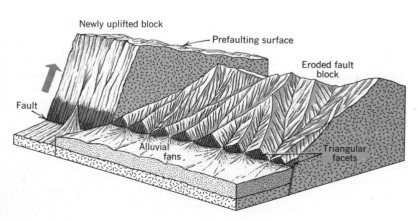

Figure 58.4   Erosion of a tilted fault block produces a rugged mountain range. A line of triangular facets at the mountain base marks the position of the original fault plane.

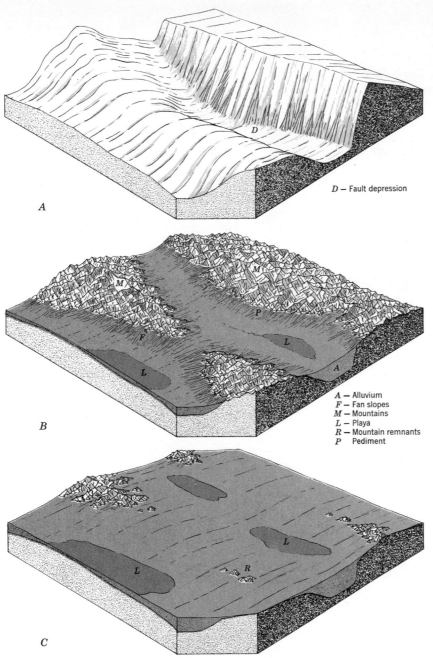

D — Fault depression

A — Alluvium
F — Fan slopes
M — Mountains
L — Playa
R — Mountain remnants
P Pediment

fans, is nothing more than a veneer perhaps 10 to 20 ft (3 to 6 m) thick, overlying a smooth sloping floor of solid bedrock. To such a rock surface, fringing a desert mountain range or cliff line, we apply the term **pediment.** On the right-hand cross section of Blocks B and C, Figure 58.5, pediment surfaces are shown in profile in a narrow zone between the thick basin alluvium and the rugged mountain masses.

Because a pediment is thinly veneered by alluvium while it is being formed, the only way to be certain that a pediment exists is to see the bedrock widely exposed to view by later erosion, as in the case of the pediment shown in Figure 58.7.

Because the old stage surface of the arid climate denudation cycle consists in part of pediments, the term **pediplain** has been introduced to describe the total land surface. A pediplain consists of alluvial fan and playa surfaces as well as pediments; it is thus partly erosional and partly depositional.

Salt Deposits of Playas

The shallow lake basins of playas are often covered with only a thin sheet of water which evaporates rapidly, leaving a white salt deposit on the surface. Most persons are

Figure 58.6   This air view of Death Valley, California, shows a mature desert landscape comparable to that shown in Figure 58.5B. (Spence Air Photos.)

familiar with the salt flats of Great Salt Lake in Utah, on which so many automobile speed records have been set.

Salts found in the various playa lakes of the southwestern United States are sodium carbonate (Na_2CO_3), borax ($Na_2B_4O_7$), calcium carbonate ($CaCO_3$), sulfates of sodium, magnesium, and potassium (Na_2SO_4, $MgSO_4$, K_2SO_4), chlorides of sodium, calcium, and magnesium ($NaCl$, $CaCl_2$, $MgCl_2$), and many others. These salts are classed as **evaporites.** Where salts are thick and pure in the inner parts of the playas, there is no soil in the true sense of the word (Figure 58.8).

Erosion by Wind

Wind performs two kinds of erosional work in the desert. Loose particles lying on the ground surface may be lifted into the air or rolled along the ground. This process is **deflation.** Where the wind drives sand and dust particles against an exposed rock or soil surface, causing it to be worn away by the impact of the particles, the process is **wind abrasion.** Abrasion requires cutting tools carried by the wind; deflation is accomplished by air currents alone.

Deflation acts whereever the ground surface is

Figure 58.7   Bedrock is widely exposed over this pediment surface at the foot of the Dragoon Mountains near Benson, Arizona. (Douglas Johnson.)

Figure 58.8 A salt flat, called The Devil's Golf Course, on the floor of Death Valley, California. Since the salt was deposited, solution by rainwater has roughened the surface. (Richard Weymouth Brooks.)

Figure 58.9 A desert pavement in Arizona. The upper view shows the boulders and gravel of an alluvial fan, on which the pavement has formed. The lower view is a detail showing the pebbles fitted closely so as to cover a sand layer beneath. (A. N. Strahler.)

thoroughly dried out and is littered with small, loose particles of soil or regolith. Dry river courses, beaches, and areas of recently formed glacial deposits are highly susceptible to deflation. In dry climates, almost the entire ground surface is subject to deflation because the soil or rock is largely bare. Wind is selective in its deflational action. The finest particles, those of clay and silt sizes, are lifted most easily and raised high into the air. Sand grains are moved only by moderately strong winds and travel close to the ground. Gravel fragments and rounded pebbles can be rolled over flat ground by strong winds, but they do not travel far. They become easily lodged in hollows or between other large grains. Consequently, where a mixture of sizes of particles is present on the ground, the finer sizes are removed; the coarser particles remain behind.

In the deserts of the southwestern United States, the floors of intermountain basins are vulnerable to deflation. The flat floors of shallow playas have in some places been reduced by deflation as much as several feet over areas of many square miles.

Where deflation has been active on an alluvial fan or alluvial terrace surface, littered with loose fragments of a wide range of sizes, the pebbles that remain behind accumulate until they cover the entire surface. By rolling or jostling about as the fine particles are blown away, the pebbles become closely fitted together, forming a **desert pavement** (Figure 58.9). The armored surface is well protected against further deflation, but it is easily disturbed by the wheels of trucks or motorcycles.

Pebbles on a desert pavement, as well as boulder surfaces acquire a black, iridescent coating of oxides of manganese and iron. This shiny coating goes by the name of **desert varnish**. Indians who inhabited the desert before the coming of European Man scratched the darkened surfaces of boulders and cliffs to produce drawings, known as **petroglyphs** (Figure 58.10).

The sandblast action of wind against exposed rock surfaces is limited to the basal few feet of a rock mass rising above a flat plain, because sand grains do not rise high

into the air. Wind abrasion produces pits, grooves, and hollows in the rock. Telephone poles on windswept sandy plains are quickly cut through at the base unless a protective metal sheathing or heap of large stones is placed around the base.

Desert Dunes

Dunes of free sand, continually shifting under the desert winds, are found at a number of places in the southern parts of the Basin and Range Province. A particularly large dune field, called the Great Sand Hills, lies just west of Yuma, Arizona, along the border between the United States and Mexico (Figure 58.11). Dune fields can also be visited on the floor of Death Valley.

One common type of sand dune is an isolated heap of free sand called a **crescent dune.** As the name suggests, this dune has a crescentic outline; the points of the cres-

Figure 58.10   Petroglyphs, crude drawings made by Indians, were scratched into the natural coating of dark desert varnish on these boulders in the Mojave Desert. (U.S. Department of the Interior, Bureau of Land Management.)

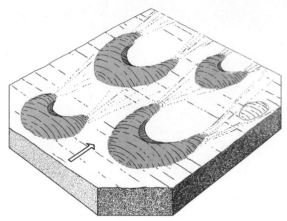

Figure 58.12   Crescent dunes. The arrow indicates wind direction.

cent are directed downwind (Figure 58.12). On the windward side of the crest the sand slope is gentle and smoothly rounded. On the lee side of the dune, within the crescent, is a steep curving dune slope, the **slip face.** This face maintains an angle of about 35° from the horizontal. Sand grains slide down the steep face after being blown

Figure 58.11   A great sand sea of transverse dunes between Yuma, Arizona and Calexico, California. A field of crescent dunes lies at the lower right. (Spence Air Photos.)

free of the sharp crest. When a strong wind is blowing, the flying sand makes a perceptible cloud at the crest.

Crescent dunes rest on a flat, pebble-covered ground surface. The sand heap may originate as a drift in the lee of some obstacle, such as a small hill, rock, or clump of brush. Once a sufficient mass of sand has formed, it begins to move downwind, taking the form of a crescent dune. For this reason, the dunes are usually arranged in chains extending downwind from the sand source.

Where sand is so abundant that it completely covers the ground, dunes take the form of wavelike ridges separated by troughlike furrows. The dunes are called **transverse dunes** because, like ocean waves, their crests trend at right angles to direction of wind (Figure 58.11). The entire area may be called a **sand sea,** because it resembles a storm-tossed sea suddenly frozen to immobility. The sand ridges have sharp crests and are asymmetrical, the gentle slope being on the windward, the steep slip face on the lee side. Deep depressions lie between the dune ridges. Sand seas require enormous quantities of sand, derived from weathering of an exposed sandstone formation or from alluvium of fans and dry stream channels.

Man's Impact on the Mountainous Desert

As we learned in opening paragraphs of this unit, the mountainous desert of the southwestern United States is being strongly impacted by human activity. The rugged mountain ranges, bouldery bajadas, and white salt flats might seem almost indestructible to the effects of recreational uses, but the truth is that desert land surfaces and ecosystems are highly vulnerable. The desert biome is said to contain 50 species of reptiles, 170 species of birds, and more than 80 species of mammals. The desert plants number over 700 species. While outwardly rugged in appearance, they are easily destroyed. Rare plant specimens are dug up and transported to the cities, even though the practice is forbidden by law. Many forms of cactus are removed by professional landscape gardeners. Sheep and cattle grazing is destroying native shrubs on the higher surfaces, while smog reaching the desert from the Los Angeles basin is threatening some areas of natural plant cover with extinction. Vandals are hacking at petroglyphs, in some cases using dynamite to break off surface slabs for transport. Archeological and paleontological sites are unprotected and open to looting by amateur collectors and fun seekers. Everywhere, the off-road vehicles (ORVs) are making new tracks, destroying plants and inducing accelerated soil erosion when torrential rains occur. Disturbance of the loose desert pavement bares underlying silt and clay, which is swept up in great dust clouds.

Besides destruction and vandalism by hordes of city people, the mountainous desert is under massive attack through prospecting and mining. For many decades ore deposits have been sought and mined in the rugged mountain ranges where ancient rocks are exposed. Death Valley National Monument is highly vulnerable to prospecting and mining, which continues to be permitted without regard for destruction of the very scenery for which the monument was set aside. Large open-pit mines for talc and borates are operating within the limits of the monument. Mining claims within the area number over 1800 and cover a total area greater than 36,000 acres. Debate continues over the legal aspects of restricting or regulating prospecting and mining within Death Valley National Monument. In 1976, the Sierra Club Legal Defense Fund filed a suit against the Department of the Interior on behalf of Death Valley National Monument, the Sierra Club, and two other plaintiffs. The suit asks that the National Park Service protect the Monument from disruption by improper mining.

SCIENCE SUPPLEMENT
Pluvial Lakes of the Great Basin

Among the nonglacial phenomena associated with Pleistocene glaciations were changes in the water balances of closed basins of the Basin and Range Province. As we explained in Unit 16, on the subject of water balance of lakes, this region has a great excess of potential evaporation over precipitation. This arid condition results today in total absence of lake water in most of these basins, in occasional stands of shallow water in others, and in a few instances such as Great Salt Lake, Utah, and Pyramid Lake, Nevada, in permanent lakes of high salinity. Runoff reaching these lakes comes by way of streams receiving discharge from neighboring mountain ranges where a water surplus occurs at high elevations. Obviously, there is a delicate equilibrium among evaporation, inflow of streams, and storage in the water balance of those closed basins presently holding water.

During Pleistocene glaciations the water balance changed in favor of small water surpluses, with the result that water occupied a large number of the intermountain basins, bringing into existence a large number of **pluvial lakes.** The word "pluvial" suggests an increase in precipitation during glaciations as the cause of the lakes. Evaporation would also have been less under a climate of lower air temperatures. We know that alpine glaciers of certain of the neighboring higher ranges, such as the Wasatch Mountains and Sierra Nevada, made major advances during glaciations to reach low altitudes, showing the effects of greater ice accumulation and reduced ablation.

Figure 58.13 is a map showing pluvial lakes as they were during maximum extent during the Wisconsinan glaciation. Altogether, there were about 120 pluvial lakes

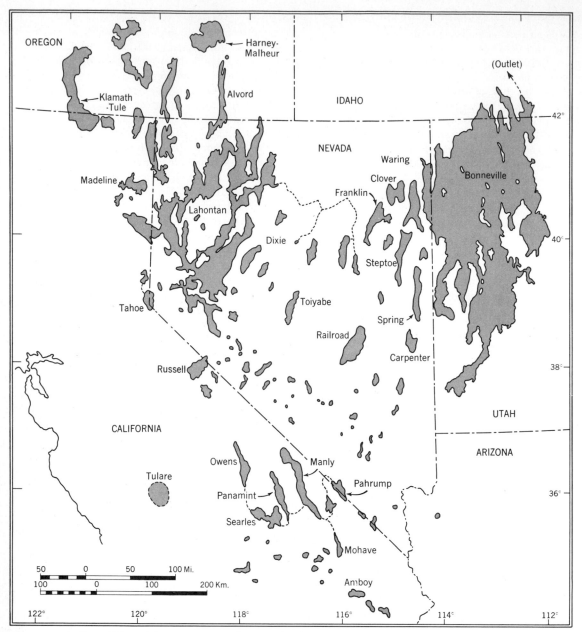

Figure 58.13 Pluvial lakes of the western United States. The dotted lines are overflow channels. (Based on a map by R. F. Flint [1957] *Glacial and Pleistocene Geology,* John Wiley & Sons, New York, p. 227, Figure 13.2.)

in existence then. Some overflowed into others and probably held fresh water at times. Largest of the pluvial lakes was Lake Bonneville, an expansion of the present-day Great Salt Lake in Utah. It reached an areal extent of 20,000 sq mi (52,000 sq km), about the same as Lake Michigan, and for a time overflowed northward into the Snake River. Its maximum depth was 1000 ft (330 m). Abandoned shorelines of Lake Bonneville can be seen today along the mountain slopes against which the lake waters rested.

Expansion, contraction, and changing salinities of the pluvial lakes constituted great swings in environmental conditions affecting ecosystems of the basins. A remarka-

ble example of adaptation of animals to changing environments is seen in the case of the desert pupfish (*Cyprinodon*). There are today some twenty populations of these tiny fish surviving in isolated spring-fed streams and tiny ponds in Death Valley, California. This tectonic basin, which lies below sea level and is one of the hottest surface environments on earth, was occupied by pluvial Lake Manly (Figure 58.13). As lake waters disappeared, the fish were forced into a few remaining spring localities and became isolated from one another. Their tolerance to a wide range of temperatures is quite phenomenal. Blue-green algae provide the fish with food.

Unit 59
Ancient Mountain Roots of Appalachia

Wilderness and the American Pioneer

When the Pilgrims first set foot on New World shores, their leader, William Bradford, described what he saw as a "hideous wilderness." Why such a negative reaction? Most other newcomers felt the same way about the forests of the eastern seaboard into which they were plunged headlong. This reaction has been studied intensively by the American historian, Roderick Nash, and discussed at length in his fascinating volume titled *Wilderness and the American Mind*. Nash writes:

> Two components figured in the American pioneer's bias against wilderness. On the direct, physical level, it constituted a formidable threat to his very survival. The transatlantic journey and subsequent western advances stripped away centuries. Successive waves of frontiersmen had to contend with wilderness as uncontrolled and terrifying as that which primitive man confronted. Safety and comfort, even necessities like food and shelter, depended on overcoming the wild environment. For the first Americans, as for medieval Europeans, the forest's darkness hid savage men, wild beasts, and still stranger creatures of the imagination. In addition civilized man faced the danger of succumbing to the wildness of his surroundings and to savagery himself. The pioneer, in short, lived too close to wilderness for appreciation. Understandably, his attitude was hostile and his dominant criteria utilitarian. The *conquest of* wilderness was his major concern.*

A new change in European attitudes toward the wilderness had its origins in the Romantic movement in Europe beginning late in the 18th Century. Revolting against the tight corsets of Classicism, many Romantics opted for a return to nature. In France Jean-Jacques Rousseau extolled the virtues of "the noble savage." One subculture among the Romantics consisted of primitivists who preached a return to the wilderness—preached, that is, from the safety of

*Roderick Nash (1973) *Wilderness and the American Mind*, revised edition, Yale University Press, New Haven, p. 24. Reproduced by permission of the author.

Asher Brown Durand, an artist of the Hudson River School, painted this Catskill mountain gorge in 1849. He included two friends: William Cullen Bryant, the poet, and Thomas Cole, his own mentor. The scene shows massive conglomeratic strata of Paleozoic age along the eastern rim of the Appalachian Plateau in New York State. (The New York Public Library Picture Collection.)

their urban environment. A handful of primitivists did, in fact, visit the New World to see at first hand what they were talking about. One was Francoise-René de Chateaubriand, who traveled through the eastern American wilderness for several months in the winter of 1791–1792. He seems to have been delighted with what he found, for he wrote that "in this deserted region the soul delights to bury and lose itself amidst boundless forests . . . to mix and confound . . . with the wild sublimities of Nature." Another Frenchman of the same persuasion was Alexis de Tocqueville, who visited the United States in 1831. He was dismayed by the pioneers' hatred of wilderness and their preoccupation with subduing nature. He wrote his commentary: "in Europe people talk a great deal of the wilds of America, but the Americans themselves never think about them; they are insensible to the wonders of inanimate nature and they may be said not to perceive the mighty forests that surround them till they fall beneath the hatchet."

One American, early in the Colonial period, expressed a primitivist view, quite unlike that of William Bradford. He was William Byrd II, a Virginian who fell heir to a large plantation. Byrd was educated in England and, upon his return to Virginia, could view the wilderness with a detached perspective. In 1728, he undertook to survey the boundary between the colonies of Virginia and North Carolina. As you know, this boundary runs straight westward, penetrating far into the Appalachians and crossing the lofty Blue Ridge Mountains. He recorded his impressions in a work titled *History of the Dividing Line*. The forested wilderness fascinated and excited him greatly and he looked upon the expedition as a delightful adventure. In October 1728, Byrd's surveying party came in sight of the Appalachian ridges, which Byrd described as "Ranges of Blue Clouds rising one above the other." Penetrating farther west, they reached a high point where Byrd found the view spectacular. He wrote "we were perpetually climbing up to a Neighbouring eminence, that we might enjoy it in more Perfection." Byrd was not one to suggest that this wilderness scenery should be preserved. As a plantation owner, he shared the views of his contemporaries that wild valleys should be converted into productive pastures. Byrd was almost alone in his time with his Romantic appreciation of wilderness. A century was to elapse before Romantics of the American school were to form a little band of devotees to the wilderness concept.

In this study unit, we will investigate the scenery of the Appalachian highlands. In comparison with the powerful mountain and canyon scenery of the West, the subdued profiles of these forested lands may prove a letdown, but there is a rare dignity in their geologic antiquity and in their dogged refusal to submit to continuous millions of years of denudation.

DATA SOURCE: Roderick Nash (1973) *Wilderness and the American Mind*, revised edition, Yale University Press, New Haven; detailed references to quotations included in this essay can be found in Chapters 2 and 3.

The Appalachians

The final American region we have selected for study in this group of units on Man and scenery is the Appalachian system of ancient mountains. Ranging in width from 75 to 150 mi (120 to 240 km), the mountainous zone of the Appalachians begins in Alabama and runs northeast, passing through New England and extending into the Maritime Provinces of Canada. In the United States, the length of this highland belt is about 1400 mi (2250 km) (Figure 59.1). Ridges and summits of the Appalachian highlands are modest in elevation—2000 to 5000 ft (600 to 1500 m)—in comparison with the great ranges of the West.

Two factors give the Appalachian highlands a distinctive character: geology and climate. Geologic control rests in the presence of a suture belt caused by continental collision at an early period in geologic time and from a very long period of crustal stability and deep erosion. The climate factor is felt through a humid continental climate with a substantial water surplus, which supports a forest biome and creates strongly leached soils, mostly Ultisols and Spodosols. Continental glaciation affected only the New England Appalachians, but those effects are not conspicuous except in a few small areas.

Continental Collision and Appalachian Structure

In Unit 23, dealing with basic concepts of plate tectonics, we showed how continental collision occurs, squeezing the sediments of continental margins into alpine structure and creating a long, narrow mountain chain (Figure 23.5). This kind of mountain range is a suture that brings together two continental lithospheric plates.

Suturing of the Appalachians occurred three times in the Paleozoic Era, a block of geologic time extending from 600 million to 225 million years before present (−600 to −225 m.y.). (Refer to Table 23.1 for names and ages of eras and periods.) After the first suture was formed, at the close of the Ordovician Period (−430 m.y.), the two lithospheric plates pulled apart on a rift zone. More sedi-

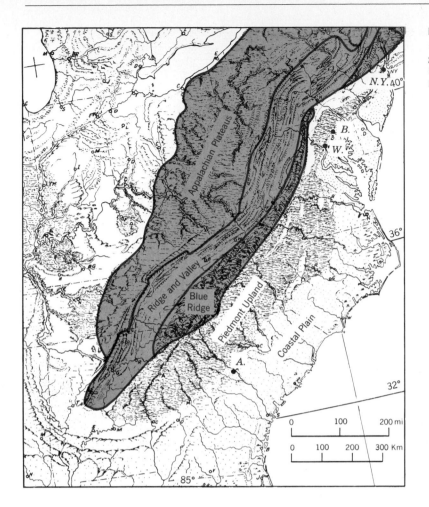

Figure 59.1 Map of the Appalachian highlands. (From A. K. Lobeck [1948] Physiographic Diagram of North America, Hammond Incorporated, New York. Reproduced by permission of Hammond Incorporated.)

ments were deposited. A second collision occurred at the end of the Devonian Period (−345 m.y.); followed by rifting and more sediment deposition. The final collision occurred in the Permian Period (−280 to −225 m.y.), forming the final suture in much the same general belt as the previous two sutures. Obviously the geology of the Appalachian highland belt is very complex. We should also add that during the entire Paleozoic Era, North America was joined with Europe as a part of the supercontinent, Pangaea. The Atlantic Ocean basin began to form by continental rifting late in the Mesozoic Era, about −150 m.y. However, the separation of the North American and Eurasian lithospheric plates created no important tectonic activity in the Appalachian region. Instead, there was continued denudation of the deformed rocks of the suture zone. Through the last time span of 150 m.y. prior to the present, the earth's crust underwent at intervals a gentle uplift; each time raising the great mass of deformed rocks with respect to sea level. As denudation progressed, deeper and deeper levels of the suture were thus exposed at the surface. What remains today are the mountain roots of the suture zone. As we noted in Unit 23, these roots consist of metamorphic rock, as well as bodies of igneous intrusive rock, which penetrated the upper crust during each of the episodes of suturing.

When we compare the geology and landforms of the Appalachians with those of the Basin and Range Province of the West, the contrast is striking. Whereas the entire western region is one of present and recent tectonic and volcanic activity, the eastern region is one of prolonged crustal stability, its present scenery shaped entirely by denudation. To understand the scenic features of the Appalachian highlands, we need first to develop a general concept of a cycle of landmass denudation in a humid climate. We then consider in turn each of three structural belts making up the Appalachian highlands: a belt of metamorphic rocks, a belt of folded strata, and an elevated plateau of flat-lying strata. The landforms in each structural belt are distinctive.

The Denudation Cycle in a Humid Climate

We introduced the general concept of denudation in Unit 26. Several units investigated the process of weathering, mass wasting, and running water that together comprise the denudation process. The denudation cycle as it applies in the Appalachians has some striking differences from the cycle of denudation in mountainous deserts, which we described in Unit 58. In the first place, the cycle in the desert began with block faulting, a form of tectonic activity missing in the past 100 m.y. in the Appalachian region. In the second place, the fluvial process in the desert region consisted of the erosion of the up-faulted blocks and the deposition of the rock waste in nearby down-faulted basins, with no connections to the sea. In the humid eastern United States, with its water surplus, runoff flows to the oceans by a continuous system of streams, converging into major rivers. In this way, sediment is carried out of the region.

The idealized denudation cycle of a geologically ancient and stable region, such as the Appalachians, begins with crustal uplift of an area that has been eroded and uplifted many times before. In other words, the beginning of one cycle marks the end of the previous cycle, when the region is reduced to a low, undulating plain lying close to sea level.

The denudation cycle can be illustrated by a series of block diagrams (Figure 59.2). The area covered by the block is many miles wide, but it is only one patch in the entire uplifted region, which might be as extensive as a subcontinental area several hundred miles across. Block A shows the undulating plain produced at the close of the previous cycle, now uplifted to an elevation of several hundreds of feet above sea level. Sea level is indicated by a color line, labeled "baselevel." The mass of crustal rock lying above sea level is the **landmass,** available for removal by fluvial action. As we enter the denudation cycle in its **initial stage,** the available landmass is at its maximum bulk, and will thereafter be diminished.

Streams flowing in broad, open valleys on the uplifted surface are not immediately affected by the uplift, but in their lower courses, near the ocean, they will begin to erode rapidly and transform their valleys into V-shaped gorges with steep rock walls and rapids. The process is called **stream rejuvenation;** it extends rapidly up the courses of the rivers and their smaller branches, finally reaching into the area of our block diagram, which is far from the sea. Now, rejuvenated streams cut V-shaped valleys into the uplifted mass, destroying the former shallow valleys. As shown in Block B, the region is now in the **young stage**—a composite of the old, undulating land surface and the new system of steep valley walls.

In time, as valleys deepen, the steep valley sides replace entirely the former land surface,so that all of the land is now in steep slopes (Block C). The landmass has now reached the **early mature stage.** The landscape is extremely rugged; ridges are sharp-crested. Little or no flat land can be found anywhere. **Relief,** which is the average elevation difference between summits and valley bottoms, is greatest at this stage. Now, as explained in Unit 55, the major streams of the area reach the graded condition and begin to form narrow floodplains.

As time passes, relief diminishes over the area. Divides are reduced in elevation and become broadly rounded. Regolith accumulates in greater thickness upon divides and valley sides. Erosion rates become slower and sediment supplied to the streams becomes smaller in quantity and finer in texture. Floodplains widen and the major

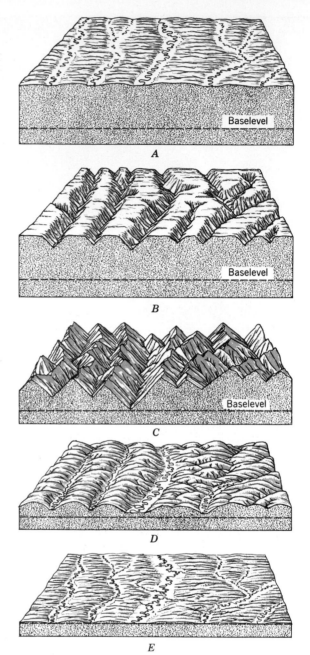

Figure 59.2   Stages in the denudation cycle in a humid climate. A. Initial stage caused by crustal uplift. B. Young stage with extensive upland and deep, steep-sided valleys, C. Early mature stage with all land in steep slopes and relief at the maximum. D. Late mature stage with lowering relief and declining slopes. E. Old stage with peneplain. Uplift at this stage will end the cycle and bring the region back to the conditions shown in Block A.

streams take on the characteristics of alluvial rivers. The subdued landscape, shown in Block D, is now in the **late mature stage.** Floors of the valleys have now approached the lower limit to which they can be reduced, which is **baselevel,** an imaginary sea-level surface extended beneath the land.

Figure 59.3 The gently rolling upland surface in the distance is part of the St. John peneplain of Puerto Rico; its elevation is about 2000 ft (600 m). The peneplain is deeply trenched by Canyon de San Cristobal *(foreground),* carved by the Rio Usabon. (U.S. Geological Survey.)

More gradually than before, relief diminishes over the area, as the erosion rate steadily diminishes. After many millions of years have elapsed, a gently undulating surface remains, shown in Block E. The landmass is now in the **old stage.** The land surface, which combines low interstream uplands with broad alluvial valleys, is called a **peneplain.** This term was coined by the geographer, W. M. Davis, combining the words "penultimate" and "plain." Professor Davis was implying that this next-to-the-last landscape would change so little with passage of time that it would most certainly never attain a hypothetical final, or ultimate stage, which would be a land surface everywhere at sea level. Instead, another episode of crustal uplift would interrupt the cycle, raising the peneplain hundreds of feet above sea level, and bringing the landscape back to the initial stage represented in Block A. The peneplain persists

through the young stage of the new denudation cycle, but is eventually entirely destroyed. Figure 59.3 shows a peneplain trenched by a deep steep-walled canyon.

The concepts of the denudation cycle and the peneplain were first developed by American geologists and geographers in the Appalachian region. Other model cycles have been worked out for other global regions where different controlling conditions of climate and geologic history prevail. The Appalachian region has had a 150-million-year history of denudation in which several cycles have been completed or partly completed. Vestiges of peneplains of at least two earlier cycles have been identified throughout the area, but interpretations of individual scientists differ and have been debated and challenged repeatedly by others.

The Blue Ridge Province

We cannot give a full and detailed description of the Appalachian highlands, but the character of the scenery can be understood in terms of three landform belts that lie side by side. The easternmost and oldest belt includes the Blue Ridge Province of Georgia, North Carolina, Tennessee, Virginia, and Maryland. A similar belt includes the ranges of western New England. The Blue Ridge consists of metamorphic rocks and intrusive igneous rocks, all of which were formed in the earliest of the continental collisions in the Paleozoic Era, or in earlier collisions. Because rocks of these types are quite strongly resistant to weathering and erosion, they form mountain ridges, many of which attain elevations well over 5000 ft (1500 m) and a few over 6000 ft (1800 m). The Great Smoky Mountains, in which a national park of that name is located, is the loftiest of the ranges of the Blue Ridge Province and lies on the boundary region of North Carolina and Tennessee. Even the highest ridges are forested, except that some summits have treeless meadows (Figure 59.4). Rock outcrops, though numerous, are not conspicuous in the landscape, as they are in the arid western lands.

Figure 59.4 Distant mountain profiles are obscured by a natural haze in this view over the Great Smoky Mountains. (National Park Service.)

Figure 59.5 Narrow parallel ridges with sharp crests extend in succession as far as the eye can see in the folded Appalachians near Warm Springs, Virginia. (Aero Service Division, Western Geophysical Company of America.)

The Ridge and Valley Province

Next to the Blue Ridge on the west is a mountain belt called the Ridge and Valley Province because it consists of long, narrow, sharp-crested ridges separated by narrow valleys (Figure 59.5). In some sections, the ridges run parallel with one another; elsewhere they loop back and forth across the land in zigzag fashion (Figure 59.6). An explanation of the ridges and valleys lies in the geology. This is a belt of sedimentary strata of Paleozoic age strongly affected by folding. Because some of the sedimentary formations are extremely durable—being of hardened sandstone—while others are weak—being of shale and limestone—long-continued erosion has etched out the weak strata from between the hard strata, much as a piece of driftwood is etched by beach sand to leave the hard layers standing in bold relief.

Some environmental aspects of the Ridge and Valley

Province in southcentral Pennsylvania are illustrated in Figure 59.7. The ridges, of resistant sandstone, rise boldly to heights of 2000 ft (600 m) above broad lowlands underlain by weak shales and limestones. Major highways run in the valleys, crossing from one valley to another through the watergaps of streams that have cut across the ridges. Important cities are situated near the watergaps of major streams. An example is Harrisburg, located where the Susquehanna River issues from a series of watergaps. Where no watergaps are conveniently located, roads must climb in long, steep grades over the ridge crests. The ridges are heavily forested; the valleys are rich agricultural belts.

The Appalachian Plateaus

The third and westernmost of the belts of the Appalachian highlands is the Appalachian Plateaus Province. All of this region is hilly or mountainous to some degree, but only the eastern portion, lying next to the Ridge and Valley Province rises to a high belt of mountainous proportions. Two high areas of partial wilderness are the Cumberland

Figure 59.6 Zigzag ridges eroded on plunging folds, south of Hollidaysburg, Pennsylvania. The nearer bend is a plunging syncline. The more distant bend *(at right)* is a plunging anticline enclosing a cove-like valley. (John S. Shelton.)

Figure 59.7 A great down-fold, involving three resistant sandstone formations and thick intervening shales, has been eroded to form bold ridges through which the Susquehanna River has cut a series of watergaps. (After A. K. Lobeck.)

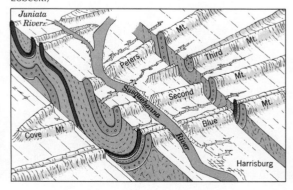

Plateau in Tennessee and Kentucky and the Allegheny Mountains in Pennsylvania, Maryland, and Tennessee.

The Appalachian Plateaus are underlain by sedimentary strata that lie nearly horizontal, or at most are very gently folded. These strata are of the same age—Paleozoic Era—as strata of the Ridge and Valley Province but, being farther from the suture zone, were little affected by tectonic activity. Here sandstone, shale, and limestone strata lie piled one layer upon the next. Denudation has reached the mature stage of the erosion cycle (see Figure 59.2C) and the relief is great (Figure 59.8). The region is extremely rugged with many deep winding gorges. Where strip mining has not laid bare the bedrock in serpentine scars, the land is forested and only in a few places can a benchlike outcrop of sandstone be followed along the contour of a mountainside.

Ridge crests and valleys in the Appalachian Plateaus show no parallel alignment, as they do in the adjacent Ridge and Valley Province. Instead, valleys show a treelike branching with a wide range of compass directions represented in the smaller valleys. This **dendritic pattern** is closely associated with regions where strata lie in a horizontal attitude.

Man and the Appalachian Wilderness

Although the Appalachian highlands still contain many wild areas, proximity to large urban population centers and easy access to many parts have invited a massive human attack upon the forest biome and its ecosystems. Highways cross the Appalachians in many places. One in particular, Route 441, bisects the Great Smoky Mountains National Park, making regulation and protection of the park almost an impossibility. The Skyline Drive and Blue Ridge Parkway follow the crest of the Blue Ridge for much of its length from Virginia to North Carolina. Shenandoah National Park on the Blue Ridge of Virginia is within a short drive of the Washington-Baltimore urban area and is heavily impacted.

The burden of public visitation on these national parks is becoming increasingly heavy, while federal funding has been inadequate to provide the personnel needed to protect these lands. Great Smoky Mountains National Park is visited by 9 million persons each year. Campgrounds are crowded to overflowing and trails are overused by the 700,000 hikers who use them each year. Park rangers are hard put to cope with these crowds and to suppress game poaching by those who unlawfully shoot bears, deer, raccoons, foxes, squirrels, and grouse, and by those who unlawfully dig up rare plants to take home. Yet, despite the obvious needs for larger ranger staffs, the permanent personnel on the staff of Great Smoky Mountains National Park decreased from 121 persons in 1971 to 107 in 1975. Seasonal employees have been increased, but the situation deteriorates steadily. Much the same story can be told of all of our national parks, but Great Smoky is particularly under stress. In few other parks is the wilderness being "loved to death" so effectively by the very public for

Figure 59.8 Seen from the air, the mature Allegheny Plateau of West Virginia appears largely forested. Relief of 700 to 800 ft (210 to 240 m) is here developed on shales of Devonian age. (J. L. Rich, *The Geographical Review.*)

whom it was created.

Dams and reservoirs have heavily impacted the wild areas of the Southern Appalachians. Many dams of the Tennessee Valley Authority (TVA) lie across streams of the Ridge and Valley Province; reservoirs penetrate the Blue Ridge Province. Farther north, proposed dams recently threatened to destroy the wild scenery of a deep gorge, The Narrows, carved by the New River in western Virginia. The Narrows is often referred to as the "Grand Canyon of the East," because a sandstone formation makes a sheer cliff along its rim. In 1976 the New River gorge achieved protection through its inclusion in the National Wild and Scenic Rivers System. The construction of new dams upstream from the gorge would have provided power for industry as well as additional flood control. These dams, by changing the flow of the river through The Narrows, would have greatly altered the ecosystems of the channel and banks of the river. It should be pointed out that the walls of the New River gorge were at one time intensively mined for coal, which outcrops in thick seams along the upper walls. The nearby forests were cut for timber. This coal mining activity ended many decades ago and small towns in the gorge were largely abandoned. New Second-growth forest has largely hidden from sight the mine working and roadbeds.

The most severely impacted region today within the Appalachian highlands is the coal-bearing portion of the Appalachian Plateaus in Pennsylvania and West Virginia. We will discuss this topic in Unit 61. The effects of strip mining upon stream channels in this area was discussed in Unit 32. Anthracite coal mines of the Ridge and Valley Province in central Pennsylvania have been largely abandoned because of depletion of the coal seams, but severe environmental damage persists in the form of strip-mined pits and the collapse of deep mine workings.

Part of the region which we have studied from the standpoint of landforms is identified with an economic region known as Appalachia. Economic depression and rural poverty are widespread in Appalachia. These conditions often tend to work against the interests of conservationists, because an improvement in the economic status of the inhabitants depends upon the arrival of new industry and an expansion of tourism and recreational use. Persons in economic distress are not as a rule avid conservationists. Employment has first priority, along with the opportunities to sell gasoline, food, and lodging to visitors from the outside. Perhaps the lesson is that conservation of the wilderness is a luxury only the affluent can afford to promote. This lesson applies in much greater force to the developing nations. In Unit 52, we saw that the economic needs of

Brazil have taken precedence over the long-range ecological benefits of preserving the rainforest of Amazonia.

We have now completed our five study units of Part VII—Man and Scenery. The final group of study units will deal with Man's energy resources. We have already found many examples of the ways in which the increased extraction and consumption of energy resources have impacted the environment in the realms of atmosphere, hydrosphere, lithosphere, and biosphere. This area of concern will receive further attention in our final study units.

SCIENCE SUPPLEMENT
Landforms of Folded Strata

In the language of geology, a troughlike downbend of strata is called a **syncline;** the archlike upbend next to it is called an **anticline.** Obviously, in a belt of folded strata,

synclines alternate with anticlines, like a succession of wave troughs and wave crests on the ocean surface.

A series of three block diagrams (Figure 59.9) shows some of the distinctive landforms resulting from fluvial denudation of a belt of folded strata. On eroded folds, the stream network is distorted into a **trellis drainage pattern** (Figure 59.10). The principal elements of this pattern are long, parallel streams occupying the narrow valleys of weak rock.

The folds illustrated in Figure 59.9 are continuous and even-crested; they produce ridges that are approximately parallel in trend and continue for great distances. In some fold regions, however, the folds are not continuous and level-crested. Instead, the fold crests rise or descend from place to place. A descending fold crest is said to plunge. Plunging folds give rise to a zigzag line of ridges. Zigzag ridges are particularly well developed in central Pennsylvania, as shown in Figure 59.6.

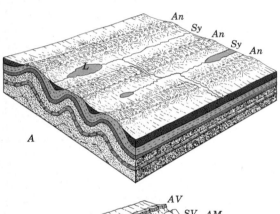

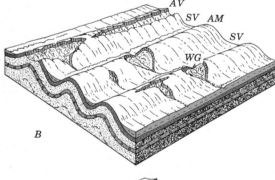

Figure 59.10   A trellis drainage pattern on folds.

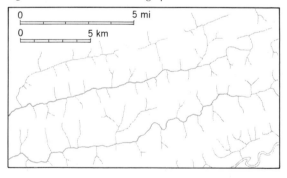

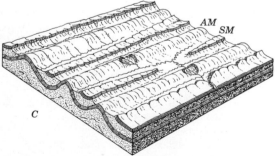

Figure 59.9 *(left)* Stages in the erosional development of folded strata. (A) While folding is still in progress, erosion cuts down the anticlines; alluvium fills the synclines, keeping relief low. An=anticline; Sy=syncline; L=lake. (B) Long after folding has ceased, erosion exposes a highly resistant layer of sandstone or quartzite. AV=anticlinal valley; SV=synclinal valley; WG=watergap. (C) Continued erosion partly removes the resistant formation but reveals another below it. AM=anticlinal mountain; SM=synclinal mountain.

facing page: Four Corners Power Plant. (Environment/Robert Charles Smith.)

PART VIII

Man's Energy Resources

Unit 60
The Fossil Fuels

Petroleum in Antiquity

Petroleum has been useful to Man since the time of earliest recorded history. Petroleum emerges naturally at the earth's surface in many places—as natural gas, crude oil, or liquid asphalt. In the cradle of civilization, that part of the Middle East that runs down through Mesopotamia and along the shores of the Persian Gulf, petroleum seepages occur in great numbers. The Old Testament has several references to these natural seepages. In the fourteenth chapter of Genesis, we read about the kings of Sodom and Gomorrah engaged in battle with their enemies in the Vale of Siddim, "which is the salt sea . . . and the vale of Siddim was full of slimepits and the kings of Sodom and Gomorrah fled, and fell there; and they that remained fled to the mountain." It is thought that the "slimepits" were pits of liquid asphalt, and this must have been a very messy place for combat and a very poor place for beating a fast retreat.

Then in Exodus we can read the familiar story of the infant Moses, whose mother hoped to save him from being thrown into the Nile and drowned by Pharaoh's soldiers. The verse says: "And when she could no longer hide him, she took for him an ark of bulrushes, and daubed it with slime and with pitch, and put the child therein; and she laid it in the flags by the river's brink." The pitch mentioned was natural asphalt, just about the only good water-proofing compound available at the time for caulking the hulls of boats. It is still used for that purpose today by many primitive peoples. Centuries ago, the Dead Sea, around which occur many seepages of petroleum, was named Lake Asphaltites, and even today one can find chunks of asphalt floating on the dense salt water of the lake.

Marco Polo, late in the thirteenth century, described a petroleum seepage in the Baku area on the shore of the Caspian Sea in these words: "On the confines toward Geirgine there is a fountain from which oil springs in great abundance, inasmuch as a hundred shiploads might be taken from it at one time." This note suggests that petroleum products were a valuable economic commodity at the time. In this same area, natural gas seepages, known as the "Eternal Fires" attracted thousands of fire-worshiping pilgrims. Perhaps this is the origin of our modern custom of the eternal gas flame, luring tourists by the thousands to the Tomb of the Unknown Soldier in Paris and to the grave of John F. Kennedy in Arlington Cemetery.

When Europeans arrived in North America, they found that Indians were using natural petroleum as a

Colonel E. L. Drake strikes a pose before his successful well at Oil Creek. The well struck oil at a depth of 69 feet and yielded 2000 barrels in its first year. (Drake Well Museum.)

438

An early gusher in the Oil Creek field. (Drake Well Museum.)

medicine and for mixing paints. American pioneers bought this oil from the Indians for medicinal use; it was called Seneca oil or Genesee oil.

Petroleum as a fuel had its first large-scale use to light lamps. As supplies of whale oil began to diminish, kerosene derived from natural petroleum emerging in seeps began to find a ready market. Spurred by this possibility, the first successful oil well was drilled in 1859 by E. L. Drake. The locality was Oil Creek in Pennsylvania, and was later known as the Titusville field. Kerosene soon replaced whale oil and candles as a lighting fuel and this was the principal economic value of petroleum until the internal combustion engine made its appearance. With the coming of the automobile, petroleum became big corporate business, much of it under the early domination of John D. Rockefeller.

Our study unit investigates both petroleum and coal and their natural occurrences. We shall be particularly interested in the reserves of all forms of hydrocarbon fuels, for at this time the survival of all industrial nations depends on these natural fuels.

Data Source: A. I. Levorsen (1967) *Geology of Petroleum,* 2nd ed., W. H. Freeman, San Francisco, pp. 17-19.

Fossil Fuels as Hydrocarbons

With this unit, we begin a study of Man's energy resources and the impacts of their extraction, processing, and use upon the environment. The first group of energy resources are hydrocarbon compounds occurring as sediments and in sedimentary rocks within the earth's crust. Because these substances represent the remains of ancient plants or animals, or have originated from those remains, they are commonly called **fossil fuels.** By this term they are distinguished from nuclear fuels (derived from the radioactive mineral uranium), from firewood, and from some lesser combustible substances such as dried cattle dung, peanut husks, or garbage, all locally important to some humans as fuel.

Hydrocarbon compounds are organic substances occurring both as solids—peat and coal—and as liquids and gases—crude oil and natural gas. Only coal qualifies physically for designation as a rock.

Peat, Lignite, and Coal

Peat, a soft, fibrous substance of brown to black color, accumulates in a bog environment where the continual presence of water inhibits decay and oxidation of plant remains. A common form of peat is of freshwater origin and represents the filling of shallow lakes, of which many thousands remained over North America and Europe after recession of the great ice sheets of the Pleistocene Epoch

(Unit 42). This peat has been used for centuries as a low-grade fuel. Peat of a different sort is formed in the saltwater environment of tidal marshes (Unit 36).

At various times and places in the geologic past, conditions were favorable for the large-scale accumulation of plant remains, accompanied by subsidence of the area and burial of the compacted organic matter under thick layers of inorganic sediments. In this way, **coal seams** interbedded with shale, sandstone, and limestone strata came into existence (Figure 60.1). Groups of strata containing coal seams are referred to as **coal measures.** Individual seams range in thickness from a fraction of an inch to as great as 50 ft (12 m) in the exceptional case.

Coal is classified into three types, representing a developmental sequence. **Lignite,** or brown coal, is soft and has a woody texture (Figure 60.2A). It represents an intermediate stage between peat and true coal. Further compaction resulting from deep burial resulted in the transformation of lignite into **bituminous coal,** often called "soft coal." In areas where the crust was compressed and folded by mountain-making forces, bituminous coal was further changed, becoming **anthracite.** Whereas bituminous coal typically breaks into blocklike fragments, anthracite exhibits a glassy type of fracture (Figure 60.2B, C).

The coals consist largely of the elements carbon, hydrogen, and oxygen, with small amounts of sulfur also present. Inorganic impurities are also present and are referred to as **ash,** the noncombustible residue after coal is completely burned.

439

Figure 60.1 This great coal seam, ranging from 60 to 90 ft (18 to 27 m) thick, is being strip-mined at Wyodak, Wyoming. The upper power shovel is removing the overburden; the shovel at the base of the seam is removing the coal. (Bureau of Mines, U.S. Department of the Interior.)

For purposes of energy analysis as fuels, the contents of lignite and coal are given in terms of percentages of fixed carbon, volatiles, and water. Figure 60.3 shows typical analyses of samples of lignite, bituminous coal, and anthracite. In the transition from lignite to bituminous coal, a large quantity of water is driven off. In the transition from bituminous coal to anthracite, most of the volatiles are driven off, with the result that anthracite is composed almost entirely of fixed carbon.

Coals are evaluated, or ranked, in order of the **fuel ratio,** which is the ratio of fixed carbon to volatile matter. Volatiles burn in the form of gas and give a long, smoky flame, whereas fixed carbon produces a short, hot, smokeless flame that is steady. The lower-ranking coals—lignite and subbituminous coal (intermediate between lignite and bituminous coal)—not only have low heating value, but also are subject to spontaneous combustion. Lignite readily disintegrates (slakes) after drying in air. Volatiles in bituminous coal are a source of gas used as a fuel. **Coke,** the fixed carbon remaining after heating has driven off the volatiles, is another form of fuel.

The Geologic Occurrence of Coal

Coal is found in all ages of sedimentary strata following the Devonian Period, when land plants evolved. (Refer to Table 23.1 for sequence and ages of geologic periods.) The Carboniferous Period is particularly noted for coals of that age having worldwide distribution. Coals of Permian age are also widespread. Triassic and Jurassic strata also con-

Figure 60.2 Specimens of coals. A. Lignite from North Dakota. (M. E. Strahler.) B. Bituminous coal, Virginia. (U.S. Geological Survey.) C. Anthracite from Pennsylvania. (M. E. Strahler.)

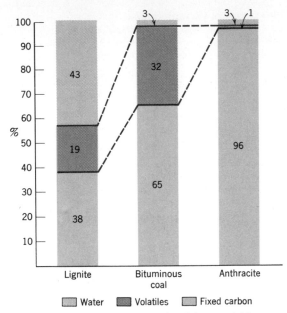

Figure 60.3 Percentage by weight of three variable constituents of representative coals. (From A. N. Strahler [1971] *The Earth Sciences,* 2nd ed., Harper & Row, New York.)

tain coals, but of limited world distribution. Cretaceous coals are second in importance only to those of the Carboniferous Period. Most of the world's lignite is from Cenozoic strata, but some high-ranking coals were also produced in that era.

Figure 60.4 shows coal fields of the 48 contiguous United States as to rank of coal. This map has a significance beyond the subject of resource distribution, since the environmental impact of mining will be felt in the areas shown as coal fields. The most important producer is the Appalachian Field, which includes some 70,000 square miles (180,000 sq km) of both flat-lying and folded strata of Carboniferous and Permian age. The Anthracite Field of northeastern Pennsylvania is very small in area, but was once a major producer. The Interior Fields of bituminous coal give particularly important production in parts of Indiana, Illinois, and Kentucky. Here the strata are of Carboniferous age and lie nearly horizontal. The Rocky Mountain Fields contain bituminous coals and lignite of Cretaceous age, while a large reserve of Cenozoic lignite occurs in the Dakotas and eastern Montana. A large area of lignite in Cenozoic strata underlies the Gulf Coastal Plain. There are minor coal fields in the Pacific Northwest. Alaska has large coal reserves of Cenozoic age.

Figure 60.4 Generalized map of coal fields of the United States and southern Canada. Anthracite fields are shown in black. (After U.S. Geological Survey, Canada Dept. of Mines & Technical Survey; and A. M. Bateman [1950] *Economic Mineral Deposits,* 2nd ed., John Wiley & Sons, New York, p. 645, Figure 16.3.)

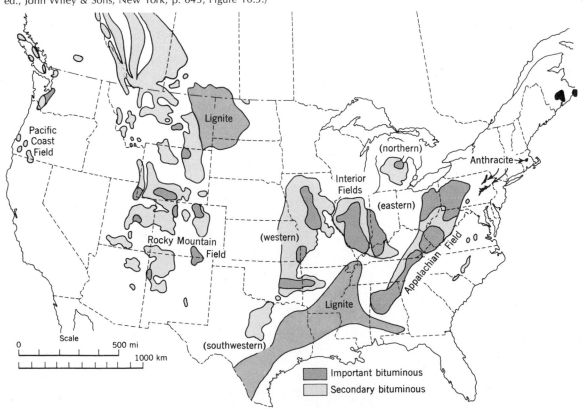

World Coal Reserves

World coal reserves are most unevenly distributed among the continents. Figure 60.5 shows a breakdown into eight world regions; figures are in billions of metric tons. This estimate shows the USSR and the United States to be in very strong positions, while Canada and Western Europe are also very favorably endowed with coal. In contrast, Africa, Australia, Japan, and the Latin American countries are poorly endowed.

Note that these figures include coal lying at depths as great as 4000 ft (1200 m) and occurring in seams as thin as 14 in. (36 cm). With present mining technologies, only about one-tenth of this amount of coal can be mined on an economically successful basis. So the figure of 1500 billion tons for the United States reduces to 150 billion tons, in terms of existing mining methods. Converted into the energy equivalent of crude oil, 150 billion tons of coal represents about 450 billion barrels of crude oil.

Petroleum

The general term **petroleum** spans the range from crude oil to natural gas in the one direction, and to asphalt and related semisolid hydrocarbon substances in the other. Table 60.1 gives the range of carbon, hydrogen, sulfur, nitrogen, and oxygen in typical analyses of the three forms of petroleum. **Crude oil** in the natural state is a mixture of a large number of hydrocarbon compounds. More than 200 compounds have been isolated and analyzed in crude oil. The range and abundance of hydrocarbon compounds differs greatly from one oil field to another.

Crude oils differ in terms of the relative abundances of various hydrocarbon groups. Generally speaking, the paraffin compounds are the most abundant of hydrocarbons in both liquid petroleum and natural gas. Crude oil is

Table 60.1   Element Composition of Typical Petroleum

Element	Percentage by Weight		
	Crude Oil	Asphalt	Natural Gas
Carbon	82–87	80–85	65–80
Hydrogen	12–15	8.5–11	1–25
Sulfur	0.1–5.5	2–8	trace–0.2
Nitrogen	0.1–1.5	0–2	1–15
Oxygen	0.1–4.5	——	——

SOURCE: A. I. Levorsen (1967) *Geology of Petroleum*, 2nd ed., W. H. Freeman and Company, San Francisco and London, p. 177, Table 5.5.
NOTE: Figures rounded to the nearest one-half percent.

described as **paraffin-base** when paraffins are dominant; it is of low density and typically yields good lubricants and a large proportion of kerosene. An example is the paraffin-base crude oil of the Pennsylvania fields. **Asphalt-base** crude oil has a high density and is referred to as a **heavy oil;** its primary yield is in the form of fuel oils.

Natural gas, found in close association with accumulations of crude oil, is a mixture of gases. The principal gas is **methane** (marsh gas, CH_4) and there are minor amounts of ethane, propane, and butane, all of which are hydrocarbon compounds. Small amounts of carbon dioxide, nitrogen, and oxygen are also present, and sometimes helium.

The amount of sulfur present in crude oil (and in coal) is a matter of great environmental importance, since during combustion of the fuel the sulfur becomes oxidized into sulfur dioxide gas (SO_2). As we learned in Unit 7, sulfur dioxide is a dangerous air pollutant. Referring to Table 60.1, you will see that the sulfur content of crude oil varies greatly; the highest percentage is 55 times greater than the lowest. Notice also that the sulfur content of natural gas is generally much lower than for crude oil. For this reason natural gas is preferred as a fuel in urban areas and is described as being "cleaner" than crude oil.

The Origin of Petroleum

While it is generally agreed that petroleum is of organic origin, the nature of the process is hypothetical. A favored explanation for crude oil is that the oil originated within microscopic floating marine plants (phytoplankton) such as the diatoms. As each diatom died, it released a minute droplet of oil, which became enclosed in muddy bottom sediment. Eventually, the mud became a shale formation, in which the oil was disseminated. Some shale formations hold petroleum in a dispersed state, and these give support to the organic hypothesis we have stated. However, the occurrence of petroleum concentrations in porous rock, such as sandstone, requires that the original oil in some manner was forced to migrate from its source region to a porous rock. The less-dense volatile gases were then segregated to occupy a position above the crude oil.

Figure 60.5   Estimated world coal reserves, in billions of metric tons. (Data of the United States Geological Survey.)

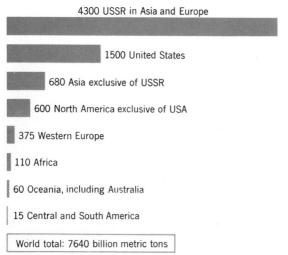

4300 USSR in Asia and Europe

1500 United States

680 Asia exclusive of USSR

600 North America exclusive of USA

375 Western Europe

110 Africa

60 Oceania, including Australia

15 Central and South America

World total: 7640 billion metric tons

Petroleum Reservoirs

Crude oil and natural gas have been concentrated into accumulations known as "oil pools," a misnomer since the oil and gas does not occupy a single large rock cavity. Instead, the oil and gas are held in pore spaces in a **reservoir rock.** Usually this is a porous sand or sandstone, but certain other rocks, such as porous carbonate rocks (limestone, dolomite), can serve as reservoirs.

One of the simplest arrangements of rock strata holding oil and gas is the **dome** or **anticline,** an up-arching of strata shown in cross section in Figure 60.6. The sandstone layer holds natural gas, crude oil, and water in layered order from top to bottom, while an impervious shale formation serves as a **cap rock.** Some details of petroleum-bearing structures, collectively called **petroleum traps,** are given in our science supplement.

Geologic ages of strata in which petroleum is found include all periods from Cambrian to present, but strata of the Paleozoic Era are of oil-bearing importance only in the United States and Canada. Most of the world petroleum production comes from strata of Cretaceous and younger age. Cenozoic strata of Eocene through Miocene age are the dominant oil sources for oil fields the world over, including those of South America, Europe, the Middle East, and Indonesia.

World Oil and Gas Reserves

Proven petroleum reserves are mostly concentrated in a few world regions. As Figure 60.7 shows, the Middle East holds more than half the known world reserves of crude oil. Of this enormous accumulation—some 350 billion barrels—Saudi Arabia has about 40% (140 billion barrels), which is almost four times as much as United States reserves (39 billion barrels). Kuwait, Iran, and Iraq hold most of the remainder of the Middle East oil. Another important center of oil accumulation is in lands surrounding the Gulf of Mexico and Caribbean Sea, with major reserves in the U.S. Gulf Coast region and Venezuela.

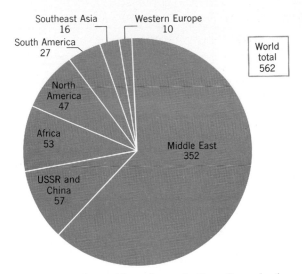

Figure 60.7 The world petroleum pie. These figures by the National Petroleum Council give proven reserves of crude oil in billions of barrels.

Many qualified specialists have made estimates of the total ultimately recoverable crude oil resources of the world. Several independent estimates made in the 1970s ranged from 1800 to 2000 billion barrels, which is over 3 times the known reserves of about 560 billion barrels shown in Figure 60.7. Figure 60.8 is a recent estimate made by Richard L. Jodry; it is based upon a detailed analysis of every potential petroleum producing area in the world. Other recent estimates give a rather similar set of data. Notice that for the United States ultimately recoverable reserves are already more than half consumed, whereas the proportion consumed is much smaller for the other geographical units.

How do natural gas reserves compare with crude oil reserves? For the United States alone, known reserves that can be produced and sold at current prices amount to about 280 trillion cubic feet, for which the crude oil equivalent is about 50 billion barrels. This quantity is somewhat larger than the proven U.S. reserves of crude oil. Undiscovered U.S. natural gas reserves have been estimated by the U.S. Geological Survey to be more than double the known reserves, but some critics feel that the Survey estimate is much too high. The United States natural gas reserves are perhaps higher than those of any nation except the U.S.S.R. (which may have more than twice as much as the U.S.) and Iran (which may have slightly more than the U.S.). Algeria and The Netherlands also rank high in gas reserves.

Oil Shale

Everyone interested in energy resources has heard of **oil shale** and of the tremendous reserve of hydrocarbon fuel it holds. The fact is that this sedimentary rock in the Rocky Mountain region is not really shale at all, and the hydro-

Figure 60.6 In this idealized cross section of a petroleum-bearing anticline or dome, Well A yields gas, Well B oil, and Well C, water. The cap rock is a shale formation; the reservoir rock is sandstone. (From A. N. Strahler [1972] *Planet Earth,* Harper & Row, New York.)

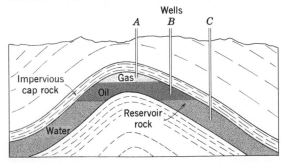

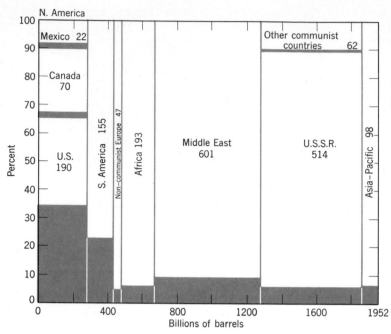

Figure 60.8   Estimated world reserves of ultimately recoverable crude oil. Figures in billions of barrels. (Data of Richard L. Jodry. Diagram after M. King Hubbert [1974] U.S. energy resources, a review as of 1972, Part I; U.S. Congress, Senate Committee on Interior and Insular Affairs, A National Fuels and Energy Policy, U.S. Govt. Printing Office, Washington, D.C.)

carbon it holds is not really petroleum. Strata of the Rocky Mountains called "oil shales" are composed of calcium carbonate and magnesium carbonate. The strata were formed as lake deposits of lime mud (marl) in a Cenozoic lake. These soft, laminated deposits belong to the Green River Formation (Figure 60.9). The oil shale beds occur largely in northeastern Utah, northwestern Colorado, and southwestern Wyoming.

The hydrocarbon matter of the Green River Formation occurs in a particular bed, the Mahogany Zone, about 70 ft (20 m) thick. It is a waxy substance, called **kerogen,** which adheres to the tiny grains of carbonate material. When the shale is crushed and heated to a temperature of 900°F (480°C) the kerogen is altered to petroleum and driven off as a liquid. The rock may be mined and processed in surface plants, or burned in underground mines, from which the oil is pumped to the surface. A pilot plant operated by the Union Oil Company along Parachute Creek in Colorado successfully extracted from 300 to 1000 tons of petroleum per day.

It is estimated that within the entire Green River Formation the fuel resource contained in beds at least 25 ft (7.6 m) thick and which average 25 gallons (95 liters) of oil per ton of shale is equivalent to 600 billion barrels of crude oil. This figure is about the same as for the ultimately recoverable crude oil from the Middle East (see Figure 60.8). By using demonstrated methods of extraction, however, only about 80 billion barrels are available at costs competitive with crude oil of comparable quality. Even so, the figure of 80 billion barrels is just about double that of U.S. known petroleum reserves.

Use of the immense resource of oil shale will be accompanied by many environmental problems, including the ravages of strip mining and the need to consume large quantities of water. These environmental factors will be evaluated in our next study unit.

Fossil Fuel Resources

The principal sources of energy expended by highly industrialized nations in the past century are the fossil fuels: coal and lignite, crude oil, and natural gas. The upper graph in Figure 60.10 shows the annual gross consumption of energy in the United States, derived from fossil fuels, hydropower, and nuclear fuel, since 1900. Energy from each source is given as equivalent to heat yield in British Thermal Units (BTU). The lower graph shows the same data converted to percentage of total annual consumption.

The two graphs tell us that the total consumption of

Figure 60.9   These cliffs of oil shale, near Rifle, Colorado, are the site of test mining operations. (U.S. Bureau of Mines.)

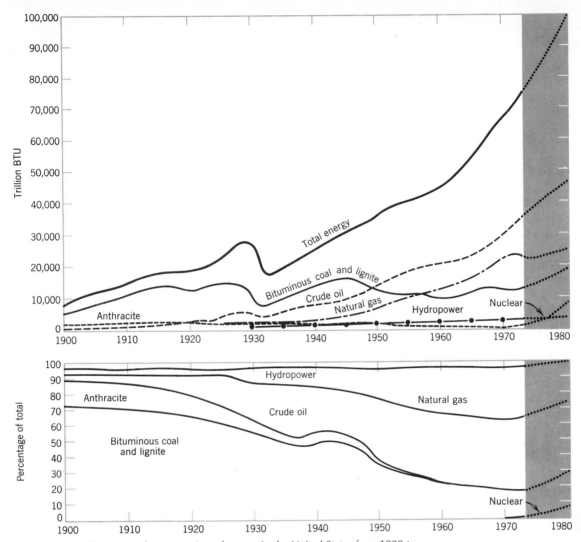

Figure 60.10 Gross annual consumption of energy in the United States from 1900 to 1973, with projections to 1980. (Data of U.S. Bureau of Mines and The Center for Strategic and International Studies.)

energy increased about tenfold from 1900 to 1973. At the same time, the contributions from each of the several sources changed markedly in ratio. Coal and lignite combined were reduced to one-quarter of the starting percentage, while anthracite declined to almost nothing. Both crude oil and natural gas increased in proportion in the same period, but of the two, natural gas greatly expanded its ratio to become nearly equal with crude oil. Hydropower, during this 73-year period, provided only about 4% of the total yearly consumption of energy.

Projections of U.S. energy consumption to the year 1980, shown on the graphs, were prepared in 1973 for use by the Joint Congressional Committee on Atomic Energy. Consumption is expected to increase in all five categories shown. Crude oil consumption will increase more rapidly than that of natural gas, while coal is also expected to show a substantial increase. Nuclear energy, which can

scarcely be shown for 1973, will make a sharp rise to an amount more than double that of hydropower. Nevertheless, fossil fuels are predicted to comprise over 90% of the total gross energy consumption by 1980.

Because the quantity of stored hydrocarbons in the earth's crust is finite, and the rate of geologic production and accumulation of new hydrocarbons is immeasurably small in comparison with the rate of their consumption, the ultimate exhaustion of this energy source is inescapable. When this event will happen is, however, a very difficult thing to predict, since we have to project into the future two independent curves. First is the rate of production, which has been increasing by about 6% per year for crude oil. Until recently discoveries of new oil reserves more than kept pace with production, so there was a moderate increase of known reserves. By 1960, however, the rate of proved discoveries of U.S. reserves began to de-

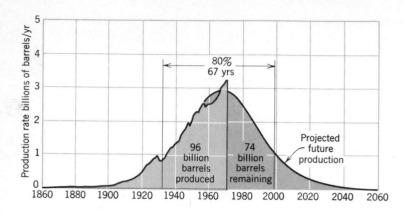

Figure 60.11 The complete cycle of crude oil production for the United States, exclusive of Alaska. (After M. K. Hubbert [1974]. Same source as Figure 60.8.)

cline. Once a decline has set in, reserves will dwindle and eventually be entirely used, after which point production itself must begin a decline and will ultimately approach zero.

The future of U.S. crude oil production has been projected by a leading geophysicist, M. King Hubbert, in the form of a bell-shaped curve, shown in Figure 60.11. The dashed line smooths out production through the year 1970, then follows a predicted rapid decline to 20% in the year 2000. A near-zero value is reached by the year 2060. The peak of production has already passed. A similar projection for natural gas gives much the same schedule, with a production peak about in 1980 and a decline to 20% by the year 2015.

The future of world crude oil production has also been predicted by Hubbert, as shown in Figure 60.12. The production peak is shown to be reached in about 1995, which is 25 years later than for the U.S., while decline to the 20% level is delayed by about the same time span.

What of the future of U.S. coal reserves, which we have set at the equivalent of 450 billion barrels of crude oil? These reserves are fully 10 times larger than the proven U.S. crude oil reserves. Using the Hubbert method, the bell-shaped production of U.S. coal production peaks about in the year 2200, which is two centuries after the peak of crude oil production. A similar curve for world coal production peaks about in the year 2150.

The conclusion we must draw from known reserves and any reasonable schedule of their depletion is that coal will become our main fossil-fuel energy resource by the year 2000, or thereabouts, and will continue in that role for perhaps another century or two, until it too is exhausted.

Other important forms of energy remain to be considered. Our next study unit deals with nuclear energy, a possible substitute for fossil fuels. In later units, we will investigate geothermal energy and solar energy. Important decisions must be made now by the American public and its government as to what measures will be taken to find a substitute for crude oil and natural gas. Shall that substitute be nuclear energy, geothermal energy, or solar energy?

Fossil Fuels as a Nonrenewable Resource

The outstanding environmental concept relating to the fossil fuels is that they have required hundreds of millions of years to accumulate, whereas they are being consumed at a prodigious rate by our industrial society. The fossil fuels are **nonrenewable resources.** Once they are gone, there will be no more, since the quantity produced in a thousand years by geologic processes is scarcely measurable in comparison to the quantity stored through geologic time.

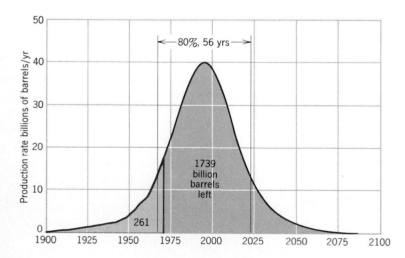

Figure 60.12 The estimated cycle of world crude oil production. (After M. K. Hubbert [1974]. Same source as Figure 60.8.)

A second environmental concept, which we will investigate in the next study unit, is that the extraction and processing of fossil fuels is a potent cause of environmental disruption. A third environmental concept, already explored in earlier units, is that the burning of the fossil fuels releases heat and pollutants into the atmosphere, with far-reaching impacts upon humans and all natural ecosystems.

SCIENCE SUPPLEMENT
Petroleum-Bearing Structures

While a few oil pools occur in structures as simple as that shown in Figure 60.6, most are more complex. A typical **stratigraphic dome** containing a valuable oil accumulation is illustrated in Figure 60.13. At the ground surface, this structure is expressed as an elliptical area of low hills and shows that at least some of the up-arching occurred quite recently. Many dome structures of this type have been important oil producers in the Rocky Mountain region.

Other arrangements and structures of sedimentary strata are capable of holding large quantities of oil and gas; these structures are known generally as **traps.** One type of trap is the **fault trap,** illustrated in Figure 60.14. The fault has displaced sedimentary strata so that petroleum has migrated up the inclined sandstone formation to accumulate against the barrier formed by shale on the opposite side of the fault surface. Another general class of trap is the **stratigraphic trap.** One trap of this class is illustrated in Figure 60.15. The sand formations become thinner from right to left as the elevation of the formation rises. The formation is said to **pinch out.** Petroleum accumulates in the highest part of the sand layer, held within impervious shales above and below. The **pinch-out trap** is particularly important in

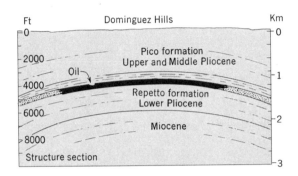

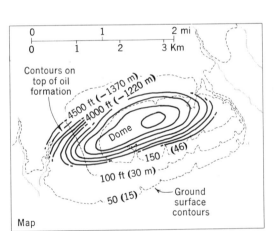

Figure 60.13   The Dominguez Hills, a low dome in an early stage of erosion, has beneath it a valuable oil pool. (After H. W. Hoots and U.S. Geological Survey.)

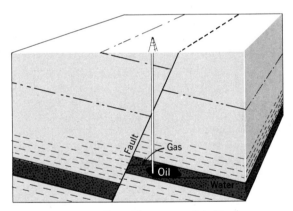

Figure 60.14   An oil pool has accumulated in the permeable sandstone beds and is prevented from escaping by the impermeable shales faulted against the edge of the sandstone layer.

Figure 60.15   Oil pools can form in the fringes of sand formations which pinch out in the direction of rise.

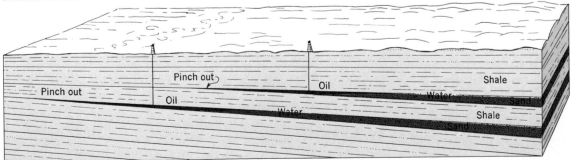

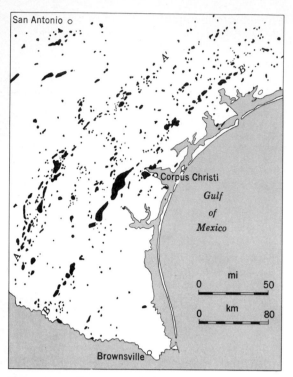

Figure 60.16 Two zones of oil pools on up-dip pinch-outs of sands of Eocene age (AA′) and Oligocene age (BB′). (After A. I. Levorsen.)

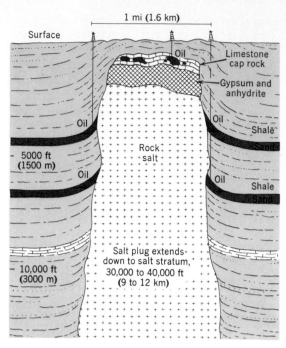

Figure 60.17 Idealized structure section of a salt dome.

Figure 60.18 Distribution of salt domes of the Gulf Coast region is indicated by dots. (After K. K. Landes.)

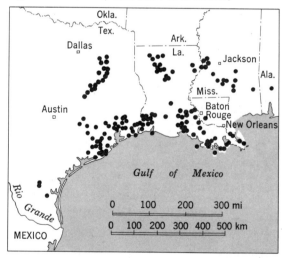

strata of the Gulf Coast region. Figure 60.16 shows the oil pools associated with two pinch-out structures in sand formations of Eocene and Oligocene ages under the coastal plain of Texas.

Another type of oil pool, abundant in the thick geosynclinal strata of the Gulf Coast, is associated with **salt domes,** or **salt plugs** (Figure 60.17). These strange, stalklike bodies of rock salt project upward through thousands of feet of strata. Apparently they were forced up by slow plastic flowage from thick salt formations lying in deep lower layers. Surrounding strata are sharply bent up and faulted against the side of the salt plug, making traps for petroleum. Salt plugs commonly have a cap rock of limestone resting upon a plate of gypsum and anhydrite. Oil may collect in cavities in the limestone. Distribution of salt domes of the Gulf Coast is shown in Figure 60.18.

Unit 61 Environmental Impacts of Fossil Fuel Extraction

Oil on the Beaches—The Santa Barbara Disaster of 1969

When you take a drive up the Pacific Coast Highway from Los Angeles to Santa Barbara, you will see them, if there happens to be no fog that day. They look at first like the bridges of large ships moored offshore, but then, as you get a better look, they turn out to be offshore drilling platforms. The two closest to shore as you near Santa Barbara are named Hilda and Hazel—the "H" stands for Humble Oil Company. By no means a tribute to the female form, a platform rises on tubular legs; it is a complex mass of steel beams, decks, derricks, rooms, and a drilling rig. The entire structure rises several stories above the ocean surface. At night the platform lights sparkle like jewels. Much farther from shore—six miles airline from Santa Barbara—you may spot more platforms, and far beyond them a chain of islands forming the other side of the Santa Barbara Channel. Two of the distant platforms belong to the Union Oil Company. They are unimaginatively designated A and B. Platform A is where the trouble began; where and when it will end nobody can guess.

Oil beneath Platforms A and B has accumulated in strata that are arched up in a wavelike fold. The oil-bearing beds are at shallow depth beneath the seabed, with only a thin caprock to hold the oil from escaping. A number of fractures, known as faults, cut through the entire structure and its caprock. Add to this situation a geologic history of numerous earthquakes, each representing a small slip along a fault, and you have all of the ingredients of chronic leakage of crude oil from the seabed.

Natural seepages of petroleum in the Santa Barbara Channel were noted and documented by the Spaniards, first of the Europeans to settle the California coast. One Franciscan monk, Father Pedro Font, wrote in 1776 that "much tar which the sea throws up is found on the shores. Little balls of fresh tar are also found. Perhaps there are springs of it which flow out of the sea." Proof that natural seepages could make large oil slicks is evident in a description written in 1792 by Vancouver, who was Captain Cook's navigator. When sailing through the channel he wrote that a layer of what seemed to be dissolved tar covered the sea in all directions within the limits of view.

Trouble came to Santa Barbara on January 28, 1969, when a new well being drilled beneath Platform A exploded with a great roar, sending up a jet

Oil reaches the sea surface from beneath Platform A off Santa Barbara, June 1969. (Santa Barbara News-Press.)

of drilling mud, crude oil, and natural gas. This was a blowout, perhaps the worst form of accident that can happen in drilling for oil. Soon the sea around the platform was "boiling" with oil rising from the ocean floor. A massive oil slick had begun to grow and within a day or two covered at least 120 square miles of ocean surface. The oil was not coming out of the well head, which had been quickly stoppered, but from a rupture in the seabed. The flow was fed by leakage through fractures starting at a point some hundreds of feet down, where the well had no protective steel casing.

Within a few days, crude oil was coming ashore at Santa Barbara, where an army of workers struggled to remove it from the beaches and harbor. Crowds of townspeople and visitors looked on in anger and dismay. Bird-cleaning stations were set up and manned around the clock by volunteers in a futile attempt to save oil-soaked grebes and other sea birds.

As the oil continued to pour out unchecked, a public reaction of monumental proportions began to build. Quickly a group of local citizens formed GOO!—Get Oil Out!. As later events proved, the environmentalists had taken on as adversaries not only the entire oil industry, but also the Nixon administration in Washington and the Department of the Interior. The ensuing interplay of all factions is incredibly complex, with charges and counter-charges flying interminably, and with representatives and committees coming and going—looking, talking, and meeting the press. Chief villain in the eyes of the environmentalists was Union Oil Company President Fred L. Hartley, who was misquoted by the *Wall Street Journal* as saying "I'm amazed at the

publicity for the loss of a few birds." Later he issued an official version reading "I'm always tremendously impressed at the publicity that the death of birds receives versus the loss of people in our country in this day and age." Interior Secretary Walter Hickel, then new at his job, appeared to the environmentalists to vacillate in the decision to shut down all channel drilling then in progress. However, on February 7, he issued the order to halt all drilling and all production from existing wells. (Platform A and its chain of neighboring platforms is located on federal leases beyond the three-mile limit and therefore beyond limits of state control.) Also under criticism was the United States Geological Survey, which, as an agency within the Interior Department, was responsible for overseeing oil production and assuring that all offshore drilling was in compliance with safety regulations.

Early in February 1969, the faulty well beneath Platform A was plugged with concrete, ending the first phase of the disaster. However, oil seepage continued from the seabed. Then on February 24, another well on the same platform blew out of control, generating a new oil spill. Again oil came ashore and again the army of workers went into action. This well was plugged, but oil continued to emerge. It was to be many months before oil seepage dropped to low levels.

Meantime, President Nixon had convened an advisory panel to consider the future of oil extraction in the Santa Barbara Channel. The panel recommended that oil extraction be continued in order to drain the oil reservoirs and thus reduce dangerous pressure. The panel's decision was protested by environmentalists on grounds that most of the panel mem-

On the Santa Barbara beach, workers spread straw to soak up oil that has drifted ashore from the blowout. (Tom Myers/De Wys.)

bers were connected with the oil industry or were from the U.S. Geological Survey.

On February 20, Secretary Hickel halted the sale of offshore oil leases, but early in April the ban on new drilling he had put into effect in February was partially lifted. Drilling operations began immediately.

Assessment of ecological damage proved to be another bone of contention. One study team was headed up by Dr. Dale Straughan, an Australian ecologist on the faculty of University of California at Santa Barbara. Her work was financed by a grant of $240,000 from the Western Oil and Gas Association. When her report eventually appeared, it was immediately suspect, particularly because her conclusion was that the damage to flora and fauna was less than predicted and that the area was recovering nicely. The controversy over the Straughan report became so highly vituperative that one person commented: "It looks as if more tempers have been lost than marine life." About 4000 dead birds were counted during the entire period of the oil spill, and perhaps twice as many died in all.

The story of oil extraction in the Santa Barbara Channel is far from reaching its end. Debate continues over sale of new oil leases, renewed drilling operations, and the establishment of shore facilities for receiving and processing new oil. In 1976 residents of Santa Barbara could see a test-drilling vessel anchored far beyond the platforms, apparently in the major shipping channel through which many oil tankers pass each week. They also learned that the world's tallest drilling platform was on its way to the Santa Barbara channel, to be placed in 850 feet of water by the EXXON Corporation.

In this study unit we will cover a broad spectrum of environmental impacts of the extraction and processing of fossil fuels. We will give coal mining, rather than petroleum extraction, the major share of our attention, because, as we learned in the previous unit, coal reserves will be the major United States fossil-fuel energy resource in decades to come.

DATA SOURCE: Carol E. and John S. Steinhart (1972) *Blowout: A Case Study of the Santa Barbara Oil Spill*, Duxbury Press, (Wadsworth Publ. Co.) North Scituate, Mass., 138 pp.; Jeffrey Potter (1973) *Disaster by Oil*, Macmillan Co., New York, pp. 153-245.

Man as an Agent of Land Scarification

Gross changes in the configuration of the land surface by extraction of the fossil fuels, particularly coal and oil shale, are simply one expression of Man's ability to bring enormous machine power and explosives to bear at concentrated points. Man in a modern technological society is capable of moving from one place to another enormous masses of soil, regolith, and bedrock for two basic purposes: first, to extract mineral resources; second, to reorganize terrain into suitable configurations for highway grades, airfields, building foundations, dams, canals, and various other large structures. Both activities involve removal of earth materials, which destroys entirely the preexisting ecosystems and habitats of plants and animals. Building up of new land upon adjacent surfaces, using those same earth materials, is a process that also destroys by burial the preexisting ecosystems and habitats.

Scarification is a general term for excavations and other land disturbances produced for purposes of extracting mineral resources. Scarification includes nearby accumulation of mineral waste (spoil, tailings). Among the forms of scarification are open-pit ore mines, coal strip mines, quarries for structural materials, borrow pits along highway grades, sand and gravel pits, clay pits, phosphate pits, scars from hydraulic mining, and stream gravel deposits reworked by dredging.

Scarification is on the increase both because demands for coal to meet energy requirements are on the rise and because of increased demands for industrial minerals used in manufacturing and construction. At the same time, as the richer and more readily available mineral deposits are consumed, industry turns to poorer grades of ores and to less easily accessible coal deposits, with the result that the rate of scarification is further increased.

Coal Mining

The mining of coal has a strong environmental impact in many ways upon the land and water of the coal fields, and upon the miners themselves. We can only understand these effects if we know something of the manner in which coal is mined. For deep-lying coal seams, vertical shafts are driven down from the surface to reach the coal, which is mined by extension of horizontal **drifts** and rooms into the face of the seam. In mountainous terrain, drifts can be driven directly into the seam where it is exposed on the mountainside.

Two underground methods are in common use in removing the coal. One is the **room-and-pillar system,** in which about half of the coal is left behind in supporting pillars. Figure 61.1 shows the plan of such a mine. A second method is the **long-wall system** in which all of the coal seam is removed inward from a large circumference, leaving a large central block to support the mine shaft. The roof above the excavated area is allowed to settle as coal is removed. Subterranean mining of coal is often followed by damage to the overlying land surface through mine collapse leading to subsidence. One example comes from the

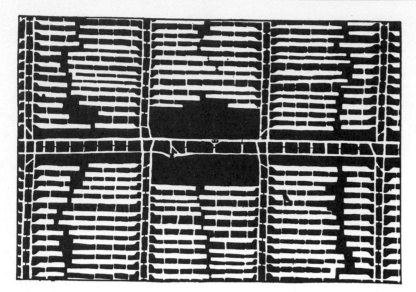

Figure 61.1   Plan (map) of a room-and-pillar mine showing rooms (white areas) and coal (black). About half of the coal remains to support the roof. (Illinois Geological Survey, Bull. 56, p. 47, Figure 17.)

city of Scranton, Pennsylvania. Here the collapse of abandoned anthracite mine workings has repeatedly caused settling and fracturing of the ground, damaging streets and houses. Near Hanna, Wyoming, the cave-in of abandoned shallow coal mines has produced many deep pits, while underground burning of the coal seam has added to progressive collapse.

Where the coal seams lie close to the surface or actually outcrop along hillsides, the **strip-mining** method is used. Here, earthmoving equipment removes the covering strata (overburden) to bare the coal, which is lifted out by power shovels. There are two kinds of strip mining, each adapted to the given relationship between ground surface and coal seam. **Area strip mining** is used in regions of nearly flat land surface under which the coal seam lies horizontally (Figure 61.2A). After the first trench is made and the coal removed, a parallel trench is made, the overburden of which is piled as a spoil ridge into the first trench. Thus the entire seam is gradually uncovered and there remains a series of parallel spoil ridges (Figure 61.3). Phosphate beds are mined extensively by the area strip mining method in Florida, and the method is also used for mining clay layers. The **contour strip mining** method is used where a coal seam outcrops along a steep hillside (Figure 61.2B). The coal is uncovered as far back into the hillside as possible and the overburden dumped on the downhill side. There results a bench bounded on one side by a steep rock cliff, or "high wall", and on the other side by a ridge of loose spoil with a steep outer slope leading down into the valley bottom. The benches form sinuous patterns following the plan of the outcrop (Figure 61.4). Strip mining is carried to depths as great as 100 ft (30 m) below the surface. Associated with contour strip mining is **auger mining** in which enormous auger drills are run horizontally into the exposed face of the coal seam after the initial strip mining is completed. Augers with cutting heads several feet in diameter are used and are capable of penetrating as far as 200 ft (60 m) into the seam.

Figure 61.2   A. Area strip mining. B. Contour strip mining.

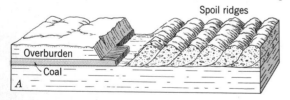

The Growth of Strip Mining

Strip mining of coal began to become a large-scale operation in the Appalachian and Interior coal fields after World War II. Some 4 million acres (1.6 million hectares) of land surface has already been affected by strip mining, and most of this area has been in the Appalachian region. There now remains an estimated 20,000 mi (32,000 km) of high wall, the inner rock wall exposed after contour strip mining has been completed. Strip mining currently affects about 5000 acres (2000 hectares) of land per week in the United States. An additional factor of change with continued strip mining in the Appalachian region is that the thickness of overburden which must be removed has steadily increased. The U.S. Geological Survey has stated that between 1946 and 1970 the average thickness of overburden increased from 32 to 55 ft (10 to 17 m) and the

Figure 61.3 Area strip mining in Ohio County, Kentucky. Dragline in background is removing overburden and piling it at the right. Loader in foreground is removing the exposed coal. (TVA.)

maximum thickness from 70 ft (21 m) in 1955 to 185 ft (56 m) in 1970. The average ratio of overburden to coal has gone from 6:1 in 1946 to 11:1 in 1970.

The major trend of change in strip-mining activity in recent years and for the future is the shift in mining activity to the Rocky Mountain coal field (see map, Figure 60.4). Here in the states of Montana, North Dakota, Wyoming, Utah, Colorado, Arizona, and New Mexico, extremely thick coal seams of Cretaceous age are readily accessible to strip mining (see Figure 60.1). The coal is of the low-sulfur type, ideally suited to firing electricity generating plants in large cities where air pollution standards are strict. Output of western coal increased by a factor of 13 in the period 1961 to 1972. Although the western strip mines are fewer in number than those of the Appalachian region, they are much larger operations. Coal seams in Wyoming and Montana reach thicknesses of 50 to 75 ft (15 to 23 m). The enormous draglines that remove the overburden weigh more than 13,000 tons and stand more than 300 ft (90 m) high. A single mine can extract several million tons of coal per year, a prodigious quantity by comparison with individual Appalachian mines. The state of Montana alone is expected to produce by 1980 some 50 million tons of coal per year from only five large strip mines.

Environmental Impact of Strip Mining

Spoil ridges left by strip mining are highly susceptible to rapid erosion under torrential rainfall. Large amounts of sediment are carried downvalley to cause aggradation of stream channels (Units 31 and 32; see Figure 32.7). On steep mountain slopes of the Appalachian area, mass wasting in the form of earthflows and mudflows affects the unstable spoil banks, while the presence of sulfur-bearing minerals in the coal seams gives rise to acid water drainage, severly impacting streams draining the local area (Unit 18).

The strip mining of semiarid lands of the Rocky Mountain coal field creates particularly serious environmental problems not found in the humid eastern states. Semidesert shrub, woodland, and grassland of this region does not regenerate rapidly if destroyed, and cannot recover unless the land surface is carefully regraded and the soil is replaced. The raw spoil, as left by mining, cannot store soil water for plant use and, moreover, in many cases exposes salts and toxic minerals unfavorable to the native plants. One successful means of adequately restoring land affected by strip mining in this region is to regrade the spoil

Figure 61.4 Contour strip mining in Wise County, Virginia. (Kenneth Murray, Kingsport, Tennessee, from Nancy Palmer Photo Agency, Inc.)

into a configuration of broadly rounded summits and gentle slopes, then to apply a soil cover. The soil can be first removed from the area to be mined and set aside until regrading has been completed. Costs of such reclamation range from $500 to $5000 per acre. Using the higher figure, the reclamation process would probably add not more than 10 cents per ton to the price of coal from the western strip mines.

Strip mining in the western region has had unfavorable side effects on ground-water resources, and these effects can be expected to become more severe as mining expands. The coal seam and its overlying and underlying strata are in some cases important aquifers in artesian ground-water systems. Not only can the aquifer be physically disrupted by strip mining, but the quality of the ground water can become impaired by the release of contaminants from the broken rock. Pumping of water out of a mine can lower the water table of the surrounding region and cause supply wells used for watering of cattle to become dry. Lowering of the water table can also cause low-lying meadows, used for summer pasture, to dry up.

Federal legislation to limit and regulate strip mining has run a turbulent course in the past decade. In 1971, there were pending at one time 19 different congressional bills on strip-mining control, including the Hechler bill that would have banned all strip mining. With the eastern United States dependent upon strip mining for nearly 50% of its coal used in generating electric power, this drastic measure died for lack of congressional and administration support. The Nixon administration favored a mild program of reclamation, strongly supported by coal-mining and power interests. The Tennessee Valley Authority (TVA)

came under strong attack from environmentalists for depending upon strip-mined coal for its power generating plants. In 1971, TVA used 60 million tons per year of strip-mined coal, but denied that the mining had contributed to poverty and depopulation of the five coal-producing states of Appalachia.

In 1972 and 1973, various highly restrictive bills were debated in committees in both the Senate and House, while the Nixon administration continued to press for a more moderate bill. In 1974, both House and Senate passed a tough bill forbidding the strip mining of coal in areas where reclamation would not be feasible. The bill would have imposed strict regulations on mining operations carried out in federally owned lands. In 1975, the Surface Mining Control and Reclamation Act, as the bill was titled, was sent to President Ford, who vetoed the bill. The Congress failed by only 3 votes to override the presidential veto. Further action seemed unlikely until at least 1977.

Land Subsidence Caused by Petroleum Withdrawal

In Unit 19, we investigated subsidence of the land surface brought about by heavy pumping of ground water. Compaction of weak strata accompanied the removal of the water from pores in the rock. A similar effect has been observed where crude oil has been pumped from strata in certain susceptible kinds of reservoir rocks.

Perhaps the best-known example of this phenomenon is that at Long Beach, California. Here the Wilmington oil field lies within the harbor area of the city (Figure 61.5).

Figure 61.5   Contours superimposed on this air view of the Long Beach, California, harbor area show the amount of subsidence in feet in the period 1928-1960. The photograph was taken in 1971, by which time all subsidence had been halted by brine injection. (Port of Long Beach.)

Oil production began in 1936 and was developed over an area of about 10 sq mi (26 sq km). Subsidence began shortly after the field was opened and continued at a rate ranging from 0.5 to 2.0 ft (0.15 to 0.6 m) per year in the center of the affected area. Figure 61.5 shows by contour lines the total subsidence by 1962, which was just over 27 ft (8 m) in the center. Subsidence is attributed to the lowering of fluid pressure, permitting the sedimentary particles to pack more closely and reduce rock volume in strata far beneath the surface. Because the subsidence brought a large land area below sea level, protective dikes and levees were built to keep out the sea. The subsidence also did much costly damage to the oil wells. In view of the prospect of continued subsidence, remedial measures have been taken in the form of water injection into deep wells to raise the underground fluid pressure. This costly procedure was successful in reversing subsidence in the southern part of the field.

Blowouts from Offshore Oil Wells

As the exploration for new oil fields and the drilling of production wells extends farther out upon the continental shelves, the prospects increase for accidents of various sorts leading to massive oil spills. One type of accident, often referred to as a **blowout,** is caused by high gas pressure within an oil well. Where the bedrock is of a weak sedimentary type, easily fractured, or where faults cut the rock, forming zones of crushed and weakened rock, the pressure of the gas rising from the oil pool beneath may force its way through the surrounding rock to reach the sea floor. Figure 61.6 shows one possible structure in which a blowout might occur. The drill hole has passed through a fault zone and oil is escaping through that passage, emerging on the sea floor as an oil seepage. Natural oil seepages are often found where such structures occur.

The Santa Barbara blowout, which we described in our opening paragraphs, seems to have resulted from the fracture of weak rock under gas pressure. This type of blowout

Figure 61.6 Schematic diagram of petroleum seepage along a fault zone penetrated by an offshore well.

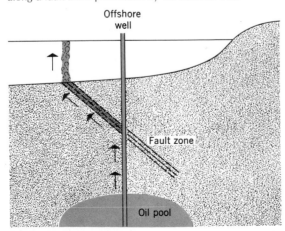

can be prevented by use of a steel well casing. In the Santa Barbara blowout, a casing was used only to a depth of about 240 ft (73 m). However, weak rock—poorly cemented sandstone and claystone—extended much deeper than the casing. It is thought by some geologists that extension of the casing for another 500 ft (150 m) might have prevented the blowout from occurring.

Water Requirements for Fossil Fuel Use

An indirect form of environmental impact caused by the extraction, processing, and consumption of fossil fuels arises from the need to consume water. In the humid eastern states and Pacific Northwest, a large water surplus is available, so that in those areas environmental problems relate primarily to air and water pollution. In the semiarid parts of the Rocky Mountain region and Colorado plateau, where large resources of coal and oil shale remain to be extracted and processed, the sources of required water are already severely limited. The flows of most large streams are already diverted to irrigation of agricultural land or to distant urban water uses.

In plans to construct gigantic electric power plants that will use local coal from the strip mines of western coal fields, provision must be made for large volumes of water to condense the steam as it passes through cooling towers after driving the turbines. Plants designed to process coal into energy forms more economical to transport can also be heavy consumers of water, depending upon the process used, whether it be coal liquefaction or coal gasification. Both strip mining and oil-shale processing use large amounts of water to irrigate the restored land surfaces created by their mineral waste. In the case of oil-shale processing, the dry, spent shale must be disposed of in large spoil banks, and these require large amounts of water to become compacted and stabilized.

Consider the case of water need versus available water supply for a large future oil-shale industry in the Piceance Basin of Colorado. The U.S. Geological Survey estimates a need for 255,000 to 295,000 acre-feet of water per year for an oil-shale industry producing one million barrels of oil per day. The Upper Colorado River Basin, from which this water would have to be taken, has an allocated total water resource of about 5 million acre-feet per year. However, the present water use, committed future uses, evaporative water losses, and other uses total all but 167,000 acre feet, a figure much less than the oil-shale industry would need. To satisfy the need of the oil-shale industry, future water commitments to other uses would have to be diverted to the oil-shale industry. For an oil-shale industry producing several million barrels of oil per day, large amounts of water presently going into agricultural use would have to be transferred to the oil industry.

Ground water cannot be counted upon as a major source of cooling water for the growth of power plants and coal-processing plants close to the coal mines, because recharge of ground water is very slow in the semiarid climate. An example is the use of ground water to supply a slurry line that carries coal from the Black Mesa coal mine in northeastern Arizona to the Mojave Power Plant in Nevada, a distance of 273 mi (440 km). The pulverized coal is mixed with water to form a slurry, which is pumped through a closed conduit. The slurry water is drawn from a deep sandstone aquifer beneath Black Mesa. The quantity of water used is 3200 acre feet (4 million cubic meters) per year. This is only about one-sixth the amount that is consumed at the other end by the Mojave Power Plant for cooling, but it represents a serious drain upon ground water resources that might otherwise be developed for future industrial growth by Indians in the Hopi and Navajo Reservations.

And so we end this study unit on a disturbing note: Vast stores of fossil fuels lie in an arid region where the water needed to convert those fuels to electric power and other energy forms is in short supply. Without the necessary water for cooling purposes, the alternative is to ship the coal out of the region by rail, an expensive form of energy transport.

Unit 62
Nuclear Energy

1976 — Year of Decision for the American Nation

The spring of 1976 held its myriad distractions for the American public, not the least of them being an orgy of patriotism called the Bicentennial. The presidential primaries were another major distraction of that period. Californians were already up to their ears in taped commercials from both the candidates and the Bicentennial people, but this was not all. In April, California radio listeners began to hear from a new line of hucksters; by May the message was grindingly familiar: "Vote NO on Proposition 15." Few listeners had any clear idea of what Proposition 15 was all about, except that it was about nuclear power in California. On June 8th, they would have to go to the polls to vote for or against Proposition 15. In many ways, this simple act of decision was a scale model of the greatest decision America must make in the 20th Century. Will America go the nuclear way, or some other way?

Proposition 15, officially known as The Nuclear Safeguards Act was placed on the California ballot by a public petition signed by more than 400,000 citizens. Like any proposed public law, the new act is a long document and not easily covered in a small capsule. The major provision of the law requires that within five years of its enactment all present and future nuclear power plants must be certified as safe in operation, along with all systems for storage or disposal of nuclear wastes. If a plant fails to meet this provision within five years, its output must be reduced to 60% of operating capacity, and each year thereafter the output further reduced by 10%. Additionally, all nuclear operations are to be provided with full compensation to citizens and businesses for any possible losses from nuclear hazards. The shutback to 60% operation applies in one year if compensation provision has not been achieved. The decision as to whether the safety provisions of the act have been met is given to the California Legislature. Approval requires a two-thirds majority of both houses of the legislature and is to be based upon

New nuclear units under construction at the San Onofre Nuclear Generating Station, near San Clemente, California. The original unit (dome in background) has been in operation since 1968. (Southern California Edison Company.)

457

recommendations of an advisory group. This group consists of at least 15 persons—"distinguished experts in the fields of nuclear engineering, nuclear weaponry, land use planning, cancer research, sabotage techniques, security systems, public health, geology, seismology, energy resources, liability insurance, transportation security, and environmental sciences, as well as concerned citizens." The advisory group is to hold public hearings and render its opinion by means of final report, the contents of which is to be made public. The Legislature is also to hold public hearings and disclose all information coming to its attention.

Support for the California Nuclear Safeguards Act came from a wide range of groups and individuals, for example, the Sierra Club, Friends of the Earth, and the California Democratic Council. Individual supporters whose names are familiar included Paul Erlich, Linus Pauling, Jack Lemmon, and San Francisco's Mayor Moscone. The Sierra Club, in a public letter described Proposition 15 quite accurately as "a carefully worded, moderate measure designed to assure that the citizens of California will have nuclear power only when proven safe, with proper storage of wastes and full insurance in case of accidents." The letter went on to say: "The Sierra Club believes it would be wiser to solve these problems before vast amounts of capital are committed to expanding this energy source."

Intense opposition to Proposition 15 came from the energy development industries—mostly electric power companies, whose donations to defeat the proposition exceeded $250,000 (according to the Sierra Club's letter). Radio and TV commercials opposed to Proposition 15 hammered away at the single theme that the Nuclear Safeguards Act would completely stop the development of nuclear power in California and that this energy source is badly needed to achieve energy independence. The speakers asserted that passage of the act would cost each California taxpayer several hundred dollars, but in what form and over what period was not stated. Speakers who gave this commercial message included a physician and an oceanographer. One of the big guns of the opposition was Edward Teller, the distinguished nuclear physicist who played a large role in developing the atom bomb and peaceful uses of the atom. Writing in a *Newsweek* editorial (May 17, 1976), Teller gave this advice:

The reactors should be deployed primarily in the advanced countries where they can be handled with the greatest safety. The energy supplied by nuclear reactors could reduce oil consumption in these advanced countries, to the world's be-

nefit. Every barrel of oil that a country like the United States imports is taken away from other countries where the need is greater. This is as strong an argument for cutting oil imports as our goal of "energy independence."

Yet, in the midst of this desperate worldwide need for energy, certain groups in California have put a referendum on the ballot in next month's election that could have disastrous consequences. Passage of this initiative would effectively forbid deployment of more reactors and would reduce the maximum permitted power of present reactors to 60 per cent of capacity (this would not enhance safety to any great extent but would make any reactor an economic fiasco). Under this proposal these consequences could be avoided only by an utterly unworkable bureaucratic procedure. Oregon and more than a dozen other states are ready to follow the lead of California. As a result, the American nuclear industry could be dead in a couple of years. If this should come to pass, America will have turned its back on the one overwhelming environmental trouble of the world—poverty.

It is remarkable and fortunate that among responsible legislative bodies no bill has been passed that would stop the building of nuclear reactors. The opponents of nuclear power are, therefore, turning to the mass of the voters. These voters are fully capable of understanding the issues, if they learn the facts. But they are subjected to sensational stories and become easy prey to scare propaganda.

Indeed, there is no better subject with which to scare people than nuclear energy. What is new, what is not completely understood, is always frightening. But nuclear energy is a special case.

It comes from a remote part of research that, in the minds of many people, borders on science fiction. It was developed in wartime and was shrouded in secrecy. It came to the attention of mankind when, in two strokes, more than 100,000 people were killed in the final days of a terrible war.

If we had demonstrated the bomb to the Japanese first, we probably would not have needed to use it on their cities. Then today we would feel safer and have a more rational attitude toward nuclear energy. The California initiative would have no chance of passing.*

On June 8, 1976 the voters of California turned down Proposition 15 by a two-to-one majority, affirming their support for further development of nuclear power in the nation's most populous state. In November elections, later that year, voters in six other states also defeated antinuclear initiatives. Only in Missouri did a consumer-oriented antinuclear issue pass, requiring power companies to wait until nuclear plants are in operation before passing on their construction costs to consumers.

In this unit and the next, we will investigate nuclear energy and some of its hazards, as well as the environmental impacts of extraction and processing of nuclear fuels.

The Position of Nuclear Energy Today

In 1954, the United States Congress voted to amend the Atomic Energy Act to allow nuclear energy to be used for the production of electricity. By 1975, about 60 nuclear plants were in operation in the United States with a total rated capacity of nearly 37,000 megawatts of power. Compared with the total U.S. 1975 electric capacity of about 215,000 megawatts, the nuclear contribution amounted to only about 17% of the total and very nearly the same capacity as for all U.S. hydroelectric generating plants combined. So nuclear energy has a long way to go to displace electrical energy produced by burning of fossil fuels. A goal of 50% contribution by nuclear energy in 1980 seemed in sight until recently.

Today, the future of nuclear energy in the United States is clouded, since the safety of nuclear energy is now much in doubt, as is the future adequacy of raw mineral supplies from which nuclear fuels are derived. In this study unit, we will review some technical aspects of nuclear energy in order to gain a background with which to evaluate the merits of the great debate on the question: Is further development of nuclear energy the wisest course of action?

Nuclear Fission

Nuclear energy plants operating today to generate electricity are all based upon the principal of **nuclear fission,** which simply means "splitting the nucleus of the atom." The important nuclear fuel that concerns us here is a particular form of the element uranium. To understand the basic issues and problems relating to nuclear energy as a resource, you will find it helpful to understand some basic facts about atoms.

The **nucleus,** or dense core of the atom, consists of two kinds of particles: **neutrons** and **protons.** The number of neutrons within a given element is only approximately constant whereas the number of protons is fixed. An example is a form of the element **uranium** (U), in which the atomic nucleus has 146 neutrons and 92 protons. The total of neutrons and protons is thus 238, a quantity known as the **mass number;** it is often designated by a superscript, thus: U^{238} (or simply U-238).

The number of protons in the nucleus (92 in uranium), is known as the **atomic number.** While the atomic number is fixed for a given named element, there is a possibility of minor variation in the number of neutrons present. Although in U-238 there are 146 neutrons, there exists another form of uranium with 143 neutrons. The latter form then has a mass number of 235 and is designated as U-235. The different varieties of the same element are known as **isotopes.**

We now focus attention upon U-235. This isotope is one of a select few isotopes of uranium and other elements which are **fissionable**—that is, the nucleus can be split apart, releasing energy in the process. The splitting of the U-235 atom was first accomplished in 1938 by Enrico Fermi, who bombarded the U-235 atoms with slow-moving neutrons. Let us investigate this process further.

Figure 62.1 is a schematic diagram showing a single U-235 atom (at the left) being struck by a neutron. Upon receiving this impact, the nucleus of the U-235 atom splits into one atom of barium (Ba) and one atom of krypton (Kr). In addition, two or three neutrons are released by the impact, and these strike the nuclei of other U-235 atoms, splitting them and releasing more neutrons. The splitting, or fission, spreads rapidly through the mass of U-235 in a **chain reaction.**

Perhaps you are familiar with the famous equation which Albert Einstein formulated to relate energy with mass; it is written $E = mc^2$. E stands for energy; m for mass. The letter c is the speed of light, which is 186,000 mi (300,000 km) per second. Now, if we convert the speed of light to centimeters per second we arrive at the number 30,000,000,000 (30 billion), which is the value of c in the Einstein equation in units of centimeters-grams-seconds. Next, we must square the value of c, giving the number 900,000,000,000,000,000,000. This fantastic number means that when one unit of matter is completely transformed into energy, the one unit of matter will produce 9-followed-by-twenty-zeroes units of energy. When U-235 atoms are split, a very small portion of the original mass of those atoms is converted to energy. Specifically, for every 1000 grams of U-235 that undergoes fission, 1 gram is converted into energy. Stated in terms of electrical energy, this single gram of mass converts into 25 million kilowatt-hours (kWh), enough electricity to supply the needs of a large city for several days.

The enormous quantity of energy released by fission of a very small quantity of U-235 is the key to both the destruction of the atom bomb and the peaceful uses of atomic energy. When the chain reaction is uncontrolled, fission consumes the entire mass of U-235 almost instantane-

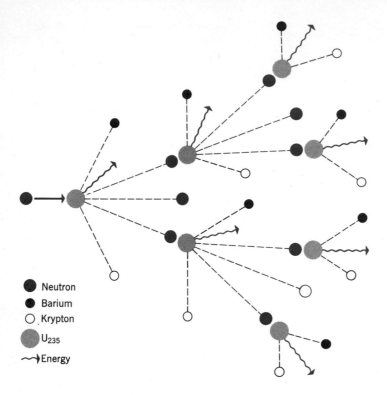

Figure 62.1 A schematic diagram of a nuclear fission chain reaction.

- ● Neutron
- ● Barium
- ○ Krypton
- ● U₂₃₅
- ⟿ Energy

ously, and we have an A-bomb. The problem of peaceful use of atomic energy is to control the rate of fission within the mass of U-235 by releasing energy as heat at a constant rate. Under these conditions, U-235 becomes a **nuclear fuel.**

Nuclear Power Plants

Controlled nuclear fission is achieved in a **nuclear reactor.** The typical power reactor consists of three parts: the core, the cooling system, and the generating system. The core consists of a large number of **fuel rods,** tubes containing uranium specially enriched in U-235, which are arranged in a hexagonal pattern (Figure 62.2). In addition to the fuel rods are **control rods,** typically made of cadmium. The control rods absorb neutrons, thus damping and controlling the fission reaction.

Cooling fluid, usually water or steam, circulates freely between the fuel and control rods, and is heated by the fission reactions occurring in the core. Heat from the reactor core is thus transferred by the cooling system to the generating system through heat exchangers, sets of coils in which the coolant fluids from the two systems pass close to one another. Steam is usually created by the heat transfer, and the steam in the generating system is used to turn a turbine to generate electricity.

The two most common types of power reactors are the boiling-water reactor (BWR) and the pressurized-water reactor (PWR). The BWR is the simpler of the two designs, and is shown in Figure 62.3. In the BWR the cooling and generating systems are combined into a single system.

The large closed vessel at the left is the reactor. Water,

Figure 62.2 A package of metal tubes, containing nuclear fuel, is being lowered into the reactor core of the San Onofre Nuclear Generating Station, near San Clemente, California. (ERDA)

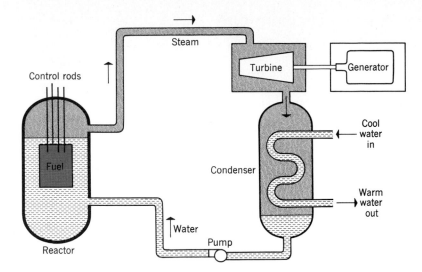

Figure 62.3 Diagram of a boiling-water reactor (BWR).

circulating through the core in which the fuel is located, turns into steam. The steam is piped through a turbine, which is a shaft fitted with finlike blades that turn at high speed under the force of the moving steam. The used steam is now passed through a condenser, in which cold water from the outside is circulated through coils to cause the steam to condense. The condensed steam now returns directly to the reactor to be reheated. Figure 62.4 shows a somewhat more complicated system, called the pressurized-water reactor (PWR). Hot water is kept under high pressure within the reactor and runs through coils to heat water in a second container. Steam generated in the second container drives the turbine.

Both the BWR and PWR are referred to as **burner-type reactors** since the nuclear fuel is steadily consumed. In time, the fuel rods have to be replaced. It is perhaps unfortunate that the word "burner" is used for these reactors, as we usually associate burning with oxidation of hydrocarbon fuels. No such oxidation process occurs in the burner-type reactor.

Cooling of the steam that has passed through the turbines in a nuclear power plant requires very large quantities of cool water. Invariably, then, the nuclear power plant is placed close to a large water source, which may be the ocean, an estuary or large river, or a lake. In this way the nuclear power plant becomes involved with the natural environment. The withdrawal of cool water and its return to the same water body as heated water strongly impacts the environment as a form of thermal pollution.

Safety of Nuclear Power Plants

Safety of nuclear power plants, the major point of issue in the great debate over the future of nuclear energy, relates to the possibility that accidents can release to the environment extremely dangerous isotopes that are radioactive. Although many persons unfamiliar with nuclear reactors fear that the entire plant will blow up like an A-bomb through an accidental chain reaction in its fuel system, the

Figure 62.4 Diagram of a pressurized-water reactor (PWR).

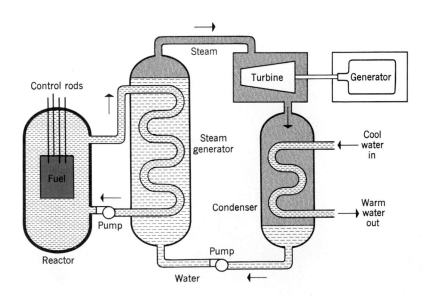

possiblity of this event actually occurring is considered by scientists to be too remote to consider seriously. Instead, the safety issues relate to possible explosions of the water and steam within the high-pressure reactor chamber, or other types of explosions or physical disruptions of the system that would release dangerous radioactive isotopes into the surrounding environment.

One possible cause for explosion, feared by opponents of nuclear energy, is the overheating of the core by a catastrophic failure of the cooling system. Water remaining in the core would quickly boil to steam at a very high pressure, possibly rupturing the reactor vessel. Without cooling, the fuel cores could become so hot from heat released in the spontaneous decay of their radioactive contents that they would melt, forming a large mass of molten material which could melt its way through the bottom of the reactor vessel. To prevent such a possibility, all water-cooled reactors (except those in the U.S.S.R.) are enclosed in a **containment shell,** the top of which forms the dome so conspicuous in a nuclear power plant. If the main reactor tank should be ruptured, the containment shell would prevent contamination of the atmosphere as well as the ground, unless that shell, too, were ruptured.

The debate about safety of nuclear power plants concerns itself largely with the probabilities of various forms of accidents occurring, the nature of those accidents, and the possible effects of release of radioactive substances into the surrounding environment. In our next unit, we will investigate the nature of radioactivity and its environmental effects.

Uranium Ore

Uranium occurs in nature in the form of uranium oxide, UO_2. One form of uranium ore, uraninite, goes by the common name of pitchblende; it is largely uranium oxide. Another uranium ore is carnotite, a mineral of complex composition including uranium oxide. Uranium ores occur in many localities of the world. The greatest known reserves outside the Sino-Soviet bloc, in order of abundance, are in the United States, Canada, Australia, the Republic of South Africa, and France. Other important uranium ore resources lie in Niger, Gabon, Argentina, Central African Republic, Yugoslavia, Zaire, and Czechoslovakia. Deposits of the United States are largely within sedimentary strata of the Colorado Plateau (Figure 62.5). After uranium ore is mined, it must be processed and concentrated into an oxide with the formula U_3O_8, known as "yellow cake."

An important fact about uranium as a natural resource is that it occurs in the form of three isotopes, U-238, U-235, and U-234. The proportion of each of these isotopes in uranium ores is very different. Percentages are as follows:

U-238		99.283%
U-235		0.711%
U-234		0.006%
	Total	100.000%

Although a reactor can be constructed to use natural uranium fuel, containing less than one percent fissionable U-235, modern reactors use fuel that has been enriched in U-235 to the level of several percent. Weapons-grade uranium is even more highly enriched.

Figure 62.5 An open-pit uranium mine in New Mexico. The richest United States uranium ore deposits occur in sedimentary strata—sandstones and shales of Triassic and Jurassic age, such as those shown here. The ore was concentrated in ancient stream channel deposits, now enclosed beneath younger strata. (ERDA)

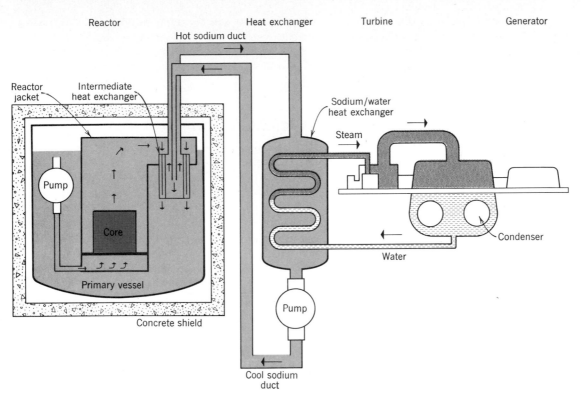

Figure 62.6 Schematic diagram of the British-type breeder reactor with its heat exchanger and power generator. (United Kingdom Atomic Energy Authority.)

The Breeder Reactor

Although only about 0.7% of all uranium is in the fissionable form of U-235, there is a way to convert the much more common isotope U-238 to a fissionable form, plutonium-239 (Pu-239). The conversion, or **transmutation,** is accomplished by bombarding U-238 with neutrons. Since U-238 is always present in reactors, and since neutrons are always released in the fission process, all reactors produce some Pu-239. This means that a reactor consumes fissionable U-235 but also produces fissionable Pu-239. The production of Pu-239 from U-238 is also referred to as **breeding** plutonium from uranium. A conventional power reactor only breeds about half as much plutonium fuel as U-235 consumed, so that there is a net loss of fissionable material in normal operation.

It is possible, however, to design a power reactor which will breed more fuel than it consumes. This type of reactor is referred to as a **breeder reactor.** At the present time, only a few large breeder reactors are in operation, and all of these are experimental. In order to maximize the breeding reaction, breeder reactors are designed quite differently from conventional power reactors (Figure 62.6). The reactor core is surrounded by a breeding blanket—an arrangement of fuel rods around the outside of the core. These outer rods contain nearly pure U-238 to be bred and little or no fissionable material. The core itself, however, is fueled with uranium enriched in U-235 or plutonium to a

level as high as 15%. Such a highly enriched core is needed to maximize the flow of neutrons needed for breeding. The neutrons must also be moving much faster than in a conventional reactor, since only fast-moving neutrons can breed plutonium. This fact means that water cannot be used to cool the reactor, since water serves to slow the neutrons. Instead, liquid sodium metal is used as the coolant fluid. Thus, the common breeder reactor design is the liquid metal fast breeder reactor, or LMFBR. (Here, "fast" refers to the use of fast neutrons rather than to the rate of breeding.)

The importance of the breeder reactor lies in its potential to greatly increase our supply of nuclear fuel. Instead of relying on the tiny fraction of U-235 present in natural uranium for our fissionable fuel, we can increase that supply one-hundredfold by converting nonfissionable U-238 to fissionable plutonium. Although most present research concerns the breeding of plutonium from U-238, there is at least one other feasible breeding cycle. This cycle involves thorium-232, an isotope often found along with naturally occurring uranium, which can be bred to U-233 under neutron bombardment. U-233, like U-235, is fissionable and can serve as a reactor fuel.

Because of the need to maximize the breeding reaction, the design of the breeder reactor is inherently less safe than that of a conventional reactor. First, because the core is highly enriched in fissionable material, fission proceeds more rapidly, producing higher core temperatures and the need for a higher volume of coolant flow. Thus, breeders run "hotter" than conventional reactors. Second, the use of liquid sodium as a coolant is inherently more difficult to control than water. It is opaque and highly reactive, and becomes intensely radioactive as it is exposed to neutron bombardment in the core. Further, a large-scale power-producing breeder will have nearly a ton of plutonium in its core. And, plutonium is one of the most toxic substances known to Man, producing lung cancer when inhaled in even the most minute of quantities.

Debate Over the Breeder Reactor

At one time, almost all scientists familiar with nuclear energy strongly urged that breeder reactors be developed with utmost speed under a high national priority. Today this course of action has come under serious doubt by many responsible scientists. Issues of reactor safety and environmental impact have risen in importance to an extent that they now overshadow the need to conserve uranium fuel. Opponents of the breeder program include the Union of Concerned Scientists, of Cambridge, Massachusetts. One statement issued in 1971 by that group concluded that a major reactor accident might easily bring a peacetime catastrophe whose scale might well exceed anything this nation has ever known. They stated further: "The gaps in basic knowledge concerning the effectiveness of the safety features of large power reactors, the surprising scarcity of adequate tests—amounting nearly to a total lack—has astonished our group, especially in view of the large number of (reactors of) apparently hazardous design that are already operating."

Besides these safety issues, many opponents of nuclear energy development now point to facts and figures which show that nuclear fission is not by any means a low-cost energy resource. These objectors are turning more strongly to the development of solar energy as the best of all possible choices for the future. We shall discuss solar energy in Unit 65.

The debate over construction of breeder reactors seems to be reaching a peak of intensity. In its 1976 report a subcommittee of the congressional Joint Committee on Atomic Energy concluded: "The time has come to end the discussion over whether or not this nation should have a breeder research and development program." The report went on to say that emphasis "should not be on the issue of 'should we do the job,' but on 'how best to get the job done'."

Nuclear Fusion

No discussion of nuclear energy would be complete without some discussion of **nuclear fusion.** The fusion process forces two hydrogen atoms to fuse into a single helium atom and to release as well a large amount of energy. In order to achieve fusion, a hydrogen isotope, deuterium, must be subjected to intense heat and pressure. At present, these temperatures and pressures can only be achieved during the explosion of an atomic bomb. The hydrogen, or thermonuclear, bomb consists of a conventional A-bomb which is used to set off a fusion reaction that releases an immense amount of energy in a very short time. As yet, however, controlled release of fusion energy in a usable fashion has not yet been achieved. Research is proceeding rapidly in this area, however, and scientists expect to have a controlled fusion reactor yielding more energy than it consumes by the early 1980s or sooner.

Fusion power has two unique features. First, it is inherently less dangerous. If the reactor malfunctions, high temperatures and confining pressures drop, and the reaction stops abruptly. Further, no radioactive waste is produced in the fusion process (although the materials of which the reactor is composed will eventually become radioactive and present a minor disposal problem). The second advantage of fusion power is that it is essentially limitless. The hydrogen isotope used—deuterium—is present in seawater, and the world's supply is sufficient to meet our power needs for millions of years at present levels of consumption.

Given these facts about the possibilities of fusion power, and the safety problems of fission power, many environmentalists are urging the use of coal to meet our energy needs until fusion power becomes practical. Still other persons believe that we can, and should, safely exploit our fission resources. Our next study unit deals specifically with the environmental hazards posed by the nuclear-fission fuel cycle.

Unit 63 Environmental Hazards from Nuclear Fuels

A Witches' Brew on the Nuclear Menu

The nuclear house that Man built has not just one chamber of horrors, but many of them. Open one door, and you see civilization consumed in a nuclear holocaust. Open another, and you see a new member of the nuclear club using its first deadly toy to blackmail a bloated American public into sending a huge ransom of food and weapons. Another door we are tempted to slam shut after one quick glance is the chamber in which seething, boiling radioactive wastes are stored. In huge witches' cauldrons of thick stainless steel, each resting upon a heavy steel 'saucer' and surrounded by prestressed, reinforced concrete are tens of millions of gallons of lethal fluids—the by-products of the processing of nuclear fuels used in warheads or consumed in the reactors of nuclear power plants. If, by some chance, a cauldron would spring a leak and discharge its waste into the ground, there would be no way to contain its spread. Traveling in the ground water system and emerging in streams, the waste could only be monitored as it raced downvalley, perhaps toward a great metropolitan region. Tens of thousands of humans might have to abandon their homes forever, leaving a deserted city that could not be reoccupied for centuries.

The great cauldrons of radioactive waste must remain intact for hundreds of years, for their deadly radiation will persist by the inexorable laws of matter and energy. As if that were not a big enough nightmare to face, the deadly wastes continue to arrive from nuclear reactors all over the country, as spent fuel rods are reprocessed and replaced by new fuel rods.

Our story concerns an attempt by Atomic Energy Commission scientists to plant accumulated radioactive wastes deep in the earth. The place they chose was Lyons, Kansas. The reason they chose it is that the sedimentary strata which lie beneath Lyons include thick beds of rock salt. At a depth of 1000 feet below Lyons is a single salt bed 300 feet thick, extending many miles in all directions. The AEC had kept its eye on the Lyons salt bed since 1955, when the prestigious National Academy of Sciences pointed out that rock salt has some remarkable properties making it a likely medium in which to store "hot" nuclear wastes. The salt has a high melting point (about 1450°F) and is able to heal any fresh fractures by slow plastic flowage of the salt under

A view down the main corridor of the Carey Salt Company mine in Lyons, Kansas. The ceiling height here is 14 feet. (AEC)

465

Canisters are placed in holes bored in the floor of the salt mine to show how the waste would be stored. (AEC)

pressure. Salt also has good shielding properties to absorb nuclear radiation.

In 1971, the AEC made its move to secure the Lyons salt bed for its nuclear burial ground. AEC officials laid out a 1000-acre surface site and sought from the congressional Joint Committee on Atomic Energy authorization for a $3½ million appropriation to purchase the site and to begin investigations and tests. The AEC had already played with the idea through a 19-month experiment carried out in the Carey Company salt mines near Lyons. As the accompanying illustrations show, cannisters containing the radioactive waste would be placed in holes in the floors of large open rooms excavated in the salt. Each hole would be 12 feet deep and lined with stainless steel. Once the cannisters had been emplaced, the room would be filled with crushed salt. In time the crushed salt would compact itself into rock salt, sealing the cannisters safely for all time to come.

At this time the Kansas Geological Survey began to become greatly concerned about the safety of the salt mine venture. The Survey's director, William H. Hambleton, pointed out a number of questionable features of the plan. Heat buildup might be a serious problem, causing the surrounding salt to become soft and plastic. Once the radioactive material corroded through its cannister walls, it would react chemically with the salt, forming new compounds with the element chlorine. If the salt should expand and lift the overlying strata, cracks might be formed into which ground water would enter. Representative Joe Skubits, a Kansas Republican, was also alarmed and

incensed by the AEC's plan. He and Hambleton both urged that the $3½ million be used for basic research on the storage of wastes in salt beds, so that there would be no unpleasant surprises after the storage was completed. A Kansas Geological Survey report pointed out that the AEC had no plans for the withdrawal of the nuclear waste if unforeseen events made that necessary. Skubits suggested that the AEC stop "playing God" and listen to the voice of the local residents. He added: "Kansas has some rights. We are not country bumpkins who can be taken for granted." The 5000 residents of Lyons, however, seemed unable to catch the spirit of their Congressman. Perhaps the thought of 200 new permanent jobs what would become available brought on a lethargy that remained unruffled by the knowledge that beneath their homes some 38,000 tons of lethal radioactive waste would be on deposit by the year 2000. To date, the AEC has been held at bay and is looking for someone else's backyard to dig its hole.

In this study unit, we explore in some detail the unpleasant side of the brave new world that is promised to us through the peaceful uses of the atom. Decisions must yet be made on how much farther nuclear energy is to be developed and where we can put that 38,000 tons of witches' brew.

DATA SOURCE: Charles H. Fox *Radioactive Wastes*, U.S. Atomic Energy Commission, Division of Technical Information, Oak Ridge, Tennessee, pp. 33-36; Constance Holden (1971) Nuclear waste; Kansans riled by AEC plans for atom dump, *Science*, vol. 172, pp. 249-250; William W. Hambleton (1972) The unsolved problem of nuclear wastes, *Technology Review* vol. 74, no. 5, pp. 15-19.

Natural Radioactivity

Quite apart from the physical effects of explosion of a nuclear generating plant, the full range of environmental impacts and hazards to Man associated with nuclear fuel processing and use arise from **radioactivity.** This phenomenon continually generates a form of energy which can be harmful to life forms.

Natural radioactivity was discovered in 1896 by a French physicist, Henri Becquerel. Quite by accident at first, he found that photographic plates, even though completely sealed off from any light, became exposed when placed close to fragments of minerals containing the element uranium. Invisible energy was obviously radiating from the mineral matter. Becquerel was able to measure the intensity of this energy but could not identify its precise source. Marie Curie took up the investigation and began to search for the mysterious agent of radiation in a large quantity of a form of uranium ore known as pitchblende. She was joined in her research by her husband, Pierre, and together they finally succeeded in isolating minute quantities of two previously unknown elements—radium and polonium. For this discovery the Curies were awarded the Nobel Prize in Physics in 1903, an honor they shared with Henri Becquerel. So great is the importance of the natural phenomenon these scientists discovered and isolated to the environment of life on earth that we should make every attempt to understand its workings. We present here a simple explanation that we hope will be within the range of understanding of those who have had very little previous science study.

In Unit 62, we explained the structure of the nucleus of an atom and the nature of isotopes. Certain isotopes of a number of naturally occurring elements are unstable. In atoms of these unstable elements, a small part of the nucleus flies off and thus transmutes the atom into another element with a different mass number, or a different atomic number, or both. In this process, called **radioactive decay,** a very small amount of mass is converted into energy in the proportion required by Einstein's equation, just as we explained in Unit 62 for the process of nuclear fission, and is released as heat.

Radioactive decay is a spontaneous process that cannot be influenced by external factors. However, Man is able to create new radioactive isotopes in nuclear reactors. Under neutron bombardment inside a reactor, the nuclei of a wide variety of elements can absorb neutrons to form new isotopes. But, since most such isotopes are unstable and undergo decay, they release dangerous radiation as well as heat and energy.

Much of the information presented in this study unit deals with Man-made radioactive isotopes and their impact upon the life environment. Naturally occurring radioactive elements are so thinly diffused through the environment that their radiation is not harmful to life. When Man extracts uranium ores and greatly concentrates the natural radioactive elements, however, the intensity of radiation in a small area can be enormously increased. This potentially dangerous type of situation is another topic we will cover in our study unit.

Radioactive Decay

Radioactive decay gives off both atomic particles and electromagnetic radiation. When an atomic nucleus breaks down an **alpha particle** is emitted; it consists of two neutrons and two protons. Consequently, the mass number decreases by 4 and the atomic number by 2. A second form of nuclear emission is the **gamma ray,** an energy form similar to that of electromagnetic radiation (Unit 1). A third form of nuclear emission is the **beta particle,** a high-velocity electron. Beta emission does not change the mass number, but results in a new element of atomic number 1 greater than before the emission (because a proton has been formed from a neutron).

Figure 63.1 shows the steps in radioactive decay of uranium-238. Recall from Unit 62 that, although U-238 is not a fissionable isotope, it is one of the naturally radioactive isotopes. In the diagram, emission of an alpha (α) particle is indicated by a horizontal arrow pointing left. The emission of a beta (β) particle is indicated by a short arrow slanting down to the right. The full names of the elements are given at the bottom of the graph. In each box, the isotope is given by its element symbol and its mass number.

During radioactive decay, the three forms of emission are absorbed in the surrounding matter after a short distance of travel and converted to heat.

Spontaneous radioactive disintegration begins with a parent isotope, such as U-238, and leads to the formation of another unstable isotope, called a **daughter product.** As shown in Figure 63.1, the daughter product of U-238 is thorium-234 (Th-234) produced by emission of an alpha particle. One daughter product leads to another in a series that may produce a number of elements in succession, as Figure 63.1 shows. Ultimately, however, the chain ends in a stable isotope, which in this case is lead-206 (Pb-206).

From the standpoint of environmental impact, it is very important to realize that the rate at which radioactive decay takes place is always constant for a given isotope, but that decay rates are different for different isotopes.

As time passes, a given original mass of the parent isotope is transmuted at a constant rate into its daughter products, so that the quantity of the parent isotope diminishes with time. The stable end product also accumulates steadily. After a certain interval of time has elapsed the quantity of parent isotope remaining will be reduced to exactly one-half the original quantity; this interval is known as the **half-life.** When a second interval of time of the same length has passed, the mass is again halved, and so on.

Figure 63.2 is a graph showing the decay of U-238 with the passage of time. The vertical bar gives the percentage of mass of the parent isotope, starting with 100%. The half-life of U-238 is 4½ billion years (b.y.). After the first 4½ b.y. have elapsed, the amount of U-238 remaining has been reduced to 50%; after a second interval of 4½ b.y., the amount remaining is 25%, and so forth. Connecting the series of points by smooth line gives us a **decay curve** for U-238. This type of decay schedule is called **exponential decay.** There will always remain a small quantity

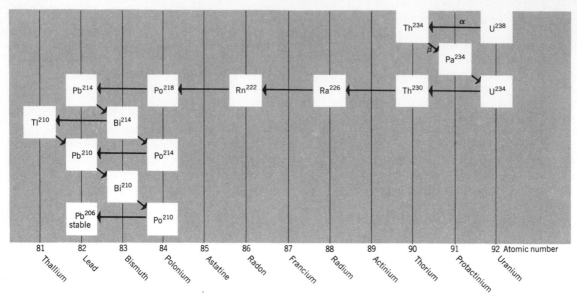

Figure 63.1   Radioactive decay series beginning with U-238 and ending in Pb-206. (After P. M. Hurley [1959] *How Old is the Earth?*, Doubleday, Garden City, N.Y., p. 62, Figure 9.)

of the parent isotope, no matter how long the decay continues.

The length of the half-life of a radioactive isotope is often of concern from the viewpoint of environmental health. Because the half-life time of an isotope is determined by the stability of its nuclear structure, the half-life cannot be changed by any external process, whether natural or Man-made. If the half-life is quite long (say, hundreds of thousands of years), then the isotope will be quite persistent, posing a constant hazard on the time scale of human life. On the other hand, because its half-life is so long, the isotope decays only very slowly, releasing radiation at a very low level. Isotopes with short half-lives release their energy much more rapidly, but then are unlikely to persist, for they change rapidly into other isotopes that may or may not pose significant health hazards.

Another important point concerns the chemical properties of the isotope. If it is an isotope of an element that is important to life processes, it can rapidly become incorpo-

rated into living tissue and create a major health problem. Take for example the dangerous radioactive isotope strontium-90, which is one of the by-products of a nuclear bomb explosion. The half-life of strontium-90 is 25 years. After it is blasted into the upper atmosphere, it spreads widely in prevailing winds and reaches the earth's surface by fallout. When consumed by cows grazing in a pasture, the strontium-90 enters their milk and finally reaches the systems of humans who consume dairy products from such herds. Because strontium is an element very much like calcium, the radioactive isotope moves to human bones, where it remains and may eventually produce cancer. There is no way that the half-life of this isotope can be shortened; the human race can only wait out its slow decay to less toxic forms.

Ionizing Radiation

Let us now broaden our view beyond the process of radioactivity to include many other sources of harmful radiation besides that produced by the spontaneous decay of isotopes. This broad range of activity is called **ionizing radiation.** Any form of ultrashortwave electromagnetic radiation or particle emission capable of tearing electrons off of other atoms is included in the definition of ionizing radiation. Gamma rays given off in radioactive decay are only one form of ionizing radiation. Enormously powerful ionizing radiation is given off in an atom bomb explosion. The effects of this radiation on the Japanese cities of Hiroshima and Nagasaki are well known—the searing of exposed human flesh and the setting of building fires at long distances from the point of bomb explosion. Any concentrated mass of a highly radioactive isotope, such as the spent fuel rod of a nuclear reactor, gives off intense ionizing radiation.

Figure 63.2   As the amount of U-238 decreases with time, the amount of lead-206 increases. The smooth line is the decay curve.

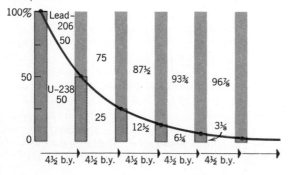

Rocks of the earth's crust, because they contain very small quantities of radioactive minerals, give off a continuous but very weak ionizing radiation to which we are all exposed. Ionizing radiation also comes naturally through the atmosphere because of the arrival of cosmic particles from outer space. These high-energy particles strike atoms in the atmosphere, shattering the atomic nuclei and producing a shower of various forms of ionizing radiation. This natural form of ionizing radiation, together with radiation from the solid earth is referred to as **background radiation,** part of the natural environment. The X rays, gamma rays, and shorter ultraviolet rays of the solar electromagnetic spectrum are also natural forms of ionizing radiation, but these are almost entirely absorbed in the upper atmosphere, as we explained in Unit 1.

X rays generated by the x-ray tube and used in medicine for diagnostic purposes and for cancer treatment are a concentrated and intense form of ionizing radiation. Even the television tube (a cathode-ray tube) emits some ionizing radiation, to which viewers can be exposed. So we see that there are both natural and Man-made forms of ionizing radiation and that the intensity can range from a very weak background radiation, always present, to lethal doses from nuclear fuels and nuclear explosions.

Biological Effects of Ionizing Radiation

What effect has ionizing radiation on humans and other life forms? We know, of course, that intense radiation can maim and kill. What about the normal environmental levels of background radiation from crustal rock and cosmic rays? Here the effects are very subtle.

A single radiation particle, traveling at high speed, can physically damage the genetic material within a living cell. By genetic materials, we are referring to the DNA molecules by means of which the genetic code operates to govern the structure and function of organisms. Changes in these molecules can affect life in two ways. First, the genetic heritage of an organism can be changed by what is known as a gene mutation. Some forms of birth defects fall into this category. Second, cell activity can be radically changed to result in uncontrolled multiplication of the affected cells to produce the diseases we know as cancer and leukemia. In other words, ionizing radiation is known to be a **carcinogenic agent.** Carcinogenic effects, together with direct tissue damage, are referred to as **somatic effects,** to distinguish them from **genetic effects** that can be passed along to future generations.

For purposes of evaluating somatic effects of ionizing radiation upon living tissues, a unit of dose called the **rem** is used. For very small doses the unit used is the **millirem,** which is one-thousandth of a rem. Somatic effects of radiation are shown in Table 63.1. Genetic effects occur at values very much lower than those shown in the table. Actually, there is no threshold value below which no genetic effects occur. In other words, even the smallest X-ray dose can produce some genetic damage. In addition, radiation effects accumulate with time during the lifetime of an indi-

Table 63.1 Somatic Effects of Radiation in Man

Dose (in rems)	Somatic Effect
100	Reduced life expectancy from cancer and leukemia; temporary to permanent sterility.
200	Death within months for 10% of those exposed; 90% survive.
700	Death within months for 90% of those exposed; 10% survive.
1,000	Death within days.
10,000	Death within hours.
100,000	Death within minutes.

SOURCE: After Earl Cook, in W. W. Murdoch, ed. (1971) *Environment,* Sinauer Associates, Inc., Stamford, Conn., p. 257.

vidual. This fact may explain the medical observation that incidence of cancer in humans increases steadily with age level, all other things being equal.

Scientists have attempted to establish an annual limit to the total annual radiation dose a human being should be allowed to absorb in an occupation dealing with radioactive materials, such as work with nuclear fuels. The natural background radiation, which is on the order of 100 millirems per year (mrem/yr), is not counted in setting this limit. Medical X rays are not counted; a single X-ray examination may give a patient a dose of several hundred millirems. The International Commission on Radiological Protection in 1966 established a value of 500 mrem/yr as the maximum to which the public should be exposed. However, the limit has been greatly lowered in recent years. In 1975, the Environmental Protection Agency (EPA) set a new annual limit of 25 mrem/yr for workers dealing with processing of nuclear fuels and working in nuclear energy plants.

Radiation Hazards from Uranium Ore Mining and Processing

In Unit 62, we explained that uranium ore must be processed and refined to produce yellow cake (U_3O_8), the concentrate sent on to plants that separate U-235 from U-238. Health hazards from ionizing radiation are encountered at all these steps, from mining to final separation of the nuclear fuel.

Within uranium mines, radiation doses can exceed 5600 mrem/yr, a quantity some 40 to 70 times the average background radiation dose from all sources. Besides direct gamma radiation from uranium ore, inhalation of radon gas poses a radiation hazard. (Radon is a radioactive product of uranium decay; see Figure 63.1.) The gas rapidly produces other radioactive daughter products, that lodge in the lungs.

Miners of pitchblende (an ore of uranium and radium) in Germany and Czechoslovakia were the first groups to show the effects of this form of ionizing radiation. Some 50% of these miners ultimately died of lung cancer attributable to radiation exposure. The lesson went unheeded, however, for when uranium mining boomed in the United States during World War II and after, standards of individual exposure and mine ventilation were set too low. In a study group of about 3400 uranium miners, 46 had died of lung cancer by the year 1967, and some 600 to 1100 out of the 6000-odd men who were uranium miners are expected to die ultimately from lung cancer because of their exposure to radiation.

Tailings (rock wastes) from uranium mines are another source of ionizing radiation since they contain radium-226 and other radioactive isotopes. Radium is particularly toxic in stream waters derived from leaching of the tailings, while radon gas, the daughter product, can accumulate to hazardous levels in buildings resting on tailings. In recent years dangerous radon-gas levels have been discovered or suspected in homes in Uravan and Grand Junction, Colorado.

Figure 63.3 Burial of containers of radioactive wastes in a trench, Oak Ridge National Laboratory, Tennessee. (AEC)

The Hazards of Nuclear Wastes

Nuclear wastes are produced in three basic phases of activity. The first, which we have just explained, are wastes from the mining and concentration of the uranium ores and involve natural radioactivity. A second category of wastes comes from **fission products** that nuclear reactors create. Chemical reprocessing of spent fuel rods to collect unfissioned U-235 and newly formed plutonium also releases from these rods the many unwanted isotopes that were produced by fission and neutron irradiation of fission products. These isotopes constitute highly dangerous radioactive wastes. At present, reprocessing is done solely by Energy Resources Development Agency (ERDA) plants, although some privately owned reprocessing plants will be operating in the near future.

A third class of wastes comes from **activation products,** which are radioactive isotopes produced by exposure of nonfuel material to radiation from fuels. The coolant liquids used in nuclear power plants may be activated, along with structural materials surrounding the fuels. In addition, many radioactive isotopes are created for specialized uses in industry, scientific research, and medicine. An example is cobalt-60 used in cancer treatment. These isotopes eventually require disposal.

With respect to levels of radioactivity, wastes are classified as low-level, intermediate-level, and high-level. **Low-level** liquid wastes generally can be treated to remove radioactive isotopes, diluted, and released into the environment. Release consists of pouring the waste into the ground or into streams. The AEC has undertaken studies to evaluate the effects of low-level waste disposal upon the environment into which the diluted liquids are dispersed.

One study area is the Clinch-Tennessee River system below Oak Ridge, Tennessee. Physical, chemical, and biological effects of the radioactivity are evaluated. Water-sampling stations extend as far as 125 mi (38 km) downstream from the Oak Ridge plant.

Intermediate-level wastes cannot be diluted sufficiently to be released but can be processed in a variety of ways for safe disposal or storage. Intermediate- and low-level solid wastes can be buried and held indefinitely in storage. For example, at the Oak Ridge National Laboratory, Tennessee, the AEC practices shallow land burial of waste containers in unlined pits and trenches (Figure 63.3). For some wastes of higher activity levels, burial in concrete-lined wells is required. Storage at the surface is also practiced to allow radioactivity to decay to lower levels.

At the government's Hanford Plant in Washington, some intermediate-level liquid wastes are discharged into trenches and allowed to infiltrate the zone of aeration, which is here 200 to 600 ft (60 to 180 m) thick. Mineral colloids permanently hold the radioactive ions and other chemicals. Retention zones for various components are shown in Figure 63.4. Depth of penetration is monitored with a system of wells. Another method of intermediate-level waste disposal under study is to inject the waste in a cement mixture into a deep well drilled in a shale formation. The mixture then solidifies in place in fractures in the rock.

High-level liquid wastes, produced in reprocessing of nuclear fuels, present the greatest environmental hazard, particularly since they contain biologically active radioactive isotopes (strontium-90 and cesium-137) that will not decay to safe levels for hundred of years. The production

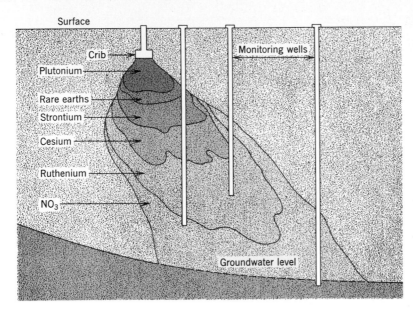

Surface

Crib

Plutonium

Rare earths

Strontium

Cesium

Ruthenium

NO₃

Monitoring wells

Groundwater level

Figure 63.4 Cross section showing retention zones of various types of radioactive liquid wastes allowed to percolate downward through the zone of aeration. Depth to water table varies from 200 to 600 ft (60 to 180 m). (After C. H. Fox [1969] *Radioactive Wastes,* U.S. Atomic Energy Commission. Understanding the Atom Series, p. 21, Figure 10.)

of heat by these wastes presents a serious problem. As shown in Figure 63.5, total heat production drops rapidly with time but strontium-90 and cesium-137 heat production diminishes very slowly and is ultimately the principal

Figure 63.5 Decline with time in heat production from various high-level radioactive wastes produced during fuel processing. Scales are logarithmic. (After C. H. Fox [1969] *Radioactive Wastes,* U.S. Atomic Energy Commission, Understanding the Atom Series, p. 24, Figure 12.)

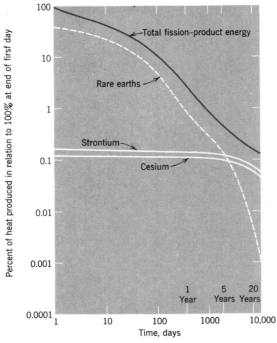

heat producer. The high-level liquid wastes are contained in elaborate, concrete-encased steel tanks set in massive retaining basins (Figure 63.6). It is of course, absolutely essential that these storage facilities function perfectly for centuries. The tanks will require periodic replacement.

Research is now being directed to conversion of the high-level liquid wastes to solid form for safer permanent containment. Interest is turning to storage of these solid wastes in underground locations. One proposal, which we explained in opening paragraphs of this unit, is to store the containers in thick layers of rock salt (halite) in sedimentary strata. Salt has a favorable quality of closing fractures by mineral flowage, should ruptures occur. Also under study is storage in bedrock tunnels in dense crystalline bedrock. Not surprisingly, scientists of many diverse backgrounds have put their minds to work on the problem of permanent storage of high-level nuclear wastes.

Underground disposal in the desert region of the southwestern United States is seriously weighed and several methods are available in this area. The principal advantage to storage in the arid environment is that evaporation completes the hydrologic cycle. Rivers carrying waste to the ocean and ground-water movement by seepage to reach distant urban centers are reasonably ruled out in these areas. Subsurface disposal sites in the ice sheet of Antarctica, or in cavities excavated in bedrock of that continent have been seriously considered, for here all water is permanently frozen. More fanciful proposals are that we shoot the wastes into space in vehicles that will never return to earth, or that we implant the wastes in subduction zones where the oceanic crust is being carried down into the mantle. As yet, the horrendous problem of containing high-level nuclear wastes remains unsolved and hangs like the legendary Sword of Damocles over the human race and countless generations as yet unborn.

Figure 63.6   Construction of high-level waste storage tanks in ERDA's Savannah River Plant in South Carolina. The upper photograph shows the steel tanks, 30 ft (9 m) high, each resting upon a massive reinforced concrete base. The lower photograph shows pouring of a surrounding sheath of reinforced concrete, which may contain cooling coils. (E. I. DuPont DeNemours & Co., S.C./ERDA.)

Unit 64
Geothermal and Tidal Energy

The Geysers

Imagine a beautiful California valley, its verdant slopes clothed in oak trees, chaparral, and pasture. Before your eyes, great jets of steam begin to arise, one by one, from scattered points on the valley bottom. The pure white plumes reach upward hundreds of feet. What is going on here? Has nature gone mad?

What you are witnessing is a geothermal energy field. The steam, which is a natural phenomenon, issues in jets from wells driven deep into the rock beneath. Normally, the steam is take by pipes to an electricity generating plant, but periodically the steam must be released directly from the well heads to remove accumulated debris. This geothermal field, called The Geysers, is located about 90 miles north of San Francisco. Here some very hot rock lies not far below the surface, and water, saturating the rock, is raised to the boiling point. Deeper down, there is undoubtedly a magma body, slowly cooling to become igneous rock.

In this day of energy shortages, we are looking to geothermal energy to contribute to the total supply. At The Geysers, total electrical production from a steam-powerd generating plant is about 600 megawatts. This is only a little less than the output of a typical large generating plant using coal, oil, or natural gas. The Geysers has one major advantage over the plant burning fossil fuels—there is little air pollution to contend with. The energy source will continue its supply, moreover, for many decades to come.

Opportunities for further development of geothermal power are considered very good for certain parts of the West. Under the Imperial Valley, within a 2000-square-mile area, is an underground reservoir of water heated to over 500°F. This field alone could perhaps produce enough electric power to meet the needs of all of Southern California for several dec-ades. Water from the condensing steam, after being used in power generating plants, could be a major source of irrigation for crops in the area.

In this study unit, we will describe the various occurrences of geothermal energy and evaluate their potential contributions to the national energy resource.

The Geysers power plant in Sonoma County, California. (Pacific Gas and Electric Company.)

Geothermal and Tidal Energy Sources

Of the earth's energy sources that are not powered by the sun, either through incoming solar rays or through storage of solar energy as fossil fuels, two deserve attention: geothermal energy and tidal energy. Both, for all practical purposes, are without any time limit for significant reduction or expiration. Geothermal energy is generated within the earth in such enormous quantities as to be practically inexhaustible. Tidal energy will continue to flow with no appreciable reduction for millions of years. Neither geothermal energy nor tidal energy has the potential, however, for supplying a large share of Man's needs in the near future. Of the two, geothermal energy holds by far the greater potential for future development on a global scale.

The Geothermal Gradient

From observations made in deep mines and boreholes, we know that the temperature of rock increases steadily with depth. This rate of increase, called the **geothermal gradient,** averages about 1 F° per 50 ft (3 C° per 100 m) for at least the uppermost two or three miles of the crust. Although the rate of increase falls off quite rapidly with increasing depth, temperatures do attain very high values in the upper mantle. For example, at a depth of 60 mi (100 km) rock temperature is estimated to be about 2000°F (1100°C). In this region, rock is close to its melting point. Locally, pockets of molten rock, or magma, are formed in the upper mantle and make their way toward the surface, as we explained in Unit 22. The rise of magma to positions near the surface, and the actual extrusion of magma in volcanoes and lava flows, are of extremely great importance in understanding geothermal energy. Obviously, if highly heated magma, or igneous rock recently solidified from magma, lies near the surface, it can provide an enormous reservoir of heat for Man's use.

Although the internal heat of the earth flows very slowly upward to the earth's surface, the quantity is extremely small. In one year, the amount of heat reaching the surface is just enough to melt an imaginary ice layer 1/5 in. (6 mm) thick. This small heat flow is insignificant compared with the amount of solar energy reaching the ground in one year. Heat within the earth's crust and mantle is produced by radioactive decay, a subject we explained in Unit 63. The radioactive elements largely responsible for heat production are uranium, thorium, and potassium. As slow as this internal heat production is, it scarcely diminishes with time and the basic energy resource can be regarded as limitless.

Occurrences of Geothermal Energy

For geothermal energy to be useful and practical as an energy source, it must be concentrated in high-temperature occurrences within range of being reached by modern well-drilling techniques. We begin with those places where steam and hot water are emitted from vents at the surface, namely, hot springs and geysers. At other locations very hot water, capable of being flashed into steam, lies within easy range of drilled wells. Still deeper, beneath some selected areas, the rock is dry but hot enough that if water is pumped down from the surface through drilled wells, it can be brought back up hot enough to flash into steam. An entirely different set of conditions occurs in some thick sequences of sedimentary strata in which water that is under pressure of natural gas can be tapped. We will describe briefly each of these types of occurrences and evaluate their present and future importance as sources of energy.

Geysers and Hot Springs

At some widely separated places over the globe, ground water reaches the surface in **hot springs** at temperatures not far below the boiling point of water, which is 212°F (100°C) at sea-level atmospheric pressure. At some of these same places, jetlike emissions of steam and hot water occur at intervals from small vents; these are **geysers** (Figure 64.1). The water that emerges from hot springs and geysers is largely ground water that has been heated in contact with hot rock and forced to the surface. In other words, this water is recycled surface water. Little, if any, is water that was originally held in rising bodies of magma.

A related phenomenon to hot springs and geysers is the **fumarole,** a jet of gases issuing from a small vent. Gas temperatures in fumaroles are extremely high, up to 650°F (320°C). Most of the gas (over 99%) is water. In other words, the fumarole emits largely superheated steam. Fumaroles are common in regions of current and recent volcanic activity.

The natural hot water and steam localities were the first type of geothermal energy source to be developed and at present account for nearly all production of electrical

Figure 64.1   The Waikite Geyser, Rotorua, North Island, New Zealand. (New Zealand Tourist Bureau.)

Figure 64.2 An electricity generating plant at The Geysers, California. Steam pipes in the foreground lead to the plant. After use in generating turbines, the steam is condensed in the large cylindrical towers. (Pacific Gas & Electric Company.)

power. Wells are drilled to tap the hot water, which flashes into steam as it reaches the surface under reduced atmospheric pressure. The steam is separated from the water in large towers and fed into generating turbines to produce electricity (Figure 64.2). The hot water is usually released into surface stream flow, where it may create a pollution problem.

The larger steam fields have sufficient energy to generate at least 15 megawatts of electric power, and a few can generate 200 megawatts or more. Table 64.1 lists the world's existing geothermal power developments with their 1975 generating capacities. The total capacity of these fields is only about 1400 megawatts, about twice what a single nuclear power plant develops, and about the same as the hydropower output of Hoover Dam. When planned additions are completed at the localities listed in Table 64.1, and a number of new power developments are completed at other sites, the added power output will be about 640 megawatts, for a total world output of just over 2000 megawatts—about the same as the hydropower output of the Grand Coulee Dam by itself. Obviously, energy contributions from shallow hot-water and steam fields are very small, and prospects for substantial increases are indeed poor. We must turn to other occurrences of geothermal energy in search of larger energy supplies.

Deep Hot-Water Sources

Much greater energy sources than those we have just described lie in deeper zones of hot ground water, but these must be tapped by deep drilling. One region of deep, hot ground water, currently under investigation, is beneath the Imperial Valley of southern California. An area of 2000 sq mi (5200 sq km) is involved, and extends over the border into Mexico in the Mexicali Valley. This region is tectonically active and has been interpreted as a zone of crustal

spreading in which the lithospheric plate is being fractured. Rising basalt magma, found elsewhere in active spreading zones such as Iceland in the North Atlantic, may be responsible for the geothermal condition, but this interpretation is speculative. Test wells show that a large reservoir of extremely hot ground water—500 to 700°F (260 to 370°C)—is present here. This water readily flashes into steam when penetrated by a drill hole. Steam pressure forces both steam and hot water to the surface, much like the action of a coffee percolator. Near Mexicali, Mexico, this resource has already been developed, with the daily flow of steam and water amounting to 2000 tons. The

Table 64.1 Geothermal Generating Capacity*

Country	Name of Field	Capacity (megawatts)
El Salvador	Ahuachapan	30
Iceland	Namafjell	3
Italy	Larderello	400
	Monte Amiata	25
Japan	Matsukawa	20
	Otake	11
	Hachimantai	10
Mexico	Pathé	3
	Cerro Prieto	75
New Zealand	Wairakei	190
	Kawerau	10
United States	The Geysers	600
U.S.S.R.	Pauzhetsk	5
	Paratunka	1
	Total	1383

SOURCE: A. J. Ellis (1975) *American Scientist,* vol. 63, p. 515, Table 1.

prospect of a large power development beneath Imperial Valley looks very good, while the salinity of the hot water is quite low. If fully developed, the Imperial Valley geothermal field could probably produce as much as 20,000 megawatts of electricity, which is an amount equal in 1975 to about 10% of the total U.S. production of electricity, or about 50% of the power output of U.S. nuclear power plants. The needs of southern California could be fully met by this source alone. Heat remaining in the water after it has been used to generate electricity could be used to distill the waste water and produce a substantial yield of irrigation water, a valuable commodity in this desert agricultural region.

Hot Dry-Rock Energy Sources

In certain areas, the intrusion of magma has been sufficiently recent that solid igneous rock of a batholith is still hot in a depth range of perhaps 1 to 3 mi (2 to 5 km). At this depth, the rock is strongly compressed and contains little, if any, ground water. Rock in this zone may be as hot as 600°F (300°C) and could supply an enormous quantity of heat energy. The planned development of this resource includes drilling into the hot zone and then shattering the surrounding rock by hydrofracture—a method using water under pressure which is widely used in petroleum development. Surface water would be pumped down one well into the fracture zone and heated water pumped up another well.

An experimental hole in northern New Mexico was drilled in 1971, and the dry granite rock at the bottom fractured by water injected under pressure. This successful experiment has led to optimism that deeper zones of hot rock can be developed. Promising locations have been found in Montana and Idaho. The potential for electrical power generation from deep hot-rock areas is believed to be many times greater than for hot water areas. One recent guess places the output of these dry-rock wells at a possible 130,000 megawatts by 1985 and nearly 400,000 megawatts by the year 2000. The latter figure is about double the entire electric generating capacity of the U.S. for 1975.

Geopressurized Energy Resources

Finally, on the list of occurrences of geothermal energy, we come to an energy source trapped in thick continental shelf sediments of the continental margin. Recall from Unit 35 that these sediments form a wedge, thickening toward the ocean basin, as shown in Figure 35.1. Rich petroleum deposits have been developed in the continental shelf wedge of the Gulf Coast region. Here, in a region extending from Texas to Louisiana, the strata in some areas have been found to hold hot water under high pressure and to contain dissolved natural gas. Subsurface bodies of this type are described as being **geopressurized.** They are avoided in drilling for petroleum because the high pressure makes it difficult to control the well. These geopressurized

areas should be explored, according to recent proposals, as sources of hot water for generating electricity. One estimate of the total energy resource in the Gulf area alone is a generating capability of between 30,000 and 115,000 megawatts of power. Development of this resource is probably not economically feasible at this time, but the ultimate potential is large.

In summary of the geothermal energy resources of the United States, a 1975 report by the U.S. Geological Survey concludes that at least 12,000 megawatts of electric generating capacity can be developed from known geothermal systems with the prevailing technology and current energy prices. This amount is about 15 times greater than the existing geothermal output. Even the expanded output would be only a very small part of our electric power needs.

Tidal Power

Tidal power, a very small contributor to the world's energy needs, makes use of the tidal rise and fall of ocean level, an unending source of energy. We explained tides and tidal currents in Unit 36. To harness the power of the tides a bay must be located along a coast subject to a large range of tide. An ideal location is to be found on the Atlantic Coast of Maine, New Brunswick, and Nova Scotia, around the Bay of Fundy. Here the tide range is greater than 10 ft (3 m). The rugged coast near the boundary of Maine and Nova Scotia is deeply indented by narrow bays, with constricted places where the bays empty into the ocean. These constrictions can be closed off by dams and the tidal flow passed through conduits connecting the bay and the ocean. Turbines placed in the conduits can be turned by the swift tidal current.

Plans for a tidal power plant at Passamaquoddy Bay, at the entrance to the Bay of Fundy, were developed and modified over a long span of years. Work on a small part of the total project was begun in 1935 and suspended in 1937. Today, only two important tidal power plants are in operation. One is the La Rance plant on the Brittany coast of France. Opened in 1966, the maximum generating capacity of the plant, which has 24 conduits, is 240 megawatts when the turbines are running at full speed. The average output for the year is only 60 megawatts, which is about the output of one small nuclear power station. A second tidal power plant is operating in the Soviet Union.

The potential for tidal power development is not great. For the world the annual tidal energy potentially available by exploitation of all suitable coastal sites is only about 1% of the total energy potentially available through hydropower development. For the United States, the developable tidal energy resources are about two-thirds as great as the hydropower resources. The prospects of huge capital expenditures being made for tidal power development are, however, extremely poor, and we can figure that the tidal energy contribution to the United States will be effectively zero in the foreseeable future.

Unit 65
Energy from the Sun

Firepower from the Sun

Everyone knows that an ordinary magnifying lens can be used as a burning glass. Within a few seconds, smoke will stream from the intense light spot you focus upon a sheet of paper. You have been playing with the same toy used by Archimedes at Syracuse in 212 B.C. Remember, Archimedes was the eccentric Greek scientist who is reputed to have leaped from his bathtub and run down the street nude shouting, "I've found it!". His bathtub discovery of the principle of buoyant suspension of solids in liquids was indeed a worthy contribution. His playing with a burning glass was perhaps more spectacular, but less practical in the long run. During the Second Punic War, a Roman fleet under Claudius Marcellus had laid siege to Syracuse, a port city on Sicily. It is fairly well documented that Archimedes invented several weapons of war to help fight off the Romans. One of these interests us particularly, since our subject is solar energy. Legend, repeated by the 12th-century writer Johannes Tzetzes, has it that "Archimedes set fire to Marcellus' navy by means of a burning glass composed of small square mirrors moving every way upon hinges which when placed in the sun's direct rays directed them upon the Roman fleet so as to reduce it to ashes at the distance of a bowshot." Whether this actually happened is quite doubtful, but we are told that Archimedes' inventions so impressed General Marcellus that he ordered the scientist's life to be spared when Syracuse fell to the Romans.

The Archimedes legend kept recurring in later centuries as a topic for debate: "Did he or didn't he?" Finally, Georges Buffon, a Frenchman, decided to stop the bickering once and for all. In 1747, Buffon assembled 168 small flat mirrors and directed their rays on a single spot, which easily set wood afire. Buffon then went on to melt lead at a distance of 130 feet and silver at 60 feet. It was not long before a fellow Frenchman, an optician, had constructed a practical solar furnace with which he could smelt

This solar engine, used to run a printing press, was exhibited in France in 1884. A parabolic reflector (right) generated the steam, which powered an ordinary steam engine (center). The man at the far left holds the product, labeled *Soleil Journal*. (New York Public Library Picture Collection.)

The solar furnace at Odeillo, in the Pyrenees. The array of mirrors, resembling billboards, reflects the sun's rays so as to strike the great parabolic reflector, which forms the north-facing wall of the building at the far left. (Claude Gazuit/Rapho-Photo researchers.)

iron, copper, and other metals.

A little later, the distinguished French scientist, Antoine Lavoisier, designed a super-furnace using solar rays. His device used two large lenses in line to gather the sun's rays. Each lens consisted of two convex glass disks, the space between being filled with wine. He got the lenses from the Saint Gobain glassworks, a firm that still supplies glass units for solar furnaces. The larger of Lavoisier's lenses was 52 inches in diameter, the second, 8 inches. The furnace developed a temperature of 3200° Fahrenheit (1750° Centigrade), which could melt just about anything known including platinum. The furnace could even reduce a diamond to graphite. Unhappily for science, Lavoisier had purchased from the royal government the right to collect taxes, and for this he was guillotined during the extreme phase of the French Revolution.

A modern French tribute to Lavoisier is the fantastic solar furnace at Odeillo, a place high in the Pyrenees Mountains. Built by Dr. Felix Trombe shortly after World War II, it consists of massed mirrors forming a giant parabolic reflector taking up the entire face of an eight-story building. The parabola faces north—a direction that receives no sun. On the mountainside in front of it are south-facing mirrors, called heliostats, which reflect the sun's rays onto the parabolic surface. Each heliostat must turn by it-

self to give precise reflection, an operation controlled by electronic computer. The 9500 mirrors of the parabola focus to a point 60 feet away where temperatures up to 6800°F (3800°C) can be obtained. The solar beam can melt through a steel plate half an inch thick in a few seconds. The Odeillo furnace is not just a curiosity; it is used for many kinds of high-temperature experiments. The great advantage of a solar furnace is that the heat can be turned off or on in an instant, using shutters in front of the furnace. In this way, bursts of intense energy can be applied, a phenomenon called "thermal shocking." Solar furnaces come in many sizes. You can buy a solar cooker that uses a reflecting parabola to heat a skillet. A folding model can be taken on a camping trip.

Our nation is now girding itself for a great debate: What form of energy shall we develop as a substitute for petroleum? Now that we have looked at several possibilities, including nuclear fuel, we turn our attention to solar energy. Does our salvation lie in the abundant, limitless, and nonpolluting energy from the sun?

DATA SOURCE: D. S. Halacy, Jr. (1973) *The Coming of Age of Solar Energy*, revised ed., Harper & Row, New York, 231 pp.; John H. Douglas (1976) Solar furnace: image of a thousand suns, *Science News*, vol. 109, pp. 235-236.

The Scope of Solar Energy

Planet earth intercepts solar energy at the rate of 1½ quadrillion megawatt-hours per year. This quantity of energy amounts to about 28,000 times as much as all the energy presently being consumed each year by Man. Thus, we realize that there is an enormous source of energy near at hand waiting to be used. That use would simply mean bypassing some of the flow of solar energy through Man-made subsystems within the natural global energy system. Another remarkable virtue of solar energy is that its use by Man cannot increase the amount of heat load upon the atmosphere and hydrosphere. A major worry we expressed in Unit 4 is that the combustion of fossil fuels will raise the global average temperature, both by emitting large amounts of heat and by raising the level of the carbon dioxide content of the atmosphere. Neither of these concerns need be felt about using solar energy. Add to these advantages the lack of environmental pollution when solar energy is used—no emissions of sulfur dioxide or carbon particles. The fact that solar energy is in endless supply—a renewable resource—should perhaps be placed at the beginning rather than at the end of the list of its virtues.

Your first thought about using solar energy is that it consists simply of catching the sun's rays on some sort of receiving surface which becomes heated, and in this way water or air is warmed. You also know that space vehicles derive electrical energy from solar cells exposed to the sun's rays. These direct interception methods are, to be sure, a major aspect of solar energy use, but there are many more when we consider the indirect ways in which solar energy is absorbed and transformed in natural earth systems.

Going one step further, take note that the ocean surface is warmed by solar radiation and that this warm water layer overlies a deep, cold layer. This water temperature difference can be used to generate electrical power. One more step takes us to the realization that solar energy drives the hydrologic cycle and lifts water vapor to high altitudes on the lands where it can condense and start its downhill path as runoff from rainfall. Viewed in this way, hydropower is a form of solar energy. Winds are generated by unequal heating of the atmosphere, therefore wind power, using windmills, is also a form of solar energy. Ocean waves, sustained by wind might also be harnessed as an indirect solar energy source, and so, perhaps, could ocean currents that are set in motion by those winds.

We begin to visualize the true scope of solar energy when we realize that biological systems use and store solar energy. The plants, as primary producers, store solar energy; the animals, as consumers, convert that stored energy into heat and locomotion. Thus **biomass energy systems** comprise a vast and varied group of sources of stored solar energy. Wood and other plant tissue as a fuel are one such source; algae cultivated in ponds would be another.

Our review of the total scope of solar energy for Man's use will be descriptive and nontechnical. It is a subject that makes use of many of the principles developed in earlier units dealing with the workings of the atmosphere, hydrosphere, and biosphere.

Direct Capture of Solar Rays

Oldest and simplest of the forms of solar energy conversion is the direct interception of the warming rays of the sun by some kind of receiving surface or medium. Applications of this principle range from simple heating of buildings and domestic hot-water supplies, to the intense heating of boilers and furnaces by focusing the solar rays upon a small target. A quite different application of direct-ray capture is to generate electricity in the receiving element.

A great saving of expenditure of fossil fuels can be achieved through solar heating of buildings. Each home, school, or office building can have its own solar collecting system so that expensive energy transport, whether by pipeline, truck, or power line can be eliminated. In most cases, the goal of this application is to supplement, rather than to replace the use of fuels.

The simplest form of solar heating is the use of large glass panes to admit sunlight into a room—the greenhouse principle. Figure 65.1 shows a cross section of a room in which solar rays are admitted during the winter, when the sun's path is low in the sky, but excluded in summer by a suitable roof overhang. Of course, the same large glass panes will result in high heat losses at night and on cold, cloudy days by outgoing longwave radiation, unless thermal drapes or shutters are also used.

Practical solar heating of interior building space and hot water systems makes use of **solar collectors.** One type of collector consists of network of metal tubes carrying circulating water. Aluminum tubes, painted black, are efficient absorbers of solar energy. Water is pumped through the tubes to heat a large body of water in a storage tank. A reflective sheet of foil under the panel may be used to intensify the heating, while an underlying insulating layer of

Figure 65.1 A simple method of solar heating makes use of the principle that short-length waves can enter a glass wall, but the heated air is trapped in the room. By careful design of the roof overhang, sun is admitted in winter and excluded in summer.

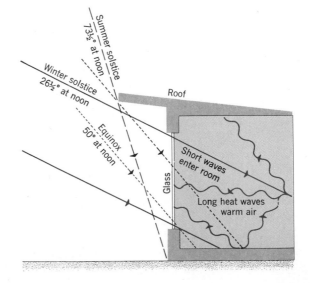

Figure 65.2 This new solar house is designed to convert the sun's energy into both heat and electricity. It was designed and constructed by the University of Delaware. The system should provide up to 80% of the total energy need of the household. (University of Delaware.)

foam plastic can decrease heat losses. A cover of glass or clear plastic is used to reduce heat loss to the atmosphere. Panels of solar collectors are usually placed on the roof of the building. If a house is designed around the solar heating system, the roof may be oriented and pitched at the optimum angle to intercept solar rays (Figure 65.2). Water can be heated to a temperature of 150°F (65°C) and can be used to transfer heat to a hot water supply for washing and bathing, as well as to a conventional space-heating system.

Where more intense heating of water, or other conducting fluids is required, parabolic reflectors can be used. The reflector focuses the solar rays upon a pipe, in which temperatures up to 950°F (550°C) can be attained (Figure 65.3). This temperature is sufficient to supply steam to a turbine that drives an electric generator. The waste heat can be used for space heating and hot-water heating. Parabolic reflector systems can be effectively used for industrial plants and shopping centers which not only need large amounts of energy during the day, but also have

large, low buildings with flat roofs on which the reflectors can be installed.

Solar energy power plants have been designed to use reflecting mirror systems, like those of the solar furnace we described in opening paragraphs of this unit. A large number of movable mirrors placed on the ground can reflect solar rays to the top of a central tower where a boiler and electric generator are located (Figure 65.4). The extremely high temperatures and pressures produced in this way allow a number of kinds of gases and fluids to be used in the boiler. Hydrogen gas, which can be generated by this process, provides an ideal medium in which to store energy for later conversion to electricity when the solar input is cut off.

An estimate has been made of the feasibility of supplying all energy needs of the United States in the year 2000 through a system of mirror-reflector power plants. The power plants would be located in the southwestern United States, where the annual number of hours of sunshine is greatest (Figure 65.5). In this region, a system with a 30% efficiency for converting solar energy into electrical energy would require a total land area equivalent to the area of a single square plot 175 mi (280 km) on a side. The area would represent 0.86% of the area of the United States. Although the ecosystem of the entire area would be destroyed, there would be no output of pollutants, and there would be no significant water consumption. Scientists who have planned this system and computed its costs are of the opinion that it will become economically competitive in the near future with systems that depend on fossil fuels and nuclear energy. They are also of the opinion that the state of technology of this form of power production is sufficiently developed to make the system function effectively.

Direct heat absorption from solar rays can have an important energy-saving application in systems for distilling seawater to produce freshwater supplies. This prospect is particularly appealing because the tropical deserts in which the greatest intensity of solar energy is available are also the regions where pure, freshwater for urban and agricultural uses is in shortest supply. A solar energy system placed in the southwestern desert of the United States, for example, could supply enough electrical energy to desalinate seawater of the Pacific Ocean in a quantity sufficient for the needs of a population of 120 million people.

Figure 65.3 Schematic design of a parabolic reflector for supplying steam to generate electricity on a small scale.

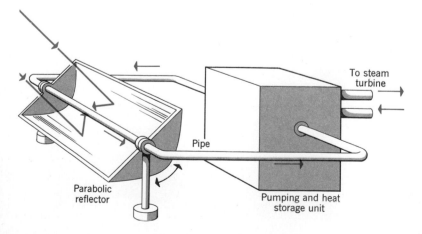

To steam turbine

Pipe

Parabolic reflector

Pumping and heat storage unit

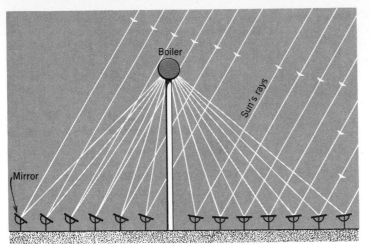

Figure 65.4 Design for a solar power plant using an array of movable mirrors to concentrate the sun's rays upon a boiler.

Electricity from the Sun's Rays

We turn now to the technology of generating electricity directly from the impact of the sun's rays. The **photovoltaic effect** is known to amateur photographers through the light meter. As you move the glass window of the meter across a scene, a small hand wavers over a calibrated dial to tell you the varying intensities of the incoming light. The sensing device in this meter is a photovoltaic cell; it transforms light energy into electricity. The hand on the meter is actually showing you the amount of electric current generated by the cell. Certain crystalline substances pro-

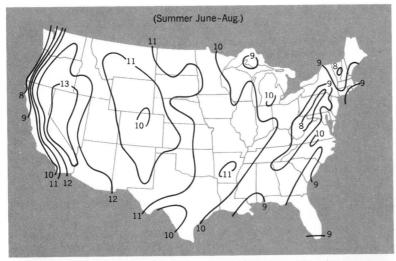

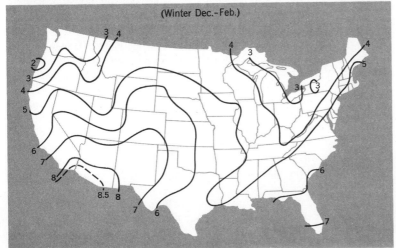

Figure 65.5 Maps of the United States showing the number of hours of sunshine to be expected in summer and winter seasons. (National Weather Service.)

duce the photovoltaic effect. The problem is to construct from these substances solar cells that are high in efficiency and low in cost. Cells of crystalline silicon are the most widely used today, with an efficiency of about 13%, although this may be in time increased to 20%. Silicon cells have been used effectively in our space vehicles, where cost is not a significant factor. Solar cells can also be made using cadmium sulfide or gallium arsenide. Because a single silicon cell generates only about one-half volt of electricity, a large number must be connected in an array to produce a high voltage output. Also, the current that is produced is direct current (DC) and requires transformation into alternating current (AC) for use in conventional power applications. A new manufacturing process, in which silicon cells are produced from a continuous ribbon of molten silicon, is being developed and may eventually reduce costs materially. The silicon used in solar cells, however, must be of extremely high purity, a factor that makes mass production difficult.

As with direct heat-gathering solar panels, arrays of photovoltaic solar cells would occupy large areas of ground surface to produce important outputs of energy. Storage of the electricity is another problem, since the system does not work at night. Storage as hydrogen fuel is an attractive possibility for large-scale systems, while batteries can be used to store power in small systems such as those of homes, farms, and ranches. One suggested small-scale use is to turn electric water pumps used for irrigation of fields in the sunny dry season of tropical countries, e.g., on wheat farms of Pakistan and northern India.

A startling proposal has been made to use orbiting space satellites as power stations. The satellite solar power station (SSPS) is visualized as a space vehicle bearing a large

array of solar cells (Figure 65.6). Power generated by the space station would be sent to earth in the form of microwave beams. Since the SSPS would be situated in a synchronous orbit, it would hover over a fixed earthpoint on the equator and feed its power to a single receiving station on the ground. The ground station could be situated as close as possible to the area served, and thus reduce the need for long transmission lines. The receiving antenna on the ground would be large—covering a circle at least 4 mi (7 km) in diameter.

Solar Sea Power

Solar sea power makes use of the temperature gradient from the surface downward in tropical waters. The temperature difference between the warm surface water layer and the cold deep water is on the order of 40F° (22C°). This does not seem like much of a difference to convert into energy, but the total solar heat input into the warm water layer is more than 10,000 times greater than needed for all Man's uses. A floating towerlike structure is planned to project from the warm layer into the cold layer (Figure 65.7). Ammonia would be used as the heat exchanger, since it would boil into a gas at the temperature of the upper warm layer but condense into a liquid upon reaching the cold lower layer. The expanding gas would be used to drive a turbine and thus generate electricity. Although the scheme seems workable in theory, many problems would need to be solved to make it a producer of energy.

Hydropower, Wind Power, and Wave Power

We will make only very brief mention of three energy forms indirectly powered by the sun: hydropower, wind power, and wave power.

Hydropower (water power) has been important to Man for centuries as the driving agent in mills for grinding grain to make flour. The slowly turning water wheel in its rustic setting is familiar to all. Later, hydropower became important in turning the factory wheels of the Industrial Revolution. Dozens of manufacturing towns and cities in New England flourished along the natural falls and rapids of rivers whose courses had been dislocated 10,000 years earlier by the ice sheets of the Pleistocene Epoch. The era of high concrete dams, producing large outputs of electricity, followed in the late 1900s and reached its culmination in the mid-1900s under domination by the U.S. Bureau of Reclamation. In the United States, only about one-fifth of the total electric power is now generated by hydroelectric plants. Their further development is severely limited both for lack of new sites and because of mounting opposition from environmentalist groups (Unit 55). In the U.S.S.R. and in other nations, many large hydroelectric plants are at present still under construction. A serious drawback to the development of hydropower, however, is that the life span of a reservoir is limited by the accumulation of sediment.

Figure 65.6   Artist's conception of an orbiting power station. The satellite beams its power to the earth in microwave form. (Arthur D. Little, Inc.)

Figure 65.7 An artist's conception of a proposed floating ocean thermal plant, designed to generate 160 million watts of electric power—enough to supply the needs of a city with 100,000 residents. The long tubular shaft reaches down to a layer of cold ocean water. (Lockheed Missiles & Space Co., Inc./ERDA.)

Eventually, filling will occur to the point that the water storage volume is inadequate.

Wind power is another indirect form of solar energy that has been used for centuries. The windmill of the Low Countries of Europe played a major role in pumping water from the polders as they were reclaimed from tidal land. The windmill was also used to grind grain in low, flat areas where streams could not be adapted to waterpower. The design of new forms of windmills has intrigued inventors for many decades. The total supply of wind energy is enormous. The World Meteorological Organization has estimated that the combined electrical-generating wind power of favorable sites throughout the world comes to about 20 million megawatts, a figure about 100 times greater than the total electrical generating capacity of the United States. Many problems must be solved in developing wind power as a major resource, and the extent of its future contribution remains in doubt. A successful medium-scale facility in operation in Denmark consists of a three-bladed propellor 80 ft (24m) in radius driving a generator capable of an output of 200 kilowatts of power. It is said to require little maintenance and to offer bright prospects for replacing a large share of Denmark's fuel-burning electric generating system. Small windmills are a promising source of supplementary electric power for countless farms and ranches, where windmills for pumping

well water were for so long ubiquitous features of the American landscape.

Wave power we mention only in passing. Waves arriving at the ocean shore bring with them an enormous flow of energy. All of it is dissipated as the waves feel bottom, steepen, and break. While the possibility of harnessing this energy has been seriously considered, it is not likely to be a source of usable energy in the foreseeable future.

Biomass Energy Systems

Finally, we come to the biological process as a working energy storage system. Some writers have called it The Green Machine. The primary producers—plants—convert sunlight, carbon dioxide, and water into carbohydrate on a vast scale. This matter, which is the biomass, consists largely of cellulose; it can be burned to release energy.

Wood fuel, which used to be the principal source of energy for the human race, is now being considered in a new role as a biomass energy system. Trees, grasses, or other crops might be extensively cultivated on plantations for use as fuel. Estimates show that in terms of cost, the combustion energy from such energy plantations might be competitive with coal in some parts of the United States, and substantially cheaper than fuel oil generally. Like any agricultural ecosystem, plantations cultivated for fuel would substitute a one-crop ecosystem for enormous expanses of natural ecosystems. One estimate places the space requirement for such plantations at 100 million acres to provide the fuel for an electric-generating plant system of 200,000 megawatts capacity, or about equal to the total 1974 United States electric generating capacity. The land area mentioned is about the same as the area of the state of California.

The production of methane gas from the biomass of plants and animals has been developed on a substantial scale as an energy source in European countries. Two important raw materials for this purpose are sewage and animal wastes. When these materials are decomposed by bacteria under anaerobic conditions (without oxygen) methane gas is given off. Methane, often called marsh gas, is an efficient clean-burning fuel and has been widely used to power small combustion engines. Since these raw materials already contain the necessary bacteria, all that is required is a closed container from which the atmospheric oxygen is excluded. Even sawdust and paper can be used in this process.

In much larger operations, methane from sewage effluent can be produced in urban sewage treatment plants. The sewage is first digested by aerobic (oxygen-using) bacteria, providing nutrients for algae to grow. The algae in turn are decomposed by anaerobic bacteria to yield methane gas, which provides fuel for generating electricity. A more direct method has been suggested, in which the algae are dried and burned as fuel. Marine kelp, a variety of algae growing in thick beds in shallow water, has also been suggested as a source of cellulose for conversion into energy.

Those who have evaluated algae as an energy resource judge that it will not be able to make an important contribution to world needs for some three to four decades to come, and that in the meanwhile the direct use of physical systems of solar power can be developed to meet human energy needs. If so, photosynthesis will remain in its present role as a food-provider.

The Global Balance of Energy

In six study units, we have reviewed the major energy resources available for Man's use. The entire scope of energy resources can now be placed in perspective by examining the natural global balance of energy.

Figure 65.8 is a flow chart showing the natural earth-energy system without any impact by Man. Energy entering the earth system is overwhelmingly solar energy, of which about 30% is reflected directly back to space and the remaining 65% is cycled through various paths before eventually leaving the earth as longwave radiation. The other two energy inputs are energy leaking out of the solid earth and tidal energy. Energy coming out of the earth by slow conduction and from a few hot spots, such as volcanoes and hot springs, is extremely small—less than 0.02% as much as solar energy. Tidal energy is only about one-tenth as much as that leaking out of the crust. The diagram shows that some energy stored in plants and animals enters the realm of storage as fossil fuels. Although not evaluated, this quantity is extremely small. In the life span of all human civilization, the quantity of energy placed in storage as fossil fuels would be too trivial to show, and in any case, it would be balanced off by the oxidation of petroleum and coal that would be gradually exposed to the atmosphere by erosion processes.

How has the energy picture changed since Man's appearance on earth? The diagram would need to be modified by showing some arrows originating in the storage boxes containing fossil fuels, nuclear energy, and geothermal energy. These arrows would feed into the escape route as outgoing longwave energy. But recall that the quantity of solar energy intercepted annually by the earth is many thousands of times greater than the energy Man consumes annually by burning fossil and nuclear fuels. The additional quantity of geothermal energy brought out of the earth by Man is also extremely small.

When we have exhausted most of the earth's store of fossil fuels and the concentrated ores of uranium, the remaining sustained natural energy resources will be solar energy, geothermal energy, and tidal energy. There is, of course, the distant prospect of fusion energy, but it does not fall within the natural system we are viewing here. The great thrust of our analysis of the planetary energy-resource systems seems to point squarely at one course of action: Make maximum use of solar energy by all available processes and as soon as possible. In solar energy lies our largest source of free, inexhaustible, nonpolluting energy. A second such source lies in tapping the deep dry-rock sources of geothermal energy, but an important contribution from that source must wait upon technological advances not yet within our grasp.

Our final unit ends where the first unit began, with the omniscient power of the sun—power to sustain life and the workings of the life environment, power perhaps to bail out the human race from a sorry fate brought on by an insatiable appetite for greater affluence.

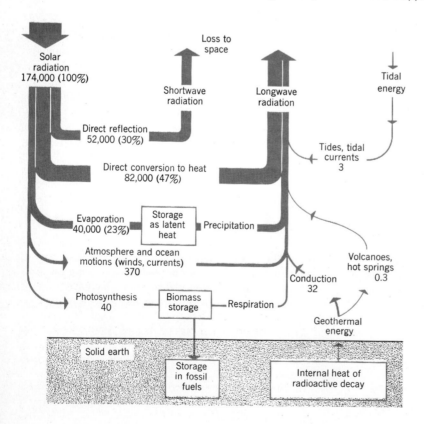

Figure 65.8   The natural energy system of the earth. The unit used is equal to one trillion watts. (From M. K. Hubbert [1974] U.S. Energy resources, a review as of 1972, Part I: U.S. Congress, Senate Committee on Interior and Insular Affairs, A National Fuels and Energy Policy Study, U.S. Govt. Printing Office, Washington, D.C.)

Epilogue

Environmental Perspectives

We have laid the scientific foundation for a general understanding of environmental problems. Many of the physical problems we analyzed seem upon first encounter to have fairly simple physical solutions. For example, one way to stop sulfur oxide air pollution is simply to stop burning fossil fuels; to cut water pollution levels, all we need to do is seal off the outfall pipes of sewage treatment plants. Yet both these actions have detrimental effects—without access to fossil fuels, our power and transportation industries would shut down, and without functional sewage treatment plants, disease would spread. These drastic remedial actions would thus produce a net loss in the total quality of our environment, rather than the gain intended. Implementation of such patently desirable environmental management procedures therefore can lead to complex reactions which arise from the structure and institutions of our society. These institutional reactions are simultaneous, and moreover, they interact.

One institution is economic. Free enterprise depends upon the reality of profit-making. Almost all measures necessary to reduce levels of pollution and intensities of environmental degradation are costly. In the long run these costs must be met; they will ultimately be absorbed by the consumer through increased prices of goods and services, or through increased taxes, or both. Small wonder that individuals as well as corporations are reluctant to take action!

Another institution of society is public law. Environmental improvements require new laws. Once placed on the books, laws must be enforced. Enforcement leads to conflict with freedom of enterprise. Obviously, effective environmental management involves some added constraints to the freedom of individuals and organizations to do as they please. Conflicts are compounded and confused by interaction of laws and law enforcement on at least three governmental levels: federal, state, and local.

Another institution is cultural. It encompasses long-standing beliefs and practices related to religious and ethnic backgrounds. Population control provides an example. Some persons believe that society as a whole has the right to limit its numbers by controlling family size. Still others feel that the family unit should make the choice for itself. Even among those who agree that some form of control is necessary, methods are still disputed—for example, some oppose abortion; others advocate it.

The cultural institution imposes its problems in many other ways, some of them quite subtle. Lifestyles differ. Attitudes about environmental standards differ. Urban groups may have a different outlook upon environmental priorities than conservationist groups. Which problem should be given first priority? Air pollution may rank high in the judgment of inner-city dwellers, while at the same time, they may show little concern as to where their sewage is discharged and in what condition. Some other citizens may live in a region where air pollution is a secondary problem; instead, water pollution from an urban area may be foremost in their minds.

The step from environmental science, which analyzes problems in terms of cause and effect, to environmental management, which seeks viable solutions to problems, is a big step. Your understanding of environmental processes and natural resources will come to nothing if you fail to follow up with an inquiry into methods of environmental and resource management. We strongly recommend that you look about in your available curriculum for a course or program that deals with these areas.

Further study of environmental management will lead to insights into action programs based upon multiple options. For example, you may find that there are nonstructural approaches to meeting demands for more water, more fuels, and more metals. There may be viable alternatives to consumptive use of materials through such procedures as substitution and recycling. A further study of urban air pollution will doubtless lead you into the area of public transportation. What alternatives are there to imposing severe controls on pollutant emissions of the passenger car? These and many, many other questions

485

arise at the level of environmental and resource management. Further study is mandatory if you, as a citizen and a voter, are to prepare yourself adequately for the decision-making process.

And now, to stimulate your thinking and enlarge your horizons, we offer a variety of questions, assertions, and opinions that relate to certain broad aspects of Man's place in the environment. Judge them on their merits as you see fit. Among the basic questions asked will be these: Do we face an environmental crisis? Do we face a shortage in supplies of materials and energy? What is our present status with respect to these problems? What will the future bring for the human race?

Is There an Environmental Crisis?

Many voices have been raised in alarm over the degraded state of the environment and threats to the well-being of ecosystems. Is the human race really threatened by the consequences of its own action? Degrees of alarm vary substantially. Which voice do we heed?

Throughout innumerable recent publications, we find statements referring to a crisis or to multiple crises arising to plague our planet. Often the authors are not explicit in giving any clear picture of what constitutes a crisis, what part of the biosphere will be affected, and whether the crisis exists now, or will arise in the future. One basic form of crisis deals with shortages of food or mineral resources, or both, in the face of a rising global population of humans. Another form of crisis deals with the unfavorable impact of pollution—broadly defined to include all forms of environmental deterioration—upon the biosphere. In other words, crises can take the form of biospheric destruction by such processes as poisoning by toxic substances, genetic damage from ionizing radiation, reduction of nutrient substances from the primary producers, and physical destruction of ecosystems and their habitats by release of mechanical or heat energy. A third crisis, in a class by itself, is catastrophic global disruption by use of nuclear weapons.

If we define an environmental crisis as a situation demanding immediate corrective action—if such be possible—to avert deterioration, damage, or destruction of the affected system, we can point to crises on various scales. Some crises will be current and local. A simple example would be a city beset by worsening smog and a static weather situation. Another would be a case of rising chlorinity in public water-supply wells of a coastal community. Signs of eutrophication of a lake signal an approaching crisis in the environment of an aquatic ecosystem.

Perhaps what most environmentalists mean when they refer to an environmental crisis of global proportions is the total situation reached at that point in time when the global demand for vital forms of energy or matter catches up with the available supply. Energy, in this sense, can take the form of food for organisms, or heat and power for industrial uses. Matter can also take the form of food for organisms, or it may consist of essential materials for industrial uses.

A global crisis involving energy or matter, or both, is inherent in one basic fact that few will dispute: the earth's resources of energy and matter are finite; whereas the demand for these resources is rising, with no limit in sight except the total finite resource itself.

To sum it up, the environmental crisis, of which so many voices warn us, is an event of many dimensions. Crisis presents itself on an areal scale ranging from local to global, and on a time scale ranging from the present to an indeterminate future point in time. The threat of crisis ranges in magnitude from deterioration of small ecosystems to total destruction of the biosphere.

While population growth of the human species has not been presented in this book, that growth is a vital ingredient in a global crisis, since greater population means both greater demand for usable energy and matter and a greater potential to pollute and degrade the environment. Therefore, we turn next to a brief review of some current views on population growth in relation to environment.

Population, Food Resources, and Environment

The current debate over population growth and its consequences can scarcely have escaped your attention. "Zero Population Growth" has joined the long list of bumper-sticker slogans of a growing ecology-conscious group of citizenry. Perhaps in no other debate on great issues of humanity has so much emotionalism been injected by so many participants. We have rarely witnessed such bitterness as is expressed by those whose positions lie at the two extremes of the debate. On the one hand there are some who claim we can sustain an almost indefinite rise in global population, since our ingenuity and technology will rise to meet any challenge. After all, they say, are there not enormous untapped food resources in the sea? And are we not experienceing a "green revolution" in crop production? At the other extreme are those who warn of wholesale destruction of human life by starvation in several of the developing nations within a few decades, despite the green revolution. They have even gone so far as to warn that once mass starvation sets in, it will be futile for food-rich industrial nations even to attempt to provide relief supplies.

The phenomenal rise in total world population, together with a sharp increase in the rate of that rise, is a fact on which there can be no debate. When population is plotted against time on arithmetic scales, the rising curve steepens so sharply that it becomes almost perpendicular in the time interval of the past half-century. In contrast, that part of the curve representing the first millenium A.D. appears almost flat, so slow is the increase. Consider that during the entire course of human history, up to the year 1850, human population had reached only one billion persons. The present world population is about 3.6 billion. Currently the rate of increase is such that a doubling of the population can take place in about thirty-five years. One recent summary of population trends states that, allowing for some decline in birth rates, the world population for the year 2000 will be 6.5 to 7.0 billion.[1] This same source goes on to say:

> Failing that reduction we may have 7.5 billion. A continued decline in death rates and progress toward a net reproduction rate of one* by the year 2040 (an optimistic assumption) would still yield a population leveling off at 15 billion late in the next century. Thus, considering demographic factors alone and leaving aside questions of resource adequacy or environmental tolerances, our best prospect would be for a stationary world population of between 15 and 20 billions. . . . The best estimate of demographers is that rapid growth is sure to continue for some time, probably more than a hundred years, even on optimistic assumptions about controlling fertility rates. (1)

Predictions relating to leveling off of population growth in developing nations experiencing rapid growth are subject to considerable disagreement. Demographers recognize that, as a nation becomes heavily industrialized, the birth rate falls to a relatively low level compared with that of the preceding agrarian period. This change is referred to as the **demographic transition.** It was observed in the case of certain industrial regions, and took place largely prior to 1940. The more optimistic debaters of the population issue predict that, as each developing nation arrives at an advanced industrial condition, it will experience a demographic transition. In this way, it is hoped, the world population growth can be stabilized, or at worst, held to a manageable rate. But even the demographic transition does not alone produce a balanced population except when there is also depletion by emigration. The best that has happened is a reduction to a doubling time of about 70 years. Consequently, the more pessimistic debaters feel it would be a tragic mistake to count upon the arrival of the demographic transition as a natural means to prevent a runaway increase.

On the subject of the ability of the earth to furnish enough food to sustain a much larger population, Professor Preston Cloud, a noted biogeologist, has stated:

> The Committee on Resources and Man of the National Academy of Sciences, which I chaired, has examined the ultimate capability of an efficiently managed world to produce food, given the cultivation of all potentially arable lands and an optimal expression of scientific and technological innovation. Its results imply that 1968 world food supplies might eventually be increased by as much as nine times, provided that sources of protein

were essentially restricted to plants, and to seafood mostly from a position lower in the marine food chain than customarily harvested and provided metal resources, agricultural water, and risky pesticides and mineral fertilizers are equal to the task and do not create intolerable side effects, and that agricultural land is not unduly preempted for other purposes. Such an ultimate level of productivity might, therefore, sustain a world population of 30 billion. Most of these, of course, would live at a level of chronic malnutrition unless distribution were so regulated as to be truly equitable, in which case all would live at a bare subsistence level, although with protein deficiency. . . .

> That seems to place a maximal limit on world populations, at a figure that could be reached by little more than a century from now at present rates of increase. Of course, many students of the problem do not believe that it is possible to sustain 30 billion people—especially considering the variety and extent of demands on water, air, and earth materials, and the psychic stresses that would arise with such numbers. I have no dispute with them. Here I seek simply to establish some theoretical outside limit, based on optimistic assumptions about what might be possible. More important attributes than a starvation diet would be sacrificed by a world that full! (2)

As we noted earlier, an increasing world population places a heavy strain upon the planet in two ways. First, more people cause more pollution and more environmental degradation. Second, more people require more of the earth's resources besides food (for example water supplies and plant fiber); they place heavier demands upon the nonrenewable energy resources we have discussed at length.

Pollution and Economics

Pollution of the environment can be viewed in a somewhat different perspective than that of biological impact upon ecosystems. There is an economic aspect to consider. The economist views pollutant wastes as **residuals.** When Man produces and consumes the wide variety of things we have become accustomed to having, there is finally left something that has no economic value on the existing market. In other words, unwanted matter and energy are generated at the terminus of the economic chain. These unwanted residuals must be disposed of, and of course, they have always been dumped upon the environment. It has been assumed that air, water, and soil are in the public domain and that these media of the environment can absorb free of charge the unwanted residuals. Writing on the subject of economics and the environment, a group of researchers with Resources for the Future (a nonprofit corporation) has analyzed the problem of residuals and the environment as follows:

> Water and air are traditionally examples of free goods in economics. But in reality in developed economies they are common property resources of great and increasing

*Synonymous with zero population growth.

value, which present society with important and difficult allocation problems that exchange in private markets cannot solve. These problems loom larger as increased population and industrial production put more pressure on the environment's ability to dilute, chemically degrade, and simply accumulate residuals from production and consumption processes. Only the crudest estimates of present external costs associated with residuals discharge exist, but it would not be surprising if these costs were already in the tens of billions of dollars annually. Moreover, as we shall emphasize again, technological means for processing or purifying one or another type of residuals do not destroy the residuals but only alter their form. Thus, given the level, patterns, and technology of production and consumption, recycle of materials into productive uses or discharge into an alternative medium are the only general operations for protecting a particular environmental medium such as water. Residual problems must be seen in a broad regional or economy-wide context rather than as separate and isolated problems of disposal of gaseous, liquid, solid, and energy waste products . . .

Yet we persist in referring to the "final consumption" of goods as though material objects such as fuels, materials, and finished goods somehow disappear into a void—a practice which was comparatively harmless only so long as air and water were almost literally "free goods." Of course, residuals from both the production and consumption processes remain, and they usually render disservices (like killing fish, increasing the difficulty of water treatment, reducing public health, soiling and deteriorating buildings, etc.) rather than services. These disservices flow to consumers and producers whether they want them or not, and except in unusual cases they cannot control them by engaging in individual exchanges. (3)

These writers propose that economic theory be revised to include the environmental media as part of the economic system. They call for a **materials balance approach** in which costs of all raw materials are traced from the time of their withdrawal from the environment to their return to that environment. They point out that residual materials do not necessarily have to be put back into the environment, where they incur costs through impact as pollutants. Instead, recycling may prove feasible and even profitable. The same can be said of some fraction of the residual energy, which may also be a source of public cost when thermal pollution results.

Resources and Their Management

Some basic facts and principles of occurrence and use of nonrenewable earth resources were covered in Units 25 and 60. Emphasis was placed on mineral substances that represent the results of accumulated geological activity of hundreds of millions of years. Consumption of these resources has skyrocketed in the past century, just as the world population itself has shot precipitously upward. Let us examine the consequences of this prodigious consump-

tion of resources which can never be renewed in the lifetime of Man on earth.

A number of authorities in a good position to know the facts have attempted to appraise the public of what the future holds in store. Walter R. Hibbard, Jr., formerly Director of the U.S. Bureau of Mines, puts it this way;

A requisite for affluence, now or in the future, is an adequate supply of minerals—fuels to energize our power and transportation; nonmetals, such as sulfur and phosphates to fertilize farms; and metals, steel, copper, lead, aluminum, and so forth, to build our machinery, cars, buildings, and bridges. These are the materials basic to our economy, the multipliers in our gross national product. But the needed materials which can be recovered by known methods at reasonable cost from the earth's crust are limited, whereas their rates of exploitation are not. This situation cannot continue. (4)

Differences exist, as one would expect, in the best estimates of reserves of mineral resources remaining in the earth's crust. More optimistic than most authorities in the field is Vincent E. McKelvey, Director of the U.S. Geological Survey. In a paper presented at Harvard University in 1971, McKelvey pointed out that dire predictions of mineral shortages have been made at intervals over the past sixty years. Nevertheless, as economic growth has moved rapidly ahead and mineral consumption has risen, the intensified research for new mineral reserves has been thus far able to keep pace with demands. McKelvey stated:

Personally, I am confident that for millennia to come we can continue to develop the mineral supplies needed to maintain a high level of living for those who now enjoy it and to raise it for the impoverished people of our own country and the world. My reasons for thinking so are that there is a visible underdeveloped potential of substantial proportions in each of the processes by which we create resources and that our experience justifies the belief that these processes have dimensions beyond our knowledge and even beyond our imagination at any given time.(5)

However, McKelvey takes a cautious position. He recognizes that many do not share his views. He feels that a searching review of resource adequacy may be required. He then goes on to say:

If our supply of critical materials is enough to meet our needs for only a few decades, a mere tapering off in the rate of increase of their use, or even a modest cutback, would stretch out these supplies for only a trivial period. If resource adequacy cannot be assured into the far distant future, a major reorientation of our philosophy, goals, and way of life will be necessary. And if we do need to revert to a low resource-consuming economy, we will have to begin the process as quickly as possible in order to avoid chaos and catastrophe.(5)

Although finite, our nonrenewable resources, including fossil fuels and uranium, the principal energy sources, allow us some options with respect to the program of depletion. Preston Cloud analyzes this concept in the following words:

Thus it is possible to think of man in relation to his renewable resources of food, water, and breathable air as limited in numbers by the sustainable annual crop. His non-renewable resources—metals, petrochemicals, mineral fuels, etc.—can be thought of, in somewhat over-simplified but valid terms, as some quantity which may be withdrawn at different rates, but for which the quantity beneath the curve of cumulative total production, from first use to exhaustion of primary sources, is largely independent of the shape of the curve. In other words, the depletion curve of a given non-renewable raw material, or of that class of resources, may rise and decline steeply over a relatively short time, or it may be a flatter curve that lasts for a longer time, depending on use rates and conservation measures such as recycling. This is a choice that civilized, industrialized man expresses whenever his collective aspirations, efforts, and ideals express themselves in a given general density of population, per capita rate of consumption, and conservation practice.(2)

Stretching of our limited earth resources to the utmost is a conservation procedure strongly endorsed by all who study resource problems. We have stressed in earlier statements in this book that pollution and environmental degradation are usual by-products of development and use of raw materials. Thus the various means available to conserve mineral use simultaneously serve two vital functions. One is to make the resource last as long as possible; the other is to minimize environmental impact.

One of the options available for stretching resources is the substitution of natural and synthetic materials, the latter made available by technological advances. For example, in electrical conductors aluminum (an abundant element in the crust) is being substituted for copper (a scarce element in the crust). For a few metals, mercury among them, no effective substitution is now possible. Plastics are being widely substituted for metals in many applications. Keep in mind, however, that plastics are synthesized from compounds which are themselves mineral resources, namely, petroleum and coal.

Recycling is another option urgently requiring intensive research and development. We have not yet begun to exploit fully the opportunities for recycling of solid wastes, which pose in themselves an environmental problem as sources of water pollution and as consumers of valuable urban land.

Energy resources, together with matter resources, comprise the total natural resource picture. While various aspects of energy resources have been included in the foregoing paragraphs, it is useful to make a further analysis of energy consumption problems.

Consumption of Energy

Do we face an energy crisis? Along with other natural resources, the consumption of energy has taken the same sharp upturn as the global population. In 1972, testifying before the House Committee on Interior and Insular Affairs, Vice Admiral Hyman G. Rickover, a leading author-

ity on technical applications of nuclear energy, had this to say:

I can think of no public issue confronting us today that will touch the lives of our children and grandchildren—if not ourselves—more closely than the ability of the U.S. to command the energy resources that are needed to sustain our economy. . . . A realistic assessment of our energy resources position would stress the fact that it is not important exactly *when* our fossil fuels give out. We may find better ways to extract oil and gas from coal, tar sands, shale; we may discover more reserves than we know of at present on the Continental Shelf surrounding our country or elsewhere in the sea. What is important is to comprehend that some day the fossil fuels will be gone; that renewable energy resources are unlikely to provide more than a small percentage of our needs; that even atomic energy, since it requires uranium, is finite; and that we cannot be certain that some man-made alternative as yet undeveloped will arrive in time—or ever—to supply our energy needs.(6)

As in the case of materials resources, Vincent E. McKelvey, Director of the U.S. Geological Survey, presents a more optimistic outlook upon the future of energy resources:

Most important to secure our future is an abundant and cheap supply of energy, for if that is available we can obtain materials from low-quality sources, perhaps even country rocks, as Harrison Brown has suggested. Again, I am personally optimistic on this matter, with respect both to the fossil fuels and particularly to the nuclear fuels. Not only does the breeder reactor appear to be near enough to practical reality to justify the belief that it will permit the use of extremely low-grade sources of uranium and thorium that will carry us far into the future, but during the last couple of years there have been exciting new developments in the prospects for commercial energy from fusion.(5)

Whatever may be the shades of opinion on this question of future supplies of energy, there is no question that the prodigious increase in energy consumption poses many problems, including serious threats to the environment. The present rate of increase of energy consumption is such that the doubling time is about fifteen years. We can anticipate a corresponding increase in the frequency and severity of environmental problems in years to come.

Discussing the environmental impact of energy use, Philip H. Abelson had this to say in an editorial in the journal *Science,* of which he is editor:

Consumption of energy is the principal source of air pollution, and energy production, transportation, and consumption are responsible for an important fraction of all our environmental problems. Use of energy continues to rise at the rate of 4.5 percent per year. Even if fuel supplies were infinite, such an increase could not be tolerated indefinitely. But fuel supplies are not inexhaustible, and this combined with the need to preserve the environment will force changes in patterns of energy production and use.

Our economy has been geared to profligate expenditure of energy and resources. Much of our pollution problem would disappear if we drove 1-ton instead of 2-ton automobiles. Demand for space heat and cooling could be reduced if buildings were properly insulated. Examples of needless use of electricity are everywhere. Promotional rates and advertising tend to encourage excessive consumption.

Slowing down the rate of increase in use of energy will not be easy. Public habits of energy consumption will not be quickly altered, and a sudden change in the rate of growth of energy consumption would cause major additional unemployment.(7)

What are the prospects of achieving success in reducing the environmental impacts of energy consumption? Abelson concludes his editorial in this way:

Measures to cut excessive use of energy are likely to come only after a long time, if ever. We should face the possibility that increased consumption of energy will continue and prepare to meet that possibility. Atmospheric pollution is not an inevitable consequence of production of energy. In the use of fossil fuels, production of sulfur dioxide is not an essential by-product. Destruction of the environment is not a necessary consequence of strip mining. Pollution from almost every method of producing and utilizing energy could be sharply attenuated either through better practices or through development of new methods. In view of the importance of energy to society, present expenditures on research and development related to energy are small and these are not well apportioned.(7)

The Prospect for a Steady-State Existence

Increasingly, in the past few years, members of the scientific community have been voicing the concept that the survival of the human race on our planet will be contingent upon achievement of an overall steady state in the total global system of flux of energy and matter, including Man and all human institutions within the framework of the biosphere.

The concept of a steady state in the total global system is a fitting one with which to close this book. Let us read what others have had to offer on this subject:

We need to concentrate our orientation of knowledge on the human-society-plus-environment level of integration because of its relevance to the central world problem of achieving a reasonably steady state between human societies and the finite resources of our planet. We are as much concerned with human society itself as with the environments in which men live; both are parts of an interacting whole that evolves as a unit through time.—S. Dillon Ripley and Helmut K. Buechner.(8)

The use of the environment is a necessary and acceptable concept. The difference is that future use must be in the recycle context of perpetual renewal and reuse, not in the old pattern of use and discard. A sort of stable state between civilization and the environment is called for—not a balance of nature (for nature is always changing in its own right) but a harmony of society and the environment within natural laws of physics, chemistry, and biology.—Committee on Scientific Astronautics.(9)

Very likely a steady-state economy may come about eventually as the result of increased scarcity and higher costs of environmental protection, which will also encourage the recovery and recycling of materials. If a more or less steady level of consumption can be maintained and can be accompanied by a stable population, technological advance may permit some small but steady gain in level of living.

The way in which we approach a steady-state economy is most important. If it can be done through the operation of market forces, the steady state would bring a high quality of life for a maximum population. On the other hand, if the steady state is approached by way of social upheavals, sudden shortages of energy and mineral resources may produce a catastrophe that will find us with a steady-state economy but at a much lower level. If the catastrophe results in world-wide nuclear war then the level may well be at or close to zero.—V. E. McKelvey and S. Fred Singer.(10)

Over three billion years of history, read from the geological record, make it clear that the question is not whether man will come into balance with nature or not. The only question is whether this will happen as a result of self-imposed restraints of natural catastrophes over which he has no control. Nor is there any question that man can, if he chooses, determine his own destiny—at least to a very large degree and for a very long time. The question is, "will he choose to do so?". . . . In all his long history man has never faced a worthier or a more critical challenge than that of achieving a lasting balance with his environment—and I mean the total human ecosystem, including the city, the sea, and the wilderness. That is the challenge primarily of the generation now entering maturity. Population control, sensible resource management, and continuous surveillance of all components of a thoroughly researched global ecosystem, including its various sociopolitical components, are the essential steps toward such a balance. A principal goal of higher education should be to discover and to communicate the basic knowledge and comprehensive understanding that will lead to those steps being taken in a well-informed, humane, and orderly manner, and as soon as practicable.—Preston Cloud.(2)

References Cited

1. Sterling Brubaker (1972) *To live on earth; man and his environment in perspective,* published for Resources for the Future, Inc., by The Johns Hopkins Press, Baltimore and London, p. 38.
2. Preston Cloud (1971) This finite earth, *A. & S. Review,* Indiana University, Spring 1971, p. 17–32.
3. A. V. Kneese, R. U. Ayers, and R. C. d'Arge (1970) *Economics and the environment,* The Johns Hopkins Press, pp. 6–7. Copyright © 1970 by Resources for the Future, Inc., Washington, D.C.
4. Walter R. Hibbard, Jr. (1968) Mineral resources: challenge or threat?, *Science,* vol. 160, p. 143. Copyright 1968 by the American Association for the Advancement of Science.
5. Vincent E. McKelvey (1972) Mineral resource estimates and public policy, *American Scientist,* vol. 60, p. 39.
6. Hyman G. Rickover (1972) Statement to House Committee on Interior and Insular Affairs regarding fuel and energy resources, April 18, 1972.
7. Philip H. Abelson (1971) Continuing increase in use of energy, *Science,* vol. 172, p. 795. Copyright 1971 by the American Association for the Advancement of Science.
8. S. Dillon Ripley and Helmut K. Buechner (1967) Ecosystem science as a point of synthesis, Reprinted by permission of *Daedalus,* Journal of the Academy of Arts and Sciences, Boston, Mass., Fall 1967, *America's Changing Environment.*
9. *Managing the environment* (1968) Publ. Committee on Scientific Astronautics, 90th. Congress, 2nd. Session, 1968, U.S. Government Printing Office, Washington, D.C., pp. 14–15.
10. Vincent E. McKelvey and S. Fred Singer (1971) Conservation and the minerals industry—a public dilemma, *Geotimes,* vol. 16, no. 12, p. 21.

Bibliography– Selected Readings in Environmental Geography

This bibliography consists of 542 carefully selected articles, book chapters, and government circulars. Nearly all of the materials can be found in a college or university library, or are currently available for library purchase. Most selections are of recent date; a few older items are included because they remain interesting and useful, or deal with history. Most selections deal with environmental topics. Case studies as well as current issues are included.

This bibliography can be used to extend your knowledge of a given topic in greater breadth and depth than your textbook permits. Individual topics can be selected for developing unit reports or a term paper. The list of references usually found at the end of each article can lead you to a deeper probe of the topic.

A clue to the level of difficulty of the selection is given by a capital letter at the end of each entry:

(P) *Popular.* These selections are nontechnical and can be fully appreciated by persons with little science training.

(M) *Middle level.* These selections have substantial environmental science content, but are largely nontechnical; they can be understood after you have mastered the information in your textbook.

(T) *Technical.* These selections contain material requiring some knowledge of basic physics, chemistry, biology, or mathematics; they are challenging to environmental science majors.

Where hyphenated letters are used (P-M, M-T) the selection contains material covering a wider range of difficulty. A selection rated P-M will have some worthwhile information easily understood by all readers.

Most articles have been selected from the following periodicals: *American Scientist, Annals Association of American Geographers, Bulletin of the Atomic Scientists, Environment, Environmental Science and Technology, Geographical Magazine, Geographical Review, National Parks and Conservation Magazine, Science, Science News, Scientific American, Technology Review of M.I.T.*

Introduction

1 The historical roots of our ecologic crisis. Lynn White, Jr., *Science,* vol. 155, pp. 1203-1207, 1967. Reprinted as Selection 6, pp. 27-35, in *Man's Impact on the Environment,* T. R. Detwyler, ed., McGraw-Hill, New York, 1971. Influence of the Judeo-Christian tradition on environmental views of Western Man. (P)

2 Man's use of the earth: Historical background. Max Nicholson, Selection 2, pp. 10-21, in *Man's Impact on the Environment,* T. R. Detwyler, ed., McGraw-Hill, New York, 1971. A leading conservationist explains Man's impact on environment from prehistory to the modern era. (P)

3 Modern Man and environment. Thomas R. Detwyler, Selection 1, pp. 2-9, in *Man's Impact on the Environment,* T. R. Detwyler, ed., McGraw-Hill, New York, 1971. A geographer's approach to the science of the environment. (P)

4 Geography as the study of environment: An assessment of some old and new commitments. Marvin W. Mikesell, Chapter 1, pp. 1-23, in *Perspectives on Environment,* Association of American Geographers, Washington, D.C., 1974. How geography as a discipline is involved in environmental science. (P)

5 Geography and the environmental crisis. Gene Wilhelm, Jr., *Nat. Parks and Conservation Mag.,* vol. 48, no. 1, p. 20, 1974. Role of geography in the environmental movement. (P)

Unit 1
Man's Impact on the Ozone Layer

6 Stratospheric pollution: Multiple threats to earth's ozone. A. L. Hammond and T. H. Maugh II, *Science,* vol. 186, pp. 335-338, 1974. Review of research findings; explanation of effects of ozone depletion. (P-M)

7 Freons and ozone in the stratosphere. J. Basuk, *Bull. Amer. Meteorological Soc.,* vol. 56, pp. 589-592, 1975. Review of facts, problems, and conclusions. (M-T)

8 Ozone destruction: Problem's scope grows, its urgency recedes. Allen L. Hammond, *Science,* vol. 187, pp. 1181-1183, 1975. New concerns are raised by finding of a variety of compounds in stratosphere. (P-M)

9 Ozone verdict: On faith or fact? Janet H. Weinberg, *Science News,* vol. 107, pp. 322-324, 1975. News review of fluorocarbon controversy. (P-M)

10 Stratospheric ozone—fragile shield? M. I. Hoffert and R. W. Stewart, *Astronautics & Aeronautics,* vol. 13, no. 10, pp. 42-55, 1975. Comprehensive review article. (T)

11 Unshielding the sun—human effects. A. Karim Ahmed, *Environment,* vol. 17, no. 3, pp. 6-14, 1975. Biological effects of ultraviolet radiation. (P-M)

12 Unshielding the sun—environmental effects. Joseph Eigner, *Environment,* vol. 17, no. 3, pp. 15-18, 1975. Ultraviolet effects on plants and animals. (P-M)

Unit 2
Remote Sensing and Environmental Studies

13 Remote sensing as an aid to the management of earth resources. Robert N. Colwell, *American Scientist,* vol. 61, pp. 175-183, 1973. Examples of uses of remote sensing imagery. (P-M)

14 Remote sensing and water resources—U.S. space program. M. W. Molloy and V. V. Salomonson, pp. 6-38, in *Remote Sensing and Water Resources Management,* Amer. Water Resources Assn., Urbana, Ill., 1973. Remote sensing hardware and programs. (P)

15 Developing geographical remote sensing. Kirk H. Stone, Chapter 1, pp. 1-13, in *Remote Sensing Techniques for Environmental Analysis,* J. E. Estes and L. W. Senger, eds., Hamilton Publ. Co. (John Wiley & Sons, New York), 1974. Past, present, and future of remote sensing. (P)

16 Remote sensing of environmental quality: Problems and potential. H. Aschmann and L. W. Bowden, Chapter 12, pp. 293-301, in *Remote Sensing Techniques for Environmental Analysis,* J. E. Estes and L. W. Senger, eds., Hamilton Publ. Co. (John Wiley & Sons, New York), 1974. (P)

17 Remote sensing of natural resources. Robert D. Rudd, Chapter 4, pp. 83-103, in *Remote Sensing Techniques for Environmental Analysis,* J. E. Estes and L. W. Senger, eds., Hamilton Publ. Co. (John Wiley & Sons, New York), 1974. Overview of remote sensing research potential. (P-M)

18 Remote sensing techniques in geographical research, Appendix V, pp. 632-643, in *Physical Geography,* 4th ed., Arthur N. Strahler, John Wiley & Sons, New York, 1975. Review of basic principles, methods, and applications of remote sensing. (M)

Units 3, 4
Global Climate Change—Natural and Man-Induced

19 Climatic modification. Werner H. Terjung, Chapter 5, pp. 105-151, in *Perspectives on Environment,* Association of American Geographers, Washington, D.C., 1974. Broad-scale review of Man's possible influence on urban and global climates. (M-T)

20 Climate change: Chilling possibilities. John H. Douglas, *Science News,* vol. 107, pp. 138-140, 1975. Review of scientists' current views on causes and directions of global climate change. (P)

21 Climatic change: Are we on the brink of a pronounced global warming? Wallace S. Broecker, *Science,* vol. 189, pp. 460-463, 1975. Possible future effect of carbon dioxide increase. (M-T)

22 Past climatic variations and the projection of future climates; survey of past climates, Chapter 4, pp. 35-45 and Appendix A, pp. 127-195, in *Understanding Climatic Change,* National Academy of Sciences, Washington, D.C., 1975. In-depth summary of scientific evidence of climate changes. (M-T)

23 Physical basis of climate and climatic change. Chapter 3, pp. 13-34, in *Understanding Climatic Change,* National Academy of Sciences, Washington, D.C., 1975. A systems approach to global climate. (M-T)

24 Global cooling? P. E. Damon and S. M. Kunen, *Science,* vol. 193, pp. 447-453, 1976. Northern and southern hemispheres have experienced opposite changes in air temperatures. (M-T)

25 The sun as a maker of weather and climate. Hurd C. Willett, *Technology Review,* vol. 78, no. 3, pp. 47-55, 1976. Solar cycles as a possible cause of climatic change. (P-M)

Unit 5
Cloud Seeding; Induced Precipitation

26 Weather modification: A technology coming of age. Allen L. Hammond, *Science,* vol. 172, pp. 548-549, 1971. General review of cloud-seeding methods and results. (P)

27 Planned (weather) modification. Chapter 3, pp. 41-67, in *Weather and climate modification,* National Academy of Sciences, Washington, D.C., 1973. Cloud-seeding principles and techniques. (M-T)

28 Politics and weather modification. Matthew Holden, Jr., Chapter 8, pp. 261-322, in *Modifying the Weather,* Univ. of Victoria, British Columbia, 1973. Social and political interactions of weather modification. (P)

29 Summaries of selected precipitation modification programs. Chapter 4, pp. 68-92, in *Weather and climate modification,* National Academy of Sciences, Washington, D.C., 1973. Detailed case studies and evaluation of results. (M-T)

30 Survey of weather modification in the Soviet Union: 1973. Louis J. Battan, *Bull. Amer. Meteorological Soc.,* vol. 54, pp. 1019-1030, 1973. Methods used in Soviet Union to induce precipitation. (M-T)

31 Weather modification: Social concerns and public policies. W. R. Derrick Sewell, Chapter 1, pp. 1-49, in *Modifying the Weather,* W. R. D. Sewell, ed., Univ. of Victoria, British Columbia, 1973.

History and social impacts of weather modification. (P-M)

Rainmaking as a Weapon of War

32 Weather warfare: Pentagon concedes 7-year Vietnam effort. Deborah Shapley, *Science,* vol. 184, pp. 1059-1061, 1974. Senate committee disclosures of Vietnam rainmaking effort. (P)

33 Weather modification as a weapon. Gordon J. MacDonald, *Technology Review,* vol. 78, no. 1, pp. 57-63, 1975. The Vietnam experience and its aftermath. (P)

34 Environmental warfare. Frank Barnaby, *Bull. of the Atomic Scientists,* vol. 32, no. 5, pp. 36-43, 1976. Review of the whole spectrum of military modification of the atmosphere, oceans, and lands. (P)

Unit 6
Late Pleistocene-Holocene Environments and Man

35 Man faces the ice; Man in the waning ice age. Chapters 10 and 11, pp. 79-94, in *Glaciers and the Ice Age,* Gwen Schultz, Holt, Rinehart and Winston, New York, 1963.

36 Ice-age hungers of the Ukraine. Richard G. Klein, *Scientific American,* vol. 230, no. 6, 1974. Mammal hunters of the periglacial steppe, bordering the Scandinavian ice sheet. (P)

37 Twenty-five years of radiocarbon dating. E. K. Ralph and H. N. Michael, *American Scientist,* vol. 62, pp. 553-560, 1974. Explains how Holocene events are dated back to 5500 B.C. (M-T)

38 17,000 years of Greek prehistory. Thomas W. Jacobsen, *Scientific American,* vol. 234, no. 4, pp. 76-87, 1976. Ice-age cave habitations extending into the Holocene. (P)

39 The final paleolithic settlements of the European plain. Romuald Schild, *Scientific American,* vol. 234, no. 5, pp. 88-99, 1976. Human occupation and vegetation changes in northern Europe following ice retreat. (P)

40 The surface of the ice-age earth. CLIMAP project members, *Science,* vol. 191, pp. 1131-1144, 1976. Global physical geography at 18,000 years before present. (M-T)

41 When the sun went strangely quiet. Kendrick Frazier, *Science News,* vol. 109, pp. 154-156, 1976. Correlation of solar activity with warm and cold periods since 1100 A.D. (P)

Units 7, 8
Air Pollutants; Urban Smog

42 Nitrogen oxides: A subtle control task. Charles N. Satterfield, *Technology Review,* vol. 75, no. 1, pp. 10-18, 1972.

How nitrogen oxides are formed and controlled. (M-T)

43 Episode 104. Virginia Brodine, pp. 2-29, in *Air Pollution,* Harcourt Brace Jovanovich, New York, 1973. Case study of an air pollution event in the eastern United States. (P-M)

44 Carbon monoxide and smog. L. D. Bodkin, *Environment,* vol. 16, no. 4, pp. 34-41, 1974. Sources and health effects of carbon monoxide. (P-M)

45 Dark days in Ankara. Walter W. Haines, *Environment,* vol. 16, no. 8, pp. 6-13, 1974. Urban air polution in the capital city of Turkey. (P-M)

46 Smog alert for our southwestern national parks. Marga Raskin, *Nat. Parks and Conservation Mag.,* vol. 49, no. 7, pp. 9-15, 1975. Possible impact of proposed giant coal-fired power plants on air quality. (P)

47 The origin and influence of airborne particulates. Paul F. Fennelly, *American Scientist,* vol. 64, pp. 46-56, 1976. Comprehensive description of particulates and their deleterious effects. (P-M-T)

48 Photochemistry of the polluted troposphere. B. J. Finlayson and J. N. Pitts, Jr., *Science,* vol. 192, pp. 111-119, 1976. Detailed chemistry of photochemical smog. (T)

Air Pollution; Impact on the Biosphere

49 The burdened human. Virginia Brodine, pp. 112-149, in *Air Pollution,* Harcourt Brace Jovanovich, New York, 1973. Health effects of air pollution. (P)

50 Will dirty air do you in? John Arehart-Treichel, *Science News,* vol. 104, pp. 280-281, 1973. Problem of assessing health impacts of urban air pollution. (P)

51 Air pollution vs. food production: An illogical trade. Ian C. T. Nisbet, *Technology Review,* vol. 76, no. 3, p. 5, 1974. Crop damage from air pollution. (P)

52 Air pollution: Effects on plants. Jean L. Marx, *Science,* vol. 187, pp. 731-733, 1976. Crop damage from urban air pollution. (P-M)

Air Pollution; Legal, Political, Social Aspects

53 Enforcing the Clean Air Act of 1970. Noel de Nevers, *Scientific American,* vol. 228, no. 6, pp. 14-21, 1973. Court actions challenge enforcement of the Clean Air Act. (P)

54 Reducing the burden. Virginia Brodine, pp. 150-187, in *Air Pollution,* Harcourt Brace Jovanovich, New York, 1973. Pollution control legislation and techniques; the economic impacts. (P)

55 Cars, fuel, and pollution. Janice Crossland, *Environment,* vol. 16, no. 2, pp. 15-20, 25-27, 1974. Alternative auto engines and their emissions. (P-M)

56 EPA's role in ambient air quality monitoring. A. J. Hoffman and others, *Science,* vol. 190, pp. 243-248, 1975. National ambient air quality standards and their monitoring explained. (P)

57 Clean Air Act: Congress deliberates on amendments. Constance Holden, *Science,* vol. 192, pp. 533-535, 1976. Delays in compliance schedules. (P)

58 Discriminatory air pollution. Julian McCaull, *Environment,* vol. 18, no. 2, pp. 26-31, 1976. Case study of air pollution distribution and social factors in Washington, D.C. (P)

59 Social impact of pollution control legislation. Wallace H. Johnson, *Science,* vol. 192, pp. 629-631, 1976. Ripple effect of compliance with the Clean Air Act. (P)

Unit 9
Urban Climate; Effects of Urbanization

60 The climate of the city. R. A. Bryson and J. E. Ross, Chapter 3, pp. 51-68, in *Urbanization and Environment,* T. R. Detwyler and M. G. Marcus, eds., Duxbury Press, Belmont, Calif., 1972. General survey of urban effects on weather and climate. (P)

61 Urban climate, air pollution, and planning. Wilfred Bach, Chapter 4, pp. 69-96, in *Urbanization and Environment,* T. R. Detwyler and M. G. Marcus, eds., Duxbury Press, Belmont, Calif., 1972. Recommendations for urban planning to minimize pollution and weather effects. (M)

62 Atmospheric alterations from Man-made biospheric changes. Stanley A. Changnon, Jr., Chapter 5, pp. 135-184, in *Modifying the Weather,* Univ. of Victoria, British Columbia, 1973. Man-induced climatic changes in both urban and nonurban areas. (P-M)

63 The atmospheric environment of cities. William R. Frisken, Chapter 1, pp. 9-48, in *The Atmospheric Environment,* The Johns Hopkins Univ. Press, Baltimore, 1973. Effects of urbanization on air temperatures and winds. (M-T)

64 The meteorologically utopian city. Helmut Landsberg, *Bull. Amer. Meteorological Soc.,* vol. 54, pp. 86-89, 1973. New urban design can reduce air pollution and conserve energy. (P)

65 Inadvertent weather modification. Stanley A. Changnon, Jr., *Water Resources Bull.,* vol. 12, pp. 695-715, 1976. Review of data on urban effects on weather and climate. (M-T)

Units 10, 11, 12
Reduction of Weather Hazards

66 How to subdue a hurricane. Louise

Purrett, *Science News,* vol. 100, pp. 128-129, 1971. Project Stormfury. (P)

67 The search for a way to suppress hail. Kendrick Frazier, *Science News,* vol. 99, pp. 200-202, 1971. Review of hail-suppression research and methods. (P)

68 The decision to seed hurricanes. R. A. Howard, J. E. Matheson, D. W. North, *Science,* vol. 176, pp. 1191-1202, 1972. Hurricane seeding, reply by Myron Tribus, *Science,* vol. 180, pp. 425-426, 1973. Cost-benefit and legal considerations of seeding hurricanes. (P-M-T)

69 Hurricane prediction and control: Impact of large computers. Allen L. Hammond, *Science,* vol. 181, pp. 643-645, 1973. Review of hurricane forecasting and seeding techniques. (P)

70 Review of the modification of certain weather hazards. Chapter 5, pp. 93-113, in *Weather and Climate Modification,* National Academy of Sciences, Washington, D.C., 1973. Fog dissipation, hail suppression, hurricane seeding, tornado prediction. (P-M)

71 Social choice and weather modification: Concepts and measurement of impact. James A. Crutchfield, Chapter 6, pp. 187-226, in *Modifying the Weather,* Univ. of Victoria, British Columbia, 1973. Benefit-cost considerations of weather modification. (P)

72 Weather modification: Colorado heeds voters in valley dispute. Luther J. Carter, *Science,* vol. 180, pp. 1347-1350, 1973. Case study of legislation enacted to control weather modification. (P)

Units 13, 14, 17
Water Resources, General

73 *Estimated Use of Water in the United States in 1970.* C. R. Murray and E. B. Reeves, U.S. Geological Survey, Circular 678, Washington, D.C., 37 pp., 1972. Explains the use categories for fresh water in the United States. (P-M)

74 The control of the water cycle. J. P. Peixoto and M. Ali Kettani, *Scientific American,* vol. 228, no. 4, pp. 46-61, 1973. Details of the global hydrologic cycle and various schemes to modify it. (P)

75 *Large Rivers of the United States.* K. T. Iseri and W. B. Langbein, U.S. Geological Survey, Circular 686, Washington, D.C., 10 pp., 1974. Stream gauging; data of discharge of United States rivers. (P)

76 Wringing out the West. Julian McCaull, *Environment,* vol. 16, no. 7, pp. 10-17, 1974. Increased demands upon the limited water supplies of the Colorado and Missouri river systems. (P)

Urban Water Supplies

77 *Water for the Cities—the Outlook.* W. J. Schneider and A. M. Spieker, U.S. Geological Survey, Circular 601-A,

Washington, D.C., 6 pp., 1970. Water-supply problems faced by Miami, Florida, and New York City. (P)

78 California: The new Romans. T. H. Watkins, Part II, pp. 133-201, in *The Water Hustlers,* Sierra Club, San Francisco, 1971. Highly critical account of the California Water Project. (P)

79 New York: Down the drain. Robert H. Boyle, Part III, pp. 203-253, in *The Water Hustlers,* Sierra Club, San Francisco, 1971. Highly critical account of the development of New York City's water supply system. (P)

80 *Role of Water in Urban Planning and Management.* W. J. Schneider, D. A. Rickert, A. M. Spieker, U.S. Geological Survey, Circular 601-H, Washington, D.C., 10 pp., 1973. Washington-Baltimore urban area as a case study in hydrological planning. (P)

81 *Water Facts and Figures for Planners and Managers.* J. H. Feth, U.S. Geological Survey, Circular 601-I, Washington, D.C., 30 pp., 1973. Water quantity and water quality as applied to urban water supply systems. (P-M-T)

82 Water resources planning and policy-making: Challenges and responses. W. R. Derrick Sewell, Chapter 13, pp. 259-286, in *Priorities in Water Management,* F. M. Leversedge, ed., Univ. of Victoria, British Columbia, 1974. An overview of water management problems and their solution. (P)

Large-Scale Water Transfers

83 Water transfers: Must the American West be won again? Frank Quinn, *Geographical Review,* vol. 58, pp. 108-132, 1968. Should alternative solutions be investigated? (P)

84 Australian-American interbasin water transfer. M. John Loeffler, *Annals, Assoc. of Amer. Geog.,* vol. 60, pp. 493-516, 1970. Comparison of water transfer projects in the United States and Australia in the light of new standards of evaluation. (P-M)

85 Soviet plans to reverse the flow of rivers: The Kama-Vychegda-Pechora Project. Philip P. Micklin, Selection 23, pp. 302-331, in *Man's Impact on Environment,* T. R. Detwyler, ed., McGraw-Hill, New York, 1971. Benefits and consequences of proposed major drainage diversions. (P-M)

86 Optimizing the operation of Israel's water system. Uri Shamir, *Technology Review,* vol. 74, no. 7, pp. 41-48, 1972. Details of Israel's main water supply system. (P-M)

87 Environmental hazards of large-scale water developments. Raymond L. Nace, Chapter 1, pp. 3-18, in *Priorities in Water Management,* F. M. Leversedge, ed., Univ. of Victoria, British Columbia, 1974. Description of several proposed major water transfers and their probable environmental effects. (P-M)

88 Water across the American continent. W. R. Derrick Sewell, *Geographical Mag.,* vol. 46, pp. 472-479, 1974. Grandiose water transfer schemes for North America. (P)

Unit 15
Ground-Water Resources, General

89 Water under the Sahara. Robert P. Ambroggi, *Scientific American,* vol. 214, no. 5, pp. 21-29, 1966. Ground-water basins of North Africa and their potential for development. (P)

90 *Long Island Water Resources.* Divison of Water Resources, New York State, State Office of Planning Coordination, Albany, N.Y., 56 pp., 1970. Overview of Long Island water supply problems and policies. (P)

91 The aqueous underground. Lynn W. Gelhar, *Technology Review,* vol. 74, no. 5, pp. 45-53, 1972. General review of ground-water occurrence, use, and contamination. (P-M)

Units 16, 18
Fresh-Water Pollution, General

92 The nation's rivers. M. Gordon Wolman, *Science,* vol. 174, pp. 905-918, 1971. Review of several forms of stream pollution and degradation. (P-M-T)

93 *Real-Estate Lakes.* D. A. Rickert and A. M. Spieker, U.S. Geological Survey, Circular 601-C, Washington, D.C., 19 pp., 1971. Many environmental problems arise from creating small lakes in real-estate developments. (P)

94 Agricultural sources of water pollution. Berlie L. Schmidt, pp. 80-87, in *Water Quality in a Stressed Environment,* W. A. Pettyjohn, ed., Burgess Publ. Co., Minneapolis, 1972. Explains how pollutants enter surface waters from croplands. (M)

95 Constituents and properties of water. C. J. Durfor and E. Becker, pp. 24-41, in *Water Quality in a Stressed Environment,* W. A. Pettyjohn, ed., Burgess Publ. Co., Minneapolis, 1972. Chemical and physical properties of fresh water for municipal use. (M-T)

96 Some basic issues in water pollution control legislation. Walter E. Westman, *American Scientist,* vol. 60, pp. 767-773, 1972. Problems in implementing federal water pollution control legislation. (P)

97 Stream quality in Appalachia as related to coal-mine drainage, 1965. J. E. Biesecker and J. R. George, pp. 45-60, in *Water Quality in a Stressed Environment,* W. A. Pettyjohn, ed., Burgess Publ. Co., Minneapolis, 1972. Acid mine drainage explained. (M-T)

98 Public eye on pollution. Christopher G. Trump, *Environment,* vol. 16, no. 10, 1974. Federal Water Pollution Control Act amendments in 1972 and role of EPA activity. (P)

99 Salt on the earth. C. T. Nisbet, *Technology Review,* vol. 76, no. 6, pp. 6-7, 1974. Deicing salt on roadways as a major pollutant. (P)

100 The people's lake. Karen Townsend Carlson, *Environment,* vol. 17, no. 2, pp. 16-26, 1975. Asbestos pollution of Lake Superior by a mining company. (P)

101 Paying to pollute. Organisation for Economic Cooperation and Development (OECD), *Environment,* vol. 18, no. 5, pp. 16-20, 1976. Europe faces problems of levying pollution charges. (P)

Thermal Pollution

102 Thermal pollution: A threat to Cayuga's waters? Luther J. Carter, *Science,* vol. 162, pp. 649-650, 1968. Possible effects of discharge of nuclear plant waste water into Lake Cayuga. (P)

103 Finding a place to put the heat. Richard H. Gilluly, *Science News,* vol. 98, pp. 98-99, 1970. Effects of thermal pollution from power plant water discharges. (P)

Acid Rain

104 Acid rain: Fossil sulfur returned to earth. Ian C. T. Nisbet, *Technology Review,* vol. 76, no. 4, pp. 8-9, 1974. Harmful effects of acid rain upon wildlife and forests. (P)

105 Acid rain: A serious regional environmental problem. G. E. Likens and F. H. Bormann, *Science,* vol. 184, pp. 1176-1179, 1974. Sources and possible adverse environmental effects of acid rain. (M-T)

Unit 19
Environmental Impacts of Ground-Water Withdrawal

106 *The Changing Pattern of Ground-Water Development on Long Island, New York.* R. C. Heath, B. L. Foxworthy, P. Cohen, U.S. Geological Survey, Circular 524, Washington, D.C., 10 pp., 1966. Nontechnical explanation of Long Island's ground-water system. (P)

107 *Water for the Future of Long Island, New York.* P. Cohen, O. L. Franke, B. L. Foxworthy, New York Water Resources Bulletin 62A, State of New York, 36 pp., 1970. Nontechnical account of Long Island's ground water problems. (P)

108 *Summary of the Hydrologic Situation on Long Island, New York, As a Guide to Water-Management Alternatives.* O. L. Franke and N. E. McClymonds, U.S. Geological Survey, Professional Paper 627-F, U.S. Government Printing Office, Washington, D.C., 59 pp., 1972. Technical review of total Long Island ground-water system. (M-T)

109 Land subsidence due to withdrawal of fluids. J. F. Poland and G. H. Davis, Selection 27, pp. 370-382, in *Man's Impact on Environment,* T. R. Detwyler, ed., McGraw-Hill, New York, 1971. General review of land subsidence, with case studies (Long Beach, Mexico City, San Joaquin Valley). (P-M)

Unit 20
Ground-Water Pollution

110 *Disposal of Liquid Wastes by Injection Underground—Neither Myth nor Millennium.* Arthur M. Piper, U. S. Geological Survey, Circular 631, Washington, D.C., 15 pp., 1969. Problems and environmental impact of forcing liquid wastes deep underground. (P-M-T)

111 Environmental framework of ground-water contamination. H. E. LeGrand, pp. 90-98, in *Water Quality in a Stressed Environment,* W. A. Pettyjohn, ed., Burgess Publ. Co., Minneapolis, 1972. General review of causes and consequences of ground-water pollution. (P)

112 Good coffee water needs body. Wayne A. Pettyjohn, pp. 194-199, in *Water Quality in a Stressed Environment,* W. A. Pettyjohn, ed., Burgess Publ. Co., Minneapolis, 1972. Case studies of pollution of supply wells. (P-M)

113 Water pollution by oil-field brines and related industrial wastes in Ohio. Wayne A. Pettyjohn, pp. 166-180, in *Water Quality in a Stressed Environment,* W. A. Pettyjohn, ed., Burgess Publ. Co., Minneapolis, 1972. Case study of chloride contamination of ground water and streams. (M-T)

114 Natural controls involved in shallow aquifer contamination. Morris Deutsch, pp. 99-106, in *Water Quality in a Stressed Environment,* W. A. Pettyjohn, ed., Burgess Publ. Co., Minneapolis, 1972. How aquifers and aquicludes affect movement of contaminants. (P-M)

115 Deep mystery. Liz Forrestal, *Environment,* vol. 17, no. 8, pp. 25-31, 1975. Problems of liquid waste disposal by injection into deep wells. (P)

Caverns and Karst

116 Hydrological and ecological problems of karst regions. H. E. LeGrand, *Science,* vol. 179, pp. 859-864, 1973. Broad-based description of karst and its hydrologic characteristics. (P-M)

117 Hydrogeologic constraints on Yucatán's development. D. O. Doehring and J. H. Butler, *Science,* vol. 186, pp. 591-595, 1974. Ground water in karst is highly susceptible to contamination and disease spread. (P-M)

118 New cave: A new look. Edwards Hay, *Nat. Parks and Conservation Mag.,* vol. 48, no. 6, pp. 21-24, 1974. Description of a newly opened cave in Carlsbad Caverns National Park. (P)

Unit 22
Volcanic Eruptions and Hazards

119 Peléan type of volcanic eruption. Chapter 7, pp. 97-127, in *Volcanoes,* Fred M. Bullard, Univ. of Texas Press, Austin, 1962. Descriptions of great eruptions of Mt. Pelée and La Soufrière in the West Indies. (P)

120 Vulcanian type of volcanic eruption. Chapter 8, pp. 128-190, in *Volcanoes,* Fred M. Bullard, Univ. of Texas Press, Austin, 1962. Descriptions of eruptions of Mt. Vesuvius and Vulcano from ancient times to recently. (P)

121 Caldera collapse in the Galapagos Islands, 1968. T. Simkin and K. A. Howard, *Science,* vol. 169, pp. 429-437, 1970. Detailed description of the formation of a great caldera. (M)

122 Life studies flow from live volcanoes. Richard H. Gilluly, *Science News,* vol. 97, pp. 411-413, 1970. Ecological succession on basaltic lava surfaces on Kilauea, Hawaii. (P)

123 Back home to work on a volcanic island. Chalmers M. Clapperton, *Geographical Mag.,* vol. 46, no. 2, pp. 83-90, 1973. Human adaption to the eruption of Heimaey, an Icelandic volcano. (P)

124 Iceland chills a lava flow. R. S. Williams, Jr., and J. G. Moore, *Geotimes,* vol. 18, no. 8, pp. 14-17, 1973. Story of Heimaey volcanic eruption. (M)

125 Eruption of Soufriere volcano on St. Vincent Island, 1971-1972. W. P. Aspinall, H. Sigurdsson, J. B. Shepherd, *Science,* vol. 181, pp. 117-124, 1973. History of Soufrière eruptions; details of a recent eruption. (P-M)

126 Mount Baker eruptions. Don J. Easterbook, *Geology,* vol. 3, no. 12, pp. 679-682, 1975. Eruptive history of a volcano in the Cascades and its potential hazards. (P-M)

127 Mauna Loa threatening. J. P. Lockwood and others, *Geotimes,* vol. 21, no. 6, pp. 12-15, 1976. How an active volcano is monitored to predict its eruptions. (P-M)

Unit 23
Plate Tectonics

128 Plate tectonics. John F. Dewey, *Scientific American,* vol. 227, pp. 56-68, 1972. Overview of global lithospheric plates, plate boundaries, subduction zones, triple junctions. (P-M)

129 Plate tectonics and sea-floor spreading. Dan P. McKenzie, *American Scientist,* vol. 60, pp. 425-435, 1972. Transform faults, triple junctions, convection in mantle. (M-T)

130 Alfred Wegener and the hypothesis of continental drift. A. Hallam, *Scientific American,* vol. 232, no. 2, pp. 88-97, 1975. Biographical sketch of Wegener; his theory confirmed. (P-M)

131 The floor of the mid-Atlantic rift. J. R. Heirtzler and W. B. Bryan, *Scientific American,* vol. 233, no. 2, pp. 79-89, 1975. Operation FAMOUS and its fantastic pillow lavas. (P-M)

Unit 24
Earthquake Hazards

132 *Toward Reduction of Losses from Earthquakes.* Committee on the Alaska Earthquake, National Academy of Sciences, Washington, D.C., 34 pp., 1969. Conclusions from the great Alaska earthquake of 1964. (P)

133 *The Alaska Earthquake, March 27, 1964: Lessons and Conclusions.* Edwin B. Eckel, U.S. Geological Survey, Professional Paper 564, U.S. Govt. Printing Office, Washington, D.C., 57 pp., 1970. (P-M)

134 Human impact of the Managua earthquake. R. W. Kates and others, *Science,* vol. 182, pp. 981-990, 1973. Sociological aspects of Managua, Nicaragua, earthquake. (P)

135 *Goals, Strategy, and Tasks of the Earthquake Hazard Reduction Program,* Robert E. Wallace, U.S. Geological Survey, Circular 701, U.S. Govt. Printing Office, Washington, D.C., 26 pp., 1974. (P-M)

136 *Seismic Hazards and Land-Use Planning.* D. R. Nichols and J. M. Buchanan-Banks, U.S. Geological Survey, Circular 690, U.S. Govt. Printing Office, Washington, D.C., 33 pp., 1974. Earthquakes, earthquake damage, urban planning for earthquakes. (P-M)

137 Earthquake shaking and damage to buildings. R. A. Page, J. A. Blume, W. B. Joyner, *Science,* vol. 189, pp. 601-608, 1975. New data raise questions about adequacy of current construction standards. (M-T)

138 Reconstruction after disaster: The Gediz earthquake of 1970. William A. Mitchell, *Geographical Review,* vol. 66, pp. 296-313, 1976. Problem of designing safe houses in high-hazard localities in Turkey, where traditional masonry buildings are death traps. (P)

Man-Induced Earthquakes

139 Man-made earthquakes in Denver. David. M. Evans, *Geotimes,* vol. 10, no. 9, pp. 11-18, 1966. Injection of fluid wastes triggers earthquakes. (M)

140 Ground rupture in the Baldwin Hills. D. H. Hamilton and R. L. Meehan, *Science,* vol. 172, pp. 333-344, 1971. Fluid injection triggers a fault. (M-T)

141 An experiment in earthquake control at Rangely, Colorado. C. B. Raleigh, J. H. Healy, J. D. Bredehoeft, *Science*, vol. 191, pp. 1230-1236, 1976. Earthquake control demonstrated in a special case. (M-T)

Earthquake Prediction

142 Earthquake prediction. Frank Press, *Scientific American*, vol. 232, no. 5, pp. 14-23, 1975. Survey of technical advances in earthquake prediction. (M)

143 *Earthquake Prediction and Public Policy*. Panel on the Public Policy Implications of Earthquake Prediction, National Research Council, National Academy of Sciences, Washington, D.C. 142 pp., 1975. Comprehensive review of social, economic, and political aspects of earthquake prediction. (P)

144 The physical basis for earthquake prediction. William F. Brace, *Technology Review*, vol. 77, no. 5, pp. 26-29, 1975. Explains dilatancy theory. (M)

Seismic Sea Waves (Tsunamis)

145 Tsunamis. Joseph Bernstein, *Scientific American*, vol. 191, no. 2, pp. 60-64, 1954. (Freeman Offprint No. 829.) Tsunami warning system. (P)

146 *Tsunami! The Story of the Seismic Sea-Wave Warning System*. Coast and Geodetic Survey, U.S. Dept. of Commerce, U.S. Govt. Printing Office, 46 pp., 1965. (P)

147 Earthquakes and tsunamis. Chapter 16, pp. 251-261 in *Volcanoes in the Sea: The Geology of Hawaii*, G. A. Macdonald and A. T. Abbott, Univ. of Hawaii Press, Honolulu, 1970. Describes Hilo destruction by tsunamis of 1946, 1950. (M)

Unit 25
Mineral Resources

148 Human materials production as a process in the biosphere. Harrison Brown, Chapter 11, pp. 117-124, in *The Biosphere*, W. H. Freeman, San Francisco, 1970. Consumption of mineral resources in relation to world reserves. (P)

149 *Mineral Resources off the Northeastern Coast of the United States*. Frank T. Manheim, U.S. Geological Survey, Circular 669, U.S. Govt. Printing Office, Washington, D.C., 28 pp., 1972. Sea-bed minerals of the continental shelf. (M)

150 Plate tectonics and mineral resources. Peter A. Rona, *Scientific American*, vol. 229, no. 1, pp. 86-95, 1973. Ore deposits and plate tectonics. (P-M)

151 Manganese nodules. Allen L. Hammond, *Science*, vol. 183, pp. 502-503, 644-646, 1974. Mineral resources of the sea bed. (P-M)

152 *Mineral Resources: Potentials and Problems*. W. P. Pratt and Donald A. Brobst, U.S. Geological Survey, Circular 698, U.S. Govt. Printing Office, Washing-

ton, D.C., 20 pp., 1974. U.S. resources of 27 major mineral commodities. (M)

153 The depletion of geologic resources. Earl Cook, *Technology Review*, vol. 77, no. 7, pp. 15-27, 1975. Economic aspects of ores and ore depletion. (M)

154 Discovery of natural resources. Philip W. Gould, *Science*, vol. 191, pp. 709-723, 1976. Modern mineral exploration techniques, including plate tectonics. (M-T)

155 Mineral resources on the ocean floor. Gustaf Arrhenius, *Technology Review*, vol. 77, no. 5, pp. 22-25, 1975. Manganese nodules. (P-M)

156 Minerals and plate tectonics. Allen L. Hammond, *Science*, vol. 189, pp. 779-781, 868-869, 915, 1975 (P-M)

157 New techniques in geophysical exploration for minerals. David W. Strangway, *Technology Review*, vol. 77, no. 6, pp. 35-37, 1975 (M)

158 Plate tectonics and mineral deposits. Patrick M. Hurley, *Technology Review*, vol. 77, no. 5, pp. 15-21, 1975. (M)

159 Railroading scrap. Peter Kakela, *Environment*, vol. 17, no. 2, pp. 27-33, 1975. Energy savings through use of scrap metals instead of virgin ores. (P)

Unit 27
Mass Wasting Hazards

160 Landslide in San Antonio Canyon. Chapter 28, pp. 328-329, in *Geology Illustrated*, John S. Shelton, W. H. Freeman, San Francisco, 1966. Toe of earthflow blocking valley. (P)

161 Debris avalanches—a geomorphic hazard. G. P. Williams and H. P. Guy, Chapter 2, pp. 25-46, in *Environmental Geomorphology*, D. R. Coates, ed., Publ. in Geomorphology, State Univ. of New York, Binghamton, 1971. Case study of mass wasting caused by rains of Hurricane Camille. (P-M)

162 Impact of highways on the hydrogeologic environment. Richard J. Parizek, Chapter 9, pp. 151-199, in *Environmental Geomorphology*, D. R. Coates, ed., Publ. in Geomorphology, State Univ. of New York, Binghamton, 1971. Highway cuts invite many forms of mass wasting. (M-T)

163 Landslides. D. M. Morton and R. Streitz, Chapter 14, pp. 64-73, in *Man and His Physical Environment*, G. D. McKenzie and R. O. Utgard, eds., Burgess Publ. Co., Minneapolis, 1972. Destructive forms of mass wasting; natural and Man-induced. (P)

164 The hazard of sensitive clays: A case study of the Ottawa-Hull area. J. G. M. Parkes and J. C. Day, *Geographical Review*, vol. 65, pp. 198-213, 1975. Human adjustment to hazards of massive earthflows in quick clays. (P)

165 Lasen's silent threat. Robert G. Holt, *Nat. Parks and Conservation Mag.*, vol. 50, no. 6, pp. 4-6, 1976. Threat of rockfall avalanche hangs over national park. (P)

166 Natural hazards in mountain Colorado. J. D. Ives and others, *Annals, Assoc. of Amer. Geog.*, vol. 66, pp. 129-144, 1976. Avalanche, landslide, mudflow, rockfall, and mountain flood as hazards to human life. (P-M)

Unit 28
Urbanization and Stream Flow

167 *Hydrology for Urban Land Planning—A Guidebook on the Hydrologic Effects of Urban Land Use*. Luna B. Leopold, U.S. Geological Survey, Circular 554, Washington, D.C., 18 pp., 1968.

168 *Sediment Problems in Urban Areas*. Harold P. Guy, U.S. Geological Survey, Circular 601-E, Washington, D.C., 8 pp., 1970. Sediment accumulations in a variety of environments, including urban areas. (P)

169 *Water as an Urban Resource and Nuisance*. H. E. Thomas and W. J. Schneider, U.S. Geological Survey, Circular 601-D, Washington, D.C., 9 pp., 1970. How urbanization affects stream flow and load. (P)

170 Water and the city. John C. Schaake, Jr., Chapter 5, pp. 97-133, in *Urbanization and Environment*, T. R. Detwyler and M. G. Marcus, eds., Duxbury Press, Belmont, Calif., 1972. Effects of urbanization on runoff, flooding, and sediment yield. (P-M)

171 Channel changes. William W. Emmett, *Geology*, vol. 2, no. 6, pp. 271-272, 1974. Channel of a Maryland stream shows clearly the impact of urbanization. (M-T)

Unit 29
Flood Hazards

172 *Flood Information for Flood-Plain Planning*. Conrad D. Bue, U.S. Geological Survey, Circular 539, U.S. Govt. Printing Office, Washington, D.C., 10 pp., 1967. (P-M)

173 *Flood-Hazard Mapping in Metropolitan Chicago*. J. R. Sheaffer, D. W. Ellis, and A. M. Spieker, U.S. Geological Survey, Circular 601-C, U.S. Govt. Printing Office, Washington D.C., 14 pp., 1970. Geological Survey program of evaluating flood hazards. (P-M)

174 The hard-learned lessons of Agnes. Science Staff, *Science News*, vol. 102, pp. 5-6, 1972. Damage from floods of Hurricane Agnes in the Northeast. (P)

175 *Effects of the May 5-6, 1973, Storm in the Greater Denver Area, Colorado*. Wallace R. Hansen, U.S. Geological Survey, Circular 689, 20 pp., 1973. Case study, detailing stream erosion and mass wasting. (P-M)

176 Deluge in Australia. I. Douglas and J. Hoffs, *Geographical Magazine*, vol. 46, no. 9, pp. 465-470, 1974. Detailed description of a major flood in New South Wales and Queensland. (P-M)

177 *Extent and Development of Urban Flood Plains*. W. J. Schneider and J. E. Goddard, U.S. Geological Survey, Circular 601-J, U.S. Govt. Printing Office, Washington, D.C., 14 pp., 1974. Flood-hazard mapping, zoned use of flood-plains. (P-M)

Unit 30
River Regulation and Flood Control

178 Geomorphology and decision-making in water resource engineering. Joseph H. Butler, Chapter 5, pp. 81-89, in *Environmental Geomorphology*, D. R. Coates, ed., Publ. in Geomorphology, State Univ. of New York, Binghamton, 1971. Environmental factors must be given greater weight in planning new water engineering projects. (P)

179 Man's impact on stream regimen and quality. Jack P. Mrowka, Chapter 4, pp. 79-104, in *Perspectives on Environment*, Association of American Geographers, Washington, D.C., 1974. Effects of dams, reservoirs, irrigation, and urbanization. (P-M)

180 Dams of pork. Julian McCaull, *Environment*, vol. 17, no. 1, pp. 11-16, 1975. Questioning the cost-benefit ratios in construction of various dams. (P)

181 The 1973 flood and Man's constriction of the Mississippi River. C. B. Belt, Jr., *Science*, vol. 189, pp. 681-684, 1975. Evidence that channel engineering was responsible for the record flood stage of 1973. (M-T)

182 Wasting a river. B. T. Parry and R. B. Norgaard, *Environment*, vol. 17, no. 1, pp. 17-20, 25-27, 1975. Case study of enviromental effects of a new California dam. (P)

183 The sinking city. F. W. Wagner and E. J. Durabb, *Environment*, vol. 18, no. 4, pp. 32-39, 1976. Flood control problems facing New Orleans on the lower Mississippi River. (P)

Channelization

184 Stream regimen and Man's manipulation. Robert V. Ruhe, Chapter 1, pp. 9-23, in *Environmental Geomorphology*, D. R. Coates, ed., Publ. in Geomorphology, State Univ. of New York, Binghamton, 1971. Case studies of channel straightening, channel contraction, and curvature control. (M-T)

185 Stream channelization: Conflict between ditchers, conservationists, Robert Gillette, *Science*, vol. 176, pp. 890-894, 1972. Environmental damage from channelization. (P)

186 Channelization: A search for a better way. E. A. Keller, *Geology*, vol. 3, no. 5, pp. 246-248, 1975. Natural processes must be included in channel modifications. (M)

Units 31, 32
Man-Induced Soil Erosion and Sedimentation

187 The deforestation of Mount Lebanon. Marvin W. Mikesell, *Geographical Review*, vol. 59, pp. 1-28, 1969. Forest destruction throughout a 5000-year history in this Mediterranean coastal land. (P)

188 Interrelationships of forest, soils, and terrane in watershed planning. Chapter 4, pp. 71-89, in *Environmental Geomorphology*, D. R. Coates, ed., Publ. in Geomorphology, State Univ. of New York, Binghamton, 1971. Watershed planning must recognize the interaction of vegetation, soils, and streams. (P)

189 Soil and the city. Donald H. Gray, Chapter 6, pp. 135-168, in *Urbanization and Environment*, T. R. Detwyler and M. G. Marcus, eds., Duxbury Press, Belmont, Calif., 1972. Urban erosion and sedimentation, mass wasting, and soil stability. (P-M)

190 Accelerated soil erosion: A problem of Man-land relationships. Karl W. Butzer, Chapter 3, pp. 57-58, in *Perspectives on Environment*, Association of American Geographers, Washington, D.C., 1974. Soil erosion processes and historical perspectives. (P-M)

191 Nature provides, Man erodes. R. P. C. Morgan, *Geographical Mag.*, vol. 46, no. 10, pp. 528-534, 1974. Accelerated soil erosion in the British Isles. (P)

192 Effects of agriculture on erosion and sedimentation in the Piedmont Province, Maryland. John E. Costa, *Bull. Geol. Soc. of Amer.*, vol. 86, pp. 1281-1286, 1975. Estimates of soil eroded and held in depositional landforms. (P-M)

193 Impact of clear-cutting and road construction on soil erosion by landslides in the western Cascade Range, Oregon. F. J. Swanson and C. T. Dyrness, *Geology*, vol. 3, no. 7, pp. 393-396, 1975. Clear-cut logging causes devastation to certain soil surfaces. (M)

Unit 34
Coastal Change — Natural and Man-Induced

194 Influence of Man upon coast lines. John H. Davis, Selection 25, pp. 332-347, in *Man's Impact on Environment*, T. R. Detwyler, ed., McGraw-Hill, New York, 1971. Human factor in modifying the coastal zone. (P)

195 Shoreline erosion and the Lost Colony. R. Dolan and K. Bosserman, *Annals*, *Assoc. of Amer. Geog.*, vol. 62, pp. 424-426, 1972. The famous Lost Colony of Roanoke may have disappeared through coastal erosion. (P)

196 The coastal challenge. D. L. Inman and B. M. Brush, *Science*, vol. 181, pp. 20-32, 1973. California costal processes and forms, Man-induced environmental impact. (M-T)

197 Monitoring the coastal environment. M. Morisawa and C. A. M. King, *Geology*, vol. 2, no. 8, pp. 385-388, 1974. Man-induced shoreline changes can be assessed only if monitoring is constantly practiced. (M)

198 Barton does not rule the waves. M. J. Clark, P. J. Ricketts, R. J. Small, *Geographical Mag.*, vol. 48, no. 10, pp. 580-588, 1976. Property destruction by wave erosion at an English seaside resort. (P)

Unit 35
Man's Impact on Low Sandy Coasts

199 *The Human Ecology of Coastal Flood Hazard in Megalopolis*. I. Burton, R. W. Kates, R. E. Snead, Dept. of Geography, Research Paper No. 115, Univ. of Chicago, 196 pp., 1969. Integrated approach to problems of human occupance of low-lying sandy coasts. (M)

200 As the seashore shifts. Dietrick E. Thomsen, *Science News*, vol. 101, pp. 396-397, 1972. Barrier-island changes caused by dune stabilization on Cape Hatteras. (P)

201 Comparison of ecological and geomorphic interactions between altered and unaltered barrier island systems in North Carolina. P. J. Godfrey and M. M. Godfrey, Chaper 11, pp. 239-257, in *Coastal Geomorphology*, D. R. Coates, ed., Publ. in Geomorphology, State Univ. of New York, Binghamton, 1973. Man's interference with natural processes on the Outer Banks. (M)

202 Man's impact on the barrier islands of North Carolina. R. Dolan, P. J. Godfrey, and W. E. Odum, *American Scientist*, vol. 61, pp. 152-162, 1973. (P-M)

203 Adjusting to nature in our national seashores. R. Dolan and B. Hayden, *Nat. Parks and Conservation Mag.*, vol. 48, no. 6, pp. 9-14, 1974. Change in policy on managment of barrier island coasts. (P)

204 Assateague, jewel of the East Coast. Judith Colt Johnson, *Nat. Parks and Conservation Mag.*, vol. 49, no. 1, pp. 4-11, 1975. Assateague Island National Seashore faces pressures for intensive development. (P)

205 How to live on a barrier island. Dietrick E. Thomsen, *Science News*, vol. 108, pp. 237-238, 1975. Changing viewpoints in human adaptation to low sandy coasts of the eastern United States. (P)

Unit 36
Man's Impact on Tidelands and Estuaries

206 The East Coast floods, 31 January-1 February 1953. J. A. Steers, Chapter 10, pp. 198-223, in *Applied Coastal Geomorphology,* J. A. Steers, ed., The M.I.T. Press, Cambridge, Mass., 1971. Disastrous flooding of English fenlands during a great storm. (M-T)

207 The role of Man in estuarine processes. L. Eugene Cronin, Selection 21, pp. 266-294, in *Man's Impact on Environment,* T. R. Detwyler, ed., McGraw-Hill, New York, 1971. Broad-scale review of Man's impact on tidelands and estuaries. (P-M-T)

208 The estuarine environment. J. R. Schubel and D. W. Pritchard, *Journal of Geologic Education,* vol. 20, pp. 60-68, 179-188, 1972. Overview of estuaries and environmental impact. (M)

209 Unnatural shoreline. Raymond Pestrong, *Environment,* vol. 16, no. 9, pp. 27-35, 1974. Changes in the San Francisco Bay shoreline by natural and Man-induced sedimentation and by filling. (P)

210 New hope for Bay area wildlife. Stanley Medders, *Nat. Parks and Conservation Mag.,* vol. 48, no. 7, pp. 20-24, 1974. Environmental destruction of San Francisco Bay tidal lands. (P)

211 Wetlands: Denial of Marco permits fails to resolve the dilemma. Luther J. Carter, *Science,* vol. 192, pp. 641-644, 1976. Controversy over dredge-and-fill alteration of Florida tidelands. (P)

Units 38, 39, 40
Flow of Energy and Materials in Ecosystems

212 The biosphere. G. Evelyn Hutchinson, Chapter 1, pp. 2-11, in *The Biosphere,* W. H. Freeman, San Francisco, 1970. Basic concepts of the biosphere, its major cycles and early evolution. (P-M)

213 The carbon cycle. Bert Bolin, Chapter 5, pp. 49-56, in *The Biosphere,* W. H. Freeman, San Francisco, 1970. Traces the circulation of carbon and its storage in carbonate rocks and fossil fuels. (P)

214 The energy cycle of the biosphere. George M. Woodwell, Chapter 3, pp. 26-36, in *The Biosphere,* W. H. Freeman, San Francisco, 1970. Net productivity of various natural and agricultural ecosystems. (P-M)

215 Mineral cycles. Edward S. Deevey, Jr., Chapter 8, pp. 83-92, in *The Biosphere,* W. H. Freeman, San Francisco, 1970. Element cycling; eutrophication of the biosphere. (M-T)

216 The nitrogen cycle. C. C. Delwiche, Chapter 7, pp. 71-80, in *The Biosphere,* W. H. Freeman, San Francisco, 1970.

Nitrogen cycle and nitrogen fixation processes. (M-T)

217 The oxygen cycle. P. Cloud and A. Gibor, Chapter 6, pp. 59-68, in *The Biosphere,* W. H. Freeman, San Francisco, 1970. History of free oxygen through geologic time. (M-T)

218 The water cycle. H. L. Penman, Chapter 4, pp. 39-45, in *The Biosphere,* W. H. Freeman, San Francisco, 1970. Properties of water; the global water balance; water and plant growth. (P-M)

219 The flow of energy in the biosphere. David M. Gates, Chapter 8, pp. 78-86, in *Chemistry in the Environment,* W. H. Freeman, San Francisco, 1973. Photosynthesis and respiration; net productivity of varied environments. (P-M)

220 Biogeochemical cycles and energy flows in environmental systems. David Watts, Chapter 2, pp. 24-56, in *Perspectives on Environment,* Association of American Geographers, Washington, D.C., 1974. Systems approach to cycling of energy and matter in ecosystems. (P-M)

221 The steady state of the earth's crust, atmosphere, and oceans. Raymond Siever, *Scientific American,* vol. 230, no. 6, pp. 72-79, 1974. Geochemical cycling of elements of the earth's crust. (M-T)

222 The cycles of plant and animal nutrition. J. Janick, C. H. Noller, and C. L. Rhykerd, *Scientific American,* vol. 35, no. 3, pp. 75-84, 1976. How plants and animals cycle energy and inorganic nutrients for human consumption. (P-M)

Units 41, 42
Man's Impact on Terrestrial Ecosystems

223 Barrier fencing for vermin control in Australia. Tom L. McKnight, *Geographical Review,* vol. 59, pp. 330-347, 1969. Much-debated use of fences to protect food crops and livestock from animal predators. (P)

224 The nutrient cycles of an ecosystem. F. H. Bormann and G. E. Likens, *Scientific American,* vol. 223, no. 4, pp. 92-101, 1970. Impact of deforestation upon an experimental forest watershed. (P-M)

225 The American chestnut, 1973. Eyvind Thor, *Nat. Parks and Conservation Mag.,* vol. 47, no. 9, pp. 9-12, 1973. Genetic selection as a means to save the American chestnut. (P)

226 The deflowering of Hawaii. F. R. Fosberg, *Nat. Parks and Conservation Mag.,* vol. 49, no. 10, pp. 4-10, 1975. Man's impact on the flora of the Hawaiian Islands. (P)

227 Forest succession. Henry S. Horn, *Scientific American,* vol. 232, no. 5, pp. 90-98, 1975. Predictive model of succession of trees in a mixed forest. (M-T)

228 Placer County Big Tree Grove. Harold Biswell, *Nat. Parks and Conservation Mag.,* vol. 49, no. 8, pp. 14-17, 1975. A stand of giant sequoia trees in northern California. (P)

229 Farming the Everglades. Michael F. Toner, *Nat. Parks and Conservation Mag.,* vol. 50, no. 8, pp. 4-9, 1976. Agricultural development in Florida Everglades threatens wildlife of a national park. (P)

Biome Research

230 Ecosystem analysis: Biome approach to environmental research. Allen L. Hammond, *Science,* vol. 175, pp. 46-48, 1972. Scientists converge upon six major biomes to study ecosystem interaction. (P)

231 This is the forest primeval. Joan Arehart-Treichel, *Science News,* vol. 102, pp. 78-79, 1972. Research on the eastern deciduous forest biome. (P)

232 IBP: The last lap. Joan Arehart-Treichel, *Science New,* vol. 104, pp. 156-157, 1973. Review of progress on global biome research. (P)

233 An evaluation of three biome programs. R. Mitchell, R. A. Mayer, J. Downhower, *Science,* vol. 192, pp. 859-865, 1976. Review of progress made in the International Biological Program (IBP). (P-M)

Forest Resources and Management

234 Forest fuel accumulation — a growing problem. Marvin Dodge, *Science,* vol. 177, pp. 139-142, 1972. Fire prevention leads to hazardous buildup of fuel. (P)

235 Smokey's other problems. John H. Douglas, *Science News,* vol. 104, pp. 138-140, 1973. Environmentalists and industry battle over clear-cutting of the nation's forests. (P)

236 Redwood National Park; controversy and compromise. John Graves, *Nat. Parks and Conservation Mag.,* vol. 48, no. 10, pp. 14-19, 1974. Logging threatens a redwood forest. (P)

237 To save the Big Trees. Douglas H. Strong, *Nat. Parks and Conservation Mag.,* vol. 49, no. 3, pp. 10-14, 1975. Story of the preservation of the Big Tree groves of the Sierra Nevada. (P)

238 Forest resources: An overview. J. S. Bethel and G. F. Schreuder, *Science,* vol. 191, pp. 747-752, 1976. Evaluation of total United States forest resources. (P)

239 National forests: Court ruling spurs clear-cutting controversy. Constance Holden, *Science,* vol. 192, pp. 36-38, 1976. Congressional activity on timber management in national forests. (P)

240 The national forests. Marion Clawson, *Science,* vol. 191, pp. 762-767, 1976. Major reforms are needed in forest management. (P)

241 The third forest. Donald Dahlsten, *Environment,* vol. 18, no. 6, pp. 35-42, 1976. Modern forestry techniques; pest control. (P)

242 Timber: Biological and economic potential. S. H. Spurr and H. J. Vaux, *Science*, vol. 191, pp. 752-756, 1976. Potential of United States commercial forest land. (M)

Military Use of Herbicides

243 Defoliation in Vietnam. Fred H. Tschirley, *Science*, vol. 163, pp. 779-786, 1969. An adviser to the U.S. Department of State reports on ecologic consequences of the defoliation program. (M-T)

244 Herbicides in Vietnam: AAAS study finds widespread devastation. Philip M. Boffey, *Science*, vol. 171, pp. 43-47, 1971. Report of Herbicide Assessment Commission. (P)

245 Herbicides: AAAS study finds dioxin in Vietnamese fish. Deborah Shapley, *Science*, vol. 180, pp. 285-286, 1973. Dioxin from Agent Orange has turned up in fish and shrimp in south Vietnam rivers. (P)

246 Herbicides: Academy finds damage in Vietnam after a fight of its own. Deborah Shapley, *Science*, vol. 183, pp. 1177-1180, 1974. National Academy of Sciences committee report sets off internal disputes. (P)

Unit 43
Agricultural Ecosystems

247 Ecological balance in tropical agriculture. Matthias U. Igbozurike, *Geographical Review*, vol. 61, pp. 519-529, 1971. A model of mixed-crop farming suitable to low-latitude regions. (M-T)

248 Microclimate management by traditional farmers. Gene C. Wilken, *Geographical Review*, vol. 62, pp. 544-560, 1972. Farmers the world over control climate near the ground with a variety of agricultural techniques. (P)

249 Energy and land constraints in food protein production. D. Pimentel, and others, *Science*, vol. 190, pp. 754-761, 1975. Energy inputs into protein production; the ultimate necessity of population control. (M-T)

250 Agricultural production and energy resources. G. H. Heichel, *American Scientist*, vol. 64, pp. 64-72, 1976. Analysis of energy consumed in United States agricultural systems. (P-M)

251 Agricultural systems. Robert S. Loomis, *Scientific American*, vol. 235, no. 3, pp. 99-105, 1976. Dominant cereals — wheat, rice, corn — and prospects for their increased production. (P)

252 The plants and animals that nourish Man. Jack R. Harlan, *Scientific American*, vol. 235, no. 3, pp. 89-97, 1976. Early history of major food crops and meat sources. (P)

253 The requirements of human nutrition. N. S. Scrimshaw and V. R. Young, *Scientific American*, vol. 51, pp. 51-64, 1976. Biochemistry and physiology of nutrient metabolism; nutrient requirements. (M-T)

The Green Revolution

254 Green revolution in India. A. K. Chakravarti, *Annals, Assoc. Amer. Geog.*, vol. 63, pp. 319-330, 1973. An early assessment of the value of the green revolution. (P-M)

255 Green Revolution (I): A just technology, often unjust in use; (II): Problems of adapting a Western technology. Nicholas Wade, *Science*, vol. 186, 1093-1096, 1186-1192, 1974. A critical review of the Green Revolution. (P)

256 Green Revolution: Creators still quite hopeful on world food. Nicholas Wade, *Science*, vol. 185, pp. 844-845, 1974. Views expressed by two leaders in the Green Revolution. (P)

257 Agriculture in China. Sterling Wortman, *Scientific American*, vol. 232, no. 6, pp. 13-21, 1975. China has adopted improved strains of rice and wheat. (P)

258 The agriculture of India. John W. Mellor, *Scientific American*, vol. 235, no. 3, pp. 155-163, 1976. Political and social factors are important in increasing India's agricultural production. (P)

259 The agriculture of Mexico. Edwin J. Wellhausen, *Scientific American*, vol. 235, no. 3, pp. 129-150, 1976. Mexico prepares to implement a second agricultural revolution. (P)

260 The amplification of agricultural production. Peter R. Jennings, *Scientific American*, vol. 235, no. 3, pp. 181-194, 1976. Plant breeding as a key to the green revolution. (P-M)

261 Rice breeding and world food production. Peter R. Jennings, *Science*, vol. 186, pp. 1085-1088, 1974. Role of plant breeders in developing agriculture. (P)

World Food Resources

262 The omens of famine: Confronting famine. John H. Douglas, *Science News*, vol. 105, pp. 306-308, 322-323, 1974. Review of growing threats of worldwide food shortages. (P)

263 The worldwide confrontation of population and food supply. Nevin S. Scrimshaw, *Technology Review*, vol. 77, no. 2, pp. 13-19, 1974. A nutritionist looks at the world food crisis. (P)

264 Increasing the harvest. Edward Groth III, *Environment*, vol. 17, no. 1, pp. 28-39, 1975. How world food production can be increased; pitfalls to be anticipated. (P)

265 The world food prospect. Lester R. Brown, *Science*, vol. 190, pp. 1053-1059, 1975. Ominous change is occurring in the world food economy. (P)

266 The agriculture of the U.S. Earl O. Heady, *Scientific American*, vol. 235, no. 3, pp. 107-127, 1976. How American contributions to world grain supplies can be increased. (P)

267 Balancing energy and food production, 1975-2000. W. R. Chancellor and J. R. Gross, *Science*, vol. 192, pp. 213-218, 1976. Fossil fuel energy inputs cannot continue indefinitely. (P-M)

268 The development of agriculture in developing countries. W. David Hopper, *Scientific American*, vol. 235, no. 3, pp. 197-205, 1976. This optimistic appraisal ignores factors of climate and soils. (P)

269 The dimensions of human hunger. Jean Mayer, *Scientific American*, vol. 235, no. 3, pp. 40-49, 1976. Global assessment of extent of malnutrition and hunger. (P)

270 Food and agriculture. Sterling Wortman, *Scientific American*, vol. 235, no. 3, pp. 31-39, 1976. General review of trends in worldwide food production. (P)

271 The resources available for agriculture. Roger Revelle, *Scientific American*, vol. 235, no. 3, pp. 165-178, 1976. Optimistic appraisal of possible increases in world food production. (P)

272 The world food problem and the role of climate. Timothy M. Laur, *EOS-Trans. Amer. Geophysical Union*, vol. 57, no. 4, pp. 189-195, 1976. Climate, population growth, and technology as factors in world food production. (P-M)

Units 44, 45
Biological Water Pollution, Eutrophication

273 Agriculture: The seeds of a problem. William E. Small, *Technology Review*, vol. 73, no. 6, pp. 49-53, 1971. Impact of animal and plant wastes — agriculture-related pollution. (P)

274 Effluence of the Eternal City. Shari Steiner, *Geographical Mag.*, vol. 43, pp. 820-822, 1971. Pollution of the Tiber River, passing through the city of Rome, Italy. (P)

275. Environmental hazards: Water pollution. Richard L. Woodward, Chapter 3, pp. 16-23, in *Understanding Environmental Pollution*, M. A. Strobbe, ed., C. V. Mosby Co., St. Louis, 1971. Overview of water pollution and health. (P)

276 Farm pollution and a nation's future. Robert C. Cowen, *Technology Review*, vol. 73, no. 6, pp. 6-7, 1971. Agriculture-related environmental pollution. (P)

277 The role of nitrogen in eutrophication processes. John J. Goering, Chapter 3, pp. 43-68, in *Water Pollution Microbiology*, R. Mitchell, ed., Wiley-Interscience, John Wiley & Sons, New York, 1972. Technical review of nitrogen pollution. (M-T)

278 The role of phosphorus in eutrophication. W. Stumm and E. Stumm-Zollinger, Chapter 2, pp. 11-42, in *Water Pollution Microbiology*, R. Mitchell, ed., Wiley-Interscience, John Wiley & Sons,

New York, 1972. Technical review of phosphorus pollution. (M-T)

279 What is a river? — Zoological description. Kenneth W. Cummins, pp. 33-52, in *River Ecology and Man*, R. T. Oglesby et al., eds., Academic Press, New York, 1972. Detailed, basic description of stream ecosystem. (M-T)

280 Restoring lakes in Sweden. Sven Björk, *Technology Review*, vol. 76, no. 2, pp. 53-60, 1973. Case studies of restoration of lakes after eutrophication occurred. (M-T)

281 Thermal alteration of aquatic ecosystems. J. Whitfield Gibbons and R. R. Sharitz, *American Scientist*, vol. 62, pp. 660-670, 1974. Ecological impact of effluent from the Savannah River Plant. (M-T)

Pollution of the Great Lakes

282 The aging Great Lakes. C. F. Powers and A. Robertson, *Scientific American*, vol. 215, no. 5, pp. 95-104, 1966. General review of eutrophication of Great Lakes and its effect on fisheries. (P)

283 The cause of pollution in Lake Erie. Federal Water Pollution Control Administration, pp. 61-79, in *Water Quality in a Stressed Environment*, W. A. Pettyjohn, ed., Burgess Publ. Co., Minneapolis, 1972. Detailed analysis of pollutants entering Lake Erie and their sources. (M-T)

284 Lake Erie's fish community: 150 years of cultural stress. H. A. Regier and W. L. Hartman, *Science*, vol. 180, pp. 1248-1255, 1973. Impact of commercial fishing and Man-induced eutrophication on Lake Erie's biotic community. (P-M)

285 The decision to control eutrophication. Terence R. Lee, Chapter 5, pp. 79-97, in *Priorities in Water Management*, F. M. Leversedge, ed., Univ. of Victoria, British Columbia, 1974. Planning by the United States and Canada to control pollution of the Great Lakes. (P)

286 The Great Lakes rediscovered. Robert A. Ragotzkie, *American Scientist*, vol. 62, pp. 454-464, 1974. General description of Great Lakes, their origin, and environmental problems. (P)

287 Management of the international Great Lakes. Leonard B. Dworsky, Chapter 11, pp. 217-239, in *Priorities in Water Management*, F. M. Leversedge, ed., Univ. of Victoria, British Columbia, 1974. Results of a seminar on problems of Great Lakes management. (P)

Unit 46
Marine Ecosystems

288 The nature of oceanic life. John D. Isaacs, *Scientific American*, vol. 221, no. 3, pp. 146-162, 1969. The marine food chain. (P)

289 Ship canals and aquatic ecosystems. W. I. Aron and S. H. Smith, *Science*, vol.

174, pp. 13-20, 1971. Effects of the Erie, Welland, and Suez canals, and possible effects of a Central American canal. (P-M)

290 Seaweeds: Their productivity and strategy for growth. K. H. Mann, *Science*, vol. 182, pp. 975-980, 1973. Review of the ecology of large marine algae. (M-T)

291 Claims to the ocean. Holger Rotkirch, *Environment*, vol. 16, no. 5, pp. 34-41, 1974. Review of territorial sea laws. (P)

292 Salt marshes: Ecosystems in danger. John Hay, *Nat. Parks and Conservation Mag.*, vol. 48, no. 3, pp. 17-21, 1974. A naturalist stresses the vulnerability of salt marsh ecosystems. (P)

293 Glacier Bay: Icy home to whales. W. S. Home, *Nat. Parks and Conservation Mag.*, vol. 49, no. 5, pp. 12-16, 1975. Whales are threatened with extinction by commercial whaling. (P)

294 The impact of Man on seagrass systems. G. W. Thayer, D. A. Wolfe, R. B. Williams, *American Scientist*, vol. 63, pp. 288-296, 1975. Threats to seagrass, a basic primary production system in the marine ecosystem of coastal zones. (P-M)

Marine Food Resources

295 The food resources of the ocean. S. J. Holt, *Scientific American*, vol. 221, no. 3, pp. 178-194, 1969. World fisheries and their production. (P)

296 Bringing back the Atlantic salmon. Robert E. Lennon, *Nat. Parks and Conservation Mag.*, vol. 50, no. 8, pp. 15-19, 1976. Efforts to restore the Atlantic salmon fisheries, despite poaching. (P)

297 El Niño 1972: Its climatic, ecological, human, and economic implications. César N. Caviedes, *Geographical Review*, vol. 65, pp. 493-509, 1975. Invasion of warmer surface waters severely impacts the fishing industry of Peru. (M-T)

298 Oysters, algae, and sewage. John H. Douglas, *Science News*, vol. 106, pp. 170-171, 1974. Raising shellfish in sea water enriched with sewage. (P)

299 The anchovy crisis. C. P. Idyll, *Scientific American*, vol. 228, no. 6, pp. 22-29, 1973. Ecological disturbance by El Niño; its ecological and economic impacts. (P)

300 The top millimeter of the ocean. Ferren MacIntyre, *Scientific American*, vol. 230, no. 5, pp. 62-77, 1974. Floating microorganisms as a possible supply of protein-rich food. (P)

301 The Chesapeake oyster fishery. John J. Alford, *Annals, Assn. Amer. Geog.*, vol. 65, pp. 229-239, 1975. Impact of predators, disease, and pollution on the oyster fishery of Chesapeake Bay. (P-M)

Unit 47
Pesticides and the Environment

302 The imported fire ant in the southern

United States. Howard G. Adkins, *Annals, Assoc. of Amer. Geog.*, vol. 60, pp. 578-592, 1970. Problems of attempted control and containment of a serious insect infestation. (P)

303 After D.D.T., what? George A. W. Boehm, *Technology Review*, vol. 74, no. 8, pp. 26-31, 1972. Controversy over continued use of DDT. (P-M)

304 Insect control (I): Use of pheromones; (II): Hormones and viruses. Jean L. Marx, *Science*, vol. 181, pp. 736-737, 833-835, 1975. Alternatives to DDT use different biological mechanisms. (P)

305 The environmental impact of modern agricultural technologies. Ian R. Manners, Chapter 7, pp. 181-212, in *Perspectives on Environment*, Association of American Geographers, Washington, D.C., 1974. Impact of fertilizers and pesticides on ecosystems. (P-M)

306 The last boll weevil. Kevin P. Shea, *Environment*, vol. 16, no. 5, pp. 6-10, 1974. The boll weevil eradication program in the South. (P)

307 Global pollutants; persistent pesticides and wildlife; pesticides and breeding failure in birds. Ian C. T. Nisbet, *Technology Review*, vol. 77, no. 3, pp. 6-7; no. 6, pp. 8-9, 69; no. 7, pp. 8-9, 1975. Series of reports on environmental effects of DDT, DDE, and PCBs on wildlife. (P-M)

308 Pesticide residues and field workers. R. C. Spear, D. L. Jenkins, T. H. Milby, *Envir. Science and Technology*, vol. 9, no. 4, pp. 308-313, 1975. Hazards of exposure to organophosphorus chemicals. (P-M)

309 Pesticides and you. NPCA Staff, *Nat. Parks and Environmental Mag.*, vol. 49, no. 11, pp. 20-22, 1975. Environmental impact of pesticides. (P)

310 Poisoning farmworkers. Joel Schwartz, *Environment*, vol. 17, no. 4, pp. 26-33, 1975. Exposure of farmworkers to dangerous pesticides. (P)

311 Pest control: NAS panel warns of possible technological breakdown. *Science*, vol. 191, pp. 836-837, 1976. Genetic resistance and other factors point to the need of alternatives to present pesticide practices. (P)

312 Pesticide standards. *Environment*, vol. 18, no. 3, pp. 18-20, 1976. Pesticide testing standards and the EPA. (P)

Ocean Pollution, Ecological Impact

313 *Marine Pollution — Potential for Catastrophe*. O. Schacter and D. Serwer, UNITAR Research Report, United Nations Office of Public Information, 24 pp., 1971. General review of global marine pollution and remedies. (P)

313 The disposal of waste in the ocean. Willard Bascomb, *Scientific American*, vol. 231, no. 2, pp. 16-25, 1974. Optimistic view on ability of oceans to absorb wastes without damage to marine life. (P)

315 Oil on the seas. Dennis Livingston, *Environment,* vol. 16, no. 7, pp. 38-43, 1974. Marine oil pollution reviewed. (P)

316 Prescription for the Mediterranean. S. J. Holt, *Environment,* vol. 16, no. 4, pp. 28-33, 1974. Pollution of the Mediterranean Sea by oil and other wastes. (P)

317 Offshore drilling: Fishermen and oilmen clash in Alaska. Mark Panitch, *Science,* vol. 189, pp. 204-206, 1975. Drilling for oil threatens a valuable fishery in Kachemak Bay. (P)

318 Pelagic tar. James N. Butler, *Scientific American,* vol. 232, no. 6, pp. 90-97, 1975. Floating black lumps are widely distributed over the world's oceans. (P)

319 Offshore oil spills and the marine environment. Stephen F. Moore, *Technology Review,* vol. 78, no. 5, pp. 61-67, 1976. Biological impact of an oil spill. (P-M)

Chemical Pollutants in the Environment

320 Trace elements: A growing appreciation of their effects on Man. Thomas H. Maugh II, *Science,* vol. 181, pp. 253-254, 1973. Summary of scientific studies of effects of trace metals on organisms. (P)

321 Trace pollutants: The hidden villains. Joan Arehart-Treichel, *Science News,* vol. 104, pp. 44-45, 1973. Environmental effects of trace metals, including cadmium and lead. (P)

322 Nerve damage. Kevin P. Shea, *Environment,* vol. 16, no. 9, pp. 6-10, 1974. Case study of nerve poisoning in Morocco by a toxic synthetic chemical. (P)

323 New hope in Japan. Kenneth R. Stunkel, *Environment,* vol. 16, no. 8, pp. 18-20, 1974. Court cases following mercury poisoning at Minamata Bay and elsewhere in Japan. (P)

324 Chemical pollutants: Polychlorinated biphenyls still a threat. Thomas H. Maugh II, *Science,* vol. 190, p. 1189, 1975. Succinct review of PCB pollution and its control. (P)

325 Environmental mutagenic hazards. Committee of the Council of the Environmental Mutagen Society, *Science,* vol. 187, pp. 503-514, 1975. Comprehensive review of environmental mutagens and their regulation. (M-T)

326 Fluoride pollution. Edward Groth III, *Environment,* vol. 17, no. 3, pp. 29-38, 1975. Possible ecological effects of fluoride pollution of air and water. (P-M)

327 PCBs in food. Joseph Highland, *Environment,* vol. 18, no. 2, pp. 13-16, 1976. Determining acceptable levels of PCBs in dietary intake. (P)

328 PCBs in the environment. A. Karim Ahmed, *Environment,* vol. 18, no. 2, pp. 6-11, 1976. Polychlorinated biphenyls (PCBs); their toxic effects and control. (P-M)

Species Extinction by Humans

329 Breaking the web. G. Uetz and D. L. Johnson, *Environment,* vol. 16, no. 10, pp. 31-39, 1974. Extinctions of animal species by human activities. (P)

330 The human predator: A survey. Robin W. Doughty, Chapter 6, pp. 152-180, in *Perspectives on Environment,* Association of American Geographers, Washington, D.C., 1974. Endangered wildlife; causes of wildlife decline. (P)

331 An expanded approach to the problem of disappearing species. Norman Myers, *Science,* vol. 193, pp. 198-202, 1976. Conservation of species viewed from economic and institutional perspectives. (P-M)

332 Wildlife of Indochina: Tragedy or opportunity? Ronald M. Nowak, *Nat. Parks and Conservation Mag.,* vol. 50, no. 6, pp. 13-18, 1976. Man's impact on wild animal species during Vietnam war. (P)

Units 48, 49
Alfisols, Ultisols, Spodosols

333 The boreal bioclimates. F. K. Hare and J. C. Ritchie, *Geographical Review,* vol. 62, pp. 333-365, 1972. Climate of the boreal forest region of North America. (M-T)

334 Classification and geography of the world's soils. H. D. Foth and L. M. Turk, Chapter 10, pp. 237-271, in *Fundamentals of Soil Science,* 5th ed., John Wiley & Sons, New York, 1972. Basic review of the United States soil taxonomy. (M)

335 The demise of the Piedmont cotton region. M. C. Prunty and C. S. Aiken, *Annals, Assoc. of Amer. Geog.,* vol. 62, pp. 283-306, 1972. History of rise and decline of cotton production in the South. (P)

336 The Middle West. John Fraser Hart, *Annals, Assoc. of Amer. Geog.,* vol. 62, pp. 258-282, 1972. Settlement and agriculture in the Middle West. (P)

337 Population change in northern New England. George K. Lewis, *Annals, Assoc. of Amer. Geog.,* vol. 62, pp. 307-322, 1972. Social and economic changes accompany population change. (P)

338 Spodosols; Alfisols; Ultisols. S. W. Buol, F. D. Hole, R. J. McCracken, Chapters 20, 21, 22, pp. 252-281, in *Soil Genesis and Classification,* Iowa State Univ. Press, Ames, 1973. (M-T)

Unit 50
Arctic Environment, Permafrost

339 Tundra and taiga. J. Ross Mackay, pp. 156-171, in *Future Environments of North America,* F. F. Darling and J. P. Milton, eds., The Natural History Press, Garden City, N. Y., 1966. Limited prospects for future economic and agricultural development. (P)

340 Natural and Man-induced disturbances of permafrost terrain. R. K. Haugen and J. Brown, Chapter 8, pp. 139-149, in *Environmental Geomorphology,* D. R. Coates, ed., Publ. in Geomorphology, State Univ. of New York, Binghamton, 1971. Severe thermal and water erosion follows disturbance of the arctic tundra. (P)

341 Land under refrigeration. Peter James, *Geographical Mag.,* vol. 44, no. 12, pp. 853-857, 1972. Processes in arctic and alpine tundra. (P)

342 *The Periglacial Environment, Permafrost, and Man.* Larry W. Price, Resource Paper No. 14, Commission on College Geography, Assoc. of Amer. Geog., Washington, D.C., 88 pp., 1972. Comprehensive description of arctic climate, soils, geomorphic processes, biologic processes, and their implications to Man. (P-M)

343 The world of underground ice. J. Ross Mackay, *Annals, Assoc. of Amer. Geog.,* vol. 62, pp. 1-22, 1972. Permafrost of the arctic region and its environmental management. (P-M)

344 Inceptisols; Histosols. Chapters 17 and 24, pp. 226-231, 291-299, in *Soil Genesis and Classification,* S. W. Buol, F. D. Hole, R. J. McCracken, Iowa State Univ. Press, Ames, 1973. Soil orders widespread in arctic and subarctic lands. (M-T)

Trans-Alaska Pipeline

345 Reaction of reindeer to obstructions and disturbances. David R. Klein, *Science,* vol. 173, pp. 393-398, 1971. Experience in Scandinavia is evaluated for application to environmental impact of the Trans-Alaska Pipeline. (P)

346 Alaska pipeline regardless of costs. W. R. Derick Sewell, *Geographical Mag.,* vol. 46, pp. 383-387, 1974. Comparison of Trans-Alaska and proposed Mackenzie pipelines. (P)

347 *Environmental Impact Analysis: The Example of the Proposed Trans-Alaska Pipeline.* David A. Brew, U.S. Geological Survey, Circular 695, Washington, D.C., 16 pp., 1974. (P-M)

348 Oil on ice. Rene O. Ramseier, *Environment,* vol. 16, no. 4, pp. 6-14, 1974. Possible environmental effects of development of oil reserves on Arctic Ocean coasts. (P)

349 Alaska's pipeline road: New conflicts loom. Mark Panitch, *Science,* vol. 189, pp. 30-32, 1975. Conflict over proposed recreational use of the pipeline service road. (P)

Unit 51
Grasslands of the Great Plains

350 The rangelands of the western U.S. R. Merton Love, *Scientific American,* vol. 222, no. 2, pp. 89-96, 1970. How our rangelands could be made more productive. (P)

351 The Dust Bowl in the 1970s. John R. Borchert, *Annals, Assoc. of Amer. Geog.,* vol. 61, pp. 1-22, 1971. Physical and human interaction in the Great Plains during drought cycles. (P-M)

352 Grasslands biome network: Results of first year. John Lynn Arehart, *Science News,* vol. 100, pp. 282-283, 1971. Biome research on the Great Plains. (P)

353 The modification of mid-latitude grasslands and forests by Man. John T. Curtis, Selection 36, pp. 507-521, in *Man's Impact on Environment.* T. R, Detwyler, ed., McGraw-Hill, New York, 1971. (M)

354 The American Great Plains. E. Cotton Mather, *Annals, Assoc. of Amer. Geog.,* vol., 62, pp. 237-257, 1972. Physical and economic geography of the Great Plains. (P)

355 Landscape meteorology in the Plains area. W. Kollmorgen and J. Kollmorgen, *Annals, Assoc. of Amer. Geog.,* vol. 63, pp. 424-441, 1973. Historical review of beliefs concerning weather, climate, soils, and agriculture of the Great Plains. (P)

356 Mollisols: Grassland soils of steppes and prairies. Chapter 19, pp. 240-251, in *Soil Genesis and Classification,* S. W. Buol, F. D. Hole, R. J. McCracken, Iowa State Univ. Press, Ames, 1973. (M-T)

357 Bison trails and their geologic significance. Lee Clayton, *Geology,* vol. 3, no. 9, pp. 498-500, 1975. Comment by E. A. Babcock and reply by L. Clayton, *Geology,* vol. 4, no. 1, pp. 4-6, 1976. Bison trails persist on the Great Plains, despite agriculture. (P-M)

358 Prairies without much grass. J. G. Nelson, *Geographical Mag.,* vol. 47, no. 10, pp. 614-620, 1975. The prairie provinces of Canada. (P)

359 Time to save the vanishing prairie. Jan S. Garton, *Nat. Parks and Conservation Mag.,* vol. 49, no. 9, pp. 4-9, 1975. Efforts to create a Tallgrass National Park in the Kansas Flint Hills. (P)

360 Center-pivot irrigation. William E. Splinter, *Scientific American,* vol. 234, no. 6, pp. 90-99, 1976. Pivoting sprinkler pipes irrigate large circular plots. (P)

361 Losing ground. Erik Eckholm, *Environment,* vol. 18, no. 3, pp. 6-11, 1976. Dust Bowl of the Great Plains, yesterday and today. (P)

Unit 52
Rainforest: Ecology and Soils

362 The tropical rain forest: A nonrenewable resource. A. Gómez-Pompa, C. Vázquez-Yanes, S. Guevara, *Science,* vol. 177, pp. 762-765, 1972. Species extinction accompanies destruction of the rainforest. (P-M)

363 Oxisols: Sesquioxide-rich, highly weathered soils of the intertropical regions. Chapter 23, pp. 282-290, in *Soil Genesis and Classification,* S. W. Buol, F. D. Hole, R. J. McCracken, Iowa State Univ. Press, Ames, 1973. (M-T)

364 Trans-Amazonica, the rain forest route. Edward P. Leahy, *Geographical Mag.,* vol. 45, no. 4, pp. 298-303, 1973. Construction methods and problems of the Brazilian highway. (P)

365 The tropical rain forest. Paul W. Richards, *Scientific American,* vol. 229, no. 6, pp. 59-67, 1973. The rainforest ecosystem; consequences of its destruction. (P)

366 Twilight of Brazilian tribes. Edwin Brooks, *Geographical Mag.,* vol. 45, no. 4, pp. 304-310, 1973. Genocide as the price of economic development. (P)

367 National park in the Amazon rain forest. Jon Tinker, *Geographical Mag.,* vol. 47, no. 1, pp. 33-39, 1974. A Peruvian tract of virgin rainforest in the Amazon basin. (P)

368 Last stand of the tropical forest. M. J. Eden, *Geographical Mag.,* vol. 47, no. 9, pp. 578-582, 1975. Forest destruction, cultivation, and soil erosion in the wet low-latitude zones. (P)

369 The reluctant Amazon Basin. J. C. Jahoda and D. L. O'Hearn, *Environment,* vol. 17, no. 7, pp. 16-20, 25-30, 1975. Exploitation of the Amazon basin to boost the Brazilian economy. (P)

370 Soils of the tropics and the world food crisis. P. A. Sanchez and S. W. Buol, *Science,* vol. 188, pp. 598-603, 1975. Clearing up many misconceptions about soils of low latitudes. (P-M)

Agriculture in Wet, Low-Latitude Climates

371 The agricultural potential of the humid tropics. Jen-Hu Chang, *Geographical Review,* vol. 58, pp. 333-361, 1968. Many problems must be faced in attempts to expand agriculture in rainforest lands. (M-T)

372 The ecology of swidden cultivation in the Upper Orinoco rain forest, Venezuela. David R. Harris, *Geographical Review,* vol. 61, pp. 475-495, 1971. An example of slash and burn agriculture in the equatorial rainforest. (P-M)

373 The origins of agriculture in the tropics. David R. Harris, *American Scientist,* vol. 60, pp. 180-193, 1972. Plant domestication and vegeculture in the wet low-latitude zones. (R)

374 The shading cycle in shifting agriculture. Ronald E. Seavoy, *Annals, Assoc. of Amer. Geog.,* vol. 63, pp. 522-528, 1973. Case study of slash and burn agriculture in rainforest of Indonesia. (P-M)

375 Tropical agroecosystems. David H. Janzen, *Science,* vol. 182, pp. 1212-1219,

1973. Taking a hard look at the environmental constraints upon expanded agriculture of the wet low-latitude zones. (P-M)

376 Bringing the green revolution to the shifting cultivator. D. J. Greenland, *Science,* vol. 190, pp. 841-844, 1975. Ways to improve crop yields in the wet, low-latitude zones. (P-M)

Unit 53
Savanna Biome

377 A grazing ecosystem in the Serengeti. Richard H. V. Bell, *Scientific American,* vol. 225, no. 1, pp. 86-93, 1971. Migrations follow the annual climatic cycle. (P)

378 National parks in savanna Africa. Norman Myers, *Science,* vol. 178, pp. 1255-1263, 1972. Difficult management problems faced by Africa's animal preserves. (P)

379 When elephants destroy a valley. John R. Giardino, *Geographical Mag.,* vol. 47, no. 3, pp. 175-181, 1974. Overcrowding by large animals in a Zambian national park leads to destruction of vegetation. (P)

380 The savanna biome: A case study of human impact on biotic communities. Theo L. Hills, Chapter 12, pp. 342-373, in *Perspectives on Environment,* American Geographical Society, Washington, D.C., 1974. Summary of savanna characteristics, followed by details of the Guiana Highlands-Amazon savanna. (P-M)

381 The Gir Forest: An endangered ecosystem. Stephen Berwick, *American Scientist,* vol. 64, pp. 28-40, 1976. Humans, domestic and wild animals, and plants form a working ecosystem. (P)

Southeast Asian Environments

382 The Chinese monsoon. Jen-Hu Chang, *Geographical Review,* vol. 61, pp. 370-395, 1971. Technical analysis of dynamics of Asiatic monsoon phenomena. (M-T)

383 The concept of laterite. T. R. Paton and M. A. J. Williams, *Annals, Assoc. of Amer. Geog.,* vol. 62, pp. 42-56, 1972. Varied interpretations of the nature and origin of soils rich in oxides of aluminum and iron. (M-T)

384 India's agriculture. A. K. Chatravarti, *Focus* (Amer. Geographical Soc.), vol. 23, no. 5, pp. 1-8, 1973. Environmental assets and hazards in a monsoon land. (P)

385 Vertisols: Shrinking and swelling dark clay soils. Chapter 16, pp. 218-225, in *Soil Genesis and Classification,* S. W. Buol, F. D. Hole, R. J. McCracken, Iowa State Univ. Press, Ames, 1973. (M-T)

386 Population pressures in Bangladesh. A. K. Dutt and N. Ahmed, *Focus* (Amer. Geographical Soc.), vol. 24, no. 3, pp. 1-10, 1974. Climate and water problems; landscape, soils, and agricultural difficulties. (P)

387 China's agriculture: Institutional and technological changes. Laurence J. C. Ma, *Focus* (Amer. Geographical Soc.), vol. 25, no. 7, pp. 1-7, 1975. General review of China's agriculture with its regional contrasts. (P)

Unit 54
Desert Biome

388 Desert species and adaptation. Neil F. Hadley, *American Scientist*, vol. 60, pp. 338-347, 1972. Plants and animals adapt to heat load and water loss under adverse conditions. (P-M)

389 Aridisols: Soils of arid regions. Chapter 18, pp. 232-239, in *Soil Genesis and Soil Classification*, S. W. Buol, F. D. Hole, R. J. McCracken, Iowa State Univ. Press, Ames, 1973. (M-T)

390 Shrubs — a neglected resource of arid lands. Cyrus N. McKell, *Science*, vol. 187, pp. 803-809, 1975. Virtues and limitations of arid land shrubs. (P-M)

Desert Irrigation and Salinization

391 Water in the desert. George B. Cressey, *Annals, Assn. of Amer. Geog.*, vol. 47, pp. 105-124, 1957. Limits to which deserts can suppored agriculture; salinization. (P)

392 Salt and silt in ancient Mesopotamian agriculture. T. Jacobsen and R. M. Adams, *Science*, vol. 128, pp. 1251-1258, 1958. Reprinted as Selection 28, pp. 383-394, in *Man's Impact on Environment*, T. R. Detwyler, ed., McGraw-Hill, New York, 1971. (P)

393 The qanats of Iran. H. E. Wulff, *Scientific American*, vol. 218, no. 4, pp. 94-105, 1968. Remarkable subterranean water supply system still in use after 3000 years. (P)

394 Irrigation and salt problems in Remnark, South Australia. Charles H. V. Ebert, *Geographical Review*, vol. 61, pp. 355-369, 1971. Case study of salinization of irrigated soils. (P-M)

395 The development of Israel's water resources. Aaron Wiener, *American Scientist*, vol. 60, pp. 466-473, 1972. Management of Israel's limited water supply for desert irrigation. (P-M)

396 Water importation. AAAS Committee on Arid Lands, *Science*, vol. 175, pp. 667-669, 1972. Summary of committee conclusions on large-scale water importation to desert areas of the United States. (P)

397 Aswan Dam revisited. Henry Van der Schalie, *Environment*, vol. 16, no. 9, pp. 18-20, 25-26, 1974. Spread of schistosomiasis as a result of a new irrigation system in the Nile Valley. (P)

398 Desert food factories. Carl N. Hodges, *Technology Review*, vol. 77, no. 3, pp. 33-39, 1975. Experimental greenhouse agriculture in deserts. (P)

399 Irrigation without waste. Kevin P. Shea, *Environment*, vol. 15, no. 5, pp. 12-15, 1975. Development of new drip-irrigation systems. (P)

400 Salting the earth. Erik P. Ekholm, *Environment*, vol. 17, no. 7, pp. 9-15, 1975. Salinization in irrigation projects in various parts of the world. (P)

401 Shall the Negev bloom? Kendrick Frazier, *Science News*, vol. 107, pp. 29-30, 1975. Israel's efforts to increase desert agriculture, using new technologies. (P)

Unit 55
Conservation and the Wilderness Ethic

402 Man in America. Raymond F. Dasmann, pp. 326-334, in *Future Environments of North America*, F. F. Darling and J. P. Milton, eds., Natural History Press, Garden City, N.Y., 1966. "It may well be too late to save more than token pieces of our natural environment." (P)

403 Reflections on the Man-nature theme as a subject for study. Clarence J. Glacken, pp. 355-371, in *Future Environments of North America*, F. F. Darling and J. P. Milton, eds., Natural History Press, Garden City, N.Y., 1966. (P)

404 The special role of national parks. Noel D. Eichhorn, pp. 335-341, in *Future Environments of North America*, F. F. Darling and J. P. Milton, eds., Natural History Press, Garden City, N.Y., 1966. Wilderness values, scientific uses under stress of visitors. (P)

405 Recreation habits and values: Implications for landscape quality. David Lowenthal, pp. 103-117, in *Challenge for Survival*, P. Dansereau, ed., Columbia Univ. Press, New York, 1970. (See also Commentary, pp. 118-128, by Charles C. Morrison, Jr.) (P)

406 *Wilderness and the American Mind.* Roderick Nash, rev. ed., Yale Univ. Press, New Haven, Conn., 1973. Chapters 1-4 trace the evolution of the wilderness concept from the Old World to the New World. (P)

407 Recreation and the environment. J. G. Nelson and R. W. Butler, Chapter 10, pp. 290-310, in *Perspectives on Environment*, Association of American Geographers, Washington, D.C., 1974. National parks and recreation systems. (P)

Scenic River Gorges

408 *Quantitative Comparison of Some Aesthetic Factors Among Rivers.* Luna B. Leopold, U.S. Geological Survey, Circular 620, Washington, D.C., 16 pp., 1969. Ranking factors and systems to indicate aesthetic value of gorges and their rivers. (P)

409 Evaluating riverscapes. Marie Morisawa, Chapter 6, pp. 91-106, in *Environmental Geomorphology*, D. R. Coates, ed., Publ. in Geomorphology, State Univ. of New York, Binghamton, 1971. Analysis of aesthetics of rivers, based upon human perception. (P)

410 Running a desert river. Virginia McConnell Simmons, *Nat. Parks and Conservation Mag.*, vol. 47, no. 12, pp. 4-9, 1973. Gorge of the Rio Grande in Big Bend National Park. (P)

411 Last stand at Red River Gorge. Alton Marsh, *Nat. Parks and Conservation Mag.*, vol. 48, no. 8, pp. 18-22, 1974. Environmental impacts of a proposed federal dam. (P)

412 Man's impact on the Colorado River in the Grand Canyon. R. Dolan, A. Howard, A. Gallenson, *American Scientist*, vol. 62, pp. 392-401, 1974. Flow control by an upstream dam caused marked changes in channel and banks. (P)

413 Canyon country: Profile of the ages. C. J. Burkhart, *Nat. Parks and Conservation Mag.*, vol. 49, no. 7, pp. 5-8, 1976. Geological description of Grand Canyon, Zion Canyon, and Bryce Canyon. (P)

414 The St. John at a critical crossroad. P. Neill and M. M. Smith, *Nat. Parks and Conservation Mag.*, vol. 49, no. 4, pp. 15-19, 1975. A proposed hydroelectric dam threatens wild scenery of the St. John River in northern Maine. (P)

Unit 56
The Alpine Environment

415 *The Incomparable Valley: A Geological Interpretation of the Yosemite.* Francois E. Matthes (edited by F. Fryxell), Univ. of Calif. Press, Berkeley, 168 pp., 1950. (P)

416 John Muir: Publicizer. Chapter 8, pp. 122-140, in *Wilderness and the American Mind*, Roderick Nash, rev. ed., Yale Univ. Press, New Haven, Conn., 1973. (P)

417 Triple jeopardy at Glacier National Park. N.P.C.A. staff, *Nat. Parks and Conservation Mag.*, vol. 49, no. 9, pp. 20-22, 1975. Proposed strip mining threatens scenery of a national park. (P)

418 Yosemite Valley Railroad; highway of history, pathway of promise. Alfred Runte, *Nat. Parks and Conservation Mag.*, vol. 48, no. 12, pp. 4-9, 1974. Solving transportation problems in national parks. (P)

419 Glacier: Beleaguered park of 1975. Gene Albert, *Nat. Parks and Conservation Mag.*, vol. 49, no. 11, pp. 4-10, 1975. Glacier National Park endangered by proposed mining operations. (P)

420 Northernmost national park: Gates of the Arctic. M. Woodbridge Williams, *Nat. Parks and Conservation Mag.*, vol. 50, no. 4, pp. 4-9, 1976. Alpine scenery in the Brooks Range of Alaska. (P)

421 Yosemite's crystal cascades. Maggie Hillert, *Nat. Parks and Conservation Mag.*, vol. 50, no. 3, pp. 4-8, 1976. Waterfalls of Yosemite National Park. (P)

Unit 57
Scenery of Rugged Coasts

422 Shores of the Apostles. Gilbert F. Stucker, *Nat. Parks and Conservation Mag.*, vol. 48, no. 7, pp. 4-9, 1974. Coastal landforms of the Apostle Islands in Lake Superior. (P)

423 Acadia: Public and private preservation. Robert O. Binnewies, *Nat. Parks and Conservation Mag.*, vol. 49, no. 4, pp. 4-9, 1975. Maine Coast Heritage Trust seeks to protect private lands for conservation purposes. (P)

424 California's Channel Islands. Stanley Medders, *Nat. Parks and Environmental Mag.*, vol. 49, no. 10, pp. 11-15, 1975. Man's impact on a group of offshore islands. (P)

425 Glacier Bay: Wilderness or mining boom? K. Jettmar and C. Summers, *Nat. Parks and Conservation Mag.*, vol. 49, no. 5, pp. 6-11, 1975. Mining activities threaten Glacier Bay National Monument. (P)

Unit 58
Desert Environment of the American Southwest

426 Crisis in a ravaged land: The California desert. Stanley Medders, *Nat. Parks and Conservation Mag.*, vol. 47, no. 12, pp. 14-19, 1973. Problems of desert protection faced by the Bureau of Land Management. (P)

427 Death Valley: Desert wilderness in danger. Harold W. Wood, Jr., *Nat. Parks and Conservation Mag.*, vol. 48, no. 2, pp. 5-9, 1974. Environmental devastation in Death Valley from mining and off-road vehicles. (P)

428 Guadelupe: Barrier reef in the desert. Annette Richards Parent, *Nat. Parks and Conservation Mag.*, vol. 48, no. 10, pp. 4-9, 1974. Capitan barrier reef forms a great desert escarpment. (P)

429 Off-road vehicle use. AAAS Committee on Arid Lands, *Science*, vol. 184, pp. 500-501, 1974. Recommendations to control exploitation of arid lands. (P)

430 Off road vehicles: A compromise plan for the California desert. Luther J. Carter, *Science*, vol. 183, pp. 396-399, 1974. Recreation vehicle lobby versus the Bureau of Land Management and organized conservationists. (P)

431 Cacti: Bizarre, beautiful, but in danger. Lyman Benson, *Nat. Parks and Conservation Mag.*, vol. 4, no. 7, pp. 17-21, 1975. Need for action to protect rare desert species from extinction. (P)

432 Organ Pipe: Trouble along the Dev-

il's Road. J. Y. Bryan, *Nat. Parks and Conservation Mag.*, vol. 49, no. 12, pp. 4-9, 1975. Mineral prospecting and cattle grazing threaten a national monument. (P)

433 The battle for Death Valley. Alan Cranston, *Nat. Parks and Conservation Mag.*, vol. 50, no. 1, pp. 4-9, 1976. United States Senator campaigns on behalf of the Death Valley National Monument. (P)

434 The mining of America's parks. NPCA Staff, *Nat. Parks and Conservation Mag.*, vol. 50, no. 1, pp. 18-20, 1976. An appeal to protect our national parks from degradation by mining. (P)

Unit 59
Appalachia

435 The Shenandoah Valley frontier. Robert D. Mitchell, *Annals, Assoc. of Amer. Geog.*, vol. 62, pp. 461-486, 1972. Case study of an evolving Appalachian frontier area. (P-M)

436 Cataloochee—a sense of place. Elizabeth Powers, *Nat. Parks and Conservation Mag.*, vol. 48, no. 12, pp. 9-14, 1974. Description of a pristine valley in Great Smoky Mountains National Park. (P)

437 Chattahoochee, river of flowered stones. Andrew Young, *Nat. Parks and Conservation Mag.*, vol. 49, no. 12, pp. 14-16, 1975. A scenic river gorge in the Southern Appalachians. (P)

438 New River country, wild and scenic. Elizabeth Watson, *Nat. Parks and Conservation Mag.*, vol. 49, no. 2, pp. 10-14, 1975. The New River gorge in the National Wild and Scenic Rivers System. (P)

439 Shadows of the past in the Great Smokies. Charlton Ogburn, *Nat. Parks and Conservation Mag.*, vol. 49, no. 8, pp. 4-7, 1975. Forests of the Great Smoky Mountains and their human history. (P)

440 Canals in America. John S. McNown, *Scientific American*, vol. 235, no. 1, pp. 117-124, 1976. Canal systems penetrated far into the Appalachian barrier. (P)

441 Coping with parsimony at Great Smoky. Boyd Evison, *Nat. Parks and Conservation Mag.*, vol. 50, no. 4, pp. 13-17, 1976. Overuse by visitors threatens a national park. (P)

442 Shortchanging the national park system. *Nat. Parks and Conservation Mag.*, vol. 50, no. 2, pp. 11-16; no. 3, pp. 9-14, 1976. Survey of budgetary and manpower problems afflicting our national parks. (P)

Unit 60
Energy Resources, General

443 Human energy production as a process in the biosphere. S. Fred Singer, Chapter 10, pp. 107-114, in *The Biosphere*, W. H. Freeman, San Francisco, 1970. Consumption of fossil fuels with future projections. (P)

444 The energy resources of the earth. M. King Hubbert, *Scientific American*, vol. 224, no. 3, pp. 61-70, 1971. (M-T)

445 World energy resources: Survey and review. Trevor M. Thomas, *Geographical Review*, vol. 63, pp. 246-258, 1973. Comparison of all major energy sources and their future prospects. (P)

446 Energy policy in the U.S. David J. Rose, *Scientific American*, vol. 230, no. 1, pp. 20-29, 1974. Overview of energy demands and energy resources. (P-M)

447 Energy self-sufficiency: An economic evaluation. Policy Study Group of the M.I.T. Energy Laboratory, *Technology Review*, vol. 76, no. 6, pp. 23-58, 1974. Comprehensive report on all major forms of energy, with policy conclusions. (P-M-T)

448 Meeting energy needs. Philip H. Abelson, *EOS, Transactions Amer. Geophysical Union*, vol. 55, no. 7, pp. 644-647, 1974. Steps the United States must take to meet future energy needs. (P)

449 A systems approach to energy. Wolf Häfele, *American Scientist*, vol. 62, pp. 438-447, 1974. Need for more efficient ways to handle energy. (M-T)

450 U.S. energy resources: limits and future outlook. Eric S. Cheney, *American Scientist*, vol. 62, pp. 14-22, 1974. Need for zero growth of population and energy use. (P-M)

451 Energy conservation and the consumer. Brice Hannon, *Science*, vol. 189, pp. 95-102, 1975. A tax placed on energy would ease a change to a more labor intensive economy. (P-M)

452 U.S. energy: The plan that can work. Manson Benedict, *Technology Review*, vol. 78, no. 6, pp. 53-59, 1976. M.I.T. professor gives his formula for supplying future energy needs. (P)

Coal as an Energy Resource

453 The challenge and promise of coal. Edmund A. Nephew, *Technology Review*, vol. 76, no. 2, pp. 21-29, 1973. Coal mining technology; impact of strip mining. (P-M)

454 Coal and the present energy situation. Elburt F. Osburn, *Science*, vol. 183, pp. 477-481, 1974. Problems of coal use as an energy source. (M)

455 The cost of coal. G. E. Dials and E. C. Moore, *Environment*, vol. 16, no. 7, pp. 18-24, 30-37, 1974. General review of economic and environmental costs of expanding coal production. (P)

456 A black mark. J. D. Leshy and T. R. Lash, *Environment*, vol. 17, no. 9, pp. 6-13, 1975. Criticism of federal coal-leasing policy in western fields. (P)

457 Oil and gas from coal. Neal R. Cochran, *Scientific American*, vol. 234, no. 5, pp. 24-29, 1976. Technology and costs of coal conversion. (P-M)

458 What is pure coal? Russell Boulding,

Environment, vol. 18, no. 1, pp. 12-17, 35-36, 1976. Energy and sulfur content, trace elements in coal. (P-M-T)

Petroleum Resources

459 Oil shale and the energy crisis. G. U. Dinneen and G. L. Cook, *Technology Review,* vol. 76, no. 3, pp. 27-33, 1974. Describes United States shale oil deposits and oil extraction technology. (M-T)

460 *The Worldwide Search for Petroleum Offshore—A Status Report for the Quarter Century, 1947-72.* Henry L. Berryhill, Jr., U.S. Geological Survey, Circular 694, 27 pp., 1974. (P-M)

461 New Opportunities for offshore petroleum exploration. Kenneth O. Emery, *Technology Review,* vol. 77, no. 5, pp. 31-33, 1975. Oil resources of continental shelves. (P-M)

462 Petroleum resources: How much oil and where? J. D. Moody and R. E. Geiger, *Technology Review,* vol. 77, no. 5, pp. 39-45, 1975. (M-T)

463 U.S.G.S. re-estimates reserves, FEA reports on proved reserves. *Geotimes,* vol. 20, no. 8, pp. 20-23, 1975. Review of revised government estimates of oil and gas reserves. (M-T)

464 Natural gas: United States has it if the price is right. Thomas H. Maugh II, *Science,* vol. 191, pp. 549-550, 1976. Natural gas reserves; methane from coal. (P)

465 The world oil industry. Christopher T. Rand, *Environment,* vol. 18, no. 3, pp. 12-17, 25-26, 1976. The big oil corporations, OPEC, and oil prices. (P)

Oil Shale Resources

466 Development of oil shale in the Green River Formation. Committee on Environment and Public Planning, Geol. Society of Amer., *The Geologist,* vol. 9, no. 4 (supplement), 8 pp., 1974. Environmental impacts and water use are detailed. (P)

467 Fossil fuels. Dietrick E. Thomsen, *Science News,* vol. 105, pp. 76-77, 1974. Origin of petroleum; occurrence of oil shale and extraction technology. (P)

468 Oil shale and the energy crisis. G. U. Dinneen and G. L. Cook, *Technology Review,* vol. 76, no. 3, pp. 27-33, 1974. Oil shale occurrence, reserves, and extraction technology. (P-M)

469 Oil shale: A huge resource of low-grade fuel. William D. Metz, *Science,* vol. 184, pp. 1271-1275, 1974. Technical and environmental problems will be difficult to solve. (P)

Unit 61
Environmental Impacts of Fossil Fuel Use

470 Black lung: Dispute about diagnosis of miners' ailment. Joe Pichirallo, *Science,* vol. 174, pp. 132-134, 1971. Victims of coal workers' disease (pneumoconiosis) seek additional benefits. (P)

471 *Water Demands for Expanding Energy Development.* G. H. Davis and L. A. Wood, U.S. Geological Survey, Circular 703, 14 pp., 1974. Water consumption required for development of geothermal, nuclear, fossil-fuel, and oil-shale power sources. (M-T)

472 Energy: Plan to use peat as fuel stirs concern in Minnesota. Philip M. Boffey, *Science,* vol. 190, pp. 1066-1070, 1975. Peat bogs threatened with destruction. (P)

473 A southwest power plant saga. Stan Miller, *Environmental Science and Technology,* vol. 10, no. 6, pp. 532-537, 1976. Problem of preserving environmental quality as great coal-burning power plants are developed in the southwestern United States. (P)

Strip Mining of Coal

474 Chewing it up at 200 tons a bite: Strip mining. William Greenburg, *Technology Review,* vol. 75, no. 4, pp. 46-55, 1973. (P)

475 The strip-mining of western coal. Genevieve Atwood, *Scientific American,* vol. 233, no. 6, pp. 23-29, 1975. Environmental impact of strip mining. (P)

476 Destroy to save? James Branscome, *Environment,* vol. 17, no. 6, pp. 6-11, 1975. TVA's impact on environment through strip mining and power plant operation. (P)

477 Left behind—Soviet mine wastes. Norman Precoda, *Environment,* vol. 17, no. 8, pp. 15-20, 1975. Widespread scarification from mining in the Soviet Union. (P)

478 Strip mining legislation: The tug of war continues. Luther J. Carter, *Science,* vol. 188, pp. 813-814, 1975. Conflicting interests slow progress toward drafting a surface mining control bill. (P)

Hazards of Offshore Oil Production

479 *Blowout: A Case Study of the Santa Barbara Oil Spill.* C. E. Steinhart and J. S. Steinhart, Duxbury Press (Wadsworth Publ. Co.), North Scituate, Mass., 138 pp., 1972.

480 Key issues in offshore oil. John W. Devanney III, *Technology Review,* vol. 76, no. 3, pp. 21-25, 1974. Ocean pollution and economic benefits. (P-M)

481 Marine oil pollution control. William E. Lehr, *Technology Review,* vol. 75, no. 4, pp. 13-22, 1976. Review of the state of oil spill abatement technology. (P)

482 Natural marine oil seepage. R. D. Wilson and others, *Science,* vol. 184, pp. 857-865, 1974. Natural oil seepages and their geologic distribution, with world map. (P-M)

483 Offshore oil: Technology . . . and emotion. Kenneth O. Emery, *Technology Review,* vol. 78, no. 5, pp. 31-37, 1976. A marine geologist tries to clear up misconceptions on dangers of offshore oil production. (P)

484 Oil spills and offshore petroleum. Robert J. Stewart, *Technology Review,* vol. 78, no. 5, pp. 47-57, 1976. Estimating probabilities of oil spills and their impact on coasts. (P-M)

Unit 62
Nuclear Energy Development

485 Soviet nuclear power. P. R. Pryde and L. T. Pryde, *Environment,* vol. 16, no. 3, pp. 26-34, 1974. Review of nuclear power development in the Soviet Union. (P)

486 The maturity and future of nuclear energy. Alvin M. Weinberg, *American Scientist,* vol. 64, pp. 16-21, 1976. Problems of public acceptance of nuclear power plants. (P-M)

487 The necessity of fission power. H. A. Bethe, *Scientific American,* vol. 234, no. 1, pp. 21-31, 1976. Uranium resources; hazards of nuclear power. (P-M)

488 Nuclear power—compared to what? D. J. Rose, P. W. Walsh, L. L. Leskovjan, *American Scientist,* vol. 64, pp. 291-299, 1976. Arguments in favor of nuclear power development over alternative energy sources. (P-M)

489 Uranium: Will there be a shortage or an embarrassment of enrichment? Allen L. Hammond, *Science,* vol. 192, pp. 866-867, 1976. Private sector participation in uranium enrichment. (P)

Hazards of Nuclear Power Plants

490 Nuclear power risks. R. Philip Hammond, *American Scientist,* vol. 62, pp. 155-160, 1974. Views of a leading nuclear scientist on hazards of atomic reactor operation. (P)

491 Report card on nuclear power. Sheldon Novik, *Environment,* vol. 16, no. 10, pp. 6-12, 1974. Risks and costs of further development of nuclear power. (P)

492 The failsafe risk. Kurt H. Hohenemser, *Environment,* vol. 17, no. 1, pp. 6-10, 1975. Evaluating the probabilities of nuclear power reactor accidents. (P)

493 An explosive reactor possibility. Kevin P. Shea, *Environment,* vol. 18, no. 1, pp. 6-11, 1976. Discussion: K. P. Shea, L. D. Buxton, L. S. Nelson, *Environment,* vol. 18, no. 5, pp. 6-8, 1976. Possibility of steam explosion in a nuclear power plant. (P-M)

494 Nuclear initiative: Californians vote "No," but Legislature acts. Luther J. Carter, *Science,* vol. 192, pp. 1317-1319, 1976. New bills were enacted to promote nuclear plant safety. (P)

Breeder Reactor Controversy

495 Nuclear breeders. Sheldon Novik, *Environment,* vol. 16, no. 6, pp. 6-15, 1974. Costs, benefits, and hazards of the breeder reactor. (P)

496 A poor buy. T. B. Cochran, J. G. Speth, A. R. Tamplin, *Environment,* vol. 17, no. 4, pp. 12-20, 1975. Economic factors in breeder reactor developments; alternative energy resources. (P-M)

497 Statement of the Executive Committee of the Scientists' Institute for Public Information. *Environment,* vol. 17, no. 4, pp. 6-7, 1975. The Scientists' Institute critcizes the liquid metal fast breeder program. (P)

498 A troublesome brew. Sheldon Novik, *Environment,* vol. 17, no. 4, pp. 8-11, 1975. Hazards connected with the liquid metal fast breeder reactor program. (P-M)

499 Toxicity of plutonium and some other actinides. John T. Edsall, *Bull. of the Atomic Scientists,* vol. 32, no. 7, pp. 27-37, 1976. Highly poisonous plutonium will be a major environmental hazard if the breeder reactor is developed. (P-M)

Unit 63
Disposal of Nuclear Wastes

500 Nuclear waste: Kansans riled by AEC plans for atom dump. Constance Holden, *Science,* vol. 172, pp. 249-250, 1971. Plan to store nuclear waste in a salt formation met with opposition. (P)

501 The unsolved problem of nuclear wastes. William W. Hambleton, *Technology Review,* vol. 74, no. 5, pp. 15-19, 1972. Underground storage of nuclear wastes; salt-mine storage. (M)

502 Disposal of nuclear wastes. A. S. Kubo and D. J. Rose, *Science,* vol. 182, pp. 1205-1211, 1973. Various options are examined. (P-M-T)

503 Expensive enrichment. Marvin Resnikoff, *Environment,* vol. 17, no. 5, pp. 28-35, 1975. Problems of radioactive wastes produced by nuclear reactors. (P-M)

Unit 64
Geothermal Energy

504 Geothermal energy: An emerging major resource. Allen L. Hammond, *Science,* vol. 177, pp. 978-980, 1972. Review of various forms of geothermal energy and their development. (P)

505 Geothermal power. Joseph Barnea, *Scientific American,* vol. 226, no. 1, pp. 70-77, 1972. Explains geologic principles of steam and hot water occurrences. (P)

506 Dry geothermal wells: Promising experimental results. Allen L. Hammond, *Science,* vol. 182, pp. 43-44, 1973. Hydraulic fracturing of hot igneous rock. (P)

507 Power from the Salton trough. Dietrick E. Thomsen, *Science News,* vol. 106, pp. 28-29, 1974. Hot brines beneath the Imperial Valley of California. (P)

508 Geothermal systems and power development. A. J. Ellis, *American Scientist,* vol. 63, pp. 510-521, 1975. New Zealand's geothermal localities. (P-M)

Unit 65
Solar Energy, General

509 Solar technologies. F. von Hippel and R. H. Williams, *Bull. of the Atomic Scientists,* vol. 31, no. 9, pp. 25-31, 1975. Overview of varied systems of using solar energy. (P)

510 Space colonies and energy supply to the earth. Gerald K. O'Neill, *Science,* vol. 190, pp. 943-947, 1975. Satellite solar power stations (SSPS). (M-T)

511 The sun in a drawer. Bruce Anderson, *Environment,* vol. 17, no. 7, pp. 36-41, 1975. Direct solar heating systems for use in buildings. (P)

512 The long-range prospects for solar energy. William G. Pollard, *American Scientist,* vol. 64, pp. 424-429, 1976. Solar electricity can make only a small contribution. (P)

513 Solar energy and rural development for the Third World. Arjun Makhijani, *Bull. of the Atomic Scientists,* vol. 32, no. 6, pp. 14-24, 1976. Special requirements must be met if solar energy is to be widely used in India. (P)

514 Storing the sun. Julian McCaull, *Environment,* vol. 18, no. 5, pp. 9-15, 1976. Technology of solar-energy storage. (P-M)

Biological-Solar Energy Systems

515 Power, fresh water, and food from cold, deep sea water. D. F. Othmer and O. A. Roels, *Science,* vol. 182, pp. 121-125, 1973. Ocean thermal gradient and nutrients put to use. (P-M)

516 The green machine. Janet H. Weinberg, *Science News,* vol. 107, pp. 228-229, 1975. Four basic systems of energy conversion through biologic processes. (P)

517 Flower power. A. D. Poole and R. H. Williams, *Bull. of the Atomic Scientists,* vol. 32, no. 5, pp. 48-58, 1976. Biomass of plants as a potential energy source. (P-M)

518 Photosynthesis as a resource for energy and materials. Melvin Calvin, *American Scientist,* vol. 64, pp. 270-278, 1976. Plants as converters of solar energy. (P-M-T)

Windpower and Seapower Systems

519 Windmills: The resurrection of an ancient energy technology. Nicholas Wade, *Science,* vol. 184, pp. 1055-1058, 1974. Windmills to generate electric power. (P-M)

520 Windmills in the history of technology. Volta W. Torrey, *Technology Review,* vol. 77, no. 5, pp. 8-9, 1975. All kinds of windmills in history. (P)

521 Power from the sea. Mark Swann, *Environment,* vol. 18, no. 4, pp. 25-31, 1976. Technology of sea-thermal energy systems. (P)

522 Wind energy. Bent Sørensen, *Bull. of the Atomic Scientists,* vol. 32, no. 7, pp. 38-45, 1976. Cost analysis of windpower systems. (M-T)

Epilogue
Population, Resources, Technology

523 The geography of human survival. William W. Bunge, *Annals, Assoc. of Amer. Geog.,* vol. 63, pp. 275-295, 1973. A geographer evaluates the prospects for survival of the human species. (P-M)

524 Mineral resources in fact and fancy. Preston Cloud, Chapter 2, pp. 50-75, in *Toward a Steady-State Economy,* H. E. Daly, ed., W. H. Freeman, San Francisco, 1973. Realities to be faced as mineral demands increase. (P)

525 The prospects for a stationary world population. Tomas Frejka, *Scientific American,* vol. 228, no. 3, pp. 15-23, 1973. Projections of the human population to the year 2150. (P-M)

526 Human population and the global development. J. P. Holdren and Paul R. Erlich, *American Scientist,* vol. 62, pp. 282-292, 1974. Rising population and per capita consumption lead to environmental damage. (P)

527 The quality of growth. Russell E. Train, *Science,* vol. 184, pp. 1050-1053, 1974. We are going to have to learn to live within our limits. (P)

528 The ancient roots of our ecological crisis. J. Donald Hughes, *Nat. Parks and Environmental Mag.,* vol. 49, no. 10, pp. 16-17, 1975. The ancient Greeks and Romans perceived and caused environmental destruction. (P)

529 Population: The forgotten crisis. Russell W. Peterson, *Nat. Parks and Conservation Mag.,* vol. 49, no. 9, pp. 15-18, 1975. Population growth and the quality of human life. (P)

530 Population vs. the environment: A crisis of too many people. James R. Echols, *American Scientist,* vol. 64, pp. 165-173, 1976. Drastic population control measures needed. (P)

531 Symbiosis between the earth and humankind. Rene Dubos, *Science,* vol. 193, pp. 459-462, 1976. Humans in creative partnership with other natural systems. (P)

532 World resources and the world middle class. Nathan Keyfitz, *Scientific*

American, vol. 235, no. 1, pp. 28-35, 1976. Limits of economic development set by limits to world resources. (P)

Environmental Planning and Legislation

533 Environmental law: (I) Maturing field for lawyers and scientists; (II) A strategic weapon against degradation? Luther J. Carter, *Science,* vol. 179, pp. 1205-1209, 1310-1350, 1973. (P)

534 Land use law: (I) Congress on verge of a modest beginning; (II) Florida is a major testing ground. Luther J. Carter, *Science,* vol. 182, pp. 691-697, 902-908, 1973. Land use policy legislation in the making. (P)

535 Future environmental needs and costs. S. Fred Singer, *EOS, Trans. Amer. Geophysical Union,* vol. 55, no. 11, pp. 948-954, 1974. Cost of a clean environment in relation to the GNP. (P-M)

536 Shaking the institutions in Sweden. Lennart J. Lundqvist, *Environment,* vol. 16, no. 8, pp. 27-35, 1974. Sweden's environmental quality protection program. (P)

537 United States environmental legislation and energy resources: A review. Daniel P. Beard, *Geographical Review,* vol. 65, pp. 229-244, 1975. Relationship between environmental quality objectives and the need for energy. (P)

538 Adjustment to new physical environments beyond the metropolitan fringe. James K. Mitchell, *Geographical Review,* vol. 66, pp. 18-31, 1976. Rising environmental concerns and new environmental attitudes characterize suburban and recreational expansion. (P)

Steady-State Existence

539 The tragedy of the commons. Garret Hardin, *Science,* vol. 162, pp. 1243-1248, 1968. Reprinted as Chapter 6, pp. 133-147, in *Toward a Steady-State Economy,* H. E. Daly, ed., W. H. Freeman, San Francisco, 1973. Conscience and coercion in the new society. (P)

540 The economics of the coming Spaceship Earth. Kenneth Boulding, Chapter 5, pp. 121-132, in *Toward a Steady-State Economy,* H. E. Daly, ed., W. H. Freeman, San Francisco, 1973. (P)

541 The steady-state economy. Herman E. Daly, Chapter 7, pp. 148-174, in *Toward a Steady-State Economy,* H. E. Daly, ed., W. H. Freeman, San Franciso, 1973. Toward a political economy of biophysical equilibrium and moral growth. (P)

542 *Toward a Steady-State Economy.* Herman E. Daly, Introduction, pp. 1-29, W. H. Freeman, San Francisco, 1973. An economist explains basic concepts of the steady-state economy. (P)

Index